PATTERN CLASSIFICATION

PATTERN CLASSIFICATION

A Unified View of Statistical and Neural Approaches

Jürgen Schürmann

Daimler-Benz Research Center Ulm

A WILEY-INTERSCIENCE PUBLICATION

JOHN WILEY & SONS, INC.

New York / Chichester / Brisbane / Toronto / Singapore

This text is printed on acid-free paper.

Library of Congress Cataloging in Publication Data:

Schürmann, Jürgen.
Pattern classification: a unified view of statistical and neural approaches / Jürgen Schürmann.
p. cm.
"A Wiley-Interscience publication."
Includes bibliographical references and index.
ISBN 0-471-13534-8 (cloth: alk. paper)
1. Pattern recognition systems. 2. Pattern perception. 3. Neural networks (Computer Science) 4. Statistical decision. I. Title.
Q327.S29 1996 95-4733
006.4—dc20

10 9 8 7 6 5 4 3 2 1

To Astrid, Carsten and Jens

CONTENTS

PREFACE

Pattern classification is a very general concept with innumerable applications in science and engineering. The development of the relevant theory evolved with the first serious attempts to recognize printed and written character images and to recognize spoken words using computer technology and has until now given rise to a complex web of theories, ideas, and inventions exhibiting numerous interrelations with such scientific disciplines as statistics, approximation theory, calculus of variations, control theory, communications technology, neurobiology, and others.

The fundamental approach chosen is to consider the pattern as having two different views like the two sides of a coin. A pattern is a pair comprising an observation and a meaning. Pattern classification is inferring meaning from observation. Designing a pattern classification system is establishing a mapping from measurement space into the space of potential meanings, whereby the different meanings are represented in this space as discrete target points. In artificial intelligence terms, pattern classification marks the step from the subsymbolic to the symbolic level of representation.

From this point of view, it makes no difference at all what kind of observations are considered and to what kind of meanings they may be linked. The identical approach applies for recognizing written text, spoken language, camera images, or any other variety of multidimensional signal interpretation. Even the types of measurements need not be restricted. They may come from distinctly different sources. Thus, the approach to be developed intrinsically embraces the data fusion problem.

The pattern classification task is basically statistic. The very core of the problem lies in the fact that the observations—describing the appearance of the pattern—may widely change without affecting the pattern meaning. The patterns to be encountered in a given application task, and hopefully to be correctly recognized by the pattern classifier, are modeled as coming from a stochastic source.

Following these lines of thought, we arrive at the three basic constituents of every pattern recognition problem: First, we have the stochastic pattern source modeling the application; second, we design some kind of generic mapping in the form of a certain mathematical function containing a number of free parameters and mapping the observed measurement vector into the most probable meaning; and third, we need an optimization criterion to force the estimations generated by the adjustable mapping to come as close as possible to the true meaning.

From this point of view all of the presently known techniques for designing pattern classification systems drop into their place within a common theoretical framework. It is shown that this holds for the classical solutions of statistical pattern classification as well as for the connectionist and neural approaches tackling the same kind of problem but starting from different motivations. It is also true for those approaches that try to completely avoid statistical terminology and argumentation.

In order to provide the necessary theoretical foundations the text starts with an outline of the decision-theoretic approach to pattern classification, which shows that all we need to know to solve a given problem are the probability functions ruling the pattern source. In practical pattern classification these statistical laws are never known but must be, in some way or other, approximately reconstructed from sets of training samples drawn from the pattern source. This is the approach of *learning from example* underlying all of the pattern classification techniques. Learning extracts knowledge from sets of learning samples. It makes no fundamental difference whether the learning process takes place separate from the recognition process or is integrated into the running recognition system.

The book develops in detail a number of competing approaches for building up the necessary estimating functions: statistical modeling, least mean-square techniques such as polynomial regression and multilayer perceptron regression, and radial basis functions. In particular, the chapter on polynomial regression contains considerable mathematical material not to be found in present textbooks or at least not in as unified a form. Both traditional statistics-based pattern classification techniques as well as connectionist and neural approaches are coherently treated and shown to be inextricably fused.

Emphasis is put on helping the reader develop an intuitive understanding of the basic properties of these approaches and the features of the resulting pattern classifier that derive therefrom. An extremely simplified two-dimensional example is used throughout the book to illustrate the different techniques in a unified way. Thus, the third dimension is used to represent functions in 2-space as they are encountered in the pattern classification system. Having understood what happens in the simplified two-dimensional case, the reader will be able to transfer these views to higher dimensions.

Viewed from the application point of view, designing the pattern classifier is only part of the story. The three chapters on measurement, features and feature selection, reject criteria and classifier performance, and combining classifiers compile a valuable amount of proven ideas and serve as an additional exercise showing how the different approaches fit together.

The book is the result of years of practical experience and hands-on work in pattern classification, predominantly but not exclusively on the background of character recognition and document understanding. Wherever possible, connections are drawn from the theoretical results derived within the chapters of this book to practical examples taken from the field of character recognition. At the same time, the book reflects two decades of teaching experience in statistical pattern classification at the Technical University of Darmstadt, Germany.

During years of close cooperation many members of my research team at Daimler-Benz Research Center Ulm (the former AEG Research Center Ulm) have contributed to the development of the ideas presented in the following pages. It would be difficult to mention them all. I wish to express my gratitude to Eberhard Mandler, Matthias Oberländer, and Norbert Bartneck for numerous fruitful discussions and to Ulrich Kressel and Jürgen Franke for critically reading the manuscript, for helpful suggestions for improvement, and for providing several of the illustrations. I especially want to acknowledge the patience of my wife, Astrid, who had to tolerate long evenings and weekends while I cared for nothing else but writing and editing the text and preparing the illustrations.

JÜRGEN SCHÜRMANN

March 1995

Ulm JÜRGEN SCHÜRMANN

March 1996

1 INTRODUCTION

The ability of pattern classification is certainly one of the key features of intelligent behavior, be it of humans or animals. This ability emerged with the biogenetic evolution as a mere matter of survival not only for the individual but also for the species. The individual receives visual, auditory, and other sensory information that must be processed to make perception and ultimately action possible for orientation in the environment, distinction between edible and poisonous food, or detecting dangerous enemies.

Pattern classification as a feature of technical systems serves similar but in general much more constrained purposes. Technical pattern classification aims at providing technical systems with the capability of reacting purposefully to a situation and to signals coming from the environment. Pattern classification must thus be a fundamental building block of any technical system designed to exhibit a certain application-specific intelligence. This book is concerned with pattern classification as a technical problem.

Though we will look at what is known about how nature solves pattern recognition tasks and consider how humans tackle problems of this kind, we need not understand completely how natural intelligence works nor should we try to. Rather, we will deal with pattern classification solely as a technical task and will make no explicit efforts to understand how natural intelligent systems work.

The term *pattern* is a word of our everyday vocabulary and means something exhibiting certain regularities, something able to serve as a model, something representing a concept of what was observed. A pattern is never an isolated observation, but rather a collection of observations connected in time or space or both. The pattern exhibits, as a whole, a certain structure indicative of the underlying concept.

The methodology of pattern classification takes up this intuitive understanding and states it more formally. In the notion of pattern two different worlds are linked that belong together like two sides of a coin—the world of physical observations accessible to any kind of measurements and the world of concepts and ideas. For our purposes the pattern is a pair of variables

$$\text{Pattern} = [\mathbf{v}, \omega]$$

where $\mathbf{v}$ is the collection of observations that can, at least in principle, be executed by some technical apparatus and ω is the concept behind the observations. Whereas $\mathbf{v}$ may be drawn from a multidimensional continuum of values, the variable ω comes from a discrete and finite set Ω of concepts. To each of the potential values $\omega \in \Omega$ a distinct name is associated.

The individual pattern, from this point of view, is one of the numerous possible incarnations of the concept ω represented by a certain constellation of observables with values given by $\mathbf{v}$:

- Pattern classification is the process of inferring ω from $\mathbf{v}$, in other words, it is the process of giving names ω to observations $\mathbf{v}$.

The most well-known and most widely discussed pattern classification tasks, among a wide variety of others, are the recognition of characters from their images on paper and the recognition of spoken words from the corresponding microphone signals. These applications explicitly illustrate that pattern classification is giving names to observations.

In both cases the observations come from the same kind of source and are of the same type: light intensities at different but neighboring locations in two-dimensional space and signal intensities at different but neighboring points of time. Words written on paper or words transferred by microphone signals have their names in common language. There are, however, many other applications where the observations combined in $\mathbf{v}$ may come from totally different physical areas and where also the set Ω of concepts contains a collection of possible reactions for which colloquial language may not even have explicit names.

A characteristic of patterns in the context of pattern classification is that every concept ω may have numerous possible incarnations $\mathbf{v}$. Think of the character recognition task: There exists an unbounded plurality of ways of designing character images that represent one single character meaning, as exemplified by the collection of *A*'s in Fig. 1.1. But even if the task is restricted to recognizing characters belonging to only one font, one of the character images will hardly equal the other due to uncontrollable variations in the character's pixel image.

Therefore, the very core of pattern classification is to cope with variability, to call an *A* an *A* and a *B* a *B*, irrespective of how it looks. The difficulty of that task depends on the degree to which the incarnations of the pattern

Figure 1.1. Variety of different images all representing the same character *A* (from Hofstadter's *Metamagical Themes*: *Questing for the Essence of Mind and Pattern* [HOF1985]).

are allowed to vary and how they are distributed in V-space. This is where statistics comes in together with the principle of *learning from examples*.

The two worlds identified above of physical observations on the one hand and concepts, names, and meanings on the other correspond, in the mathematical sense, to two spaces. First, we have the measurement space

V, the vector space spanned by the vector **v** of observations describing how the pattern looks, and second, we have the set Ω of possible meanings. Each of the imaginable patterns establishes a link $[\mathbf{v}, \omega]$ between both spaces which may be passed in either direction; if the considered patterns are characters, then the following are true:

From ω to **v**: rendering the character image from the character meaning
From **v** to ω: recognition of the character meaning from the character image

These links are relations in the mathematical sense, or mappings, if we put it a bit more illustratively, going from one of the two spaces into the other. The mapping $\omega \rightarrow \mathbf{v}$ is one to many due to the variability of patterns representing the same concept. The elements ω of Ω are therefore called classes and Ω is the set of classes. Depending on the variability of the mapping $\omega \rightarrow \mathbf{v}$ the opposite mapping $\mathbf{v} \rightarrow \omega$ may or may not be unique since in general it cannot be excluded that the same observation **v** may be linked to different concepts in Ω.

From this point of view, pattern classification is the task of establishing a mapping from **v** to ω in order to recognize the concept ω—the class—behind the observation **v** when only the observation **v** is known. This mapping must take into account what is known about the variability of patterns. And this variability is best described by the notion of class-specific distributions in **V**-space, which may or may not penetrate.

Knowledge about these distributions in **V**-space is a kind of knowledge that can hardly be acquired other than by learning from examples. And learning from examples is an intrinsically statistical concept. For this purpose, in any practical application, a collection of patterns $[\mathbf{v}, \omega]$ is assembled that shows how patterns **v** of the different classes $\omega \in \Omega$ have to look, or in other words, what the correct meanings ω of those patterns are that look like the given examples **v**.

1.1 RECOGNITION OF ENTITIES VERSUS MODEL-BASED RECOGNITION

We have dealt so far with patterns as entities in the sense that the concepts they represent are on the lowest level of the conceptual hierarchy. They are the atoms of the conceptual world that is constructed in order to model a certain problem domain, notwithstanding the fact that the pattern itself is described by a normally large number of measurement observations.

Consider, for example, the problem of recognizing spoken utterances as complete words: The set Ω of classes may be the set of the 10 numerals $0, \ldots, 9$ and the observation on which the recognition process is based is the section of the sampled microphone signal spanning from the beginning of the speech utterance to its end. Thus a measurement vector **v** is defined that obviously contains enough information for the job to be done, since the original speech can be reconstructed from **v** to any degree of perfection and can in this form reliably be recognized by a human listener.

This example is intended to clarify what is meant by the term *recognized as entity*. The recognition process aims at the whole word. There is no modularization, no breaking down of the entire task into subtasks.

This is in contrast to another approach in which word subunits are introduced as logical entities and words are constructed from these subunits according to a certain set of rules, be it in the form of a complete enumeration or a grammar. The recognition process would then run in a sequence of two steps, the first being recognition of the word subunits according to the recognition-as-entity paradigm and the second being recognition of the admissible words by symbolic reasoning employing the knowledge of how words are formed from word subunits.

Structuring the problem area and the design of the conceptual apparatus for developing solutions to technical problems is a matter of design ingenuity. The example task of word recognition may be solved in either of the ways just discussed. However, it should be clear that every subdivision of arbitrary recognition tasks into subtasks ends up with elementary patterns to be recognized as entities and a normally complex system of rules defining how higher level concepts are formed from the elementary concepts.

Pattern classification and pattern recognition are often viewed as subfields of artificial intelligence (AI). In this context the process of dealing with concepts from a conceptual hierarchy is called *symbolic reasoning*, and a discrimination is made between the symbolic and the *subsymbolic level*. What here is called observation and measurement belongs to the subsymbolic level and what is called concept or class is part of the symbolic one. Pattern classification is positioned exactly between the subsymbolic and the symbolic worlds. The task of pattern classification is building a bridge between both worlds, generating symbols from subsymbolic observations.

There are numerous practical applications that can be successfully tackled by the *recognition-of-entities* approach. Examples are recognition of isolated character images, recognition of whole words in speech, diagnosis of technical systems from operational signals, to cite only a few. There are, however, a multitude of complex tasks that cannot be solved without layers of symbolic reasoning above the recognition-of-entities level.

This fact becomes obvious even from the example of character and text recognition. In this application the single character is the appropriate elementary pattern. But does the single character convey any semantic content in the sense of the application? In many cases it does not. Instead, characters form words, and these have meanings that cannot be derived from their constituents but must be declared separately, the terminology laid down in dictionaries and encyclopedias. The concept of the whole being more than the sum of its parts is here specifically valid. But as humans we deal with characters and words without being aware of these complications.

Above the level of words there is a boundless hierarchy of notions and concepts. But also in the opposite direction no clear-cut bounds are to be found. What prevents us from breaking down the single-character image into pieces such as line endings, crossings, bows, and inclusions and to define rules that allow us to recognize character images from their constituents?

Recognition and understanding in all but the most trivial cases deal with interwoven networks of concepts and semantic relations. This fact, becoming already visible just in the simple example of recognizing characters and text, is all the more true when it comes to recognition and understanding of speech and natural scenes. On that level recognition of entities is no longer the adequate instrument. Looking, for example, at a real-world scene, it is not the question of identifying this scene as item number *xyz* from a catalog of known images. Instead, what we are often interested in is a description of the scene in terms of our own language, in knowing what objects are in the scene, their positions and orientations, and their geometric relations. Scene analysis must compile a database of information holding answers for potential questions about what is visible in the scene.

The foregoing discussion has shed light on the position of pattern classification in the context of other disciplines concerned with cognition, recognition, and perception. In this light we are able to give the theme of this book, that pattern classification is the task of giving names or labels to objects or events based on a set of measurements appropriately taken from the physical world.

Pattern classification in this sense is an indispensable subtask in every image, speech, or other understanding system and one that must be combined with knowledge-based reasoning in all but trivial cases in order to come to a complete solution for most realistic application tasks. Pattern classification and symbolic reasoning are thus natural complements, rather than competing approaches, for designing and implementing technical perception and understanding systems. However, the question that remains to be answered in each specific case is where to position the boundary between subsymbolic and symbolic reasoning, between pattern classification and knowledge-based techniques.

1.2 STATISTICAL APPROACH

We have already seen that patterns belonging to the same class are subject to variations. These need not be caused by random processes, but it is very useful to treat them as if they were. Statistics is an adequate means for describing variations, random or not, in terms of which variations may occur at all and with which frequencies. The statistical approach is even applicable to variations such as those in Fig. 1.1, where the selection of one of the manifestations of the character A will be guided by the aesthetic sense and other preferences of the human originator of the text, as it is applicable to cases where the variations are indeed caused by statistical reasons, for example, if the patterns come from a unique model and are distorted by some random noise.

A useful picture for illustrating the concept of variation in pattern classification is the notion of the *measurement space*. All of the physical observations describing the pattern are combined in the measurement vector $\mathbf{v}$, which corresponds to one certain point in the N-dimensional vector space $\mathbf{V}$, with N the number of measurements taken. Different patterns with different measurement vectors $\mathbf{v}$ correspond to different points in measurement space and patterns with similar appearance are lying closely together. The space $\mathbf{V}$ is called $\mathbf{V}$-space or *pattern space*.

The set of all conceivable patterns to be encountered in a certain application forms a collection of points in measurement space that can, at least in principle, be described by some statistical distribution function. Since the pattern is a pair $[\mathbf{v}, \omega]$ of values with $\mathbf{v}$ describing how it looks and ω what it means, or in other words, to which class it belongs, the pattern points in measurement space are labeled by ω. With K the number of classes to be distinguished, we thus have a multitude of K class-specific distributions in measurement space, each labeled with the corresponding class label ω.

Pattern classification is the task of recognizing the class label ω from the measurement vector $\mathbf{v}$. This task is equivalent to establishing a mapping $\mathbf{v} \rightarrow \mathbf{d}$ from the measurement space $\mathbf{V}$ into the decision space $\mathbf{D}$, containing K discrete points each of which represents one of the K classes $\omega \in \Omega$ (see Fig. 1.2).

Obviously, the mapping $\mathbf{v} \rightarrow \mathbf{d}$ should in as many cases as possible point to that point in $\mathbf{D}$ carrying the true class label ω. This requirement determines a *statistical optimization problem* since the probability of error is a statistical measure. The optimum among all conceivable mappings $\mathbf{v} \rightarrow \mathbf{d}$ is that which guarantees the maximum recognition rate. Although the ultimate optimization criterion is the probability of error connected with the specific mapping $\mathbf{v} \rightarrow \mathbf{d}$, it often must for practical reasons be substituted by some kind of approximation.

The difficulty of the classification task, expressed in terms of the minimum achievable error rate, depends on the nature of the distributions in measurement space, on whether these distributions are locally concentrated or spread out over wide regions of $\mathbf{V}$, and specifically on the degree of their mutual penetration.

The design of a pattern classification system requires knowledge of the specific statistical situation in pattern space either in the form of knowledge of the relevant distribution functions in $\mathbf{V}$-space or at least in the form of a sufficiently large set of learning samples drawn from these distributions.

Acquiring this kind of knowledge, at least in approximate form, is crucial for every pattern classification task. Since, except for synthetic recognition

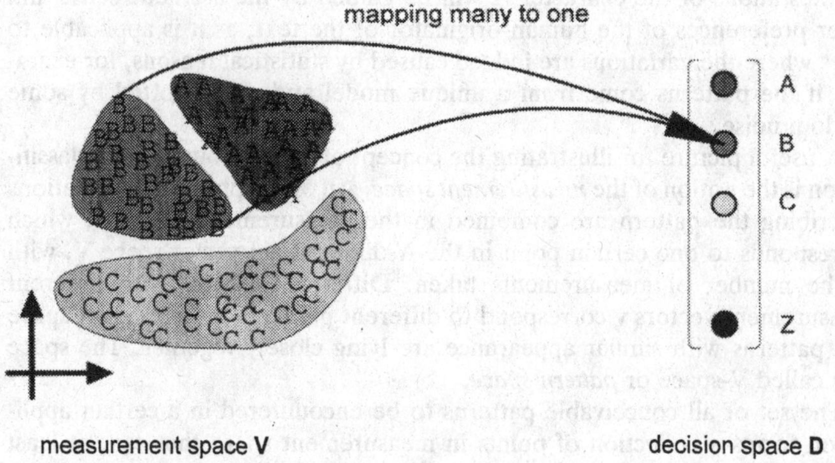

Figure 1.2. Pattern classification viewed as establishing a mapping $\mathbf{v} \rightarrow \mathbf{d}$ from measurement space **V** to decision space **D**.

problems, the distributions in measurement space are unknown, the only practical way to the design of recognition systems is to rely on the paradigm of *learning from examples*.

Thus, the basic components of any pattern classification task are as follows:

- A general concept of how to structure the mapping $\mathbf{v} \rightarrow \mathbf{d}$
- An optimization criterion for optimizing the mapping $\mathbf{v} \rightarrow \mathbf{d}$
- A learning sample drawn from the current recognition task on which to base the optimization procedure

1.3 NEURAL NETWORK APPROACH

The course of argumentation we have followed so far puts the pattern classification theme into a technical-mathematical framework. This has not been the only way of looking at the problem. Since the ability for pattern classification is an essential feature of natural intelligent systems, it is interesting to study how nature solves problems of this kind and try to copy the solutions.

This kind of approach has attracted enormous attention, especially during the last decade, and is centered around the neuron as the basic building block of natural brains. The unrivaled computational power and versatility of the biological brain are due to a complicated network of vast numbers of neurons. Biologists estimate that the human brain consists of about 10^{11}

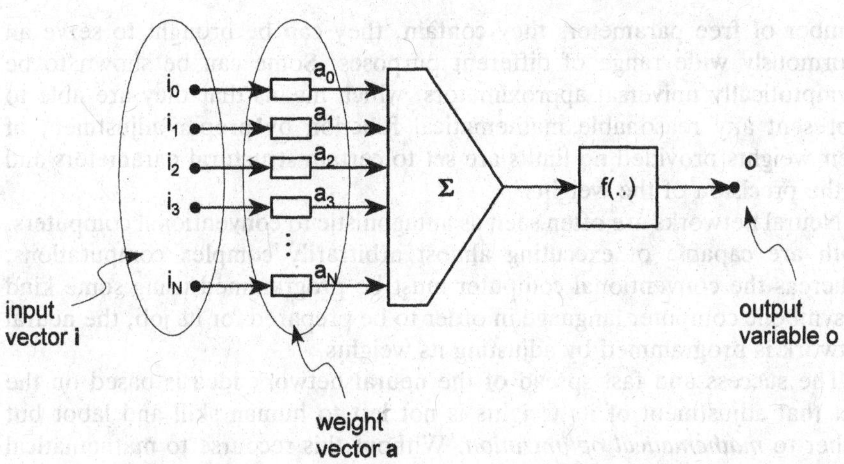

Figure 1.3. Artificial neuron. The *N*-dimensional input vector **i** is mapped into the scalar output variable *o* by means of the scalar product $\mathbf{a}^T\mathbf{i}$ followed by a nonlinear functional mapping $f(\cdot)$.

neurons and that each of them is on the average connected to about 10^4 others.

For the single artificial neuron, compared to the biological model, a rather simple mathematical model has been generally accepted consisting of a number of input nodes and one output node (Fig. 1.3). The mathematical operations connecting the input nodes to the output node are the scalar product of the neuron input vector **i** with a vector **a** of weights, associated with the neuron, followed by an in general nonlinear mapping $f(\cdot)$ of the result into the neuron output variable $o = f(\mathbf{a}^T\mathbf{i})$.

Even the individual artificial neuron is a powerful mathematical structure exhibiting an enormously wide functionality. By proper adjustment of the activation function $f(\cdot)$ and weight vector **a** it can be made to serve a number of different purposes, such as implementing Boolean threshold logic for large numbers of Boolean input variables or providing high-dimensional basis functions for nonlinear functional approximation. All the more powerful are networks of artificial neurons that, due to the simple and regular structure of the single neuron, may be composed of more than 10,000 individual artificial neurons without becoming blocked by the limitations of present-day technology.

Using the artificial neuron as the basic building block, a variety of different design concepts have been developed for arranging individual neurons in neural networks, often inspired by insights into how biological systems work or by imagining how they are supposed to work.

A feature common to all of these different designs is that they constitute flexible, adjustable mathematical structures. Due to the normally large number of free parameters they contain, they can be brought to serve an enormously wide range of different purposes. Some can be shown to be asymptotically universal approximators, which means that they are able to represent any reasonable mathematical function by proper adjustment of their weights provided no limits are set to certain structural parameters and to the precision of the weights.

Neural networks are often seen as antagonistic to conventional computers. Both are capable of executing almost arbitrarily complex computations. Whereas the conventional computer must be programmed using some kind of symbolic computer language in order to be prepared for its job, the neural network is programmed by adjusting its weights.

The success and fast spread of the neural network idea is based on the fact that adjustment of its weights is not left to human skill and labor but rather to *mathematical optimization*. Without this recourse to mathematical optimization weight adjustment for neural networks would indeed be unaffordable in view of the size and complexity of typical neural network designs.

Mathematical optimization establishes the connection to the specific purpose the neural network serves and makes use of an optimization criterion indicating how well it does with the present set of weights. A gradient descent technique or some other kind of optimization procedure modifies the set of weights until an, in general, local optimum is found. This process is called neural network training.

The task to be solved—employing the neural network—is for this purpose represented by samples taken from the current application. Thus we find that *learning from examples* and *parameter adjustment by mathematical optimization* are the main characteristics of neural network approaches.

Another driving force behind the neural network idea is that neural networks lend themselves to implementation in analog technology. Indeed, neural network technology can be viewed as the rebirth of the techniques of analog computation.

Despite these motivations, which seem so contrasting to conventional computing, it must be understood that nothing happens with neural networks outside the scope of conventional computing. Instead, almost all current work in neural network research and experimentation runs on ordinary computers.

Neural networks have much in common with the structures needed for pattern classification. Pattern classification and neural networks go back to the same roots in the historic evolution of artificial intelligence (AI) techniques. The idea of neural networks is taken from biological systems performing pattern classification functions. It is no wonder that neural networks are considered to be predestined pattern classifiers. In this role they agree with the concepts developed in conventional pattern classification. The purpose of this book is to treat the topic of pattern classification in a unified way, relating conventional and neural network approaches to the same basic concepts that lie in mathematics and statistics.

The connection to what was stated before as the essence of pattern classification, namely establishing a mapping $\mathbf{v} \rightarrow \mathbf{d}$ from measurement space $\mathbf{V}$ to decision space $\mathbf{D}$, is provided by viewing the individual neuron and the neural network as functional approximators.

The single artificial neuron implements a mathematical function $\mathbf{i} \rightarrow o$. Depending on the weight vector $\mathbf{a}$, this function can be widely varied. Correspondingly, larger artificial neural networks composed of typically large numbers of single neurons represent mathematical mappings that, in the general case, can be arbitrarily formed by appropriately adjusting the set $\mathbf{A} = \{\mathbf{a}_n\}$ of all weight vectors $\mathbf{a}_n$ contained in the construction. Hence, neural networks establish generic mappings that obviously can be applied for the kind of mappings $\mathbf{v} \rightarrow \mathbf{d}$ we need for pattern classification tasks.

From this point of view the neural network approach becomes part of the statistical approach. However, it has provided families of novel mapping functions not previously considered (see Chapters 7 and 8).

1.4 CONCEPTUAL FRAMEWORK

Some of the key terms necessary for the evolution of the pattern classification methodology have been introduced in the foregoing discussions. In the following we will explain the fundamental notions of pattern classification.

Classes

Pattern classification deals with objects or events to be classified. There exists a finite set of possible events

$$\Omega = \{\omega_1, \omega_2, \ldots, \omega_k, \ldots, \omega_K\} \tag{1.1}$$

The elements ω_k of Ω are called *classes* and Ω the *set of classes*. The number of classes to be distinguished is

$$K = \text{card}(\Omega) = \text{number of classes} \tag{1.2}$$

The K classes ω_k are mutually exclusive and complete. We are operating here under a *closed-world assumption*: Whenever an event ω occurs, it must be uniquely one element of the set Ω of classes. No other events are allowed to happen. With respect to practical applications, this is a severe limitation. In Chapter 10 we will discuss how to circumvent the consequences of this assumption.

The idea of a set of classes is convincingly illustrated by the example of character recognition. Let Ω be the letters $A, \ldots, Z$. The pattern classification task is then the task of recognizing the capital letters. This specific definition of Ω excludes every other character, lowercase letters and numerals are not to be presented.

The set Ω of classes may, depending on the application, be defined quite differently, confined to numerals only or embracing the complete set of characters on a typewriter. The definition of Ω is predominantly a question of application.

However, sometimes it can be advantageous to treat different-shape variations, as for example **a** and *a*, of the same character class *a* as different classes. This possibility turns what is at first glance the seemingly straightforward procedure of determining Ω into a complex design procedure since it applies not only to *a* but also to a number of other classes.

It is often convenient to associate numeric types to the elements of the set Ω. Two different associations are common, which can be viewed as mappings of the set Ω into either the one-dimensional scale of integer values or the K-dimensional vector space.

The first kind of mapping leads to the *class label k*, which is simply the index of the elements ω_k of Ω:

$$\begin{array}{cccccccc} \Omega = \{\omega_1 & \omega_2 & \cdots & \omega_k & \cdots & \omega_K\} \\ \Updownarrow & \Updownarrow & & \Updownarrow & & \Updownarrow \\ k \in \{1 & 2 & \cdots & k & \cdots & K\} \end{array} \tag{1.3}$$

The second kind of mapping introduces the concept of the *target vector* $\mathbf{y}$, a K-dimensional vector variable that can assume only K discrete values $\mathbf{y}_1$ to $\mathbf{y}_K$,

$$\begin{array}{cccccccc} \Omega = \{\omega_1 & \omega_2 & \cdots & \omega_k & \cdots & \omega_K\} \\ \Updownarrow & \Updownarrow & & \Updownarrow & & \Updownarrow \\ \mathbf{y} \in \{\mathbf{y}_1 & \mathbf{y}_2 & \cdots & \mathbf{y}_k & \cdots & \mathbf{y}_K\} \end{array} \tag{1.4}$$

which are defined to be the K columns of the K-dimensional identity matrix

$$\mathbf{I} = \begin{bmatrix} 1 & 0 & \cdots & 0 & \cdots & 0 \\ 0 & 1 & \cdots & 0 & \cdots & 0 \\ \vdots & \vdots & & \vdots & & \vdots \\ 0 & 0 & \cdots & 1 & \cdots & 0 \\ \vdots & \vdots & & \vdots & & \vdots \\ 0 & 0 & \cdots & 0 & \cdots & 1 \end{bmatrix} = [\mathbf{y}_1 \quad \mathbf{y}_2 \quad \cdots \quad \mathbf{y}_k \quad \cdots \quad \mathbf{y}_K] \tag{1.5}$$

This kind of association between ω and the vector-valued variable $\mathbf{y}$ represents a "one out of K" coding scheme for the classes to be distinguished.

Whereas in (1.3) the class labels k, representing the K classes, inherit the

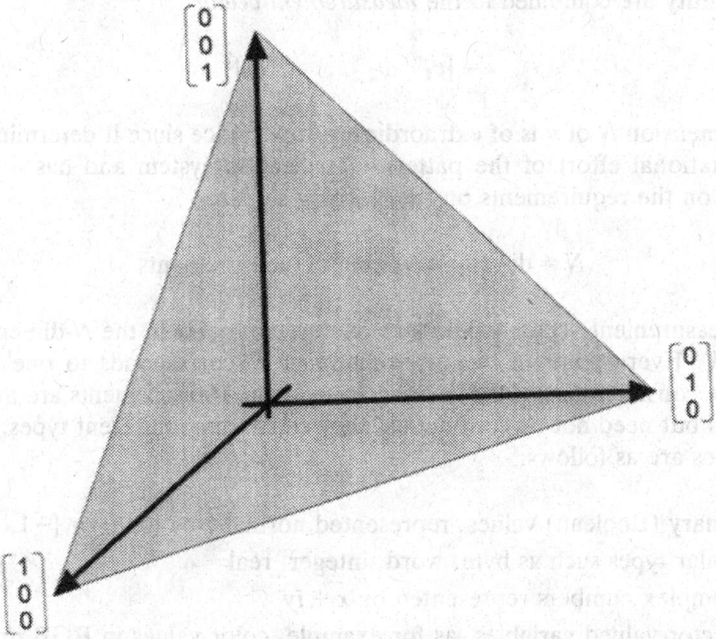

Figure 1.4. Three-dimensional decision space spanned by three target vectors $\mathbf{y}_1$, $\mathbf{y}_2$, $\mathbf{y}_3$. Tops of three vectors form two-dimensional equilateral triangle in 3-space. Picture can be generalized to equilateral tetrahedron for $K = 4$ classes and to similar configurations in higher dimensional spaces.

neighborhood relations of the integer values on the scale of integers, the introduction of the target vector $\mathbf{y}$ as in (1.5) removes all neighborhood imbalances. All mutual distances between different target vectors become equal. The tops of the K target vectors in $\mathbf{Y}$-space form a so-called simplex that itself is a $(K - 1)$-dimensional object. In the case, for example, of $K =$ 3 classes the three target vectors form an equilateral triangle that actually is a two-dimensional figure (see Fig. 1.4).

We call the K-dimensional continuous space spanned by the K target vectors $\mathbf{y}_1, \ldots, \mathbf{y}_K$ the *decision space* $\mathbf{D}$. It contains the K embedded target points.

Measurements and Features

Pattern classification is the task of giving names to objects based on observations. These observations may have arbitrary, even quite different origins and are called measurements. The set of all measurements referring to the same entity are combined in the *measurement vector*

$$\mathbf{v} = [v_1 \quad v_2 \quad \ldots \quad v_n]^T \tag{1.6}$$

The dimension N of $\mathbf{v}$ is of extraordinary importance since it determines the computational effort of the pattern classification system and has a strong impact on the requirements on the learning set size

$$N = \dim(\mathbf{v}) = \text{number of measurements} \tag{1.7}$$

The measurement vector $\mathbf{v}$ points to one certain point in the N-dimensional space $\mathbf{V}$. Every point in *measurement space* $\mathbf{V}$ corresponds to one of the possible constellations of the measurement data. Measurements are numerical data but need not be continuous; they can assume different types. Some examples are as follows:

- Binary (Boolean) values, represented normally by $\{0, 1\}$ or $\{-1, +1\}$
- Scalar types such as byte, word, integer, real
- Complex numbers represented by $x + iy$
- Vector-valued variables, as for example, color values in RGB or other multichannel data

The different types may be arbitrarily mixed. The ordering scheme of the components of $\mathbf{v}$ is arbitrary but must be fixed.

The question of which measurements to choose is a design decision and must be decided by human insight into the field of application. Measurements should have the potential of giving hints as to which class the observed event belongs. We will return to the question of measurement and feature selection in Chapter 9 and will deal there also with the possibilities for extracting powerful feature sets from larger sets of feature candidates.

The term *feature* is used here almost synonymously with the term *measurement*. Measurements are simply observations, hopefully useful for the recognition task, whereas features are appropriately constructed, normally from simpler measurements, and should therefore have more discriminative power. The transition is fluid since every combination of elementary measurements renders a new measurement, the difference lying only in the more or less complicated prescription.

In many cases the discriminative power of feature sets can, to a remarkable degree, be improved by properly chosen transformations. Such transformations are, for example, the short-term Fourier transform and the wavelet transform often used when dealing with time series or images or normalizing operations such as size, slant, and line thickness when dealing with character images. The design of appropriate feature sets is an engineering task of eminent importance in most of the applications.

An interesting question to ask is whether the set of measurements is complete with respect to reconstruction. Consider the problem of recognizing characters. The basic set of measurements normally is the collection of pixels of the character's scanned image. From the pixel data the original character image can be reconstructed with sufficient detail if only the resolution of the scanning raster is high enough. If the reconstructed image is recognizable to humans in the same way as the original, nothing important can have been lost when the real-world event was described by the set of pixel features.

When the set of measurements has the potential for reconstruction, we are on the safe side. It should be noted that for recognition rather than for reconstruction often only a fraction of that information is needed. Nevertheless, the principle of checking the reconstructive power is very useful in feature evaluation and feature selection.

Observation Vector

The two variables thus defined, $\mathbf{v}$ and $\mathbf{y}$, describe how the pattern looks and what it represents. These are two aspects of a single pattern:

$$\text{Pattern} = [\mathbf{v}, \mathbf{y}] \tag{1.8}$$

It is therefore adequate to concatenate both measurement vector $\mathbf{v}$ and target vector $\mathbf{y}$ to form a single vector, the *vector* $\mathbf{z}$ of *observations*:

$$\mathbf{z} = \begin{pmatrix} \mathbf{v} \\ \mathbf{y} \end{pmatrix} \tag{1.9}$$

The vector variable $\mathbf{z}$ contains all that is known about the single pattern. The learning set from which the pattern classification system is to be derived according to the learning-from-examples paradigm contains collections $\{\mathbf{z}\}$ of observation vectors $\mathbf{z}$.

Once the pattern classification system is successfully trained, it is confronted with only that part of $\mathbf{z}$ containing the measurement information with only the measurement vector $\mathbf{v}$. The pattern classifier accepts the measurement vector $\mathbf{v}$ as its input variable and generates an output $\hat{\mathbf{y}}$ that most likely should be the target vector $\mathbf{y}$. Thus from the partial information $\mathbf{v}$ the complete observation vector $\mathbf{z}$ is at least approximately reconstructed.

Pattern Classification System

We have identified the task of pattern classification with the task of establishing a mapping from measurement space $\mathbf{V}$ into decision space $\mathbf{D}$. This

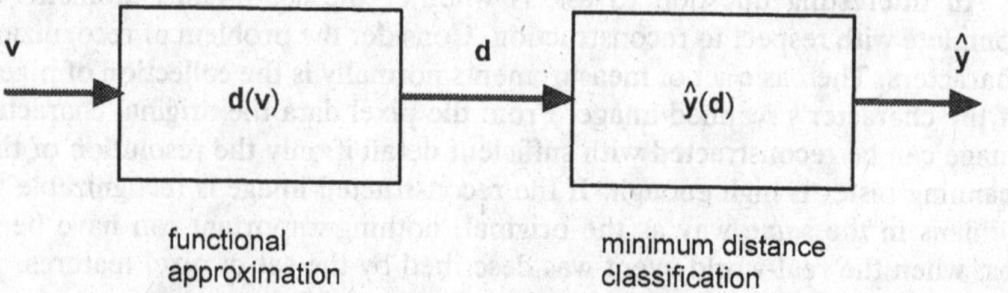

Figure 1.5. Two-step procedure for mapping **v** into **ŷ**. First step generates estimation **d(v)** and second step performs minimum-distance decision **d** → **ŷ**.

mapping is implemented in two steps, combining the two fundamental principles of recognition (Fig. 1.5):

- *Functional Approximation*: Mapping **v** → **d** from **V** to **D** subject to the optimization goal that **d** should come as close as possible to the associated target vector **y**.
- *Nearest-Neighbor Principle – Minimum Distance Classification*: Given **d**, search for the target vector **ŷ** nearest to **d** among the set of target vectors {**y**} and output **ŷ** or, equivalently, its class label $\hat{k}$.

Already the first of the two steps leads from measurement space **V** into decision space **D** and is often called *estimation* since, in an obvious sense, **d** is an estimate for **y** based on the knowledge contained in **v**. The second of the two steps is called *decision* since it generates a logical predicate, namely, "**v** belongs to class $\hat{k}$."

The estimation function **d(v)** shall be capable of generating estimates **d** coming as close as possible to the desired values **y** as they are given by the patterns [**v**, **y**], which are to be encountered in the pattern classification application

$$\begin{array}{lcl} [\mathbf{v} & \quad \mathbf{y}] & \Leftrightarrow \text{pattern} \\ \downarrow & \quad | & \\ \mathbf{d}(\mathbf{v}) & \quad | & \Leftrightarrow \text{estimation} \\ \downarrow & \quad \downarrow & \\ \mathbf{d} & \approx \ \mathbf{y} & \Leftrightarrow \text{goal} \end{array} \tag{1.10}$$

The design of that function **d(v)** is the very core of pattern classification, and there are numerous approaches possible, ranging from those totally based on human insight into the problem and designing sophisticated, hand-crafted decision rules on the one hand to completely statistical ones on the other. However, it should be understood that the concept of (1.10) is powerful enough to describe any conceivable type of pattern recognition system regardless of the underlying design principles.

Learning

The concept of an estimation function **d**(**v**) offers the opportunity to come to *automated learning procedures* if the estimation function is defined to have a predetermined structure and embedded in this structure a number of adjustable parameters allowing to form the function as a whole. There exist several different approaches to defining the predetermined structure, leading to different families of estimating functions. We will discuss the most important of them in the chapters to follow.

The learning process is organized according to (1.10). What is to be learned is defined by the learning set containing a collection of patterns representative for the application, each of which is a pair **z** of **v** and **y**; see (1.8), (1.9). Based on this set of learning samples an optimization feedback loop is installed consisting of the *pattern classification system* to be trained, an *evaluation system* comparing the generated estimation **d** with the desired value **y**, and the *error feedback*, which changes the system parameters of the estimating function thus that the error is decreased until an optimum is found (Fig. 1.6).

Following this argument, we are led to a statistical point of view. The application is considered to be a *pattern source* capable of providing an unlimited number of patterns [**v**, **y**]. Both variables **v** and **y** are accessible during learning, but after having been trained, the recognition system has henceforth only access to the measurement vector **v**.

The pattern source is a statistical process, and every collection of patterns taken from this source is a statistical set of samples. This is especially true for the learning set. Although it may be nice and often also useful to know how perfectly the elements of the learning set are recognized by the trained system, this is not what we really need to know about its performance. What counts is the error rate in actual application, and this can only be estimated by checking the system performance with newly collected test samples.

These considerations naturally lead to the *distinction* between *learning* and *test sets*. The procedure of checking the system performance based on the learning set is often called *reclassification*, and the procedure of checking it with an independent test set is called *generalization*. Obviously, what is relevant for the application is generalization.

A question of utmost importance relates to the necessary size of learning and test sets:

- The more parameters the estimation function contains, the larger the size of the training sample must be.

The only way to reduce the requirements on the sample set size is to introduce

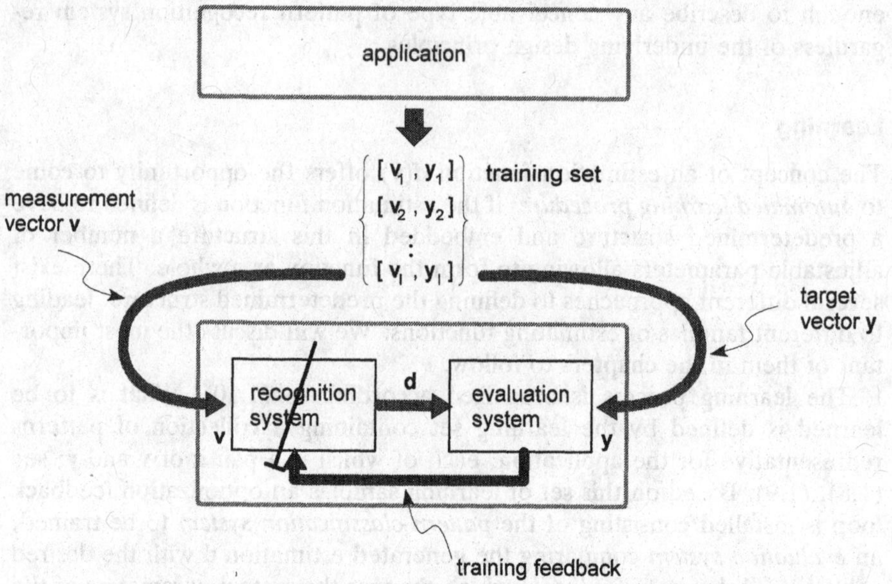

Figure 1.6. Learning from examples: In principle, the application provides an unlimited number of sample patterns [**v**, **y**]. Measurement vector **v** goes into estimating function **d**(**v**), which generates **d**. An evaluation system compares **d** and **y**. Based on remaining error, parameters of estimating function are modified until no further improvements can be achieved.

plausible statistical assumptions consistent with the properties of the application. For increasing sizes of learning and test sets the reclassification and generalization error rates should converge from different sides to the actual value.

Unfortunately these asymptotically converging curves of performance versus sample set size are difficult to achieve since any performance score gained from a certain test set is simply a random observation exhibiting a stochastic behavior. The stochastic variation of such performance measurements can be described by the mean and variance. Typically the variance increases with decreasing sample set size such that large numbers of experiments have to be undertaken to come to reliable estimations.

Of the two steps every recognition system has to perform—functional approximation and minimum-distance classification—the first is dominant and deserves most of our interest since learning happens in this step. Therefore, pattern classification can be viewed essentially as a special problem of functional approximation comprising minimum-distance classification as a necessary ingredient.

2

STATISTICAL DECISION THEORY

We will treat patterns as stochastic variables governed by certain stochastic rules that are able to mirror adequately the conditions of the application.

Stochastic variables x may be continuous or discrete. This makes no difference in principle but does make a difference in mathematical detail since discrete stochastic events are described by probabilities and continuous events by probability densities.

To any potential value x that a discrete stochastic variable can assume there is a probability $P(x)$ associated with it indicating the probability that just that value x will occur. The sum over all of these probabilities is 1.

For a continuous stochastic event the notion of probability must be substituted by the notion of a probability density. The probability density $p(x)$ means that the probability for the continuous event of falling into the interval $[x \cdots x + dx]$ is $p(x)\,dx$, where dx is the infinitesimally small width of the interval on the x scale. Thus in the continuous case the product $p(x)\,dx$ is the logical equivalent to $P(x)$. The sum over all $p(x)\,dx$ again is 1, but this summation in mathematical terms is integration.

This is the point where the distinction between discrete and continuous stochastic events concerns our argumentation; it changes probabilities into probability densities and summations into integrations. For simplicity, in the following explanations we will treat all stochastic variables as if they were discrete variables and use the sum operator Σ as a symbol for the sum in the discrete case and for the integral in the continuous case.

2.1 THE PATTERN SOURCE

The *pattern source* is a stochastic model representing the situation for which the pattern classification system is to be developed (Fig. 2.1). It is capable of generating unlimited numbers of varying patterns, pairs $[\mathbf{v}, \mathbf{y}]$, according to a stochastic law given by the *joined probability*

$$\text{prob}(\mathbf{v}, \mathbf{y}) \tag{2.1}$$

whereby $\text{prob}(\mathbf{v}, \mathbf{y})$ indicates the probability of the combination of $\mathbf{v}$ and $\mathbf{y}$ to happen.

The relations between $\mathbf{v}$ and $\mathbf{y}$ become clearer if we derive some further probabilities from (2.1) such as the *marginal distributions*

$$\text{prob}(\mathbf{v}) = \sum_{\mathbf{y}} \text{prob}(\mathbf{v}, \mathbf{y}) \tag{2.2}$$

$$\text{prob}(\mathbf{y}) = \sum_{\mathbf{v}} \text{prob}(\mathbf{v}, \mathbf{y}) \tag{2.3}$$

and the *conditional probabilities*

$$\text{prob}(\mathbf{v}|\mathbf{y}) = \frac{\text{prob}(\mathbf{v}, \mathbf{y})}{\text{prob}(\mathbf{y})} = \frac{\text{prob}(\mathbf{v}, \mathbf{y})}{\sum_{\mathbf{v}} \text{prob}(\mathbf{v}, \mathbf{y})} \tag{2.4}$$

$$\text{prob}(\mathbf{y}|\mathbf{v}) = \frac{\text{prob}(\mathbf{v}, \mathbf{y})}{\text{prob}(\mathbf{v})} = \frac{\text{prob}(\mathbf{v}, \mathbf{y})}{\sum_{\mathbf{y}} \text{prob}(\mathbf{v}, \mathbf{y})} \tag{2.5}$$

In all of the above expressions the target vector $\mathbf{y}$ can be replaced by its synonym class label k or class ω if appropriate.

The marginal distribution $\text{prob}(\mathbf{v})$ (2.2) describes the probability of occurrence of a certain $\mathbf{v}$ when the class membership is left unconsidered. The reverse expression $\text{prob}(\mathbf{y}) = \text{prob}(\mathbf{k}) = \text{prob}(\omega)$ (2.3) states the probability of occurrence of patterns belonging to class ω irrespective of how they look in terms of the measurement vector $\mathbf{v}$.

The probability $\text{prob}(\omega)$ is called *a priori probability* since that is the only

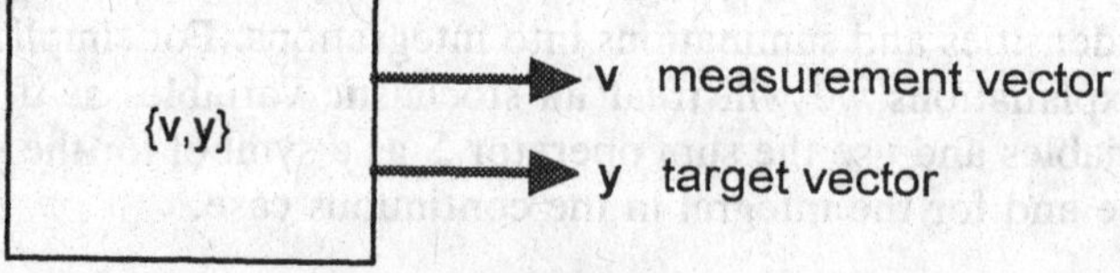

Figure 2.1. Pattern source as statistical model for pattern-generating process. Joint probability prob(**v**, **y**) matches conditions of specific application.

knowledge a recognition system has at its disposal as long as it does not know the measurement vector $\mathbf{v}$. After having taken note of how the pattern to be recognized looks, that is, with the knowledge of $\mathbf{v}$, the situation changes. The relevant probability is then the conditional probability $\text{prob}(\mathbf{y}|\mathbf{v}) = \text{prob}(k|\mathbf{v}) = \text{prob}(\omega|\mathbf{v})$ (2.5). This term is called *a posteriori probability* since it states how probable is the class ω after $\mathbf{v}$ has been observed.

The opposite conditional probability $\text{prob}(\mathbf{v}|\mathbf{y}) = \text{prob}(\mathbf{v}|k) = \text{prob}(\mathbf{v}|\omega)$ (2.4) describes how patterns look if they are known to belong to class ω. It is therefore called the *class-specific probability*.

It should be noted that the a posteriori probability (2.5) exists only for those $\mathbf{v}$ for which $\text{prob}(\mathbf{v}) > 0$ and is otherwise left completely undefined since then not only the denominator but also the numerator of (2.5) is zero. In order to allow all of the probability functions introduced above to exist for arbitrary $\mathbf{v}$, we define $\text{prob}(\mathbf{y}|\mathbf{v}) = 0$ for $\text{prob}(\mathbf{v}) = 0$.

The four probabilities are connected by *Bayes's rule*:

$$\text{prob}(\mathbf{v}, \mathbf{y}) = \text{prob}(\mathbf{y}|\mathbf{v})\text{prob}(\mathbf{v}) = \text{prob}(\mathbf{v}|\mathbf{y})\text{prob}(\mathbf{y}) \tag{2.6}$$

Again $\mathbf{y}$ may be replaced by its synonym class label k or class ω.

Bayes's rule allows us to compute the joined probability from a priori and class-specific probabilities, which is a quite common form of describing the pattern source. In contrast, Bayes's rule allows us to derive the a posteriori probability from the pattern source statistical model $\text{prob}(\mathbf{v}, \mathbf{y}) = \text{prob}(\mathbf{v}, \omega) = \text{prob}(\mathbf{v}, k)$.

Statistical independence between $\mathbf{y}$ and $\mathbf{v}$ would have the consequence that $\text{prob}(\mathbf{v}, \mathbf{y}) = \text{prob}(\mathbf{v})\text{prob}(\mathbf{y})$ and would make both a posteriori and a priori probabilities equal:

$$\text{prob}(\mathbf{y}|\mathbf{v}) = \frac{\text{prob}(\mathbf{v}, \mathbf{y})}{\text{prob}(\mathbf{v})} = \frac{\text{prob}(\mathbf{v})\text{prob}(\mathbf{y})}{\text{prob}(\mathbf{v})} = \text{prob}(\mathbf{y})$$

That means that in the case of statistical independence between $\mathbf{v}$ and $\mathbf{y}$ no pattern classifier is able to improve the knowledge about the class label k of $\mathbf{v}$ beyond what was already known before.

2.2 RISK MINIMIZATION

The decision-theoretic approach to the pattern classification problem deals with system optimization on the level of classes. The recognition system has to make decisions among the members ω of the set Ω. In order to also allow a special treatment of ambiguous cases, the possibility of *reject* is introduced, which means that any decision is refused as to which class ω the input vector $\mathbf{v}$ belongs.

A reject, however, indicates ambiguity only with respect to the set Ω of admissible classes and does not account for the situation when anything other than one of the elements of Ω may have been observed. This situation is explicitly excluded by the *closed-world assumption*.

The classifier deciding on the class membership ω of its input vector $\mathbf{v}$ may be right or wrong with its decision. We must therefore distinguish the classifier output $\hat{\omega}$ from the true class ω accompanying $\mathbf{v}$. Due to the introduction of rejection the range of $\hat{\omega}$ is given by

$$\hat{\Omega} = \Omega \cup \{\omega_0\} = \{\omega_0, \omega_1, \omega_2, \ldots, \omega_k, \ldots, \omega_K\} \tag{2.7}$$

The Cartesian product between the two sets Ω and $\hat{\Omega}$ defines the set of different constellations of ω and $\hat{\omega}$ that are able to occur. To each of it a *cost* or *loss value*

$$C(\omega, \hat{\omega}) = \text{loss} \quad \text{if pattern of class } \omega \text{ is classified as } \hat{\omega} \tag{2.8}$$

is assigned describing the loss to be suffered if just that case happens. The $K(K+1)$ loss values are entered in the *loss matrix* $\mathbf{C}$

$$\mathbf{C} = \left[\begin{array}{c|cccc} C(\omega_1, \omega_0) & C(\omega_1, \omega_1) & C(\omega_1, \omega_2) & \cdots & C(\omega_1, \omega_K) \\ C(\omega_2, \omega_0) & C(\omega_2, \omega_1) & C(\omega_2, \omega_2) & \cdots & C(\omega_2, \omega_K) \\ \vdots & \vdots & \vdots & \vdots & \vdots \\ C(\omega_K, \omega_0) & C(\omega_K, \omega_1) & C(\omega_K, \omega_2) & \cdots & C(\omega_K, \omega_K) \end{array}\right] \tag{2.9}$$

The first column of $\mathbf{C}$ holds the K reject losses whereas the rest of the matrix represents the losses for the K^2 possible interclass confusions including the K cases of correct decision.

How to fill the loss matrix $\mathbf{C}$ remains a question of the specific application. Often a simple and regular loss assignment scheme will be used, as for example,

$$\mathbf{C} = \begin{bmatrix} C_r & 0 & C_f & \cdots & C_f \\ C_r & C_f & 0 & \cdots & C_f \\ \vdots & \vdots & \vdots & \vdots & \vdots \\ C_r & C_f & C_f & \cdots & 0 \end{bmatrix} \tag{2.10}$$

where a constant loss C_f is associated with any kind of error, another smaller loss C_r with a reject, and no loss at all with a correct decision.

The possibility of arbitrary cost assignments, however, is a valuable tool for modeling applications where certain types of confusion have more undesired and more expensive consequences than others.

Based on the three conceptual entities, pattern source, classifier, and

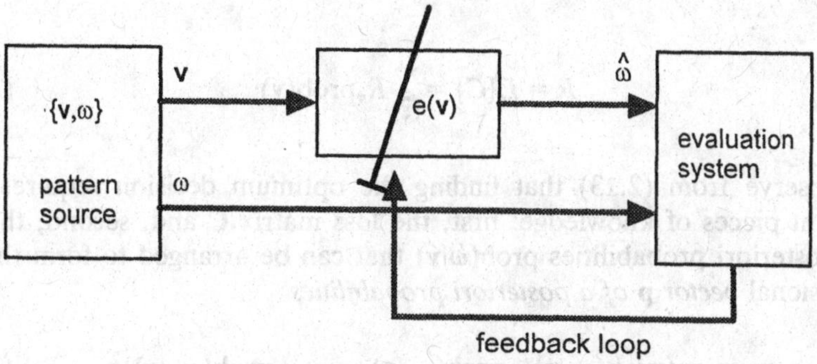

Figure 2.2. Optimization loop for finding optimum decision rule.

evaluation system—implementing the loss matrix—an optimization feedback loop is arranged with the goal of minimizing the overall classification loss (Fig. 2.2).

What is to be minimized is not the loss, which itself is a random variable driven by the stochastic pattern source, but rather the mathematical expectation $E\{\cdot\}$ of the loss, in other words, its long time average, called the *risk*:

$$R = E\{C\} = \sum_{\mathbf{v}} \sum_{\omega} C(\omega, \hat{\omega})\text{prob}(\mathbf{v}, \omega) \tag{2.11}$$

The estimated class $\hat{\omega}$ is generated by the pattern classifier by virtue of some function $\hat{\omega} = e(\mathbf{v})$. This function $e(\mathbf{v})$ is the very objective of the optimization procedure

$$R = E\{C\} = \sum_{\mathbf{v}} \sum_{\omega} C(\omega, e(\mathbf{v}))\text{prob}(\mathbf{v}, \omega)$$
$$= \sum_{\mathbf{v}} \left[\sum_{\omega} C(\omega, e(\mathbf{v}))\text{prob}(\omega|\mathbf{v}) \right] \text{prob}(\mathbf{v}) = \min_{e(\mathbf{v})} \tag{2.12}$$

What we are looking for is the risk-minimizing decision function $e(\mathbf{v})$.

The risk R as given by (2.12) is minimized whenever the expression in square brackets is minimized

$$R_{\mathbf{v}} = \sum_{\omega} C(\omega, e(\mathbf{v}))\text{prob}(\omega|\mathbf{v}) = \min_{e(\mathbf{v})} \tag{2.13}$$

We call $R_{\mathbf{v}}$ the *local risk*—the risk at position $\mathbf{v}$ in measurement space. Averaging over all of the possible values $\mathbf{v}$ renders the risk as defined in

(2.12):

$$R = E\{C\} = \sum_{\mathbf{v}} R_{\mathbf{v}} \text{prob}(\mathbf{v}) \tag{2.14}$$

We observe from (2.13) that finding the optimum decision requires two different pieces of knowledge: first, the loss matrix **C** and, second, the set of a posteriori probabilities prob($\omega|\mathbf{v}$) that can be arranged to form the K-dimensional *vector* **p** *of a posteriori probabilities*

$$\mathbf{p} = (\text{prob}(\omega_1|\mathbf{v}) \quad \text{prob}(\omega_2|\mathbf{v}) \quad \cdots \quad \text{prob}(\omega_K|\mathbf{v}))^T \tag{2.15}$$

With this vector **p** of a posteriori probabilities and the loss matrix **C** a $(K+1)$-dimensional risk vector **r** can be computed

$$\mathbf{r} = \mathbf{C}^T\mathbf{p} = \begin{bmatrix} \sum_{\omega} C(\omega, \hat{\omega} = \omega_0)\text{prob}(\omega|\mathbf{v}) \\ \sum_{\omega} C(\omega, \hat{\omega} = \omega_1)\text{prob}(\omega|\mathbf{v}) \\ \sum_{\omega} C(\omega, \hat{\omega} = \omega_2)\text{prob}(\omega|\mathbf{v}) \\ \vdots \\ \sum_{\omega} C(\omega, \hat{\omega} = \omega_K)\text{prob}(\omega|\mathbf{v}) \end{bmatrix} \tag{2.16}$$

whose $K+1$ components correspond to the $K+1$ potential decisions of the pattern classifier. In order to find the optimum decision, we have only to search the minimum component of **r** and output the corresponding $\hat{\omega}$.

The local risk $R_{\mathbf{v}}$ of (2.13) can be written shortly as

$$R_{\mathbf{v}} = \text{minimum component } [\mathbf{r}] \tag{2.17}$$

The lesson taught by these considerations is that all the optimum pattern classifier needs to know are the vector **p** of a posteriori probabilities and the scheme of losses **C** with which its decisions are evaluated. Thus the problem is solved in generality if only **p** is known since knowledge of the loss matrix **C** should be taken for granted. And whenever **p** is unknown, it must be at least approximately reconstructed from the learning sample set.

2.3 BAYES CLASSIFIER

We will now specialize on the simplified loss matrix of (2.10). The relevant loss matrix entries are

$$C(\omega, \hat{\omega}) = \begin{cases} 0 & \text{for } \hat{\omega} = \omega \quad \text{correct decision} \\ C_r & \text{for } \hat{\omega} = \omega_0 \quad \text{reject} \\ C_f & \text{otherwise} \quad \text{false decision} \end{cases} \tag{2.18}$$

With these values the risk vector of (2.16) becomes

$$\mathbf{r} = \mathbf{C}^T\mathbf{p} = \begin{bmatrix} C_r \\ C_f(1 - \text{prob}(\omega_1|\mathbf{v})) \\ C_f(1 - \text{prob}(\omega_2|\mathbf{v})) \\ \vdots \\ C_f(1 - \text{prob}(\omega_K|\mathbf{v})) \end{bmatrix} \tag{2.19}$$

This expression can be simplified further due to the fact that the rank order of a certain set of numbers is not affected by strictly monotonic mappings. The maximum remains the maximum if the mapping is monotonically increasing and is changed into the minimum if the mapping is decreasing.

By suitable monotonic operations such as multiplication with a constant term (in this case $-1/C_f$), addition of another constant (in this case $+1$) the collection of numbers to be compared for the minimum (2.19) is recalculated and the maximum is now searched among the components of the vector

$$\begin{bmatrix} 1 - \dfrac{C_r}{C_f} \\ \text{prob}(\omega_1|\mathbf{v}) \\ \text{prob}(\omega_2|\mathbf{v}) \\ \vdots \\ \text{prob}(\omega_K|\mathbf{v}) \end{bmatrix} = \begin{pmatrix} \beta \\ \mathbf{p} \end{pmatrix} \tag{2.20}$$

Therefrom we get the decision rule valid for the simple loss assignment of (2.18) and known as the *Bayes's decision rule*:

$$\text{Decide for } \hat{\omega}: \begin{cases} \text{if } (\text{prob}(\hat{\omega}|\mathbf{v}) = \max_{\omega}\{\text{prob}(\omega|\mathbf{v})\} \text{ and } \text{prob}(\hat{\omega}|\mathbf{v}) > \beta) \\ \\ \text{otherwise reject} \end{cases} \tag{2.21}$$

This is an intuitively convincing result. In the given situation, with all the evidence provided by $\mathbf{v}$, decide the most likely $\hat{\omega}$ in terms of the a posteriori probability $\text{prob}(\omega|\mathbf{v})$. The reject check tests whether the maximum a posteriori probability found is above the threshold

$$\beta = 1 - \frac{C_r}{C_f} \tag{2.22}$$

Since both C_r and C_f are positive, and by assumption $C_r < C_f$, the reject threshold β is bound to lie in the interval $\beta \in [0\,..\,1]$. The K a posteriori probabilities $\text{prob}(\omega|\mathbf{v})$ sum to 1. Hence, the minimum possible value of $\text{prob}(\hat{\omega}|\mathbf{v})$ is $1/K$. Therefore, rejects can only occur for values of β stemming from the interval

$$\frac{1}{K} \leq \beta < 1 \tag{2.23}$$

The cost assignment scheme of (2.18) evaluates every kind of substitution error with the same loss value. This is equivalent to counting the number of errors. The Bayes classifier, being optimum for this cost assignment, guarantees the minimum error rate:

- The Bayes classifier marks the reference point of optimum performance that can at best be approximated by any practical pattern classification system having no access to the true a posteriori probability distributions but instead being forced to rely on approximations.

It should be noted that the term *Bayes's classifier* is used here in a strict sense, rather than when this term is used to mean this type of classifier in combination with the assumption of class-specific normal distributions. We will discuss this type of pattern classification system later in Chapter 4.

The a posteriori probabilities needed for the optimum decision rule (2.21) can, according to (2.5), be expressed by a priori and class-specific probabilities

$$\text{prob}(\omega|\mathbf{v}) = \frac{\text{prob}(\mathbf{v}, \omega)}{\text{prob}(\mathbf{v})} = \frac{\text{prob}(\mathbf{v}|\omega)\text{prob}(\omega)}{\text{prob}(\mathbf{v})} \tag{2.24}$$

Since in this expression the nominator does not depend on the class ω, it can be discarded when substituting (2.24) in (2.21). We then get a completely equivalent form of the *Bayes decision rule*:

$$\text{Decide for } \hat{\omega}: \begin{cases} \text{if } \text{prob}(\mathbf{v}|\hat{\omega})\text{prob}(\hat{\omega}) = \max\limits_{\omega}\{\text{prob}(\mathbf{v}|\omega)\text{prob}(\omega)\} \\ \quad \text{and} \quad \text{prob}(\mathbf{v}|\hat{\omega})\text{prob}(\hat{\omega}) > \beta\,\text{prob}(\mathbf{v}) \\ \text{otherwise reject} \end{cases} \tag{2.25}$$

In this formulation the role of the a priori probability prob(ω) becomes evident. We need to know how probable the different classes are a priori. This seems at first glance to be an insignificant detail but turns out to be a difficult question to answer in many applications. Imagine that the pattern classification system is intended to be applied in an automatic fault diagnosis system. What then is the a priori probability of a system fault to occur?

Determining a priori probabilities is an intricate problem. From a practical point of view the a priori probabilities prob(ω) can hardly be distinguished from conditional probabilities prob($\omega|\mathbf{v}$). They describe the probabilities of occurrence of the different classes, but only provided we are in a situation for which they are valid. The question of whether they are valid or not finally leads to the question of whether the pattern classifier actually operates under the conditions for which it was trained.

Problems of this kind do not occur with another type of decision rule that does not contain any a priori probabilities, the *maximum-likelihood decision rule*. There are different derivations possible linking the maximum-likelihood rule with Bayes's rule.

A simple assumption is to treat the K classes ω as equiprobable. In this case the a priori probability prob(ω) is $1/K$ for each of the classes and no longer influences the decision rule (2.25) and can hence be completely omitted:

$$\text{Decide for } \hat{\omega}: \begin{cases} \text{if prob}(\mathbf{v}|\hat{\omega}) = \max\limits_{\omega}\{\text{prob}(\mathbf{v}|\omega)\} \\ \quad \text{and} \quad \text{prob}(\mathbf{v}|\hat{\omega}) > \beta K \, \text{prob}(\mathbf{v}) \\ \text{otherwise reject} \end{cases} \tag{2.26}$$

Another approach is to operate with a loss assignment scheme punishing recognition errors for rare classes with higher losses, inverse to their probability of occurrence prob(ω):

$$C(\omega, \hat{\omega}) = \begin{cases} 0 & \text{for } \hat{\omega} = \omega \quad \text{correct decision} \\ C_r & \text{for } \hat{\omega} = \omega_0 \quad \text{reject} \\ \dfrac{C_f}{K\,\text{prob}(\omega)} & \text{otherwise} \quad \text{false decision} \end{cases} \tag{2.27}$$

With respect to the decision for the K classes $\omega_1, \ldots, \omega_K$, this cost assignment has the same effect as the equal probability assumption leading to (2.26):

$$\text{Decide for } \hat{\omega}: \begin{cases} \text{if prob}(\mathbf{v}|\hat{\omega}) = \max\limits_{\omega}\{\text{prob}(\mathbf{v}|\omega)\} \\ \quad \text{and} \quad \text{prob}(\mathbf{v}|\hat{\omega}) > \sum\limits_{\omega} \text{prob}(\mathbf{v}|\omega) - K\dfrac{C_r}{C_f}\text{prob}(\mathbf{v}) \\ \text{otherwise reject} \end{cases} \tag{2.28}$$

The only difference is that the reject check comes out slightly different since in (2.27) only the loss term for false decisions is defined to be inverse proportional to prob(ω) whereas the loss term for the reject case is the same for all of the classes $\omega \in \Omega$. If in (2.27) also the reject loss is made inverse proportional to prob(ω) then again (2.26) holds.

2.4 GENERAL STRUCTURE OF PATTERN CLASSIFIER

The decision-theoretic approach provides a clear-cut guideline to classifier design. All we have to do is to compute the risk vector **r** (2.16) and search for the minimum component. With the loss assignment of (2.18) this simplifies to the sequence of three steps: first, calculation of the K a posteriori probabilities prob(ω|**v**), or equivalently the products prob(**v**|ω)prob(ω); second, a search for the maximum of these values; and third, execution of some kind of reject check.

The general structure of the pattern classification system derived from these considerations is outlined in Fig. 2.3. We use the notion of a discriminant vector **d** for the K-dimensional vector variable, the components of which are searched for maximum or minimum depending on the type of monotonic mapping applied, increasing or decreasing.

The individual class-specific discriminant functions d_k (components of the discriminant vector **d**) may be probability functions, as in the decision rules

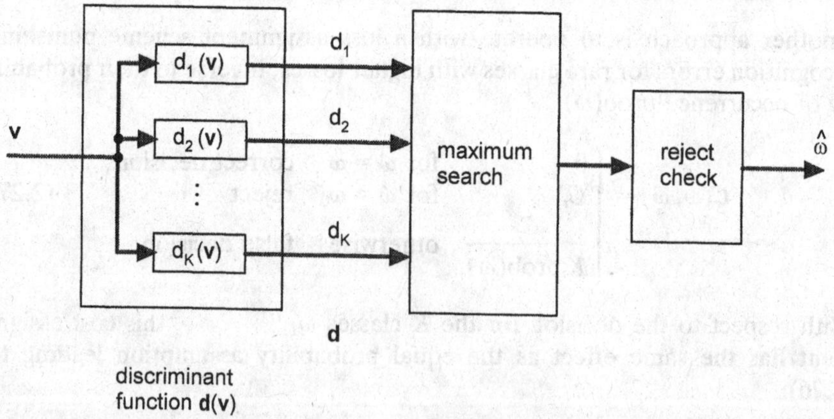

Figure 2.3. General structure of pattern classification system consisting of three steps: First step maps input vector **v** into K-dimensional discriminant vector **d**, second step finds maximum component of **d** together with its position within vector, and third step performs reject check by comparing maximum component of **d** with certain threshold. It may be necessary to replace maximum search by minimum search depending on type of monotonic mapping identically applied to all components of **d**.

of Section 2.3 or estimates thereof; risk values, as in (2.16); any other kind of class membership function; or some kind of distance-measuring function evaluating the dissimilarity of **v** with each of the K classes. The structure is general enough to embrace them all.

The first of the three steps outlined above plays the dominant role in the pattern classification system. Here it is where all the learning takes place. The search for the minimum or maximum among a given number of values in the second step is a simple and straightforward operation, as is the reject check in the last step.

It becomes obvious from Fig. 2.3 that the reject check executed in the third step can be completely separated from the first two. This allows us to postpone the discussion of the possibility of rejects and the necessary reject criteria until later. We will return to this problem in Chapter 10 and until then exclude the possibility of reject from our consideration.

The K discriminant functions $d_k(\mathbf{v})$ are in general continuous functions over the N-dimensional measurement space, which is illustrated in Fig. 2.4 for the one-dimensional case. The maximum search applied to the K discriminant functions $d_k(\mathbf{v})$ marks a whole region in measurement space as belonging to one class $\omega \in \Omega$. This region is called a *class region* or *domain* of that specific class. The class regions need not be connected but may be split into several subregions enclosed by regions of other classes. Class regions belonging to different classes are separated by *class borders* or *class boundaries*, which in the general case of an N-dimensional measurement space are $(N-1)$-dimensional, in general nonlinear, subspaces.

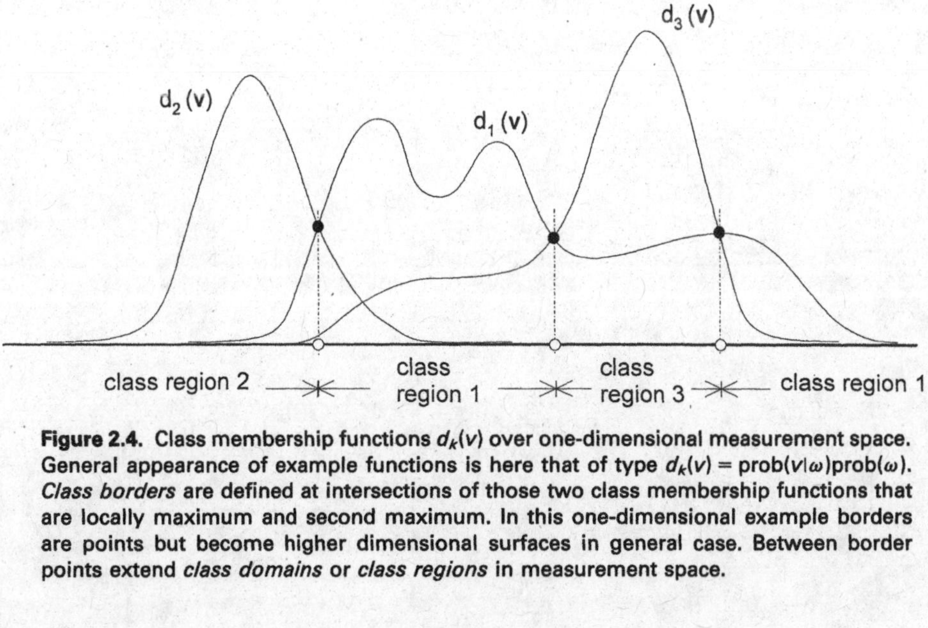

Figure 2.4. Class membership functions $d_k(v)$ over one-dimensional measurement space. General appearance of example functions is here that of type $d_k(v) = \text{prob}(v|\omega)\text{prob}(\omega)$. *Class borders* are defined at intersections of those two class membership functions that are locally maximum and second maximum. In this one-dimensional example borders are points but become higher dimensional surfaces in general case. Between border points extend *class domains* or *class regions* in measurement space.

The class membership functions $d_k(\mathbf{v})$ may or may not extend across the whole measurement space with nonzero values. Typically they have larger values only in certain regions of the measurement space and vanish in others. Special complications occur if there are regions in **V**-space, where all of the class-specific probabilities prob($\mathbf{v}|\omega$) are zero. In those regions the a posteriori probabilities prob($\omega|\mathbf{v}$) remain undefined and are arbitrarily set to zero (see Section 2.1).

The common situation is that the class membership functions penetrate each other, which makes classification errors principally unavoidable since then the same point $\mathbf{v}$ in measurement space belongs with nonzero probability to more than one class $\omega \in \Omega$. It is the achievement of the decision-theoretic approach to provide a solution for exactly that case and to minimize the resulting error rate.

3 NEED FOR APPROXIMATIONS: FUNDAMENTAL APPROACHES

The foregoing considerations were based on the assumption that the stochastic laws ruling the pattern source are known. For that case the solution is simple and already given in Section 2.3. In all practical cases these laws are just not known. What is known then is a collection of learning samples drawn from the application.

When probability laws are given, we possess a model pattern source that can be used to generate unlimited numbers of synthetic patterns fully representative of the application. However, what we are facing here is just the inverse problem. What we are given is a certain number of incarnations, namely those taken more or less randomly from the real application as the learning sample set, and what we have to do is try to recover the unknown probability laws of the statistical model from this learning set.

The situation at this point of the discussion is not as unfamiliar as it at first glance may seem. There are many examples where our conceptions are based on some continuous function but all we have at hand is a selection of points taken from that function. Recovering the continuous function from the given set of sample points is the task of interpolation, or to a certain degree extrapolation, and this has much in common with the task of *learning* in pattern classification.

Think of the way one- or two-dimensional continuous functions are represented by sequences or arrays of numbers for the purpose of digital signal processing. In that case, the samples are typically taken at regular intervals along the coordinate axes and the conditions are known under which the continuous functions can be recovered from the sample points without any error. The sampling theorem of information theory [GAL1968] states precisely these conditions.

The task of reconstructing probability laws from the learning sample set in pattern classification has certain peculiarities making it somewhat more complicated than reconstructing continuous functions from their sampled versions in digital signal processing. The dominant impediments come, first, from the difference in dimensionality, second, from the fact that the samples are taken at random and not at regular intervals and, third, from a normally small learning set size compared with the wide variety of potential incarnations $\{\mathbf{v}\}$ the pattern source is able to render—sparse sampling.

The learning set is only a small selection taken at random from the often infinite or practically infinite set of potential pattern vectors $\{\mathbf{v}\}$. Another random selection of the same size taken from the same pattern source would have a quite different content. With respect to *generalization*, this fact raises the question of the degree of reliable learning from learning sets of limited size, in other words, how large the learning set size must be for sufficiently perfect learning.

We know from Sections 2.1 and 2.3 that the probability laws governing the pattern source can be written differently and that there exist two equivalent versions of the optimum decision rule, (2.21) making use of the a posteriori probabilities prob($\omega|\mathbf{v}$) and (2.25) making use of the product of class-specific probabilities prob($\mathbf{v}|\omega$) and a priori probabilities prob(ω).

Since the a priori probabilities prob(ω) are either simply set to $1/K$ or otherwise replaced by plausible estimates the main task left is to build up approximations for either

(a) a posteriori probabilities prob($\omega|\mathbf{v}$) or
(b) class-specific probabilities prob($\mathbf{v}|\omega$)

from the learning set. Depending on the starting point chosen, (a) or (b), the development of learning algorithms is driven into quite different directions.

Approach (a), approximating the a posteriori probabilities prob($\omega|\mathbf{v}$), is optimally suited for functional approximations. We will see in Section 3.1 that developing regression functions with the goal of estimating $\mathbf{y}$ from $\mathbf{v}$ directly results in estimations for prob($\mathbf{y}|\mathbf{v}$) $\equiv$ prob($\omega|\mathbf{v}$). The concept of functional approximation needs a set of basis functions, and there are many different choices possible.

We will follow two ways, using two different families of basis functions: polynomials (in Chapter 6), leading to *polynomial regression*, and multilayer perceptron basis functions (in Chapter 7), leading to *multilayer perceptron regression*. In both cases learning is accomplished by parameter adjustment whereby the parameters are the coefficients of the linear combination and possibly parameters controlling the appearance of the basis functions themselves.

In contrast, approach (b), approximating the class-specific probabilities prob($\mathbf{v}|\omega$), is optimally suited for working with established statistical models such as the multidimensional Gaussian model for representing the class-specific stochastic processes $\{\mathbf{v}|\omega\}$.

Learning, in this case, is accomplished by parameter fitting such that certain statistical moments of the statistical model become equal to the empirical moments as they are observed in the learning set. Making use of certain mathematical simplifications, a whole variety of *distance-measuring pattern classification techniques* can therefrom be derived. This kind of approach is introduced in Section 3.2 and treated in more detail in Chapter 4.

A third approach, applicable to both goals (a) and (b) of approximating prob($\omega|\mathbf{v}$) or prob($\mathbf{v}|\omega$) from the learning set, is the *radial basis functions* approach combining aspects of both of the above two techniques.

Radial basis functions are unimodal local functions in **V**-space centered at arbitrary points $\mathbf{r} \in \mathbf{V}$ and vanishing with increasing distance between **r** and **v**. By linear combination of a whole set of such radial basis functions with different centers **r** and possibly different decay functions, estimates for prob($\omega|\mathbf{v}$) can be gained following the functional approximation approach.

Radial basis functions, however, may also be viewed as statistical models representing subsets of the class-specific stochastic process $\{\mathbf{v}|\omega\}$ (submodels). This is especially interesting since typically Gaussian kernels are chosen to construct these functions. The approximation for prob($\mathbf{v}|\omega$) is then gained from linear combination of the individual submodels. We will return to this approach in Chapter 8.

The following sections of this chapter introduce the fundamental approaches of least mean-square functional approximation, statistical modeling of class-specific distributions, and minimum-distance classification and discuss their general properties.

In Chapter 4 we will discuss in some detail statistical modeling applied to the pattern classification problem. This discussion serves a twofold purpose. First, considering the statistical model as the true description of the pattern classification task, it provides a reference solution for comparison with the approximate solutions to be treated in the chapters to follow. Second, the approach renders approximate solutions if the statistical model is known not to be valid but is treated as if it is.

3.1 LEAST MEAN-SQUARE FUNCTIONAL APPROXIMATIONS

The basic idea of functional approximation is easily explained. Consider the simple case of two scalar variables v and y. We are given a set of examples in the form of the pair $[v, y]$ showing how y is related to v and we want to fit a continuous function $d(v)$ to the given set of samples (see Fig. 3.1). To do this task, $d(v)$ must be taken from an appropriate family of functions capable of being formed to assume the desired shape under the control of some suitable optimization criterion.

The most widely used optimization criterion is the least mean square.

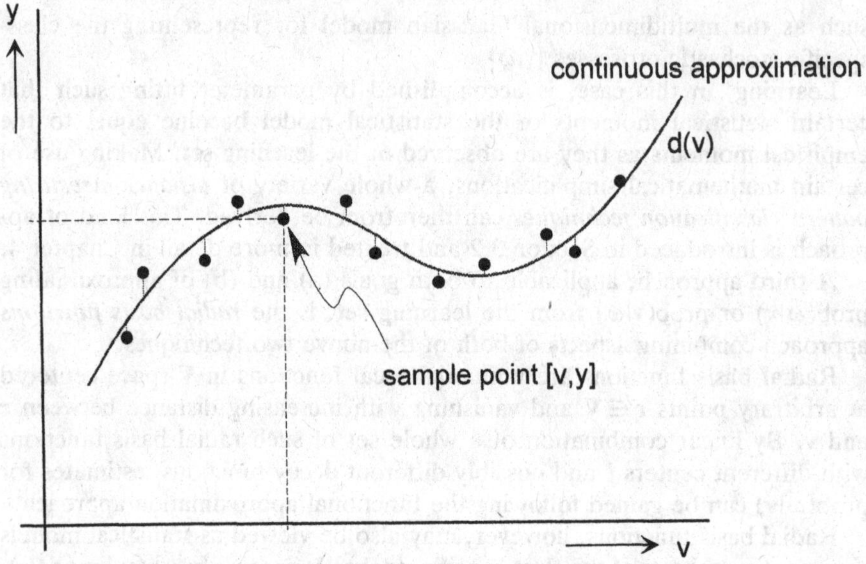

Figure 3.1. Functional approximation. Relation between two variables v and y as described by given set of examples $[v, y]$ is approximately represented by continuous function $d(v)$.

With $d(v)$ a member of the family of linear functions we arrive at the concept of *linear regression*, which is a standard operation on every scientific pocket calculator. This concept is easily generalized to *nonlinear regression*. The example of Fig. 3.1 corresponds to cubic regression.

The same concept works also for pattern classification tasks with the difference that in pattern classification $\mathbf{v}$ and $\mathbf{y}$ are vector variables. It should also be mentioned that for most pattern classification applications nonlinearity of the mapping $\mathbf{d}(\mathbf{v})$ is crucial. These circumstances make the mathematical procedures somewhat more complicated. The principles, however, remain the same.

Least mean-square optimization is only one of the possible optimization criteria that may be applied to the problem of functional approximation. It has the advantage of leading to systems of linear equations when the approximating function $d(v)$ is built up as a linear combination from a set of given basis functions. Throughout this book we will concentrate on least mean-square optimization since this is of utmost importance in the practical application of pattern classification.

Hard and Soft Labeling

We have stated above that the concept of functional approximation is optimally suited for approximating the K unknown a posteriori probabilities prob(ω|**v**). These are the components of the vector **p** of a posteriori probabilities (2.15):

$$\mathbf{p} = (\text{prob}(\omega_1|\mathbf{v}) \quad \text{prob}(\omega_2|\mathbf{v}) \quad \cdots \quad \text{prob}(\omega_K|\mathbf{v}))^T$$

so that our goal is to recover the function **p**(**v**) from the given learning set. If the learning set would be composed of pairs [**v**, **p**] this would be a straightforward interpolation and extrapolation task.

But the learning set here is composed of pairs [**v**, **y**], whereby **v** describes how the pattern looks and **y** what it means in the sense of to which class it belongs. This fact makes our task somewhat different from interpolation and extrapolation, and we are led to the question what really is the difference between using {**v**, **y**} or {**v**, **p**} as a learning set. Let us therefore look into the roles the variables **p** and **y** play in this context and what we are going to do.

Both **y** and **p** represent the class membership of **v** but in a quite different way. Whereas the target vector **y** represents a *hard labeling* scheme stating that **v** belongs to one of the K classes and to none of the others, **p** does just the same but in a *soft labeling* mode with the ability of expressing ambiguities. In other words, the difference between the two is that **y** distinctly marks to which of the K classes in Ω the pattern **v** belongs whereas **p** reflects the fuzziness of the pattern classification task and tells us about the likelihood of **v** to come from any of the different classes contained in Ω.

Following the concept of functional approximation (compare also Fig. 1.6), what we are going to do here is to recover or at least approximate **p**(**v**) from observations **y**(**v**) as contained in the learning sample set {**v**, **y**}. At first glance it is not so clear that fitting a continuous function **d**(**v**) into the given collection of points {**v**, **y**} will render **p**(**v**); however, we will soon see that this is indeed the case; see (3.10).

In this context often the question is raised whether it would not be advantageous to use some kind of soft labeling to explicitly express the ambiguities of the specific pattern classification task. We will return to this point later in Section 6.3. In the following we will discuss how labeling is at all possible in practical applications and which variations exist.

From the strict viewpoint of learning nothing else seems to be possible than to rely on hard labeling and to deal with patterns as pairs [**v**, **y**]. These pairs are taken from the application, and within the application the intended meaning should be definitely clear.

Think, for example, of the recognition of spoken words and of a learning sample collected from human speakers. When uttering a word the speaker has a certain intended meaning in mind. This intention is coded into the target vector **y** and the utterance itself is coded, after suitable signal processing, into the measurement vector **v**. We call the process of labeling patterns according to the intended meaning *labeling by intention*.

At the time of generation of this pattern [**v**, **y**] it is completely unknown whether earlier or later in the process of collecting the learning sample a pattern may be uttered with identical measurement vector **v** but with a different intended meaning. Ambiguities of this kind can become noticeable only after a statistical analysis, that is, after learning has taken place.

There are, however, applications where we are given observations **v** but do not know the true class membership **y**. But there are human experts capable of producing reliable guesses with respect to the true class membership (in many applications, such as in speech or script recognition, almost everybody is an expert).

Consider the above example of speech recognition and the case that all we have is a tape with the recorded utterances and we are unable to ask the test person what he or she really had in mind for each of the utterances. A human listener, however, can hear the recorded words and label them according to what was understood. This kind of labeling is called *labeling by guess*, and the human expert providing the label is the *teacher* from which the pattern classifier learns.

It is then possible to recover the true meaning only to the degree to which the teacher is able to do so. When using the guess to generate the target vector **y**, the teacher's error is introduced into the learning process. The pattern classifier trained from such a learning sample can at best approach the performance of its teacher.

In this situation of labeling by guess, the teacher generally knows about the possible conflicts. Thus it is at least imaginable that he or she provides not the hard label **y** but a soft label in the form of a guess on the vector **p** of a posteriori probabilities.

Regression Function

After this short excursion into the problem of pattern labeling we return to the task of functional approximation with the pattern being a pair:

$$\text{Pattern} = [\mathbf{v}, \mathbf{y}]$$

where **v** is the measurement vector and **y** the target vector indicating the true class membership. What we are now looking for is a function **d(v)** able to recover **y** if only **v** is known (Fig. 3.2).

The most general way of selecting an estimating function **d(v)** for functional fitting is to take **d(v)** from the family of arbitrary functions of **v** and to search among them for that individual function that best complies with the *least mean-square* criterion

$$S^2 = E\{|\mathbf{d}(\mathbf{v}) - \mathbf{y}|^2\} = \min_{\mathbf{d}(\mathbf{v})} \tag{3.1}$$

From the mathematical point of view (3.1) defines a problem in the calculus of variations.

The solution is found starting from the assumption that **d** would already

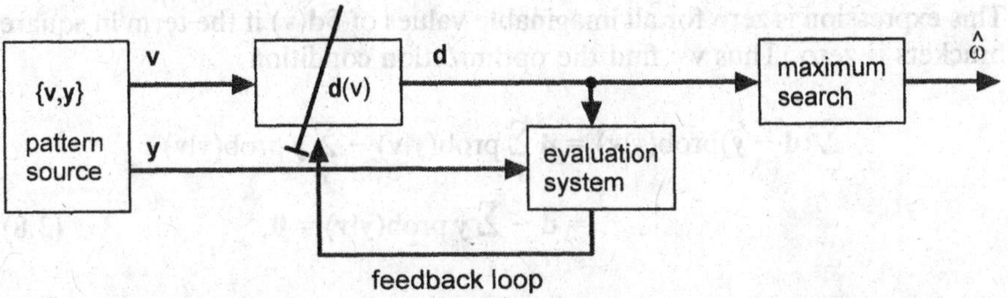

Figure 3.2. Least mean-square optimization of estimating function **d(v)** based on stochastic law prob(**v**, **y**) ruling pattern source. Figure resembles fundamental optimization loop of Fig. 2.2, but here operations of pattern classifier are broken into two steps of first functional approximation and second decision, as in Fig. 1.5, and optimization loop includes only estimating function **d(v)** and not entire system.

be the optimum with the consequence that any deviation $\delta\mathbf{d}$ must result in degradation of the optimization criterion

$$S^2(\mathbf{d} + \delta\mathbf{d}) > S^2(\mathbf{d}) \qquad \text{for all } \forall\, \delta\mathbf{d} \neq \mathbf{0} \tag{3.2}$$

In (3.2) both **d** and $\delta\mathbf{d}$ are functions of **v**. We use (3.1) to express both sides of the inequality (3.2) and get

$$\begin{aligned} S^2(\mathbf{d} + \delta\mathbf{d}) &= E\{|\mathbf{d} + \delta\mathbf{d} - \mathbf{y}|^2\} \\ &= E\{|\mathbf{d} - \mathbf{y}|^2\} - 2E\{\delta\mathbf{d}^T(\mathbf{d} - \mathbf{y})\} + E\{|\delta\mathbf{d}|^2\} \end{aligned} \tag{3.3}$$

$$S^2(\mathbf{d}) = E\{|\mathbf{d} - \mathbf{y}|^2\} \tag{3.4}$$

Inserting this in (3.2) results in the inequality

$$E\{|\delta\mathbf{d}|^2\} - 2E\{\delta\mathbf{d}^T(\mathbf{d} - \mathbf{y})\} > 0 \qquad \forall\, \delta\mathbf{d} \neq \mathbf{0} \tag{3.5}$$

which is necessarily satisfied if the second term vanishes. Hence we find the optimization condition defining the optimum estimation function $\mathbf{d}(\mathbf{v})$:

$$E\{\delta\mathbf{d}^T(\mathbf{d} - \mathbf{y})\} = \mathbf{0} \tag{3.6}$$

The mathematical expectation of (3.6) refers to the stochastic law prob(**v**, **y**) of the pattern source; hence

$$\begin{aligned} E\{\delta\mathbf{d}^T(\mathbf{d} - \mathbf{y})\} &= \sum_{\mathbf{v}} \sum_{\mathbf{y}} \delta\mathbf{d}^T(\mathbf{d} - \mathbf{y})\,\text{prob}(\mathbf{v}, \mathbf{y}) \\ &= \sum_{\mathbf{v}} \delta\mathbf{d}^T\left[\sum_{\mathbf{y}} (\mathbf{d} - \mathbf{y})\,\text{prob}(\mathbf{y}|\mathbf{v})\right]\text{prob}(\mathbf{v}) = \mathbf{0} \end{aligned} \tag{3.7}$$

This expression is zero for all imaginable values of $\delta\mathbf{d}(\mathbf{v})$ if the term in square brackets is zero. Thus we find the optimization condition

$$\begin{aligned}\sum_{\mathbf{y}} (\mathbf{d} - \mathbf{y})\text{prob}(\mathbf{y}|\mathbf{v}) &= \mathbf{d} \sum_{\mathbf{y}} \text{prob}(\mathbf{y}|\mathbf{v}) - \sum_{\mathbf{y}} \mathbf{y}\,\text{prob}(\mathbf{y}|\mathbf{v}) \\ &= \mathbf{d} - \sum_{\mathbf{y}} \mathbf{y}\,\text{prob}(\mathbf{y}|\mathbf{v}) = \mathbf{0} \end{aligned} \tag{3.8}$$

The optimum estimation function, with respect to (3.1), is the so-called *regression function*

$$\mathbf{d}(\mathbf{v}) = \sum_{\mathbf{y}} \mathbf{y}\,\text{prob}(\mathbf{y}|\mathbf{v}) = E\{\mathbf{y}|\mathbf{v}\} \tag{3.9}$$

The result of (3.9) has an intuitively convincing interpretation: It simply refers to the fact that among a set of vectors $\{\mathbf{y}\}$ the mean $E\{\mathbf{y}\}$ has the property of being in the average $E\{|\mathbf{y} - E\{\mathbf{y}\}|^2\}$ closest to all members of the set. Equation (3.9) states the same fact for the conditional stochastic process of $\{\mathbf{y}|\mathbf{v}\}$.

This result is valid for any arbitrary choice of the target vector $\mathbf{y}$ since we have so far made no use at all of the special arrangements laid down in (1.5). However, with the special convention that the target vector $\mathbf{y}$ is K-dimensional with only one of its components equal to 1 and all the others equal to 0, the regression function simplifies to the *vector* $\mathbf{p}$ of *a posteriori probabilities* as defined in (2.15):

$$\begin{aligned}\mathbf{d}(\mathbf{v}) &= \sum_{\mathbf{y}} \mathbf{y}\,\text{prob}(\mathbf{y}|\mathbf{v}) \\ &= \begin{pmatrix}1\\0\\ \vdots \\0\end{pmatrix}\text{prob}(\omega_1|\mathbf{v}) + \begin{pmatrix}0\\1\\ \vdots \\0\end{pmatrix}\text{prob}(\omega_2|\mathbf{v}) + \cdots + \begin{pmatrix}0\\0\\ \vdots \\1\end{pmatrix}\text{prob}(\omega_K|\mathbf{v}) \\ &= \begin{pmatrix}\text{prob}(\omega_1|\mathbf{v})\\ \text{prob}(\omega_2|\mathbf{v})\\ \vdots \\ \text{prob}(\omega_K|\mathbf{v})\end{pmatrix} = \mathbf{p}\end{aligned} \tag{3.10}$$

Comment

This result is worth a comment: We started the undertaking of building an approximation for $\text{prob}(\omega|\mathbf{v})$ with the concern of whether the target vector

y would be the appropriate goal to rely on for the estimation. This question is now positively settled:

- Least mean-square approximation of a function $\mathbf{d}(\mathbf{v})$ to $\mathbf{y}$ renders the vector of a posteriori probabilities $\mathbf{p}$.

Relations between Minimum Distance and Maximum A Posteriori Decisions

When looking back on the achievements reached so far we note that a little incoherence seems to be left; compare Figs. 1.5 and 2.3. In Chapter 1 it was stated that the general structure of the pattern classifier would consist of the two steps functional approximation $\mathbf{d}(\mathbf{v})$ and minimum-distance classification $\min\{|\mathbf{d} - \mathbf{y}|\}$ (Fig. 1.5). In contrast, we arrive here at the result that the optimum classifier consists of the two steps estimation $\mathbf{d}(\mathbf{v})$ followed by search for the maximum component of $\mathbf{d}$ (Fig. 2.3).

It is easily shown that this is no contradiction at all.

Therefore, we calculate the K distances r_k^2 between the estimation $\mathbf{d}$ and the set of K target vectors $\{\mathbf{y}_k\}$:

$$r_k^2 = |\mathbf{d} - \mathbf{y}_k|^2 = |\mathbf{d}|^2 - 2\mathbf{y}_k^T\mathbf{d} + |\mathbf{y}_k|^2 \tag{3.11}$$

According to (1.5) each of the $\mathbf{y}_k$ has unity length and only the kth component with value 1 and all the others with values 0. This results in

$$r_k^2 = 1 + |\mathbf{d}|^2 - 2d_k \tag{3.12}$$

Equation (3.12) defines a strictly monotonic decreasing mapping between r_k^2 and d_k, which leaves, apart from reversing the direction, the rank order among the K values $\{d_k\}$ unaffected.

Thus, searching for the minimum of $\{r_k^2\}$ is equivalent to searching for the maximum of $\{d_k\}$ for $k \in \{1, \ldots, K\}$.

Need for Approximations

What we have gained so far from the functional approximation point of view (3.1) with which we started is a nice result fitting fully into our conceptual framework. But a thorough look at (3.10) shows that what we found is somewhat puzzling. We observe that the optimum estimation function $\mathbf{d}(\mathbf{v})$ established in this way consists of just those a posteriori probabilities $\text{prob}(\omega|\mathbf{v})$ for which we started to search practicable approximations.

This result, however, provides a most valuable insight since it shows that least mean-square functional approximation is able to render the optimum discriminant function $\mathbf{d}(\mathbf{v}) = \mathbf{p}(\mathbf{v})$ if only $\mathbf{d}(\mathbf{v})$ is taken from a sufficiently general family of functions. Remember that we started with the choice of

$\mathbf{d}(\mathbf{v})$ being any arbitrary function of $\mathbf{v}$ and ended thus with an optimization problem belonging to the field of calculus of variations.

This was the least restrictive conceivable choice, and under these circumstances least mean-square optimization exactly reaches the goal.

For practical purposes we are bound to take $\mathbf{d}(\mathbf{v})$ from less powerful families of functions but with the property of being practically treatable. This leads us to use such functions $\mathbf{d}(\mathbf{v})$ being composed of a set of suitably selected basis functions and containing a more or less large number of free coefficients by which the actual appearance of the function can be properly tailored.

The most common constructions of this type are the following:

- Polynomial functions
- Multilayer perceptron functions
- Radial basis functions

We will deal with these functions separately in Chapters 6–8.

One fact, however, deserves to be noted at this point in the discussion: Any type of functional approximation based on the least mean-square approach of (3.1) effectively renders some kind of approximation to the optimum estimation function $\mathbf{d}(\mathbf{v}) = \mathbf{p}(\mathbf{v})$ [regression function (3.10)] subject to the restrictions of the family of functions chosen for constructing the estimation.

3.2 STATISTICAL MODELING OF CLASS-SPECIFIC DISTRIBUTIONS

We have stated at the beginning of this chapter that there were two equivalent ways of constructing approximations to the unknown stochastic laws ruling the application: either to approximate $\text{prob}(\omega|\mathbf{v})$, as we have tried to do above, or to approximate the reverse probability, the class-specific probability $\text{prob}(\mathbf{v}|\omega)$.

The learning sample is a collection of pairs $[\mathbf{v}, \mathbf{y}]$. For the purpose of the considerations to follow it is convenient to use the class label k instead of the target vector $\mathbf{y}$ for characterizing class membership ω. Therefore, the pattern in this context is represented by the pair of values

$$\text{Pattern} = [\mathbf{v}, k]$$

The total learning set $\{\mathbf{v}, k\}$ can, by sorting with respect to k, easily be divided into K subsets,

$$\{\mathbf{v}|k\} = \text{class-specific learning set, subset of total learning set}$$

each containing incarnations $[\mathbf{v}|k]$ of only one of the classes $k = 1, \ldots, K$.

The class-specific probability $\text{prob}(\mathbf{v}|\omega) \equiv \text{prob}(\mathbf{v}|k)$ we are looking for tells how these patterns of class k are distributed in measurement space. This task would be rather simple if the dimension of the measurement space $\mathbf{V}$ would be small, say 1 or 2, which, however, is rarely true.

One common approach particularly useful in these low-dimensional cases is to divide the range of possible values into regular intervals and to collect *histograms* showing how often $[\mathbf{v}|k]$ falls into each of the bins. Then, in a second step continuous functions can be fitted to the measured histogram counts rendering empirical model distribution functions that approximate $\text{prob}(\mathbf{v}|k)$. We will pick up this idea again in Chapter 8.

Seen from the viewpoint of practical realizability, there is one problem with the histogram approach, namely, that the number of histogram bins grows exponentially with the dimension N of the measurement space. Imagine that each of the N coordinate axes is divided into 10 intervals, which would be rather sparse for $N = 1$ or $N = 2$. For a typical pattern classification task N is on the order of 1 to several hundreds, which would lead to the gigantic and absolutely unrealistic number of 10^N histogram bins.

The curse of *dimensionality* has similarly dramatic effects on other conceivable approaches. Whereas for one-dimensional random variables numerous different types of probability functions can be found in statistics textbooks, for high-dimensional variables almost solely the N-dimensional normal distribution is left, and for larger values of N even this can only be handled in a simplified form.

Thus, a common way of modeling class-specific probabilities in N-space is to assume *normal distributions* (*Gaussian distributions*):

$$N(\mathbf{v}, \boldsymbol{\mu}, \mathbf{K}) = \frac{1}{\sqrt{(2\pi)^N \det \mathbf{K}}} \exp[-\tfrac{1}{2}(\mathbf{v} - \boldsymbol{\mu})^T \mathbf{K}^{-1} (\mathbf{v} - \boldsymbol{\mu})] \qquad (3.13)$$

The notation $N(\mathbf{v}, \boldsymbol{\mu}, \mathbf{K})$ with the three arguments $\mathbf{v}$, $\boldsymbol{\mu}$, and $\mathbf{K}$ expresses the fact that, on the one hand, $N(\mathbf{v}, \boldsymbol{\mu}, \mathbf{K})$ is the probability density function of some random variable $\mathbf{v}$ and therefore must have $\mathbf{v}$ as its argument and, on the other hand, the specific form of this density function $N(\mathbf{v}, \boldsymbol{\mu}, \mathbf{K})$ is determined by the two parameters mean vector $\boldsymbol{\mu}$ and covariance matrix $\mathbf{K}$. These two parameters allow us to position the center of $N(\mathbf{v}, \boldsymbol{\mu}, \mathbf{K})$—the point of maximum probability density—anywhere in N-space and to control the width together with the form of the density function. We will discuss this type of distribution in more detail in Section 4.1.

For the purpose of the present discussion it suffices to describe the K different class-specific probabilities by K normal distribution functions each with its own set of parameters $\boldsymbol{\mu}_k$, $\mathbf{K}_k$:

$$\text{prob}(\mathbf{v}|k) = N(\mathbf{v}, \boldsymbol{\mu}_k, \mathbf{K}_k) \qquad (3.14)$$

If one single distribution of the type (3.13) is not flexible enough to fit the empirical distribution of the corresponding class k to the desired degree of precision, then a *linear combination* of a certain, usually small, number of normal distribution functions can be employed to render a better fitting mixture distribution. This possibility is considered in Section 8.3.

Whereas in the case of modeling prob($\mathbf{v}|k$) by one single normal distribution the estimation of the parameters $\boldsymbol{\mu}$ and $\mathbf{K}$ is a straightforward task and is performed by calculating *sample mean* and *sample covariance* as simple arithmetic averages from the class-specific learning set, the task of fitting mixture distributions is much more complicated. It leads to nested optimization loops but can be speeded up by suitable design decisions about the number of component distributions or about their respective positions $\boldsymbol{\mu}_i$ and covariance matrices $\mathbf{K}_i$.

This task of modeling, based on mixture distributions, introduces the aspect of *unsupervised learning* into the otherwise completely *supervised task* of *learning from examples*. The *decomposition of a given distribution* into component distributions is a specific pattern classification task of its own.

In a certain sense the notion of a *subclass* is introduced here. Since the decomposition shall be performed automatically, without a teacher's intervention, the labeling of members of a certain class as members of one of the subclasses is not given beforehand but must be found during the decomposition process. This process of automatically finding subclasses within the learning set $\{\mathbf{v}|k\}$ of one single class k is called *clustering*. These ideas will be taken up in Section 8.2.

3.3 MINIMUM-DISTANCE CLASSIFICATION

We have already seen that minimum-distance classification is an integral part of any pattern classification system. The general two-stage pattern classifier of Fig. 1.5 consists of two modules: functional approximation and minimum-distance decision. Both are essential in making the whole system effective, but the question remains of how to organize the task sharing between them, whether the first or second module has to carry the major part of the workload.

The task assignment between the two stages resulting from our foregoing consideration put the main workload on the functional approximation module and left for the decision module only the comparably simple task of searching the maximum among a set of numbers (Fig. 2.3). This result was the consequence of an optimization-directed systematic approach founded on the prerequisite of sufficient knowledge about to the stochastic properties of the pattern source, either given in the form of probability laws ruling the pattern source or approximately gained from the learning sample.

However, when it comes to approximations, because the optimum solution turns out to be unachievable, a completely new situation is encountered, and it is also appropriate to reconsider task sharing between the two modules of

Fig. 1.5. Indeed, in the extreme case the functional approximation can be completely left out—replaced by the identity mapping—and the decision searched directly in measurement space **V** by applying suitable distance metrics.

At first glance, minimum-distance classification as derived from this point of view seems to open a whole new field of approaches. Actually, however, it is tightly related to the techniques already developed in the foregoing section on statistical modeling of class-specific distributions (Section 3.2).

Remember the functional form of the normal distribution given in (3.13), which is frequently employed for modeling the class-specific probability prob($\mathbf{v}|k$). This probability function represents the probability of **v** being a member of class k. We observe that it is determined by the quadratic form

$$Q = (\mathbf{v} - \boldsymbol{\mu})^T \mathbf{K}^{-1} (\mathbf{v} - \boldsymbol{\mu})$$

in the exponent of the exponential function exp(·).

This quadratic form Q can be regarded as a distance metric, measuring the distance between the measurement vector **v** to be classified and a reference vector $\boldsymbol{\mu}$. The distance measured is non-Euclidean since those points in measurement space **V**, being equidistant to the reference $\boldsymbol{\mu}$, lie on an elliptic instead of a circular hull around $\boldsymbol{\mu}$.

This non-Euclidean metric is called the *Mahalanobis metric* and the corresponding minimum-distance classifier the *Mahalanobis classifier*, to be distinguished from the *Euclidean classifier*, which relies simply on the squared Euclidean norm as its distance metric [DUH1973]:

$$Q = (\mathbf{v} - \boldsymbol{\mu})^T (\mathbf{v} - \boldsymbol{\mu}) = |\mathbf{v} - \boldsymbol{\mu}|^2$$

In Section 3.2 we have considered the possibility of decomposing the class-specific distribution into several subclass distributions that can again be modeled by normal distribution functions. In terms of minimum-distance classification this approach leads to the so-called *multireference minimum distance classifier* with each of the subclasses contributing one of the multireferences.

The principal idea of distance measuring can easily be elaborated on by referring to application-dependent heuristics and by developing distance measures that are more sophisticated than simple Euclidean or Mahalanobis distances. We will not go into these details. It is sufficient to have shown how the numerous ideas of approaching the goal of minimum error rate pattern classification are related and that their right to exist derives from the fact that the optimum solution can only be approached by some kind of approximation.

4

CLASSIFICATION BASED ON STATISTICAL MODELS DETERMINED BY FIRST- AND SECOND-ORDER STATISTICAL MOMENTS

In this chapter we will follow the approach of modeling prob($\mathbf{v}|k$) and will use the N-dimensional normal distribution for that purpose. There are two different motivations possible for doing so. The first one is that outlined already in Section 3.2: We are facing a practical problem described by the learning set {$\mathbf{v}$, k} and have no knowledge at all about the underlying stochastic properties of the pattern source. Especially, there exists no theoretical justification that the class-specific probabilities prob($\mathbf{v}|k$) are of the type considered, but we treat them as if they were and let the practical success decide whether this assumption was sensible or not. It should be marked that this pragmatic approach may work well even in situations where the assumption that all the prob($\mathbf{v}|k$) are normally distributed is considerably violated.

The second motivation is that we intend to investigate a model situation for which we really know the probabilities prob($\mathbf{v}|k$). From this point of view the class-specific probabilities we will consider really are the true ones. Since we thus know all we need to know, we are able to apply the optimum decision rules of Chapter 2 and to derive from them the optimum classifier.

In such a situation it is indeed interesting to explore how the optimum classifier looks and how it is able to cope with the considered pattern classification problem. Additionally, this approach provides us with an optimum reference system, a kind of gauge, to compare the different approximate approaches that will be developed in subsequent chapters.

This synthetic model situation is the point of view we will adopt in this chapter.

4.1 MULTIDIMENSIONAL NORMAL DISTRIBUTION

The N-dimensional normal distribution was already given in (3.13),

$$N(\mathbf{v}, \boldsymbol{\mu}, \mathbf{K}) = \frac{1}{\sqrt{(2\pi)^N \det K}} \exp[-\tfrac{1}{2}(\mathbf{v} - \boldsymbol{\mu})^T \mathbf{K}^{-1}(\mathbf{v} - \boldsymbol{\mu})]$$

where $N(\mathbf{v}, \boldsymbol{\mu}, \mathbf{K})$ is the probability density function of an N-dimensional continuous vector variable $\mathbf{v}$ [RAO1973].

For $N = 1$ this reduces to the well-known one-dimensional Gaussian distribution

$$N(v, \mu, \sigma^2) = \frac{1}{\sqrt{2\pi}\sigma} \exp\left[-\frac{1}{2}\left(\frac{v - \mu}{\sigma}\right)^2\right] \tag{4.1}$$

with its bell-shaped form, one single peak at $v = \mu$ and the smooth decay to both sides of the maximum but nowhere really vanishing in the range $[-\infty < v < +\infty]$, at least not in the mathematical sense (see Fig. 4.1).

Mean μ and *variance* σ^2 are the first- and second-order statistical moments of the random process $\{v\}$:

$$\mu = E\{v\} \qquad \text{mean value of } \{v\} \tag{4.2}$$

$$\sigma^2 = E\{|v - \mu|^2\} \qquad \text{variance of } \{v\} \tag{4.3}$$

The square root $\sigma = \sqrt{E\{|v - \mu|^2\}}$ of the variance is called the *standard deviation*.

The N-dimensional normal distribution looks, with the necessary generalizations, quite similar. This distribution function again is *unimodal* (it exhibits one single peak in $\mathbf{V}$-space positioned at $\mathbf{v} = \boldsymbol{\mu}$) and decays in all directions from $\boldsymbol{\mu}$ according to the exponential law of (3.13) but does not really vanish to $N(\mathbf{v}, \boldsymbol{\mu}, \mathbf{K}) = 0$ at any point of the measurement space $\mathbf{V}$. The N-dimensional appearance of this distribution is determined by the quadratic form $Q = (\mathbf{v} - \boldsymbol{\mu})^T \mathbf{K}^{-1}(\mathbf{v} - \boldsymbol{\mu})$ in the argument of the exponential function.

In two dimensions $\mathrm{N}(\mathbf{v}, \boldsymbol{\mu}, \mathbf{K})$ is really bell shaped with the peculiarity that the bell may be deformed such that its cross section is elliptic instead of circular. The form of this cross section is defined by the matrix $\mathbf{K}$ of the quadratic form. (See Fig. 4.2; compare Figs. 4.3 and 4.4.).

The two parameters of the N-dimensional normal distribution are again the first- and second-order statistical moments

$$\boldsymbol{\mu} = E\{\mathbf{v}\} \qquad \text{mean value of } \{\mathbf{v}\} \tag{4.4}$$

$$\mathbf{K} = E\{(\mathbf{v} - \boldsymbol{\mu})(\mathbf{v} - \boldsymbol{\mu})^T\} \qquad \text{covariance matrix of } \{\mathbf{v}\} \tag{4.5}$$

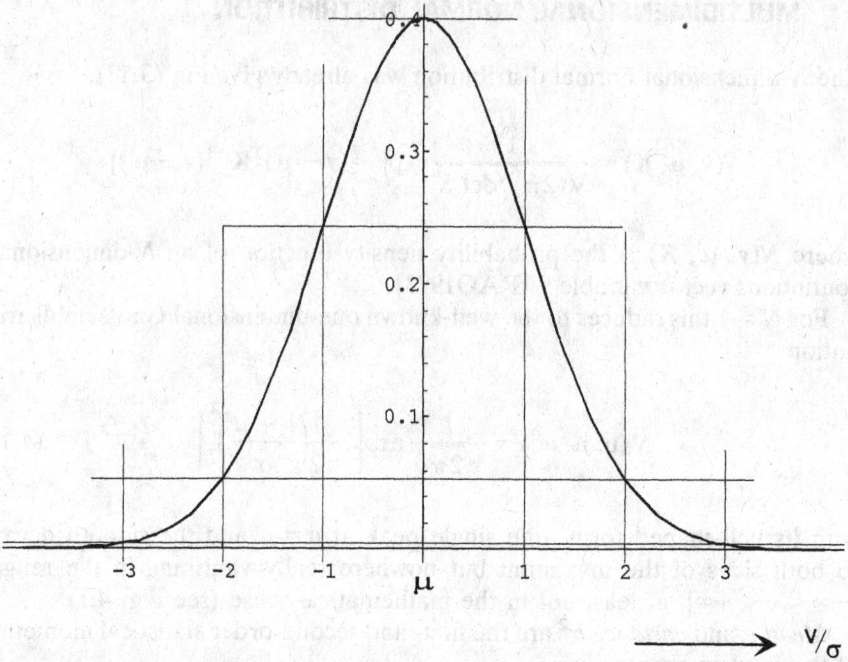

Figure 4.1. One-dimensional normal distribution function $N(v, \mu, \sigma^2)$ according to (4.1). Parameters μ and σ determine position of peak of $N(v, \mu, \sigma^2)$ on v-scale and width of bell-shaped curve, respectively.

The covariance matrix **K** has two important properties that directly derive from (4.5):

$$\mathbf{K} \text{ is } \textit{symmetric} \tag{4.6}$$

$$\mathbf{K} \text{ is } \textit{positive definite} \tag{4.7}$$

Symmetry means that **K** is left unchanged by matrix transposition: $\mathbf{K}^T = \mathbf{K}$. Positive definiteness means that the quadratic form Q formed with **K** and an arbitrary nonvanishing vector **x** is definitely positive:

$$Q = \mathbf{x}^T\mathbf{K}\mathbf{x} > 0 \qquad \forall \mathbf{x} \neq \mathbf{0} \tag{4.8}$$

In the case that zero must be included ($Q \geqq 0$) both the quadratic form and matrix **K** are called *positive semidefinite*. This, however, does not happen as long as **K** is nonsingular.

For the discussions to follow we will consider only the regular case—**K** positive definite—and will comment on the extension of semidefiniteness where appropriate.

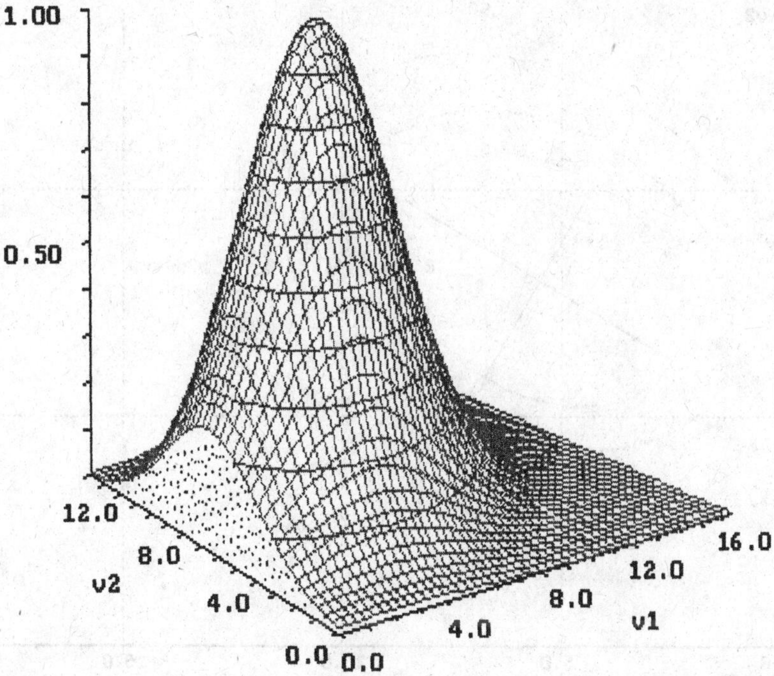

Figure 4.2. Two-dimensional normal distribution. Position of peak in two-dimensional v-plane is given by mean vector $\boldsymbol{\mu}$ whereas covariance matrix **K** determines form of the cross section (in general elliptic, in exceptional case circular). Vertical axis of three-dimensional-plot is scaled relative to peak value.

Definiteness of Quadratic Form

The definiteness of **K** is easily shown by inserting the definition (4.5) of **K** into (4.8),

$$\begin{aligned} Q &= \mathbf{x}^T E\{(\mathbf{v}-\boldsymbol{\mu})\mathbf{v}-\boldsymbol{\mu})^T\}\mathbf{x} \\ &= E\{\mathbf{x}^T(\mathbf{v}-\boldsymbol{\mu})(\mathbf{v}-\boldsymbol{\mu})^T\mathbf{x}\} \\ &= E\{[(\mathbf{v}-\boldsymbol{\mu})^T\mathbf{x}]^2\} \geq 0 \end{aligned} \tag{4.9}$$

since the term in square brackets $w = (\mathbf{v}-\boldsymbol{\mu})^T\mathbf{x}$ is scalar and the expectation $E\{w^2\}$ of the square of some scalar random variable w must be positive. The singular case of $Q = 0$ indicates that the random process $\{\mathbf{v}-\boldsymbol{\mu}\}$ is orthogonal to $\mathbf{x}$, that is, fills only a linear subspace of the entire N-dimensional measurement space **V**.

The fact of **K** being positive definite has the following consequences:

- The term **K** is regular (nonsingular) and has an inverse $\mathbf{K}^{-1}$.

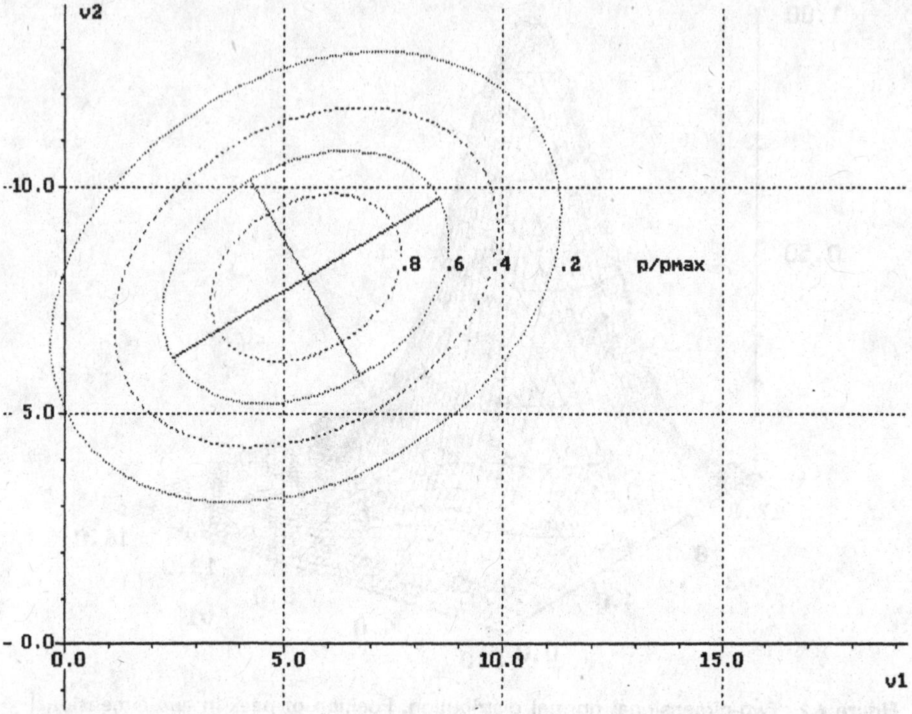

Figure 4.3. Contour plot of same two-dimensional normal distribution as in Fig. 4.2. Two orthogonal lines mark directions given by eigenvectors **b** with lengths according to square root of corresponding eigenvalues λ. Four concentric ellipses show loci of constant probability density p for fixed ratios p/p_{max} relative to peak value p_{max} of the probability density at center of distribution.

- The determinant of **K** is positive definite, det $\mathbf{K} > 0$.
- The inverse $\mathbf{K}^{-1}$ is positive definite.
- The determinant of $\mathbf{K}^{-1}$ is positive definite, det $\mathbf{K}^{-1} > 0$.
- All of the main diagonal elements of **K** are positive definite.
- All of the eigenvalues of **K** are positive definite.

Going back to the elements v_n of the measurement vector **v**, we find that the covariance matrix **K** consists of the variances

$$\begin{aligned} E\{|v_n - \mu_n|^2\} &= \text{variance of } \{v_n\} \\ &= \text{var}\{v_n\} \end{aligned} \tag{4.10}$$

and the covariances between v_n and all other measurements v_m:

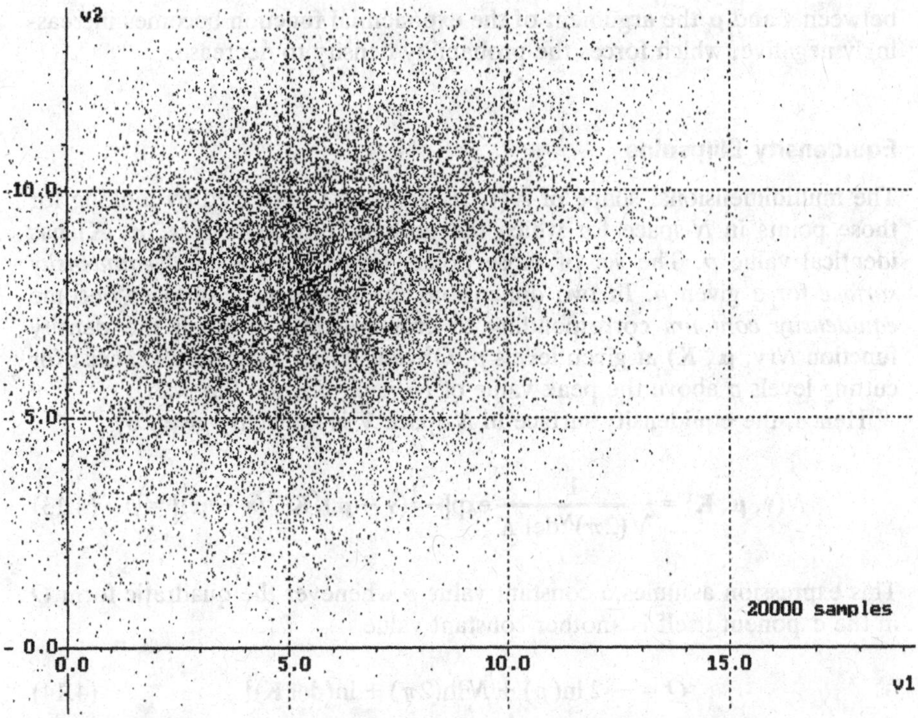

Figure 4.4. Scatterplot corresponding to Fig. 4.3 for 20,000 samples drawn from two-dimensional normal distribution of Fig. 4.2. Two orthogonal lines mark eigenvectors **b** with lengths according to square root of corresponding eigenvalues λ.

$$\begin{aligned} E\{(v_n - \mu_n)(v_m - \mu_m)\} &= \text{covariance between } \{v_n\} \text{ and } \{v_m\} \\ &= \text{cov}\{v_n, v_m\} \end{aligned} \tag{4.11}$$

$$\mathbf{K} = \begin{bmatrix} \text{var}\{v_1\} & \text{cov}\{v_2, v_1\} & \cdots & \text{cov}\{v_N, v_1\} \\ \text{cov}\{v_2, v_1\} & \text{var}\{v_2\} & \cdots & \text{cov}\{v_N, v_2\} \\ \vdots & \vdots & \ddots & \vdots \\ \text{cov}\{v_N, v_1\} & \text{cov}\{v_N, v_2\} & \cdots & \text{var}\{v_N\} \end{bmatrix} \tag{4.12}$$

The above-mentioned properties of symmetry and positive definiteness of the main diagonal elements are clearly visible.

The definiteness of **K**, together with the properties of the exponential function, is responsible for the unimodality of the N-dimensional normal distribution $N(\mathbf{v}, \boldsymbol{\mu}, \mathbf{K})$. The argument of the exponential function of (3.13) is, due to the minus sign, strictly negative. The maximum value that $N(\mathbf{v}, \boldsymbol{\mu}, \mathbf{K})$ can assume is that for $Q = 0$ or $\mathbf{v} = \boldsymbol{\mu}$. For larger distances between $\mathbf{v}$ and $\boldsymbol{\mu}$ the argument of the exponential function becomes increasingly negative, which forces the probability density to decrease.

Equidensity Ellipsoids

The multidimensional shape of $N(\mathbf{v}, \boldsymbol{\mu}, \mathbf{K})$ is best described by looking for those points in N-space for which the probability density $N(\mathbf{v}, \boldsymbol{\mu}, \mathbf{K})$ has identical value p. The set of those points forms the so-called *equidensity surface* for a given p. In two dimensions the equidensity surfaces become *equidensity contours* corresponding to cross sections through the density function $N(\mathbf{v}, \boldsymbol{\mu}, \mathbf{K})$ at given levels p. Obviously, no cross sections exist for cutting levels p above the peak value of $N(\mathbf{v}, \boldsymbol{\mu}, \mathbf{K})$; see Fig. 4.3.

Hence, the equidensity surface in N-space $\mathbf{V}$ is implicitly given by

$$N(\mathbf{v}, \boldsymbol{\mu}, \mathbf{K}) = \frac{1}{\sqrt{(2\pi)^N \det K}} \exp[-\tfrac{1}{2}(\mathbf{v} - \boldsymbol{\mu})^T \mathbf{K}^{-1}(\mathbf{v} - \boldsymbol{\mu})] = p \quad (4.13)$$

This expression assumes a constant value p whenever the quadratic form Q in the exponent itself is another constant value

$$Q = -[2\ln(p) + N\ln(2\pi) + \ln(\det \mathbf{K})] \quad (4.14)$$

Thus the equidensity surface in N-space $\mathbf{V}$ is determined by

$$Q = (\mathbf{v} - \boldsymbol{\mu})^T \mathbf{K}^{-1}(\mathbf{v} - \boldsymbol{\mu}) = \text{const} \quad (4.15)$$

whereby the cutting constraint becomes $Q > 0$.

A quadratic form set to a constant value defines a *quadric surface* in N-space. In two dimensions, as in Fig. 4.2, the quadric is an ellipse, in three and more dimensions an ellipsoid or hyperellipsoid. Since every value of p within the admissible range leads to the same expression (4.15) with only different values of Q, all of the quadrics are concentric with center $\boldsymbol{\mu}$.

Orientation and Size of Ellipsoids

What must be determined now is the orientation and form of the ellipsoids. To do this we will make a short excursion into what is called *spectral decomposition of matrices*.

To the symmetric matrix $\mathbf{K}$ (4.6) belongs a pair of matrices $\mathbf{B}$ and $\mathbf{D}$ whereby $\mathbf{B}$ is the *matrix of eigenvectors* of $\mathbf{K}$ and $\mathbf{D}$ is the *diagonal matrix of eigenvalues* of $\mathbf{K}$:

$$\mathbf{B} = (\mathbf{b}_1 \quad \mathbf{b}_2 \quad \cdots \quad \mathbf{b}_n) \quad (4.16)$$

$$\mathbf{D} = \begin{bmatrix} \lambda_1 & 0 & \cdots & 0 \\ 0 & \lambda_2 & \cdots & 0 \\ \vdots & \vdots & \ddots & \vdots \\ 0 & 0 & \cdots & \lambda_N \end{bmatrix} \tag{4.17}$$

The eigenvectors $\mathbf{b}_n$ are mutually orthogonal and hence the matrix $\mathbf{B}$ of eigenvectors is an orthogonal matrix with the property

$$\mathbf{B}^T\mathbf{B} = \mathbf{B}\mathbf{B}^T = \mathbf{I} \tag{4.18}$$

where $\mathbf{I}$ is the N-dimensional identity matrix.

Using the matrices $\mathbf{B}$ and $\mathbf{D}$, the covariance matrix $\mathbf{K}$ can be written

$$\mathbf{K} = \mathbf{B}\mathbf{D}\mathbf{B}^T \tag{4.19}$$

Inserting $\mathbf{B}$ and $\mathbf{D}$ as given above, (4.16) and (4.17), and multiplying from the right with $\mathbf{B}$, we get

$$\mathbf{K}(\mathbf{b}_1 \quad \mathbf{b}_2 \quad \cdots \quad \mathbf{b}_N) = (\mathbf{b}_1 \quad \mathbf{b}_2 \quad \cdots \quad \mathbf{b}_N) \begin{bmatrix} \lambda_1 & 0 & \cdots & 0 \\ 0 & \lambda_2 & \cdots & 0 \\ \vdots & \vdots & \ddots & \vdots \\ 0 & 0 & \cdots & \lambda_N \end{bmatrix} \tag{4.20}$$

$$= (\lambda_1\mathbf{b}_1 \quad \lambda_2\mathbf{b}_2 \quad \cdots \quad \lambda_N\mathbf{b}_N)$$

This leads to the so-called *eigenvalue problem*

$$\mathbf{K}\mathbf{b}_i = \lambda_i\mathbf{b}_i \quad \Leftrightarrow \quad (\mathbf{K} - \lambda_i\mathbf{I})\mathbf{b}_i = \mathbf{0} \quad \text{for } i = 1, \ldots, N \tag{4.21}$$

having N solutions in the form of the corresponding *eigenvalue–eigenvector* pairs $[\lambda_i, \mathbf{b}_i]$.

The decomposed form of $\mathbf{K}$, according to (4.19), can easily be inverted:

$$\mathbf{K}^{-1} = \mathbf{B}\mathbf{D}^{-1}\mathbf{B}^{\mathrm{T}} \tag{4.22}$$

Inserting that into the quadratic form Q of (4.15) renders

$$Q = (\mathbf{v} - \boldsymbol{\mu})^T\mathbf{B}\mathbf{D}^{-1}\mathbf{B}^T(\mathbf{v} - \boldsymbol{\mu})$$

$$= (\mathbf{v} - \boldsymbol{\mu})^T\mathbf{B} \begin{bmatrix} \lambda_N^{-1} & 0 & \cdots & 0 \\ 0 & \lambda_2^{-1} & \cdots & 0 \\ \vdots & \vdots & \ddots & \vdots \\ 0 & 0 & \cdots & \lambda_N^{-1} \end{bmatrix} \mathbf{B}^T(\mathbf{v} - \boldsymbol{\mu}) \tag{4.23}$$

A change of the coordinate system from $\mathbf{v}$ to $\mathbf{w}$, where $\mathbf{w}$ is given by

$$\mathbf{w} = \mathbf{B}^T(\mathbf{v} - \boldsymbol{\mu}) \tag{4.24}$$

decisively simplifies Q to a form where the orientation and the length of the ellipsoid's half axes are easily read:

$$\begin{aligned} Q &= \mathbf{w}^T\mathbf{D}^{-1}\mathbf{w} \\ &= (w_1 \quad w_2 \quad \cdots \quad w_N) \begin{bmatrix} \lambda_1^{-1} & 0 & \cdots & 0 \\ 0 & \lambda_2^{-1} & \cdots & 0 \\ \vdots & \vdots & \ddots & \vdots \\ 0 & 0 & \cdots & \lambda_N^{-1} \end{bmatrix} \begin{bmatrix} w_1 \\ w_2 \\ \vdots \\ w_N \end{bmatrix} \\ &= \sum_{i=1}^{N} \frac{w_i^2}{\lambda_i} \end{aligned} \tag{4.25}$$

The coordinate transformation $\mathbf{v} \rightarrow \mathbf{w}$ of (4.24) necessary to bring the quadratic form into standard notation consists of the following:

- Translation of the coordinate system's origin into the ellipsoid's center $\boldsymbol{\mu}$
- Rotation of the coordinate system by the rotation matrix $\mathbf{B}$

Thus we find that the principal axes of the ellipsoid defined by (4.15) are given by the eigenvectors $\mathbf{b}_i$ of $\mathbf{K}$ and the length of the half axes by the square root $\sqrt{\lambda_i}$ of the corresponding eigenvalues λ_i.

Some Further Properties of Normal Distribution

It is worthwhile noting that the property of a random variable $\mathbf{v}$ of coming from a normal distribution is *invariant with respect to linear transformations*. If $\mathbf{v}$ comes from a normal distribution with parameters $\boldsymbol{\mu}$ and $\mathbf{K}$ and is mapped into another random variable $\mathbf{w}$ by

$$\mathbf{w} = \mathbf{C}^T(\mathbf{v} - \mathbf{v}_0) \tag{4.26}$$

then $\mathbf{w}$ has also a normal distribution $N(\mathbf{w}, \boldsymbol{\mu}_w, \mathbf{K}_w)$ with parameters

$$\boldsymbol{\mu}_w = \mathbf{C}^T(\boldsymbol{\mu} - \mathbf{v}_0) \qquad \mathbf{K}_w = \mathbf{C}^T\mathbf{K}\mathbf{C} \tag{4.27}$$

This property is unique for the normal distribution insofar as it is valid for all $\mathbf{C}$. However, this does not allow us to infer normality of an arbitrary N-dimensional distribution from the fact that it has a normal projection.

Another unique property of this specific type of distribution is that if all of the elementary random variables v_n contained in $\mathbf{v}$ are mutually uncorrelated, that is, have zero covariance (4.11), they are also mutually statistically independent since then the joined probability prob($\mathbf{v}$) can be factorized into the product

$$\text{prob}(\mathbf{v}) = \text{prob}(v_1, v_2, \ldots, v_N) = \text{prob}(v_1) \cdot \text{prob}(v_2) \cdots \text{prob}(v_N) \qquad (4.28)$$

Although the normal distribution has a comparably smooth and regular form, in the sense that it is not very likely for an empirical random variable $\mathbf{v}$ observed in some pattern classification application to behave in this way, it has a fast with the dimension N of $\mathbf{v}$ increasing number of parameters:

$$\text{Number of parameters of } N(\mathbf{v}, \boldsymbol{\mu}, \mathbf{K}) = \tfrac{1}{2}[N(N+1)] + N = \tfrac{1}{2}[N^2 + 3N] \qquad (4.29)$$

Also for moderate N this number of parameters soon becomes prohibitive, especially in view of the fact that all of them must, with sufficient reliability, be estimated from the learning set.

Therefore, for larger values of N often simplifications of the general normal distribution are employed. These simplifications concern the covariance matrix $\mathbf{K}$ and typically, in the order of restrictiveness, are as follows:

- Assumption of statistical independence among components of $\mathbf{v}$
- Assumption of equal variances: white Gaussian process

4.2 BAYES CLASSIFIER FOR NORMALLY DISTRIBUTED CLASSES

We stay with the perspective of dealing with a model situation. There are K classes to be discriminated. The pattern source is a stochastic process $\{\mathbf{v}, k\}$ composed of K class-specific subprocesses $\{\mathbf{v}|k\}$ driven by another stochastic process $\{k\}$. The probabilities governing $\{\mathbf{v}|k\}$ and $\{k\}$ are known.

The a priori probability prob(k) is a given set of numbers $\{P_k\}$, $k = 1, \ldots, K$, and the K class-specific probabilities are normal distributions (3.14) with known parameters $\boldsymbol{\mu}_k$, $\mathbf{K}_k$:

$$\text{prob}(k) = \text{a priori probability of class } k = P_k$$

$$\text{prob}(\mathbf{v}|k) = \text{class-specific probability of class } k = N(\mathbf{v}, \boldsymbol{\mu}_k, \mathbf{K}_k)$$

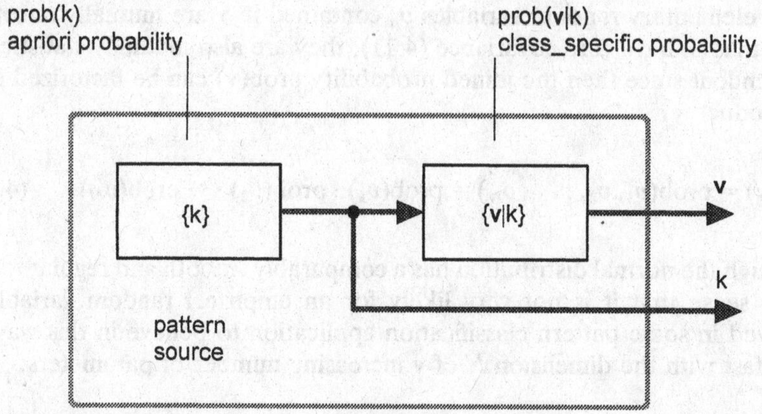

Figure 4.5. Model of pattern source composed of two stochastic processes $\{k\}$ and $\{\mathbf{v}|k\}$; compare Section 2.1. Stochastic process $\{k\}$ generating class labels k is described by set of numbers P_k, $k = 1, \ldots, K$, whereas class-specific probabilities are normal distributions $N(\mathbf{v}, \boldsymbol{\mu}_k, \mathbf{K}_k)$. Two random variables k and $\mathbf{v}$ are forwarded to the outside world.

Thus the joined probability (2.6) governing the pattern source becomes

$$\text{prob}(\mathbf{v}, k) = \text{prob}(\mathbf{v}|k)\text{prob}(k) = P_k N(\mathbf{v}, \boldsymbol{\mu}_k, \mathbf{K}_k) \tag{4.30}$$

This situation is illustrated by Fig. 4.5.

In this model situation we know all we need to know to design the optimum classifier. Building on the results of Section 2.3 and ignoring the possibility of reject, we get the *minimum error rate decision* from the *Bayes decision rule* (2.21):

$$\text{Decide for } \hat{k}\text{:} \quad \text{if } d_{\hat{k}}(\mathbf{v}) = \max_k\{d_k(\mathbf{v})\} \tag{4.31}$$

where the K discriminant functions $d_k(\mathbf{v})$ are the a posteriori probabilities

$$\begin{aligned} d_k(\mathbf{v}) &= \text{prob}(k|\mathbf{v}) \\ &= \frac{\text{prob}(\mathbf{v}|k)\text{prob}(k)}{\text{prob}(\mathbf{v})} = \frac{\text{prob}(\mathbf{v}|k)\text{prob}(k)}{\sum_{k=1}^{K} \text{prob}(\mathbf{v}|k)\text{prob}(k)} \\ &= \underset{k}{\text{NormalizeToUnity}}[\text{prob}(\mathbf{v}|k)\text{prob}(k)] \end{aligned} \tag{4.32}$$

In order to come to a more compact notation, we have introduced a special operation NormalizeToUnity$[\cdot]$ that accepts a set of K functions $f_k(\mathbf{v})$ and normalizes them with respect to k; thus the sum of the resulting K normalized functions $f_{k,\text{normalized}}(\mathbf{v})$ is unity for all values of $\mathbf{v}$,

$$\sum_{k=1}^{K} \underset{k}{\text{NormalizeToUnity}}[f_k(\mathbf{v})] = 1 \qquad \forall \mathbf{v} \tag{4.33}$$

Note that the so defined mapping $f_k(\mathbf{v}) \rightarrow f_{k,\text{normalized}}(\mathbf{v})$ is nonlinear. Together with (4.30) we finally get the discriminant functions $d_k(\mathbf{v})$ of the *Bayes classifier for normally distributed classes*:

$$d_k(\mathbf{v}) = \underset{k}{\text{NormalizeToUnity}}[P_k N(\mathbf{v}, \boldsymbol{\mu}_k, \mathbf{K}_k)] \tag{4.34}$$

The K expressions $d_k(\mathbf{v})$ are the components of the discriminant vector $\mathbf{d}$, which have to be compared for the maximum (see also Fig. 2.3). It should be remarked that these class membership functions $d_k(\mathbf{v})$ are the true a posteriori probabilities prob($k|\mathbf{v}$) and not approximations, as long as the model conditions hold.

Due to the nonlinear mapping performed by the NormalizeToUnity operation the appearance of the functions $d_k(\mathbf{v})$ differs considerably from that of the normal distributions from which they originate.

Example

These relations will be illustrated by a simple two-dimensional, three-class example that will be consistently used throughout the following chapters:

Number of classes	$K = 3$
A priori probability	Uniform $\rightarrow P_k = 1/K = \frac{1}{3}$
Class-specific probabilities	Normal, with the parameters given in (4.35)

$$\begin{aligned}
&\text{Class 0:} \quad \boldsymbol{\mu}_0 = \begin{pmatrix} 4.0 \\ 9.0 \end{pmatrix} \quad \mathbf{K}_0 = \begin{pmatrix} 2.0 & 2.0 \\ 2.0 & 5.0 \end{pmatrix} \\
&\text{Class 1:} \quad \boldsymbol{\mu}_1 = \begin{pmatrix} 8.5 \\ 7.5 \end{pmatrix} \quad \mathbf{K}_1 = \begin{pmatrix} 2.0 & -2.0 \\ -2.0 & 5.0 \end{pmatrix} \\
&\text{Class 2:} \quad \boldsymbol{\mu}_2 = \begin{pmatrix} 6.0 \\ 3.5 \end{pmatrix} \quad \mathbf{K}_2 = \begin{pmatrix} 7.0 & -4.0 \\ -4.0 & 7.0 \end{pmatrix}
\end{aligned} \tag{4.35}$$

The relevant expression for the purpose of classification according to (4.30) is the joined probability prob($\mathbf{v}$, k) = $P_k N(\mathbf{v}, \boldsymbol{\mu}_k, \mathbf{K}_k)$, which, for $k =$

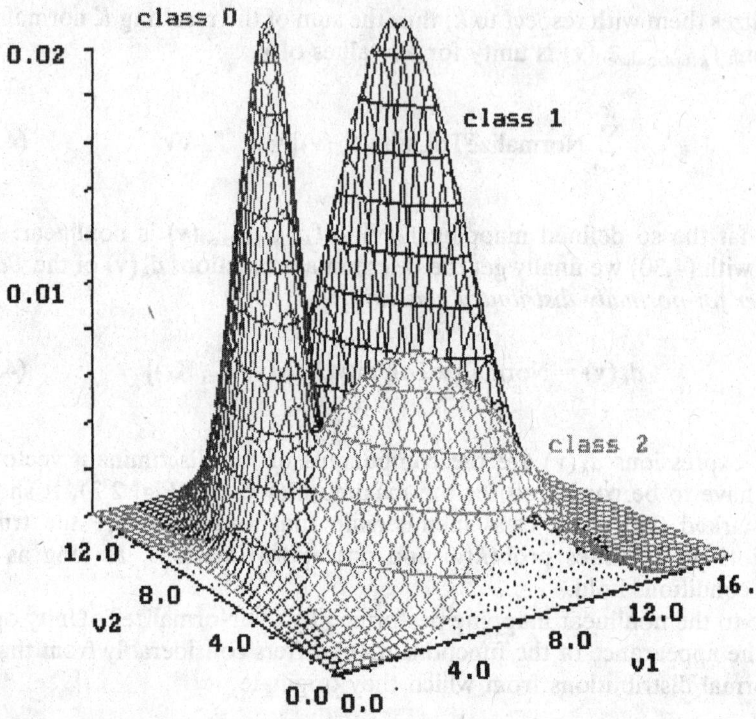

Figure 4.6. Three-dimensional plot of three class-specific normal distribution functions in form of $\max_k[P_k N(\mathbf{v}, \boldsymbol{\mu}_k, \mathbf{K}_k)]$ as defined by example of (4.35). Vertical axis is scaled to represent prob(**v**, k).

0, 1, 2, defines three different functions of **v**. Except for the factor P_k, these functions are the three normal distributions given by the example.

These three class-specific distributions are displayed as functions of the two-dimensional measurement space in Fig. 4.6. The vertical axis is scaled to represent prob(**v**, k). Since the three covariance matrices are different, the three normal distributions have different orientations of their principal axes. Two of the covariance matrices (for classes 0 and 1) have equal determinants resulting in a similar shape and equal height of the peak values. The distribution for class 2 has a larger width than the two others and therefore a lower peak value.

The three functions are mutually penetrating. The three-dimensional plot shows only the unhidden parts of the three surfaces. This is accomplished by plotting

$$\text{plot}(\mathbf{v}) = \max_k[\text{prob}(\mathbf{v}, k)]$$

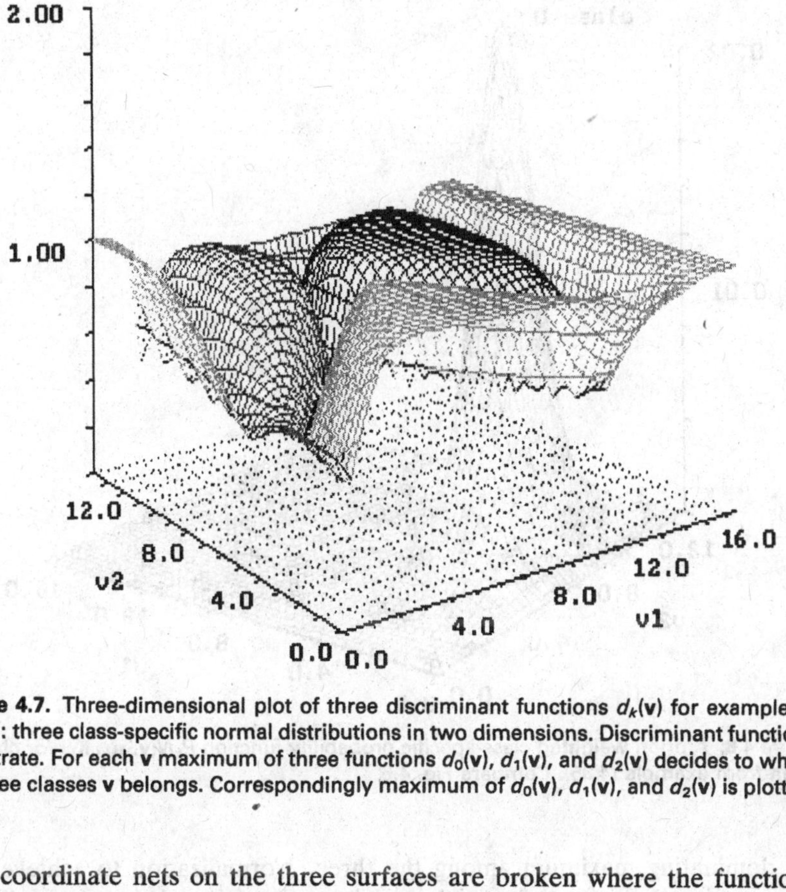

Figure 4.7. Three-dimensional plot of three discriminant functions $d_k(\mathbf{v})$ for example of (4.35): three class-specific normal distributions in two dimensions. Discriminant functions penetrate. For each **v** maximum of three functions $d_0(\mathbf{v})$, $d_1(\mathbf{v})$, and $d_2(\mathbf{v})$ decides to which of three classes **v** belongs. Correspondingly maximum of $d_0(\mathbf{v})$, $d_1(\mathbf{v})$, and $d_2(\mathbf{v})$ is plotted.

The coordinate nets on the three surfaces are broken where the functions intersect in order to highlight the intersection curves.

In the form of (4.34) the decision rule requires the NormalizeToUnity operation to be applied on $\text{prob}(\mathbf{v}, k) = P_k N(\mathbf{v}, \boldsymbol{\mu}_k, \mathbf{K}_k)$. The resulting functions $d_k(\mathbf{v})$ are displayed in Fig. 4.7. The plot shows again the maximum of the three functions $d_k(\mathbf{v})$, but compared to Fig. 4.6 the general appearance has drastically changed.

All three functions are limited to the range of [0 . . 1] simply by the fact that they represent a posteriori probabilities. The curves of intersection are now buried in deep furrows. The most dominant difference, however, is that whereas in Fig. 4.6 the three functions $\text{prob}(\mathbf{v}, k) = P_k N(\mathbf{v}, \boldsymbol{\mu}_k, \mathbf{K}_k)$ fall to zero with increasing distances from the class centers, in Fig. 4.7 one of the three functions approaches the value 1 in these outer areas.

This effect, again, results from the property of the $d_k(\mathbf{v})$ to represent a posteriori probabilities or, in other words, is the direct result of the NormalizeToUnity operation. In those far-off regions of measurement space all of the class-specific probabilities decrease to zero, but at different rates. Although itself finally becoming extremely small, one of these values remains

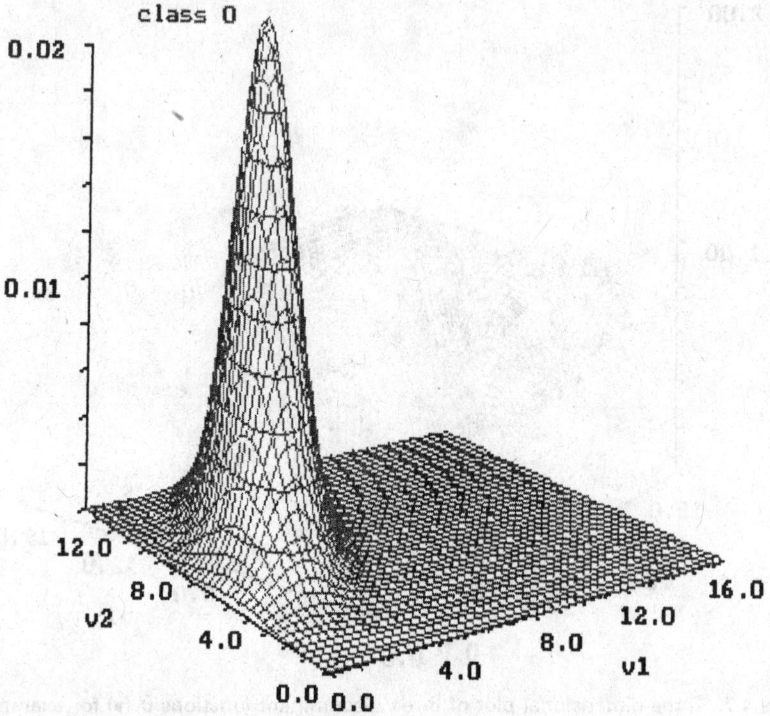

Figure 4.8. A priori weighted class-specific probability function $P_k N(\mathbf{v}, \boldsymbol{\mu}_k, \mathbf{K}_k)$ for class 0 taken from example (4.35). Compare Fig. 4.6.

the dominating maximum among the three. Normalization to achieve the *sum-equal-unity property* forces the maximum to approach 1.

These observations are closely related to the mathematical characteristics of the normal distribution function, which nowhere in the measurement space totally vanishes. From a practical point of view this is quite unlikely behavior. Any stochastic process $\{\mathbf{v}|k\}$ of patterns representing a real application will rather exhibit certain limits beyond which no measurement vectors $\mathbf{v}$ may be encountered.

The two three-dimensional plots Figs. 4.6 and 4.7 convey a clear idea of what is effected by the NormalizeToUnity operation of (4.34). The fact, however, that the functions for all three classes are combined by the $\max[\cdot]$ operation somewhat obscures what happens to the single functions. In order to provide this view too, in Figs. 4.8 and 4.9 only the functions corresponding to class 0 are shown.

Confidences

The discriminant functions $d_k(\mathbf{v})$ of (4.34) have the property of being a posteriori probabilities. After having utilized all the evidence contained in

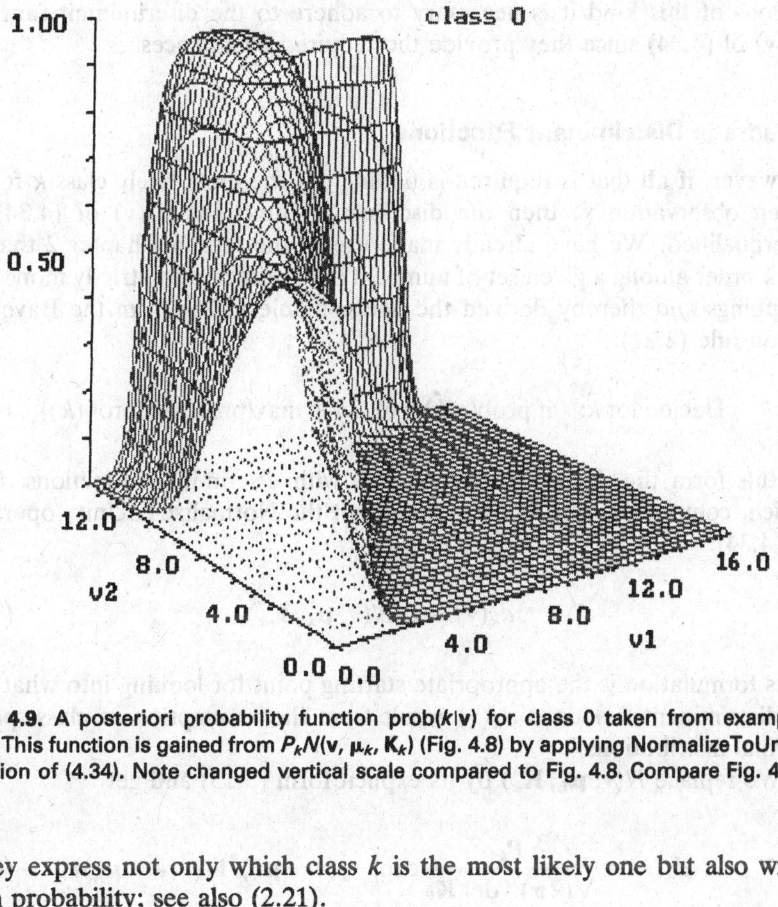

Figure 4.9. A posteriori probability function prob(k|**v**) for class 0 taken from example (4.35). This function is gained from $P_k N(\mathbf{v}, \boldsymbol{\mu}_k, \mathbf{K}_k)$ (Fig. 4.8) by applying NormalizeToUnity operation of (4.34). Note changed vertical scale compared to Fig. 4.8. Compare Fig. 4.7.

v, they express not only which class k is the most likely one but also with which probability; see also (2.21).

In other words,

- $d_k(\mathbf{v}) = \text{prob}(k|\mathbf{v})$ is the probability of being right with the assertion that k would be the correct class.

The value of $d_k(\mathbf{v})$ indicates the trustworthiness of that claim and, therefore, makes $d_k(\mathbf{v})$ the best of all imaginable *confidence values*. This interpretation is valid not only for the maximum of the K values $d_k(\mathbf{v})$ but also for all of them. A value $d_k(\mathbf{v}) > 0$ for any of the nonmaximum components of **d** certifies that there is a measurable chance for the corresponding class k to be the true one, measured in terms of the a posteriori probability $d_k(\mathbf{v})$.

As discussed in Section 1.1 there are many applications for which mere classification of entities is not everything but rather the base on which a whole edifice of symbolic reasoning may be constructed. Constructions of this kind often must rely on uncertain decisions and on sets of alternatives remaining from unfinished classifications on the lower levels. These systems need to know how much credit to give to low-level classifications. For applications of this kind it is necessary to adhere to the discriminant functions $d_k(\mathbf{v})$ of (4.34) since they provide the required confidences.

Quadratic Discriminant Functions

However, if all that is required is finding out the most likely class k for the given observation $\mathbf{v}$, then the discriminant functions $d_k(\mathbf{v})$ of (4.34) are overqualified. We have already made use of the fact in Chapter 2 that the rank order among a given set of numbers is not affected by strictly monotonic mappings and thereby derived the decision rule (2.25) from the Bayes decision rule (2.21):

$$\text{Decide for } \hat{k}: \quad \text{if } \text{prob}(\mathbf{v}|\hat{k})\text{prob}(\hat{k}) = \max_k\{\text{prob}(\mathbf{v}|k)\text{prob}(k)\} \tag{4.36}$$

In this form the decision rule operates with discriminant functions $d_k(\mathbf{v})$, which, compared with (4.34), simply omit the NormalizeToUnity operation of (4.34):

$$d_k(\mathbf{v}) = P_k N(\mathbf{v}, \boldsymbol{\mu}_k, \mathbf{K}_k) \tag{4.37}$$

This formulation is the appropriate starting point for looking into what type of discriminant functions $d_k(\mathbf{v})$ result from the assumption of class-specific normal distributions.

We replace $N(\mathbf{v}, \boldsymbol{\mu}_k, \mathbf{K}_k)$ by its explicit form (3.13) and get

$$d_k(\mathbf{v}) = \frac{P_k}{\sqrt{(2\pi)^N \det \mathbf{K}_k}} \exp[-\tfrac{1}{2}(\mathbf{v} - \boldsymbol{\mu}_k)^T \mathbf{K}_k^{-1}(\mathbf{v} - \boldsymbol{\mu}_k)] \tag{4.38}$$

The trick with the monotonic mappings not affecting the outcome of the decision rule can be applied again and gives, after multiplication by $\sqrt{(2\pi)^N}$ and taking the logarithm, the new discriminant function

$$d_k(\mathbf{v}) = \ln(P_k) - \tfrac{1}{2}\ln(\det \mathbf{K}_k) - \tfrac{1}{2}(\mathbf{v} - \boldsymbol{\mu}_k)^T \mathbf{K}_k^{-1}(\mathbf{v} - \boldsymbol{\mu}_k) \tag{4.39}$$

Equation (4.39) cannot be further simplified by monotonic mappings.

We find that this discriminant function $d_k(\mathbf{v})$ consists of a term a_{0k} that does not depend on $\mathbf{v}$ and therefore is computable in advance, together with a quadratic form in $\mathbf{v}$ determined by the inverse covariance matrix $\mathbf{K}_k^{-1}$ and centered at the class mean $\boldsymbol{\mu}_k$:

$$d_k(\mathbf{v}) = a_{0k} + Q_k(\mathbf{v}) \tag{4.40}$$

with

$$a_{0k}(\mathbf{v}) = \ln(P_k) - \tfrac{1}{2}\ln(\det \mathbf{K}_k) \tag{4.41}$$

and

$$Q_k(\mathbf{v}) = -\tfrac{1}{2}(\mathbf{v} - \boldsymbol{\mu}_k)^T \mathbf{K}_k^{-1}(\mathbf{v} - \boldsymbol{\mu}_k) \tag{4.42}$$

The most important result of these deliberations is that the discriminant functions $d_k(\mathbf{v})$ of the Bayes classifier for normally distributed classes are *quadratic functions*. Surfaces of constant value d_k in N-space $\mathbf{V}$ are positive-definite quadrics: ellipsoids and hyperellipsoids. This type of classifier is therefore called a *quadratic classifier*:

- The Bayes classifier for normally distributed classes is a quadratic classifier.

Class Regions and Borders

The border between classes k and j is defined by the intersection of the two corresponding discriminant functions $d_k(\mathbf{v})$ and $d_j(\mathbf{v})$:

$$d_k(\mathbf{v}) = d_j(\mathbf{v}) \quad \Leftrightarrow \quad d_k(\mathbf{v}) - d_j(\mathbf{v}) = 0 \tag{4.43}$$

and hence implicitly given by a function $g_{kj}(\mathbf{v}) = 0$ that for mathematical convenience is derived from $d_k(\mathbf{v}) - d_j(\mathbf{v})$ by multiplication with -2.

Inserting (4.39) we get

$$g_{kj}(\mathbf{v}) = \ln\left(\frac{\det \mathbf{K}_k}{\det \mathbf{K}_j}\right) - 2\ln\left(\frac{P_k}{P_j}\right) + [(\mathbf{v} - \boldsymbol{\mu}_k)^T \mathbf{K}_k^{-1}(\mathbf{v} - \boldsymbol{\mu}_k)$$
$$- (\mathbf{v} - \boldsymbol{\mu}_j)^T \mathbf{K}_j^{-1}(\mathbf{v} - \boldsymbol{\mu}_j)] \tag{4.44}$$

This is mainly the difference between two positive-definite quadratic forms and can be made to become one quadratic form by suitable transformations including quadratic completion

$$g_{kj}(\mathbf{v}) = g_0 + (\mathbf{v} - \mathbf{v}_0)^T \mathbf{M}^{-1}(\mathbf{v} - \mathbf{v}_0) \tag{4.45}$$

The abbreviations g_0, $\mathbf{v}_0$, and $\mathbf{M}$ are defined as follows:

$$\mathbf{M} = [\mathbf{K}_k^{-1} - \mathbf{K}_j^{-1}]^{-1} = \mathbf{K}_k[\mathbf{K}_j - \mathbf{K}_k]^{-1}\mathbf{K}_j = \mathbf{K}_j[\mathbf{K}_j - \mathbf{K}_k]^{-1}\mathbf{K}_k$$
$$\mathbf{v}_0 = \mathbf{M}[\mathbf{K}_k^{-1}\boldsymbol{\mu}_k - \mathbf{K}_j^{-1}\boldsymbol{\mu}_j] \tag{4.46}$$
$$g_0 = \ln\left(\frac{\det \mathbf{K}_k}{\det \mathbf{K}_j}\right) - 2\ln\left(\frac{\mathrm{P}_k}{\mathrm{P}_j}\right) + [\boldsymbol{\mu}_k^T \mathbf{K}_k^{-1}\boldsymbol{\mu}_k - \boldsymbol{\mu}_j^T \mathbf{K}_j^{-1}\boldsymbol{\mu}_j - \mathbf{v}_0^T \mathbf{M}^{-1}\mathbf{v}_0]$$

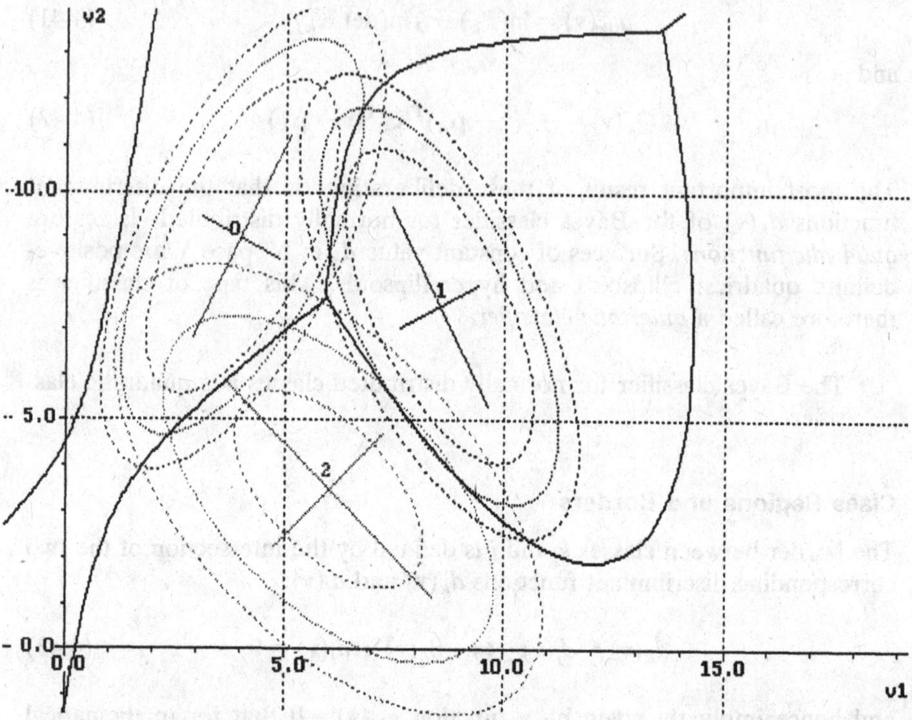

Figure 4.10. View into two-dimensional measurement space of example (4.35). Three class-specific distributions are each represented by their principal axes and a collection of equidensity contours corresponding to values {0.020, 0.010, 0.005} of prob(v|k); compare Fig. 4.6. Crossing points of equidensity ellipses are points on class boundary. Network of pairwise borders is shown by solid lines, but only for those sections that actually separate different classes.

Whether the function $g_{kj}(\mathbf{v})$, defining the boundary between the two classes k and j, and the matrix $\mathbf{M}$ are definite or not depends on the situation and is determined by the definiteness of the difference $[\mathbf{K}_k^{-1} - \mathbf{K}_j^{-1}]$ of the two inverse covariance matrices.

Hence the class boundaries may be any type of quadric: ellipsoids, paraboloids, or hyperboloids. In any case, the center of the quadric is given by $\mathbf{v}_0$, whereas type and shape of the class boundary are achieved from analyzing $\mathbf{M}$.

These relations shall be exemplified for the two-dimensional three-class example of (4.35). Figure 4.10 shows how the network of pairwise class borders separates the measurement space into class regions.

The different types of class boundaries become better visible if the presentation of Fig. 4.10 is somewhat zoomed out, as is shown in Fig. 4.11.

The separation of two classes by an ellipsoid divides the measurement

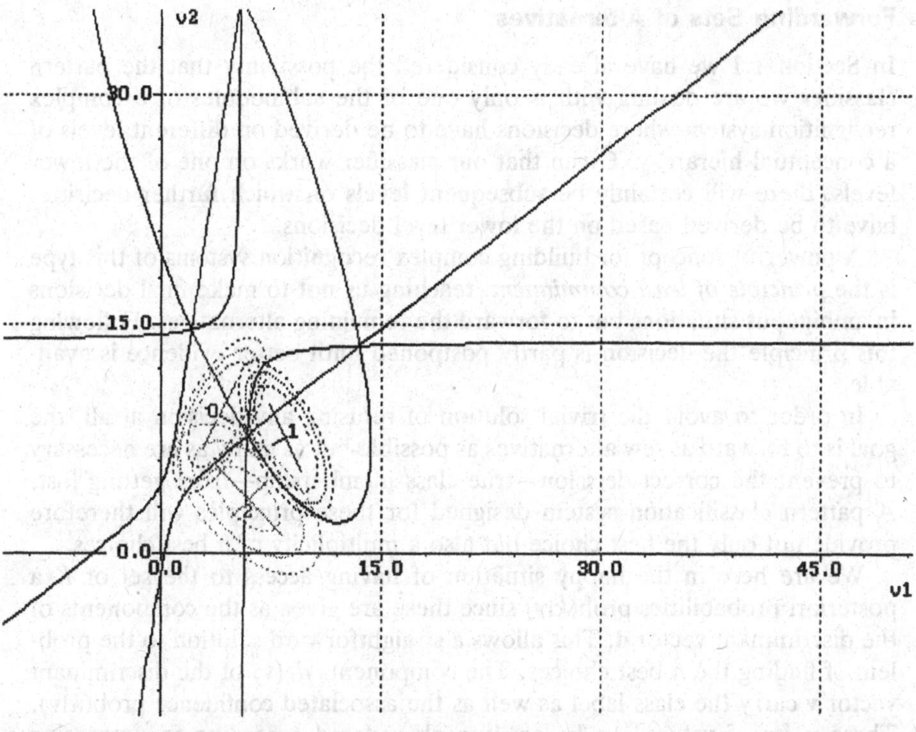

Figure 4.11. Zoomed-out view of Fig. 4.10. It can clearly be seen that borders between classes 0/2 and classes 0/1 are hyperbolas and border between classes 1/2 is ellipse. Complete system of class boundaries is shown by light grey solid lines. Those sections that actually separate classes are shown in dark.

space into two separate regions: inside and outside the ellipsoid. Separation by an hyperboloid generates three separate regions: one between the two cups and two on both of the outer sides of the cups. In general the measurement space **V** is divided into a number of cells distinctly exceeding the number of classes.

The class borders already became visible in Figs. 4.6 and 4.7. The latter shows the borderlines buried in deep furrows. These result from the fact that the maximum a posteriori probability approaches the value 1 within the more centered parts of the respective class regions but falls to considerably lower values along the class boundaries. The bottom of the furrows lies on the $\text{prob}(k|\mathbf{v}) \approx \frac{1}{2}$ level in regions where two classes dominantly compete and decreases to $\frac{1}{3}$ at boundary crossing points where three classes meet.

The pattern classifier can produce decisions of high certainty only in the center parts of the class regions. Along the class border the decisions remain ambiguous.

Forwarding Sets of Alternatives

In Section 1.1 we have already considered the possibility that the pattern classifier we are dealing with is only one of the submodules of a complex recognition system where decisions have to be derived on different levels of a conceptual hierarchy. Given that our classifier works on one of the lower levels, there will certainly be subsequent levels on which further decisions have to be derived based on the lower level decisions.

A powerful concept for building complex recognition systems of this type is the *principle of least commitment*, teaching us not to make final decisions in ambiguous situations but to forward the remaining alternatives. Following this principle the decision is partly postponed until better evidence is available.

In order to avoid the trivial solution of refusing any decision at all, the goal is to forward as few alternatives as possible but as many as are necessary to prevent the correct decision—true class membership—from getting lost. A pattern classification system designed for these principles will therefore provide not only the best choice but also a multiplicity of n best choices.

We are here in the happy situation of having access to the set of K a posteriori probabilities prob($k|\mathbf{v}$) since these are given as the components of the discriminant vector $\mathbf{d}$. This allows a straightforward solution to the problem of finding the n best choices. The components $d_k(\mathbf{v})$ of the discriminant vector $\mathbf{v}$ carry the class label as well as the associated confidence prob($k|\mathbf{v}$). These pairs of values can be easily rank ordered according to decreasing confidences.

The generation of alternatives is controlled by a confidence threshold CnfThrsh that may assume any value within the range of $[1/K\,..\,1]$. The pattern classifier forwards as many alternatives as necessary to bring the accumulated confidence of the forwarded choices above the given threshold CnfThrsh.

With CnfThrsh = $1/K$ only one single alternative is generated that corresponds to the traditional one-best classifier – winner takes all. The minimum $1/K$ of the threshold value relates to the fact that the minimum value that can be assumed by the maximum of the K a posteriori probabilities prob($\omega|k$) is $1/K$ in the case of a uniform distribution of the a posteriori probabilities.

On the other hand, with CnfThrsh = 1 the complete discriminant vector $\mathbf{v}$ is forwarded since the total accumulated confidence cannot exceed the value 1. For the application, this case resembles very much the case of reject since then the decision is left completely open. With intermediate values of CnfThrsh a variable number a of alternatives is generated depending on the input vector $\mathbf{v}$ to the pattern classifier.

This defines the *n best classifier* with variable number a of choices. Applying this technique to the two-dimensional, three-class example of (4.35), we arrive at the situation in measurement space $\mathbf{V}$ shown in Fig. 4.12.

We have considered here the possibility of generating alternatives from the

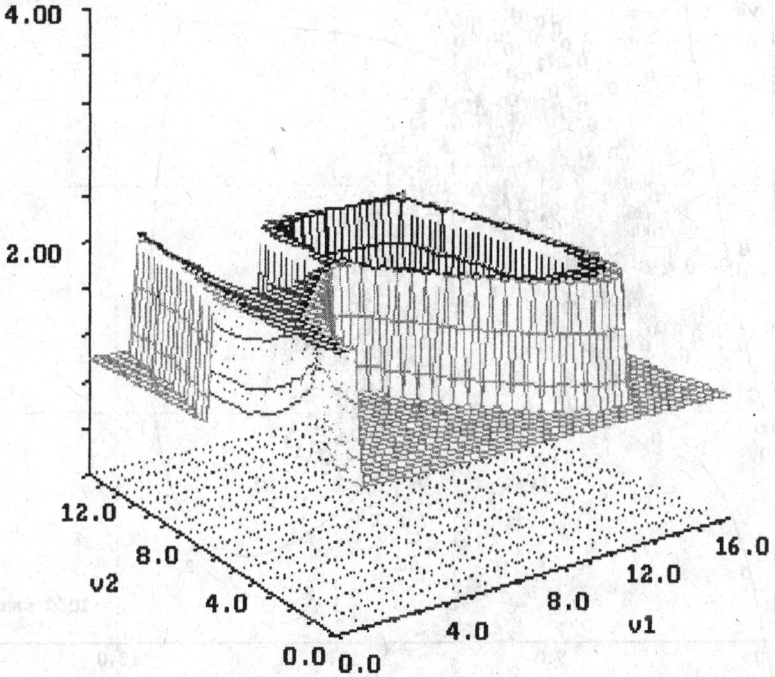

Figure 4.12. Number of alternatives generated by *n* best classifier applied to example of (4.35) plotted as function above measurement space. For this picture confidence threshold was set to CnfThrsh = 0.7. Class boundaries become clearly visible as steep walls separating class regions. These walls are erected on a wide plain on level $a = 1$ and reach level $a = 2$. Between walls basins are formed for class regions, well separated from each other by bordering walls.

viewpoint of Bayes classification based on the assumption of the a posteriori probabilities being known. The same topic will be discussed for the realistic case of estimated a posteriori probabilities in Chapter 10.

Scatterplots in Measurement and in Decision Space

The main task of the pattern classifier is to establish a mapping $\mathbf{v} \rightarrow \mathbf{d}$ from measurement space $\mathbf{V}$ into decision space $\mathbf{D}$. For the two-dimensional, three-class example of (4.35) this mapping can be easily visualized by scatterplots showing how the distribution of points in $\mathbf{V}$-space is mapped into a corresponding distribution of points in $\mathbf{D}$-space, whereby each of the points represents one single pattern.

Figure 4.13 shows the view into the measurement space $\mathbf{V}$ and Fig. 4.14 the corresponding view into the decision space $\mathbf{D}$. Whereas the $\mathbf{V}$-space picture is directly understandable, the $\mathbf{D}$-space picture needs some interpretation. For this purpose we refer to the considerations of Section 1.4, where

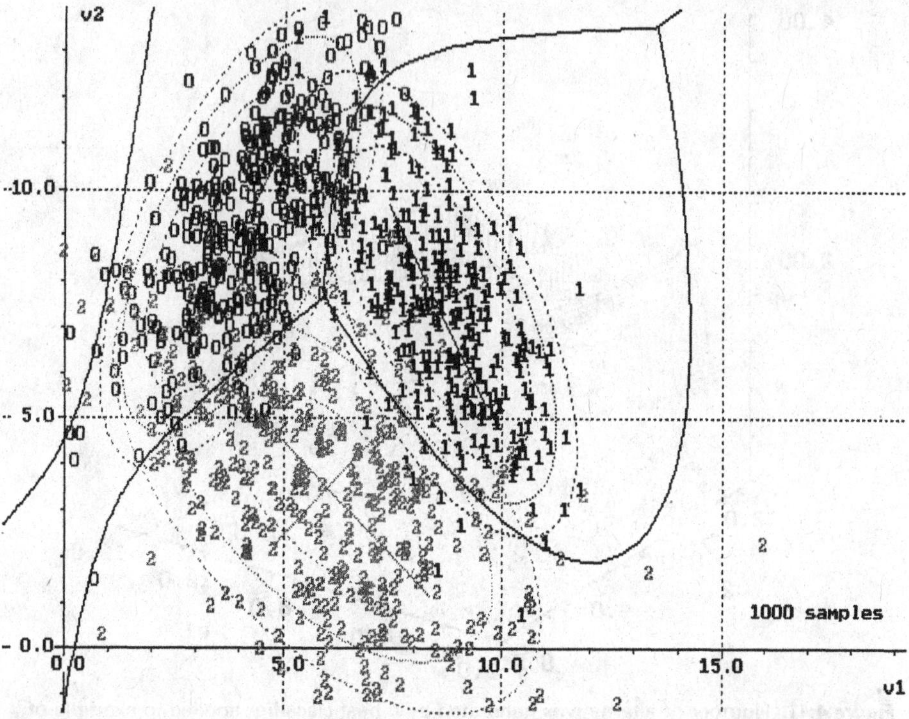

Figure 4.13. Scatterplot for example of (4.35) in measurement space **V** based on total sample size of 1000 patterns. Three classes 0, 1, 2 are equiprobable: $P_0 = P_1 = P_2 = \frac{1}{3}$. Patterns are represented by symbols 0, 1, and 2 and plotted on background of Fig. 4.10.

the decision space **D** was introduced as spanned by the K target vectors **y** of (1.5). In the example of (4.35) considered here, with $K = 3$ classes, the decision space **D** is the common three-dimensional space and the three target vectors form an orthogonal tripod. The tops of the target vectors mark the corner points of an equilateral triangle that can be represented in the two-dimensional plane. This equilateral triangle is shown in Fig. 4.14 together with the set of patterns projected from **V**-space into **D**-space by **d**(**v**).

We observe that the projected patterns in **D**-space are crowded along the triangle's sides and that the center region of the triangle remains almost empty. This is due to the situation in **V**-space shown in Fig. 4.13. The three class-specific distributions in **V**-space of this example are arranged so that penetrations of the class-specific distributions occur almost exclusively between pairs of classes. These penetrations happen along the pairwise borders and predominantly cause ambiguities between class pairs. Only a small portion of the total stochastic process happens to lie in that region of **V**-space where all three classes are intermixed.

The distribution of patterns in decision space **D** has a quite peculiar

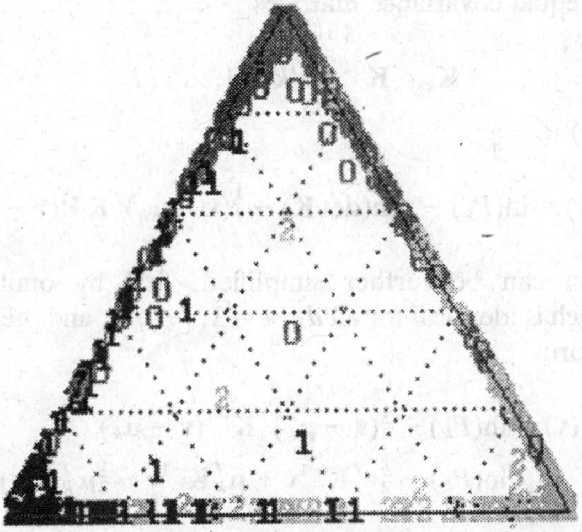

Figure 4.14. Scatterplot for same situation as in Fig. 4.13 in decision space **D**. Decision space **D** is spanned by three target vectors $\mathbf{y}_0, \mathbf{y}_1, \mathbf{y}_2$, which define an equilateral triangle in **D**-space; see Fig. 1.4. This equilateral triangle is put into the drawing plane with the three corners representing the tops of the three target vectors. The patterns are represented by symbols 0, 1, and 2 as in Fig. 4.13 and appear crowded along triangle's sides. Only a few patterns are mapped into triangle's center region.

form. The mass of the patterns is concentrated in the lower dimensional subsimplices into which the decision space simplex can be partitioned. This effect is not unique for the example used here but is rather common also in practical applications.

4.3 SIMPLIFICATION TO EQUAL COVARIANCE MATRICES

We found in the foregoing section that the general case of arbitrarily different covariance matrices for normally distributed classes led to quadratic discriminant functions (4.39):

$$d_k(\mathbf{v}) = \ln(P_k) - \tfrac{1}{2}\ln(\det \mathbf{K}_k) - \tfrac{1}{2}(\mathbf{v} - \boldsymbol{\mu}_k)^T \mathbf{K}_k^{-1}(\mathbf{v} - \boldsymbol{\mu}_k)$$

We will now consider the case of equal covariance matrices for the K class-specific normal distributions and will see that this kind of assumption leads to remarkable savings in computational expenses, especially for higher dimensional cases, that is, for larger values of N.

The case of equal covariance matrices

$$\mathbf{K}_k = \mathbf{K} \quad \forall k = 1, \ldots, K \tag{4.47}$$

simplifies (4.39) to

$$d_k(\mathbf{v}) = \ln(P_k) - \tfrac{1}{2}\ln(\det \mathbf{K}) - \tfrac{1}{2}(\mathbf{v} - \boldsymbol{\mu}_k)^T \mathbf{K}^{-1}(\mathbf{v} - \boldsymbol{\mu}_k) \tag{4.48}$$

This expression can be further simplified, first by omitting the term $\frac{1}{2}\ln(\det \mathbf{K})$, which is identical for all d_k, $k = 1, \ldots, K$, and then by evaluating the quadratic form

$$\begin{aligned} d_k(\mathbf{v}) &= \ln(P_k) - \tfrac{1}{2}(\mathbf{v} - \boldsymbol{\mu}_k)^T \mathbf{K}^{-1}(\mathbf{v} - \boldsymbol{\mu}_k) \\ &= \ln(P_k) - \tfrac{1}{2}\mathbf{v}^T\mathbf{K}^{-1}\mathbf{v} + \boldsymbol{\mu}_k^T\mathbf{K}^{-1}\mathbf{v} - \tfrac{1}{2}\boldsymbol{\mu}_k^T\mathbf{K}^{-1}\boldsymbol{\mu}_k \end{aligned} \tag{4.49}$$

Again a constant term $\frac{1}{2}\mathbf{v}^T\mathbf{K}^{-1}\mathbf{v}$ not influencing the rank order of the $d_k(\mathbf{v})$ can be omitted until we finally get

$$d_k(\mathbf{v}) = \ln(P_k) - \tfrac{1}{2}\boldsymbol{\mu}_k^T\mathbf{K}^{-1}\boldsymbol{\mu}_k + \boldsymbol{\mu}_k^T\mathbf{K}^{-1}\mathbf{v} \tag{4.50}$$

We observe that the simplification introduced by the equal covariance assumption has changed the quadratic decision function of (4.39) into a *linear discriminant function*. Using

$$a_{0k} = \ln(P_k) - \tfrac{1}{2}\boldsymbol{\mu}_k^T\mathbf{K}^{-1}\boldsymbol{\mu}_k \qquad \mathbf{a}_k = \mathbf{K}^{-1}\boldsymbol{\mu}_k \tag{4.51}$$

we get a nicely compact notation for the linear discriminant function

$$d_k(\mathbf{v}) = a_{0k} + \mathbf{a}_k^T\mathbf{v} \tag{4.52}$$

The resulting classifier is called a *linear classifier*

- The Bayes classifier for normally distributed classes with equal covariance matrices is a *linear classifier*:

Although the conditions leading to this result at first glance seem to be rather restrictive, there indeed exist practical situations where these conditions hold and (4.52) is the adequate discriminant function. This is the case when the class-specific stochastic processes $\{\mathbf{v}|k\}$ are generated by additive superposition of fixed data vectors $\boldsymbol{\mu}_k$ representing the K classes with a class-independent correlated, nonwhite, Gaussian random process $\{\mathbf{r}\}$:

$$\{\mathbf{v}|k\} = \boldsymbol{\mu}_k + \{\mathbf{r}\} \quad \text{for } k = 1, \ldots, K \tag{4.53}$$

White Covariance Matrix

With the additional assumption of the common covariance matrix **K** being proportional to the N-dimensional identity matrix $\mathbf{K} = \alpha\mathbf{I}$, these expressions can be further simplified. Starting from (4.50) we get

$$d_k(\mathbf{v}) = \ln(P_k) - \frac{1}{2\alpha}\boldsymbol{\mu}_k^T\boldsymbol{\mu}_k + \frac{1}{\alpha}\boldsymbol{\mu}_k^T\mathbf{v} \tag{4.54}$$

Multiplying the whole expression with α yields

$$d_k(\mathbf{v}) = \alpha\ln(P_k) - \tfrac{1}{2}|\boldsymbol{\mu}_k|^2 + \boldsymbol{\mu}_k^T\mathbf{v} \tag{4.55}$$

The coefficients of the linear discriminant function of (4.52) now simplify to

$$a_{0k} = \alpha\ln(P_k) - \tfrac{1}{2}|\boldsymbol{\mu}_k|^2 \quad \mathbf{a}_k = \boldsymbol{\mu}_k \tag{4.56}$$

In terms of the *prototype plus additive Gaussian noise model* of (4.53), the case considered here is that of white, uncorrelated and class-independent Gaussian noise $\{\mathbf{r}\}$ with variance α equal for all components r_n of $\mathbf{r}$,

$$\alpha = \text{var}\{r_n\} = \text{var}\{v_n\} \tag{4.57}$$

additively superimposed on the K given prototype vectors $\boldsymbol{\mu}_k$. In this case the coefficient vector $\mathbf{a}_k$ of the linear discriminant function $d_k(\mathbf{v})$ of (4.52) comes out to be the prototype vector $\boldsymbol{\mu}_k$ itself, in digital signal processing this kind of classifier is called a *matched filter*

Class Regions and Borders

Similar to the question asked in Section 4.2 of how the borders between the different class regions in measurement space look, we will now consider the class borders for the simplified case of equal covariance matrices.

The class borders are again defined by (4.43):

$$d_k(\mathbf{v}) = d_j(\mathbf{v}) \quad \Leftrightarrow \quad d_k(\mathbf{v}) - d_j(\mathbf{v}) = 0$$

The $d_k(\mathbf{v})$ are here linear functions in **V**-space. Therefore, their differences

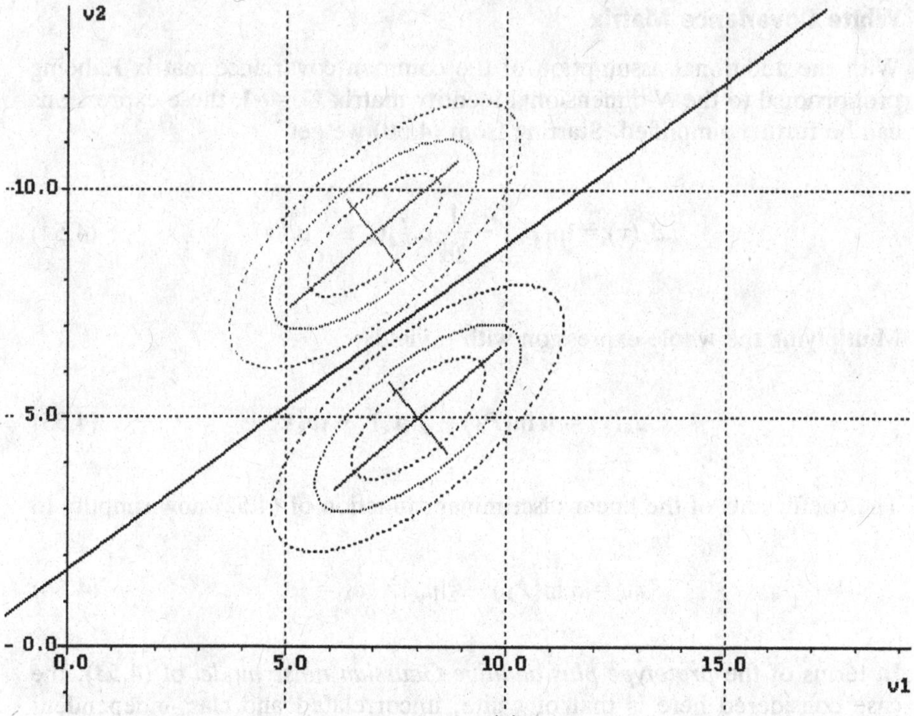

(*a*)

Figure 4.15. Two normally distributed classes with identical covariance matrices and equal a priori probabilities. (a–c) Orientation of separation as it follows rotation of covariance matrices.

are bound to be linear functions as well and the borders in N-space as (N-1)-dimensional planes: straight lines in 2-space.

From (4.52) we get the implicit representation of the separating plane

$$g_{kj}(\mathbf{v}) = d_k(\mathbf{v}) - d_j(\mathbf{v}) = a_0 + \mathbf{a}^{\mathrm{T}}\mathbf{v} = 0 \tag{4.58}$$

$$\begin{aligned} a_0 = a_{0k} - a_{0j} &= \ln\left(\frac{P_k}{P_j}\right) - \tfrac{1}{2}(\boldsymbol{\mu}_k^T\mathbf{K}^{-1}\boldsymbol{\mu}_k - \boldsymbol{\mu}_j^T\mathbf{K}^{-1}\boldsymbol{\mu}_j) \\ &= \ln\left(\frac{P_k}{P_j}\right) - \tfrac{1}{2}(\boldsymbol{\mu}_k - \boldsymbol{\mu}_j)^T\mathbf{K}^{-1}(\boldsymbol{\mu}_k + \boldsymbol{\mu}_j) \end{aligned} \tag{4.59}$$

$$\mathbf{a} = \mathbf{a}_k - \mathbf{a}_j = \mathbf{K}^{-1}(\boldsymbol{\mu}_k - \boldsymbol{\mu}_j) \tag{4.60}$$

Putting both together gives

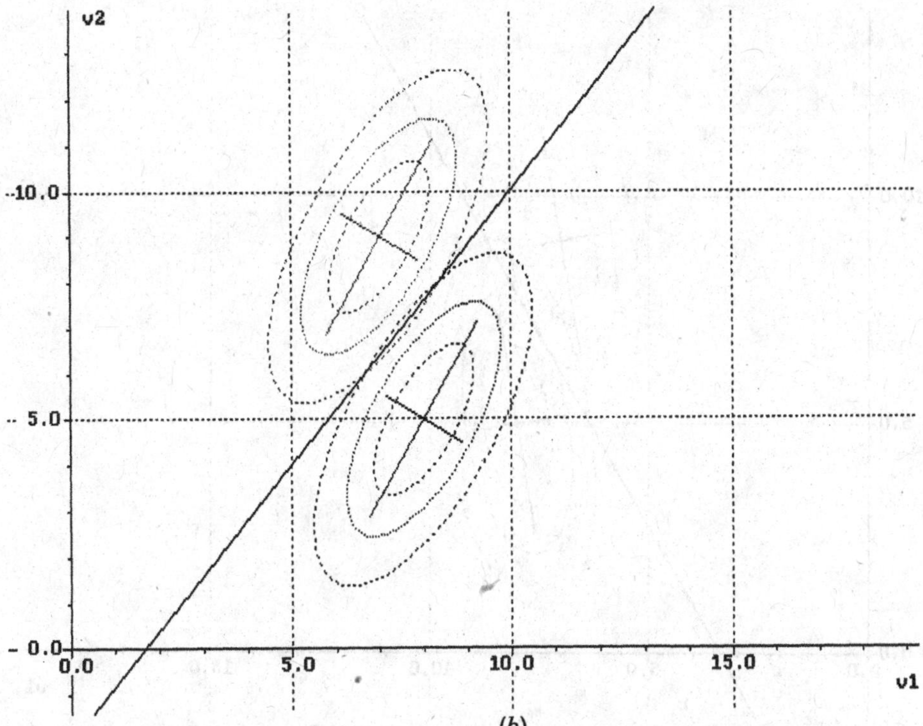

(b)

Figure 4.15. (*Continued*)

$$g(\mathbf{v}) = \ln\left(\frac{P_k}{P_j}\right) + (\boldsymbol{\mu}_k - \boldsymbol{\mu}_j)^T \mathbf{K}^{-1}[\mathbf{v} - \tfrac{1}{2}(\boldsymbol{\mu}_k + \boldsymbol{\mu}_j)] = 0 \qquad (4.61)$$

We find that the normal vector $\mathbf{a}$ of the separating plane in general does not coincide with the difference vector $\boldsymbol{\mu}_k - \boldsymbol{\mu}_j$ between the two class means but is instead rotated by the inverse covariance matrix $\mathbf{K}^{-1}$.

In case of equal a priori probabilities $P_k = P_j$ the mean $\frac{1}{2}(\boldsymbol{\mu}_k + \boldsymbol{\mu}_j)$ between the two class centers becomes a point of the bordering plane. In the general case of unequal a priori probabilities the crossing point between the difference vector $\boldsymbol{\mu}_k - \boldsymbol{\mu}_j$ and the bordering plane is moved toward the center of the less probable class.

In the special case of covariance matrices $\mathbf{K}$ equal or at least proportional to the N-dimensional identity matrix I the difference vector $\boldsymbol{\mu}_k - \boldsymbol{\mu}_j$ coincides with the plane normal. Beyond that, if the a priori probabilities are equal, then the separating plane becomes the perpendicular bisector between the class centers $\boldsymbol{\mu}_k$ and $\boldsymbol{\mu}_j$.

These relations will be illustrated in Figs. 4.15 and 4.16. Figure 4.15 shows

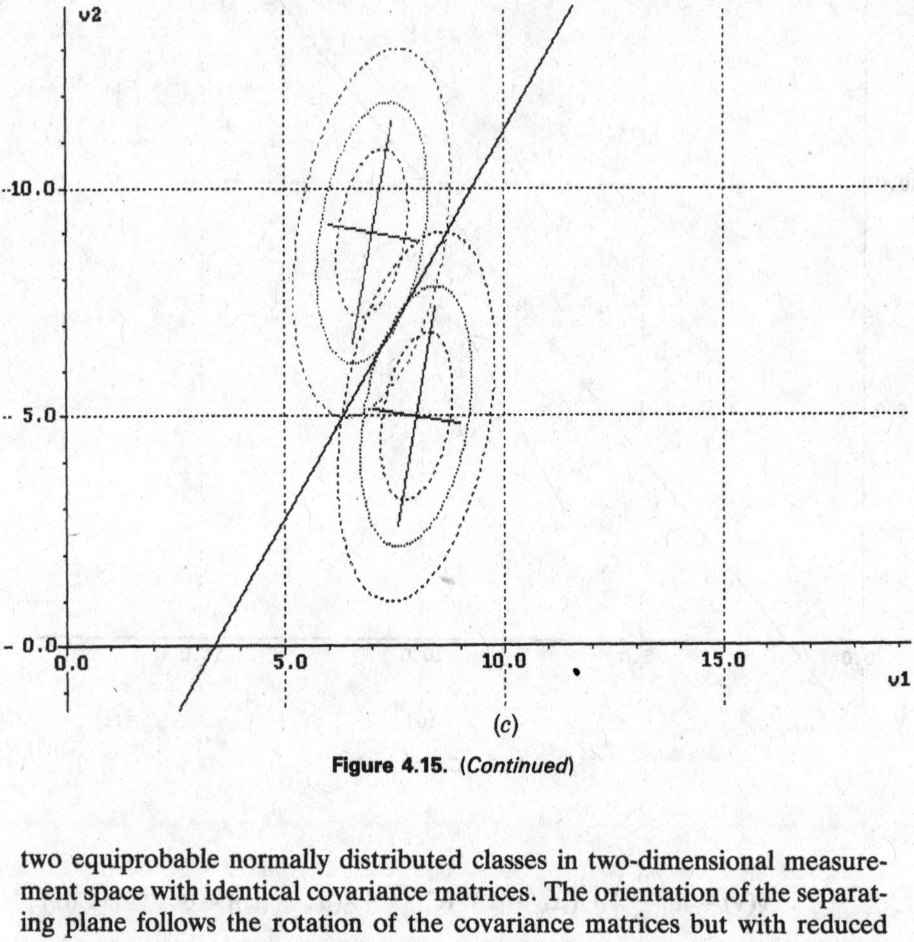

(c)

Figure 4.15. (*Continued*)

two equiprobable normally distributed classes in two-dimensional measurement space with identical covariance matrices. The orientation of the separating plane follows the rotation of the covariance matrices but with reduced angle of rotation. The special case of covariance matrices proportional to the identity matrix is illustrated by Fig. 4.16.

4.4 EUCLIDEAN AND MAHALANOBIS DISTANCE CLASSIFIERS

From the results of Section 4.3 it is a small step to the concept of *minimum-distance classification*.

We start with the optimum discriminant function $d_k(\mathbf{v})$ for normally distributed classes for the equal covariance case (4.49):

$$d_k(\mathbf{v}) = \ln(P_k) - \tfrac{1}{2}(\mathbf{v} - \boldsymbol{\mu}_k)^T \mathbf{K}^{-1}(\mathbf{v} - \boldsymbol{\mu}_k)$$

The resulting class membership estimations have to be compared for maximum (4.31). The additional assumption of uniform a priori probabilities

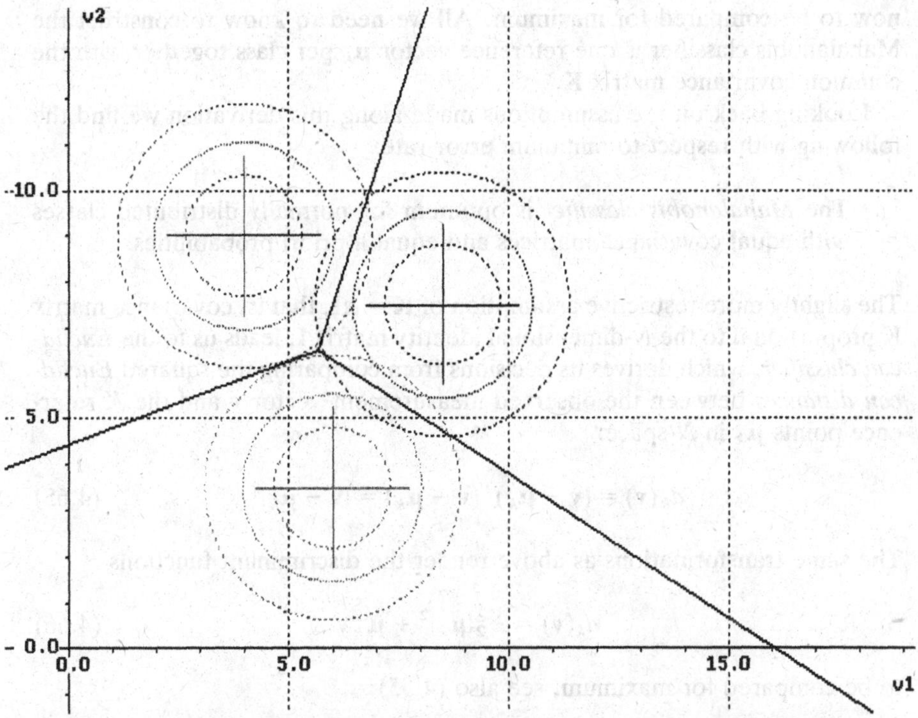

Figure 4.16. Three classes with covariance matrixes identical and proportional to identity matrix and with equal a priori probabilities. Three class separating planes are perpendicular bisectors between class centers.

($P_k = 1/K$) allows us to omit the term $\ln(P_k)$. Multiplication with -2 finally renders the discriminant functions $d_k(\mathbf{v})$ of the *Mahalanobis classifier* utilizing the squares of the so-called *Mahalanobis distances* as classification criteria,

$$d_k(\mathbf{v}) = (\mathbf{v} - \boldsymbol{\mu}_k)^T \mathbf{K}^{-1} (\mathbf{v} - \boldsymbol{\mu}_k) \tag{4.62}$$

which now, however, must be compared for minimum.

This expression is quadratic but can be simplified in the same way as in the last section to

$$d_k(\mathbf{v}) = \mathbf{v}^T \mathbf{K}^{-1} \mathbf{v} - 2\boldsymbol{\mu}_k^T \mathbf{K}^{-1} \mathbf{v} + \boldsymbol{\mu}_k^T \mathbf{K}^{-1} \boldsymbol{\mu}_k \tag{4.63}$$

The pure quadratic term $\mathbf{v}^T\mathbf{K}^{-1}\mathbf{v}$ has no influence on the decision and can be omitted. Hence we get, after multiplication with $-\frac{1}{2}$, the discriminant functions

$$d_k(\mathbf{v}) = -\tfrac{1}{2}\boldsymbol{\mu}_k^T \mathbf{K}^{-1} \boldsymbol{\mu}_k + \boldsymbol{\mu}_k^T \mathbf{K}^{-1} \mathbf{v} \tag{4.64}$$

now to be compared for maximum. All we need to know to construct the Mahalanobis classifier is one reference vector $\boldsymbol{\mu}_k$ per class together with the common covariance matrix **K**.

Looking back on the assumptions made along this derivation we find the following with respect to minimum error rate:

- The *Mahalanobis classifier* is optimum for normally distributed classes with equal covariance matrices and equal a priori probabilities.

The slightly more restrictive assumption of $\mathbf{K} = \alpha\mathbf{I}$, that is, covariance matrix **K** proportional to the N-dimensional identity matrix **I**, leads us to the *Euclidean classifier*, which derives its decisions from comparing the squared *Euclidean distances* between the observed measurement vector **v** and the K reference points $\boldsymbol{\mu}_k$ in N-space:

$$d_k(\mathbf{v}) = (\mathbf{v} - \boldsymbol{\mu}_k)^T(\mathbf{v} - \boldsymbol{\mu}_k) = |\mathbf{v} - \boldsymbol{\mu}_k|^2 \tag{4.65}$$

The same transformations as above render the discriminant functions

$$d_k(\mathbf{v}) = -\tfrac{1}{2}|\boldsymbol{\mu}_k|^2 + \boldsymbol{\mu}_k^T\mathbf{v} \tag{4.66}$$

to be compared for maximum, see also (4.55):

- The Euclidean classifier is optimum for normally distributed classes with equal covariance matrices proportional to the identity matrix and equal a priori probabilities.

It should again be noted that the essence of (4.66) is to compute the scalar product of reference vector $\boldsymbol{\mu}_k$ and measurement vector **v**:

- Both Euclidean and the Mahalanobis classifiers are linear classifiers.

Both classifiers rely on linear discriminant functions $d_k(\mathbf{v})$ of type (4.52). Since the constant term a_{0k} as well as the coefficient vector $\mathbf{a}_k$ can be computed beforehand, they require both the same computational effort for classification but differ in their effort for learning. The difference lies in the excess demand on statistical data—covariance matrix **K**—for the Mahalanobis classifier.

Comments

The foregoing considerations have shown how some of the most popular conceptions for classifier design can be derived from decision-theoretic foundations, from the assumption of the normal distribution for the class-specific probabilities and, potentially, from some additional restrictions. We should be aware of the fact that using the simple idea of minimum Euclidean distance classification implicitly corresponds to certain statistical assumptions that, if they hold, make this classifier the unsurpassable optimum.

The crucial question whether these statistical assumptions hold or not can almost never be definitely answered in any practical application. The question that then remains is to which degree these assumptions are valid, a question still more difficult to answer in view of the fact that no means exist to measure the degree of validity.

The only possible way to overcome these difficulties, therefore, is to cut the Gordian knot, using some kind of assumption as a working hypothesis and checking whether the resulting classifier is able to do the intended job. It should be clear that there exists only a minor difference between this way of proceeding and totally ignoring all statistical assumptions and simply checking which of the different classifier types from the pattern classification arsenal is powerful enough and adequate from the cost/performance point of view.

It should be mentioned that the normal distribution is a member of a whole family of N-dimensional probability functions that with minor additional restrictions lead to the same results as the normal distribution itself. These are the family of functions

$$P(\mathbf{v}, \boldsymbol{\mu}, \mathbf{K}) = \frac{1}{F\sqrt{\det \mathbf{K}}} f[-\tfrac{1}{2}(\mathbf{v} - \boldsymbol{\mu})^T \mathbf{K}^{-1}(\mathbf{v} - \boldsymbol{\mu})] \tag{4.67}$$

for arbitrary monotonically decreasing functions $f(\cdot)$. What these generalized distribution functions have in common with the normal distribution is that they depend on a quadratic form; their difference lies only in the monotonic law of decay $f(\cdot)$. The term F in the denominator cares for the fact that integrating this function over the total measurement space $\mathbf{V}$ must render unity. Hence, F depends on the function $f(\cdot)$ and becomes $F = \sqrt{(2\pi)^N}$ if $\exp(-\frac{1}{2}r^2)$ is chosen for $f(r^2)$ [SCH1977].

4.5 STATISTICALLY INDEPENDENT BINARY MEASUREMENTS

We have so far considered the single measurements v_n (components of the measurement vector $\mathbf{v}$) to be real values. There are, however, many cases where the measurements can assume only two different values; think, for example, of a character recognition application where the black or white pixel values are directly used as measurements.

We need an assignment of numbers to the discrete values True and False of the measurement domain that can be accomplished quite differently:

$$\mathbf{v} = \begin{cases} 0 & \text{for False} \\ 1 & \text{for True} \end{cases} \quad \text{or} \quad \mathbf{v} = \begin{cases} -1 & \text{for False} \\ +1 & \text{for True} \end{cases} \tag{4.68}$$

to quote only the most obvious two. Both representations are equivalent and lead to identical results.

We treat the components v_n of $\mathbf{v}$ as binary-valued variables $v_n \in \{0, 1\}$, $n = [1, \ldots, N]$. As in the foregoing there are K classes to be discriminated.

The case to be considered here is that of *statistically independent binary measurements*, in the sense that for each of the K classes there exists a class-specific probability $\text{prob}(\mathbf{v}|k)$ having the property of statistical independence among the components v_n of $\mathbf{v}$:

$$\text{prob}(\mathbf{v}|k) = \prod_{n=1}^{N} \text{prob}(v_n|k) \tag{4.69}$$

It must be mentioned that even if in many cases this assumption of statistical independence is not especially realistic, it may be well suited for rendering reasonably good classifiers.

The probability function $\text{prob}(v_n)$ of the single binary variable v_n has only two distinct values

$$\text{prob}(v_n) = \begin{cases} 1 - \mu_n & \text{for } v_n = 0 \\ \mu_n & \text{for } v_n = 1 \end{cases} \tag{4.70}$$

that directly depend on $\mu_n = E\{v_n\}$. Using exponentials $\text{prob}(v_n)$ can be written in closed form

$$\text{prob}(v_n) = \mu_n^{v_n}(1 - \mu_n)^{1-v_n} \tag{4.71}$$

Inserting that into the above expression for $\text{prob}(\mathbf{v}|k)$ gives

$$\text{prob}(\mathbf{v}|k) = \prod_{n=1}^{N} \mu_{nk}^{v_n}(1 - \mu_{nk})^{1-v_n} \tag{4.72}$$

The Bayes decision rule (2.25) requires us to compute the discriminant functions

$$d_k(\mathbf{v}) = \text{prob}(\mathbf{v}|k)\text{prob}(k) = P_k\text{prob}(\mathbf{v}|k) \tag{4.73}$$

and to compare the resulting values $d_k(\mathbf{v})$ for a maximum.

We again make use of the fact that monotonic mappings do not disturb the rank order among the values to be compared and simplify this expression to

$$d_k(\mathbf{v}) = \ln(P_k) + \sum_{n=1}^{N} [v_n \ln(\mu_{nk}) + (1 - v_n) \ln(1 - \mu_{nk})] \qquad (4.74)$$

by taking the logarithm. With respect to **v**, again we achieve a linear function of the same type as in (4.52),

$$d_k(\mathbf{v}) = a_{0k} + \mathbf{a}_k^T \mathbf{v}$$

but with differently defined coefficients a_{0k}, $\mathbf{a}_k$,

$$a_{0k} = \ln(P_k) + \sum_{n=1}^{N} \ln(1 - \mu_{nk}) \qquad (4.75)$$

$$a_{nk} = \ln\left(\frac{\mu_{nk}}{1 - \mu_{nk}}\right)$$

compared to the linear classifiers of Section 4.3. Thus the a_{nk} are the components of the coefficient vector $\mathbf{a}_k$:

- The optimum classifier for binary, class-specific statistical independent measurements is a linear classifier.

The closest relationship exists to the case of normally distributed classes with covariance matrices **K** proportional to the identity matrix **I**; compare (4.56):

$$a_{0k} = \alpha \ln(P_k) - \tfrac{1}{2}|\boldsymbol{\mu}_k|^2 \qquad a_{nk} = \mu_{nk}$$

In both cases the assumptions on the statistical properties of $\{\mathbf{v}|k\}$ are so restrictive that the coefficient vectors $\mathbf{a}_k$ of the linear discriminant function (4.52) are completely determined by the class-specific first-order statistical moments $\boldsymbol{\mu}_k = E\{\mathbf{v}|k\}$. It must be noted, however, that the resulting algorithmic rules for deriving the coefficients a_{nk} from μ_{nk} are different.

Impact of Variances of Binary Variables

The variance of any stochastic variable can be computed by

$$\text{var}\{v_n\} = E\{v_n^2\} - E^2\{v_n\} \qquad (4.76)$$

Binary variables $v_n \in \{0, 1\}$, such as the measurements considered here, have the property of $v_n^2 = v_n$. Thus we get

$$\mathrm{var}\{v_n\} = \mu_n - \mu_n^2 = \mu_n(1 - \mu_n) \tag{4.77}$$

By definition, the N measurements v_n are statistically independent. Thus the covariance matrix $\mathbf{K}_k$ of the class-specific stochastic process $\{\mathbf{v}|k\}$ becomes

$$\mathbf{K}_k = \begin{bmatrix} \mu_{1k}(1-\mu_{1k}) & 0 & \cdots & 0 \\ 0 & \mu_{2k}(1-\mu_{2k}) & \cdots & 0 \\ \vdots & \vdots & \ddots & \vdots \\ 0 & 0 & \cdots & \mu_{Nk}(1-\mu_{Nk}) \end{bmatrix} \tag{4.78}$$

It is quite interesting to observe that the coefficients a_{nk} of (4.75) vanish to zero for $\mu_{nk} \to \frac{1}{2}$. This is the value indicating the maximum conceivable unreliability of a binary measurement $v_n \in \{0, 1\}$ indicating the fact that in half of the occurrences in class k the measurement v_n takes on the value $v_n = 0$ and the value 1 in the other half of the cases.

Reliable observations v_n are those with small variance, usually either 0 or

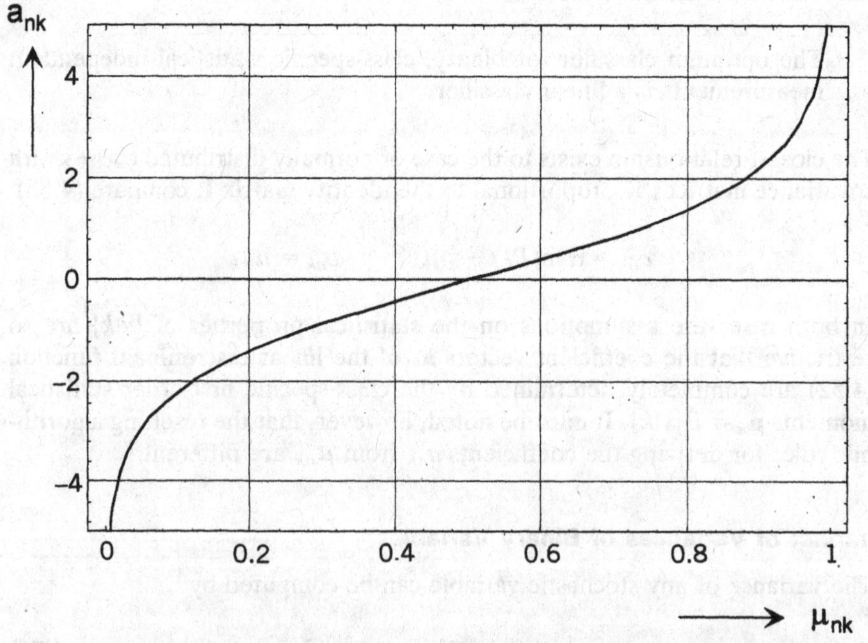

Figure 4.17. Relationship between weight a_{nk} in the linear discriminant function $d_k(\mathbf{v})$ (4.75) and class-specific mean μ_{nk} of nth measurement v_n for the case of statistically independent binary variables $v_n \in \{0, 1\}$.

1. The more discriminative power the v_n gain, the more their weight increases in (4.52). The weights of reliable measurements v_n dominate the weights of all others when μ_{nk} asymptotically approaches 0 or 1. See Fig. 4.17.

4.6 PARAMETER ESTIMATION

We started this chapter by emphasizing the fact that there are two different roles possible for statistical models in pattern classification.

What we have followed so far is the idea that the statistical model actually describes the situation in measurement space **V**. When this is true, everything we need to know about the stochastic processes $\{\mathbf{v}|k\}$ and $\{k\}$ is known and we can derive from this knowledge how the optimum classifier looks.

The other view is to take one of the conceivable statistical models as a sufficiently fitting description of the situation in measurement space and to use it as approximation to the actual but unknown situation. All of the statistical models we have considered here are generic in the sense that they provide a number of free parameters that allow us to adapt the functions $\text{prob}(\mathbf{v}|k)$ they represent to the requirements of the application.

The degree of performance this model fitting process is able to achieve depends on the general properties of the model and on the properties of the pattern source $\{\mathbf{v}, k\}$ representing the current application (even if these properties are unknown). This gives rise to the question of how to select the appropriate model from the arsenal of known statistical models.

This question is extremely difficult to answer since for almost all practical applications there exists no basic axiom from which an appropriate model can be derived. Hence, the common procedure in practical pattern classification is to choose one of the potential models based on the designer's past experience and to test empirically whether this is capable of yielding a pattern classifier with the desired cost/performance ratio.

It is also possible, and quite successful, to use statistical models that, from a strictly mathematical point of view, ought to be excluded from consideration. Think of an application where the N-dimensional measurement vector **v** represents the black and white pixel image of characters to be recognized. Due to the binary nature of the single measurements, the measurement space **V** in this case is the N-cube. The distribution $\{\mathbf{v}|k\}$ of points in N-space belonging to one certain class k can, strictly speaking, never be governed by an N-dimensional normal distribution, since the argument **v** of such a distribution function $\text{prob}(\mathbf{v}|k)$ is an N-dimensional continuous variable. Nevertheless, the normal distribution model may also be a good choice in such a case.

The situation does not fundamentally change when the measurement vector **v** is continuous and no objections can be raised from the viewpoint of distinction between discrete and continuous variables. Also, then, some unanswerable questions remain: Does the N-dimensional normal distribution really fit? Must the general case of different covariance matrices **K** be treated or can simplifications be applied?

These questions can only be answered if we know more about the properties of the pattern source $\{\mathbf{v}, k\}$ introduced in Section 2.1 in order to represent the statistical characteristics of the application. All we may really know about the statistics of $\{\mathbf{v}, k\}$ must be derived from the learning set containing a large number J of sample patterns $[\mathbf{v}, k]$:

$$\begin{aligned}&\text{Learning set} = \{[\mathbf{v}, k]_1, [\mathbf{v}, k]_2, [\mathbf{v}, k]_3, \ldots, [\mathbf{v}, k]_J\}\\&\text{Sample size} = J\end{aligned} \tag{4.79}$$

The learning set may be divided into class-specific subsets $\{\mathbf{v}|k\}$ with corresponding sizes J_k, $k = 1, \ldots, K$.

It should be possible, at least in principle, first to analyze the learning set with respect to the adequate statistical model and, after having solved this problem, perform the model fitting by adjusting the model parameters. This technique works only for very low dimension N of $\mathbf{v}$ since then statistical tests for normality can be applied. For dimensions N of realistic size no practical tests of this kind are available. Hence classifier development based on one statistical hypothesis or the other is the appropriate way of testing whether the hypothesis works.

Statistical Moments

The process of model fitting completely relies on the given learning set. Since the models are class specific, we need the class-specific learning set,

$$\text{Learning set} = \{[\mathbf{v}|k]_1, [\mathbf{v}|k]_2, [\mathbf{v}|k]_3, \ldots, [\mathbf{v}|k]_{Jk}\} \tag{4.80}$$

with sample size J_k.

The statistical models considered in this chapter have as their parameters *statistical moments* defined by the mathematical expectation operator $E\{\cdot\}$ directly applied either to the stochastic variable $\mathbf{v}$ or to the higher order terms thereof.

If only a sample set $\{\mathbf{v}\}$ is available, the mathematical expectation operator $E\{\cdot\}$ is to be replaced by the arithmetic mean applied to that expression $f(\mathbf{v})$ of $\mathbf{v}$ for which the expectation is to be computed:

$$E_{\text{estimated}}\{f(\mathbf{v})\} = \frac{1}{J}\sum_{j=1}^{J} f(\mathbf{v}_j) \tag{4.81}$$

In the context of the present deliberations, what is needed are the first- and second-order statistical moments

$\boldsymbol{\mu} = E\{\mathbf{v}\}$ first-order moment

$\mathbf{K} = E\{(\mathbf{v}-\boldsymbol{\mu})(\mathbf{v}-\boldsymbol{\mu})^T\}$ central second-order moment, covariance matrix

Model fitting simply consists in estimating these statistical moments from the given learning set:

$$\boldsymbol{\mu}_{\text{estimated}} = \frac{1}{J}\sum_{j=1}^{J} \mathbf{v}_j \tag{4.82}$$

$$\mathbf{K}_{\text{estimated}} = \frac{1}{J}\sum_{j=1}^{J} (\mathbf{v}_j - \boldsymbol{\mu}_{\text{estimated}})(\mathbf{v}_j - \boldsymbol{\mu}_{\text{estimated}})^T$$

It should be noted that the definition given in (4.82) for the empirical covariance matrix $\mathbf{K}_{\text{estimated}}$ slightly differs from the standard statistical definition as the sum is divided by J and not by $J-1$, which would make $\mathbf{K}_{\text{estimated}}$ an unbiased estimate of $\mathbf{K}$. So the estimation is only asymptotically unbiased. With respect to the normally large sample size J this makes only a minor difference that could be easily corrected by multiplying the estimation $\mathbf{K}_{\text{estimated}}$ with $J/(J-1)$.

The reason for our deviation from the standard statistical definition is that we will compute statistical moments of different order in the same moment matrix scheme using augmented input vectors; see (4.84) and (4.85).

Whenever it is clear from the context whether what is meant are the true values $\boldsymbol{\mu}$ and $\mathbf{K}$ or their estimates, the index "estimated" is omitted in order to shorten the expressions.

Statistical moments of the kind discussed here not only are the relevant parameters of statistical models but have equal importance for the classifier design strategies based on functional approximation to be considered in the chapters to follow.

The notation of (4.82) suggests that a sequence of two steps is necessary to compute both $\boldsymbol{\mu}$ and $\mathbf{K}$. This process can however be performed by running through the learning set only once. This is accomplished by computing the moment matrix $\mathbf{M}$ of the same statistical process $\{\mathbf{v}\}$:

$\mathbf{M} = E\{\mathbf{v}\mathbf{v}^T\}$ noncentral second-order moment, moment matrix

The three statistical moments $\boldsymbol{\mu}$, $\mathbf{K}$, and $\mathbf{M}$ are connected by

$$\mathbf{K} = \mathbf{M} - \boldsymbol{\mu}\boldsymbol{\mu}^T \tag{4.83}$$

The same relation holds for the corresponding estimations. Hence with one run through the sample set both $\boldsymbol{\mu}$ and $\mathbf{M}$ are determined and then $\mathbf{K}$ is computed.

Augmented Measurement Vector

These relations can be written slightly differently by introducing an augmented measurement vector $\mathbf{x}$ with one additional component with value 1:

$$\mathbf{x} = \begin{pmatrix} 1 \\ \mathbf{v} \end{pmatrix} \tag{4.84}$$

The moment matrix $E\{\mathbf{x}\mathbf{x}^T\}$ of the augmented variable $\mathbf{x}$ contains both $\boldsymbol{\mu}$ and $\mathbf{M}$:

$$E\{\mathbf{x}\mathbf{x}^T\} = \begin{pmatrix} 1 & \boldsymbol{\mu}^T \\ \boldsymbol{\mu} & \mathbf{M} \end{pmatrix} \tag{4.85}$$

From the viewpoint of matrix inversion, computation of $\mathbf{K}$ according to (4.83) corresponds to a partial inversion of $E\{\mathbf{x}\mathbf{x}^T\}$ such that just the leftmost column of this expression is transformed to unity form:

$$E\{\mathbf{x}\mathbf{x}^T\} = \begin{pmatrix} 1 & \boldsymbol{\mu}^T \\ \boldsymbol{\mu} & \mathbf{M} \end{pmatrix} \xrightarrow[\text{row manipulations}]{\text{elementry matrix}} \begin{pmatrix} 1 & \boldsymbol{\mu}^T \\ 0 & \mathbf{M} - \boldsymbol{\mu}\boldsymbol{\mu}^T \end{pmatrix} = \begin{pmatrix} 1 & \boldsymbol{\mu}^T \\ 0 & \mathbf{K} \end{pmatrix} \tag{4.86}$$

The moment matrix $\mathbf{M}$ or their augmented variant $E\{\mathbf{x}\mathbf{x}^T\}$ is estimated from the learning set, in analogy to (4.82), by

$$\begin{aligned} \mathbf{M}_{\text{estimated}} &= \frac{1}{J}\sum_{j=1}^{J} \mathbf{v}_j\mathbf{v}_j^T \\ E_{\text{estimated}}\{\mathbf{x}\mathbf{x}^T\} &= \frac{1}{J}\sum_{j=1}^{J} \mathbf{x}_j\mathbf{x}_j^T \end{aligned} \tag{4.87}$$

Moment matrices as well as covariance matrices are symmetric. Utilizing this fact allows savings in storage space and processing time.

Both $\boldsymbol{\mu}$ and $\mathbf{K}$ represent statistical properties of the respective learning set, be it the total learning set $\{\mathbf{v}\}$ irrespective of class membership k or one of the collection of class-specific learning sets $\{\mathbf{v}|k\}$.

Parameter Estimation from Subsets

Since $E\{\cdot\}$ and its estimates (4.81) are linear operators, there exists an isomorphism between sets and subsets of patterns $\{[\mathbf{v}, k]\}$ on the one side and statistical moments of these sets and subsets on the other.

Think of a pattern source PatSource = $\{\mathbf{v}, k\}$ being composed of a number

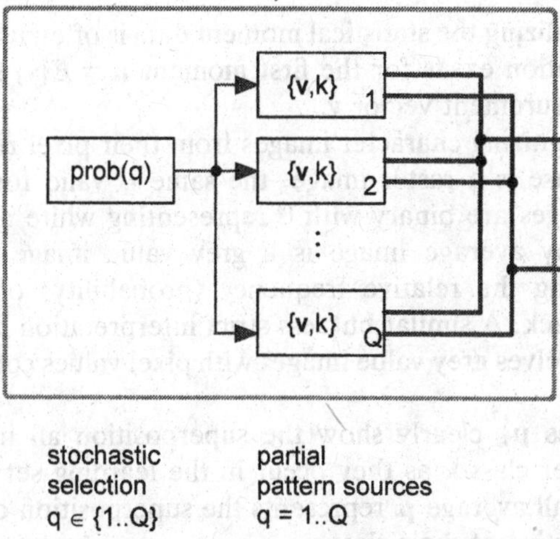

Figure 4.18. Pattern source composed of a number of partial stochastic processes stochastically activated with known probabilities α_q. Each of the partial pattern sources PatSource$_q$, $q = 1, \ldots, Q$, can be described by its own learning set. The total learning set $\{\mathbf{v}, k\}$ is then the corresponding mixture of all the individual learning sets with mixing weights α_q.

of elementary pattern sources PatSource$_q$, $q = 1, \ldots, Q$, stochastically activated with prob(PatSource$_q$) $= \alpha_q$, as illustrated by Fig. 4.18.

In such a situation each of the individual pattern sources is empirically described by its corresponding learning set. The total learning set can equivalently be accumulated either from observing the composed stochastic process or from mixing the partial learning sets with weights α_q. Isomorphically, the statistical moments of the total learning set also can be gained either from applying the estimation (4.81) to the total learning set or from first applying (4.81) to the partial learning sets separately and then computing the linear combination of the partial moments with the same set of mixing weights α_q. It should be mentioned that these possibilities are not at all restricted to the case of class-specific subsets but are applicable to any subdivision of the stochastic process $\{\mathbf{v}, k\}$ into arbitrary subprocesses.

This possibility of mixing, editing, and manipulating partial pattern sources and their relevant statistical parameters on the level of *statistical moments* is most advantageous from a practical point of view and the key to economic classifier development. The time-consuming task of extracting the required statistical moments from learning sets needs to be performed only once. The resulting statistical data are stored in a suitably organized database and from there retrieved for classifier development using different design strategies or within different application contexts.

Visualization of Statistical Parameters

In practical applications visualizing the statistical moment data is often useful. The most obvious interpretation exists for the first moment $\boldsymbol{\mu} = E\{\mathbf{v}\}$ since $\boldsymbol{\mu}$ is simply the average measurement vector $\mathbf{v}$.

Consider the case of recognizing character images from their pixel representation. Since $\mathbf{v}$ in that case is a raster image, the same is valid for the average $\boldsymbol{\mu}$. If the raster images are binary with 0 representing white and 1 representing black, then any average image is a grey value image with the shades of grey indicating the relative frequency (probability) of the corresponding pixel being black. A similar but less strict interpretation holds if the raster images are themselves grey value images with pixel values coming from the range of $[0\,.\,.\,1]$.

The class-specific averages $\boldsymbol{\mu}_k$ clearly show the superposition all incarnations on a certain character class k as they occur in the learning set (see Fig. 4.19), whereas the overall average $\boldsymbol{\mu}$ represents the superposition of all the character images irrespective of their class.

Another kind of statistical data even easily represented in the same form are the variances of the individual measurements. These variances either are separately measured or are taken from the main diagonal of the respective covariance matrices $\mathbf{K}_k$, or directly derived from the means $\boldsymbol{\mu}_k$ if the measurements are binary. We remember Equation (4.77) teaching that the variance $\text{var}\{v\}$ of a binary stochastic variable v exclusively depends on its mean $\mu = E\{v\}$. Figure 4.20 shows the variances $\text{var}\{v_n\}$ of the components of $\mathbf{v}$ for the same example as Fig. 4.19.

Visualization of covariance matrices $\mathbf{K}$ is slightly more complicated [FRA1991b]. The covariance matrix is a square two-dimensional array of numbers. Its organization is determined by the organization of the measurement vector $\mathbf{v}$. All rows and columns of $\mathbf{K}$ have the same data structure as $\mathbf{v}$: If $\mathbf{v}$ represents a pixel raster image, then so do the rows and columns of $\mathbf{K}$. The symmetry of $\mathbf{K}$ allows us to transfer any interpretation of its columns to its rows.

In terms of its columns $\mathbf{k}_n$ the covariance matrix $\mathbf{K}$ can be written

$$\mathbf{K} = (\mathbf{k}_1, \mathbf{k}_2, \ldots, \mathbf{k}_N) \tag{4.88}$$

The nth column $\mathbf{k}_n$ represents the covariance between the scalar variable v_n (the nth measurement) and the complete measurement vector $\mathbf{v}$:

$$n\text{th column}(\mathbf{K}) = \text{cov}\{v_n, \mathbf{v}\} \tag{4.89}$$

In the case of $\mathbf{v}$ being a raster image, v_n represents one of the pixels and $\mathbf{k}_n$ the covariance between that certain nth pixel v_n (positioned at row r and column c in the raster image) and the entire image $\mathbf{v}$. These relations are illustrated by Fig. 4.21.

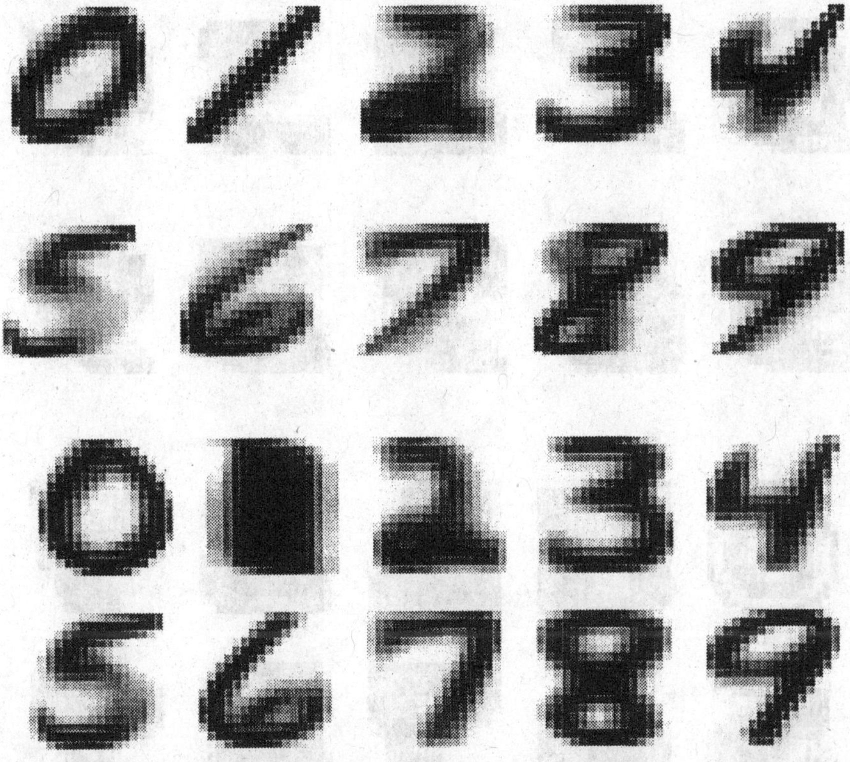

Figure 4.19. Collection of class-specific averages $\boldsymbol{\mu}_k$ of pixel raster images representing handprinted isolated numerals. Character images of upper block are registered according to their rectangular bounding boxes and then size normalized to standard size of 16 × 16 pixels whereas those of lower block are additionally shear normalized. Original traster images were originally black and white binary images but are changed into grey value images by size and shear normalization procedures. Typical variations of handprint become visible in fuzziness of resulting average shapes. This fuzziness is to a certain degree reduced by additional shear normalization.

There exist as many covariance images $\mathbf{k}_n$, $n = 1, \ldots, N$, as there are pixels in the pixel map. They can, altogether, be arranged to again form a complete raster image where the $\mathbf{k}_n$ subimage is positioned according to its pixel position $[r, c]$. Thus, we arrive at a kind of fractal raster image, itself a large $R \times C$ raster image composed of small $R \times C$ raster images.

Figure 4.22 shows what we get from reordering the covariance matrix **K** in comparison with the original covariance matrix **K**.

In this case the covariance matrix **K** is computed for only one class, the handprinted numeral 2. The covariances $\text{cov}\{v_n, v_m\}$ may be positive or negative. Positive values are shown in light grey and negative in dark grey; black corresponds to vanishing values.

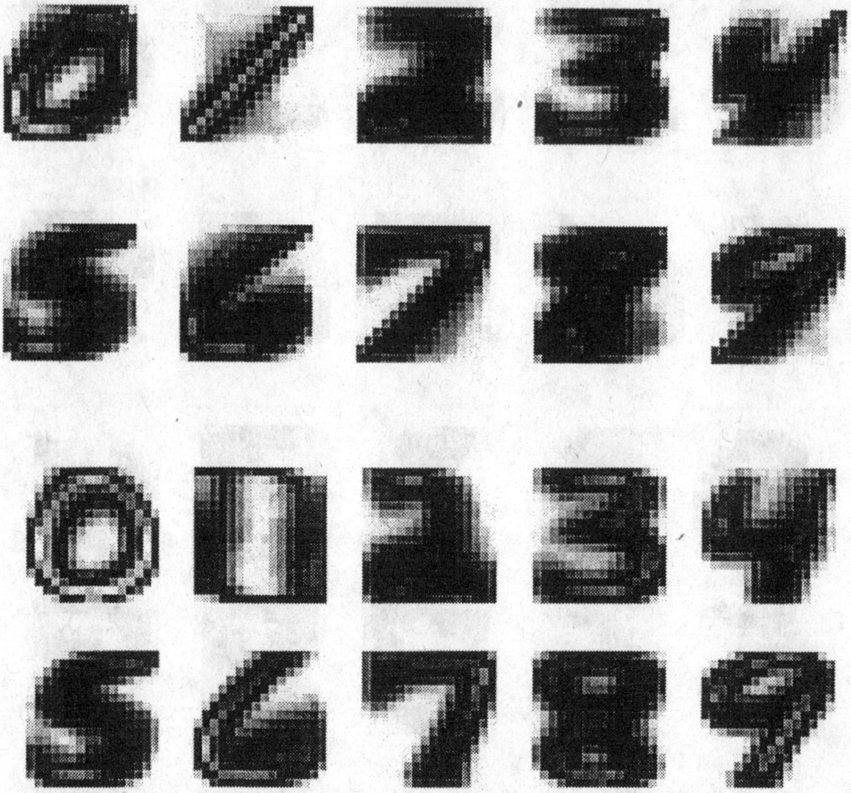

Figure 4.20. Collection of raster images showing class-specific variances var$\{v_{nk}\}$ for same application as Fig. 4.19. Pixel variations, toggling from black to white, are most likely to occur along stroke edges whereas variance vanishes to zero in those regions of pixel image consistently black or white. Thus character images appear as a kind of smeared outline image. Effect of additional shear normalization becomes visible in sharpened outline images. Note that typically slanted stroke of handprint numeral 1 is changed into vertical bar by shear normalization and almost completely fills 16 × 16 raster image since bounding box size normalization procedure here did not keep aspect ratio constant.

Fig. 4.22*a* clearly reflects the raster image structure. The covariance matrix is far from representing a "white" process, which would have one light grey line along the main diagonal. Nonvanishing positive and negative covariances appear distributed over the whole matrix since there are many pixel pairs in the raster image having, in a substantial portion of cases, either the same (covariance positive) or opposite colors (covariance negative) if, as here is done, only the character class 2 is considered.

The reordering of the rows and columns of **K** leads to the result shown

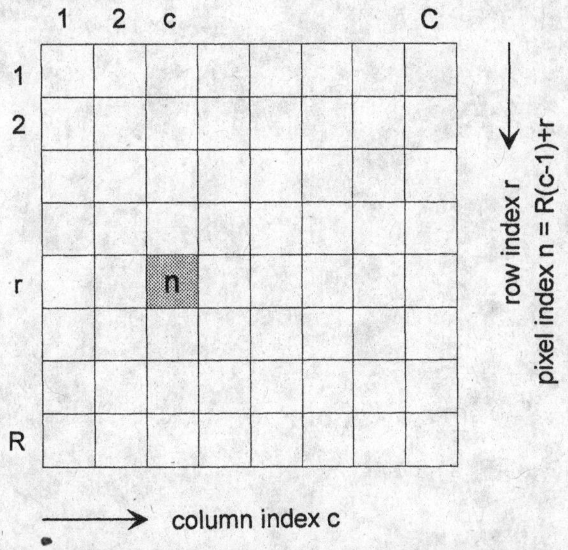

Figure 4.21. Interpretation of the nth column $\mathbf{k}_n$ of covariance matrix $\mathbf{K}$ when measurement vector $\mathbf{v}$ represents a raster image. The illustration shows rectangle $R \times C$ pixel map with nth pixel at position $[r, c]$ shaded. The nth column $\mathbf{k}_n$ of $\mathbf{K}$ is again a raster image and contains covariances between highlighted pixel v_n and entire pixel image $\mathbf{v}$, including covariance with itself $[\text{cov}\{v_n, v_n\} = \text{var}\{v_n\}]$, at highlighted position.

in Fig. 4.22*b*. This image is a systematic reordering of rows and columns of $\mathbf{K}$ and shows the complete data contained in the covariance matrix.

Interpretation

Figure 4.22 convincingly demonstrates that the stochastic process $\{\mathbf{v}|k\}$ from which the covariance matrix $\mathbf{K}$ was gained is to a high degree correlated since the whole image ought to be composed of only N isolated pixels with values that do not equal zero, namely those corresponding to the var$\{v_n\}$ terms.

The correlations among the N pixels becoming visible in this representation are mostly due to the fact that a character image is a kind of line drawing. Whenever one of the pixels is swapped from white to black, mostly because the whole character stroke was moved in that direction, other pixels behave in a more or less predictable manner.

The neighbors of the considered pixel along the stroke's edge tend to become black also (are positively correlated) whereas the pixels along the opposite edge of the stroke are likely to be swapped from black to white (are negatively correlated). These effects give the covariance image the appearance of an arrangement of edge-enhanced subimages, emphasizing

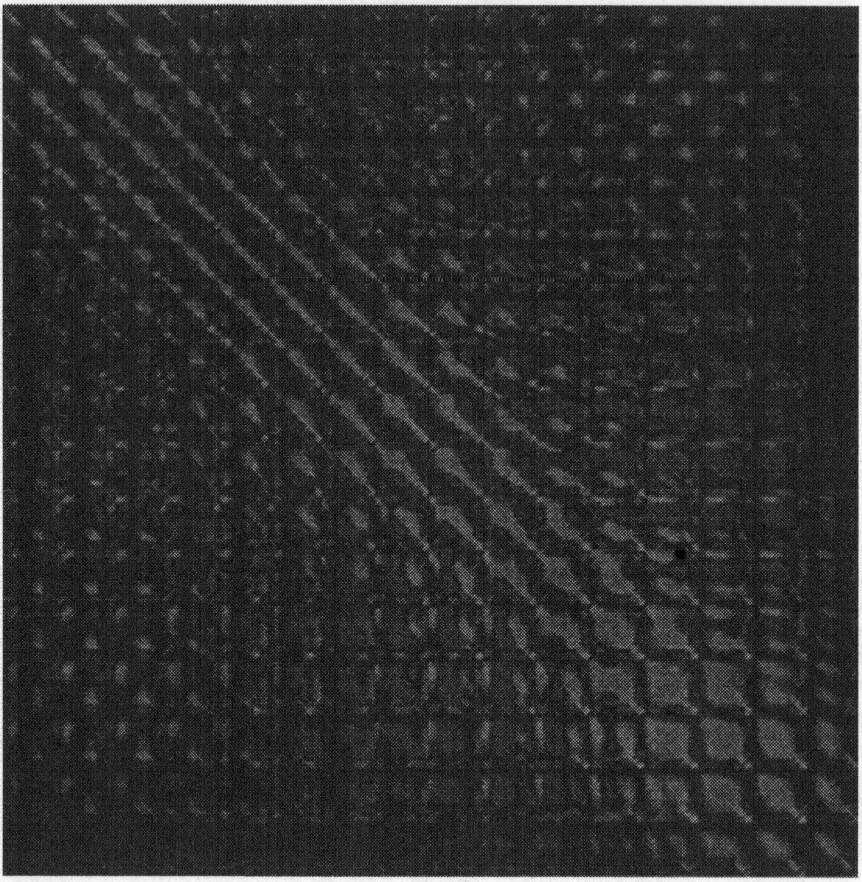

(a)

Figure 4.22. Visualization of covariance matrix **K** with (*a*) rows and columns in natural order and (*b*) rearranged so that subimages $\mathbf{k}_n$ are positioned according to their pixel coordinates [*r*, *c*]. Data comes from character recognition application, handprinted numeral 2. Character images are preprocessed as in Fig. 4.19. Positive values are coded in light grey, negative in dark grey; black represents zero.

local structures of positive and negative correlation, which suggests a kind of local feature.

The representation has a certain touch of fractal self-similarity, in the sense that the image of Fig. 4.22 is an image composed of subimages similar to the whole. This is due to the fact that **K** contains second-order moments $\text{cov}\{v_n, v_m\}$ addressed by two indices n and m, both running over the whole range $1, \ldots, N$. Thus the total set of N^2 data elements can be regularly arranged in two nested levels of first $n = 1, \ldots, N$ and for each n again for $m = 1, \ldots, N$. In Fig. 4.22 self-similarity is restricted to two levels since **K**

(b)

Figure 4.22. *(Continued)*

contains only second-order moments. Higher order moment matrices exhibit self-similarity on as many levels as correspond to their order.

The self-similarity would even be stronger if what would be considered is not the case of a handprinted character but that of a printed one, exhibiting much less variation than handprinting.

4.7 RECURSIVE PARAMETER ESTIMATION

The techniques we have discussed in the foregoing section for parameter estimation implement what could be called *off-line*, *blockwise*, or *batch learning*. They require the total learning set to be available and compute the statistical moments [according to Equation (4.81) and the formulas derived therefrom] by summation over all elements of the learning set.

This is not the only way to arrive at estimations for statistical moments. A competing approach is the technique of *on-line learning*, changing the accumulated statistical knowledge whenever new evidence becomes available, that is, with every new incoming element of the learning set.

This technique has the special appeal of being closely related to the concept of learning as it is commonly understood in colloquial language, where "learning" means the capability of continuously improving one's skills by being taught or simply by doing. There are different names for this kind of learning—such as *incremental learning*, *on-line learning*, *iterative learning*, *recursive learning*—all referring to its organization as a continuous process of repetitive improvement of what was learned so far.

At first glance, recursive learning seems to be a contrasting concept compared with the techniques of batch learning as introduced in the foregoing section. The rules for recursive parameter estimation are, however, best directly derived from the already introduced *off-line learning rules* of (4.81) and (4.82).

Recursive Learning of Means

The learning sample is a sequence of observations

$$\{\mathbf{v}_1, \mathbf{v}_2, \mathbf{v}_3, \mathbf{v}_4, \ldots, \mathbf{v}_J, \ldots\}$$

The mean value $\boldsymbol{\mu}_J$ of the first J items can easily be derived from the corresponding value $\boldsymbol{\mu}_{J-1}$ valid for the first $J-1$ items and the present observation $\mathbf{v}_J$:

$$\boldsymbol{\mu}_J = \frac{1}{J}\sum_{j=1}^{J} \mathbf{v}_j = \frac{1}{J}\left[\sum_{j=1}^{J-1} \mathbf{v}_j + \mathbf{v}_J\right]$$

$$= \left(1 - \frac{1}{J}\right)\boldsymbol{\mu}_{J-1} + \frac{1}{J}\mathbf{v}_J \tag{4.90}$$

Equation (4.90) has the form of a *learning rule for the mean value* of a stochastic sequence $\{\mathbf{v}\}$. The recursion for $\boldsymbol{\mu}$ is started with a first rough estimation $\boldsymbol{\mu} = \boldsymbol{\mu}_0$ or even with $\boldsymbol{\mu} = \mathbf{0}$ and is then continuously improved by updating it with the incoming observations. After having seen a sufficient large number of observations $\mathbf{v}$ the estimation asymptotically approaches the true mean.

Since (4.90) is derived from the standard notation of the arithmetic mean we need not care about its convergence. If initialized with a consistent estimation, as $\boldsymbol{\mu}_0 = \mathbf{0}$, the recursion generates the identical estimations for all values of J as the standard formula employing the sum operator.

The updating rule can be written slightly differently,

$$\boldsymbol{\mu}_J = \boldsymbol{\mu}_{J-1} + \frac{1}{J}(\mathbf{v}_J - \boldsymbol{\mu}_{J-1}) \tag{4.91}$$

showing that (4.90) has the property of being an *error correction rule*. The estimation is modified in each updating step proportional to the deviation between the present estimation and the present observation. Whenever $\mathbf{v}_J = \boldsymbol{\mu}_{J-1}$, no corrections occur.

The recursive estimation (4.90) for the mean value contains a continuously decreasing sequence of weights α_J:

$$\alpha_J = \frac{1}{J} \tag{4.92}$$

This is not the only possible assignment. There exists a whole theory of stochastic approximation [AGA1966], [DVO1956] showing the admissible range for the sequence of $\alpha = \alpha_J$ to make the recursion

$$\boldsymbol{\mu} \Leftarrow \boldsymbol{\mu} + \alpha(\mathbf{v} - \boldsymbol{\mu}) \quad \Leftrightarrow \quad \boldsymbol{\mu} \Leftarrow (1 - \alpha)\boldsymbol{\mu} + \alpha\mathbf{v} \tag{4.93}$$

a consistent estimate for the mean $\boldsymbol{\mu}$ of $\{\mathbf{v}\}$.

With $\alpha = 1/J$ the recursive estimation renders what may be called the *long-term mean* of $\{\mathbf{v}\}$. All observations contained in the learning sample regardless of their time of presentation get the same weight within the process of computing the mean value. The earliest have the same influence as the latest.

This corresponds to the fact that the weight with which the present observation goes into the calculation of the mean is continuously decreased the longer the sequence of observations grows. Since $\alpha \to 0$ for ever-increasing sample size J, new observations finally lose any influence, at least in a practical sense. The variance of the estimated mean decreases to zero for $J \to \infty$.

These considerations of convergence and consistency refer to the idealized situation of a stationary stochastic process $\{\mathbf{v}\}$ with parameters constant in time. This is not the situation with which practical pattern classification has to deal.

In practice we can never be sure whether the statistical properties of the given pattern source are *stationary* or not. In order to determine a sensible engineering problem they should at least be what is called *quasistationary*. They are allowed to change with time but only so slowly that the estimations gained within a certain interval of time are allowed to be transferred to the

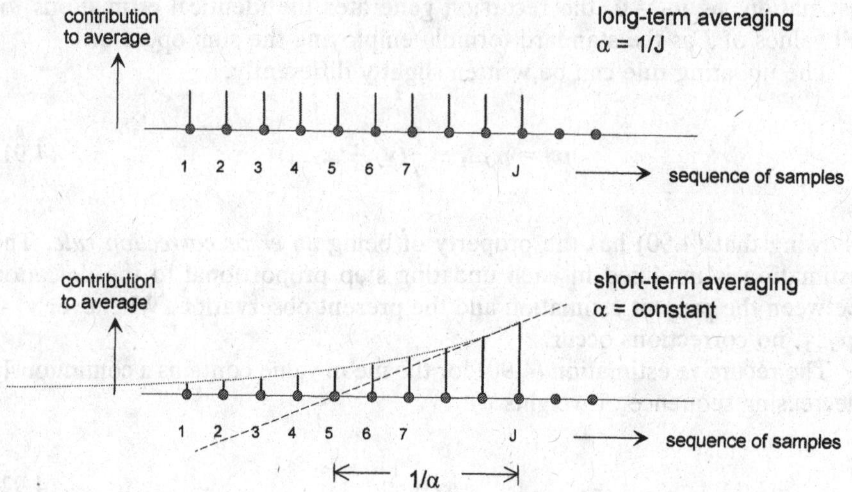

Figure 4.23. Long- and short-term averaging by recursive mean estimation according to (4.93).

following time interval and then be applied in the pattern classifier's decision rule.

What we are looking for in such a situation is the *short-term* rather than the *long-term* mean. The recursive estimate of (4.93) becomes a short-term estimate when the sequence of weights α is set to a constant value:

$$\alpha = \begin{cases} \dfrac{1}{J} & \text{long-term average} \\ \text{const} & \text{short-term average} \end{cases} \tag{4.94}$$

With $\alpha = \text{const}$ (4.93) performs what also is called *exponential smoothing* since then the contribution of each observation $\mathbf{v}$ to the estimated average exponentially decreases toward the past. The latest observation has the strongest influence.

The corresponding sequence of weights that are exponentially decreasing into the past can be viewed as a kind of time-dependent window through which the sequence of samples is observed. This exponential window is characterized by its width $1/\alpha$. Compare Fig. 4.23.

Recursive Learning of Moment Matrices

The recursive technique of estimating means can easily be transferred to estimating second-order moments, as, for example, the moment matrix $\mathbf{M} = E\{\mathbf{v}\mathbf{v}^T\}$:

$$\mathbf{M} \Leftarrow (1-\alpha)\mathbf{M} + \alpha\mathbf{v}\mathbf{v}^T \tag{4.95}$$

where α retains the interpretation of above.

In order to establish a recursive estimation for the covariance matrix $\mathbf{K}$, it must be taken into account that $\boldsymbol{\mu}$ is unknown and must be estimated by a second recursive estimation interwoven into the estimation of $\mathbf{K}$:

$$\begin{aligned}
\mathbf{K}_J &= \mathbf{M}_J - \boldsymbol{\mu}_J\boldsymbol{\mu}_J^T \\
&= [(1-\alpha)\mathbf{M}_{J-1} + \alpha\mathbf{v}_J\mathbf{v}_J^T] - [(1-\alpha)\boldsymbol{\mu}_{J-1} + \alpha\mathbf{v}_J][(1-\alpha)\boldsymbol{\mu}_{J-1} + \alpha\mathbf{v}_J]^T \\
&= (1-\alpha)\mathbf{M}_{J-1} + \alpha\mathbf{v}_J\mathbf{v}_J^T - (1-\alpha)^2\boldsymbol{\mu}_{J-1}\boldsymbol{\mu}_{J-1}^T - \alpha(1-\alpha)[\boldsymbol{\mu}_{J-1}\mathbf{v}_J^T + \mathbf{v}_J\boldsymbol{\mu}_{J-1}^T] \\
&\quad - \alpha^2\mathbf{v}_J\mathbf{v}_J^T \\
&= (1-\alpha)[\mathbf{M}_{J-1} - \boldsymbol{\mu}_{J-1}\boldsymbol{\mu}_{J-1}^T + \alpha(\mathbf{v}_J\mathbf{v}_J^T - \boldsymbol{\mu}_{J-1}\mathbf{v}_J^T + \mathbf{v}_J\boldsymbol{\mu}_{J-1}^T + \boldsymbol{\mu}_{J-1}\boldsymbol{\mu}_{J-1}^T)] \\
&= (1-\alpha)[\mathbf{K}_{J-1} + \alpha(\mathbf{v}_J - \boldsymbol{\mu}_{J-1})(\mathbf{v}_J - \boldsymbol{\mu}_{J-1})^T]
\end{aligned}$$

Hence we get the twofold recursion for $\boldsymbol{\mu}$ and $\mathbf{K}$:

$$\begin{aligned}
\mathbf{K} &\Leftarrow (1-\alpha)[\mathbf{K} + \alpha(\mathbf{v} - \boldsymbol{\mu})(\mathbf{v} - \boldsymbol{\mu})^T] \\
\boldsymbol{\mu} &\Leftarrow (1-\alpha)\boldsymbol{\mu} + \alpha\mathbf{v}
\end{aligned} \tag{4.96}$$

Recursive Learning of Inverse Covariance Matrix

It is specially important to know that the techniques of recursive estimation are not only applicable to mean, moment, and covariance matrices but also to expressions calculated therefrom. This shall be exemplified for the recursive estimation of the inverse moment matrix $\mathbf{M}^{-1}$ and the inverse covariance matrix $\mathbf{K}^{-1}$.

For this purpose we will make use of the following matrix inversion theorem [WES1968]:

$$[\mathbf{A} + \mathbf{B}\mathbf{C}\mathbf{D}^T]^{-1} = \mathbf{A}^{-1} - \mathbf{A}^{-1}\mathbf{B}[\mathbf{C}^{-1} + \mathbf{D}^T\mathbf{A}^{-1}\mathbf{B}]^{-1}\mathbf{D}^T\mathbf{A}^{-1} \tag{4.97}$$

where $\mathbf{A}$ and $\mathbf{C}$ are regular quadratic $n \times n$ and $m \times m$ matrices, respectively, and $\mathbf{D}$ and $\mathbf{B}$ are nonquadratic $m \times n$ matrices.

Starting from the recursion (4.95) for the moment matrix itself,

$$\mathbf{M}_J = (1-\alpha)\mathbf{M}_{J-1} + \alpha\mathbf{v}_J\mathbf{v}_J^T \tag{4.98}$$

we will derive a recursion for its inverse $\mathbf{M}^{-1}$. With the assignments

$$\mathbf{A} = (1-\alpha)\mathbf{M}_{J-1} \qquad \mathbf{B} = \mathbf{v}_J \qquad \mathbf{C} = \alpha \qquad \mathbf{D} = \mathbf{v}_J$$

and application of the above matrix inversion theorem, we get a recursion for the inverse moment matrix:

$$\begin{aligned}\mathbf{M}_J^{-1} &= [(1-\alpha)\mathbf{M}_{J-1} + \alpha \mathbf{v}_J \mathbf{v}_J^T]^{-1} \\ &= \frac{1}{1-\alpha}\mathbf{M}_{J-1}^{-1} - \frac{1}{(1-\alpha)^2}\mathbf{M}_{J-1}^{-1}\mathbf{v}_J\left(\frac{1}{\alpha} + \frac{1}{1-\alpha}\mathbf{v}_J^T\mathbf{M}_{J-1}^{-1}\mathbf{v}_J\right)^{-1}\mathbf{v}_J^T\mathbf{M}_{J-1}^{-1} \\ &= \frac{1}{1-\alpha}\left(\mathbf{M}_{J-1}^{-1} - \alpha\frac{\mathbf{M}_{J-1}^{-1}\mathbf{v}_J\mathbf{v}_J^T\mathbf{M}_{J-1}^{-1}}{1+\alpha(\mathbf{v}_J^T\mathbf{M}_{J-1}^{-1}\mathbf{v}_J - 1)}\right) \end{aligned} \tag{4.99}$$

Practical application of this recursion requires the following sequence of steps:

- The preliminary value for $\mathbf{M}^{-1}$ is given or already estimated.
- The present sample $\mathbf{v}$ is observed.
- First calculate $\mathbf{w} = \mathbf{M}^{-1}\mathbf{v}$.
- Update the inverse moment matrix $\mathbf{M}^{-1}$ according to

$$\mathbf{M}^{-1} \Leftarrow \frac{1}{1-\alpha}\left[\mathbf{M}^{-1} - \alpha\frac{\mathbf{w}\mathbf{w}^T}{1+\alpha(\mathbf{w}^T\mathbf{v} - 1)}\right] \tag{4.100}$$

Similarly we can derive a recursion for $\mathbf{K}^{-1}$. We start from (4.96), apply the matrix inversion theorem of (4.97) with the substitutions

$$\mathbf{A} = \mathbf{K}_{J-1} \qquad \mathbf{B} = \mathbf{v}_J - \boldsymbol{\mu}_{J-1} \qquad \mathbf{C} = \alpha \qquad \mathbf{D} = \mathbf{v}_J - \boldsymbol{\mu}_{J-1}$$

and get

$$\begin{aligned}\mathbf{K}_J^{-1} &= \frac{1}{1-\alpha}[\mathbf{K}_{J-1} + \alpha(\mathbf{v} - \boldsymbol{\mu}_{J-1})(\mathbf{v} - \boldsymbol{\mu}_{J-1})^T]^{-1} \\ &= \frac{1}{1-\alpha}\left[\mathbf{K}_{J-1}^{-1} - \alpha\frac{\mathbf{K}_{J-1}^{-1}(v - \boldsymbol{\mu}_{J-1})(v - \boldsymbol{\mu}_{J-1})^T\mathbf{K}_{J-1}^{-1}}{1+\alpha(v - \boldsymbol{\mu}_{J-1})^T\mathbf{K}_{J-1}^{-1}(v - \boldsymbol{\mu}_{J-1})}\right]\end{aligned} \tag{4.101}$$

This expression can be simplified in the same way as the recursion for the inverse moment matrix of (4.100):

- The preliminary value for $\mathbf{K}^{-1}$ is given or already estimated.
- The present sample $\mathbf{v}$ is observed.
- First calculate $\mathbf{w} = \mathbf{K}^{-1}(\mathbf{v} - \boldsymbol{\mu})$.
- Update the inverse moment matrix $\mathbf{K}^{-1}$ according to

$$\mathbf{K}^{-1} \Leftarrow \frac{1}{1-\alpha}\left[\mathbf{K}^{-1} - \alpha\frac{\mathbf{w}\mathbf{w}^T}{1+\alpha\mathbf{w}^T(\mathbf{v}-\boldsymbol{\mu})}\right] \tag{4.102}$$

- Update the mean $\boldsymbol{\mu}$ according to (4.90):

$$\boldsymbol{\mu} \Leftarrow (1-\alpha)\boldsymbol{\mu} + \alpha\mathbf{v}$$

In Chapter 6 we will make use of these formulas.

Comments

The foregoing deliberations should have made clear that from the mathematical point of view no fundamental difference exists between *batch estimates* derived from (4.81) and *recursive estimates* as those given by (4.90), (4.95). and (4.96).

A most interesting property is that the principle of recursive learning can be applied not only to the statistical moments $\boldsymbol{\mu}$ and $\mathbf{K}$, which represent the necessary statistical knowledge for classifier adaptation, but also to mathematical expressions containing $\boldsymbol{\mu}$ and $\mathbf{K}$.

The time characteristics of the learning process (short-time or long-time learning) can easily be adjusted by proper use of a constant or a time-dependent learning factor α.

Recursive learning is an attractive technique capable of keeping pace with the stream of incoming observations. This feature can be easily combined with pattern classification. The recognition system works with its already accumulated knowledge and simultaneously improves itself by recursive learning.

We should, however, not forget that recursive learning as discussed in this section needs the class label. The human teacher cannot leave the pattern classification system alone with its capability of recursive learning. For every pattern $[\mathbf{v}, k]$ arriving, the class label k must be known such that the correct class mean $\boldsymbol{\mu}_k$ and class covariance matrix $\mathbf{K}_k$ can be updated.

In certain cases, the teacher may be substituted by the application, which often has the possibility of checking whether the classifications derived by the pattern classifier are plausible or not. Plausible decisions can be taken for true and used in the updating rules.

The obvious advantage of recursive learning is that the pattern classifier, starting from some default initialization, is able to improve on the job and to follow changes in the statistical properties of the pattern source, especially if the possibility of employing some plausibility check provided by application as the teacher is used.

In contrast, there is the risk of drifting away from a thoroughly adjusted sophisticated optimum since recursive learning can only follow the current properties of the pattern source and is sensible only if these properties change slowly and consistently. However attractive the properties of recursive learning may be, in each application it must be considered whether they are appropriate or not.

A fundamental problem lies in the fact that basing classifier adaptation on recursive learning on the job makes it unclear who the teacher really is—from whom and what the pattern classifier learns.

5

CLASSIFICATION BASED ON MEAN-SQUARE FUNCTIONAL APPROXIMATIONS

The essence of *learning from examples* in pattern classification is building estimations for the unknown probability laws that govern the application. We have learned in Chapter 3 that there are two different possible approaches to reach this goal, namely deriving estimations from the learning set for either of the following:

- Class-specific probabilities $\text{prob}(\mathbf{v}|\omega)$
- A posteriori probabilities $\text{prob}(\omega|\mathbf{v})$

Chapter 4 was concerned with the first of the two approaches and used the idea of parameterized statistical models. We will now follow the second approach and derive approximations for $\text{prob}(\omega|\mathbf{v})$ based on the idea of functional approximation.

The starting point of the argumentation is the fact that least mean-square approximation (3.1) of an arbitrary function $\mathbf{d}(\mathbf{v})$ to the target vector $\mathbf{y}$,

$$S^2 = E\{|\mathbf{d}(\mathbf{v}) - \mathbf{y}|^2\} = \min_{\mathbf{d}(\mathbf{v})}$$

renders the so-called regression function $\mathbf{d}(\mathbf{v}) = E\{\mathbf{y}|\mathbf{v}\}$ (3.9), which for the case considered here of $\mathbf{y}$ being defined according to (1.5), directly becomes the vector $\mathbf{p}$ of a posteriori probabilities (3.10):

$$\mathbf{p} = [\text{prob}(\omega_1|\mathbf{v}) \quad \text{prob}(\omega_2|\mathbf{v}) \quad \cdots \quad \text{prob}(\omega_K|\mathbf{v})]^T$$

At first glance, this result seems to be of more mathematical rather than of practical relevance. The vector **p** of a posteriori probabilities is just what we do not have but what we want to have.

This result, however, opens a broad way for constructing approximations to **p**(**v**) from the set of learning samples. All that we need to do is fitting some function **d**(**v**) to the learning set {**y**, **v**} such that the squared Euclidean norm $|\mathbf{d}(\mathbf{v}) - \mathbf{y}|^2$ of the difference between estimation **d**(**v**) and observation **y**(**v**), as taken from the learning set {**y**, **v**}, becomes minimum in the average.

Compared with the ideal solution **p**(**v**) of the above, the result of such a procedure is approximative in a twofold sense: First, we cannot actually work with functions having the flexibility and adaptability of "any arbitrary function of **v**" but must instead use some more constrained type of function. Second, we must replace the mathematical expectation $E\{\cdot\}$ with the empirical mean taken over a limited size learning set {**y**, **v**} randomly drawn from the pattern source.

What we will get, then, are approximations **d**(**v**) to the true vector **p** of a posteriori probabilities. These approximations are subject to the specific constraints chosen, accidentalness and limited size of the learning set and type of estimating function used.

The basic idea is to employ for the estimate **d**(**v**) some type of parameterized function **d**(**v**, **A**) whose parameter set **A** is optimized under the least mean-square criterion

$$S^2 = E\{|\mathbf{d}(\mathbf{v}, \mathbf{A}) - \mathbf{y}|^2\} = \min_{\mathbf{A}} \tag{5.1}$$

The most obvious approach is to construct **d**(**v**) by linear combination from a suitable set of basis functions $f_l(\mathbf{v})$, $i = l, \ldots, L$, in **V**-space, whereby the parameter set **A** becomes the set of coefficientsnecessary for the linear combination. In this simplest case the basis functions $f_l(\mathbf{v})$ are completely defined functions of **v** and do not themselves depend on any parameters.

But it is also possible to make these basis functions $f_l(\mathbf{v}) = f_l(\mathbf{v}, \mathbf{A}_l)$ themselves dependent on an individual parameter set $\mathbf{A}_l$. The parameters $\mathbf{A}_l$ control the shapes of the individual basis functions and are part of the overall parameter set **A** to be optimized by the least mean-square optimization procedure.

In both cases **d**(**v**) can be written

$$\mathbf{d}(\mathbf{v}) = \mathbf{d}(\mathbf{v}, \mathbf{A}) = \sum_{l=1}^{L} \mathbf{c}_l f_l(\mathbf{v}, \mathbf{A}_l) \quad \text{where} \quad \mathbf{A} = \bigcup_{l=1}^{L} \{\mathbf{c}_l, \mathbf{A}_l\} \tag{5.2}$$

where the parameter set $\mathbf{A}_l$ contained in $f_l(\mathbf{v})$ may also be empty, resulting in

$$\mathbf{d}(\mathbf{v}) = \mathbf{d}(\mathbf{v}, \mathbf{A}) = \sum_{l=1}^{L} \mathbf{c}_l f_l(\mathbf{v}) \quad \text{where} \quad \mathbf{A} = \bigcup_{l=1}^{L} \{\mathbf{c}_l\} \tag{5.3}$$

There exist a multitude of systems of basis functions in **V**-space having the capability of representing, in the form of a weighted sum, any reasonable function of **v** to any degree of accuracy if only their number is large enough. Basing the least mean-square approximation of $\mathbf{d}(\mathbf{v})$ to $\{\mathbf{y}, \mathbf{v}\}$ on such a system of basis functions, therefore, results in a procedure which must with increasing number of basis functions asymptotically approach the optimum, namely $\mathbf{d}(\mathbf{v}) \to \mathbf{p}(\mathbf{v})$.

Learning, here, is performed by adjusting the set **A** of parameters—the coefficients $\mathbf{c}_l$ of the linear combination together with the parameters $\mathbf{A}_l$ contained within the basis functions—by least mean-square optimization. This kind of approach moves the optimization problem from the domain of calculus of variations into the domain of standard parameter optimization.

The objective function $S^2 = S^2(\mathbf{A})$ (5.1) depends on the set **A** of all parameters contained in $\mathbf{d}(\mathbf{v})$. The fundamental difference between the two types of estimating functions is that in the general case (5.2) $\mathbf{d}(\mathbf{v})$ depends nonlinearly on **A** whereas in the simplified case (5.3) $\mathbf{d}(\mathbf{v})$ is linearly dependent on **A**.

The optimum is found by setting the first derivative of $S^2(\mathbf{A})$ with respect to **A** to zero. Since the objective function is least mean square, $S^2(\mathbf{A})$ is for the simplified case (5.3) quadratic in **A** and its derivative with respect to **A** is linear. This has the remarkable effect that finding the optimum set of parameters **A** in the simplified case (5.3) leads to solving a system of linear equations.

However, in the general case of (5.2) the optimum is determined by a nonlinear system of equations that may have more than one local minimum. Whereas the system of linear equations derived from (5.3) has a direct solution, the solution in the general case must be searched for by some kind of steepest descent gradient technique.

A most desirable property the employed family of functions $f_l(\mathbf{v})$ should have is to allow approximations asymptotically approaching the optimum $\mathbf{d}(\mathbf{v}) \to \mathbf{p}(\mathbf{v})$ if the number L of basis functions becomes sufficiently large. An estimating function $\mathbf{d}(\mathbf{v})$ built from a set of basis functions having this property is said to be a *universal approximator* ([HSW1989], [WHI1992]). Different families of functions $\mathbf{d}(\mathbf{v})$ derived from different sets of basis functions that have this feature in common are asymptotically equivalent.

In the following chapters we will discuss the properties of different families of discriminant functions $\mathbf{d}(\mathbf{v})$ derived from different sets of basis functions. In Chapter 6 polynomials in **v** are used as basis functions leading to polynomial regression, in Chapter 7 we will use multilayer perceptron functions leading to multilayer perceptron regression, and in Chapter 8 we will deal with radial basis functions leading to a third variety of estimating functions.

These different families of discriminant functions, although approximating the same goal of $\mathbf{d}(\mathbf{v}) \to \mathbf{p}(\mathbf{v})$, have quite different properties and their own pros and cons, which shall become clearer from the discussions in the following chapters.

The use of polynomials is a very old concept denoted as the concept of Φ-machines in the earlier literature ([SEB1962], [NIL1965]). The principles of polynomial regression, as described in Chapter 6, go back to Schürmann [SCH1968]. The introduction of multilayer perceptron functions together with the invention of the backpropagation learning rule marks the beginning of the age of neural networks ([WER1974], [RHW1986]), shortly followed by the concept of radial basis functions [POG1989].

The most important advantage of the polynomial approach is that it has a direct solution, is easy and fast to compute, and does not depend on additional parameters such as learning rate and initialization. As a most useful byproduct the computational procedure of solving the matrix equation renders a rank order of all of the polynomial terms based on their contribution to solving the pattern classification task.

Regular polynomials exhibit a fast increase in the polynomial length if the number N of dimensions of the feature vector is large. The growth of the polynomial structure must therefore be controlled by heuristic rules, for which this rank ordering property is a valuable help.

Another remarkable advantage of the polynomial concept is that the computational procedure of classifier adaptation can be split into the two phases of, first, extracting the necessary statistical moments from the learning set, which is the dominant time-consuming operation, and, second, calculating the polynomial coefficients. This separation allows economic organization of the overall learning process, which is especially advantageous if classifiers for varying applications must be routinely calculated.

In contrast to the polynomial approach, the multilayer perceptron approach leads to a nonlinear system of equations that can only be solved by steepest descent gradient search or an equivalent technique. This fact, however, makes optimization criteria other than least mean-square optimization easily applicable.

The organization of the learning process allows us to introduce constraints into the learning process, for example, the constraint that certain of the parameters shall have identical values—weight sharing. The multilayer perceptron learning procedure is quite time consuming and leads without intermediate results directly from the learning set to the trained classifier. As a consequence thereof, the learning process must be practically repeated if, for example, the composition of the set Ω of classes is changed.

The radial basis functions approach is applicable not only to approximating the vector $\mathbf{p}(\mathbf{v})$ of a posteriori probabilities but also to generating approximations for the class-specific probabilities $\text{prob}(\mathbf{v}|\omega)$. If used in the same way as the polynomial and the multilayer perceptron approach for generating an estimate $\mathbf{d}(\mathbf{v})$ for $\mathbf{p}(\mathbf{v})$ according to (5.1), the mathematical procedure becomes identical to that of polynomial regression if the radial basis functions themselves are treated as given, case (5.2). In this case the set of parameters $\mathbf{A}$ is determined by a linear matrix equation. This changes, however, if the parameters of the radial basis functions themselves are included in the least mean-square optimization procedure, case (5.3).

All three approaches allow us to construct nonlinear discriminant functions **d**(**v**). The polynomial approach concentrates the nonlinearity into a kind of preprocessing operation requiring multiplications between input variables. In the multilayer perceptron and radial basis function approaches, to implement the nonlinearity, only one type of scalar nonlinear function is needed, allowing it to be hard-wired as a fast table look-up operation. The rest are linear matrix–vector operations.

In the following, for all three approaches we will study the design conceptions, learning rules, and general properties that derive therefrom. Some of the mathematical derivations are more for the advanced reader and may be skipped at the first reading.

Based on the synthetic example of Section 4.2, the results of these considerations will be related to the "optimum" solution developed in the foregoing chapter from the assumption of having complete knowledge about the statistical properties of the pattern source.

It should be noted that some of the material presented in Chapter 4 in the context of approximating prob($\mathbf{v}|\omega$) is necessary also in the context to be considered next, especially those in Sections 4.6 and 4.7 on parameter estimation, since statistical moments gained from the learning set contain the characteristics of the pattern source and are, for some of the techniques to be described in the subsequent chapters, just the necessary data from which the parameters of the pattern classifier are to be computed.

6

POLYNOMIAL REGRESSION

The most obvious approach to designing an approximating function $\mathbf{d}(\mathbf{v})$ from a set of basis functions is to rely on the principle of polynomial approximation. It is basic mathematical knowledge that a polynomial of sufficient length is well suited to represent any reasonable function; see the Weierstrass theorem and the Taylor series expansion. The use of polynomials in pattern classification goes far back to the very beginning of this discipline ([SEB1962], [NIL1965]).

We will introduce the technique of polynomial approximation first for a scalar function $d(\mathbf{v})$ with a vector-valued argument $\mathbf{v}$ and will generalize to the case of a vector-valued function $\mathbf{d}(\mathbf{v})$ as the second step:

$$\begin{aligned} d(\mathbf{v}) = a_0 + a_1v_1 + a_2v_2 + \cdots + a_Nv_N \\ + a_{N+1}v_1^2 + a_{N+2}v_1v_2 + a_{N+3}v_1v_3 + \cdots \\ + a\ldots v_1^3 + a\ldots v_1^2v_2 + a\ldots v_1^2v_3 + \cdots \end{aligned} \tag{6.1}$$

This general polynomial consists of one constant term a_0 followed by N linear terms a_nv_n in the first line followed by $N(N+1)/2$ quadratic terms in the second line followed by a still larger number of cubic terms in the third line, and so on, up to an arbitrary degree G of the polynomial terms.

The complete polynomial with degree G and with dimension N of the argument vector $\mathbf{v}$ has

$$L = \binom{N+G}{G} \tag{6.2}$$

polynomial terms. We call L the *polynomial length*.

Each of the *polynomial terms*—products and power terms of the components of $\mathbf{v}$—constitutes one of the L basis functions $f_l(\mathbf{v})$, $l = 1, \ldots, L$, of a functional expansion. These basis functions are combined in the form of a weighted sum—in mathematical terms a linear combination. The coefficients a_l are the weights of the linear combination.

The general polynomial of (6.1) can be written in a more compact form by introducing a vector-valued mapping $\mathbf{v} \rightarrow \mathbf{x}$ generating the L-dimensional vector $\mathbf{x}$ from the N-dimensional vector variable $\mathbf{v}$:

$$\mathbf{x}(\mathbf{v}) = (1 \quad v_1 \quad v_2 \quad \cdots \quad v_N \quad v_1^2 \quad v_1v_2 \quad v_1v_3 \quad \cdots \quad v_1^3 \quad v_1^2v_2 \quad v_1^2v_3 \quad \cdots)^T \tag{6.3}$$

The function $\mathbf{x}(\mathbf{v})$ determines the type of the polynomial $\mathbf{d}(\mathbf{v})$, and therefore, $\mathbf{x}$ is called the *polynomial structure*. We introduce also an L-dimensional *coefficient vector* $\mathbf{a}$ and get the compact form for the scalar polynomial

$$d(\mathbf{v}) = \mathbf{a}^T\mathbf{x}(\mathbf{v}) \tag{6.4}$$

It must be noted that polynomials of this type need not to be complete. In practical application, polynomials of a certain degree G are often designed according to certain heuristic construction rules not employing all of the polynomial terms of that degree. We will address this topic briefly in the following but return to a more detailed discussion later in Chapter 9. Here, it may suffice to know that the structure $\mathbf{x}(\mathbf{v})$ of the polynomial is manually predetermined, similarly to how the degree G of the polynomial is fixed by a design decision.

For the purpose of pattern classification we need a vector-valued polynomial function $\mathbf{d}(\mathbf{v})$ consisting of K scalar polynomials

$$d_k(\mathbf{v}) = \mathbf{a}_k^T\mathbf{x}(\mathbf{v}) \quad \text{responsible for class } k = 1, \ldots, K \tag{6.5}$$

each belonging to one of the K classes. We combine the K class-specific coefficient vectors $\mathbf{a}_k$ into one *coefficient matrix*

$$\mathbf{A} = (\mathbf{a}_1 \quad \mathbf{a}_2 \quad \cdots \quad \mathbf{a}_K) \tag{6.6}$$

and get

$$\mathbf{d}(\mathbf{v}) = \mathbf{A}^T\mathbf{x}(\mathbf{v}) \tag{6.7}$$

Only the coefficient matrix $\mathbf{A}$ will be adjusted during the optimization procedure. The polynomial structure $\mathbf{x}(\mathbf{v})$ is predetermined and remains un-

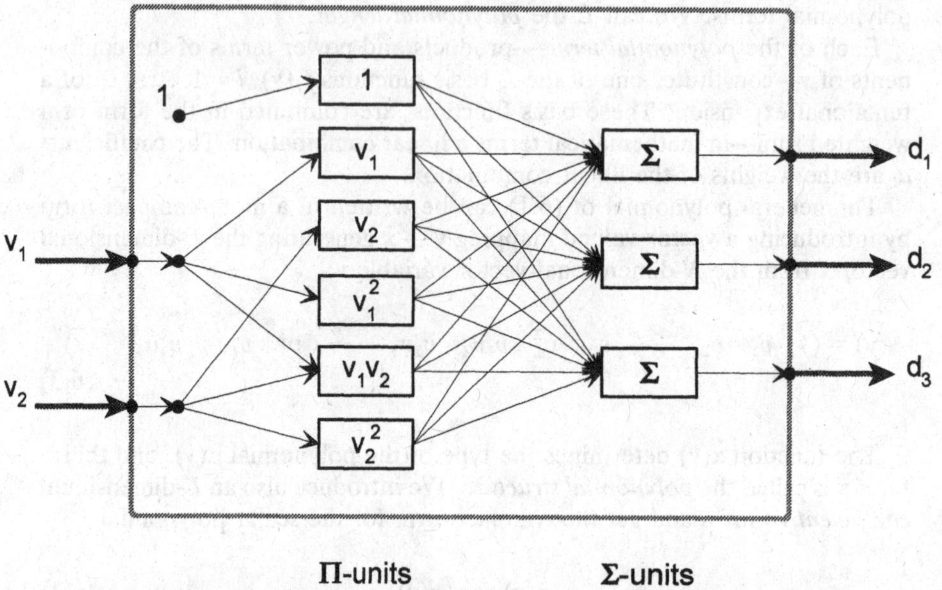

Figure 6.1. Network representation for polynomial classifier with complete polynomial of degree $G = 2$, $N = 2$ measurements, and $K = 3$ classes. In first column of processing units (first layer in direction of information flow) each unit computes product of its input variables, which are components of input vector **v**. These units are called Π-units. Their outputs are completely connected to next column of processing units. Each connecting line represents a weight a_{nk}, which are elements of coefficient matrix **A**. Processing units of this second layer are called Σ-units. They sum all their input variables and form components of output vector **d**. Whole network in neural network terms is a Π/Σ-network.

changed; if not, the whole optimization procedure is wrapped into a next level optimization process aiming also at adaptation of the polynomial structure $\mathbf{x}(\mathbf{v})$.

The polynomial approximation approach has a nice pictorial representation, which is shown in Fig. 6.1 for the simple case of $N = 2$ and $G = 2$. For larger values of N and G complete networks grow rapidly in size; thus pictorial representations become extremely complex. In practical applications N is often several tens to hundreds while G must be limited to very small numbers.

The problems of combinatorial growth are basically not due to the construction of regular polynomials but rather are intrinsic problems of high dimensionality (compare the considerations of Section 3.2) and must be overcome in some way in any practical application in order to make this concept work.

Complete polynomials exhibit rather undesired scaling properties since the polynomial length L changes for larger dimension N of the measurement vector $\mathbf{v}$ in wide steps with the polynomial degree G. With the techniques to be discussed in Chapter 9, however, the polynomial length L and thus the computational effort can be controlled in fine steps.

The most effective approach in this direction is the use of *dimensionality-reducing transformations*. The given measurement vector $\mathbf{v}$ is first transformed into a new measurement vector $\mathbf{w}$ with lower dimensionality. The intention is to compress as much as possible of the *descriptive and discriminative power* of the collection of raw measurements $\mathbf{v}$ into a hopefully much smaller number of characteristic features making up the transformed measurement vector $\mathbf{w}$.

The basic idea behind this approach corresponds to the goals of *data compression* as used for transmitting speech, images, and other data across communication channels with limited bandwidth or storing the same types of data on storage media with limited capacity. The techniques to be applied are almost the same in communication and storage as in pattern classification.

There are two points of view addressed: descriptive and discriminative power. The first one is concerned with the potential of reconstruction to retrieve the original measurement vector $\mathbf{v}$ from its compressed version $\mathbf{w}$ with maximum fidelity. The second point of view does not care for reconstructability at all but rather tries to conserve in $\mathbf{w}$ only what is necessary to come to a discrimination between the K classes of the pattern classification task. Contemplating on this last point of view leads to realizing that compression for discriminability indistinguishably merges with the final goal of classification itself and, therefore, is hardly able to give any advice on how to divide the overall task of pattern classification into the subtasks of data compression and classification. A distinction of this kind is much easier found from the reconstruction point of view.

A second approach is that of designing incomplete polynomials according to appropriate heuristics. We will return to these problems in Chapter 9.

The following considerations on design and adaptation of functions $\mathbf{d}(\mathbf{v})$ of the type given in (6.7) do not depend on whether the raw measurement vector $\mathbf{v}$ is directly input to the estimating function $\mathbf{d}(\mathbf{v})$ or if first it is mapped into a compressed feature vector $\mathbf{w}$ and then the estimation $\mathbf{d}(\mathbf{w})$ is gained from $\mathbf{w}$ in the same way as before from $\mathbf{v}$. Presently we are interested only in the second of the two consecutive mappings $\mathbf{v} \rightarrow \mathbf{w}$ and $\mathbf{w} \rightarrow \mathbf{d}$ and will therefore denote the input variable to the functional approximation by $\mathbf{v}$.

The polynomial $\mathbf{d}(\mathbf{v})$ of (6.7) can easily be generalized to represent just a wider family of approximating functions. For this purpose we need only admit for the polynomial structure $\mathbf{x}(\mathbf{v})$ functions that are not restricted to be products and power terms of the given measurement v_n but rather arbitrary functions of $\mathbf{v}$. This generalizes the polynomial classifier to the *functional classifier* of Fig. 6.2 ([PAO1989], [FRA1991b]).

The polynomial classifier, as a rule, contains the constant term $x_0 = 1$ as

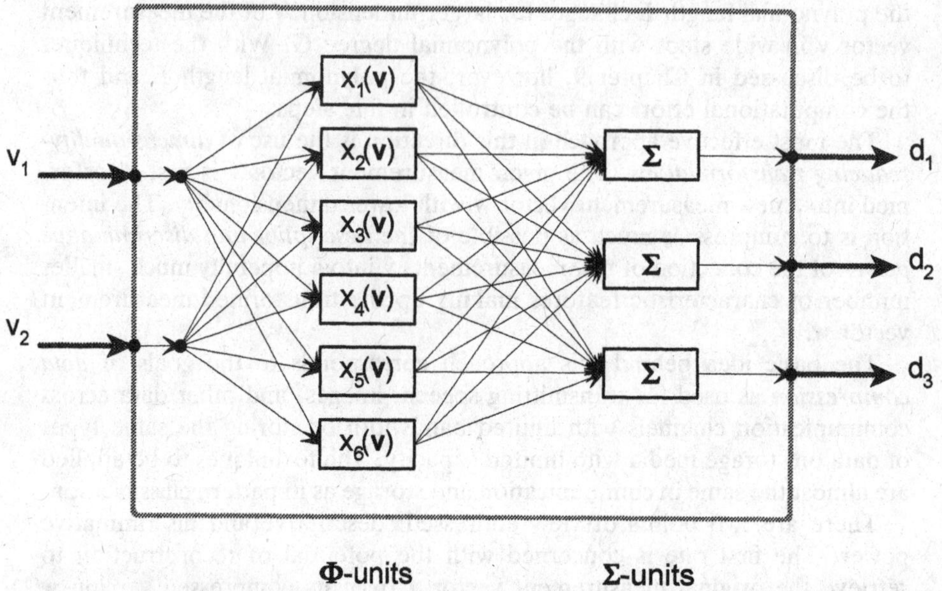

Figure 6.2. Network representation for functional classifier derived from polynomial classifier of Fig. 6.1 by generalizing mapping **x**(**v**). First layer of processing units implements set of basis functions and second layer implements linear combination necessary to achieve vector-valued output function **d**(**x**(**v**)). The N input nodes are completely connected to first-layer units in order to provide argument **v** for every functional unit. These functional units are called Φ-units and whole arrangement a Φ/Σ-network.

the first term of the vector-to-vector mapping $\mathbf{x}(\mathbf{v})$. For the functional classifier it is the design decision of whether $\mathbf{x}(\mathbf{v})$ shall contain a constant term or not.

Two prominent examples of polynomial structures are as follows:

- Complete linear polynomial structure:

$$\mathbf{x}(\mathbf{v}) = \begin{pmatrix} 1 \\ \mathbf{v} \end{pmatrix} = (1 \quad v_1 \quad v_2 \quad \cdots \quad v_N)^T \tag{6.8}$$

- Complete quadratic polynomial structure:

$$\mathbf{x}(\mathbf{v}) = (1 \quad v_1 \quad v_2 \quad \cdots \quad v_N \quad v_1^2 \quad v_1 v_2 \quad \cdots \quad v_N^2)^T \tag{6.9}$$

Generalization to higher degree polynomials is straightforward.

The most prominent structure $\mathbf{x}(\mathbf{v})$ for the functional classifier is that coming from the *radial basis function approach*. The L basis functions $x_l(\mathbf{v})$ are in this case rotational functions centered at certain preselected reference points $\mathbf{r}_l$ in **V**-space and are monotonically decreasing with increasing distance between **v** and the reference point **r**:

$$x_l(\mathbf{v}) = \exp(-|\mathbf{v} - \mathbf{r}_l|^2) \quad l = 1, \ldots, L \tag{6.10}$$

See Chapter 8.

6.1 ADAPTATION OF COEFFICIENT MATRIX

Both types of approximating functions introduced in this chapter [those of the polynomial classifier (Fig. 6.1) with $\mathbf{x}(\mathbf{v})$ according to (6.3) and those of the functional classifier (Fig. 6.2) with arbitrary structure $\mathbf{x}(\mathbf{v})$] have the same simple form of (6.7):

$$\mathbf{d}(\mathbf{v}) = \mathbf{A}^T\mathbf{x}(\mathbf{v})$$

Since the structure $\mathbf{x}(\mathbf{v})$ is considered predefined, all of the adaptability—all the *potential for learning*—lies in the coefficient matrix **A**. Learning is performed by least mean-square approximation with **A** the only adjustable parameter [compare (5.1)]:

$$S^2 = E\{|\mathbf{d}(\mathbf{v}) - \mathbf{y}|^2\} = E\{|\mathbf{A}^T\mathbf{x}(\mathbf{v}) - \mathbf{y}|^2\} = \min_{\mathbf{A}} \tag{6.11}$$

The optimization criterion S^2 of this expression is called the *residual variance* since it describes the remaining error after **y** has been best approximated by $\mathbf{d}(\mathbf{v}) = \mathbf{A}^T\mathbf{x}(\mathbf{v})$.

The residual variance S^2 is a function of **A** and can therefore be written as $S^2(\mathbf{A})$. From the foregoing expression it is obvious that S^2 depends quadratically on **A**. Hence we are looking for the minimum of a quadratic function of **A** that is known, from the fact of being quadratic, to have only one minimum. If **A** is a scalar, then the procedure for finding the minimum is straightforward: Compute the first derivative of S^2 with respect to **A** and set the result to zero. This results in a linear expression for the optimum parameter **A**.

The procedure for finding the optimum coefficient matrix **A** is quite similar. Instead of making explicit use of derivatives, we choose the same technique as in Section 3.1. The basic idea is to start from the assumption that **A** is the optimum solution to (6.11). Then any deviation $\delta\mathbf{A}$ from the optimum **A** must result in an increase of S^2:

$$S^2(\mathbf{A} + \delta\mathbf{A}) \geq S^2(\mathbf{A}) \qquad \forall\ \delta\mathbf{A} \neq \mathbf{0} \tag{6.12}$$

The right side of this inequality is already given by (6.11) and can be transformed to

$$S^2(\mathbf{A}) = E\{|\mathbf{A}^T\mathbf{x} - \mathbf{y}|^2\} = E\{[\mathbf{A}^T\mathbf{x} - \mathbf{y}]^T[\mathbf{A}^T\mathbf{x} - \mathbf{y}]\} \qquad (6.13)$$

Making use of the fact that the inner product of two vectors **a** and **b** can be written as the trace of their outer product,

$$\mathbf{a}^T\mathbf{b} = \text{trace}[\mathbf{b}\mathbf{a}^T] \qquad (6.14)$$

or more generally in terms of arbitrary matrices **P** and **Q** with matching dimensions,

$$\text{trace}[\mathbf{PQ}] = \text{trace}[\mathbf{QP}] \qquad (6.15)$$

we get

$$\begin{aligned} S^2(\mathbf{A}) &= E\{\text{trace}[[\mathbf{A}^T\mathbf{x} - \mathbf{y}][\mathbf{A}^T\mathbf{x} - \mathbf{y}]^T]\} \\ &= \text{trace}[E\{\mathbf{y}\mathbf{y}^T\}] - 2\,\text{trace}[\mathbf{A}^T E\{\mathbf{x}\mathbf{y}^T\}] + \text{trace}[\mathbf{A}^T E\{\mathbf{x}\mathbf{x}^T\}\mathbf{A}] \\ &= E\{|\mathbf{y}|^2\} - 2\,\text{trace}[\mathbf{A}^T E\{\mathbf{x}\mathbf{y}^T\}] + \text{trace}[\mathbf{A}^T E\{\mathbf{x}\mathbf{x}^T\}\mathbf{A}] \end{aligned} \qquad (6.16)$$

This result holds for any arbitrary assignment for the target vector **y**. With the special arrangements of (1.5), however (the target vector **y** being a K-dimensional unit vector with only one of its components 1 and all the others 0), the expression simplifies to

$$S^2(\mathbf{A}) = 1 - 2\,\text{trace}[\mathbf{A}^T E\{\mathbf{x}\mathbf{y}^T\}] + \text{trace}[\mathbf{A}^T E\{\mathbf{x}\mathbf{x}^T\}\mathbf{A}] \qquad (6.17)$$

Replacing therein **A** with $\mathbf{A} + \delta\mathbf{A}$ yields

$$\begin{aligned} S^2(\mathbf{A} + \delta\mathbf{A}) = 1 &- 2\,\text{trace}[(\mathbf{A} + \delta\mathbf{A})^T E\{\mathbf{x}\mathbf{y}^T\}] \\ &+ \text{trace}[(\mathbf{A} + \delta\mathbf{A})^T E\{\mathbf{x}\mathbf{x}^T\}(\mathbf{A} + \delta\mathbf{A})] \end{aligned}$$

and after performing the multiplications,

$$\begin{aligned} S^2(\mathbf{A} + \delta\mathbf{A}) = 1 &- 2\,\text{trace}[\mathbf{A}^T E\{\mathbf{x}\mathbf{y}^T\}] - 2\,\text{trace}[\delta\mathbf{A}^T E\{\mathbf{x}\mathbf{y}^T\}] \\ &+ \text{trace}[\mathbf{A}^T E\{\mathbf{x}\mathbf{x}^T\}\mathbf{A}] + 2\,\text{trace}[\delta\mathbf{A}^T E\{\mathbf{x}\mathbf{x}^T\}\mathbf{A}] \\ &+ \text{trace}[\delta\mathbf{A}^T E\{\mathbf{x}\mathbf{x}^T\}\delta\mathbf{A}] \end{aligned} \qquad (6.18)$$

By inserting both expressions into the inequality of (6.12), we get

$$\text{trace}[\delta\mathbf{A}^T E\{\mathbf{x}\mathbf{x}^T\}\delta\mathbf{A}] - 2\,\text{trace}[\delta\mathbf{A}^T(E\{\mathbf{x}\mathbf{y}^T\} - E\{\mathbf{x}\mathbf{x}^T\}\mathbf{A})] \geq 0 \qquad (6.19)$$

This inequality necessarily holds if the second term vanishes since the first term is positive definite due to the positive definiteness of the moment matrix $E\{\mathbf{xx}^T\}$. Hence the condition for $\mathbf{A}$ being the optimum solution simplifies to

$$\text{trace}[\delta\mathbf{A}^T(E\{\mathbf{xy}^T\} - E\{\mathbf{xx}^T\}\mathbf{A})] = 0 \qquad \forall\, \delta\mathbf{A}$$

which is true for all $\delta\mathbf{A}$ if $\mathbf{A}$ satisfies the linear equation

$$E\{\mathbf{xx}^T\}\mathbf{A} = E\{\mathbf{xy}^T\} \tag{6.20}$$

This result deserves to be commented on.

Comments

We started this chapter by designing a least mean-square estimate $\mathbf{d}(\mathbf{v})$ for the target vector $\mathbf{y}$ indicating the true class membership of the pattern $[\mathbf{v}, \mathbf{y}]$ to be classified. This estimating function was designed to be a linear combination of a set of given basis functions, especially a polynomial in $\mathbf{v}$, and has the simple form of (6.7):

$$\mathbf{d}(\mathbf{v}) = \mathbf{A}^T\mathbf{x}(\mathbf{v})$$

In general the estimation $\mathbf{d}(\mathbf{v})$ does not hit the target $\mathbf{y}$ precisely such that an *error vector* $\Delta\mathbf{d}$ remains:

$$\Delta\mathbf{d}(\mathbf{v}) = \mathbf{d}(\mathbf{v}) - \mathbf{y} = \mathbf{A}^T\mathbf{x}(\mathbf{v}) - \mathbf{y} \tag{6.21}$$

which is again a stochastic variable.

All the adaptability of this structure lies in the coefficient matrix $\mathbf{A}$. Least mean-square optimization of $\mathbf{A}$ requires that the residual variance S^2, the mathematical expectation $E\{|\Delta\mathbf{d}|^2\}$ of the squared Euclidean norm of the error vector $\Delta\mathbf{d}$, becomes minimum.

In (6.20) we find that the optimum coefficient matrix $\mathbf{A}$ is simply computed by solving a system of linear equations that consists of the two moment matrices $E\{\mathbf{xx}^T\}$ and $E\{\mathbf{xy}^T\}$, which describe properties of the *pattern source* from which the patterns $[\mathbf{v}, \mathbf{y}]$ come (see Section 2.1).

These two statistical moment matrices $E\{\mathbf{xx}^T\}$ and $E\{\mathbf{xy}^T\}$ must be given, in the case of a pattern source with known statistical properties, or must be computed from a given set of learning samples $\{\mathbf{v}, \mathbf{y}\}$ in the same way as described in Section 4.6 for the statistical moments needed for statistical modeling.

Thus:

- *Learning from examples* for the concept of functional approximation essentially consists in collecting moment matrices from the learning set and solving a linear matrix equation.

Before we go into those details, we will look at some of the general properties of the solution found.

6.2 PROPERTIES OF SOLUTION

According to (6.20), the optimum coefficient matrix **A** leads to the following minimum value of the optimization criterion S^2:

$$\begin{aligned} S^2_{\min}(\mathbf{A}) &= S^2(\mathbf{A}_{\text{opt}}) \\ &= E\{|\mathbf{y}|^2\} - 2\,\text{trace}[\mathbf{A}^T_{\text{opt}}E\{\mathbf{x}\mathbf{y}^T\}] + \text{trace}[\mathbf{A}^T_{\text{opt}}E\{\mathbf{x}\mathbf{x}^T\}\mathbf{A}_{\text{opt}}] \end{aligned} \tag{6.22}$$

Inserting (6.20) gives either

$$S^2_{\min}(\mathbf{A}) = E\{|\mathbf{y}|^2\} - \text{trace}[\mathbf{A}^T_{\text{opt}}E\{\mathbf{x}\mathbf{y}^T\}] \tag{6.23}$$

or equivalently

$$S^2_{\min}(\mathbf{A}) = E\{|\mathbf{y}|^2\} - \text{trace}[\mathbf{A}^T_{\text{opt}}E\{\mathbf{x}\mathbf{x}^T\}\mathbf{A}_{\text{opt}}] \tag{6.24}$$

Residual Variance

This simplifies to the *residual variance* of the trained pattern classification system

$$\begin{aligned} S^2_{\min}(\mathbf{A}) &= 1 - \text{trace}[\mathbf{A}^T_{\text{opt}}E\{\mathbf{x}\mathbf{y}^T\}] \\ &= 1 - \text{trace}[\mathbf{A}^T_{\text{opt}}E\{\mathbf{x}\mathbf{x}^T\}\mathbf{A}_{\text{opt}}] \end{aligned} \tag{6.25}$$

if **y** is the unit vector defined in Section 1.4.

Orthogonality of Estimation Error Δd

Another important property of the least mean-square solution is *orthogonality* between the set of basis functions contained in **x**(**v**) and the error vector **Δd**. In statistical terms this means that the moment matrix built from **x** and **Δd** must be the null matrix

$$E\{\mathbf{x}\,\Delta\mathbf{d}^T\} = E\{\mathbf{x}(\mathbf{A}^T_{\text{opt}}\mathbf{x} - \mathbf{y})^T\} = E\{\mathbf{x}\mathbf{x}^T\}\mathbf{A}_{\text{opt}} - E\{\mathbf{x}\mathbf{y}^T\} = \mathbf{0} \tag{6.26}$$

since, according to (6.20), the last of the two equations is zero.

This orthogonality is inherited by the relation between estimation **d** and error vector $\Delta\mathbf{d}$ since $\mathbf{d}$ is a linear combination of all the basis functions contained in $\mathbf{x}(\mathbf{v})$:

$$E\{\mathbf{d}\,\Delta\mathbf{d}^T\} = E\{\mathbf{A}_{\text{opt}}^T\mathbf{x}\,\Delta\mathbf{d}^T\} = \mathbf{A}_{\text{opt}}^T E\{\mathbf{x}\,\Delta\mathbf{d}^T\} = \mathbf{0} \tag{6.27}$$

If the set of basis functions $\mathbf{x}(\mathbf{v})$ contains a constant term, as is the case with polynomials designed according to (6.3), then $\mathbf{x}(\mathbf{v})$ can be written as

$$\mathbf{x}(\mathbf{v}) = \begin{pmatrix} 1 \\ \mathbf{x}^* \end{pmatrix} \tag{6.28}$$

with $\mathbf{x}^*$ the vector of the remaining basis functions. This expression inserted into the orthogonality condition (6.26) gives

$$E\left\{\begin{pmatrix} 1 \\ \mathbf{x}^* \end{pmatrix} \Delta\mathbf{d}^T\right\} = \begin{pmatrix} E\{\Delta\mathbf{d}^T\} \\ E\{\mathbf{x}^*\,\Delta\mathbf{d}^T\} \end{pmatrix} = \mathbf{0}$$

Unbiasedness of Estimation d(v)

From the above it directly follows that

$$E\{\Delta\mathbf{d}\} = E\{\mathbf{d}(\mathbf{v}) - \mathbf{y}\} = \mathbf{0} \tag{6.29}$$

The estimation error $\Delta\mathbf{d}$ has zero mean; in other words $\mathbf{d}(\mathbf{v})$ is an unbiased estimate for the target vector $\mathbf{y}$. Both have identical means:

$$E\{\mathbf{d}(\mathbf{v})\} = E\{\mathbf{y}\} \tag{6.30}$$

Unity Sum of Components of d(v)

In the context of pattern classification $\mathbf{y}$ is the target vector indicating what the true class membership of the pattern $[\mathbf{v}, \mathbf{y}]$ is and $\mathbf{d}(\mathbf{v})$ the discriminant function of the pattern classifier (compare Fig. 2.3), producing class membership estimates $d_k(\mathbf{v})$, $k = 1, \ldots, K$, which are least mean-square estimations for the unknown a posteriori probabilities $\text{prob}(k|\mathbf{v})$ under the constraint of the given set of basis functions used for constructing $\mathbf{d}(\mathbf{v})$; compare Section 3.1.

The N-dimensional space from which the measurement vector $\mathbf{v}$ comes is called the *measurement space* $\mathbf{V}$ and the K-dimensional space spanned by $\mathbf{y}$ is the *decision space* $\mathbf{D}$. The discriminant function $\mathbf{d}(\mathbf{v})$ provides a mapping $\mathbf{V} \rightarrow \mathbf{D}$ from measurement space into decision space; compare Fig. 1.2.

When the set of target vectors $\{\mathbf{y}\}$ does not use the entire decision space, which obviously is the case with $\mathbf{y}$ defined according to (1.5), the restrictions valid for $\mathbf{y}$ are under certain circumstances inherited by the estimation $\mathbf{d}(\mathbf{v})$.

In order to make use of the definitions of (1.5), we introduce a K-dimensional vector,

$$\mathbf{e} = (1 \quad 1 \quad \cdots \quad 1)^T \tag{6.31}$$

consisting of K components equal to 1. Applying $\mathbf{e}$, the property of the target vector $\mathbf{y}$ to have components y_k that sum to 1 can be expressed by

$$\mathbf{e}^T\mathbf{y} = \sum_{k=1}^{K} y_k = 1 \tag{6.32}$$

This equation states that the K discrete target vectors $\mathbf{y}_1, \mathbf{y}_2, \ldots, \mathbf{y}_K$ representing the K classes lie in a linear subspace of the decision space spanned by the tops of these vectors; compare Fig. 1.4. The decision space origin does not belong to this subspace.

This property of the set of target vectors $\{\mathbf{y}\}$ is mirrored in the properties of the coefficient matrix $\mathbf{A}$. We refer to (6.20),

$$E\{\mathbf{x}\mathbf{x}^T\}\mathbf{A} = E\{\mathbf{x}\mathbf{y}^T\}$$

multiply both sides from the right with $\mathbf{e}$, and get

$$E\{\mathbf{x}\mathbf{x}^T\}\mathbf{A}\mathbf{e} = E\{\mathbf{x}\mathbf{y}^T\}\mathbf{e} = E\{\mathbf{x}\mathbf{y}^T\mathbf{e}\} = E\{\mathbf{x}\} \tag{6.33}$$

The special circumstances mentioned above concern the structure of the set of basis functions $\mathbf{x}(\mathbf{v})$ and require that one of the basis functions is constant, as is the case with polynomials designed according to (6.3).

Using the same denotation as in (6.28),

$$\mathbf{x}(\mathbf{v}) = \begin{pmatrix} 1 \\ \mathbf{x}^* \end{pmatrix}$$

we find that the (6.33) holds if the product $\mathbf{Ae}$ becomes an N-dimensional vector with one component 1 in the first place and $N-1$ zeros in all of the others. Inserting

$$\mathbf{A}\mathbf{e} = (1 \quad 0 \quad 0 \quad \cdots \quad 0)^T \tag{6.34}$$

we get

$$E\left\{\begin{pmatrix} 1 \\ \mathbf{x}^* \end{pmatrix}(1 \quad \mathbf{x}^*)^T\right\}\begin{pmatrix} 1 \\ 0 \\ \vdots \\ 0 \end{pmatrix} = E\left\{\begin{pmatrix} 1 \\ \mathbf{x}^* \end{pmatrix}\right\}$$

$$\begin{pmatrix} 1 & E\{\mathbf{x}^*\}^T \\ E\{\mathbf{x}^*\} & E\{\mathbf{x}^*\mathbf{x}^{*T}\} \end{pmatrix} \begin{pmatrix} 1 \\ 0 \\ \vdots \\ 0 \end{pmatrix} = \begin{pmatrix} 1 \\ E\{\mathbf{x}^*\} \end{pmatrix}$$

which is easily proved to be true.

The result of these considerations is that the coefficient matrix **A** has the property that the components of its first row sum to 1 whereas all the other rows of **A** have component sum zero. This is expressed by (6.34).

As a consequence the discriminant vector **d**(**v**) also has the property of its components summing to 1:

$$\mathbf{e}^T\mathbf{d}(\mathbf{v}) = \mathbf{e}^T\mathbf{A}^T\mathbf{x}(\mathbf{v}) = (1 \quad 0 \quad \cdots \quad 0)\begin{pmatrix} 1 \\ \mathbf{x}^* \end{pmatrix} = 1$$
$$\sum_{k=1}^{K} d_k(\mathbf{v}) = 1 \tag{6.35}$$

whereas the error vector $\Delta\mathbf{d}$ has component sum zero:

$$\mathbf{e}^T\Delta\mathbf{d}(\mathbf{v}) = \mathbf{e}^T\mathbf{d}(\mathbf{v}) - \mathbf{e}^T\mathbf{y} = 1 - 1 = 0$$
$$\sum_{k=1}^{K} \Delta d_k(\mathbf{v}) = 0 \tag{6.36}$$

It should be mentioned that these properties of **d** and $\Delta\mathbf{d}$ are due to the fact of $\mathbf{e}^T\mathbf{y} = 1$ (6.32), which is true not only for the case of **y** being one of the K unit vectors, as defined in (1.5), but also if the vector **p** of a posteriori probabilities would be used as target vectors (see the deliberations of Section 3.1 on this topic) or any other soft labeling target vector **y** with the property of its components summing to 1.

6.3 FUNCTIONAL APPROXIMATION WITH y VERSUS p AS TARGET VECTORS

We will here again discuss the difference between using either **y** (1.5) or **p** (3.10) as target vector for the functional approximation $\mathbf{d}(\mathbf{v}) = \mathbf{A}^T\mathbf{x}(\mathbf{v})$. The two approaches lead to two different optimization problems,

$$S_{\mathbf{y}}^2 = E\{|\mathbf{A}^T\mathbf{x}(\mathbf{v}) - \mathbf{y}|^2\} = \min_{\mathbf{A}} \tag{6.37}$$

versus

$$S_{\mathbf{p}}^2 = E\{|\mathbf{A}^T\mathbf{x}(\mathbf{v}) - \mathbf{p}|^2\} = \min_{\mathbf{A}} \tag{6.38}$$

but can be shown to have one common solution **A**. For this purpose we transform the second of the two problems $S_{\mathbf{p}}^2 = \min_{\mathbf{A}}$ into

$$\begin{aligned} S_{\mathbf{p}}^2 &= E\{|\mathbf{A}^T\mathbf{x} - \mathbf{p}|^2\} = E\{|(\mathbf{A}^T\mathbf{x} - \mathbf{y}) - (\mathbf{p} - \mathbf{y})|^2\} \\ &= E\{|\mathbf{A}^T\mathbf{x} - \mathbf{y}|^2\} - 2E\{(\mathbf{A}^T\mathbf{x})^T(\mathbf{p} - \mathbf{y})\} + 2E\{\mathbf{y}^T(\mathbf{p} - \mathbf{y})\} + E\{|\mathbf{p} - \mathbf{y}|^2\} \\ &= \min_{\mathbf{A}} \end{aligned} \tag{6.39}$$

While the first of the four terms in this expression turns out to be $S_{\mathbf{y}}^2$, the second can be shown to be zero due to the definition of **p** (3.10):

$$\mathbf{p} = \sum_{\mathbf{y}} \mathbf{y}\,\mathrm{prob}(\mathbf{y}|\mathbf{v}) \quad \text{leading to} \quad \sum_{\mathbf{y}} (\mathbf{p} - \mathbf{y})\mathrm{prob}(\mathbf{y}|\mathbf{v}) = \mathbf{0} \tag{6.40}$$

Writing the expectation operator in its explicit form renders

$$\begin{aligned} E\{(\mathbf{A}^T\mathbf{x}(\mathbf{v}))^T(\mathbf{p} - \mathbf{y})\} &= \sum_{\mathbf{v}}\sum_{\mathbf{y}} \mathbf{x}^T(\mathbf{v})\mathbf{A}(\mathbf{p} - \mathbf{y})\mathrm{prob}(\mathbf{y}|\mathbf{v})\mathrm{prob}(\mathbf{v}) \\ &= \sum_{\mathbf{v}} \mathbf{x}^T(\mathbf{v})\mathbf{A}\left[\sum_{\mathbf{y}} (\mathbf{p} - \mathbf{y})\mathrm{prob}(\mathbf{y}|\mathbf{v})\right]\mathrm{prob}(\mathbf{v}) = \mathbf{0} \end{aligned} \tag{6.41}$$

This as a whole is zero since the expression in square brackets is zero.

The third and fourth terms of (6.39), on the other hand, can together be simplified to

$$\begin{aligned} 2E\{\mathbf{y}^T(\mathbf{p} - \mathbf{y})\} + E\{|\mathbf{p} - \mathbf{y}|^2\} &= \sum_{\mathbf{v}}\sum_{\mathbf{y}} [2\mathbf{y}^T(\mathbf{p} - \mathbf{y}) + |\mathbf{p} - \mathbf{y}|^2]\mathrm{prob}(\mathbf{y}|\mathbf{v})\mathrm{prob}(\mathbf{v}) \\ &= \sum_{\mathbf{v}}\sum_{\mathbf{y}} [\mathbf{p}^T\mathbf{p} - \mathbf{y}^T\mathbf{y}]\mathrm{prob}(\mathbf{y}|\mathbf{v})\mathrm{prob}(\mathbf{v}) \\ &= \sum_{\mathbf{v}} |\mathbf{p}|^2\mathrm{prob}(\mathbf{v}) - \sum_{\mathbf{v}}\sum_{\mathbf{y}} |\mathbf{y}|^2\mathrm{prob}(\mathbf{y}|\mathbf{v})\mathrm{prob}(\mathbf{v}) \\ &= E\{|\mathbf{p}|^2\} - E\{|\mathbf{y}|^2\} \end{aligned} \tag{6.42}$$

This expression turns out to be the negative of the mean $E\{\mathrm{var}\{\mathbf{y}|\mathbf{v}\}\}$ of the conditional variance var{y|v}:

$$\begin{aligned}E\{\text{var}\{\mathbf{y}|\mathbf{v}\}\} &= \sum_{\mathbf{v}}\left[\sum_{\mathbf{y}} |\mathbf{y}-\mathbf{p}|^2 \text{prob}(\mathbf{y}|\mathbf{v})\right]\text{prob}(\mathbf{v}) = E\{|\mathbf{y}-\mathbf{p}|^2\} \\ &= \sum_{\mathbf{v}}\sum_{\mathbf{y}} [|\mathbf{y}|^2 - 2\mathbf{p}^T\mathbf{y} + |\mathbf{p}|^2]\text{prob}(\mathbf{y}|\mathbf{v})\text{prob}(\mathbf{v}) \\ &= E\{|\mathbf{y}|^2\} - 2\sum_{\mathbf{v}} \mathbf{p}^T\left[\sum_{\mathbf{y}} \mathbf{y}\,\text{prob}(\mathbf{y}|\mathbf{v})\right]\text{prob}(\mathbf{v}) + E\{|\mathbf{p}|^2\} \\ &= E\{|\mathbf{y}|^2\} - E\{|\mathbf{p}|^2\} \end{aligned} \tag{6.43}$$

With these results equation (6.39) simplifies to

$$\begin{aligned} S_{\mathbf{p}}^2 &= S_{\mathbf{y}}^2 - E\{\text{var}\{\mathbf{y}|\mathbf{v}\}\} \\ &= S_{\mathbf{y}}^2 - E\{|\mathbf{y}-\mathbf{p}|^2\} \\ &= S_{\mathbf{y}}^2 - (E\{|\mathbf{y}|^2\} - E\{|\mathbf{p}|^2\}) \end{aligned} \tag{6.44}$$

The mean conditional variance $E\{\text{var}\{\mathbf{y}|\mathbf{v}\}\}$, first, is a property of the pattern source and, second, does not depend on **A**. Therefore, it needs not be considered when minimizing $S_{\mathbf{p}}^2$ with respect to **A**. Thus, solving the optimization problem $S_{\mathbf{p}}^2 = \min_{\mathbf{A}}$ has exactly the same solution **A** as solving the optimization problem $S_{\mathbf{y}}^2 = \min_{\mathbf{A}}$. The residual variance $S_{\mathbf{y}}^2$ with respect to **y** is necessarily by $E\{\text{var}\{\mathbf{y}|\mathbf{v}\}\} \geq 0$ larger than the residual variance $S_{\mathbf{p}}^2$ with respect to **p**.

Here, **y** is the K-dimensional unit vector (1.5) with $E\{|\mathbf{y}|^2\} = 1$, whereas **p** is the vector of a posteriori probabilities (3.10) with $E\{|\mathbf{p}|^2\} < 1$ if the different classes overlap in measurement space. Hence, the difference between the residual variance $S_{\mathbf{y}}^2$ with respect to **y** and the residual variance $S_{\mathbf{p}}^2$ with respect to **p** comes out to be

$$S_{\mathbf{y}}^2 - S_{\mathbf{p}}^2 = 1 - E\{|\mathbf{p}|^2\} \geq 0 \quad \text{since} \quad E\{|\mathbf{p}|^2\} \leq 1 \tag{6.45}$$

Comments

- We find that the above two approaches of using either **p** or **y** as target vector for calculating the coefficient matrix **A** of the functional approximation $\mathbf{d}(\mathbf{v}) = \mathbf{A}^T\mathbf{x}(\mathbf{v})$ are equivalent in the sense that they result in the same **A**.

This result has an interesting interpretation: The K class-specific discriminant functions $d_k(\mathbf{v})$ being the components of the K-dimensional discriminant function $\mathbf{d}(\mathbf{v})$ are at the same time least mean-square estimates for the

Boolean class membership indicators y_k as well as least mean-square estimates for the a posteriori probabilities prob($k|\mathbf{v}$).

These considerations cast a light on the question of whether a pattern classifier can be improved by replacing the *hard labels* **y** by *soft labels* **p** in the learning set; compare the discussions on hard and soft labeling in Chapter 3. From the mathematical point of view it cannot, provided the learning set size is not limited. In the case of soft labeling knowledge about the fuzziness of the classification task to be solved is explicitly expressed by using the vector **p** of a posteriori probabilities as target vector. In the case of hard labeling this same knowledge is equivalently expressed by the set of patterns with identical **v** but contradictory labels **y**.

From a practical point of view, however, employing soft labeling can indeed be advantageous over hard labeling since then the fuzziness of the application can be adequately expressed with smaller learning set sizes.

It must be mentioned that for the human labeler soft labeling is considerably harder than hard labeling, not only in view of the requirements to reliably guess the vector **p** of a posteriori probabilities but also in view of the mere input volume. In the case of hard labeling only the correct label has to be manually keyed in or at least confirmed if the labeling is performed in cooperation with an already existing pattern classifier. In contrast, in the case of soft labeling the numeric values of all or at least the dominant components of **p** have to be manually keyed in.

Another lesson to be learned from these considerations is the following: It is essential that, using **y** as target vector, conflicting patterns are not withheld from the learning set. Conflicting patterns mark the boundary between different classes in measurement space and are just those that must be learned with special care.

6.4 MEAN AND COVARIANCE OF ESTIMATION ERROR

Based on the principle of mean-square polynomial approximation, we have derived the discriminant function $\mathbf{d}(\mathbf{v})$, being the core of any pattern classifier. This discriminant function has the form of $\mathbf{d}(\mathbf{v}) = \mathbf{A}^T\mathbf{x}(\mathbf{v})$ (6.7). Classifier training is accomplished by solving the linear matrix equation (6.20).

We will now look into the properties of the stochastic process $\{\Delta\mathbf{d}\}$ of the estimation error (6.21) occurring when the classifier employing the optimum coefficient matrix **A** is connected to the pattern source for which **A** was optimized; compare Fig. 6.3.

The estimation error $\Delta\mathbf{d}$ is the difference between the estimation **d** and the true target vector **y**:

$$\Delta\mathbf{d} = \mathbf{d} - \mathbf{y} \tag{6.46}$$

We have already seen that the stochastic process $\{\Delta\mathbf{d}\}$ has zero mean (6.29),

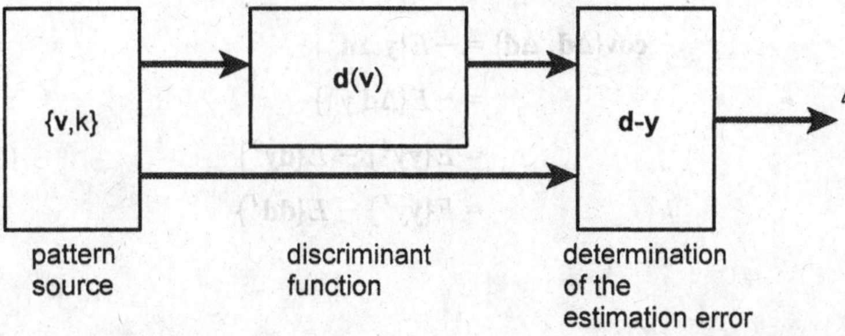

Figure 6.3. Pattern classifier with optimum coefficient matrix **A** connected to pattern source {**v**, **y**}. Discriminant vector **d** produced by classifier is compared to target vector **y** and resulting estimation error $\Delta\mathbf{d} = \mathbf{d} - \mathbf{y}$ is being observed. Whole configuration constitutes stochastic process {Δ**d**} of error vectors whose properties are studied in this section.

$$E\{\Delta\mathbf{d}\} = \mathbf{0}$$

which results in the fact that the covariance matrix $\mathbf{cov}\{\Delta\mathbf{d}, \Delta\mathbf{d}\}$ and the moment matrix $E\{\Delta\mathbf{d}\,\Delta\mathbf{d}^T\}$ are identical:

$$\mathbf{cov}\{\Delta\mathbf{d}, \Delta\mathbf{d}\} = E\{\Delta\mathbf{d}\,\Delta\mathbf{d}^T\} = E\{(\mathbf{d}-\mathbf{y})(\mathbf{d}-\mathbf{y})^T\} \tag{6.47}$$

Breaking up the left bracket we get

$$\begin{aligned}\mathbf{cov}\{\Delta\mathbf{d}, \Delta\mathbf{d}\} &= E\{\mathbf{d}(\mathbf{d}-\mathbf{y})^T\} - E\{\mathbf{y}(\mathbf{d}-\mathbf{y})^T\} \\ &= E\{\mathbf{d}\,\Delta\mathbf{d}^T\} - E\{\mathbf{y}\mathbf{d}^T\} + E\{\mathbf{y}\mathbf{y}^T\}\end{aligned} \tag{6.48}$$

Making use of the orthogonality condition (6.27),

$$E\{\mathbf{d}\,\Delta\mathbf{d}^T\} = E\{\mathbf{d}(\mathbf{d}-\mathbf{y})^T\} = \mathbf{0}$$

we find that

$$E\{\mathbf{d}\mathbf{d}^T\} = E\{\mathbf{d}\mathbf{y}^T\} = E\{\mathbf{y}\mathbf{d}^T\} \tag{6.49}$$

Inserting the last two expressions in (6.48) finally renders three equivalent notations for the covariance matrix of the estimation error Δ**d** valid for the case of the optimum coefficient matrix **A** being used in the polynomial discriminant function $\mathbf{d}(\mathbf{v}) = \mathbf{A}^T\mathbf{x}(\mathbf{v})$:

$$\begin{aligned} \mathbf{cov}\{\Delta\mathbf{d}, \Delta\mathbf{d}\} &= -E\{\mathbf{y}\,\Delta\mathbf{d}^T\} \\ &= -E\{\Delta\mathbf{d}\,\mathbf{y}^T\} \\ &= E\{\mathbf{y}\mathbf{y}^T\} - E\{\mathbf{d}\mathbf{y}^T\} \\ &= E\{\mathbf{y}\mathbf{y}^T\} - E\{\mathbf{d}\mathbf{d}^T\} \end{aligned} \tag{6.50}$$

Class-Specific Means of Estimation Error

The first of these expressions can be further transformed by utilizing the possibility of changing between the symbolic and explicit form of the expectation operator $E\{\cdot\}$:

$$\begin{aligned} \mathbf{cov}\{\Delta\mathbf{d}, \Delta\mathbf{d}\} &= -E\{\Delta\mathbf{d}\,\mathbf{y}^T\} \\ &= -\sum_{\mathbf{y}}\sum_{\mathbf{v}} \Delta\mathbf{d}\,\mathbf{y}^T \mathrm{prob}(\mathbf{v}|\mathbf{y})\mathrm{prob}(\mathbf{y}) \\ &= -\sum_{k=1}^{K} P_k E\{\Delta\mathbf{d}|k\}\mathbf{y}_k^T \end{aligned} \tag{6.51}$$

Therein, P_k is the a priori probability prob(k) of class k, $E\{\Delta\mathbf{d}|k\}$ the class-specific mean of the estimation error $\Delta\mathbf{d}$, and $\mathbf{y}_k$ the target vector $\mathbf{y}$ belonging to class k. This vector $\mathbf{y}_k$ has only one component unequal to zero, namely the kth component with value 1. This makes the kth item of the sum in (6.51) a matrix consisting of all columns zero except the kth, which becomes $-P_k E\{\Delta\mathbf{d}|k\}$. Hence the whole covariance matrix becomes

$$\mathbf{cov}\{\Delta\mathbf{d}, \Delta\mathbf{d}\} = (-P_1 E\{\Delta\mathbf{d}|1\} \quad -P_2 E\{\Delta\mathbf{d}|2\} \quad \cdots \quad -P_K E\{\Delta\mathbf{d}|K\}) \tag{6.52}$$

Since the covariance matrix is symmetric, a similar interpretation is valid for its rows:

$$\mathbf{cov}\{\Delta\mathbf{d}, \Delta\mathbf{d}^T\} = \begin{pmatrix} -P_1 E\{\Delta\mathbf{d}^T|1\} \\ -P_2 E\{\Delta\mathbf{d}^T|2\} \\ \vdots \\ -P_K E\{\Delta\mathbf{d}^T|K\} \end{pmatrix} \tag{6.53}$$

Row and Column Sums of Estimation Error Covariance Matrix

Carrying out the summation over all K columns gives

$$\sum_{k=1}^{K} P_k E\{\Delta\mathbf{d}|k\} = E\{\Delta\mathbf{d}\} = \mathbf{0} \tag{6.54}$$

which is the null vector, according to (6.29). The consequence is that all of the rows as well as all of the columns of $\mathbf{cov}\{\Delta\mathbf{d}, \Delta\mathbf{d}\}$ sum up to zero:

$$\begin{aligned} \text{SumOfRows}[\mathbf{cov}\{\Delta\mathbf{d}, \Delta\mathbf{d}\}] &= \mathbf{0} \\ \text{SumOfColumns}[\mathbf{cov}\{\Delta\mathbf{d}, \Delta\mathbf{d}\}] &= \mathbf{0} \end{aligned} \tag{6.55}$$

Error Bounds on Class-Specific Estimations

Covariance matrices are positive definite. This is true also for $\mathbf{cov}\{\Delta\mathbf{d}, \Delta\mathbf{d}\}$ and results in all of its principal diagonal terms being positive since they represent the variances $\text{var}\{\Delta d_k\}$ of the corresponding component of $\Delta\mathbf{d}$. From (6.52) we conclude that the kth principal diagonal element is

$$-P_k E\{\Delta d_k|k\} = \text{var}\{\Delta d_k\} \geq 0 \tag{6.56}$$

which shows that the class-specific mean $E\{\Delta\mathbf{d}|k\}$ of the error vector $\Delta\mathbf{d}$ has a negative kth component.

It should explicitly be noted that the left side of (6.56) is the class-specific mean $E\{\Delta d_k|k\}$ whereas the right side $\text{var}\{\Delta d_k\}$ represents the variance of the kth component of $\Delta\mathbf{d}$ regardless of the class.

We have already seen that the kth component $d_k(\mathbf{v})$ of the discriminant function $\mathbf{d}(\mathbf{v})$ plays the double role of being a least mean-square estimate for the Boolean class membership indicator $y_k(\mathbf{v})$ as well as for the a posteriori probability $p_k(\mathbf{v}) = \text{prob}(\mathbf{v}|k)$.

The estimation error Δd_k measures the difference between $d_k(\mathbf{v})$ and $y_k(\mathbf{v})$:

$$\Delta d_k(\mathbf{v}) = d_k(\mathbf{v}) - y_k(\mathbf{v})$$

with

$$y_k(\mathbf{v}) = \begin{cases} 1 & \text{for } \mathbf{v} \text{ from class } k \\ 0 & \text{for } \mathbf{v} \text{ from class } j \neq k \end{cases}$$

where $k = 1, \ldots, K$. The class-specific mean $E\{\Delta d_k|k\}$ is the average of this class-k-related estimation error valid for the case that only patterns $[\mathbf{v}, k]$, belonging to class k, are input to the discriminant function. In that case $y_k = 1$ and hence

$$E\{d_k|k\} = 1 + E\{\Delta d_k|k\}$$

We see from (6.56) that $E\{\Delta d_k|k\} \leq 0$ and that therefore

$$E\{d_k|k\} = 1 - \frac{1}{P_k}\operatorname{var}\{\Delta d_k\} \leq 1 \tag{6.57}$$

The class membership function $d_k(\mathbf{v})$ targeted to 1 for measurement vectors $\mathbf{v}$ coming exclusively from class k misses that goal in the average, given by $E\{d_k|k\}$, by an amount that directly depends on the overall variance $\operatorname{var}\{\Delta d_k\}$ of that class membership function. The average necessarily stays below the goal.

The principal diagonal elements of $\mathbf{cov}\{\Delta\mathbf{d}, \Delta\mathbf{d}\}$ are not only limited by a lower bound zero but also have an upper bound. The worst conceivable estimation is one that uses no measurements at all: zero-degree polynomial. In that case $\mathbf{x}(\mathbf{v}) = 1$ with dimension 1. Inserting that into (6.20) yields $\mathbf{A} = E\{\mathbf{y}\}$ and, with (6.7), $\mathbf{d} = E\{\mathbf{y}\}$.

The optimum estimation $\mathbf{d}$ for $\mathbf{y}$ in that case is simply the mean of $\mathbf{y}$. With (6.50) we get

$$\mathbf{cov}_{\mathbf{x}(\mathbf{v})=1}\{\Delta\mathbf{d}, \Delta\mathbf{d}\} = E\{\mathbf{y}\mathbf{y}^T\} - E\{\mathbf{y}\}E\{\mathbf{y}^T\} = \mathbf{cov}\{\mathbf{y}, \mathbf{y}\} \tag{6.58}$$

which is the covariance matrix of the target vector $\mathbf{y}$.

Due to the definitions of (1.5)

$$E\{\mathbf{y}\mathbf{y}^T\} = \begin{bmatrix} P_1 & 0 & \cdots & 0 \\ 0 & P_2 & \cdots & 0 \\ \vdots & \vdots & \ddots & \vdots \\ 0 & 0 & \cdots & P_K \end{bmatrix} \tag{6.59}$$

and therefore

$$\mathbf{cov}\{\mathbf{y}, \mathbf{y}\} = \begin{bmatrix} P_1(1-P_1) & -P_1P_2 & \cdots & -P_1P_K \\ -P_1P_2 & P_2(1-P_2) & \cdots & -P_2P_K \\ \vdots & \vdots & \ddots & \vdots \\ -P_1P_K & -P_2P_K & \cdots & P_K(1-P_K) \end{bmatrix} \tag{6.60}$$

The principal diagonal elements of $\mathbf{cov}\{\mathbf{y}, \mathbf{y}\}$ are the variances of the components y_k of $\mathbf{y}$ and have the values

$$\text{var}\{y_k\} = P_k(1 - P_k) \tag{6.61}$$

Together with (6.56) we find that the variance $\text{var}\{\Delta d_k\}$ of the kth component of the estimation error has upper and lower bounds,

$$0 \leq \text{var}\{\Delta d_k\} = -P_k E\{\Delta d_k | k\} \leq P_k(1 - P_k) \tag{6.62}$$

and hence the kth component of the class-specific mean $\mathbf{\Delta d}$ is bounded by

$$P_k - 1 \leq E\{\Delta d_k | k\} \leq 0 \tag{6.63}$$

whereby the lower bound (left side of the inequality) is assumed when the estimation is merely based on the constant term $\mathbf{x}(\mathbf{v}) = 1$.

Applied to the class-specific mean $E\{d_k | k\}$ of the class-specific estimate d_k itself, this yields

$$P_k \leq E\{d_k | k\} \leq 1 \tag{6.64}$$

with the lower bound valid for the same case $\mathbf{x}(\mathbf{v}) = 1$ as above.

Comments

The foregoing considerations refer to some of the general properties the stochastic process $\{\mathbf{\Delta d}\}$ of the estimation error $\mathbf{\Delta d}$ exhibits if the optimum coefficient matrix $\mathbf{A}$ is used in the polynomial discriminant function $\mathbf{d}(\mathbf{v}) = \mathbf{A}^T\mathbf{x}(\mathbf{v})$.

This situation is very similar to the case called *reclassification* in Section 1.4: The classifier is checked for some performance parameters with the same pattern source used for training. Note, however, that in the present discussion we are not speaking about learning and test sets but rather about expectation, variances, and covariances. For the present discussion we simply assume that the moment matrices from which all these results are derived reliably represent the properties of the pattern source.

The covariance matrix $\mathbf{cov}\{\mathbf{\Delta d}, \mathbf{\Delta d}\}$ is a very effective kind of performance data characterizing the degree to which the polynomial classifier has learned to cope with the challenges of its job. It is important to note that these performance data are not gained by running the classifier with a test set—as the test set may be with the learning set itself—but are derived as a byproduct of the adaptation procedure.

6.5 COVARIANCE OF ESTIMATION ERROR AND RESIDUAL VARIANCE

There exists a close relationship between the covariance matrix $\mathbf{cov}\{\Delta\mathbf{d}, \Delta\mathbf{d}\}$ of the estimation error $\Delta\mathbf{d}$ and the residual variance S^2 (6.11), minimization of which was the goal of the whole optimization approach:

$$\begin{aligned} S^2 &= E\{|\Delta d|^2\} = E\{\text{trace}[\Delta\mathbf{d}\,\Delta\mathbf{d}^T]\} = \text{trace}[E\{\Delta\mathbf{d}\,\Delta\mathbf{d}^T\}] \\ &= \text{trace}[\mathbf{cov}\{\Delta\mathbf{d}, \Delta\mathbf{d}\}] \\ &= \sum_{k=1}^{K} \text{var}\{\Delta d_k\} \\ &= -\sum_{k=1}^{K} P_k E\{\Delta d_k \,|\, k\}) \end{aligned} \tag{6.65}$$

The variances $\text{var}\{\Delta d_k\}$ are the contributions of the class-specific estimates $d_k(\mathbf{v})$ to the total mean-square error.

Another nice result is achieved from the same relationship if we write $\mathbf{cov}\{\Delta\mathbf{d}, \Delta\mathbf{d}\}$ as in the last line of expression (6.50) and at the same time make use of (6.59):

$$\begin{aligned} S^2 &= \text{trace}[\mathbf{cov}\{\Delta\mathbf{d}, \Delta\mathbf{d}\}] \\ &= \text{trace}[E\{\mathbf{y}\mathbf{y}^T\}] - \text{trace}[E\{\mathbf{d}\mathbf{d}^T\}] \\ &= 1 - E\{|\mathbf{d}|^2\} \end{aligned} \tag{6.66}$$

Since the residual variance S^2 is bound to be nonnegative, the average squared Euclidean norm of $\mathbf{d}$ has lower and upper limits $0 \le E\{|\mathbf{d}|^2\} \le 1$.

6.6 COVARIANCE AND CLASS-SPECIFIC MEANS OF DISCRIMINANT VECTOR d

We refer to the results of Section 6.4 on the statistical properties of the estimation error $\Delta\mathbf{d}$ and will now derive some of the properties of the stochastic process $\{\mathbf{d}\}$.

With (6.21) we have $\mathbf{d} = \mathbf{y} + \Delta\mathbf{d}$ and from (6.29) we know that $E\{\Delta\mathbf{d}\} = \mathbf{0}$, with the consequence that $E\{\mathbf{d}\} = E\{\mathbf{y}\}$. Hence the covariance matrix $\mathbf{cov}\{\mathbf{d}, \mathbf{d}\}$ can be written

$$\mathbf{cov}\{\mathbf{d}, \mathbf{d}\} = E\{\mathbf{d}\mathbf{d}^T\} - E\{\mathbf{d}\}E\{\mathbf{d}^T\} = E\{\mathbf{d}\mathbf{d}^T\} - E\{\mathbf{y}\}E\{\mathbf{y}^T\} \tag{6.67}$$

Correspondingly we have

$$\mathbf{cov}\{\mathbf{y},\mathbf{y}\} = E\{\mathbf{y}\mathbf{y}^T\} - E\{\mathbf{y}\}E\{\mathbf{y}^T\}$$

Both together give

$$E\{\mathbf{y}\mathbf{y}^T\} - E\{\mathbf{d}\mathbf{d}^T\} = \mathbf{cov}\{\mathbf{y},\mathbf{y}\} - \mathbf{cov}\{\mathbf{d},\mathbf{d}\}$$

and finally, with (6.50),

$$\mathbf{cov}\{\mathbf{d},\mathbf{d}\} = \mathbf{cov}\{\mathbf{y},\mathbf{y}\} - \mathbf{cov}\{\Delta\mathbf{d},\Delta\mathbf{d}\} \tag{6.68}$$

In order to develop the expression for $\mathbf{cov}\{\mathbf{d},\mathbf{d}\}$ somewhat further, we go back to (6.67) and substitute $E\{\mathbf{d}\mathbf{d}^T\}$ by (6.49)

$$\begin{aligned} E\{\mathbf{d}\mathbf{d}^T\} &= E\{\mathbf{d}\mathbf{y}^T\} \\ &= \sum_{\mathbf{y}}\sum_{\mathbf{v}} \mathbf{d}(\mathbf{v})\mathbf{y}^T \,\mathrm{prob}(\mathbf{v}|\mathbf{y})\mathrm{prob}(\mathbf{y}) \\ &= \sum_{k=1}^{K} P_k E\{\mathbf{d}(\mathbf{v})|k\}\mathbf{y}_k^T \end{aligned}$$

In analogy to (6.51) we get

$$E\{\mathbf{d}\mathbf{d}^T\} = (P_1E\{\mathbf{d}|1\} \quad P_2E\{\mathbf{d}|2\} \cdots P_KE\{\mathbf{d}|K\}) \tag{6.69}$$

Together with

$$E\{\mathbf{y}\}E\{\mathbf{y}^T\} = \begin{bmatrix} P_1 \\ P_2 \\ \vdots \\ P_K \end{bmatrix} (P_1 \quad P_2 \quad \cdots \quad P_K) = \begin{bmatrix} P_1^2 & P_1P_2 & \cdots & P_1P_K \\ P_1P_2 & P_2^2 & & P_2P_K \\ \vdots & & \ddots & \vdots \\ P_1P_K & P_2P_K & \cdots & P_K^2 \end{bmatrix} \tag{6.70}$$

the covariance matrix $\mathbf{cov}\{\mathbf{d},\mathbf{d}\}$ becomes

$$\mathbf{cov}\{\mathbf{d},\mathbf{d}\} = \begin{bmatrix} P_1(E\{d_1|1\}-P_1) & P_2(E\{d_1|2\}-P_1) & \cdots & P_K(E\{d_1|K\}-P_1) \\ P_1(E\{d_2|1\}-P_2) & P_2(E\{d_2|2\}-P_2) & \cdots & P_K(E\{d_2|K\}-P_2) \\ \vdots & \vdots & \ddots & \vdots \\ P_1(E\{d_K|1\}-P_K) & P_2(E\{d_K|2\}-P_K) & \cdots & P_K(E\{d_K|K\}-P_K) \end{bmatrix} \tag{6.71}$$

Covariance matrices are symmetric, which results in

$$\text{cov}\{d_j, d_k\} = P_k(E\{d_j|k\} - P_j) = P_j(E\{d_k|j\} - P_k) \tag{6.72}$$

The principal diagonal of **cov{d, d}** contains the variances

$$\text{var}\{d_k\} = P_k(E\{d_k|k\} - P_k) \geq 0, \tag{6.73}$$

which must be positive: compare (6.64).

6.7 SOME PROPERTIES OF MAPPING V → D FROM MEASUREMENT SPACE INTO DECISION SPACE

The discriminant function **d**(**v**) of the pattern classifier provides a mapping **V** → **D** from the *N*-dimensional measurement space **V** into the *K*-dimensional decision space **D** (see Fig. 1.2).

The decision space is spanned by the *K* target vectors $\mathbf{y}_1, \mathbf{y}_2, \ldots, \mathbf{y}_K$ whose tops define a linear subspace of **D** and form within this subspace an equilateral simplex that for $K = 3$ classes becomes a two-dimensional equilateral triangle, for $K = 4$ classes a three-dimensional tetrahedron, and for larger numbers *K* of classes one of the corresponding higher dimensional objects.

This situation was illustrated by Fig. 1.4 for the $K = 3$ case.

The pattern source generates a stochastic process {**v**, **y**} of patterns that form a certain distribution of points {**v**} in measurements space, compare Chapter 4. Since the measurement space **V** is mapped into the decision space **D** by the discriminant function **d**(**v**), we get a corresponding collection of points {**d**} in **D**-space. What we here are concerned with is to come to assertions about how the collection {**d**} is distributed in **D**-space.

Let us first consider the optimum conceivable (3.10) discriminant function **d**(**v**) = **p**(**v**) applied for the mapping **V** → **D**. Because **p**(**v**) is the vector of a posteriori probabilities

$$\mathbf{p}(\mathbf{v}) = \begin{bmatrix} \text{prob}(1|\mathbf{v}) \\ \text{prob}(2|\mathbf{v}) \\ \vdots \\ \text{prob}(K|\mathbf{v}) \end{bmatrix}$$

this optimum discriminant function has the two properties

$$0 \leq p_k(\mathbf{v}) \leq 1 \quad \forall k = 1, \ldots, K \tag{6.74}$$

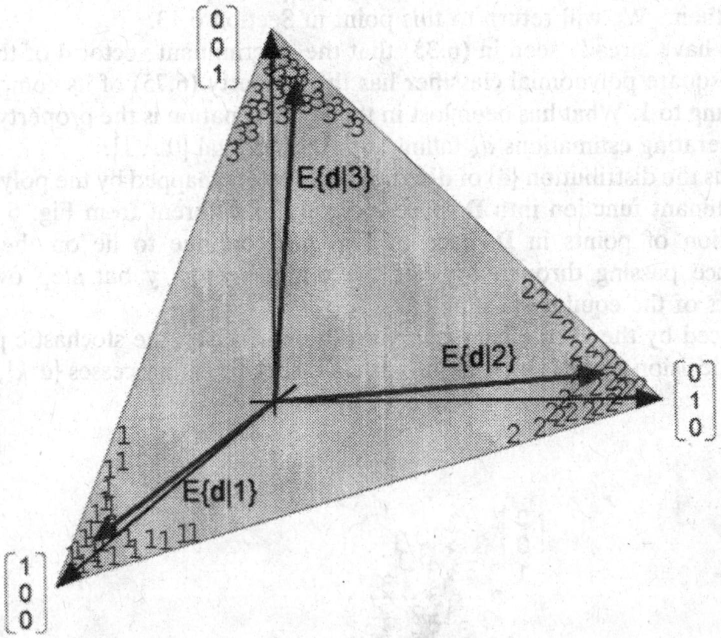

Figure 6.4. Three-dimensional decision space spanned by three target vectors $\mathbf{y}_1$, $\mathbf{y}_2$, $\mathbf{y}_3$ as in Fig. 1.4. Tops of the three vectors form two-dimensional equilateral triangle in **D**-space. Illustration shows distribution {**d**} of discriminant vectors in **D**-space as generated by *optimum discriminant function* **d**(**v**) = **p**(**v**). All points lie within triangle's plane and inside equilateral triangle.

$$\sum_{k=1}^{K} p_k(\mathbf{v}) = 1 \tag{6.75}$$

Thus the stochastic process {**d**} of patterns mapped into the decision space **D** is completely contained within the same linear subspace as the tops of the target vectors **y** and is bound to lie completely inside the equilateral simplex, for the case of three classes completely inside the equilateral triangle of Fig. 1.4, as shown in Fig. 6.4. For the two-dimensional, three-class example (4.35) of Section 4.2 such a view into the decision space was shown in Fig. 4.14.

It should be noted that properties (6.74) and (6.75), which are valid for the optimum discriminant function $\mathbf{d}(\mathbf{v}) = \mathbf{p}(\mathbf{v})$, are not at all sufficient to conclude the optimality of some given discriminant function $\mathbf{d}(\mathbf{v})$. All that can be stated is that whenever (6.74) and (6.75) do not hold, $\mathbf{d}(\mathbf{v})$ is excluded from being the optimum discriminant function $\mathbf{p}(\mathbf{v})$.

Depending on the design principles employed for classifier construction, a classifier may or may not exhibit these properties. It is, however, in most cases desirable to have estimates $\mathbf{d}(\mathbf{v})$ obeying (6.74) and (6.75); if they do not by themselves obey these constraints, special provisions are possible to force them. We will return to this point in Section 6.13.

We have already seen in (6.35) that the discriminant vector **d** of the least mean-square polynomial classifier has the property (6.75) of its components summing to 1. What has been lost in the approximation is the property (6.74) of generating estimations d_k falling into the interval [0 . . 1].

Thus the distribution {**d**} of discriminant vectors mapped by the polynomial discriminant function into **D**-space looks quite different from Fig. 6.4. The collection of points in **D**-space of Fig. 6.5 continue to lie on the linear subspace passing through tops of the target vectors **y** but step over the borders of the equilateral simplex.

Forced by the least mean-square criterion of (3.1), the stochastic process {**d**} in decision space is broken into its class-specific subprocesses {**d**|k}, which

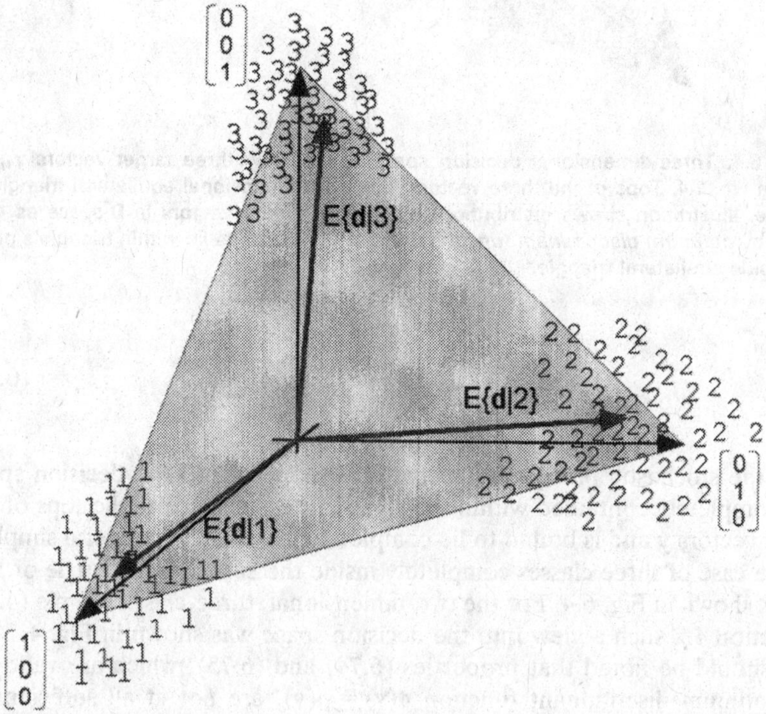

Figure 6.5. Three-dimensional decision space spanned by the three target vectors $\mathbf{y}_1$, $\mathbf{y}_2$, $\mathbf{y}_3$ as in Figs. 1.3 and 6.4. Tops of three vectors form two-dimensional equilateral triangle in **D**-space. Illustration shows distribution {**d**} of discriminant vectors in **D**-space as generated by *polynomial discriminant function* **d**(**v**). All points fall on plane passing through tops of three target vectors as in Fig. 6.4 but are no longer captured inside equilateral triangle.

are each selectively attracted by their corresponding target vectors $\mathbf{y}_k$ similar to how charged particles are attracted by charges of opposite polarity.

The patterns input to the classifier are pairs $[\mathbf{v}, k]$. By applying the discriminant function $\mathbf{d}(\mathbf{v})$, the classifier maps them into pairs $[\mathbf{d}, k]$. Those belonging to class k gather in the neighborhood of the target vector $\mathbf{y}_k$ responsible for class k.

We do not know the form that the distribution of points $\{\mathbf{d}|k\}$ coming from one certain class k will have in decision space. We can, however, compute the class-specific means $E\{\mathbf{d}|k\}$ from the corresponding means $E\{\mathbf{x}|k\}$ and the coefficient matrix $\mathbf{A}$ of the polynomial discriminant function $\mathbf{d}(\mathbf{v}) = \mathbf{A}^T\mathbf{x}(\mathbf{v})$:

$$E\{\mathbf{d}|k\} = \mathbf{A}^T E\{\mathbf{x}(\mathbf{v})|k\} \tag{6.76}$$

From the considerations of the foregoing sections [see (6.57) (6.64)], we know already that the kth component of $E\{\mathbf{d}|k\}$ is bounded by

$$P_k \leq E\{d_k|k\} \leq 1 - \frac{\text{var}\{\Delta d_k\}}{P_k} \leq 1 \tag{6.77}$$

which gives us some qualitative knowledge about the position of $E\{\mathbf{d}|k\}$, $k = 1, \ldots, K$, in decision space (Fig. 6.5).

6.8 TRAINING POLYNOMIAL CLASSIFIER: SOLVING MATRIX EQUATION

After having unfolded such a host of mathematical relationships, we should not lose sight of what we said at the beginning of this chapter and of the objectives we are pursuing: the adaptation of the polynomial regression classifier based on the concept of learning from examples. Let us therefore briefly recapitulate what our intentions were and what we have accomplished so far.

The idea was to construct a functional approximation $\mathbf{d}(\mathbf{v})$ capable of generating reliable estimations $\mathbf{d}$ for the target vector $\mathbf{y}$ belonging to the measurement vector $\mathbf{v}$ as given by the pattern $[\mathbf{v}, \mathbf{y}]$. And this approximation should work not only for one single exemplar of $[\mathbf{v}, \mathbf{y}]$ but on the average for all of the countless patterns $[\mathbf{v}, \mathbf{y}]$ the stochastic pattern source is able to generate.

These considerations led us to follow a least mean-square approach (see

Fig. 3.1),

$$S^2 = E\{|\mathbf{d}(\mathbf{v}) - \mathbf{y}|^2\} = \min_{\mathbf{d}(\mathbf{v})}$$

with the approximating function $\mathbf{d}(\mathbf{v})$ confined to be a polynomial (6.7),

$$\mathbf{d}(\mathbf{v}) = \mathbf{A}^T\mathbf{x}(\mathbf{v})$$

Learning from examples in this context means that the coefficient matrix **A** of the polynomial has to be properly adjusted with respect to the least mean-square criterion based on a given set $\{\mathbf{v}, \mathbf{y}\}$ of learning samples.

We found in (6.20) that the optimum coefficient matrix **A** is determined by a linear matrix equation

$$E\{\mathbf{x}\mathbf{x}^T\}\mathbf{A} = E\{\mathbf{x}\mathbf{y}^T\}$$

consisting of the two moment matrices $E\{\mathbf{x}\mathbf{x}^T\}$ and $E\{\mathbf{x}\mathbf{y}^T\}$. Since solving linear matrix equations constitutes no major problem, even if they are large, the essence of learning from examples here is establishing the two moment matrices from the learning sample.

Interestingly, we find ourselves confronted with exactly the same task of accumulating statistical moments we had to solve in Chapter 4 when starting from the idea of fitting statistical models to the probability laws governing the pattern source. All of the techniques discussed in Sections 4.6 and 4.7 for calculating statistical moment matrices are here also applicable.

Needless to say, that computation of **A** always leads to a linear matrix equation irrespective of how nonlinear the approximating function $\mathbf{d}(\mathbf{v})$ may be. The polynomial is linear in the coefficient matrix **A** and, in general, nonlinear in the polynomial structure $\mathbf{x}(\mathbf{v})$.

From the mathematical point of view the problem of training the polynomial classifier based on a learning set seems, at this point of the discussion, to be sufficiently well understood to leave it to a suitable mathematical package or to the computer center to take care of the rest.

Linear Dependencies

However, we will go into some of the details of linear dependency since it contains a most interesting, hidden byproduct. Remember that solving a matrix equation requires the left side of that equation, in our case $E\{\mathbf{x}\mathbf{x}^T\}$, to be nonsingular. In terms of the application this requires that there must not exist any linear dependencies among the components of $\mathbf{x}$ with respect to the given pattern source.

Whether $E\{\mathbf{x}\mathbf{x}^T\}$ is regular or not is only partly a question of the polynomial $\mathbf{x}(\mathbf{v})$ itself. Obviously, linear dependencies are inevitable if some of the components of $\mathbf{x}$ still are, by definition, linear combinations of others—in the simplest case repetitions.

But even if $\mathbf{x}(\mathbf{v})$ is constructed to contain none of these dependencies, regularity of $E\{\mathbf{x}\mathbf{x}^T\}$ can in general not be guaranteed. Here the properties of the pattern source come into the game. It may easily happen that the distribution of polynomial vectors $\mathbf{x}$ generated from the pattern source $\{\mathbf{v}, \mathbf{y}\}$ by the nonlinear mapping does not fill the entire $\mathbf{X}$-space but rather a lower dimensional subspace thereof.

Linear dependencies in systems of linear equations destroy the uniqueness of the solution. What at first glance looks like a complication really is an important alleviation. Linear dependencies do not at all prevent any solution but rather generate solution manifolds. If linear dependencies happen to occur, we are able to detect them and to reduce the resulting solution manifold to one distinct solution.

This reduction of the solution manifold to a single one is accomplished by introducing additional constraints with properties we find advantageous for the problem at hand.

Predictor and To-be-Predicted Variables

The mathematical treatment of the whole procedure can be remarkably simplified if we connect the two vectors $\mathbf{x}$ and $\mathbf{y}$ to one vector $\mathbf{z}$ containing all of the observations available for one pattern; compare (1.9):

$$\mathbf{z} = \begin{pmatrix} \mathbf{x} \\ \mathbf{y} \end{pmatrix} \tag{6.78}$$

This vector $\mathbf{z}$ is called the *vector of observations*. Its components are in a certain sense equivalent to each other regardless of whether they belong to those provided by some kind of measurement definition (subvector $\mathbf{x}$) or to those provided by a priori knowledge or a human teacher (subvector $\mathbf{y}$), since all of them are observables describing the same pattern $[\mathbf{v}, \mathbf{y}]$. It is however absolutely essential to know where in $\mathbf{z}$ the polynomial subvector $\mathbf{x}$ ends and the target subvector $\mathbf{y}$ begins.

In practical terms, $\mathbf{z}$ is an $(L + K)$-dimensional vector and is treated as such. The book-keeping information about the boundary between those terms to be used for establishing an approximation and those to be approximated is held separately and accessed if required.

For the considerations to follow $\mathbf{z}$ is simply a vector of observables, some of which, belonging to $\mathbf{x}$, are selected to be used as the basis upon which a reconstruction of all the others, contained in $\mathbf{y}$, is to be built. According to this distinction, the terms contained in $\mathbf{x}$ play the role of *predictor variables*,

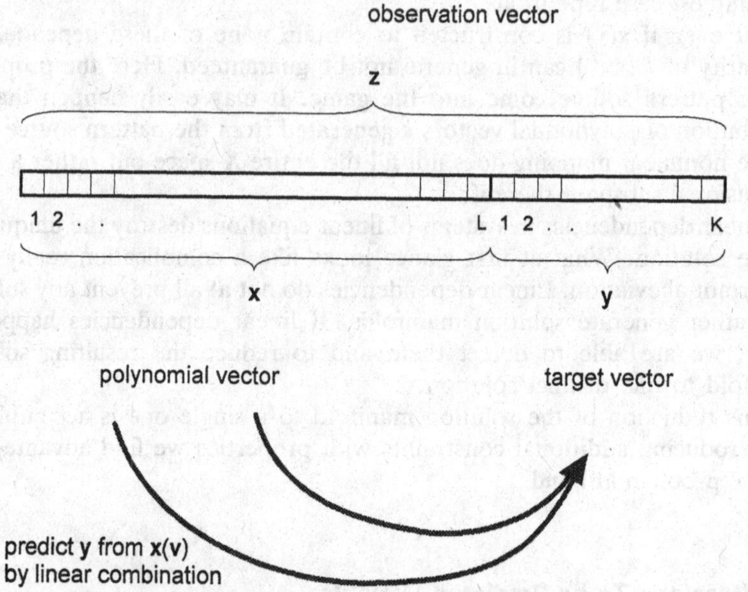

Figure 6.6. Observation vector **z** composed of two subvectors **x** and **y**. Separation between two subjectors determines roles **x** and **y** have to play in least mean-square approximation game. Those observables contained in **x** are selected to serve as input data of approximation that tries to predict by linear combination as accurately as possible all observables contained in **y**.

whereas the terms contained in **y** play the role of *variables to be predicted*; see Fig. 6.6.

In this general view, it is no longer necessary that terms that are members of the **x** community are positioned on neigboring places in **z** nor those that are members of the **y** community. With proper book-keeping about the status of the components of **z** as belonging to either **x** or **y**, they might also be completely intermingled along the $L + K$ positions of the vector data structure of **z**.

Solving Matrix Equation

Given the polynomial structure **x**(**v**) and the concatenation rule of (6.78), the learning set {**v**, **y**} is mapped into a corresponding set {**z**} of observation vectors. The moment matrix **M** of the stochastic process {**z**} contains all of the necessary statistical parameters

$$\mathbf{M} = E\{\mathbf{z}\mathbf{z}^T\} = E\left\{\begin{pmatrix}\mathbf{x}\\ \mathbf{y}\end{pmatrix}(\mathbf{x}^T \quad \mathbf{y}^T)\right\} = \begin{pmatrix} E\{\mathbf{x}\mathbf{x}^T\} & E\{\mathbf{x}\mathbf{y}^T\} \\ E\{\mathbf{y}\mathbf{x}^T\} & E\{\mathbf{y}\mathbf{y}^T\}\end{pmatrix} \tag{6.79}$$

especially in its upper half, the constituents of the matrix equation (6.20):

$$E\{\mathbf{x}\mathbf{x}^T\}\mathbf{A} = E\{\mathbf{x}\mathbf{y}^T\}$$

Matrix equations of this kind are practically solved by matrix manipulations; by adding a suitable multiple of a selected row to another row, a zero can be generated at any matrix position. Matrix manipulations applied to rows are equivalent to left-hand matrix multiplications.

Even though the matrix equation of (6.78) in reality is solved by matrix manipulations, it is most appropriate to describe the computational procedure by equivalent matrix multiplications in order to gain a better insight into what actually happens.

Thus multiplying $\mathbf{M}$ from the left with

$$\mathbf{T} = \begin{pmatrix} [E\{\mathbf{x}\mathbf{x}^T\}]^{-1} & \mathbf{0} \\ -E\{\mathbf{y}\mathbf{x}^T\} - E\{\mathbf{x}\mathbf{x}^T\}]^{-1} & \mathbf{I}\end{pmatrix}$$

gives the result

$$\mathbf{TM} = \begin{pmatrix} \mathbf{I} & [E\{\mathbf{x}\mathbf{x}^T\}]^{-1}E\{\mathbf{x}\mathbf{y}^T\} \\ \mathbf{0} & E\{\mathbf{y}\mathbf{y}^T\} - E\{\mathbf{y}\mathbf{x}^T\}[E\{\mathbf{x}\mathbf{x}^T\}]^{-1}E\{\mathbf{x}\mathbf{y}^T\}\end{pmatrix} \tag{6.80}$$

which is identical to the result we would have gained from applying the *Gauss–Jordan algorithm* of numerical mathematics to the array of numbers contained in $\mathbf{M}$ with the goal of changing the upper left submatrix $E\{\mathbf{x}\mathbf{x}^T\}$ into the L-dimensional identity matrix $\mathbf{I}$ and the lower left submatrix $E\{\mathbf{y}\mathbf{x}^T\}$ into a $K \times L$ null matrix $\mathbf{O}$.

We find that these matrix transformations have changed $\mathbf{M}$ into

$$\mathbf{M} \xrightarrow[\text{manipulations}]{\text{elementary matrix row}} \begin{pmatrix} \mathbf{I} & \mathbf{A} \\ \mathbf{0} & \mathbf{cov}\{\Delta\mathbf{d}, \Delta\mathbf{d}\}\end{pmatrix} \tag{6.81}$$

which is easily proved first for the upper half,

$$E\{\mathbf{x}\mathbf{x}^T\}\mathbf{A} = E\{\mathbf{x}\mathbf{y}^T\} \quad \Leftrightarrow \quad \mathbf{A} = [E\{\mathbf{x}\mathbf{x}^T\}]^{-1}E\{\mathbf{x}\mathbf{y}^T\}$$

as well as for the lower half with reference to (6.50),

$$\begin{aligned}\mathbf{cov}\{\Delta\mathbf{d}, \Delta\mathbf{d}\} &= E\{\mathbf{y}\mathbf{y}^T\} - E\{\mathbf{d}\mathbf{y}^T\} \\ &= E\{\mathbf{y}\mathbf{y}^T\} - \mathbf{A}^T E\{\mathbf{x}\mathbf{y}^T\} \\ &= E\{\mathbf{y}\mathbf{y}^T\} - E\{\mathbf{y}\mathbf{x}^T\}[E\{\mathbf{x}\mathbf{x}^T\}]^{-1} E\{\mathbf{x}\mathbf{y}^T\}\end{aligned}$$

This is a most important result since it provides not only the coefficient matrix **A** of the polynomial classifier but at the same time also the covariance matrix $\mathbf{cov}\{\Delta\mathbf{d}, \Delta\mathbf{d}\}$ of the estimation error $\{\Delta\mathbf{d}\}$.

We know from (6.65) that the residual variance achieved when applying the coefficient matrix **A** just derived for estimating the target vector **y** from **v** is

$$S^2 = E\{|\Delta\mathbf{d}|^2\} = \text{trace}[\mathbf{cov}\{\Delta\mathbf{d}, \Delta\mathbf{d}\}] \tag{6.82}$$

This value can be easily calculated in parallel to the process of matrix row manipulations.

A comment must be made concerning the use of the matrix inverse in the foregoing deliberations. This is allowed only if $E\{\mathbf{x}\mathbf{x}^T\}$ is nonsingular. But even in the case that there exist certain linear dependencies among the components of **x**, the foregoing derivations remain valid if they are applied to those components of **x** that are not linear dependent on others. Hence, as the process of solving the matrix equation proceeds, we have to monitor the components of **x** and detect those that turn out to be linear dependent on those already used for the prediction.

6.9 FEATURE SELECTION AND PIVOT STRATEGIES

This leads us to the *feature selection* properties of polynomial and functional regression. The given polynomial structure $\mathbf{x}(\mathbf{v})$ is to be considered as just a draft from which to select a subset of really useful terms.

Normally we have a large number of polynomial terms that may be more or less useful for the functional approximation task, into which we have transformed the given pattern classification problem. Those that turn out to be completely linear predictable from others—or, in mathematical terms, linearly dependent on them are totally useless. These relationships and dependencies, however, are not at all known in advance but must be detected with the progress of the computational procedure.

For this purpose we introduce the distinction between *candidate terms* and *accepted terms*. The polynomial terms contained in the draft polynomial structure are treated as candidates that have to first prove their independence from those already accepted before they themselves can reach the status of being accepted.

This distinction meets with another distinction, namely that introduced in the section before, of *predictor terms* being part of **x** and *terms to be predicted* being part of **y**.

The procedure is organized so that at the beginning the set of accepted terms is empty and the set of candidate terms contains the complete polynomial vector **x**. In a sequence of steps the set of accepted polynomial terms is augmented term by term after an evaluation and selection process searching for the next most promising candidate, in a sense still to be determined. The components of **y**, obviously, must be excluded from this selection process; they remain the to-be-predicted terms.

Within the set of predictor terms, thus, a distinction is introduced between those terms still staying in the status of a candidate predictor term and those already accepted and actually used as predictor terms. This distinction is dynamically evolving with the progress of the matrix inversion process.

Only the accepted predictor terms are effective as predictors. However, the computational procedure of solving the linear matrix equation treats every variable either as predictor or as to be predicted. Therefore, for all of the remaining candidate terms predictions are gained in the same way as for the actual to-be-predicted terms contained in **y**, allowing for every candidate to check the degree to which it itself is predictable from the already accepted predictor terms.

Accordingly, we have to distinguish between three different states the components of **z** may assume:

- Candidate predictor ⇔ temporarily to be predicted
- Accepted predictor
- To be predicted

Interestingly, the sequence of selection steps totally corresponds to the sequence of steps that make up the standard Gauss–Jordan algorithm for solving the matrix equation of Section 6.8. In each of these steps one of the columns of the system of linear equations is transformed into a unit vector having one component with value 1 positioned on the principal diagonal of this array of numbers and zeros elsewhere.

Equation (6.81) provides the necessary interpretations. The action of transforming one certain column into unit vector form is equivalent to changing the status of the corresponding variable from *candidate* to *accepted*.

Pivot Selection

The question to be answered now is that for the appropriate candidate selection criterion or, the other way around, the question of which column of the matrix array to transform next into unit vector form. In numerical mathematics this selection problem is known as the problem of *pivot selection*.

The pivot element is that among the matrix elements which is to be changed within the next processing step by division by itself into the value 1. Obviously matrix elements that are zero must be excluded from being selected as pivot elements.

To look somewhat closer into these details we consider the observation vector **z** as consisting of a certain selection of already accepted predictor variables **x**, one certain candidate term z, and the vector of the to-be-predicted target variables **y**:

$$\mathbf{z}^T = (\mathbf{x}^T \quad \cdots \quad z \quad \cdots \quad \mathbf{y}^T) \tag{6.83}$$

This situation is illustrated by Fig. 6.7. For the sake of convenience the already accepted variables **x** are shown as being collected at the leftmost

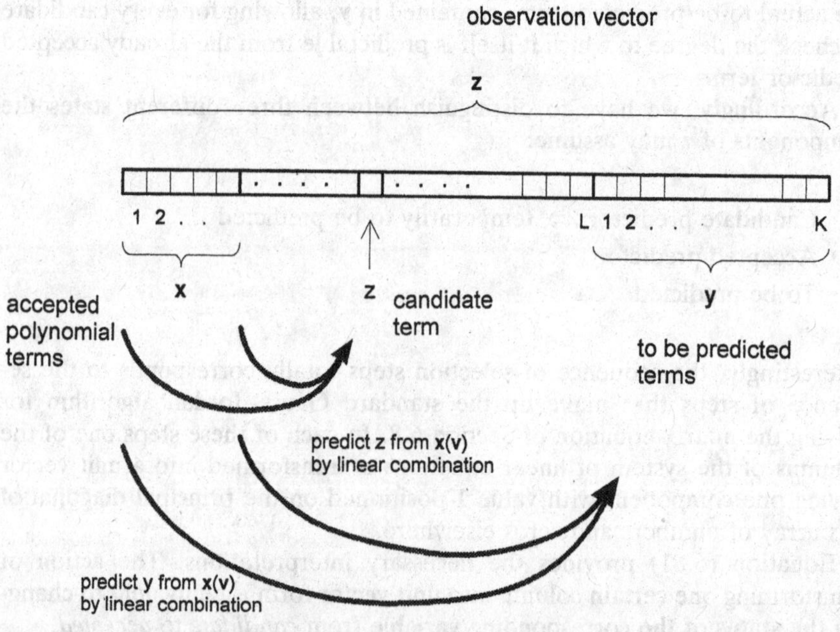

Figure 6.7. Partitioning of vector **z** of observations into subvectors having different roles in functional approximation procedure. Subvector **x** contains all accepted polynomial terms in certain intermediate state of computational procedure. Subvector **y** is original target vector, containing terms to be predicted. Vector component z is a candidate term chosen to be representative of all others. Variable z is checked for appropriateness to be accepted next. Note that denotation **x** is used here not for complete set of polynomial terms contained in draft polynomial but for those actually used as predictor terms in present state of the procedure.

vector positions of **z**. In practice that will not actually be the case since the components of **x** have been selected in earlier steps according to their appropriateness for the approximation task and not according to their position within **z**. This partitioning scheme transfers to the moment matrix **M** of (6.79) and gives

$$\mathbf{M} = E\{\mathbf{z}\mathbf{z}^T\} = \begin{bmatrix} E\{\mathbf{x}\mathbf{x}^T\} & \cdots & E\{\mathbf{x}z\} & \cdots & E\{\mathbf{x}\mathbf{y}^T\} \\ \vdots & \ddots & \vdots & \ddots & \vdots \\ E\{z\mathbf{x}^T\} & \cdots & E\{zz\} & \cdots & E\{z\mathbf{y}^T\} \\ \vdots & \ddots & \vdots & \ddots & \vdots \\ E\{\mathbf{y}\mathbf{x}^T\} & \cdots & E\{\mathbf{y}z\} & \cdots & E\{\mathbf{y}\mathbf{y}^T\} \end{bmatrix} \tag{6.84}$$

Carrying out the matrix transformation until the leftmost columns belonging to **x** are brought into unit vector form, we get, from (6.81),

$$\mathbf{M} \xrightarrow[\text{manipulations}]{\text{elementary matrix row}} \begin{bmatrix} \mathbf{I} & \cdots & \mathbf{c} & \cdots & \mathbf{A} \\ \vdots & \ddots & \vdots & \ddots & \vdots \\ 0 & \cdots & \text{var}\{\Delta z\} & \cdots & \mathbf{cov}\{\Delta z, \Delta\mathbf{d}\} \\ \vdots & \ddots & \vdots & \ddots & \vdots \\ \mathbf{0} & \cdots & \mathbf{cov}\{\Delta\mathbf{d}, \Delta z\} & \cdots & \mathbf{cov}\{\Delta\mathbf{d}, \Delta\mathbf{d}\} \end{bmatrix} \tag{6.85}$$

This is the state of affairs we meet when all components contained in **x** have the status of predictor terms.

In the upper right submatrix we find the coefficient matrix **A** that is valid for the intermediate state of the approximation procedure based on the vector **x**(**v**) of the accepted predictor terms, and in the lower right position we find the covariance matrix of the corresponding estimation error **Δd** as in (6.81).

At the same time a least mean-square approximation for $\hat{z}$ the candidate term z is established,

$$\hat{z}(\mathbf{v}) = \mathbf{c}^T\mathbf{x}(\mathbf{v}) \quad \text{where} \quad \Delta z = \hat{z} - z \tag{6.86}$$

based on the same set of accepted predictor variables **x**(**v**). We find the corresponding coefficient vector **c** in the upper middle submatrix position and the resulting estimation error var{Δz} in the center submatrix position, belonging, according to both the row and column positions, to z.

With these interpretations in mind it is easy to detect candidate terms that are linearly dependent on the already accepted predictor terms. A candidate

z is linearly dependent on $\mathbf{x}$ when the corresponding principal diagonal element in the matrix array becomes zero, since then z is predictable from $\mathbf{x}$ without any prediction error:

$$\text{var}\{\Delta z\} = 0 \quad \Leftrightarrow \quad z \text{ is linearly dependent on } \mathbf{x} \tag{6.87}$$

In practical application the question of linear dependence cannot be answered by checking var{Δz} for zero. Instead, a certain threshold MinDiagThrsh must be applied,

$$\text{var}\{\Delta z\}\begin{cases} <\text{MinDiagThrsh} & \text{exclude } z \text{ from further consideration} \\ \geq\text{MinDiagThrsh} & z \text{ retains status of candidate predictor} \end{cases} \tag{6.88}$$

excluding also almost linear-dependent terms from further consideration.

A candidate term z, having once proved to be linearly dependent on some certain set $\mathbf{x}$ of accepted predictor variables, cannot but retain this property when $\mathbf{x}$ is augmented by accepting other arbitrary candidate terms. This fact makes it senseless to try z again in any later phase of the computational procedure.

Linear dependent terms are therefore excluded from further consideration, be it by ignoring them in the subsequent steps of the procedure or by explicit elimination. In numerical mathematics such a solution to singular matrix equations is known as the *generalized inverse technique* [ALB1972].

Detection and elimination of linear dependent candidate terms are crucial for assuring a unique solution. It should be mentioned, however, that the thus excluded other solutions of the solution manifold have the same (and no better) residual variance.

We know from (6.82) that the trace of the lower right submatrix **cov{Δd, Δd}** of the matrix scheme (6.85) gives the *residual variance* S^2 for the present state of the approximation procedure. This is the least mean-square error with which $\mathbf{y}$ is predictable from $\mathbf{x}$.

Correspondingly, we can calculate the least mean-square error with which the whole set of momentary candidate predictor terms is predictable from $\mathbf{x}$:

$$R^2 = \sum_{\forall z \notin \mathbf{x} \cup \mathbf{y}} \text{var}\{\Delta z\} \tag{6.89}$$

Evaluation of this equation requires the summation over all main diagonal elements of (6.85) belonging neither to the predictor ($\mathbf{x}$) nor to the to-be-predicted ($\mathbf{y}$) variables.

Remember that $\mathbf{x}$ is a subset of the draft polynomial structure $\mathbf{x}_{\text{draft}}$ with which the whole procedure started, namely the subset of those polynomial terms already accepted as predictor terms. The above given expression R^2 can therefore also be interpreted as the *reconstruction error* with which the entire draft polynomial structure $\mathbf{x}_{\text{draft}}$ can be recovered from its subset $\mathbf{x}$ of the presently accepted polynomial terms. Obviously, this reconstruction error R^2 reduces to zero when $\mathbf{x}$ approaches $\mathbf{x}_{\text{draft}}$ since then nothing remains to be predicted.

Maximum Linear Independence (LU) Strategy

To decide which of the candidate terms to accept next, we need more than the simple exclusion criterion of (6.88). One obvious idea is to look for that candidate z with maximum var$\{\Delta z\}$, that candidate which is least predictable from the already accepted polynomial terms or, in other words, the candidate carrying *maximum novelty*. This pivot selection rule is called the *maximum linear independence* strategy.

At the beginning of this chapter we introduced the distinction between *descriptive* and *discriminative power* as general properties of features considered for the classification task. What we are just doing is looking into the candidate selection problem from the viewpoint of descriptive power.

The candidate term z with maximum var$\{\Delta z\}$ is the one contributing most, among all of the candidates, to the reconstruction error R^2 (6.89). Acceptance of that term z must reduce the reconstruction error R^2 by at least the amount of var$\{\Delta z\}$. The reservation "at least" is necessary since it may well happen that inclusion of z into the set of predictor variables $\mathbf{x}$ will make the remaining candidate predictor terms themselves better predictable.

Thus, the maximum linear independence strategy comes very close to a *minimum reconstruction error strategy* but is not really one. All that it tells is that in the present state of the procedure the variable z itself is least predictable, which allows us to draw the conclusion that removing z from the set of candidate terms and including it into the set of predictor terms will lead to a considerable reduction in reconstruction error. Truly selecting the best candidate with respect to reconstruction error reduction is possible but would require an evaluation procedure similar to that discussed in the following section.

As an interesting byproduct of the adaptation algorithm, a protocol on the reconstruction error R^2 is kept, showing the evolution of R^2 with the progress of the computational procedure. Here, R^2 is a monotonically decreasing function of the current polynomial length.

The pivot strategy controlled by the maximum var$\{\Delta z\}$ of the candidate terms z is at the same time optimum with respect to computational accuracy since in any step the largest available element is selected for division.

The maximum linear independence strategy for candidate selection must be combined with the test (6.88) for linear dependence in order to get rid of the variables that are totally or nearly totally linear dependent.

Minimum Residual Variance (MS) Strategy

We will now adopt the complementary position and look into the same problem of candidate selection from the viewpoint of discriminative power since a candidate term z may well be quite important from the viewpoint of descriptive power but may at the same time be rather useless for predicting $\mathbf{y}$.

What we need to know is which effect the inclusion of the candidate term z into the set of accepted terms will have on the overall optimization criterion S^2. This is a question simple to answer from the insights we already have into the process of stepwise building up estimations for z and $\mathbf{y}$. All we have to do is to carry the computational procedure one step further. This will change the matrix array of (6.85) into a form having one unit column more. In order to simplify the expressions, we first introduce the notation m and $\mathbf{m}$ into (6.85):

$$\mathbf{M} \xrightarrow{\text{elementary matrix row manipulations}} \begin{bmatrix} \mathbf{I} & \cdots & \mathbf{c} & \cdots & \mathbf{A} \\ \vdots & & \vdots & & \vdots \\ 0 & \cdots & m & \cdots & \mathbf{m}^T \\ \vdots & & \vdots & & \vdots \\ \mathbf{0} & \cdots & \mathbf{m} & \cdots & \mathbf{cov}\{\Delta\mathbf{d}, \Delta\mathbf{d}\} \end{bmatrix} \tag{6.90}$$

and then carry out the next step of the algorithm:

$$\mathbf{M} \xrightarrow{\text{elementary matrix row manipulations}} \begin{bmatrix} \mathbf{I} & \cdots & \mathbf{0} & \cdots & \mathbf{A} - \dfrac{\mathbf{c}\mathbf{m}^T}{m} \\ \vdots & & \vdots & & \vdots \\ 0 & \cdots & 1 & \cdots & \dfrac{\mathbf{m}^T}{m} \\ \vdots & & \vdots & & \vdots \\ \mathbf{0} & \cdots & \mathbf{0} & \cdots & \mathbf{cov}\{\Delta\mathbf{d}, \Delta\mathbf{d}\} - \dfrac{\mathbf{m}\mathbf{m}^T}{m} \end{bmatrix} \tag{6.91}$$

We find that the covariance matrix of the estimation error $\Delta\mathbf{d}$ is changed by subtraction of the outer product of $\mathbf{m}$ with itself divided by the former principal diagonal element m, the pivot element.

What we are really interested in is not the covariance matrix $\mathbf{cov}\{\Delta\mathbf{d}, \Delta\mathbf{d}\}$ but rather its trace (6.82), which after accepting z into the set of predictor variables assumes the value

$$S^2 - \Delta S^2 = \text{trace}\left[\mathbf{cov}\{\Delta\mathbf{d}, \Delta\mathbf{d}\} - \frac{\mathbf{m}\mathbf{m}^T}{m}\right] = S^2 - \frac{|\mathbf{m}|^2}{m} \tag{6.92}$$

The current value S^2 of the residual variance, being valid after having accepted $\mathbf{x}$, is decreased by the nonnegative amount

$$\Delta S^2 = \frac{|\mathbf{m}|^2}{m} \tag{6.93}$$

when the candidate term z is additionally accepted.

This pivot selection rule, controlled by the maximum of ΔS^2, is called the *minimum residual variance strategy*. Obviously the linear dependence check of (6.88) must be executed with this strategy as well in order to get rid of the totally or nearly totally linear dependent variables.

Note that the measure ΔS^2 of discriminative power evaluates the contribution of each of the remaining candidate terms in view of the specific situation, taking well into account which other terms are already used and not being misled by potential correlations between the predictor terms. Situations in which that two candidate terms are so similar with respect to their predictive power that if one is accepted the other is almost worthless are detected by the ΔS^2 criterion.

The minimum residual variance strategy is directly related to the overall optimization goal of least mean-square functional approximation and hence especially is attractive, as it promises to build the estimating function from just those candidate polynomial terms that have the maximum discriminative power.

Being a greedy algorithm, however, the selection of predictor terms $\mathbf{x}$ from the draft polynomial structure $\mathbf{x}_{\text{draft}}$ is not actually optimum but in practical application is reasonably close to optimum since selecting in each stage of the procedure the individually best term does not necessarily lead to optimum selection. Finding the actually optimum subset would require complete enumeration, which is prohibitive for a realistic length L of the draft polynomial structure.

Most remarkably, the measure ΔS^2 of discriminative power can be computed with modest additional computational effort from the status the matrix array (6.90) has after the subset $\mathbf{x}$ of the draft polynomial structure $\mathbf{x}_{\text{draft}}$ is included into the functional approximation. All we need to do is fetch the subvector $\mathbf{m}$ and the corresponding principal diagonal element m from the matrix array and compute ΔS^2 according to (6.93).

Similar to the maximum linear dependence strategy, the protocol on the residual variance S^2 can be kept showing the evolution of S^2 with the progress of the computational procedure. Again S^2 is a monotonically decreasing function of the current polynomial length.

Sequence of Intermediate Solutions and Feature Ranking

The adaptation algorithm for calculating the classifier coefficient matrix **A** from the moment matrix **M** is organized in steps. It starts with **M** the given moment matrix (6.79) and **A** empty. In a sequence of steps the specific polynomial structure $\mathbf{x}(\mathbf{v})$ is built up by selecting and accepting one candidate term z after the other from the draft polynomial structure $\mathbf{x}_{\text{draft}}$. At the same time the reconstruction error R^2 is computed for each of the steps as well as the residual variance S^2.

Hence, for each of the intermediate solutions a quintuple of results is gained and saved,

$$[\mathbf{A}, \mathbf{x}(\mathbf{v}), R^2, S^2, l] \tag{6.94}$$

where l is the number of computing step indicating the current polynomial length.

In each step the set of accepted polynomial terms is augmented by 1. Storing the counter variable l together with the just accepted candidate predictor term z gives a rank order-order list

$$[z, l] \tag{6.95}$$

evaluating all of the components of **x** with respect to either their descriptive or their discriminative power depending on which of the two pivot strategies LU or MS was applied.

These rank-order lists play an important role in feature selection and feature construction since they allow us to go into the procedure with a redundant draft polynomial structure $\mathbf{x}(\mathbf{v})$ which is then reduced to the relevant subset by the feature ranking capability of polynomial regression. Compare Section 9.2 dealing with "Rank-Order Based Feature Selection."

6.10 ESTABLISHING MOMENT MATRIX M FROM LEARNING SET OR FROM STATISTICAL MODELS

The moment matrix **M** of (6.79) contains all of the necessary information about the statistical properties of the pattern classification task to be solved. Given the learning set $\{\mathbf{v}, \mathbf{y}\}$ and the draft polynomial structure $\mathbf{x}(\mathbf{v})$ the learning set is mapped into an equivalent set $\{\mathbf{z}\}$ of observation vectors. These go into the moment matrix calculating procedure.

It is a question of practicability whether the set $\{\mathbf{z}\}$ is explicitly stored in a separate file or the observation vector is formed merely as a temporary variable and **M** is directly computed from the original learning set $\{\mathbf{v}, \mathbf{y}\}$ by a procedure using $\mathbf{x}(\mathbf{v})$ as a subroutine.

Preferably **M** is computed from the sequence of learning samples

$\{\mathbf{z}_1, \mathbf{z}_2, \mathbf{z}_3, \ldots, \mathbf{z}_J\}$ using the arithmetic mean (4.81):

$$\mathbf{M}_{\text{estimated}} = \frac{1}{J} \sum_{j=1}^{J} \mathbf{z}_j \mathbf{z}_j^T$$

The result of this averaging procedure is called an *estimation* since what we get from any learning set is always an estimation of the true moment matrix of the underlying pattern stochastic process of pattern generation: the pattern source. Compare Section 4.6 on parameter estimation.

Instead of relying on the arithmetic mean, the techniques of recursive parameter estimation (4.95) of Section 4.7 also may be applied;

$$\mathbf{M} \Leftarrow (1 - \alpha)\mathbf{M} + \alpha\, \mathbf{z}\mathbf{z}^T$$

From a practical point of view it is often advantageous to build a database of class-specific moment matrices since for classifier design based on polynomial regression calculating moment matrices is the most time-consuming task. The different moment matrices contained in the database can easily be mixed with arbitrary weights for different applications requiring, for example, different arrangements for the set of class labels,

$$\mathbf{M}_{jk} = \alpha_j \mathbf{M}_j + \alpha_k \mathbf{M}_k \quad \text{where} \quad \alpha_j + \alpha_k = 1$$

Compare the considerations of Section 4.6 on parameter estimation from subsets.

Regularities of Moment Matrices for Complete Polynomials

The moment matrix **M** contains statistical moments up to twice the degree of the polynomial structure $\mathbf{x}(\mathbf{v})$. This shall be illustrated by the moment matrix for a complete quadratic polynomial structure as given in (6.9) for the case of $N = 2$ and $K = 3$; compare Fig. 6.1. In order to shorten the expressions, the mathematical expectation is here written as $E\{x\} = \bar{x}$:

$$\left[\begin{array}{cccccc ccc}
1 & \overline{v_1} & \overline{v_2} & \overline{v_1^2} & \overline{v_1 v_2} & \overline{v_2^2} & P_1 & P_2 & P_3 \\
\hdashline
\overline{v_1} & \overline{v_1^2} & \overline{v_1 v_2} & \overline{v_1^3} & \overline{v^2 v_2} & \overline{v_1 v_2^2} & P_1\,\overline{v_1|1} & P_2\,\overline{v_1|2} & P_3\,\overline{v_1|3} \\
\overline{v_2} & \overline{v_1 v_2} & \overline{v_2^2} & \overline{v_1^2 v_2} & \overline{v_1 v_2^2} & \overline{v_2^3} & P_1\,\overline{v_2|1} & P_2\,\overline{v_2|2} & P_3\,\overline{v_2|3} \\
\hdashline
\overline{v_1^2} & \overline{v_1^2} & \overline{v_1^2 v_2} & \overline{v_1^4} & \overline{v_1^3 v_2} & \overline{v_1^2 v_2^2} & P_1\,\overline{v_1^2|1} & P_2\,\overline{v_1^2|2} & P_3\,\overline{v_1^2|3} \\
\overline{v_1 v_2} & \overline{v_1^2 v_2} & \overline{v_1 v_2^2} & \overline{v^3 v_2} & \overline{v^2 v_2^2} & \overline{v_1 v_2^3} & P_1\,\overline{v_1 v_2|1} & P_2\,\overline{v_1 v_2|2} & P_3\,\overline{v_1 v_2|3} \\
\overline{v_2^2} & \overline{v_1 v_2^2} & \overline{v_2^3} & \overline{v_1^2 v_2^2} & \overline{v_1 v_2^3} & \overline{v_2^4} & P_1\,\overline{v_2^2|1} & P_2\,\overline{v_2^2|2} & P_3\,\overline{v_2^2|3} \\
\hdashline
P_1 & P_1\,\overline{v_1|1} & P_1\,\overline{v_2|1} & P_1\,\overline{v_1^2|1} & P_1\,\overline{v_1 v_2|1} & P_1\,\overline{v_2^2|1} & P_1 & 0 & 0 \\
P_2 & P_2\,\overline{v_1|2} & P_2\,\overline{v_2|2} & P_2\,\overline{v_1^2|2} & P_2\,\overline{v_1 v_2|2} & P_2\,\overline{v_2^2|2} & 0 & P_2 & 0 \\
P_3 & P_3\,\overline{v_1|3} & P_3\,\overline{v_2|3} & P_3\,\overline{v_1^2|3} & P_3\,\overline{v_1 v_2|3} & P_3\,\overline{v_2^2|3} & 0 & 0 & P_3
\end{array}\right] \tag{6.96}$$

The regular structure of $\mathbf{x}(\mathbf{v})$ results in repetitive occurrence of the same statistical moment at different positions of the matrix array. The number of distinctly different statistical moments of degree g to be computed from N measurements is given as

$$\text{Number of moments } (N, g) = \binom{N+g-1}{g} \tag{6.97}$$

Hence the number of relevant terms in the $E\{\mathbf{x}\mathbf{x}^T\}$ submatrix of $\mathbf{M}$ for a complete quadratic polynomial is given by

$$\text{Number of relevant terms} = \sum_{g=1}^{4} \binom{N+g-1}{g} \tag{6.98}$$

which for large N asymptotically approaches $N^4/24$. In contrast, the total number of matrix positions within the square matrix $E\{\mathbf{x}\mathbf{x}^T\}$ according to (6.2) is given by

$$\text{Total number of terms} = \left[\binom{N+2}{2}\right]^2 \tag{6.99}$$

approaching $N^4/4$ for large N. Thus about only one-sixth of all terms in $E\{\mathbf{x}\mathbf{x}^T\}$ are relevant for complete quadratic polynomials and large N, a fact that, for complete polynomials, can be recoined into remarkable savings of computer time.

6.11 SECOND-DEGREE POLYNOMIAL CLASSIFIER FOR NORMALLY DISTRIBUTED CLASSES

The functional approximation approach of polynomial regression does not require any assumptions on the statistics of the pattern source. However, it also remains applicable if the statistical properties of prob($\mathbf{v}, \mathbf{y}$) are already known. From these considerations we will throw the bridge to the classifier design principles of Chapter 4, especially to the *Bayes classifier for normally distributed classes* of Section 4.2.

With the aim of establishing a kind of reference problem for testing how the different approximative techniques handle a case for which the optimum solution is already known, we designed the small two-dimensional example of (4.35) with three normally distributed classes.

The optimum classifier for the case of normally distributed classes is a quadratic classifier; compare the discussion on quadratic discriminant functions in Section 4.2. The discriminant functions $d_k(\mathbf{v})$, being the components of the discriminant vector $\mathbf{d}(\mathbf{v})$, are in this case positive-definite quadrics [compare (4.40)] whereas the class boundaries are general quadrics [compare (4.46)].

When following the polynomial regression approach, these facts suggest trying to solve the same problem again with second-degree polynomials; see (6.9). But we must be well aware of the fact that the quadratic discriminant functions $\mathbf{d}(\mathbf{v})$ deriving from this approach are, due to their mathematical construction, principally different from those derived in Chapter 4 [SCH1977].

This becomes obvious when we remember that the polynomial discriminant functions used here are least mean-square approximations to the a posteriori probability functions $\text{prob}(k|\mathbf{v})$ of (4.32) and not to the quadratic discriminant functions $d_k(\mathbf{v})$ of (4.40), which are derived from the a posteriori probability functions by nonlinear monotonic mappings. For the example of (4.35) the a posteriori probability functions $\text{prob}(k|\mathbf{v})$ are not all quadratic in $\mathbf{v}$.

These considerations lead to the clear conclusion that second-degree polynomials cannot be optimum if the pattern source is known to have normally distributed classes. In the following chapter we will nevertheless look at what happens if we try to solve such a pattern classification task with the quadratic polynomial regression classifier.

From a practical point of view these principal differences between the different quadratic discriminant functions are not serious objections against polynomial regression since one can never be sure that a practical pattern classification problem is actually governed by normal distributions. In such a case both approaches are legitimate engineering approximations.

Beyond that, we are by no means bound to stay with second-degree polynomials. Increasing the degree G of the polynomial approximation above $G = 2$ must improve the polynomial approximation, but in order to keep the example simple, this was deliberately not done here.

Deriving Up to Fourth-Order Moments for Normally Distributed Classes

We are pursuing the goal of developing a second-degree polynomial classifier for the two-dimensional three-class example of (4.35) and need for that purpose the moment matrix $\mathbf{M}$ (6.96). It would be no problem at all to estimate this moment matrix $\mathbf{M}$ from the set of training samples drawn from the model pattern source.

However, there exists a more direct way that derives the necessary statistical moments directly from the statistical model of the pattern source. Remember that the statistical model of (4.35) consists of three class-specific normal distributions. Each is determined by first-order (mean) and second-order (covariance) statistical moments.

We deal with the three classes separately and can therefore omit the class label k. Thus for each component v_n, $n = 1, \ldots, N$, of the measurement vector $\mathbf{v}$ we are given the first and second order statistical moments

$$E\{v_n\}$$
$$\operatorname{cov}\{v_n, v_m\} = E\{(v_n - E\{v_n\})(v_m - E\{v_m\})\}$$

Since these completely determine the class-specific normal distribution, they also determine any of the higher statistical moments, especially those of third and fourth order needed here.

The derivation uses central and noncentral moments for which the following notation is introduced: momj[·] for noncentral and cenj[·] for central moments of jth order, respectively. For indexing we need four different integer variables m, n, o, p each running from $1, \ldots, N$.

From the given data we find the first- and second-order moments

$$\begin{aligned} \text{mom1}[m] &= E\{v_m\} \\ \text{cen2}[m, n] &= \operatorname{cov}\{v_m, v_n\} \\ \text{mom2}[m, n] &= \text{cen2}[m, n] + \text{mom1}[m]\text{mom1}[n] \end{aligned} \tag{6.100}$$

Then the third-order noncentral moments are derived by

$$\begin{aligned} \text{mom3}[m, n, o] = {} & \text{cen2}[m, n]\text{mom1}[o] \\ & + \text{cen2}[m, o]\text{mom1}[n] \\ & + \text{cen2}[n, o]\text{mom1}[m] \\ & + \text{mom1}[m]\text{mom1}[n]\text{mom1}[o] \end{aligned} \tag{6.101}$$

and the central moments by

$$\begin{aligned} \text{cen4}[m, n, o, p] = {} & \text{cen2}[m, n]\text{cen2}[o, p] \\ & + \text{cen2}[m, o]\text{cen2}[n, p] \\ & + \text{cen2}[n, p]\text{cen2}[m, o] \end{aligned} \tag{6.102}$$

The noncentral moments of fourth order are derived by

$$\begin{aligned} \text{mom4}[m, n, o, p] = {} & \text{cen4}[m, n, o, p] \\ & + \text{cen2}[m, n]\text{mom1}[o]\text{mom1}[p] \\ & + \text{cen2}[m, o]\text{mom1}[n]\text{mom1}[p] \\ & + \text{cen2}[m, p]\text{mom1}[n]\text{mom1}[o] \\ & + \text{cen2}[n, o]\text{mom1}[m]\text{mom1}[p] \end{aligned}$$

$$+ \text{cen2}[n,p]\text{mom1}[m]\text{mom1}[o]$$
$$+ \text{cen2}[o,p]\text{mom1}[m]\text{mom1}[n]$$
$$+ \text{mom1}[m]\text{mom1}[n]\text{mom1}[o]\text{mom1}[p] \quad (6.103)$$

With these equations and the class-specific mean $\boldsymbol{\mu}_k = E\{\mathbf{v} \mid k\}$ and covariance matrix $\mathbf{K}_k = \mathbf{cov}\{\mathbf{v}, \mathbf{v} \mid k\}$, we are able to calculate all of the statistical moments necessary for establishing the class-specific moment matrix $\mathbf{M}_k = \{\mathbf{z}\mathbf{z}^T \mid k\}$ of the respective class. In a last step the K class-specific moment matrices $\mathbf{M}_k$ are combined into the overall moment matrix $\mathbf{M}$:

$$\mathbf{M} = \sum_{k=1}^{K} P_k \mathbf{M}_k$$

from which the coefficient matrix $\mathbf{A}$ of the quadratic polynomial classifier is computed by the procedures described in Section 6.8.

6.12 VISUALIZATIONS BASED ON TWO-DIMENSIONAL EXAMPLE OF CHAPTER 4

We are now prepared to go back to the *example* of (4.35) as introduced in Section 4.2 and used there for several illustrations in the context of Bayesian classification for normally distributed classes. The viewpoint chosen there was that the statistical properties of the pattern source were completely known. From the considerations of Section 4.2 we know how the classifier optimum for that statistical situation—the Bayesian classifier—managed its task. We will now adopt the same point of view and look into how the polynomial regression classifier with second-degree polynomials works on the same problem.

The Bayesian classifier is optimum for this artificial example. No other classifier can do better. It shall serve as a reference for conveying an impression of how close other classifier design techniques come to the optimum.

However, the example must not be misinterpreted in the sense that classifier design based on the normal distribution assumption leads to classifiers generally superior over those derived from other techniques. It is just the choice of the example that here makes this concept optimum. In practice we do not know either the statistical situation or the optimum type of classifier.

Remember, also, that the limitation to quadratic polynomials is an arbitrary choice inspired by the observation that in the same case the Bayesian classifier turned out to be a quadratic classifier. We know already that polynomials need higher degrees to converge to the optimum solution.

We start from the statistical data given in (4.35). With the polynomial structure

$$\mathbf{x}(\mathbf{v}) = (1 \quad v_1 \quad v_2 \quad v_1^2 \quad v_1 v_2 \quad v_2^2)^T$$

the three class-specific moment matrices for the classes 0, 1, and 2 are established according to the procedure described in the foregoing section. Since they are symmetric, they are shown here only as upper triangular matrices:

$$\mathbf{M}_0 = \begin{bmatrix} 1.00 & 4.00 & 9.00 & 18.0 & 38.0 & 86.00 & 1.00 & 0.00 & 0.00 \\ \cdot & 18.00 & 38.00 & 88.03 & 178.04 & 380.02 & 4.0 & 0.00 & 0.00 \\ \cdot & \cdot & 86.00 & 178.04 & 380.02 & 863.93 & 9.00 & 0.00 & 0.00 \\ \cdot & \cdot & \cdot & 460.26 & 900.38 & 1844.44 & 18.00 & 0.00 & 0.00 \\ \cdot & \cdot & \cdot & \cdot & 1844.44 & 3972.19 & 38.00 & 0.00 & 0.00 \\ \cdot & \cdot & \cdot & \cdot & \cdot & 9064.74 & 86.00 & 0.00 & 0.00 \\ \cdot & \cdot & \cdot & \cdot & \cdot & \cdot & 1.00 & 0.00 & 0.00 \\ \cdot & \cdot & \cdot & \cdot & \cdot & \cdot & \cdot & 0.00 & 0.00 \\ \cdot & \cdot & \cdot & \cdot & \cdot & \cdot & \cdot & \cdot & 0.00 \end{bmatrix}$$

$$\mathbf{M}_1 = \begin{bmatrix} 1.00 & 8.50 & 7.50 & 74.25 & 61.75 & 61.25 & 0.00 & 1.00 & 0.00 \\ \cdot & 74.25 & 61.75 & 665.19 & 522.86 & 490.58 & 0.00 & 8.50 & 0.00 \\ \cdot & \cdot & 61.25 & 522.86 & 490.58 & 534.32 & 0.00 & 7.50 & 0.00 \\ \cdot & \cdot & \cdot & 6100.15 & 4542.98 & 4045.33 & 0.00 & 74.25 & 0.00 \\ \cdot & \cdot & \cdot & \cdot & 4045.33 & 4173.90 & 0.00 & 61.75 & 0.00 \\ \cdot & \cdot & \cdot & \cdot & \cdot & 4925.67 & 0.00 & 61.25 & 0.00 \\ \cdot & \cdot & \cdot & \cdot & \cdot & \cdot & 0.00 & 0.00 & 0.00 \\ \cdot & \cdot & \cdot & \cdot & \cdot & \cdot & \cdot & 1.00 & 0.00 \\ \cdot & \cdot & \cdot & \cdot & \cdot & \cdot & \cdot & \cdot & 0.00 \end{bmatrix}$$

$$\mathbf{M}_2 = \begin{bmatrix} 1.00 & 6.00 & 3.50 & 43.00 & 17.00 & 19.25 & 0.00 & 0.00 & 1.00 \\ \cdot & 43.00 & 17.00 & 342.00 & 102.50 & 87.50 & 0.00 & 0.00 & 6.00 \\ \cdot & \cdot & 19.25 & 102.50 & 87.50 & 116.38 & 0.00 & 0.00 & 3.50 \\ \cdot & \cdot & \cdot & 2955.00 & 681.00 & 523.75 & 0.00 & 0.00 & 43.00 \\ \cdot & \cdot & \cdot & \cdot & 523.75 & 467.25 & 0.00 & 0.00 & 17.00 \\ \cdot & \cdot & \cdot & \cdot & \cdot & 811.56 & 0.00 & 0.0 & 19.25 \\ \cdot & \cdot & \cdot & \cdot & \cdot & \cdot & 0.00 & 0.00 & 0.00 \\ \cdot & \cdot & \cdot & \cdot & \cdot & \cdot & \cdot & 0.00 & 0.00 \\ \cdot & \cdot & \cdot & \cdot & \cdot & \cdot & \cdot & \cdot & 1.00 \end{bmatrix}$$

The three class-specific matrices $\mathbf{M}_k$ are joined with equal weights (0.333, 0.333, 0.333) according to the equal a priori probabilities of (4.35) to form the moment matrix $\mathbf{M}$ from which we then derive the coefficient matrix $\mathbf{A}$.

To demonstrate the influence of the pivot strategy when solving the matrix

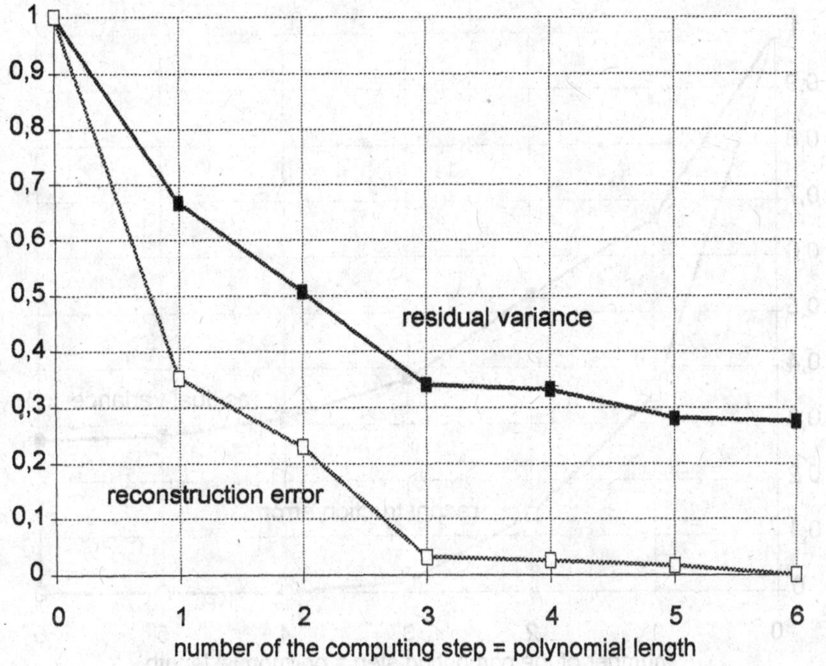

Figure 6.8. Development of reconstruction error R^2 and residual variance S^2 with progress of computing procedure when no *special strategy* is applied. Candidate terms are included into polynomial structure ordered according to their position in draft polynomial structure.

equation, Figs. 6.8–6.10 show how the two criteria R^2 and S^2 develop with increasing polynomial length. The running number of computing steps is counted beginning with zero according to the fact that this is the situation with $\mathbf{x}(\mathbf{v})$ empty corresponding to an approximation $\mathbf{d} \equiv \mathbf{0}$. In the first step of the procedure the constant term $x_0 = 1$ is included in the functional approximation $\mathbf{x}(\mathbf{v}) = 1$ resulting in an approximation function $\mathbf{d} = E\{\mathbf{y}\}$.

From the considerations of the foregoing sections we know that

$$S^2(0) = 1 \quad \text{and} \quad S^2(1) = \sum_{k=1}^{K} P_k(1 - P_k)$$

Similarly the reconstruction error of the first two steps of the procedure is

$$R^2(0) = E\{|\mathbf{x}|^2\} \quad \text{and} \quad R^2(1) = E\{|\mathbf{x} - E\{\mathbf{x}\}|^2\}$$

The illustrations represent the reconstruction error relative to $R^2(0)$. In all three figures the abscissa indicates the number of computing steps, which

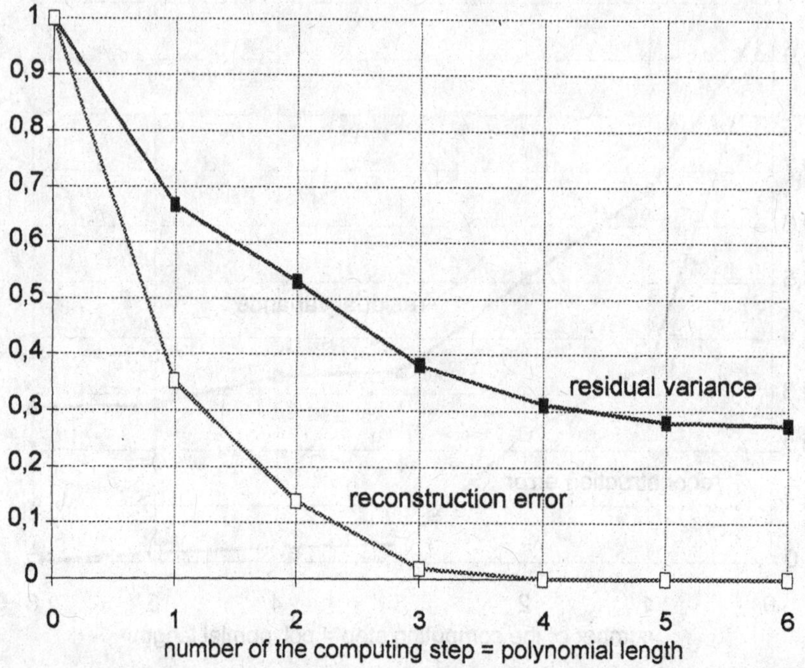

Figure 6.9. Development of reconstruction error R^2 and residual variance S^2 with progress of computing procedure when controlled by *maximum linear independence strategy* LU. Candidate terms are included in polynomial structure ordered according to their contribution to current reconstruction error. Most unpredictable term included first.

equals the polynomial length −1. This is exactly the number of polynomial terms if the constant term $x_0 = 1$ is not counted.

It should be noted that the constant term $x_0 = 1$ is treated separately: It is in any case without any check the first term included into the set of predictor terms. This shall prevent that some other constant or almost constant term is used instead to subtract the mean, that is, to eliminate the bias.

Comparing the three diagrams it can easily be seen that the minimum residual variance strategy (MS) indeed provides the fastest decrease in residual variance S^2 and the maximum linear independence strategy (LU) the fastest decrease in reconstruction error R^2. All three S^2 plots end up with the same final value since a linear system of equations has a unique result irrespective of the sequence of mathematical manipulations. The same is true for the R^2 plots, which all converge to $R^2 = 0$, since nothing remains to be predicted when all the candidate terms are included in **x**.

The three different strategies generate different rank orders among the polynomial terms:

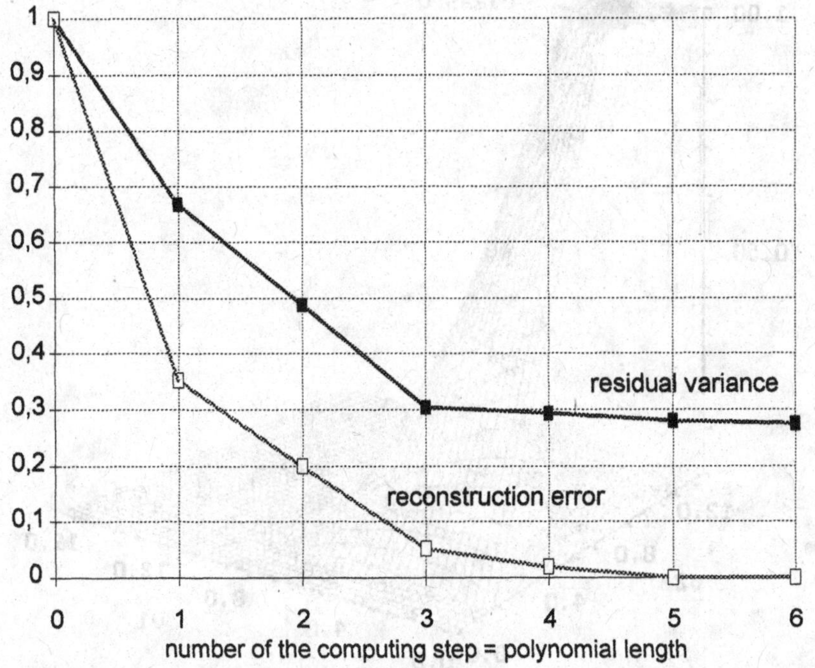

Figure 6.10. Development of reconstruction error R^2 and residual variance S^2 with progress of computing procedure when controlled by *minimum residual variance strategy* MS. Candidate terms are included in polynomial structure ordered according to their contribution to predict target vector **y** from the currently accepted predictor terms **x**.

Rank order	1	2	3	4	5	6
No strategy	1	v_1	v_2	v_1^2	$v_1 v_2$	v_2^2
LU strategy	1	v_2^2	v_1^2	$v_1 v_2$	v_2	v_1
MS strategy	1	$v_1 v_2$	v_2	v_1^2	v_2^2	v_1

The polynomial discriminant function approximates, under the constraints of the limited polynomial degree $G = 2$, the a posteriori probability prob(k|**v**). For the considered example the a posteriori probability function prob(0|**v**) for class 0 is depicted in Fig. 4.9. The polynomial approximation is shown in Fig. 6.11.

The limitation to a second-degree polynomial prevents a closer fit to the true a posteriori function of Fig. 4.9, which has a rather complicated appearance. Increase of the degree G of the approximating polynomial would have improved the approximation. Note that the differences are smaller in regions of higher probability prob(**v**) and increase in regions of vanishing prob(**v**); compare Fig. 4.6.

A three-dimensional plot of the three optimum discriminant functions was

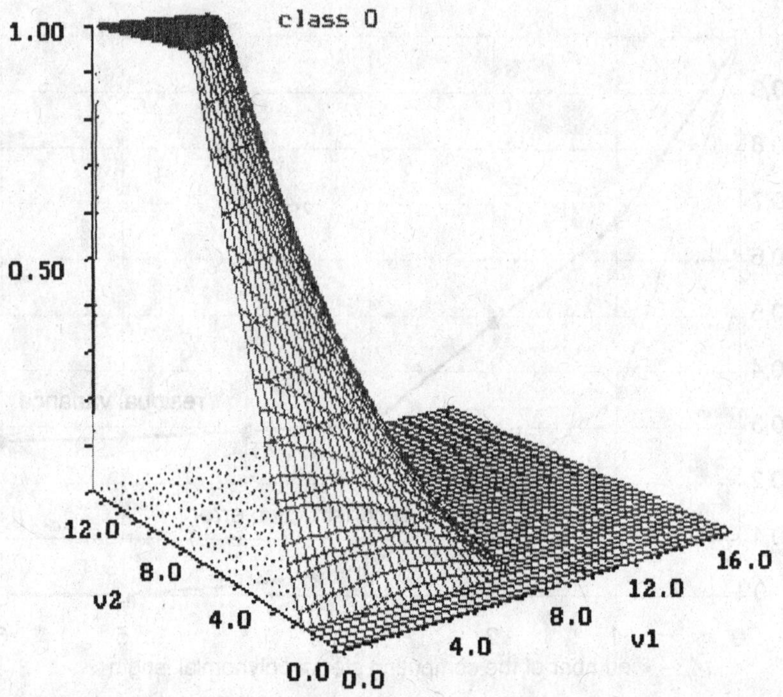

Figure 6.11. Approximation to a posteriori probability function prob(0|**v**) as shown in Fig. 4.9 by best fitting quadratic polynomial. Three-dimensional plot is clipped on levels 0 and 1 for purpose of presentation. Actually approximating function extends unbounded beyond 1 and below 0. Approximation $d_0(\mathbf{v})$ is hyperbolic function extending over entire two-dimensional measurement space.

shown in Fig. 4.7. In the same way the three polynomial approximations are shown in Fig. 6.12.

Figure 6.13 presents a view into the measurement space similar to Fig. 4.10. Obviously the system of class borders, although much simpler than that of the Bayesian classifier, is reasonably adequate.

Comparison of the two systems of class boundaries is shown in Fig. 6.14. Both systems of borders are rather similar in the more populated regions of measurement space but diverge in regions that are almost or completely unpopulated.

The effect of the approximation is also visible in the number of alternatives generated by the polynomial regression classifier shown in Fig. 6.15 for the same confidence threshold CnfThrsh = 0.7 as in Fig. 4.12. We observe that the separating walls of two alternatives between the class regions are much wider than for the Bayesian classifier. In a small center region where all three classes meet, already three alternatives are generated. In that case the pattern classifier dares no more commitment than to forward a rank-ordered list of all the classes to be discriminated.

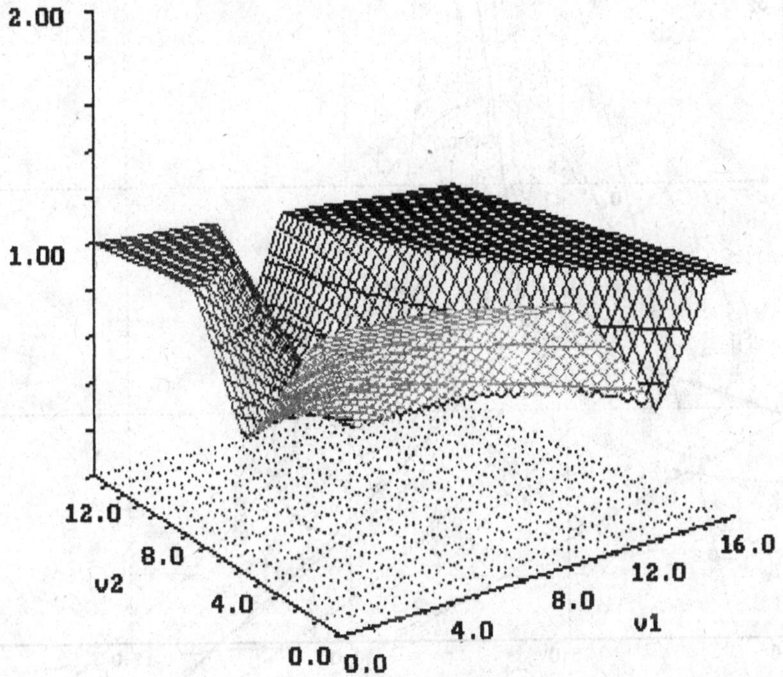

Figure 6.12. Three-dimensional plot of three polynomial discriminant functions in form of max[d_0(**v**), d_1(**v**), d_2(**v**)]. As in Fig. 6.11 three-dimensional plot is clipped at level 1. Note changed vertical scale. Picture shows simplifications introduced by limitation to quadratic polynomials. In relevant regions of measurement space, however, which are those densely populated by pattern source {**v**, *k*}, approximation is sufficiently similar to function to be approximated.

The wider walls between the class regions are caused by the insufficient steepness of the approximated a posteriori probability functions, which, as quadratic polynomials, are not as flexible as to follow precisely the true probability functions; compare Figs. 4.9 and 6.11.

The same effect becomes visible if we look into the decision space as in Fig. 4.14. Figure 6.16 confirms what was sketched in Fig. 6.5. The pattern vectors {**v**} projected into the decision space by the polynomial discriminant function **d**(**v**) are no longer captured inside the equilateral triangle as in Fig. 4.14 but are spread out in the neighborhood of their respective target points $\mathbf{y}_k$. The insufficient flexibility of the approximation results in a kind of blurring. The probability mass is smeared inside and outside the decision triangle.

6.13 CONFIDENCE MAPPING

Comparison of Figs. 4.14 and 6.16 turns our attention again upon one important difference between the discriminant function **d**(**v**) established by the

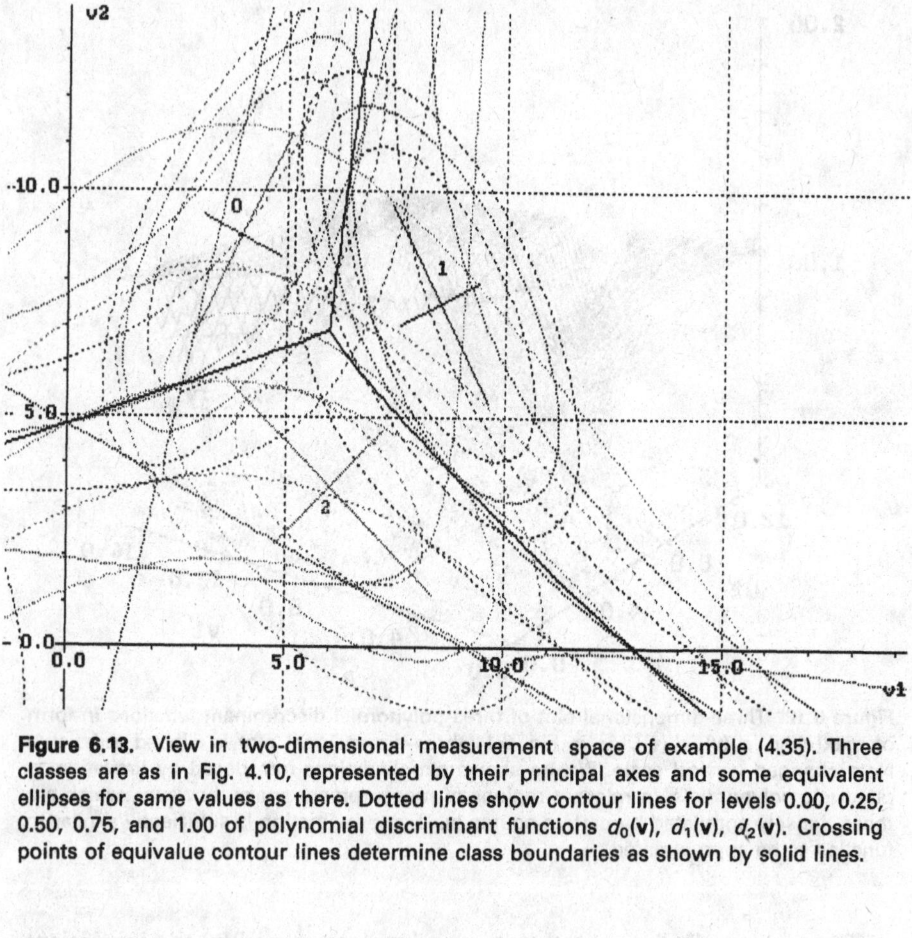

Figure 6.13. View in two-dimensional measurement space of example (4.35). Three classes are as in Fig. 4.10, represented by their principal axes and some equivalent ellipses for same values as there. Dotted lines show contour lines for levels 0.00, 0.25, 0.50, 0.75, and 1.00 of polynomial discriminant functions $d_0(\mathbf{v})$, $d_1(\mathbf{v})$, $d_2(\mathbf{v})$. Crossing points of equivalue contour lines determine class boundaries as shown by solid lines.

polynomial regression classifier and that of the optimum discriminant function $\mathbf{p}(\mathbf{v})$. Of the two properties (6.74) and (6.75) one is obviously lost—the property of generating estimations $d_k(\mathbf{v})$ coming from the closed interval $[0..1]$.

Motivation

There are many applications in pattern classification where the discriminant vector $\mathbf{d}$ is not the final result of the classification procedure to be used only for searching the largest of its components. These are the applications where the discriminant vector $\mathbf{d}$ is considered as providing a set of alternatives weighted with confidence values and going into subsequent confidence based reasoning procedures. Compare the considerations on confidence and forwarding sets of alternatives of Section 4.2.

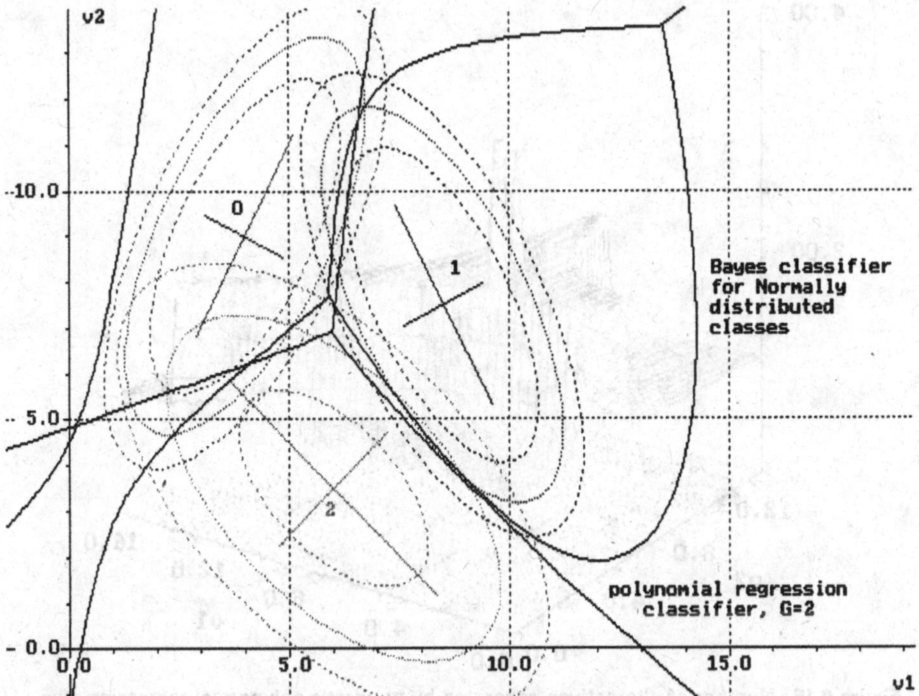

Figure 6.14. Comparison of two different systems of class boundaries as determined by Bayesian classifier, being optimum for given example, and quadratic polynomial regression classifier. Both are shown by solid lines. In regions of high probability prob(v) borders are close together whereas in lesser populated regions of measurement space quite large deviations can be observed.

For those purposes the confidence values provided should be reliable and coherent with statistical experience, which means, for example, that if the classifier evaluates a certain decision with a confidence score of 80%, then within a larger sample of similar cases (in the sense of carrying the same confidence value) this decision should turn out to be true in 80% of the cases. Negative values and values larger than 1, unavoidable when working directly with least mean-square approximations for target values 0 and 1, are undesired artefacts of the approximation technique and must be corrected one way or the other as conflicting with the conception of confidence.

The simplest, but not really satisfying, approach would be to clip the estimations d_k at the two levels of 0 and 1. This technique is able to restore the validity of (6.74) but misses the goal of providing statistical coherence.

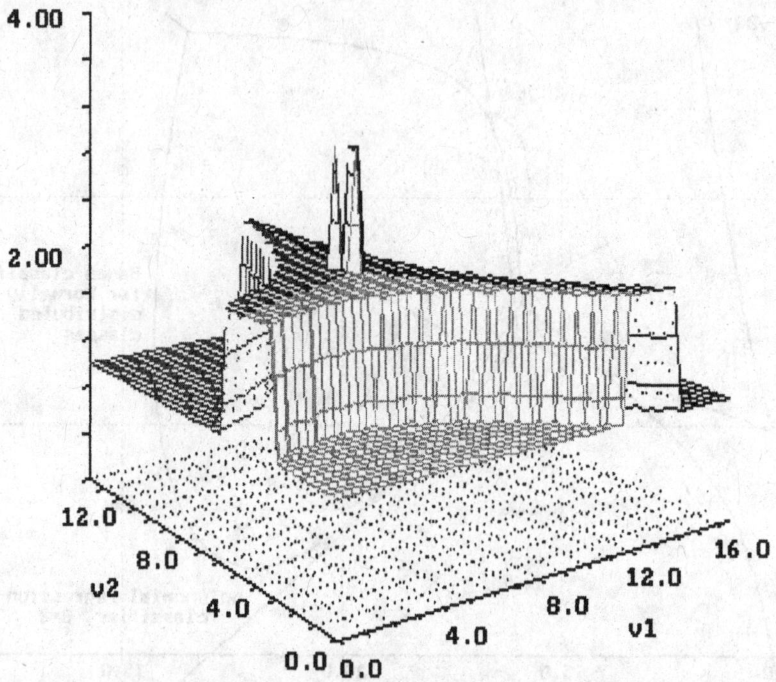

Figure 6.15. Number of alternatives generated by quadratic polynomial regression classifier driven in *n* best classification mode shown as three-dimensional plot over measurement space. Compare Fig. 4.12.

Imperfect Estimations Used as Feature Variables for Subsequent Classifier

A somewhat more intelligent approach is to treat the result of the approximation gained so far as a mere vector of feature variables on which to base again a functional approximation process with the goal of providing an improved approximation (Fig. 6.17).

We will follow this idea here in the context of polynomial classification with the discriminant vector **d** being a polynomial approximating the vector **p** of a posteriori probabilities. It should, however, be stated from the beginning that the same idea applies to any kind of classification technique with the components of the discriminant vector **d** being any kind of class membership functions measuring similarities or distances.

Each of the K components of **d** is treated individually. The kth component of **d** is a class membership function separating class k from the rest of the set Ω of the K classes. This function $d_k(\mathbf{v})$ is a least mean-square approximation to the target function $y_k(\mathbf{v})$ with the two values

$$y_k(\mathbf{v}) = \begin{cases} 1 & \text{for } \mathbf{v} \text{ from class } k \\ 0 & \text{for } \mathbf{v} \text{ from class } j \neq k \end{cases}$$

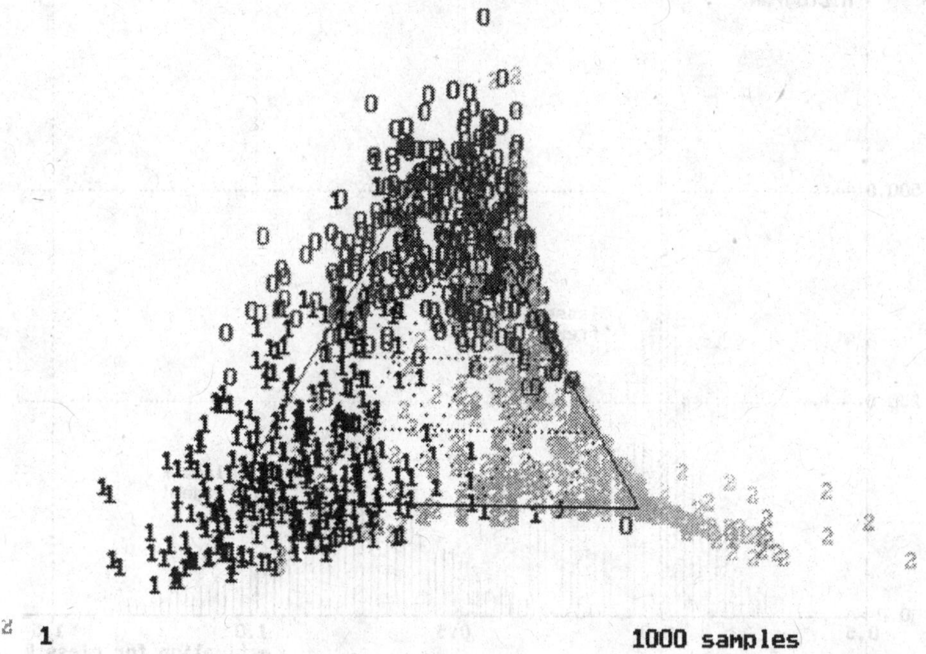

Figure 6.16. Scatterplot of same set of samples as in Fig. 4.14 in decision space **D**, here for quadratic polynomial regression classifier. Three class-specific distributions are nonlinearly distorted images of corresponding distributions in measurement space; compare Fig. 4.13. With increasing degree of polynomial discriminant function **d(v)** distribution would be more and more moved into interior of decision triangle.

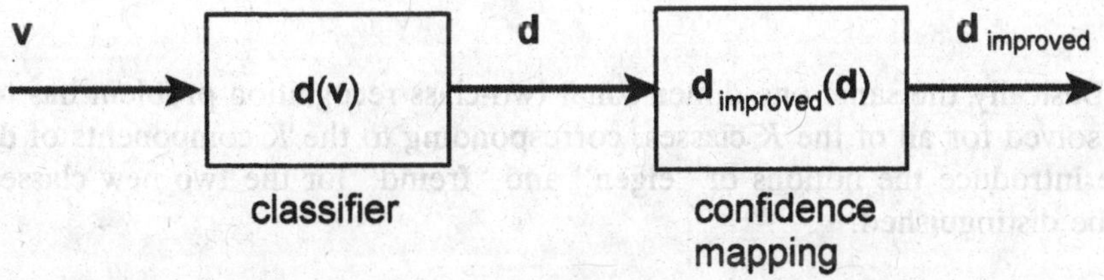

Figure 6.17. General concept of improving estimation **d(v)** generated by polynomial approximation by confidence mapping.

where $k = 1, \dots, K$. As a result of the approximation, in other words, as a result of classifier training based on the learning sample, the estimations d_k targeted to 1 fall into the neighborhood of 1 and the estimations targeted to 0 fall into the neighborhood of 0. Thus, $d_k(\mathbf{v})$ is a reasonably well suited one-dimensional feature variable for this specific two-class recognition task, namely to predict $y_k(\mathbf{v})$ reliably from d_k; see Fig. 6.18.

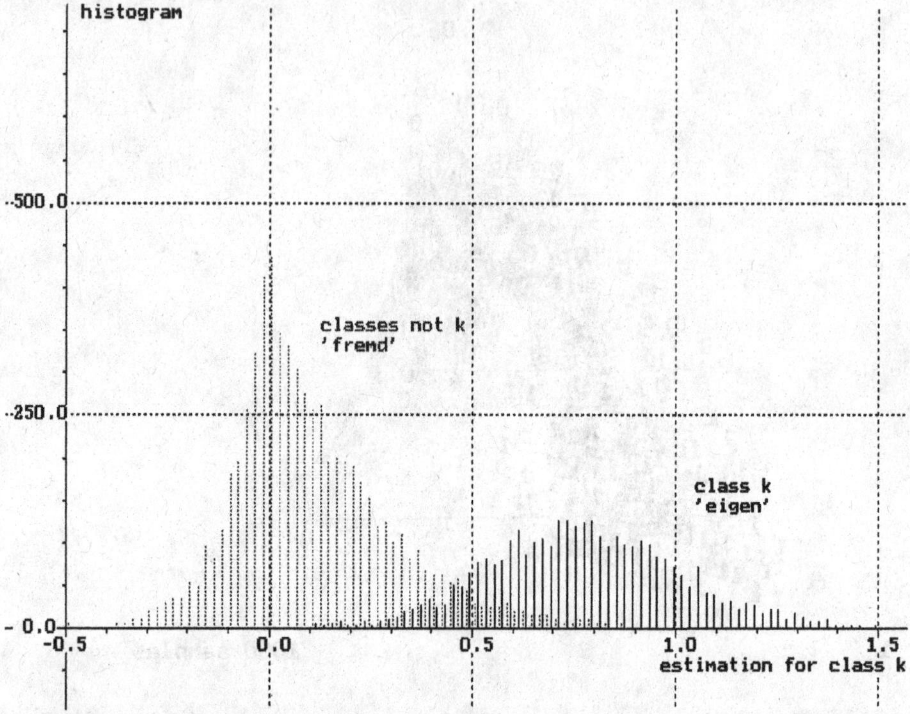

Figure 6.18. Distributions in d_k-space of two classes eigen and fremd. Both distributions are rather broad. The eigen distribution, containing estimations targeted to 1, is definitely closer to 1, and the fremd distribution is closer to zero. Data belong to two-dimensional, three-class example of (4.35) and shows distribution for class $k = 1$. It is clearly visible that eigen distribution extends into the region $d_k > 1$ as well as fremd distribution into region $d_k < 0$. Note that fremd histogram contains here twice number of events of eigen histogram, since number of classes is 3.

Basically the same one-dimensional two-class recognition problem has to be solved for all of the K classes, corresponding to the K components of $\mathbf{d}$. We introduce the notions of "eigen" and "fremd" for the two new classes to be distinguished:

- Eigen — Indicates membership to class k as far as $d_k(\mathbf{v})$ is considered, $y_k = 1$
- Fremd — Indicates membership to any class j of set of remaining $K - 1$ classes $j \neq k$ as far as $d_k(\mathbf{v})$ is considered, $y_k = 0$.

Since the feature space here is one-dimensional we do not encounter any of the difficulties typical for higher dimensional feature spaces and can apply in a most direct manner what was elaborated on in the foregoing chapters of this book on classifier design techniques.

The two classes just introduced are statistically described by prob(eigen), prob(fremd), prob(d_k|eigen), and prob(d_k|fremd), all of which can be derived from empirical data, as shown in Fig. 6.18.

What we need to know is the a posteriori probability prob(eigen|d_k), indicating the probability of the observed pattern coming from class k—and not from any of the other classes—if the kth component $d_k(\mathbf{v})$ of the polynomial discriminant function $\mathbf{d}(\mathbf{v})$ renders the value d_k.

Even if these probabilities are themselves replaced again by approximations, we gain an improved estimation of the a posteriori probability by

$$\begin{aligned} \mathrm{cnf}(d_k) &= \frac{\mathrm{prob}(\mathrm{eigen})\mathrm{prob}(d_k|\mathrm{eigen})}{\mathrm{prob}(\mathrm{eigen})\mathrm{prob}(d_k|\mathrm{eigen}) + \mathrm{prob}(\mathrm{fremd})\mathrm{prob}(d_k|\mathrm{fremd})} \\ &= \left(1 + \frac{\mathrm{prob}(\mathrm{fremd})\mathrm{prob}(d_k|\mathrm{fremd})}{\mathrm{prob}(\mathrm{eigen})\mathrm{prob}(d_k|\mathrm{eigen})}\right)^{-1} \end{aligned} \tag{6.104}$$

mapping the raw estimation d_k into the confidence cnf(d_k). The two probabilities prob(eigen) and prob(fremd),

$$\begin{aligned} \mathrm{prob}(\mathrm{eigen}) &= \mathrm{prob}(k) = P_k \\ \mathrm{prob}(\mathrm{fremd}) &= 1 - \mathrm{prob}(k) = 1 - P_k \end{aligned} \tag{6.105}$$

are either given a priori or determined by counting relative frequencies. The class-specific distributions prob(d_k|eigen) and prob(d_k|fremd) or their likelihood ratio are easily recovered from histograms, as in Fig. 6.18.

It is important to note that whereas we are able in this way to produce sensible confidence values cnf(d_k) for the K classes $k = 1, \ldots, K$ obeying (6.74) at the same time, property (6.75) may even be lost. If the closed-world assumption holds, that is, no other measurement vectors $\mathbf{v}$ are input to the recognition system than those coming from the statistical process $\{\mathbf{v}, \mathbf{y}\}$, as was described by the learning set, we are allowed to renormalize the K estimations and gain an improved estimation

$$\mathbf{d}_{\mathrm{improved}} = \frac{1}{\sum_{k=1}^{K} \mathrm{cnf}(d_k)} \begin{pmatrix} \mathrm{cnf}(d_1) \\ \mathrm{cnf}(d_2) \\ \vdots \\ \mathrm{cnf}(d_K) \end{pmatrix} \tag{6.106}$$

In Chapter 4 we called this operation Normalize To Unity[·] applied to the confidence values cnf(d_k).

Computing Confidences from Eigen- and Fremd-Histograms

The closed-world assumption is nice for developing pattern classification systems but is difficult to assure in practical applications. The closed-world assumption assumes that only samples of the admissible classes are presented to the classifier. In practical application this can not at all be guaranteed. Thus the question of *garbage patterns* is raised, that is, patterns not in accordance with the statistical experience of the classifier and coming from regions of the measurement space not populated by the pattern source {**v**, **y**} and the learning sample.

Garbage patterns must be detected prior to computing confidences since for them no sensible confidences are derivable and there is no chance left of detecting them after having gone through the confidence mapping procedure.

The problem of garbage pattern detection is again a recognition problem with the two classes "legitimate" and "garbage". Whereas for the legitimate class statistical knowledge is available, this is definitely not the case for the garbage class; otherwise we could have this included as an additional class from the beginning.

The garbage class is the universe of "everything else" that may happen "everywhere" in decision space. Thus the adequate statistical assumption is the uniformity assumption. According to what we have learned about statistical decision theory in Chapter 2, we have to compute the respective a posteriori probabilities for the two classes "legitimate" and "garbage" from their class-specific distributions and to determine the points of intersections. Practically, this kind of proceeding leads to detecting garbage patterns as "outliers" compared with the known distribution of the legitimate patterns.

The procedures of establishing the confidence mapping function must therefore be organized such that they provide all the necessary information for outlier detection as a byproduct. For this purpose the histograms representing the eigen and fremd distributions of all K classes are analyzed to define appropriate outlier-quantiles between which regions of acceptance are defined on d_k scale for both of distributions. A pattern **v** to be classified falling neither into the eigen nor into the fremd acceptance region for any of the K classes is rejected as being a garbage pattern.

The histograms of Fig. 6.18 can be considered as being sampled versions of the true probability density functions prob(d|eigen) and prob(d|fremd) distorted by a random error caused by the limited number of samples per histogram bin. This error term increases with decreasing histogram counts.

We must regard that counting the events from class k in hist[i|eigen] and those not from class k in hist[i|fremd] includes counting the class-specific frequencies and leads to the following correspondence between histogram and probability:

$$\text{hist}[d|\text{eigen}] \Leftrightarrow \text{prob}(\text{eigen})\cdot\text{prob}(d|\text{eigen})$$
$$\text{hist}[d|\text{fremd}] \Leftrightarrow \text{prob}(\text{fremd})\cdot\text{prob}(d|\text{fremd})$$

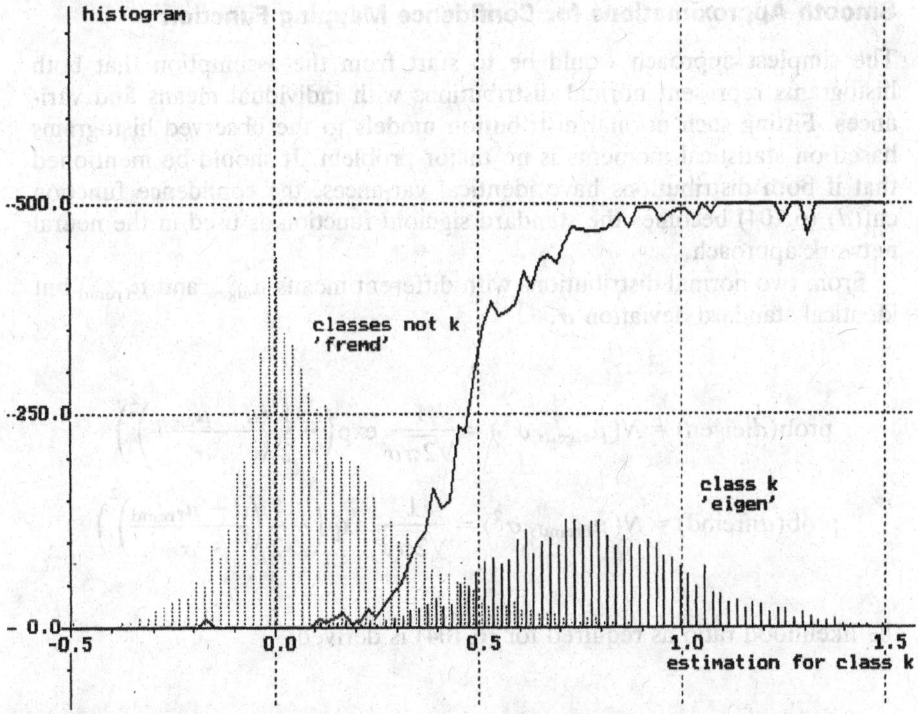

Figure 6.19. Sampled confidence function according to (6.107) for same example as Fig. 6.18. Discrete values directly derived from histograms are linearly interpolated. The sample point 500 on histogram scale corresponds to value 1 of confidence function.

Therefore, the expression

$$\mathrm{cnf}[i] = \frac{\mathrm{hist}[i \mid \mathrm{eigen}]}{\mathrm{hist}[i \mid \mathrm{eigen}] + \mathrm{hist}[i \mid \mathrm{fremd}]} = \left(1 + \frac{\mathrm{hist}[i \mid \mathrm{fremd}]}{\mathrm{hist}[i \mid \mathrm{eigen}]}\right)^{-1} \quad (6.107)$$

is a sampled approximation to (6.104), with the index i representing the position of the respective histogram bin on the d_k scale. The result is a one-dimensional array cnf[i] of the same format as the two histograms. Since the specific value d_k of a given estimation is easily mapped into the corresponding index i, this kind of confidence mapping can be simply implemented as a table look-up operation. Figure 6.19 clearly shows how the confidence function is superimposed by a random term coming from the finiteness of the sample set as used for establishing the histograms. We are therefore looking for a smooth approximation to be derived from the histograms.

Smooth Approximations for Confidence Mapping Function

The simplest approach would be to start from the assumption that both histograms represent normal distributions with individual means and variances. Fitting such normal distribution models to the observed histograms based on statistical moments is no major problem. It should be mentioned that if both distributions have identical variances, the confidence function cnf(d) (6.104) becomes the standard sigmoid function as used in the neural network approach.

From two normal distributions with different means μ_{eigen} and μ_{fremd} but identical standard deviation σ,

$$\text{prob}(d|\text{eigen}) = N(\mu_{\text{eigen}}, \sigma^2) = \frac{1}{\sqrt{2\pi}\sigma} \exp\left(-\frac{1}{2}\left(\frac{d-\mu_{\text{eigen}}}{\sigma}\right)^2\right)$$

$$\text{prob}(d|\text{fremd}) = N(\mu_{\text{fremd}}, \sigma^2) = \frac{1}{\sqrt{2\pi}\sigma} \exp\left(-\frac{1}{2}\left(\frac{d-\mu_{\text{fremd}}}{\sigma}\right)^2\right)$$

the likelihood ratio as required for (6.104) is derived:

$$\begin{aligned}\frac{\text{prob}(d|\text{fremd})}{\text{prob}(d|\text{eigen})} &= \exp\left(-\frac{1}{2\sigma^2}\left[(d-\mu_{\text{fremd}})^2 - (d-\mu_{\text{eigen}})^2\right]\right) \\ &= \exp\left[\frac{\mu_{\text{fremd}} - \mu_{\text{eigen}}}{\sigma^2}\left(d - \frac{(\mu_{\text{fremd}} + \mu_{\text{eigen}})}{2}\right)\right]\end{aligned}$$

Using

$$\alpha = \frac{\mu_{\text{eigen}} - \mu_{\text{fremd}}}{\sigma^2} \qquad \beta = \frac{\mu_{\text{eigen}} + \mu_{\text{fremd}}}{2} \qquad \gamma = \ln\left(\frac{\text{prob(fremd)}}{\text{prob(eigen)}}\right) \tag{6.108}$$

we find

$$\text{cnf}(d) = \frac{1}{1 + \exp\{-\alpha[d - (\beta + \gamma/\alpha)]\}} \tag{6.109}$$

which indeed is the classical sigmoid function with respect to d, centered at $\beta + \gamma/\alpha$ on the d scale and with steepness coefficient α.

Generic Model for Confidence Mapping Function

These considerations are a valuable justification to use a kind of sigmoid model for generating a smooth approximating function to the sampled confidence function of Fig. 6.19.

But we should also have another important point of view in mind. We do not know how perfect the classifier is, having produced the raw estimation **d** that we are just going to map into an improved estimation. It might well be that this classifier is already perfect or at least almost perfect. In such a case the normal distribution cannot be an adequate model and the sampled confidence function of (6.107) will be approximately linear within the [0 . . 1] interval on the d scale; see Fig. 6.22 below and the corresponding explanation.

Our intention is that the concept of confidence mapping should be applicable to any case of classifier without knowing how perfectly or imperfectly the classifier works. We introduce, therefore, a generic model for the confidence mapping function $\mathrm{cnf}(d)$ consisting of three pieces:

- Lower sigmoidal bow
- Straight-line segment
- Upper sigmoidal bow

The model is designed such that the first derivative exists; see Fig. 6.20. Matching this model to the given histograms is again based on least mean-square approximation,

$$F(\mathbf{c}) = \sum_i \mathrm{hist}[i](y(i, \mathbf{c}) - \mathrm{cnf}[i])^2 \tag{6.110}$$

where $\mathrm{hist}[i]$ represents the sum of the two histograms $\mathrm{hist}[i|\mathrm{eigen}] + \mathrm{hist}[i|\mathrm{fremd}]$, $\mathrm{cnf}[i]$ is the sampled confidence function derived from the histograms according to (6.107), and $y(i, \mathbf{c})$ is the model function evaluated at the center of the ith interval on the d scale with parameter vector $\mathbf{c}$.

The result of the fitting procedure is shown in Fig. 6.21. In order to show how the same procedure handles the case of **d** generated by the optimum classifier, we go back to the experimental data shown in Chapter 4. The Bayes classifier for the given example generates the distributions on the d_k scale shown in Fig. 6.22 for the class $k = 1$ to be compared with Fig. 6.18. In Fig. 6.22 we observe that in the case of already optimum estimations the confidence mapping function becomes the identity function, which obviously leaves the given estimations unchanged.

In fact it can be shown mathematically that from the proposition $d_k = \mathrm{prob}(\mathrm{class\_}k|\mathbf{v})$ directly follows $\mathrm{cnf}(d_k) = d_k$. We will make intuitively clear what happens when the estimation d_k is provided by the optimum classifier. In that case the measurement $\mathbf{v}$, for which a certain value $d_k =$

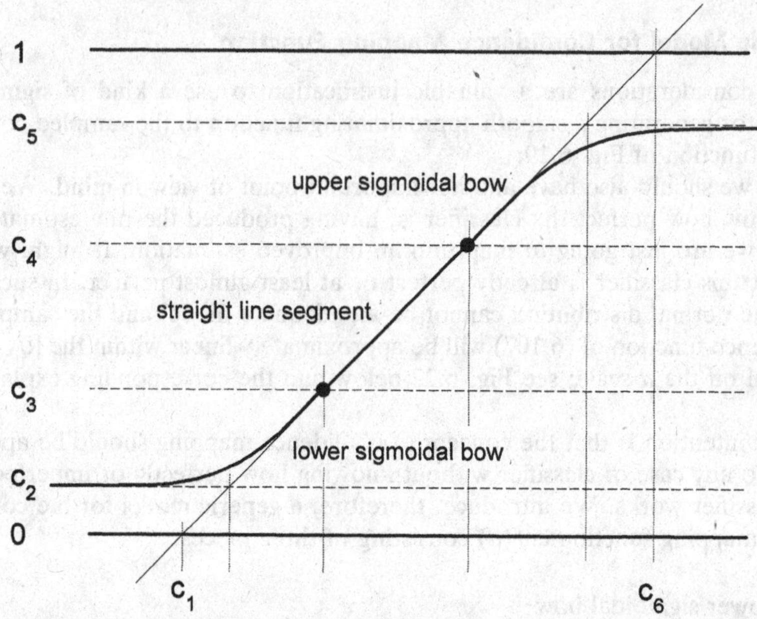

Figure 6.20. Generic model for confidence mapping function $\mathrm{cnf}(d) = y(d, c)$ consisting of three contiguous parts: lower sigmoidal bow, straight-line segment, and upper sigmoidal bow. Whole construction depends on six parameters (contained in parameter vector **c**) and is capable of representing classical sigmoid function $\sigma(d) = 1/[1 + \exp(-d)]$ as well as identity function for the [0..1] domain.

prob(class_k|**v**) is computed, stems from a point in measurement space {**v**} where the proportion of patterns belonging to class k and those not belonging to that class k are exactly given by d_k = prob(class_k|**v**) and prob(not_class_k|**v**) = 1 − prob(class_k|**v**) = $1 - d_k$.

The histogram interval on the d_k scale centered at value d_k collects all of the patterns **v** that have this property in common, irrespective of from which part of the measurement space they come. Therefore the proportion of measurement vectors **v** mapped into that specific interval and coming from class k compared to those not coming from class k must in the limit be d_k and $1 - d_k$, respectively. Inserting this into (6.107) gives

$$\mathrm{cnf}(d_k) = \frac{1}{1 + (1 - d_k)/d_k} = \frac{d_k}{d_k + 1 - d_k} = d_k$$

Confidence Mapping Applied to Examples of Section 6.12

The effect of confidence mapping shall be demonstrated by reference to the results gained from applying the second-degree polynomial classifier to the two-dimensional, three-class example of Section 4.2. The results gained di-

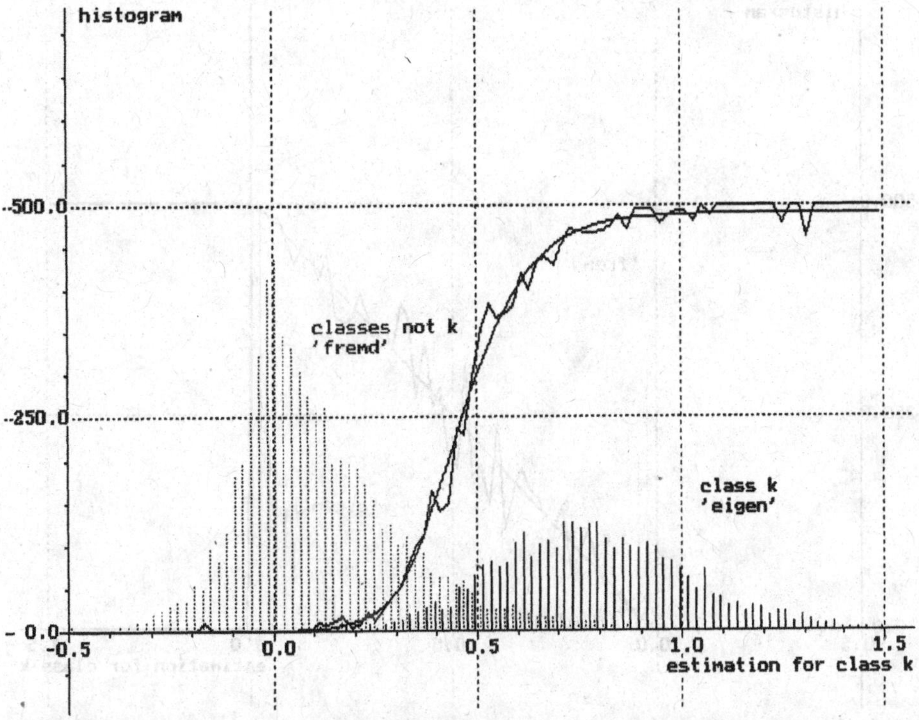

Figure 6.21. Result of fitting generic model of Fig. 6.20 to sampled confidence function of Fig. 6.19.

rectly from polynomial classification are shown in Section 6.12 in Figs. 6.11 and 6.12 and in Figs. 6.15 and 6.16.

The same diagrams are shown in Figs. 6.23–6.26 for the case when the discriminant vector **d** produced by the polynomial classifier is further processed by the confidence mapping procedure.

Comments

The most important effect of confidence mapping lies in providing confidence scores that are coherent with statistical experience in the sense that a confidence score of, say, 80% indicates that the accompanying choice is on the average true with 80% probability. As a byproduct the properties (6.74) and (6.75) are restored, having at least partially been lost in the functional approximation procedure.

This property makes the class-specific discriminant functions $d_k(\mathbf{v})$ better comparable among each other and makes the ranking of alternatives more reliable. The resulting estimations become legitimate probability estimates

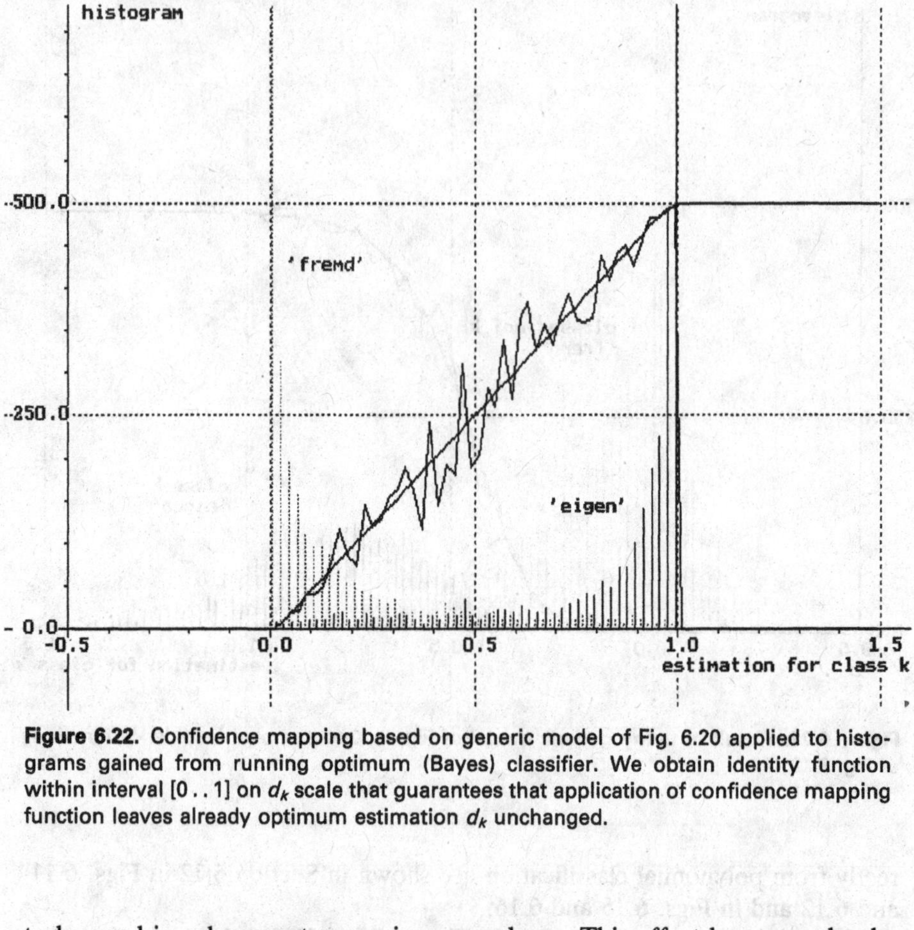

Figure 6.22. Confidence mapping based on generic model of Fig. 6.20 applied to histograms gained from running optimum (Bayes) classifier. We obtain identity function within interval [0 . . 1] on d_k scale that guarantees that application of confidence mapping function leaves already optimum estimation d_k unchanged.

to be used in subsequent reasoning procedures. This effect becomes clearly visible when comparing Figs. 6.16 and 6.26.

The positive effect of confidence mapping depends on how imperfect the discriminant function $\mathbf{d}(\mathbf{v})$ has been before with respect to the goal of approximating $\mathbf{p}(\mathbf{v})$. A typical imperfection of quadratic polynomial classification occurs in the case of one class in measurement space $\mathbf{V}$ being broadly surrounded by other classes. In this situation the polynomial discriminant function for the considered class tends to systematically underestimate the a posteriori probability. Confidence mapping is able to correct this; see Fig. 6.27.

It is most important to note that the same technique of confidence mapping based on eigen and fremd histograms is a universal scaling method making class membership estimations commensurable regardless of the scale on which they are gained and regardless of their interpretation as estimated a posteriori probabilities or arbitrary distance measures. In any case, we have the two histograms hist[i|eigen] and hist[i|fremd] of those patterns belonging

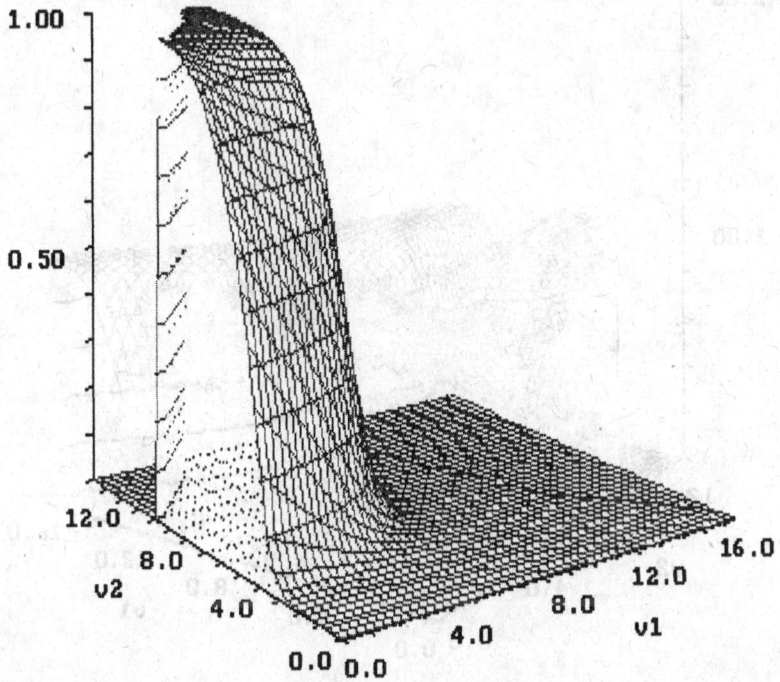

Figure 6.23. Improvement of polynomial approximation Fig. 6.11 to a posteriori probability function prob(0|v) shown in Fig. 4.9 by confidence mapping technique. Cutoff of discriminant function in leftmost corner of three-dimensional plot image is caused by outlier detection procedure.

to class *k* and those belonging to any of the remaining classes. Once these histograms are measured, the rest of the procedure remains the same.

Beyond that, the thorough view into the numerous histograms (two for each of the classes to be distinguished) allows us to define outlier-quantiles to be utilized for garbage pattern detection.

6.14 RECURSIVE LEARNING

Classifier adaptation is based on learning from examples, and these are contained in the *learning set*. We have seen in the foregoing chapters that statistical *moment matrices* derived from the learning set carry the relevant information even for different classifier design techniques such as classifier design based on statistical models as well as classifier design based on the conception of least mean-square functional approximation.

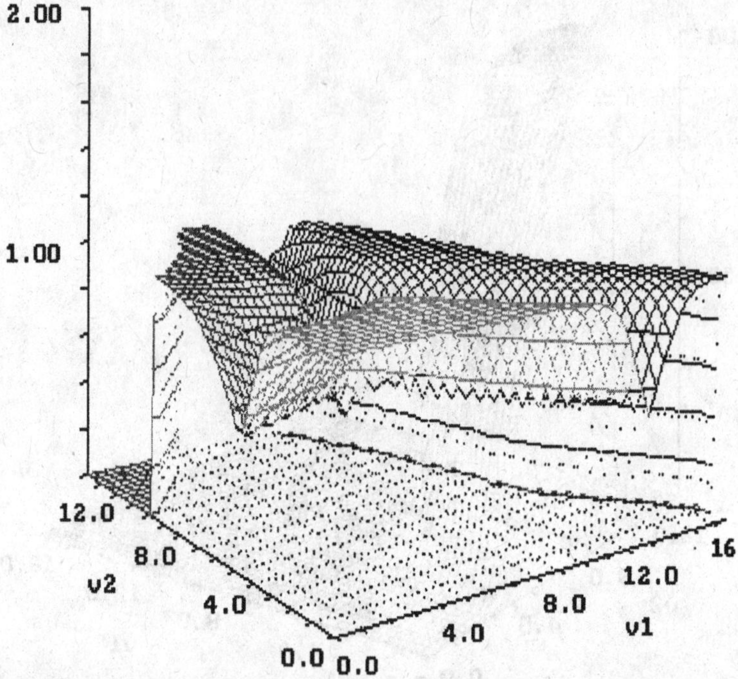

Figure 6.24. Three-dimensional plot of three discriminant functions in form of $\max[d_0(\mathbf{v}), d_1(\mathbf{v}), d_2(\mathbf{v})]$ produced from the polynomial discriminant functions of Fig. 6.12 by confidence mapping. Three functions are clipped to zero in those regions of the measurement space not populated by pattern source $\{\mathbf{v}, k\}$ (outlier detection).

We know from the considerations of Sections 4.7 and 6.10 that statistical moment matrices may either be computed in a batch processing style by

$$\mathbf{M} = \frac{1}{J}\sum_{j=1}^{J} \mathbf{z}_j\mathbf{z}_j^T$$

or recursively by

$$\mathbf{M} \Leftarrow (1-\alpha)\mathbf{M} + \alpha\,\mathbf{z}\mathbf{z}^T$$

where the learning parameter α determines the influence past samples have on the estimation. With $\alpha = \text{const}$ we get a *short term average* with the property of increasingly forgetting past observations and with $\alpha = 1/J$ the *long-term average* identical to the above sum formula for the arithmetic mean if properly initialized.

We also know from Section 4.7 that the recursive formulation is applicable not only to the statistical moments but also to expressions still to be computed

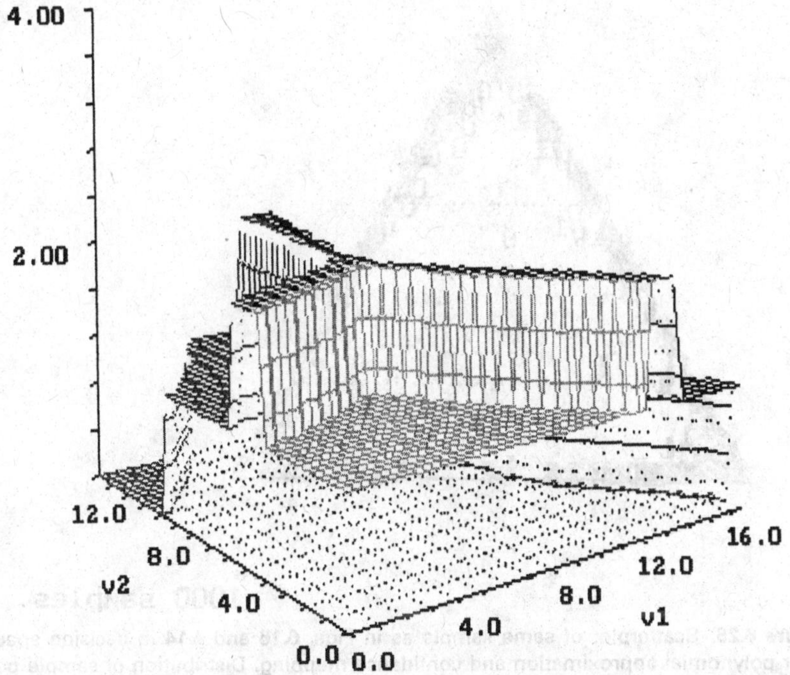

Figure 6.25. Number a of alternatives generated by quadratic polynomial classifier after confidence mapping. Compare with Fig. 6.15. Confidence threshold for n best alternatives procedure is with CnfThrsh = 0.7, as in Figs. 6.15 and 4.12. Separating walls (of two alternatives) between class regions in measurement space have become narrower than in Fig. 6.15 due to improved estimations of a posteriori probabilities. In outside regions number of alternatives a is set to zero (reject of garbage patterns).

from these moments. This was exemplified in Section 4.7 by deriving recursive learning rules for inverse moment and covariance matrices.

We will now make use of the expressions given there and derive a recursive learning rule for the coefficient matrix $\mathbf{A}$ of the least mean-square polynomial classifier [AGA1966].

The optimum coefficient matrix $\mathbf{A}_J$ based on the first J items of the learning set is given by (6.20)

$$\mathbf{A}_J = \left[\sum_{j=1}^{J} \mathbf{x}_j \mathbf{x}_j^T \right]^{-1} \sum_{j=1}^{J} \mathbf{x}_j \mathbf{y}_j^T \tag{6.111}$$

whereas the optimum coefficient matrix $\mathbf{A}_{J-1}$ based on the first $J-1$ items

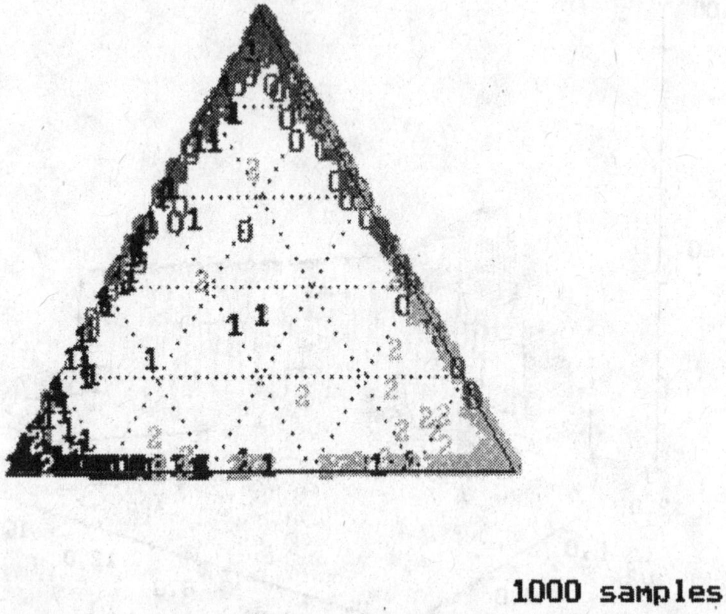

Figure 6.26. Scatterplot of same sample as in Figs. 6.16 and 4.14 in decision space **D** after polynomial approximation and confidence mapping. Distribution of sample points is completely captured inside decision triangle. Inside area, however, is almost empty; compare Fig. 4.14. Sample points gather along lines connecting two of three classes, which indicates that conflicts occur mostly between pairs of classes, not between all three.

of the learning set is given by

$$\mathbf{A}_{J-1} = \left[\sum_{j=1}^{J-1} \mathbf{x}_j\mathbf{x}_j^T\right]^{-1} \sum_{j=1}^{J-1} \mathbf{x}_j\mathbf{y}_j^T \tag{6.112}$$

Both of the two sums occurring in the equation for sample size J can be written recursively,

$$\begin{aligned} \sum_{j=1}^{J} \mathbf{x}_j\mathbf{x}_j^T &= (1-\alpha)\sum_{j=1}^{J-1} \mathbf{x}_j\mathbf{x}_j^T + \alpha\,\mathbf{x}_J\mathbf{x}_J^T \\ \sum_{j=1}^{J} \mathbf{x}_j\mathbf{y}_j^T &= (1-\alpha)\sum_{j=1}^{J-1} \mathbf{x}_j\mathbf{y}_j^T + \alpha\,\mathbf{x}_J\mathbf{y}_J^T \end{aligned} \tag{6.113}$$

and turn out to consist of just the sums needed for the equation (6.112) for sample size $J-1$ plus a correction term determined by the present observation as given by $\mathbf{x}_J$ and $\mathbf{y}_J$.

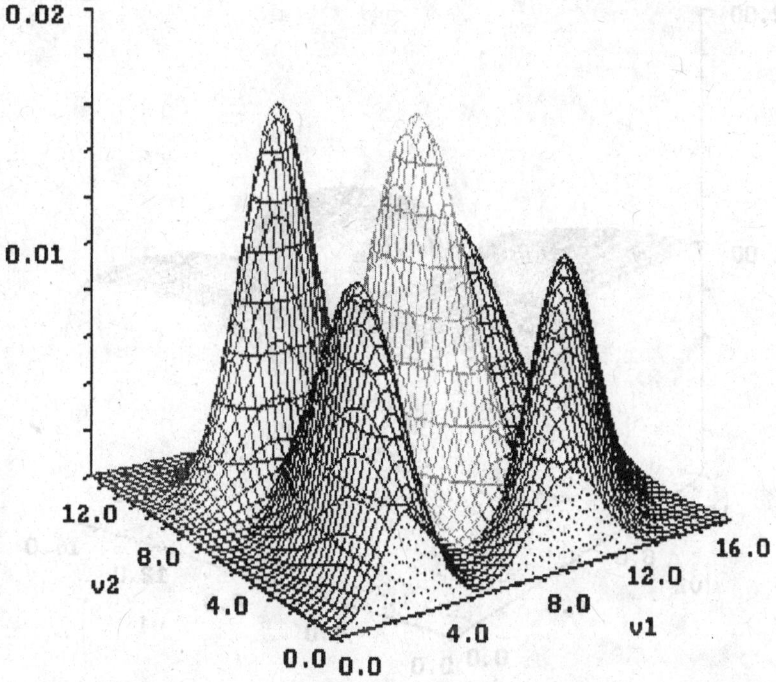

(a)

Figure 6.27. Demonstration of effect of confidence mapping in situation that one class region in measurement space is surrounded by four other class regions. (*a*) Five a priori weighted class-specific distributions P_k prob($\mathbf{v}|k$) shown as in Fig. 4.6. (*b*) True a posteriori probability functions prob($k|\mathbf{v}$). (*c*) Approximations gained by quadratic polynomial approximation. It is clearly visible that discriminant function responsible for center class does not reach value 1. (*d*) Situation is remarkably improved by confidence mapping. Main difference compared to (*b*) comes from clipping five discriminant functions to zero in unpopulated regions of measurement space by outlier detection procedure.

For the first of the two sums we need the matrix inverse, which can directly be taken from (4.101),

$$\left[\sum_{j=1}^{J} \mathbf{x}_j\mathbf{x}_j^T\right]^{-1} = \frac{1}{1-\alpha}\left[\left[\sum_{j=1}^{J-1} \mathbf{x}_j\mathbf{x}_j^T\right]^{-1} - \alpha\,\frac{\left[\sum_{j=1}^{J-1} \mathbf{x}_j\mathbf{x}_j^T\right]^{-1}\mathbf{x}_J\mathbf{x}_J^T\left[\sum_{j=1}^{J-1} \mathbf{x}_j\mathbf{x}_j^T\right]^{-1}}{1+\alpha\left(x_J^T\left[\sum_{j=1}^{J-1} \mathbf{x}_j\mathbf{x}_j^T\right]^{-1}\mathbf{x}_J - 1\right)}\right] \tag{6.114}$$

Performing the multiplication according to (6.111) gives

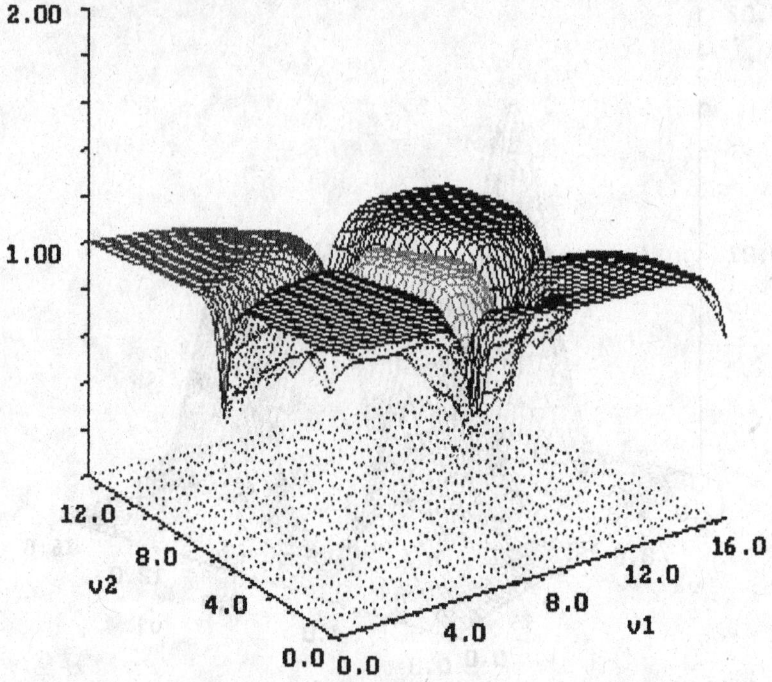

(b)

Figure 6.27. (*Continued*)

$$\mathbf{A}_J = \left[\left[\sum_{j=1}^{J-1} \mathbf{x}_j \mathbf{x}_j^T \right]^{-1} - \alpha \frac{\left[\sum_{j=1}^{J-1} \mathbf{x}_j \mathbf{x}_j^T \right]^{-1} \mathbf{x}_J \mathbf{x}_J^T \left[\sum_{j=1}^{J-1} \mathbf{x}_j \mathbf{x}_j^T \right]^{-1}}{1 + \alpha \left(\mathbf{x}_J^T \left[\sum_{j=1}^{J-1} \mathbf{x}_j \mathbf{x}_j^T \right]^{-1} \mathbf{x}_J - 1 \right)} \right]$$

$$\times \left[\sum_{j=1}^{J-1} \mathbf{x}_j \mathbf{y}_j^T + \frac{\alpha}{1-\alpha} \mathbf{x}_J \mathbf{y}_J^T \right]$$

$$= \left[\sum_{j=1}^{J-1} \mathbf{x}_j \mathbf{x}_j^T \right]^{-1} \sum_{j=1}^{J-1} \mathbf{x}_j \mathbf{y}_j^T - \alpha \frac{\left[\sum_{j=1}^{J-1} \mathbf{x}_j \mathbf{x}_j^T \right]^{-1} \mathbf{x}_J \mathbf{x}_J^T \left[\sum_{j=1}^{J-1} \mathbf{x}_j \mathbf{x}_j^T \right]^{-1} \sum_{j=1}^{J-1} \mathbf{x}_j \mathbf{y}_j^T}{1 + \alpha \left(\mathbf{x}_J^T \left[\sum_{j=1}^{J-1} \mathbf{x}_j \mathbf{x}_j^T \right]^{-1} \mathbf{x}_J - 1 \right)}$$

$$+ \frac{\alpha}{1-\alpha} \left[\sum_{j=1}^{J-1} \mathbf{x}_j \mathbf{x}_j^T \right]^{-1} \mathbf{x}_J \mathbf{y}_J^T - \frac{\alpha^2}{1-\alpha} \frac{\left[\sum_{j=1}^{J-1} \mathbf{x}_j \mathbf{x}_j^T \right]^{-1} \mathbf{x}_J \mathbf{x}_J^T \left[\sum_{j=1}^{J-1} \mathbf{x}_j \mathbf{x}_j^T \right]^{-1} \mathbf{x}_J \mathbf{y}_J^T}{1 + \alpha \left(\mathbf{x}_J^T \left[\sum_{j=1}^{J-1} \mathbf{x}_j \mathbf{x}_j^T \right]^{-1} \mathbf{x}_J - 1 \right)}$$

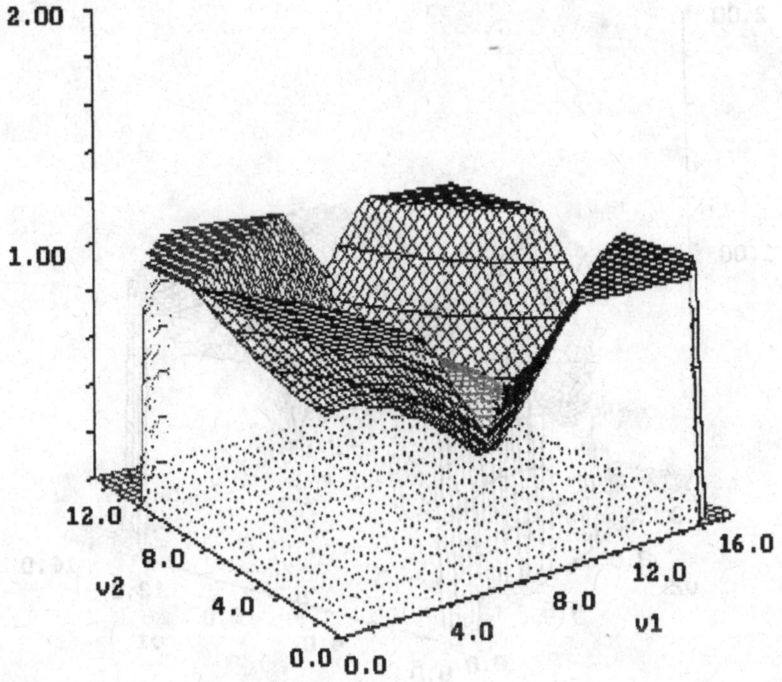

(c)

Figure 6.27. (*Continued*)

This expression can be simplified by inserting the coefficient matrix $\mathbf{A}_{J-1}$ as given above (6.112) at the appropriate positions and by introducing the equation

$$Q = \mathbf{x}_J^T \left[\sum_{j=1}^{J-1} \mathbf{x}_j \mathbf{x}_j^T \right]^{-1} \mathbf{x}_J \tag{6.115}$$

Making use of the fact that Q is a quadratic form and therefore a scalar expression, we get

$$\mathbf{A}_J = \mathbf{A}_{J-1} + \alpha \frac{-\left[\sum_{j=1}^{J-1} \mathbf{x}_j \mathbf{x}_j^T \right]^{-1} \mathbf{x}_J \mathbf{x}_J^T \mathbf{A}_{J-1}}{1 + \alpha(Q-1)}$$

$$+ \frac{\alpha}{1-\alpha} \frac{\left[1 + \alpha(Q-1) \left[\sum_{j=1}^{J-1} \mathbf{x}_j \mathbf{x}_j^T \right]^{-1} - \alpha Q \left[\sum_{j=1}^{J-1} \mathbf{x}_j \mathbf{x}_j^T \right]^{-1} \right] \mathbf{x}_J \mathbf{y}_J^T}{1 + \alpha(Q-1)}$$

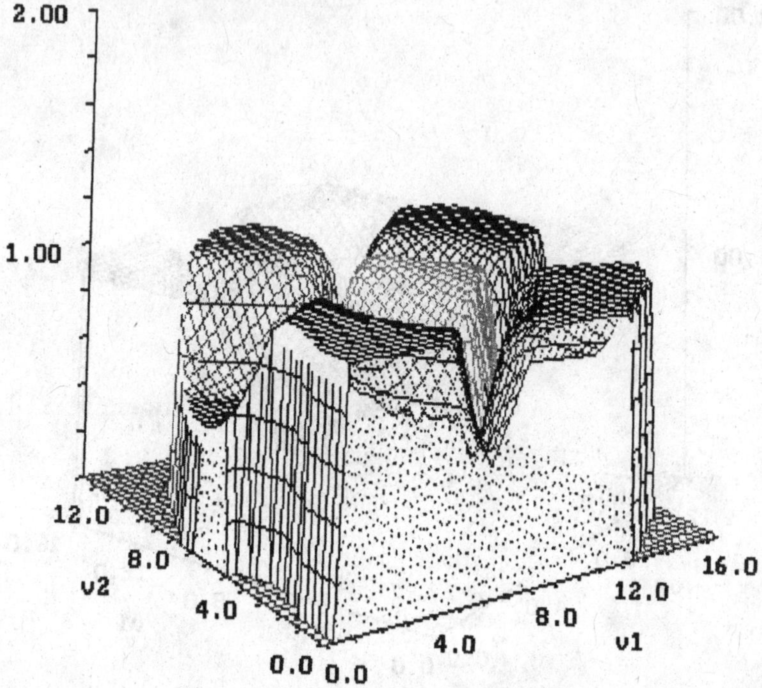

(d)

Figure 6.27. (*continued*)

which simplifies to

$$\mathbf{A}_J = \mathbf{A}_{J-1} + \alpha \frac{\left[\sum_{j=1}^{J-1} \mathbf{x}_j \mathbf{x}_j^T\right]^{-1} \mathbf{x}_J}{1 + \alpha(Q-1)} [\mathbf{y}_J^T - \mathbf{x}_J^T \mathbf{A}_{J-1}] \tag{6.116}$$

A final simplification is possible by going back to (6.114) and multiplying that expression from the right by $\mathbf{x}_J$:

$$\left[\sum_{j=1}^{J} \mathbf{x}_j \mathbf{x}_j^T\right]^{-1} \mathbf{x}_J = \frac{1}{1-\alpha} \left[\left[\sum_{j=1}^{J-1} \mathbf{x}_j \mathbf{x}_j^T\right]^{-1} \mathbf{x}_J - \alpha \frac{\left[\sum_{j=1}^{J-1} \mathbf{x}_j \mathbf{x}_j^T\right]^{-1} \mathbf{x}_J \mathbf{x}_J^T \left[\sum_{j=1}^{J-1} \mathbf{x}_j \mathbf{x}_j^T\right]^{-1} \mathbf{x}_J}{1 + \alpha\left(x_J^T \left[\sum_{j=1}^{J-1} \mathbf{x}_j \mathbf{x}_j^T\right]^{-1} \mathbf{x}_J - 1\right)} \right]$$

$$\left[\sum_{j=1}^{J} \mathbf{x}_j \mathbf{x}_j^T\right]^{-1} \mathbf{x}_J = \frac{\left[\sum_{j=1}^{J-1} \mathbf{x}_j \mathbf{x}_j^T\right]^{-1} \mathbf{x}_J}{1 + \alpha(Q-1)} \tag{6.117}$$

Recursive Learning Rule for Polynomial Classifier

We now need only put things together. Substituting (6.117) in (6.116) we gain the comparably simple updating rule for recursive learning in the context of least mean-square polynomial classification:

$$\mathbf{A}_J = \mathbf{A}_{J-1} - \alpha \left[\sum_{j=1}^{J} \mathbf{x}_j \mathbf{x}_j^T \right]^{-1} \mathbf{x}_J [\mathbf{A}_{J-1}^T \mathbf{x}_J - \mathbf{y}_J]^T \tag{6.118}$$

This recursive learning rule requires the following sequence of steps:

- A preliminary value for the coefficient matrix **A** is already given or suitably chosen when initializing the procedure.
- The present sample [**v**, **y**] is observed and mapped according to the given polynomial structure **x**(**v**) into the pair of variables [**x**, **y**].
- Compute the estimation **d** based on the given observation **x** and the present coefficient matrix **A**:

$$\mathbf{d} = \mathbf{A}^T \mathbf{x}$$

- Compute the difference $\Delta\mathbf{d}$ between estimation **d** and target **y**:

$$\Delta\mathbf{d} = \mathbf{d} - \mathbf{y}$$

- Compute the outer vector product $\mathbf{x}\,\Delta\mathbf{d}^T$ and modify it by multiplication with the inverse weight matrix **G**, $\mathbf{G}^{-1}\mathbf{x}\,\Delta\mathbf{d}^T$.
- Update **A** according to (6.118):

$$\mathbf{A} \Leftarrow \mathbf{A} - \alpha\,\mathbf{G}^{-1}\mathbf{x}\,\Delta\mathbf{d}^T \tag{6.119}$$

In Equation (6.118) the weight matrix **G** is the moment matrix $E\{\mathbf{x}\mathbf{x}^T\}$ valid for the sequence of J samples used so far for updating the coefficient matrix **A**. If strictly followed, (6.118) would require us to run an additional recursion for the inverse of this moment matrix **G** according to (6.114),

$$\mathbf{G}_J = \frac{1}{1-\alpha} \left[\mathbf{G}_{J-1} - \alpha \frac{\mathbf{G}_{J-1}\mathbf{x}_J\mathbf{x}_J^T\mathbf{G}_{J-1}}{1 + \alpha(\mathbf{x}_J^T\mathbf{G}_{J-1}\mathbf{x}_J - 1)} \right] \tag{6.120}$$

The learning rule of (6.119) has the properties of an error correction rule. No correction at all occurs when the current estimation **d**, computed from the given input vector **x** and the last valid coefficient matrix **A**, hits the target vector **y** precisely with $\Delta\mathbf{d} = \mathbf{0}$.

Modifications by Use of Simplified Weight Matrices G

It is possible to replace **G** by even drastic simplifications without sacrifying the convergence properties of the recursive learning rule. In the extreme case **G** is replaced by the identity matrix **I**, resulting in the ultimately simplified learning rule

$$\mathbf{A} \Leftarrow \mathbf{A} - \alpha \mathbf{x}\, \Delta \mathbf{d}^T \tag{6.121}$$

This is a remarkable reduction in mathematical complexity that is, however, exchanged for an increased sensitivity to the size of the updating steps, which, as was the case with (6.119), now only roughly and no longer precisely go in the correct direction. We will soon return to this topic.

Because of these properties, the classifier learning rule of (6.121) was called the Quick & Dirty rule elsewhere [AGA1966]. The imperfections in computing the direction of the updating steps must be compensated by a smaller step width (smaller values of the *learning factor* α), resulting in a slower convergence as measured in the number of those updating steps.

A useful compromise is to apply not the complete moment matrix **G** but rather the diagonal matrix **D** gained from **G** by setting all of the nondiagonal elements to zero:

$$\mathbf{D} = \begin{pmatrix} E\{x_1x_1\} & 0 & \cdots & 0 \\ 0 & E\{x_2x_2\} & \cdots & 0 \\ \vdots & \vdots & \ddots & \vdots \\ 0 & 0 & \cdots & E\{x_Lx_L\} \end{pmatrix} \tag{6.122}$$

This weight matrix is easily invertible,

$$\mathbf{D} = \begin{bmatrix} \dfrac{1}{E\{x_1x_1\}} & 0 & \cdots & 0 \\ 0 & \dfrac{1}{E\{x_2x_2\}} & \cdots & 0 \\ \vdots & \vdots & \ddots & \vdots \\ 0 & 0 & \cdots & \dfrac{1}{E\{x_Lx_L\}} \end{bmatrix} \tag{6.123}$$

and can, with little additional effort, be used in (6.119).

If a reasonable estimate for **D** is available, this can be used in the procedure from the beginning and without any change. It is, however, rather simple to establish an accompanying recursion for $\mathbf{D}^{-1}$.

The recursion (4.96) for the lth diagonal element m_l of **D**,

$$m_l \Leftarrow (1-\beta)m_l + \beta x_l^2$$

can easily be transformed into a recursion for the inverse diagonal element $q_l = 1/m_l$ of the same matrix:

$$q_l \Leftarrow q_l \frac{1}{1+\beta(qx_l^2 - 1)} \tag{6.124}$$

The learning factor here is denoted by β in order to distinguish it from the learning factor α of the main recursion (6.119).

It should be noted that the use of **D** for the weight matrix **G** in (6.119) corresponds to a componentwise normalization of the polynomial terms [SCH1977]:

$$x_l \Leftarrow \frac{x_l}{\sqrt{E\{x_l^2\}}} \qquad \forall l = 1, \ldots, L \tag{6.125}$$

Why Changes in Weight Matrix G Do Not Disturb Convergence

The fact that the recursive learning rule of (6.119) is almost unaffected by alterations applied to the weight matrix **G** shall be illustrated by looking into the details of one single updating step.

We consider the situation that $\mathbf{A}_{J-1}$ is the present state of the coefficient matrix **A**. The just-arriving sample is $[\mathbf{x}_J, \mathbf{y}_J]$. The estimation error prior to adjusting the coefficient matrix is

$$\Delta\mathbf{d}_J = \mathbf{A}_{J-1}^T\mathbf{x}_J - \mathbf{y}_J \tag{6.126}$$

and the error after having carried out the adjustments on **A** but measured with the same pair of values $[\mathbf{x}_J, \mathbf{y}_J]$ is

$$\Delta\mathbf{d}_J^* = \mathbf{A}_J^T\mathbf{x}_J - \mathbf{y}_J \tag{6.127}$$

This expression can be simplified, making use of the fact that **G** is symmetric and that the quadratic form $\mathbf{x}\mathbf{G}^{-1}\mathbf{x}$ is a scalar to

$$\begin{aligned}\Delta\mathbf{d}_J^* &= (\mathbf{A}_{J-1} - \alpha\mathbf{G}^{-1}\mathbf{x}_J\,\Delta\mathbf{d}_J^T)^T\mathbf{x}_J - \mathbf{y}_J \\ &= \mathbf{A}_{J-1}^T\mathbf{x}_J - \mathbf{y}_J - \alpha\mathbf{x}_J^T\mathbf{G}^{-1}\mathbf{x}_J\,\Delta\mathbf{d}_J \\ &= (1 - \alpha\,\mathbf{x}_J^T\mathbf{G}^{-1}\mathbf{x}_J)\,\Delta\mathbf{d}_J\end{aligned} \tag{6.128}$$

This is a remarkable finding since it states that error vectors $\Delta\mathbf{d}$ before and $\Delta\mathbf{d}^*$ after the correction are collinear and simply differ by a scalar factor

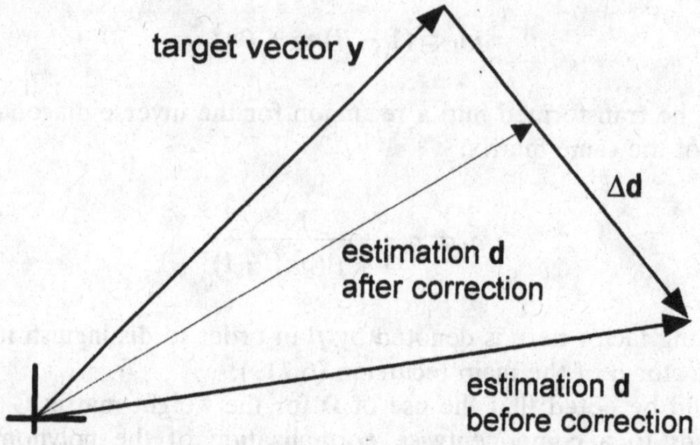

Figure 6.28. Effect of single learning step according to (6.119) on estimation error $\Delta\mathbf{d}$ before and $\Delta\mathbf{d}^*$ after correction. With $\alpha = \alpha_{\text{limit}}$ correction for last recently observed pattern [**x**, **y**] is such that estimation $\mathbf{d}(\mathbf{x})$ for resubstituted **x** precisely hits target vector **y**.

$(1 - \alpha\mathbf{x}\mathbf{G}^{-1}\mathbf{x})$, which can easily be made zero by suitable choice of the learning factor α; see Fig. 6.28.

These relations between $\Delta\mathbf{d}$ and $\Delta\mathbf{d}^*$ are valid irrespective of the weight matrix **G** used, even if it is substituted by the identity matrix **I**.

Stability Limits for Learning Factor α

In (6.128) we find that, depending on the value of the learning factor α, the individual learning step may have one of the following results:

(a) The remaining error $\Delta\mathbf{d}^*$ is decreased to a certain degree but with the property that a further increase of α leads to a further decrease in $\Delta\mathbf{d}^*$.

(b) The remaining error $\Delta\mathbf{d}^*$ is decreased to zero (full hit).

(c) The remaining error $\Delta\mathbf{d}^*$ may have been decreased or even increased but with the property that any further increase of α leads to an increase in $\Delta\mathbf{d}^*$ (overshooting the goal).

These findings determine a limit for the learning factor

$$\alpha_{\text{limit}} = \frac{1}{\mathbf{x}_J^T\mathbf{G}^{-1}\mathbf{x}_J} \tag{6.129}$$

since α_{limit} marks the strongest sensible learning mode. With $\alpha > \alpha_{\text{limit}}$ the correction overshoots the goal.

The above simplifications of **G** transfer this limit into

$$\alpha_{\text{limit}} = \begin{cases} \dfrac{1}{|\mathbf{x}_J|^2} & \text{for } \mathbf{G} = \mathbf{I} \qquad (6.130) \\[2ex] \dfrac{1}{\sum_{l=1}^{L} \dfrac{x_{l,J}^2}{E\{x_l^2\}}} & \text{for } \mathbf{G} = \mathbf{D}, \text{ according to (6.122)} \qquad (6.131) \end{cases}$$

These limits depend on the current situation and vary with the sequence of observations $\{\mathbf{x}\}$. For practical purposes we need an orientation about which range of values for the learning factor α to choose for the learning procedure. Such an estimation is gained by replacing the individual values for the Jth sample $\mathbf{x}_J$ in the above equations (6.129)–(6.131) by their respective means.

The denominator of (6.129) has the mean value of

$$E\{\mathbf{x}^T\mathbf{G}^{-1}\mathbf{x}\} = \text{trace}[\mathbf{G}^{-1}E\{\mathbf{x}\mathbf{x}^T\}] \qquad (6.132)$$

which, for the general case of $\mathbf{G}$ being the moment matrix $E\{\mathbf{x}\mathbf{x}^T\}$, simplifies to

$$E\{\mathbf{x}^T\mathbf{G}^{-1}\mathbf{x}\} = \text{trace}[E\{\mathbf{x}\mathbf{x}^T\}^{-1}E\{\mathbf{x}\mathbf{x}^T\}] = \dim[\mathbf{x}] = L \qquad (6.133)$$

and results in the practical limit for the learning factor α of

$$\alpha_{\text{limit}} = \frac{1}{L} \qquad (6.134)$$

Computing the mean of the denominator of (6.131) we arrive at exactly the same result since

$$E\left\{\sum_{l=1}^{L} \frac{x_l^2}{E\{x_l^2\}}\right\} = \sum_{l=1}^{L} \frac{E\{x_l^2\}}{E\{x_l^2\}} = \dim[\mathbf{x}] = L \qquad (6.135)$$

whereas computing the mean of the denominator of (6.130) gives

$$E\{|\mathbf{x}|^2\} = \text{trace}[E\{\mathbf{x}\mathbf{x}^T\}] \qquad (6.136)$$

Thus we find the practical limits for the learning factor α given by $1/L$ for the cases of $\mathbf{G} = E\{\mathbf{x}\mathbf{x}^T\}$ and $\mathbf{G} = \mathbf{D}$ and by $1/E\{|\mathbf{x}^2|\}$ for the Quick & Dirty case of $\mathbf{G} = \mathbf{I}$.

In practical application α must be chosen distinctly smaller in order not to strongly focus learning on just the last recently seen example.

Role of Last Seen Sample in Recursive Learning

Remember that the whole procedure of recursive learning was derived from the goal of minimizing, in the least mean-square sense and for the given pattern source, the deviation between the target vector **y** and the discriminant function **d**(**v**), as produced by the pattern classifier. [See Section 6.1 and especially (6.11).] Thus the result is principally optimum with respect to the entire set of learning samples.

All that was done here in Section 6.14 was to reformulate the mathematical procedure for computing the optimum coefficient matrix **A** from the *batch learning version* into a recursive one. In this way, the recursive learning rule (6.119) was derived directly from the solution (6.20) found for batch learning:

- If properly initialized and run with the long-term averaging choice of $\alpha = 1/J$ *recursive* learning converges to the same solution as *batch* learning (6.20).

The recursive solution, however, must in general differ from the solution gained from batch learning if what is mostly done in practice a constant learning factor α is applied. We know from Section 4.7 that recursive learning with a constant learning factor α provides short-term averaging and has the property of forgetting far past experience.

In practical application often a compromise is made toward long-term averaging by reducing the learning factor α in steps from a higher value at the beginning to a smaller but also constant value with the progress of the procedure. This technique combines a quick start with fast but rough learning in the beginning with more accurate learning in the steady state.

Thus, depending on the specific choice of the learning factor α, a more or less wide history of all the learning samples seen determines the optimization problem of finding the optimum coefficient matrix **A**. In view of this fact it is most remarkable that this optimum is found by a sequence of optimizing steps, each considering only the last recently seen sample [see (6.119)].

Visualizations Based on Example of Section 4

The technique of recursive learning shall be exemplified by Figs. 6.29 and 6.30, taken again from the two-dimensional three-class example of (4.35). The learning procedure is used with the weight matrix $\mathbf{G} = \mathbf{D}$ according to (6.122), which itself is learned recursively by an accompanying recursion with $\beta = 6\alpha$. Both recursions are initialized with zeros. These diagrams show the development of the optimization criteria residual variance S^2 and forced recognition error rate ϵ with the progress of the learning procedure.

In order to observe the transient behavior immediately after starting the recursion, a short-time observation window of 200 samples was introduced for measuring the residual variance and counting the errors. The limited size

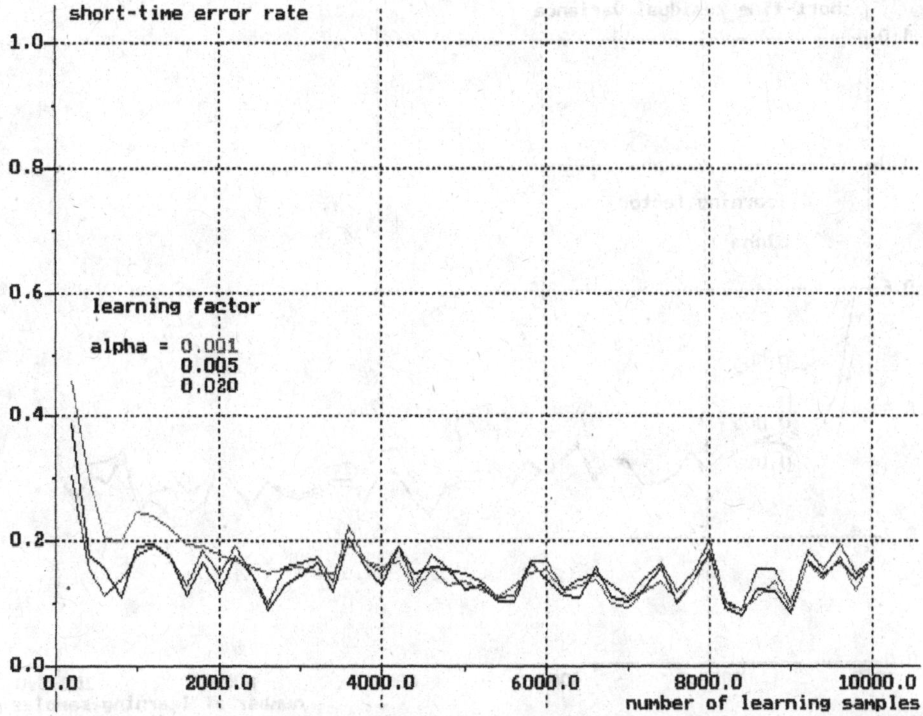

Figure 6.29. Recursive classifier adaptation of quadratic polynomial classifier according to (6.119) with weight matrix **G** = **D**. Abscissa shows number of learning samples presented to learning rule and vertical axis shows short-time error rate ϵ observed during learning procedure, blockwise measured for every 200 consecutive samples. Parameter is learning factor α = [0.02, 0.005, 0.001].

of this observation window limits the accuracy with which these statistical parameters can be estimated and results in random variations due to the randomness of the input patterns presented to the learning procedure.

It is interesting to know how the pattern classifier gained from the direct solution of the matrix equation (6.20) behaves if confronted with the same sequence of learning patterns and measured in the same way. Figures 6.31 and 6.32 show the learning transition curves for $\alpha = 0.001$ taken from Figs. 6.29 and 6.30 together with the reference curves for the fixed classifier gained from the direct solution.

After a sufficiently long period of training with a sufficiently small learning factor α the differences between the recursive and the direct solutions vanish.

Comments

It is most important to know that recursive learning under the optimization criterion of (3.1) renders approximations to the vector **p** of a posteriori

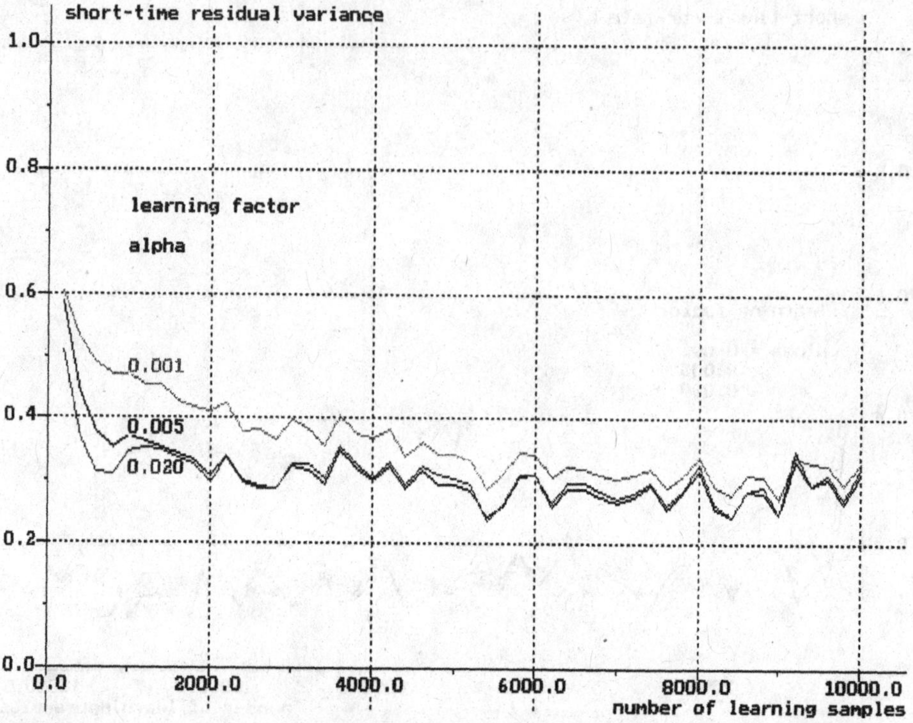

Figure 6.30. Recursive classifier adaptation of quadratic polynomial classifier according to (6.119) with weight matrix **G** = **D**. Abscissa shows number of learning samples presented to learning rule and vertical axis shows short-time residual variance S^2 observed during learning procedure, blockwise measured for every 200 consecutive samples. Parameter is learning factor $\alpha = [0.02, 0.005, 0.001]$.

probabilities prob($k|\mathbf{v}$). These themselves strongly depend on the a priori probabilities $P_k = \text{prob}(k)$; compare (4.32).

In other words:

- Learning a posteriori probabilities from the learning sample set implies learning the a priori probabilities.

In order not to come to misled results the frequencies of the different classes in the learning set must truly reflect the intentions the classifier designer has about the a priori probabilities in the pattern classification task to be solved.

Unintentional changes in the frequencies of the different classes within the learning set influence the resulting estimation function up to the effect that classes no longer occurring within the sequence of learning samples are completely forgotten. If some kind of short-term learning is applied, the frequencies of the different classes within the learning time window must correspond to the intended values.

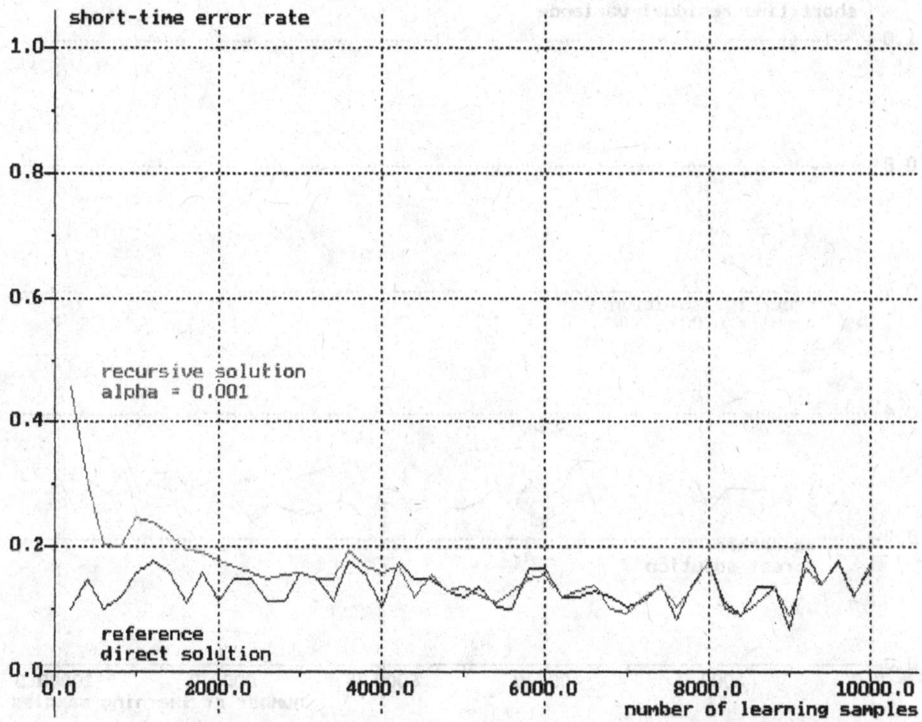

Figure 6.31. Comparison of recursive learning according to (6.119) with batch learning by directly solving matrix equation (6.20), demonstrated for short-time error rate ϵ. Fluctuations in reference curve are due to varying statistical properties of small test sets (with size 200), consecutively taken from pattern source. It can clearly be seen how recursively trained classifier approaches reference with increasing number of learned samples.

For a typical learning situation where a sufficient number of samples for each of the classes is available, these requirements are easily fulfilled by selecting learning samples randomly from the different classes, but with the required probabilities prob(k).

If, however, the learning sample is directly drawn from some practical application, the class membership k of the incoming patterns $[\mathbf{v}, k]$ must be taken as it is and can by no means be influenced. Overlearning and unlearning of classes can also be avoided in such a situation if the learning factor α is made class dependent. When the classes should be treated as equiprobable, the class-dependent learning factor α_k must be chosen inverse proportional to the frequency of observation of the respective class within the learning time window.

In Section 6.9, in the context of the direct solution (6.20), we have dealt with the problem of linear dependencies among the polynomial terms. In order to find a unique optimum, such linear dependencies had to be detected

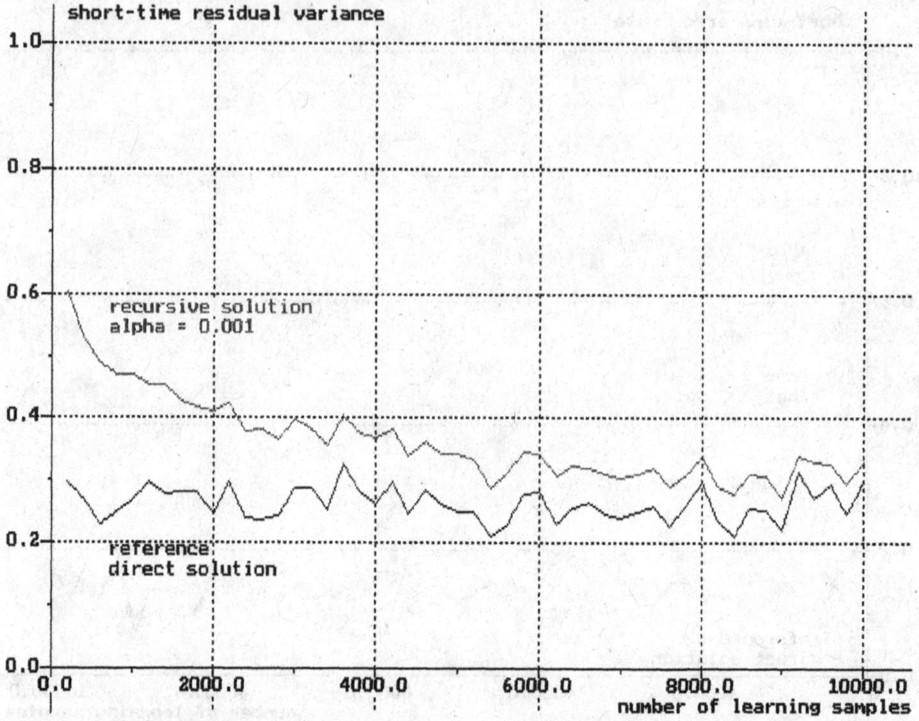

Figure 6.32. Comparison of recursive learning according to (6.119) with batch learning by directly solving matrix equation (6.20), demonstrated for short-time residual variance S^2. Fluctuations in reference curve are due to varying statistical properties of small test sets (with size 200), consecutively taken from pattern source. Compared with Fig. 6.31 it can be seen that residual variance converges somewhat slower than error rate ϵ.

prior to or at least during the computational procedure. The same question of linear dependencies does not arise at all in the context of recursive learning. Whenever such linear dependencies exist, they need not and cannot be detected. Linear dependencies generate solution manifolds. Recursive learning selects a certain solution among the potential solutions depending on the initialization and the choice of the learning parameters.

Compared with the procedures of Section 6.8, another important difference is that here no opportunity exists for feature ranking besides that of evaluating the coefficient weights after adaptation.

The mathematical structure of the recursive learning rule of (6.119) is comparably simple. The standard operation of the pattern classifier—computing the discriminant vector $\mathbf{d}(\mathbf{v})$—is already part of the operations necessary for recursive learning. Thus implementation of recursive learning is a straightforward augmentation of the standard procedure.

6.15 CLASSIFER ITERATION

We have based the whole solution of the pattern classification problem on the conception of least mean-square optimization (3.1),

$$S^2 = E\{|\mathbf{d}(\mathbf{v}) - \mathbf{y}|^2\} = \min_{\mathbf{d}(\mathbf{v})}$$

with the consequence that given the type of the discriminant function $\mathbf{d}(\mathbf{v})$ and given the pattern source with its stochastic properties, or equivalently the learning set, the whole story is mathematically settled. The rest is number crunching and must lead to a unique result in terms of the optimization criterion. If a manifold of solutions exist, then, with identical mean-square error.

Thus, the solution is completely but implicitly determined by two ingredients: type of the discriminant function and properties of the pattern source. These two determine also the final success when we take the optimization criterion for granted.

If, however, also the choice of optimization criterion is considered to be a free design parameter, we have the three ingredients determining the performance of the resulting classifier:

- Type of discriminant function
- Optimization criterion
- Properties of pattern source

These considerations show where to position the lever in order to change and ultimately improve the overall system performance.

The most obvious possibility is to vary the type of discriminant function, try higher order polynomials, and increase the polynomial length, try other types of basis functions; typically, the larger the mathematical effort, the better the performance.

Competing approaches are to modify the optimization criterion or to manipulate the properties of the given pattern source. A modified optimization criterion could take special care of those patterns that turn out to be difficult to recognize, thus forcing the pattern classifier to improvements with regard to these problem patterns. The same effect can be accomplished by manipulations applied to the pattern source, especially by intentionally changing the proportion in the learning set of problem patterns and of those easy to recognize. Thus special emphasis can be put on patterns difficult to recognize.

These last two possibilities are in a sense complementary and either one can be applied to achieve the same kind of effect. The approach of manipulating the composition of the learning set, however, offers the opportunity to come to improvements in classifier performance over the straightforward least mean-square approach without sacrificing its computational advantages.

One especially effective technique of achieving improvements in classifier performance from modifications in the learning set composition is *classifier iteration*. The idea is to let the classifier itself decide which of the patterns in its learning set are those difficult to recognize [SCH1972] and to derive a subset of problem patterns from the given learning set using the given preliminary classifier.

The basic loop of the procedure is illustrated by Fig. 6.33. It is entered with the presently available classifier **A** together with the moment matrix **M**

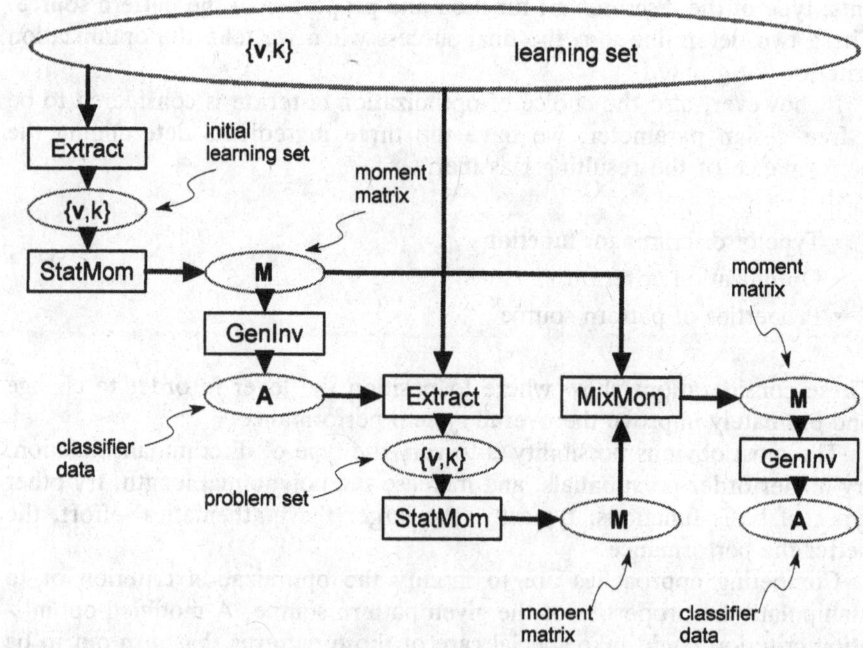

Figure 6.33. Schematic flow diagram of one basic step of classifier iteration loop. From given learning set a usually, but not necessarily, comparably small subset is separated (initial learning set). From this initial matrix **M** of statistical moments is computed as well as initial classifier **A**, applying generalized matrix inversion procedure of Section 6.8. This preliminary classifier is then used to extract from learning set first problem set for which matrix $\mathbf{M}_{\text{problem}}$ of statistical moments is computed. Both moment matrix **M** of preliminary classifier and moment matrix $\mathbf{M}_{\text{problem}}$ of problem set are mixed with appropriate weight α, resulting in moment matrix **M** of modified learning set, which is now enriched with problem samples. From this, again by generalized matrix inversion procedure, an improved classifier **A** is achieved.

from which it was computed. The fundamental four operations of one step are as follows:

- Separate the current problem set from the given learning set.
- Compute the moment matrix $\mathbf{M}_{\text{problem}}$ belonging to the current problem set.
- Update the given moment matrix **M** with that of the current problem set:

$$\mathbf{M} \Leftarrow (1 - \alpha)\mathbf{M} + \alpha \mathbf{M}_{\text{problem}} \tag{6.137}$$

- Compute the classifier from the updated moment matrix.

Mixing weights α on the order of, as a rule, some 10% in only a few classifier iteration steps, remarkable improvements can generally be achieved.

The whole procedure establishes a *recursive classifier learning* rule quite similar to those recursive learning rules discussed in the foregoing section. The difference lies in the fact that here the procedure proceeds in larger steps, not on the level of single samples but rather on the level of whole sets of learning samples, and that the corrections are applied not directly to the classifier coefficient matrix **A** but to the moment matrices **M**, which determine the classifier coefficient matrix **A**.

The procedure can equally well be applied to pattern classification tasks with *closed* and *open learning sets*. The notion of a closed learning set characterizes the situation where a fixed-size (closed) learning set is given and the sequence of problem sets is derived with the different classifiers evolving during the procedure from the identical learning set. This contrasts to the situation with an open (ever-increasing) learning set continuously taken from a running application. In such a case the sequence of evolving classifiers may even keep pace with slowly changing properties of the pattern source.

It should be mentioned that the residual variance S^2 of the least mean-square procedure (measured during classifier adaptation) must increase for the classifier computed from the modified moment matrix representing the learning set intentionally enriched with problem patterns. At first glance somewhat irritating, we also observe an increase in residual variance S^2 if the improved classifier is checked with the original learning set.

The reason is that the initial classifier with which the whole procedure of classifier iteration was started was just the minimum residual variance classifier. Any modified (improved) classifier is necessarily different and must generate an increased residual variance S^2. The improvements will show up, however, in the error rate ϵ.

These effects show that modifying the composition of the learning set is equivalent to leaving the least mean-square optimization criterion. What we have introduced here as classifier adaptation based on a learning set enriched with problem patterns can as well be viewed as classifier adaptation with an unchanged learning set but based on a different optimization criterion.

The effect of the procedure is mainly that those samples contribute to the learning process coming from close-to-the-border regions in measurement space. These are those for which ambiguous discriminant vectors **d** are generated having more than one dominant component, regardless of whether they are correctly recognized.

It remains a design decision if those samples recognized incorrectly but with reliably looking values d_j, $j \neq k$, close to 1 shall be included in the problem set. Excluding them lets the behavior of the learning procedure become quite similar to that of backpropagation learning; see Section 7.9.

It is worth mentioning that the modifications to the learning rule and optimization criterion discussed here can as well be applied to the recursive learning techniques of Section 6.14, simply by excluding samples with sufficiently unambiguous discriminant vectors **d** from the updating rule (6.119).

Comments

The considerations of this section stress the dominant importance of the learning set and emphasize the role of the human teacher being responsible for the learning set composition. Any variation in the learning set may have an impact on the resulting classifier performance. The classifier simply learns what it is trained for.

This is also true with respect to the representation of the different classes in the learning set. Often the potentially nonuniform distribution of classes in a raw learning set is equalized in order not to underrepresent rare events. A more general way is treating the different classes separately and calculating and saving class-specific moment matrices that are then linearly combined with appropriate weights to form the moment matrix **M** from which to compute the classifier matrix **A**; see Section 4.6, the discussion of parameter estimation from subsets.

7

MULTILAYER PERCEPTRON REGRESSION

The idea of learning from nature has brought about a different approach for constructing functional approximations $\mathbf{d}(\mathbf{v})$ to given sets $\{\mathbf{v}, \mathbf{y}\}$ of observations centered around the concept of the artificial neuron and, mostly larger, networks of artificial neurons.

During the last decade activities in the area of neural networks rapidly increased due to a number of different motivations. The most basic impulse came from the fact that pattern classification is an ability common to animals and humans and is localized in the brain with the neuron cell as the fundamental building block. Other forces driving the evolution of this technology have been the concept of analog information processing and, closely related to it, the principle of parallel information processing.

The first artificial neurons were designed at a time when the analog computer ruled the scene and systems of linear and differential equations and other complicated mathematical tasks were solved using networks of resistors, capacitors, and operational amplifiers. As soon as the mathematical laws behind two certain different physical effects were identified as being homomorphic, one of them could be used as a model for the other. Analog circuits can be composed of large numbers of rather inexpensive parts and all of them are perfectly working in parallel. Problems are that it is necessary to provide all of the connections in parallel, that the whole arrangement becomes thus extremely task specific, and that the numerical precision of analog computation is distinctly limited and sensitive to extraneous interferences.

With the advent of the digital (von Neumann) computer, the analog computer and thinking in continuous functions were for short interval of time superceded by logic and logical inference. Digital computing was freed from the imprecisions of analog computing and provided almost unbounded flexibility by programming. The digital computer turned out to be the genuine universal machine. Everything computable was also computable by the digital computing machine. Simultaneously, the techniques of communication developed. Addressable and switchable data connections between the components of the computer system evolved, enabling temporary connections on demand when they were needed and leaving the way free for other connections the rest of the time. These advantages were sold with the drawback that most computer components were idle most of the time.

In the field of pattern recognition, driven by the potency of logic and logical inference, the whole branch of knowledge-based reasoning grew at this time: the artificial intelligence approach.

As a countermovement, with the claim of overcoming some obvious limitations of the sequential von Neumann computer paradigm, the ideas of neural networks and parallel distributed processing, strengthened with the development of new technologies, especially in microelectronics, achieved a breakthrough when it became clear that gradient descent and the chain rule of calculus were capable of solving the problem of optimizing multilayered nonlinear networks ([WER1974], [RHW1986]).

The whole field acquired widespread attention and attracted numerous inspirations from different scientific fields such as biology, computer science, physics, and microelectronics. An enormous scientific activity was released, sometimes somewhat overemphasizing the differences to traditional scientific fields.

After this short excursion into the history of neural and conventional computing, we will concentrate in the present chapter on the multilayer perceptron. For pattern classification applications, especially from the viewpoint of establishing least mean-square estimates to the a posteriori probabilities (compare Chapter 5), this type of neural network design has proven to be the most representative of a whole variety of neural network designs.

In Chapter 8 we will look into another technique developed under the neural network brand: the radial basis function approach.

7.1 MODEL NEURON

The neuron cell is the fundamental building block of natural intelligent systems, but intelligent behavior emerges, in a manner that is admittedly not understood, only from gigantic arrangements of individual neurons. Present guesses estimate the number of neurons in the human brain as 10^{11} and the mean number of connections between one individual neuron and others as 10^4. It may ultimately well turn out that the single neuron represents not just a simple scalar product but a whole complex computing device.

Although in neurophysiology numerous different types of biological neu-

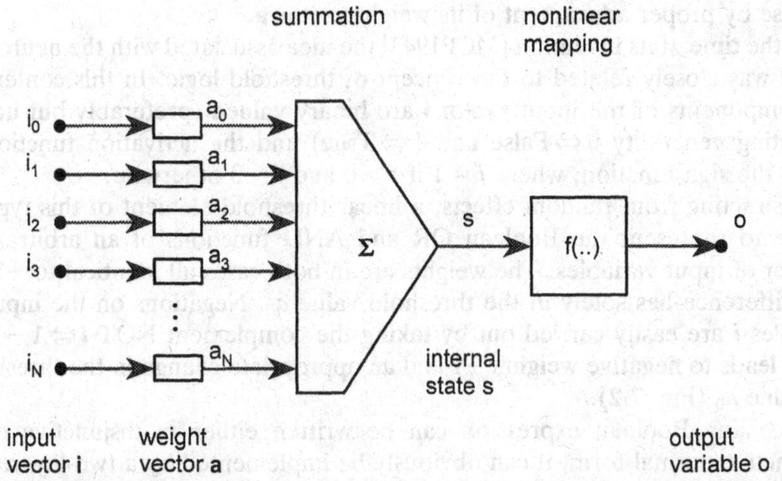

Figure 7.1. Model neuron. Vector **i** of input variables is entered into scalar product with vector **a** of weights and renders current value of internal state variable s, which is then mapped into output variable o by some in general nonlinear activation function $f(\cdot)$. For mathematical convenience vector **i** of input variables is augmented by additional term $i_0 = 1$ in its top position, which, together with corresponding component of weight vector **a**, provides threshold value for activation function.

rons are known, it became common use in the context of artificial neural networks to represent the neuron by the simplified model shown in Fig. 7.1.

The neuron consists of a large number of input nodes, representing the synaptic contacts between the considered neuron cell and the axons of those other neurons it is connected with, and one single output node representing the neuron's axon. The input nodes may be inhibitory or excitatory, corresponding to either negative or positive weights in the summation rendering the value of the internal state variable s. The nonlinear activation function $f(\cdot)$ represents the property of biological neurons to require a minimum activation before firing and to reach a certain level of saturation with increasing activation s.

The artificial neuron is completely described by its vector **a** of weights and the activation function $f(\cdot)$. In mathematical terms the neuron's operation is simply the scalar product of **i** and **a** nonlinearly mapped by $f(\cdot)$

$$o = f(\mathbf{a}^T\mathbf{i}) \tag{7.1}$$

Depending on the neural network design the activation function $f(\cdot)$ is in general predefined whereas the collection of weights contained in **a** remain free parameters of the construction. Hence the artificial neuron is a flexible structure that, within certain limitations, can be adapted to serve a certain purpose by proper adjustment of its weight vector **a**.

At the time of its invention [MCP1943] the idea associated with the neuron model was closely related to the concept of threshold logic. In this context the components of the input vector **i** are binary valued (preferably but not restricting generality 0 ⇔ False and 1 ⇔ True) and the activation function $f(s)$ is the sign function, where $f = 1$ if $s > 0$ and $f = 0$ otherwise.

Abstracting from random effects, a linear threshold element of this type is able to represent the Boolean OR and AND functions of an arbitrary number of input variables. The weights are in both cases all identical to +1. The difference lies solely in the threshold value a_0. Negations on the input variables i are easily carried out by taking the complement NOT $i \Leftrightarrow 1 - i$, which leads to negative weights −1 and an appropriate change in the threshold value a_0 (Fig. 7.2).

Since any Boolean expression can be written either in disjunctive or conjunctive normal form, it can obviously be implemented by a two-layered arrangement of linear threshold elements or artificial neurons of this type.

It should be mentioned that the original perceptron of Rosenblatt [ROS1957], which lend its name to a whole family of artificial neural network designs, was a linear threshold element implementing a logical predicate $o(\mathbf{i})$ that could be trained by adjusting its weight vector **a** to separate two given sets of Boolean vectors by rendering an output value 0 ⇔ False for all vectors $\{\mathbf{i}|0\}$ of the first set and 1 ⇔ True for all vectors $\{\mathbf{i}|1\}$ of the second. This

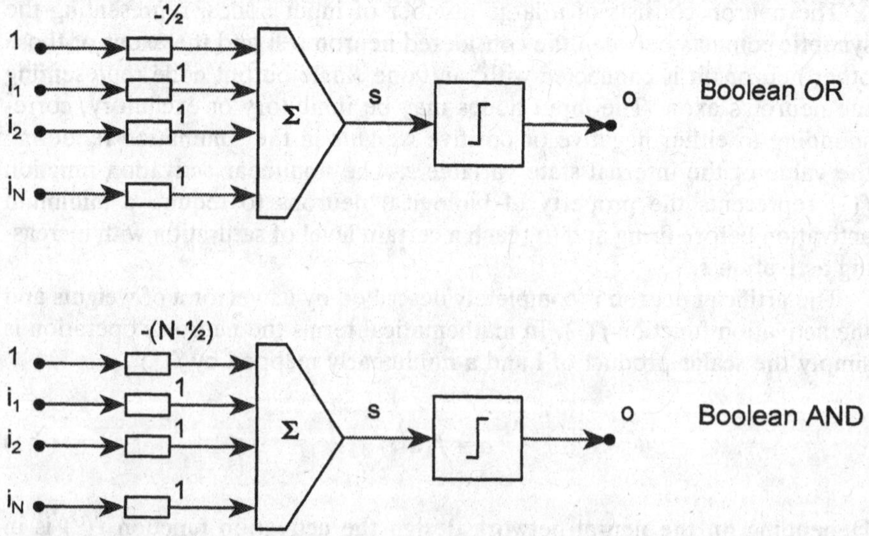

Figure 7.2. Linear threshold elements as artificial neurons implementing the Boolean OR and AND functions.

special kind of functional approximation task is equivalent to the solution of a linear system of inequalities. The perceptron learning rule

$$\mathbf{a} \Leftarrow \begin{cases} \mathbf{a} & \text{if correct} \\ \mathbf{a} + \alpha\mathbf{i} & \text{else} \quad \text{if} \quad \mathbf{i} \text{ comes from class 1} \\ \mathbf{a} - \alpha\mathbf{i} & \qquad\qquad\quad \mathbf{i} \text{ comes from class 0} \end{cases} \tag{7.2}$$

was shown to find the solution if one exists within a finite number of training steps [NOV1963].

7.2 SIGMOIDAL ACTIVATION FUNCTION

By far more important than the linear threshold element with its hard clipping activation function became the common artificial neuron with a smooth activation function. The most prominent of these functions is the so-called sigmoid function

$$\sigma(x) = \frac{1}{1 + \exp(-x)} \tag{7.3}$$

owing its name to its *s*-like shape (Fig. 7.3). The sigmoid function $\sigma(\cdot)$ is closely related to the $\tanh(\cdot)$ function

$$\tanh(x) = \frac{2}{1 + \exp(-2x)} - 1 = 2\sigma(2x) - 1 \tag{7.4}$$

The maximum slope of this function is $\frac{1}{4}$ at position $x = 0$. By adding two additional parameters ξ and ψ, a more general form of the sigmoid function is achieved:

$$\sigma_{\text{generalized}}(x) = \frac{1}{1 + \exp[-\psi(x - \xi)]} \tag{7.5}$$

with ψ controlling the slope steepness and ξ the position on the **x**-scale. In the context of artificial neurons with adjustable weight vector **a**, including the constant term, this kind of generalization is redundant since both ξ and ψ would be completely absorbed by the adjustable weights.

In another context we have already shown that the sigmoid function in its generalized form comes out to be the optimum discriminant function for two normally distributed classes on the x scale with different means but identical variances [see (6.109), Section 6.13].

In the context of its use in the neuron model, the sigmoid function has

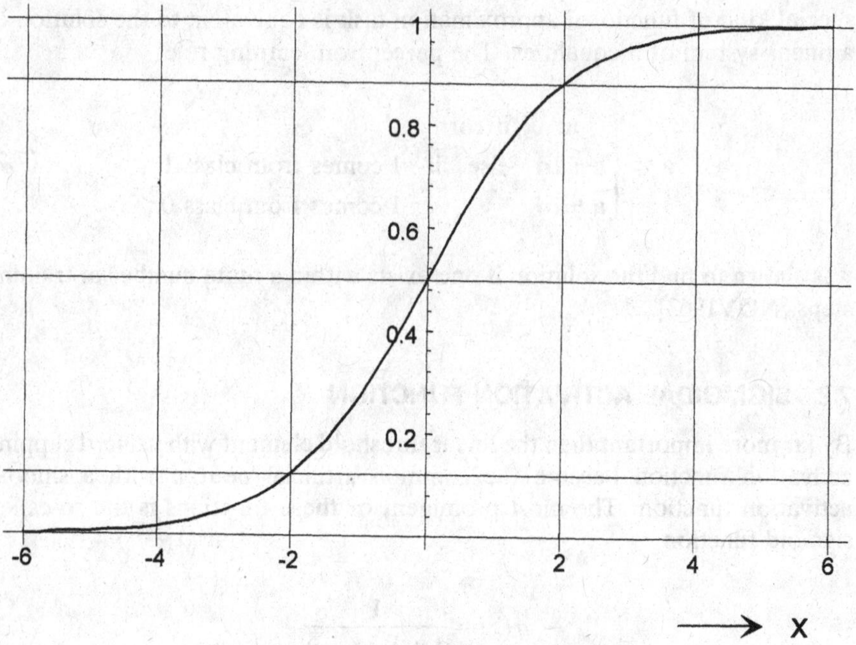

Figure 7.3. Standard sigmoid function $\sigma(\cdot)$.

In the context of its use in the neuron model, the sigmoid function has two important properties:

- Nonlinear
- Differentiable

We will see that the nonlinearity is crucial; without this property the multilayer feed-forward networks we will consider would collapse into single-layer networks. The fact that its derivative exists allows calculus to be applied to find the optimum constellation of weights.

The first derivative of (7.3) can be expressed by the sigmoid function $\sigma(\cdot)$ itself:

$$\begin{aligned}\frac{\partial \sigma}{\partial x} &= \frac{-1}{[1+\exp(-x)]^2}\exp(-x)(-1) \\ &= \frac{1}{1+\exp(-x)}\left[1-\frac{1}{1+\exp(-x)}\right] \\ &= \sigma(x)[1-\sigma(x)] \qquad (7.6)\end{aligned}$$

7.3 SINGLE LAYER OF MULTILAYER PERCEPTRON

The multilayer perceptron is an arrangement of several consecutive layers each consisting of a number of artificial neurons of the type given in Fig. 7.1 operating on the same input vector **i** and generating in parallel the same number of output variables, which are then combined into the output vector **o**.

The single layer of the multilayer perceptron shown in Fig. 7.4 is mathematically described by the coefficient matrix **A** containing all of the neuron weights and the vectorial sigmoid function $\boldsymbol{\sigma}(\cdot)$. We express the fact that before going into the matrix multiplication, the input vector **i** is augmented by a first component 1 by introducing the mapping $\mathbf{v} \rightarrow \tilde{\mathbf{v}}$:

$$\tilde{\mathbf{v}} = \begin{pmatrix} 1 \\ \mathbf{v} \end{pmatrix} \tag{7.7}$$

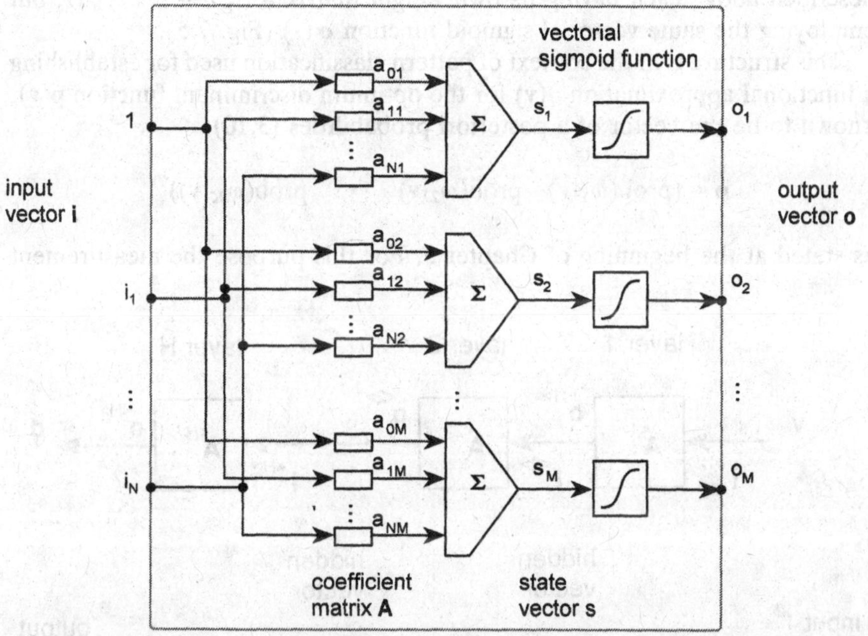

Figure 7.4. Single layer of the multilayer perceptron consisting of M artificial neurons and mapping N-dimensional input vector **i** into the **M**-dimensional output vector **o**. Set of $N \times M$ weights a_{nm} forms coefficient matrix **A** representing all adaptability of perceptron layer. The M individual sigmoid functions $\sigma(\cdot)$ corresponding to (7.3) can be combined into one vectorial sigmoid function $\boldsymbol{\sigma}(\cdot)$ applying $\sigma(\cdot)$ to all components of its vectorial argument in same manner.

Thus, there results an extremely compact notation for the operations of the single layer of neurons:

$$\mathbf{o} = \boldsymbol{\sigma}(\mathbf{A}^T\tilde{\mathbf{i}}) \tag{7.8}$$

In other words, the operations of the single layer of a multilayer perceptron neural network are a matrix multiplication followed by a vectorial nonlinear mapping identically applied to all of the components of the resulting vector.

The components of the output vector **o** depend in an obvious manner on the following:

- Weights, contained in matrix **A**
- Input variables, contained in input vector **i**

7.4 MULTILAYER PERCEPTRON

The multilayer perceptron consists of a number H of layers of the type described above each having its own weight matrix $\mathbf{A}^{\langle h \rangle}$, $h = 1, \ldots, H$, but employing the same vectorial sigmoid function $\boldsymbol{\sigma}(\cdot)$ (Fig. 7.5).

This structure is in the context of pattern classification used for establishing a functional approximation $\mathbf{d}(\mathbf{v})$ for the optimum discriminant function $\mathbf{p}(\mathbf{v})$, known to be the vector of a posteriori probabilities (3.10):

$$\mathbf{p} = (\text{prob}(\omega_1|\mathbf{v}) \quad \text{prob}(\omega_2|\mathbf{v}) \quad \cdots \quad \text{prob}(\omega_K|\mathbf{v}))^T$$

as stated at the beginning of Chapter 5. For this purpose the measurement

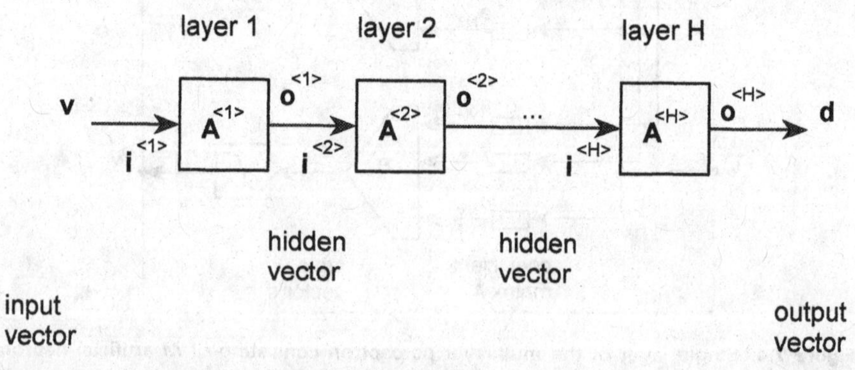

Figure 7.5. Block diagram of multilayer perceptron. Each single-layer module is organized as in Fig. 7.4 and contains matrix $\mathbf{A}^{\langle h \rangle}$ of weights. Its input vector $\mathbf{i}^{\langle h \rangle}$ is fed from its predecessor and its output vector $\mathbf{o}^{\langle h \rangle}$ becomes input of its successor. Whole structure is capable of representing a variety of different functions $\mathbf{d}(\mathbf{v})$ depending on choice of matrix coefficients $\mathbf{A}^{\langle h \rangle}$, $h = 1, \ldots, H$.

vector v of the pattern classification problem is fed into the first-layer input of the multilayer perceptron structure and a discriminant vector **d** is gained at the output of the final layer.

According to (7.8), the repetitive mapping through the H layers of the multilayer perceptron is in mathematical terms a nested application of vectorial sigmoid functions combined with linear matrix operations [POG1989]:

$$\mathbf{d}(\mathbf{v}) = \sigma(\mathbf{A}^{T\langle 3\rangle}\tilde{\sigma}(\mathbf{A}^{T\langle 2\rangle}\tilde{\sigma}(\mathbf{A}^{T\langle 1\rangle}\tilde{\mathbf{v}}))) \tag{7.9}$$

This is exemplified for the case of $H = 3$ in (7.9). The generalization to larger numbers of perceptron layers is straightforward. However, in order not to overload the presentation, this as well as the corresponding formulas that follow are given for a limited nesting depth.

The nested sigmoid function of (7.9) is a quite different type of functional approximation compared to the polynomial approximation (6.7) of Chapter 6 but is employed in exactly the same way. The adaptability of the construction—the capability for learning—lies in both cases in the weights contained in the coefficient matrix or matrices.

Learning is in both cases performed by weight adjustment controlled by the least mean square criterion, as defined by (3.1):

$$S^2 = E\{|\mathbf{d}(\mathbf{v}) - \mathbf{y}|^2\} = \min_{\mathbf{d}(\mathbf{v})}$$

We know from the considerations of Chapters 3 and 5 that this kind of approximation renders an estimate for the optimum discriminant function, the vector $\mathbf{p}(\mathbf{v})$ of a posteriori probabilities.

It should be noted that, except for a slight difference, the single-layer perceptron, $H = 1$, and the linear polynomial classifier, $G = 1$, are identical and merge into the same structure if the final sigmoidal mapping of the perceptron output variables is omitted:

- Whereas the sigmoidal mapping of the perceptron output may be omitted or not, the nonlinearities between the layers are crucial for the whole construction.

This is easily seen if the sigmoidal mappings $\sigma(\cdot)$ in (7.9) are replaced by the identity function. For that purpose, in the coefficient matrix $\mathbf{A}^{\langle h\rangle}$ of the hth layer let us separate the first row $\mathbf{a}_0^{T\langle h\rangle}$ containing the coefficients belonging to the constant term 1:

$$\mathbf{A}^{\langle h\rangle} = \begin{pmatrix} \mathbf{a}_0^{T\langle h\rangle} \\ \mathbf{A}^{*\langle h\rangle} \end{pmatrix} \tag{7.10}$$

Omitting all of the sigmoidal mappings lets the whole system of nested functions collapse into one linear operation:

$$\mathbf{d}(\mathbf{v}) = \mathbf{A}^T\tilde{\mathbf{v}} = \mathbf{A}^T\begin{pmatrix}1\\ \mathbf{v}\end{pmatrix} \tag{7.11}$$

where the matrix $\mathbf{A}$ of this expression comes out to be

$$\mathbf{A} = \begin{pmatrix}\mathbf{a}_0^{T\langle 1\rangle} + \mathbf{a}_0^{T\langle 2\rangle}\mathbf{A}^{*\langle 1\rangle} + \mathbf{a}_0^{T\langle 3\rangle}\mathbf{A}^{*\langle 2\rangle}\mathbf{A}^{*\langle 1\rangle}\\ \mathbf{A}^{*\langle 3\rangle}\mathbf{A}^{*\langle 2\rangle}\mathbf{A}^{*\langle 1\rangle}\end{pmatrix} \tag{7.12}$$

Again the mathematical expressions are given only for $H = 3$ but can appropriately be generalized for any number H of layers. We find that replacing all of the nonlinearities by identity mappings indeed renders (7.11), which we already know as the linear polynomial classifier; compare (6.7) and (6.8).

Relations to Concept of Functional Approximation Based on Linear Combination of Basis Functions

The multilayer perceptron is used here for constructing the discriminant function $\mathbf{d}(\mathbf{v})$ of pattern classification based on the concept of least mean-square functional approximation. The basic idea outlined in Chapter 5 was to generate the functional approximation by a linear combination of a suitable set of basis functions.

Whereas it is quite obvious which are the basis functions in the case of polynomial approximation, such relations to multilayer perceptron functional approximation need some explanation. There are essentially two differences between the polynomial approach and the multilayer perceptron approach.

First, in polynomial approximation the basis functions do not depend on adjustable parameters but are considered given [compare (5.3)], whereas in multilayer perceptron approximation the basis functions themselves depend on adjustable parameters [compare (5.2)].

Second, in multilayer perceptron the linear combination is not the final step in constructing the discriminant function $\mathbf{d}(\mathbf{v})$; instead, the functions gained by linear combination go through an additional nonlinear functional mapping.

Consider the two-layer perceptron shown in Fig. 7.6. The first layer maps the input vector variable $\mathbf{v}$ into the vector $\mathbf{h}$ of hidden variables. In the second perceptron layer these go into linear combinations, the outcomes of which are then nonlinearly mapped into the components of the output vector variable $\mathbf{d}$ by sigmoid functions.

In terms of functional approximation by linear combination of basis functions, the first layer of this two-layer perceptron generates the *basis functions*, which are comprised into the vector $\mathbf{h}$ of hidden variables. The second layer implements the linear combinations. Hence, the weight matrix $\mathbf{A}^{\langle 1\rangle}$ of the

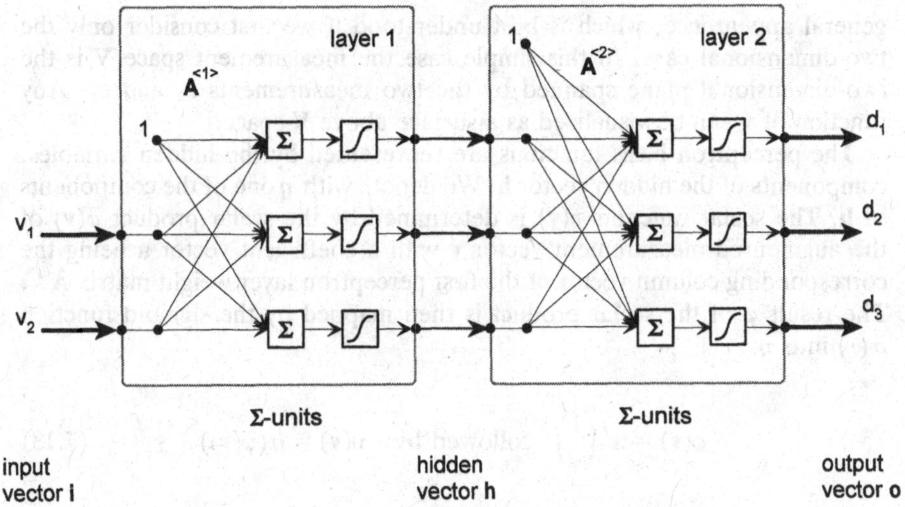

Figure 7.6. Detailed view on two-layer perceptron.

first layer determines the appearance of the basis functions, whereas the weight matrix $\mathbf{A}^{\langle 2\rangle}$ of the second perceptron layer contains the coefficients of the linear combination.

The fact that the perceptron basis functions themselves are subject to the learning procedure seems to represent a generalization over using predetermined basis functions and to offer the potential of developing a set of problem-specific basis functions. It must, however, be noted that without this capability of change during the process of functional approximation, functions of this type could only incidentally be useful.

The second difference, stated above, of nonlinear mapping the result of the linear combination is not as serious as it seems to be at first glancc. This nonlinear mapping is monotonic and identical for all of the components of **d** and does not change the rank order among the components of **d** but only changes their numerical values. Hence, omitting it after the coefficients in all of the perceptron layers are fixed does not affect the classifier's decisions. There exists a close relationship between the sigmoidal mapping at the perceptron output and the confidence mapping function considered in Section 6.13 in the context of polynomial regression.

This nonlinearity at the multilayer perceptron output has, however, an impact on the optimization procedure and on the solution found. In practical application often the last layer of nonlinearity is completely omitted.

7.5 APPEARANCE OF PERCEPTRON BASIS FUNCTIONS

The mathematical structure of the single perceptron layer (7.8) forces the basis functions generated by the first perceptron layer to exhibit all the same general appearance, which is best understood if we first consider only the two-dimensional case. In this simple case the measurement space **V** is the two-dimensional plane spanned by the two measurements v_1 and v_2. Any function of **v** can be visualized as a surface above **V**-space.

The perceptron basis functions are represented by the hidden variables, components of the hidden vector **h**. We denote with η one of the components of **h**. The scalar function $\eta(\mathbf{v})$ is determined by the scalar product $\varphi(\mathbf{v})$ of the augmented measurement vector **v** with a coefficient vector **a** being the corresponding column vector of the first perceptron layer weight matrix $\mathbf{A}^{\langle 1 \rangle}$. The result φ of the scalar product is then mapped by the sigmoid function $\sigma(\cdot)$ into η:

$$\varphi(\mathbf{v}) = \mathbf{a}^T \begin{pmatrix} 1 \\ \mathbf{v} \end{pmatrix} \quad \text{followed by} \quad \eta(\mathbf{v}) = \sigma(\varphi(\mathbf{v})) \tag{7.13}$$

The first of these two steps results in $\varphi(\mathbf{v})$ being a planar surface above **V**-space, which traces the measurement space along the straight line

$$\varphi(\mathbf{v}) = \mathbf{a}^T \begin{pmatrix} 1 \\ \mathbf{v} \end{pmatrix} = 0 \tag{7.14}$$

Going through the sigmoidal mapping $\sigma(\cdot)$, the planar surface $\varphi(\mathbf{v})$ is bent into the range of values $[0\,..1]$. The trace $\varphi(\mathbf{v}) = 0$ of the plane becomes the half-value line of the bent surface $\eta(\mathbf{v})$ since the sigmoid function $\sigma(\cdot)$ assumes the value $\sigma(0) = 0.5$ if its argument vanishes to $\varphi = 0$.

Hence we find that the perceptron basis functions in the two-dimensional case are smooth unit step functions with a sigmoidal transition from 0 to 1 along a straight borderline (Fig. 7.7). In the N-dimensional case the straight line generalizes to an $(N-1)$-dimensional linear subspace (a hyperplane) along which again a smooth transition from 0 to 1 occurs.

The most remarkable fact with the perceptron basis functions is that they are not predetermined from the beginning but, within the limits given by their general appearance, their shape is formed according to the requirements of the learning procedure.

Linear Combination of Perceptron Basis Functions

We will stay for a moment with the same example of the two-dimensional measurement space **V** to make intuitively clear how, by linear combination of a large number of different basis functions of this kind, arbitrary functions above **V**-space can be formed.

This shall be illustrated by showing the result of the simplest imaginable case of a linear combination of two different perceptron basis functions,

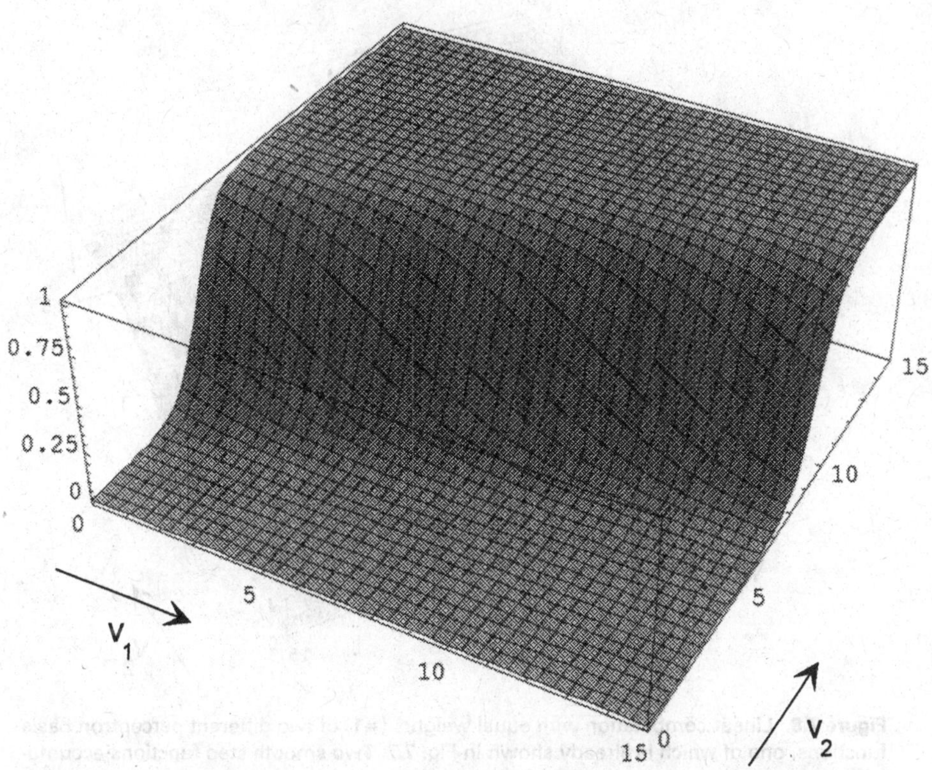

Figure 7.7. General appearance of perceptron basis functions, smooth unit step function along straight borderline. Position and orientation of step line and step steepness are determined by corresponding column vector of first-layer weight matrix $\mathbf{A}^{\langle 1\rangle}$ and are adjusted according to requirements of classification task during learning process.

namely the additive superposition of two basis functions with identical weights 1; see Fig. 7.8.

The linear combination is accomplished by the second layer of the two-layer perceptron, which we are considering here, with the coefficients of the linear combination given by the weight matrix $\mathbf{A}^{\langle 2\rangle}$ of this layer. The final sigmoidal mapping forms the landscape of Fig. 7.8, again with the goal of improving the accuracy of the functional approximation (Fig. 7.9).

It is easily imaginable that weighted superposition with properly chosen positive or negative weights of a large number of basis functions of this type, with different position, orientation, and slope of the $0 \rightarrow 1$ transition, is able to render any reasonable continuous function of $\mathbf{v}$, at least in some bounded region of the $\mathbf{V}$-space.

One specially important feature of multilayer perceptron regression in this context is that the basis functions themselves are formed by the learning procedure, which means that the $0 \rightarrow 1$ transitions they determine are moved

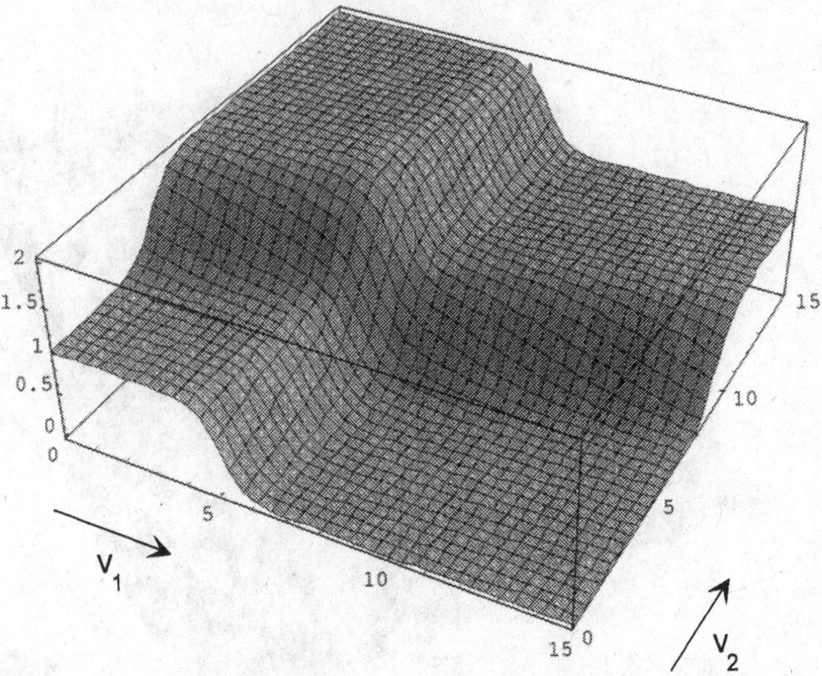

Figure 7.8. Linear combination with equal weights (=1) of two different perceptron basis functions, one of which is already shown in Fig. 7.7. Two smooth step functions accumulate to value 2 in those regions of **V** where both assume value 1. By superposition with suitable weights (positive and negative) of large number of basis functions, arbitrary landscapes above **V**-space can be formed.

in **V**-space into those positions and orientations actually needed. Typically the $0 \rightarrow 1$ transitions move into positions along the class boundaries between pairs of classes such that one of the class regions falls on the "zero" and the other on the "one" side of the transition. After all, the final sigmoidal mapping (Fig. 7.9) provides a kind of finishing operation flattening the resulting landscape and suppressing undesired details.

These conceptions, here exemplarily illustrated for a two-dimensional measurement space **V**, can be generalized to higher dimensions.

The general properties of the multilayer perceptron are not just accessible to our intuition: It has been shown that linear combination of perceptron basis functions is capable of approximating any function of interest to any desired degree of accuracy provided that sufficiently many hidden variables (basis functions) are available [HSW1989]. The multilayer perceptron thus has the property of being a *universal approximator*.

These statements refer to the two-layer perceptron and are strictly valid only if no constraints are imposed on the number of hidden variables (percep-

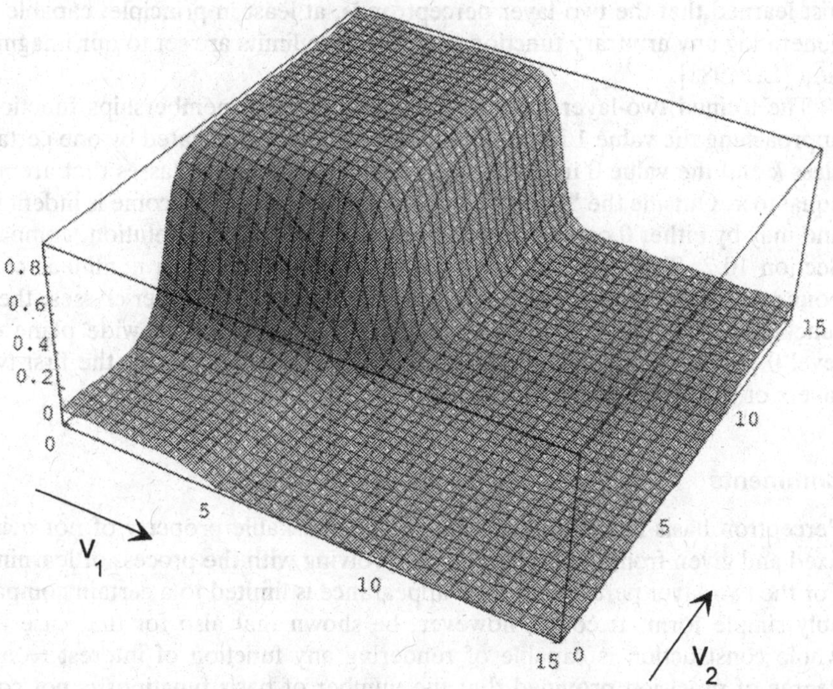

Figure 7.9. Same two-dimensional landscape as in Fig. 7.8 after sigmoidal mapping by sigmoid function $\sigma(\cdot)$ of second layer of two-layer perceptron.

tron basis functions). They do not exclude that a perceptron with more than two layers may, from a practical point of view, be superior to one with only two.

It remains an open question whether in a given situation additional effort would be better devoted to increasing the number of hidden variables of the two-layer perceptron or to increasing the number of layers. System designers often choose the number H of layers of the multilayer perceptron larger than two and justify their decision with practical success.

Perceptron Basis Functions in Multilayer Case

What we have considered in the foregoing section is the appearance of the perceptron basis functions if they are derived from a single perceptron layer. We will now look into the three-layer perceptron ($H = 3$).

Since the three-layer perceptron is nothing else than a two-layer perceptron with one additional layer that provides the linear combination of its input functions, the answer is comparably simple and straightforward. The basis functions of a three-layer perceptron come from the set of all possible functions the two-layer perceptron is able to generate. And since we have just learned that the two-layer perceptron is, at least in principle, capable of generating any arbitrary function of $\mathbf{v}$, no more limits are set to our imagination [LIP1988].

The trained two-layer perceptron generates class memberships functions approaching the value 1 in those regions of **V**-space populated by one certain class k and the value 0 in regions populated by the other classes that are not equal to k. Outside the "known" regions in **V**-space, the outcome is indefinite and may by either 0 or 1 depending on peculiarities of the solution, compare Section 10.2. Typically the $0 \rightarrow 1$ transition occurs along a nonlinear class boundary. If the class region is surrounded by regions of other classes, these functions take on the form of a mountain of height 1 on a wide plane on level 0. Functions of such a type are likely to be generated by the first two layers of the three-layer perceptron.

Comments

Perceptron basis functions have the most remarkable property of not being fixed and given from the beginning but evolving with the process of learning. For the two-layer perceptron their appearance is limited to a certain comparably simple form. It could, however, be shown that also for that case the whole construction is capable of rendering any function of interest to any degree of precision provided that the number of basis functions is not constrained.

7.6 BACKPROPAGATION LEARNING

In the context of pattern classification the multilayer perceptron is employed for establishing a discriminant function $\mathbf{d}(\mathbf{v})$ that shall come as close as possible to the true class membership indicator variable $\mathbf{y}$, the target vector of the pattern classification problem as introduced in Section 1.4. The least mean-square criterion is used for optimization (3.1):

$$S^2 = E\{|\mathbf{d}(\mathbf{v}) - \mathbf{y}|^2\} = \min_{\mathbf{d}(\mathbf{v})}$$

The discriminant function $\mathbf{d}(\mathbf{v})$ is nonlinear, not only with respect to the input variable $\mathbf{v}$, which is desired, but also with respect to the set of coefficients contained in the union of all of the weight matrices $\mathbf{A}^{\langle h \rangle}$, $h = 1, \ldots, H$, and that makes things slightly complicated:

$$S^2 = E\{|\sigma(\mathbf{A}^{T\langle H \rangle} \cdots \tilde{\sigma}(\mathbf{A}^{T\langle 2 \rangle}\tilde{\sigma}(\mathbf{A}^{T\langle 1 \rangle}\tilde{\mathbf{v}}))) - \mathbf{y}|^2\} = \min_{\mathbf{A}^{\langle 1 \rangle}, \mathbf{A}^{\langle 2 \rangle}, \ldots, \mathbf{A}^{\langle H \rangle}} \tag{7.15}$$

The *criterion function* S^2 depends on all of the H weight matrices

$$S^2 = S^2(\mathbf{A}^{\langle 1\rangle}, \mathbf{A}^{\langle 2\rangle}, \ldots, \mathbf{A}^{\langle H\rangle}) \tag{7.16}$$

and must be imagined as a complicated error surface above the high-dimensional space spanned by all of the weights contained in $\mathbf{A}^{\langle h\rangle}$, $h = 1, \ldots, H$.

What we are looking for is the global minimum of $S^2(\mathbf{A}^{\langle 1\rangle}, \mathbf{A}^{\langle 2\rangle}, \ldots, \mathbf{A}^{\langle H\rangle})$. It is possible that functions of this type generally do not exhibit just one single minimum. It is unknown if there are local minima, how many of them there are, and how they relate to the one global minimum for which we are searching.

We know, however, that due to the inherent symmetries of the construction, the criterion function has a number of symmetries and thus a number of equivalent local minima as well as a system of equivalue global minima. These symmetries come from the fact that the roles of the hidden variables are exchangeable.

There is no reason for hoping that sometimes a direct solution to the optimization problem of (7.15) will be found, which presently indeed does not exist. Optimization problems of this kind must be solved otherwise. Good candidates are *Monte Carlo search* methods and their modern successors, *genetic algorithms*, as well as all kinds of *gradient descent* procedures.

The task we are involved in when searching the minimum of the error surface $S^2(\mathbf{A}^{\langle 1\rangle}, \mathbf{A}^{\langle 2\rangle}, \ldots, \mathbf{A}^{\langle H\rangle})$ has been compared with the task of searching the deepest point on the bottom of the ocean from a ship equipped with a deap-sea lead. This situation is made worse by the fact that we here have to deal with large numbers of free parameters, whereas in the case of the ocean and the ship the search space is two dimensional.

This task, on the other hand, is somewhat alleviated since, at every point where the lead is set, we know also the direction of steepest descent, the gradient of the error surface. It is obvious to follow the direction of steepest descent until a minimum is found.

The *backpropagation algorithm* [RHW1986], being the most well-known learning rule for the multilayer perceptron and to be derived in the following, belongs to the category of gradient descent techniques. All we need to know to apply this technique to search the minimum of the criterion function is the gradient with respect to all of the trainable parameters of the construction.

Since $S^2(\mathbf{A}^{\langle 1\rangle}, \mathbf{A}^{\langle 2\rangle}, \ldots, \mathbf{A}^{\langle H\rangle})$ is a well-defined function, its partial derivatives with respect to all of the coefficients can be calculated. Once the gradient ∇S^2 is computed, we simply have to modify the current value $\mathbf{A}$ of the parameter set $\mathbf{A} = \{\mathbf{A}^{\langle 1\rangle}, \mathbf{A}^{\langle 2\rangle}, \ldots, \mathbf{A}^{\langle H\rangle}\}$ by a certain (small amount) in the opposite direction as given by the gradient ∇S^2:

$$\mathbf{A} \Leftarrow \mathbf{A} - \alpha \nabla S^2 \tag{7.17}$$

The procedure is repeated until a vanishing gradient indicates a local minimum. The appropriate choice of the learning parameter α is crucial. Large values of α alleviate escaping from local minima but hold the risk of running the hillsides up and down without finding the minimum at all, whereas too small values of α lead to unacceptable slow convergence. The problem of being trapped in local minima can be countered by randomizing the search procedure and applying sophisticated control strategies such as *simulated annealing*.

This technique applies larger stepwidths at the beginning of the minimum-search procedure to prevent the minimum search from being trapped in smaller local minima. With the progress of the procedure the stepwidth is decreased and the minimum search is allowed to settle at a better value of the criterion function. A similar effect is achieved by the common singular learning procedure; see the later section on singular and cumulative learning in this chapter.

We will in the following calculate the partial derivatives of the criterion function $S^2(\mathbf{A}^{\langle 1\rangle}, \mathbf{A}^{\langle 2\rangle}, \ldots, \mathbf{A}^{\langle H\rangle})$ with respect to all of the weights contained in $\mathbf{A} = \{\mathbf{A}^{\langle 1\rangle}, \mathbf{A}^{\langle 2\rangle}, \ldots, \mathbf{A}^{\langle H\rangle}\}$.

Computing Gradient

According to the definition (7.9) of $\mathbf{d}(\mathbf{v})$ as being a nested sequence of sigmoid functions

$$\mathbf{d}(\mathbf{v}) = \sigma(\mathbf{A}^{T\langle H\rangle} \cdots \tilde{\sigma}(\mathbf{A}^{T\langle 2\rangle}\tilde{\sigma}(\mathbf{A}^{T\langle 1\rangle}\tilde{\mathbf{v}})))$$

the chain rule of calculus will be needed for this calculation. The regular structure of the multilayer perceptron suggests a recursive way of proceeding. We will therefore first consider only one certain layer of the construction and later combine the results.

The criterion function S^2 as given above is defined using the notion of mathematical expectation $E\{\cdot\}$. Since here only a sample set $\{\mathbf{v}, \mathbf{y}\}$ is available, the expectation must be replaced by the arithmetic mean (compare Section 4.6), giving

$$S^2 = \frac{1}{J}\sum_{j=1}^{J} |\mathbf{d}(\mathbf{v}_j) - \mathbf{y}_j|^2 = \frac{1}{J}\sum_{j=1}^{J} F_j \tag{7.18}$$

where F_j denotes the contribution of the jth sample of the learning set to the average criterion function S^2:

$$F_j = |\mathbf{d}(\mathbf{v}_j) - \mathbf{y}_j|^2 \tag{7.19}$$

The gradient of S^2 comes out to be the average gradient of F_j:

$$\nabla S^2 = \frac{1}{J}\sum_{j=1}^{J} \nabla F_j \tag{7.20}$$

Although the ultimate goal of the perceptron adaptation procedure is to minimize the criterion function S^2, it turns out to be sensible sometimes to minimize each F_j individually, instead. Minimization of F_j corresponds to learning with just the last seen example $[\mathbf{v}_j, \mathbf{y}_j]$ in mind, whereas minimization of S^2 corresponds to learning with regard to the complete learning set. Compare Section 6.14, the discussion on the role of the last seen example in recursive learning.

The two variants of the learning procedure are as follows:

- Singular learning (also known as stochastic learning)
- Cumulative learning (also known as batch learning)

The notion of batch learning also in use for what we prefer to call cumulative learning is in this book otherwise occupied; compare Section 6.14. We will return to what distinguishes singular and cumulative learning later.

Here, it suffices to know that once ∇F_j is computed for each individual sample $j = 1, \ldots, J$, the value of ∇S^2 is easily gained by simple averaging, (7.20). We will therefore derive in the following the gradient ∇F, omitting the subscript j in order to simplify the notation.

Partial Derivatives for *h*th Layer

With reference to Fig. 7.4 the input and output variables of the hth layer are denoted by

$$\begin{aligned} i_n^{\langle h \rangle} &= n\text{th input variable of layer } h \\ o_m^{\langle h \rangle} &= m\text{th output variable of layer } h \end{aligned} \tag{7.21}$$

and the weights connecting the N input variables to the mth output by

$$a_{nm}^{\langle h \rangle} = \text{weight within layer } h \text{ connecting input node } n \text{ with output node } m \tag{7.22}$$

In terms of these variables the operations of the hth layer are described by

$$\begin{aligned} o_m^{\langle h \rangle} &= \sigma(s_m^{\langle h \rangle}) \\ s_m^{\langle h \rangle} &= \sum_{n=0}^{N^{\langle h \rangle}} a_{nm}^{\langle h \rangle} i_n^{\langle h \rangle} \end{aligned} \tag{7.23}$$

The hth layer shall be one of the intermediate layers of the multilayer perceptron. We assume that the partial derivatives of the criterion function

F with respect to the output variables of the hth layer are already known:

$$\frac{\partial F}{\partial o_m^{\langle h \rangle}} = \text{presently considered given}$$

Since F depends on $o_m^{\langle h \rangle}$ and $o_m^{\langle h \rangle}$ depends on $a_{nm}^{\langle h \rangle}$ and $i_n^{\langle h \rangle}$ for $n = 1, \ldots, N^{\langle h \rangle}$, according to (7.23), we get

$$\frac{\partial F}{\partial a_{nm}^{\langle h \rangle}} = \frac{\partial F}{\partial o_m^{\langle h \rangle}} \frac{\partial o_m^{\langle h \rangle}}{\partial s_m^{\langle h \rangle}} \frac{\partial s_m^{\langle h \rangle}}{\partial a_{nm}^{\langle h \rangle}} = \frac{\partial F}{\partial o_m^{\langle h \rangle}} \frac{\partial o_m^{\langle h \rangle}}{\partial s_m^{\langle h \rangle}} i_n^{\langle h \rangle} \tag{7.24}$$

We now make use of the fact that the first derivative of the sigmoid function is given by (7.6), which, together with (7.23), leads to

$$\frac{\partial o_m^{\langle h \rangle}}{\partial s_m^{\langle h \rangle}} = o_m^{\langle h \rangle}(1 - o_m^{\langle h \rangle}) \tag{7.25}$$

Hence we find

$$\frac{\partial F}{\partial a_{nm}^{\langle h \rangle}} = o_m^{\langle h \rangle}(1 - o_m^{\langle h \rangle}) i_n^{\langle h \rangle} \frac{\partial F}{\partial o_m^{\langle h \rangle}} \tag{7.26}$$

Similarly, the derivative of F with respect to $i_n^{\langle h \rangle}$ is achieved from

$$\frac{\partial F}{\partial i_n^{\langle h \rangle}} = \sum_{m=1}^{M^{\langle h \rangle}} \frac{\partial F}{\partial o_m^{\langle h \rangle}} \frac{\partial o_m^{\langle h \rangle}}{\partial s_m^{\langle h \rangle}} \frac{\partial s_m^{\langle h \rangle}}{\partial i_n^{\langle h \rangle}} = \sum_{m=1}^{M^{\langle h \rangle}} o_m^{\langle h \rangle}(1 - o_m^{\langle h \rangle}) a_{nm}^{\langle h \rangle} \frac{\partial F}{\partial o_m^{\langle h \rangle}} \tag{7.27}$$

The sum over the $M^{\langle h \rangle}$ output nodes of the considered layer is necessary to take into account all of the possibilities for $i_n^{\langle h \rangle}$ to influence the criterion function.

We thus know all of the partial derivatives for one single layer once the derivatives with respect to its output variables are known (Fig. 7.10).

Partial Derivatives with Respect to Output Variables

The output variables $o_m^{\langle H \rangle}$ of the last layer $\langle H \rangle$ are identical to the components d_k of the discriminant vector $\mathbf{d}$,

$$o_m^{\langle H \rangle} = d_k \quad \text{where} \quad M^{\langle H \rangle} = K \qquad m = k \tag{7.28}$$

and the partial derivatives corresponding to them are easily determined from (7.19) as

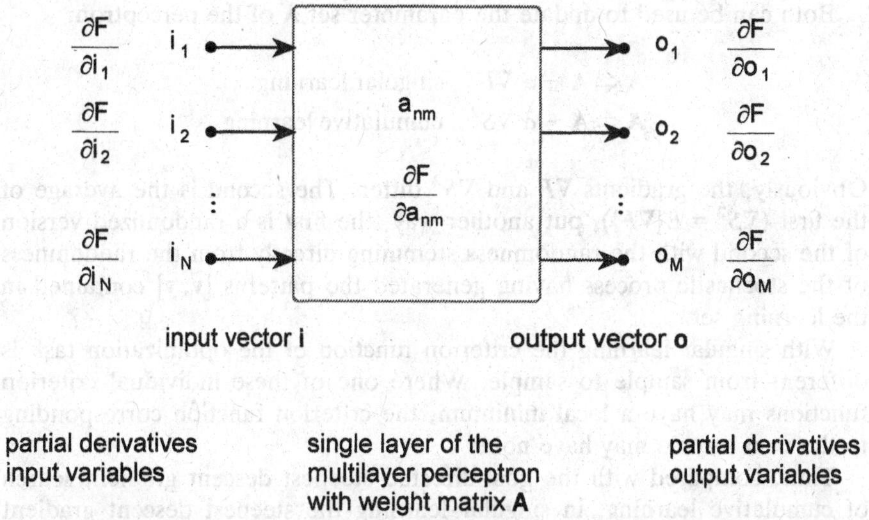

Figure 7.10. Single layer of multilayer perceptron with variables and derivatives. Arrows indicate *forward* flow of operations. To each of input and output variables belongs partial derivative of criterion function F with repect to respective variable o_m or i_n. These partial derivatives constitute *backward* flow of operations. Must be given at output side in order to be computed on input side.

$$\frac{\partial F}{\partial o_m^{\langle H \rangle}} = \frac{\partial F}{\partial d_k} = \frac{\partial}{\partial d_k} |\mathbf{d}(\mathbf{v}) - \mathbf{y}|^2 = \frac{\partial}{\partial d_k} \sum_{k=1}^{K} (d_k - y_k)^2 = 2(d_k - y_k) \quad (7.29)$$

After the present pair $[\mathbf{v}, \mathbf{y}]$ of measurement vector $\mathbf{v}$ and target vector $\mathbf{y}$ has been completely processed through the multilayer perceptron structure, the derivatives belonging to the output variables can be computed according the above equation. This fulfills the precondition for computing the partial derivatives with regard to both weights and input variables of the last layer and, recursively, for all the layers before. The computation of the gradient ∇F inverts the normal data flow going from the input to the output of the multilayer perceptron into the opposite direction. This inversion of the data flow gave the whole procedure the name *backpropagation algorithm*.

Singular and Cumulative Learning

With the two computing steps *forward propagation* for mapping the input vector $\mathbf{v}$ into the discriminant vector $\mathbf{d}$ and *backward propagation* for computing the partial derivatives with respect to all of the weights contained within the different perceptron layers, the gradient ∇F is achieved.

By going through the whole learning set without making any changes to the perceptron weights and averaging ∇F, the gradient ∇S^2 is gained.

Both can be used to update the parameter set **A** of the perceptron:

$$\mathbf{A} \Leftarrow \mathbf{A} - \alpha \nabla F \quad \text{singular learning}$$
$$\mathbf{A} \Leftarrow \mathbf{A} - \alpha \nabla S^2 \quad \text{cumulative learning}$$

Obviously, the gradients ∇F and ∇S^2 differ. The second is the average of the first ($\nabla S^2 = E\{\nabla F\}$), put another way, the first is a randomized version of the second with the randomness stemming directly from the randomness of the stochastic process having generated the patterns $[\mathbf{v}, \mathbf{y}]$ contained in the learning set.

With singular learning the criterion function of the optimization task is different from sample to sample. Where one of these individual criterion functions may have a local minimum, the criterion function corresponding to the next sample may have none.

Thus, compared with the goal-directed steepest descent gradient search of cumulative learning, in singular learning the steepest descent gradient search is superimposed by random steps in arbitrary directions. The result, as a rule, is that a useful wide minimum is actually found whereas small local minima are leapt over.

In this context it should be remembered that the closely related recursive learning rule of Section 6.14 was also of the singular learning type.

The whole singular learning procedure consists of the following sequence of steps:

- Preliminary values for the coefficient matrices $\mathbf{A}^{\langle 1 \rangle}, \mathbf{A}^{\langle 2 \rangle}, \ldots, \mathbf{A}^{\langle H \rangle}$ of all perceptron layers are already given or suitably chosen when initializing the procedure.
- The present sample $[\mathbf{v}, \mathbf{y}]$ is observed.
- Compute the discriminant vector $\mathbf{d}$ based on the given observation $\mathbf{v}$ and the present weight matrices $\mathbf{A}^{\langle 1 \rangle}, \mathbf{A}^{\langle 2 \rangle}, \ldots, \mathbf{A}^{\langle H \rangle}$ (forward propagation).
- Compute the difference $\Delta\mathbf{d}$ between estimation $\mathbf{d}$ and target $\mathbf{y}$:

$$\Delta\mathbf{d} = \mathbf{d} - \mathbf{y}$$

- Compute the gradient ∇F with respect to all of the perceptron weights (error backpropagation).
- Update the perceptron weights according to

$$a_{nm}^{\langle h \rangle} \Leftarrow a_{nm}^{\langle h \rangle} - \alpha \frac{\partial F}{\partial a_{nm}^{\langle h \rangle}} \qquad \forall h = 1, \ldots, H, n = 1, \ldots, N^{\langle H \rangle}, \quad m = 1, \ldots, M^{\langle H \rangle} \tag{7.30}$$

The difference between singular and cumulative learning is that with *singular learning* the weights $a_{nm}^{\langle h \rangle}$ are updated with ∇F for every sample of the learning set presented whereas with *cumulative learning* the complete learning set must be worked through in order to gain the averaged gradient ∇S^2 from the sequence $\{\nabla F\}$ according to (7.20) before the weights $a_{nm}^{\langle h \rangle}$ can be updated with ∇S^2:

$$a_{nm}^{\langle h \rangle} \Leftarrow a_{nm}^{\langle h \rangle} - \alpha \frac{\partial S^2}{\partial a_{nm}^{\langle h \rangle}} \quad \forall h = 1, \ldots, H, n = 1, \ldots, N^{\langle H \rangle}, m = 1, \ldots, M^{\langle H \rangle} \tag{7.31}$$

Note that the learning factor α in both types of learning rules may be chosen differently.

Comments

The backpropagation algorithm is easy to implement but computationally expensive. Classifier adaptation by backpropagation is an extremely time consuming operation, especially if the number of weights involved is large, since then also the learning set size must be adequately large. Another drawback is that the results depend on initialization, the choice of the learning factor α, and the order in which the elements of the learning set are presented.

Similar to the techniques of recursive learning for the polynomial classifier (compare Section 6.14), backpropagation ignores potential linear dependencies within the set of input variables nor does it offer the feature-ranking possibilities of the generalized inverse technique for computing the coefficient matrix of the polynomial classifier (see Section 6.9). Gradient search, however, works also for very large numbers of weights larger than can reasonably be handled by the generalized inverse approach of Section 6.8.

Initialization of the weight matrices must avoid being captured by symmetries. Such a symmetry happens if for example all the perceptron weights are zero. Typically, initialization is performed using small random values.

The resulting multilayer perceptrons are characterized by their respective numbers of input, hidden, and output variables $(N, N^{\langle 1 \rangle}, \ldots, N^{\langle H-1 \rangle}, K)$, giving the code of (2, 3, 3) for the two-layer perceptron structure of Fig. 7.6. The total number of weights is easily computed from

$$T = \sum_{h=1}^{H} (N^{\langle h-1 \rangle} + 1) N^{\langle h \rangle} \quad \text{where} \quad N^{\langle 0 \rangle} = N \qquad N^{\langle H \rangle} = K \tag{7.32}$$

where $N = \dim[\mathbf{v}]$ is the number of measurements and $K = \dim[\mathbf{d}]$ the number of classes. In the special case of the two-layer perceptron

$$T = (N+1)M + (M+1)K = (N+K+1)M + K \qquad (7.33)$$

where $M =$ is the number of hidden variables.

7.7 VISUALIZATIONS BASED ON TWO-DIMENSIONAL EXAMPLE OF CHAPTER 4

We have introduced in Chapter 4 the simple two-dimensional three-class example of (4.35) in order to make intuitively clear how the key concepts of statistical and neural pattern classification work and how they are related. Compare, therefore, what is shown in this section to the reference data of Section 4.2 and to the corresponding Sections 6.12–6.14.

In Chapter 6 we have set the design parameter polynomial degree G of the polynomial regression approach to $G = 2$, which resulted for the given example with $N = 2$ in a second-degree polynomial with length $L = 6$ and a total number $T = 18$ free parameters for the polynomial pattern classifier. To come to a multilayer perceptron classifier with comparable overall expense, the number of layers is here set to $H = 2$ and the number of hidden variables to $N^{\langle 1 \rangle} = 3$. At $T = 21$ the resulting $(2, 3, 3)$-perceptron has a slightly larger number of weights. This is exactly the perceptron structure shown in Fig. 7.6.

Backpropagation learning was performed using the singular learning rule of (7.30) and a sequence of learning factors $\alpha = [0.1, 0.2, 0.5]$ based on a learning set of size $J = 10{,}000$ generated by the statistical model described in Section 4.2. This learning set is the same as used with the recursive learning rule of polynomial regression in Section 6.14.

The convergence of simple singular backpropagation turned out to be somewhat slower than that of recursive polynomial learning. Therefore, the learning times had to be increased by running the same learning set repetitively. In backpropagation learning one complete representation of the entire learning set is usually called one epoch and the learning time needed is counted in epochs.

The perceptron network was initialized with values taken randomly from the interval $[-0.1\,..\,0.1]$. The resulting learning curves are shown in Figs. 7.11 and 7.12 for five epochs; compare with Figs. 6.29 and 6.30 achieved from the recursive learning rule of polynomial regression

The function plots of Figs. 7.11 and 7.12 exhibit a continuous exponential decay superimposed by a random distortion resulting from short-time observation. We had to compromise between this kind of randomness and the ability of the measuring technique to follow the transient behavior of the observables ϵ and S^2 during the first period of time after starting the learning process.

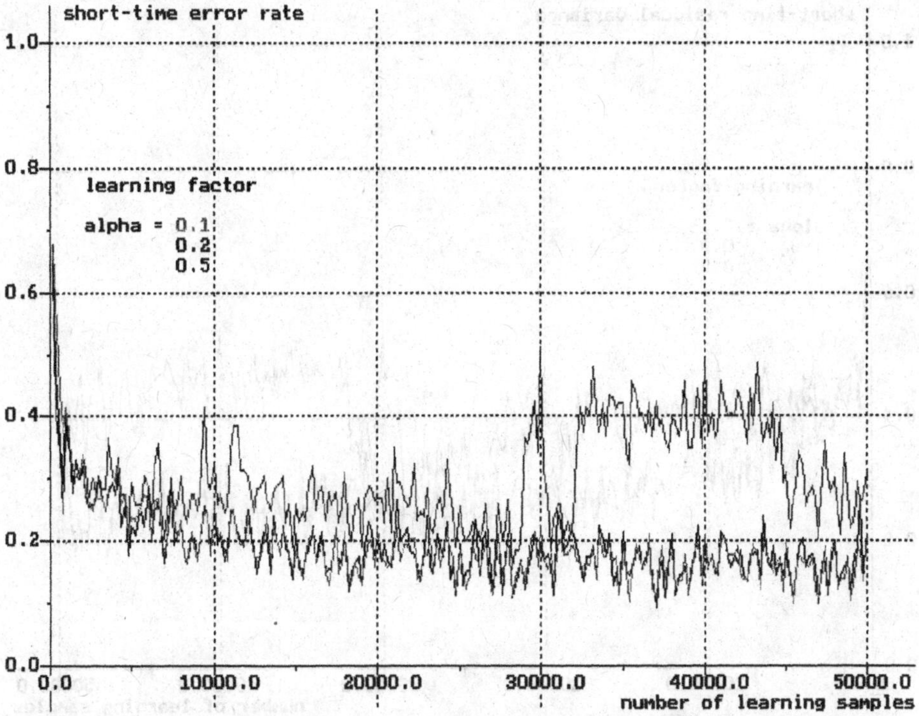

Figure 7.11. Backpropagation learning according to (7.30) using singular learning technique. Abscissa shows number of learning samples presented to learning rule and vertical axis shows short-time error rate ϵ observed during learning procedure, blockwise measured for every 200 consecutive samples as in Fig. 6.29. To match slower convergence of this learning rule, abscissa domain is five times larger. Parameter is learning factor $\alpha = [0.1, 0.2, 0.5]$.

Whereas Figs. 6.29 and 7.11 are directly comparable since they measure the same kind of data a comment must be made concerning the comparison of Figs. 6.30 and 7.12. Any nonlinear mapping identically applied to the components of the discriminant vector **d** either of the perceptron or the polynomial regression type classifier changes the value of S^2 but has no influence on ϵ. The multilayer perceptron of Fig. 7.6 contains this nonlinear mapping; the polynomial classifier from which Fig. 6.30 was achieved does not (if not followed by the confidence mapping of Fig. 6.17, which was not the case here).

Figures 7.11 and 7.12 show clearly the influence of the learning factor. With $\alpha = 0.1$ or $\alpha = 0.2$ the learning curves coincide after a certain number of learning steps, but with the larger value of $\alpha = 0.5$ no solution is found.

Whatever the state of its set of weight matrices $\mathbf{A}^{\langle 1 \rangle}, \mathbf{A}^{\langle 2 \rangle}, \ldots, \mathbf{A}^{\langle H \rangle}$ may be, the multilayer perceptron establishes a functional mapping $\mathbf{d}(\mathbf{v})$ from its

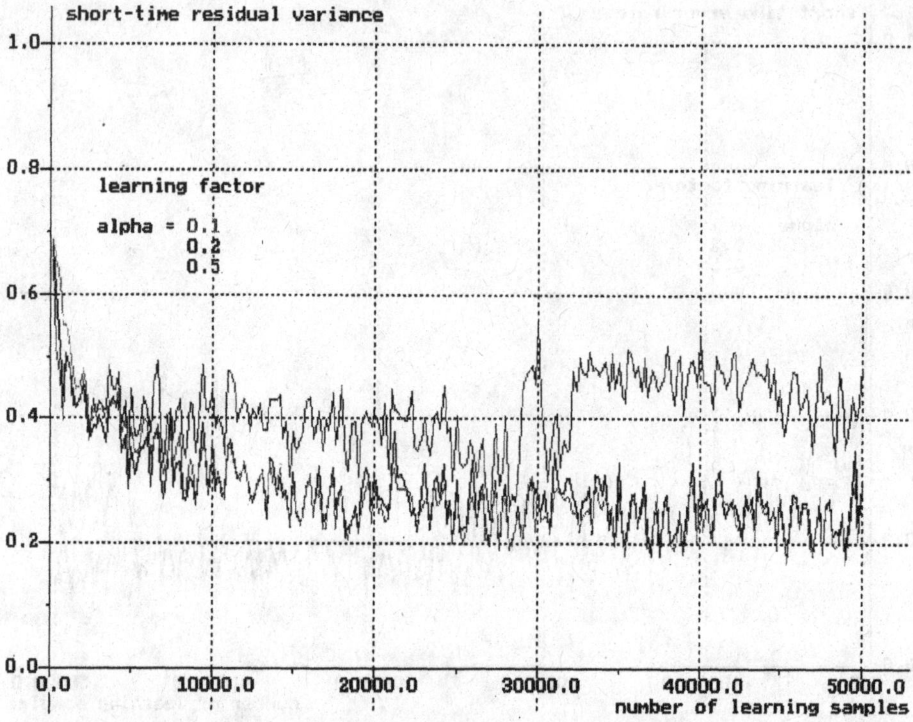

Figure 7.12. Backpropagation learning according to (7.30) using singular learning technique. Abscissa shows number of learning samples presented to learning rule and vertical axis shows short-time residual variance S^2 observed during learning procedure, blockwise measured for every 200 consecutive samples as in Fig. 6.30. To match slower convergence of this learning rule, abscissa domain is five times larger. Parameter is learning factor $\alpha = [0.1, 0.2, 0.5]$.

input space **V** to its output space **D** and thus defines a set of continuous functions $d_1(\mathbf{v}), \ldots, d_K(\mathbf{v})$ above the input space **V**.

In the case of the two-dimensional three-class example of (4.35) these functions are the three class membership functions $d_0(\mathbf{v})$, $d_1(\mathbf{v})$, $d_2(\mathbf{v})$, which have been shown in several three-dimensional plots for the different approaches discussed so far. We choose here $d_0(\mathbf{v})$ and $d_1(\mathbf{v})$ for a separate presentation in order to alleviate comparisons. The function $d_0(\mathbf{v})$ shown in Fig. 7.13 is the multilayer perceptron approximation to the a posteriori probability function prob(0|**v**) of Fig. 4.9.

Comparing Figs. 7.13 and 6.11 we observe the influence of sigmoidal mapping applied to the output variables. Whereas the estimation gained by polynomial regression of Fig. 6.11 exhibits a steep flank in the class 0 region of the measurement space, the perceptron-generated class membership function of Fig. 7.13 has a plateau in the same region. Remember, however, that

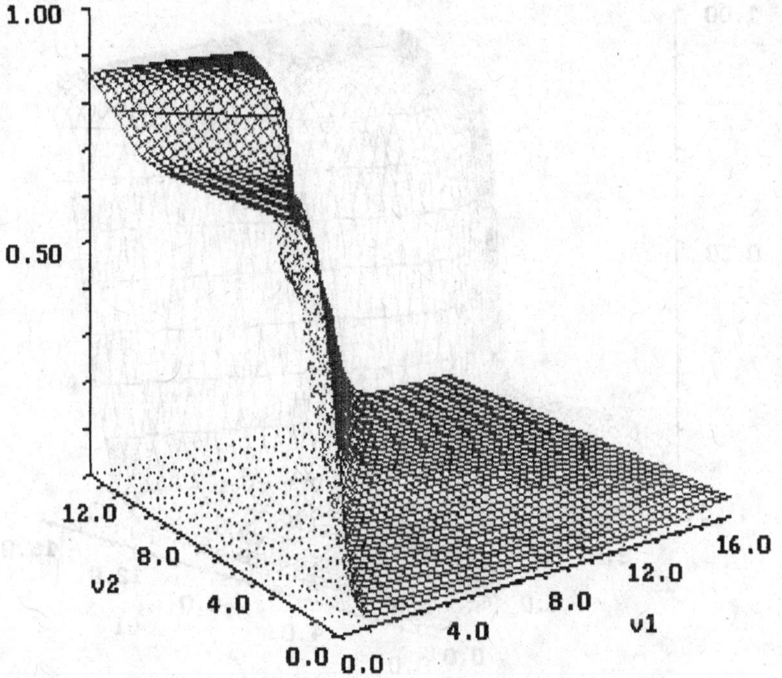

(*a*)

Figure 7.13. Three-dimensional plot of classes 0 and 1 discriminant functions $d_0(\mathbf{v})$, $d_1(\mathbf{v})$ approximating a posteriori probability functions prob(0|**v**) of Fig. 4.9 and prob(1|**v**) (not shown in Section 4.2). Functions are gained from (2, 3, 3)-perceptron for two-dimensional three-class example of (4.35) having been trained for five epochs with $\alpha = 0.1$ (endpoints of learning curves of Figs. 7.11 and 7.12).

the same effect is accomplished by applying the technique of *confidence mapping* to the output of the polynomial regression classifier (Fig. 6.23).

Figure 7.14 shows the three discriminant functions $d_0(\mathbf{v})$, $d_1(\mathbf{v})$, $d_2(\mathbf{v})$ generated by the (2, 3, 3)-perceptron to be compared with Figs. 4.7, 6.12, and 6.24 in the same representation as there.

As any pattern classifier the perceptron discriminant function $\mathbf{d}(\mathbf{v})$ provides a mapping from the measurement space **V** into the decision space **D**. Figure 7.15 shows the scatterplot of the same sample set as in Figs. 4.14, 6.16, and 6.26 for the (2, 3, 3) perceptron. We observe an irregularity that is quite different from that of Fig. 6.16. The reason for this irregularity is that of the two properties the discriminant function $d_k(\mathbf{v})$ should have, [(6.74) and (6.75)], again one is lost in the approximation procedure. Whereas (6.74) holds simply due to the construction of the multilayer perceptron Fig. 7.6

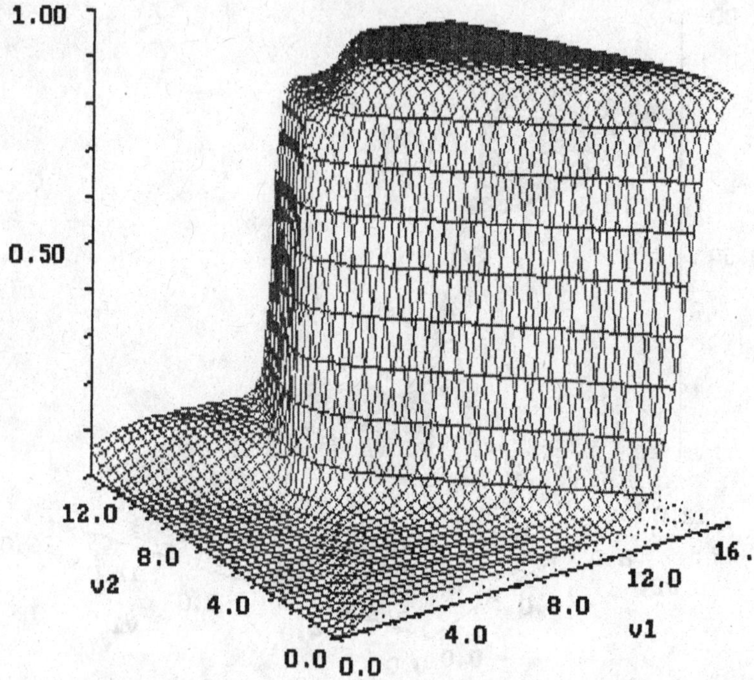

(*b*)

Figure 7.13. (*Continued*)

(sigmoidal mapping of the output variables), the condition of summing to one condition, (6.75), is no longer guaranteed.

The mapping procedure generating the decision space plots uses an orthogonal projection to get an image of the three-dimensional space **D** on the two-dimensional imaging plane. The plane passing the K target points in decision space is given by

$$\mathbf{e}^T \mathbf{d}_{\text{in plane}} - 1 = 0 \qquad (7.34)$$

with **e** defined by (6.31) being the plane normal. The orthogonal projection of some point **d** in **D**-space renders the image point $\mathbf{d}_{\text{in plane}}$. Both are distinguished by a certain length τ in direction of the plane normal **e**:

$$\mathbf{d} = \mathbf{d}_{\text{in plane}} + \tau \mathbf{e}$$

Multiplying this expression from left with $\mathbf{e}^T$ and taking into account that $\mathbf{e}^T\mathbf{e} = K$, we easily get

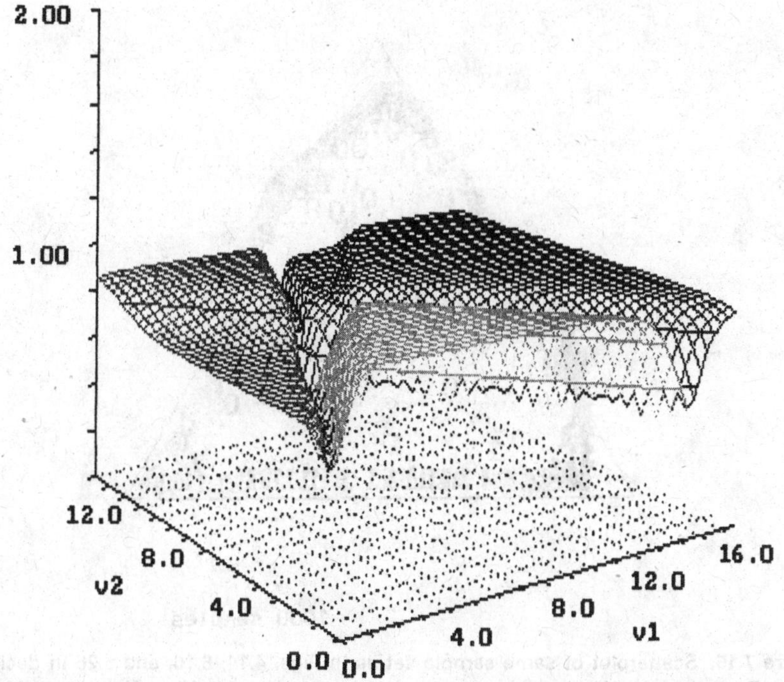

Figure 7.14. Three-dimensional plot of three discriminant functions generated by (2, 3, 3) perceptron in form of $\max[d_0(\mathbf{v}), d_1(\mathbf{v}), d_2(\mathbf{v})]$. Singular learning over five epochs of training with $\alpha = 0.1$.

$$\tau = \frac{1 - \mathbf{e}^T\mathbf{d}}{K}$$

and the projection rule

$$\mathbf{d}_{\text{in plane}} = \mathbf{d} - \frac{1 - \mathbf{e}^T\mathbf{d}}{K}\mathbf{e} \tag{7.35}$$

If the SumToUnity condition is violated, which is the fact for discriminant vectors $\mathbf{d}$ not lying in the plane passing the K target vectors, the smaller of the components of $\mathbf{d}$ may get negative values even if they had been nonnegative before. We observe in Fig. 7.15 that the distribution of points in $\mathbf{D}$-space crosses the triangle's borders and thus leaves the triangle's interior.

7.8 • CONSTRUCTIVE DESIGN OF PERCEPTRON BASIS FUNCTIONS

We have considered in Section 7.5 the general appearance of the perceptron basis functions. Those findings are confirmed by Fig. 7.13. The output func-

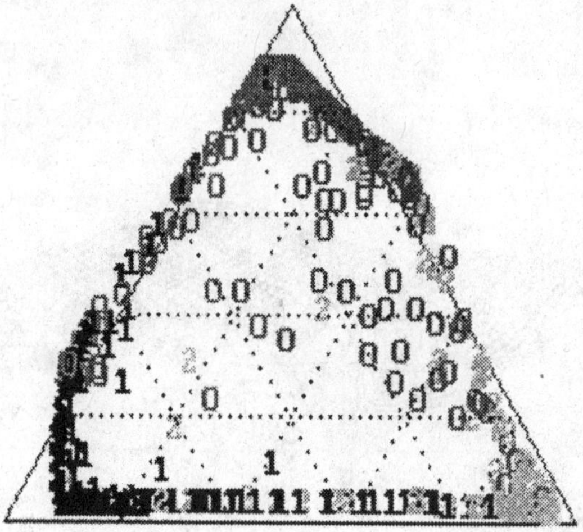

Figure 7.15. Scatterplot of same sample set as in Figs. 4.14, 6.16, and 6.26 in decision space **D** as produced by multilayer perceptron regression classifier. Distribution is captured within unit square in decision space but not within equilateral triangle shown.

tion is indeed the smooth overlay of three different ramps crossing the measurement space: What else should it be? Each of the three soft-flanked ramps corresponds to one of the three perceptron basis functions.

These ideas lead us to the questions of what would be the optimum set of basis functions for a given recognition problem and whether it might be possible to design these basis functions in advance rather than let them evolve from learning.

It is often argued that, in contrast to rule-based techniques for designing pattern classification systems, statistical learning techniques, such as learning polynomial and perceptron regression functions, suffer from the drawback of rendering uninterpretable results. The missing explanation capability is often considered a fundamental drawback and it is sometimes argued that pattern classification systems of this kind might be less trustworthy than those based on rules derived from human experts. Besides the fact that large rule-based systems generate conclusions as difficult to interpret, the following considerations show that we can indeed come to an understanding of how the perceptron derives its conclusions.

Obviously, we are not able to predict in detail which configuration of weights will eventually be the result of statistical learning. Knowing, however, that learning in essence is simply an optimization process controlled by a clear-cut and well-understood optimization criterion, we are in the position of understanding the basic principles ruling the construction of perceptron discriminant functions.

Based on this understanding, we will constructively design the weights of both perceptron layers, rather than letting them evolve under the control of the steepest descent optimization procedure, and look into the results we get comparing these with the results of conventional learning.

It is the author's intention not to replace sound and reliable mathematical optimization techniques by handcrafted heuristics but rather to demonstrate the appropriateness of the ideas presented. The deliberations shall give some insights into the mathematical operations in perceptron regression classifiers and shall shed some light on the relation between different looking approaches in pattern classification. We will for this purpose again use the example of (4.35).

Motivation

Classifiers generate class membership functions in **V**-space to be compared for a maximum; see Fig. 2.3. Thus the whole measurement space **V** is partitioned into a number of class regions with a network of borders separating them.

If the classes are reasonably compact, which is a common precondition implicitly or explicitly required for all of the simpler pattern classifiers, there will be predominantly one region per class. In more complicated cases the class regions may disintegrate into subclass regions. Regardless of how many regions belong to one class, all these class and subclass regions are separated by a kind of *Voronoi* network providing piecewise boundaries between pairs of classes.

We have seen in Section 7.5 that the *first layer* of the two-layer perceptron provides basis functions dividing the measurement space into half spaces. It is a convincing conception that these ramp functions position their smooth $0 \rightarrow 1$ transition approximately along the pairwise borders and generate a kind of "fuzzy" predicate indicating that a certain point in **v** lies on the right- or left-hand side of the borderline determined by the considered basis function.

Following this idea it is obvious that the job of the second layer is to perform logical operations on these fuzzy predicates. We know from the considerations at the beginning of this chapter that the perceptron structure is ideally suited for such a task. Thus the perceptron output functions simply must express that the class region of a certain class lies left of this and right of that borderline. If the number of basis functions becomes larger, the logical expressions correspondingly become more complicated. The whole structure, however, is able to determine the class regions by their enclosing walls.

Pairwise Borders between Classes

If this is true, it must be quite straightforward to design a two-layer perceptron solving such clear-cut classification tasks as given by the example of (4.35). Since K is the number of classes to be distinguished, the first perceptron layer has to provide $K(K-1)/2$ basis functions, each differentiating between exactly one of the possible pairs of classes. It should be noted that for $K = 10$ the number of hidden nodes comes out to be $M = 45$. This is quite consistent with the number of hidden nodes reported by many experimenters working with numeral recognition with its $K = 10$ classes [KRE1991].

Designing pairwise linear boundaries is an easy task if we know, or estimate from the learning set, the statistical parameters for the K classes $k = 1, \ldots, K$:

$$P_k = \text{a priori probability}$$
$$\boldsymbol{\mu}_k = \text{class-specific mean}$$
$$\mathbf{K}_k = \text{class-specific covariance matrix}$$

In the case of the synthetic example (4.35) considered here we have direct access to these statistical data. In any practical application P_k, $\boldsymbol{\mu}_k$, and $\mathbf{K}_k$ would have to be computed from the learning sample; see Section 4.6.

For each pair j, k of classes a separate linear classification task must be solved. The simplest way to achieve this is to compute the linear regression classifier with

$$\mathbf{x} = \begin{pmatrix} 1 \\ \mathbf{v} \end{pmatrix} \qquad y_{kj} = \begin{cases} 1 & \text{for class } k \\ 0 & \text{for class } j \end{cases} \qquad d_{kj} = \mathbf{a}_{kj}^T \mathbf{x} \tag{7.36}$$

and to use the coefficient vector $\mathbf{a}_{kj}$ as the weight vector of the corresponding hidden node. From the given parameters P_k, $\boldsymbol{\mu}_k$, and $\mathbf{K}_k$ the augmented versions of mean and moment matrix

$$\mathbf{M}_k = E\{\mathbf{x}\mathbf{x}^T | k\} = \begin{pmatrix} 1 & \boldsymbol{\mu}_k^T \\ \boldsymbol{\mu}_k & \mathbf{K}_k + \boldsymbol{\mu}_k \boldsymbol{\mu}_k^T \end{pmatrix} \quad \text{and} \quad \mathbf{m}_k = E\{\mathbf{x} | k\} = \begin{pmatrix} 1 \\ \boldsymbol{\mu}_k \end{pmatrix}$$

are easily computed.

The coefficient vector $\mathbf{a}_{kj}$ of the basis function separating classes k and j is determined by the linear matrix equation (6.20),

$$E\{\mathbf{x}\mathbf{x}^T | k, j\} \mathbf{a}_{kj} = E\{\mathbf{x} y | k, j\}$$

with the right and left side matrices of this linear matrix equation given by

$$E\{\mathbf{x}\mathbf{x}^T|k,j\} = \frac{1}{P_k + P_j}[P_k\mathbf{M}_k + P_j\mathbf{M}_j]$$
$$E\{\mathbf{x}y|k,j\} = \frac{1}{P_k + P_j}P_k\mathbf{m}_k \tag{7.37}$$

Inserting this into the matrix equation to be solved, we arrive at

$$[P_k\mathbf{M}_k + P_j\mathbf{M}_j]\mathbf{a}_{kj} = P_k\mathbf{m}_k \tag{7.38}$$

Therefrom the $K(K-1)/2$ first layer weight vectors $\mathbf{a}_{kj}$ are easily computed.

The linear estimation for d_{kj} for the class k versus class j discrimination is nonlinearly mapped by the sigmoid function into the fuzzy predicate h_{kj},

$$d_{kj} = \mathbf{a}_{kj}^T\begin{pmatrix}1\\ \mathbf{v}\end{pmatrix} \qquad h_{kj} = \sigma(d_{kj}) \tag{7.39}$$

rendering one of the basis functions for polynomial regression.

According to the definition of the target variable y_{kj} (7.36), the basis function $h_{kj}(\mathbf{v})$, which is responsible for separating the two classes k and j, generates the value $0 \Leftrightarrow$ left on the (class j) side and the value $1 \Leftrightarrow$ right on the (class k) side of the k/j-border with a smooth sigmoidal transition between both regions. The slope of the transition can be adjusted to any desired steepness by applying the generalized version (7.5) of the sigmoid function with $\xi = 0$ and a suitably chosen value of ψ.

For the example of (4.35) Fig. 7.16 shows the positions and orientations of the $0 \rightarrow 1$ transition for each of the three basis functions h_1, h_2, and h_3 as computed by (7.39). These fuzzy left/right predicates must be combined into class membership predicates, again in the range of $[0..1]$, by employing the second layer units as threshold logic units expressing the appropriate conjunctions with negated and nonnegated input variables.

The three basis functions represent fuzzy predicates with the following properties:

Basis Function	Separating Class from Class		Class on $1 \Leftrightarrow$ Right Side	Class on $0 \Leftrightarrow$ Left Side
h_1	0	1	0	1
h_2	0	2	0	2
h_3	1	2	1	2

Each of the K class regions is separated from those of the remaining $K-1$ classes by $K-1$ borders. The second layer of this perceptron must therefore perform the logical AND of each $K-1$ input variables for each of the K classes. Obviously, only those basis functions contribute to computing the estimation for class k that are at all concerned with this class. The whole

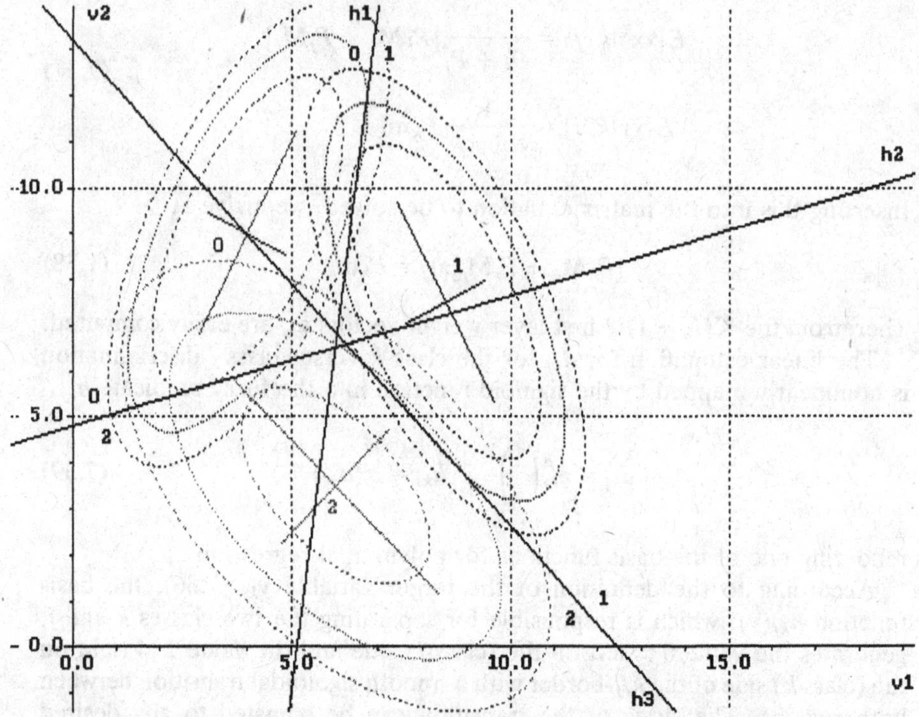

Figure 7.16. View into two-dimensional measurement space of example (4.35). Three class-specific distributions of classes 0, 1, and 2 are represented by their equidensity ellipses as in Fig. 4.10. Solid lines crossing arrangement of ellipses are half-value lines of three pairwise separating basis functions: $h_1 \Leftrightarrow h_{01}$ separating classes 0 and 1, $h_2 \Leftrightarrow h_{02}$ separating classes 0 and 2, and $h_3 \Leftrightarrow h_{12}$ separating classes 1 and 2. The left and right sides are indicated by the corresponding class labels.

construction simply defines the class region of class k as lying on the "correct" side of all pairwise borders.

For the three-class example this simplifies to the AND operation of each two basis functions. The following shows the weights contained in the weight matrix $\mathbf{A}^{\langle 2 \rangle}$ of the second perceptron layer:

Output Function	Classes on 0 ⇔ Wrong Side	Class on 1 ⇔ Correct Side	Logical Expression	$a_{0m}^{\langle 2 \rangle}$	$a_{1m}^{\langle 2 \rangle}$	$a_{2m}^{\langle 2 \rangle}$	$a_{3m}^{\langle 2 \rangle}$
o_0	1, 2	0	$h_1 \wedge h_2$	$-\frac{3}{2}$	1	1	0
o_1	0, 2	1	$\neg h_1 \wedge h_3$	$-\frac{1}{2}$	-1	0	1
o_2	0, 1	2	$\neg h_2 \wedge \neg h_3$	$\frac{1}{2}$	0	-1	-1

Since the nonlinear activation function used in the second layer is again the sigmoid function and not the threshold function of Fig. 7.2, the operations carried out by this layer are not really the logical AND but rather soft-AND functions.

Visualization

Based on the above technique of pairwise separating borders a two-layer perceptron of the same (2, 3, 3) type as in the foregoing section was designed for the example of (4.35). The sigmoid functions of both layers got an arbitrary steepness coefficient $\psi = 5$; see (7.5).

Figure 7.17 shows the resulting class membership functions for classes 0 and 1 that are directly comparable to Fig. 7.13. The set of all three discriminant functions $d_0(\mathbf{v})$, $d_1(\mathbf{v})$, and $d_2(\mathbf{v})$ is shown in Fig. 7.18, to be compared with Fig. 7.14.

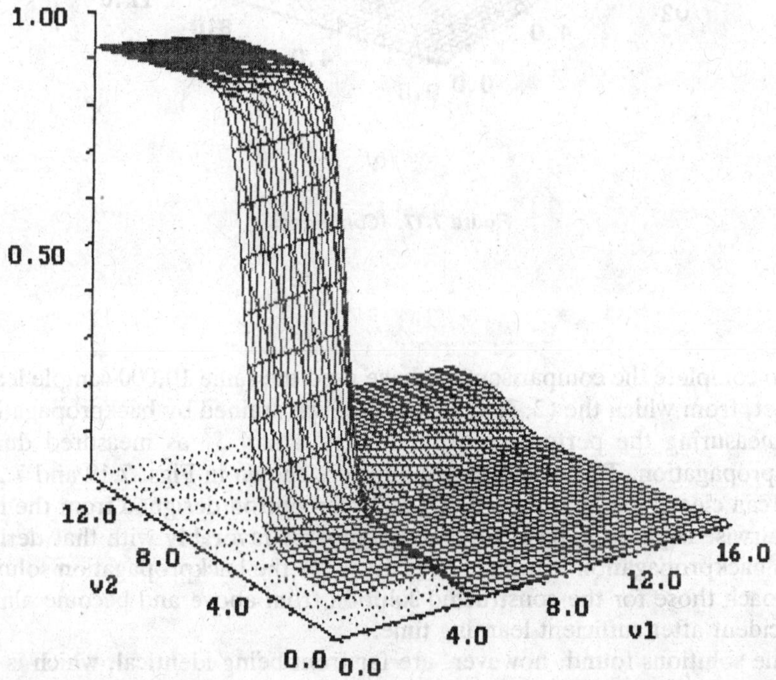

(a)

Figure 7.17. Three-dimensional plot of classes 0 and 1 discriminant functions $d_0(\mathbf{v})$, $d_1(\mathbf{v})$ approximating a posteriori probability functions prob(0|v) of Fig. 4.9 and prob(1|v) gained from (2, 3, 3) perceptron constructed from idea of pairwise separating borders between class regions. Compare with Fig. 7.13.

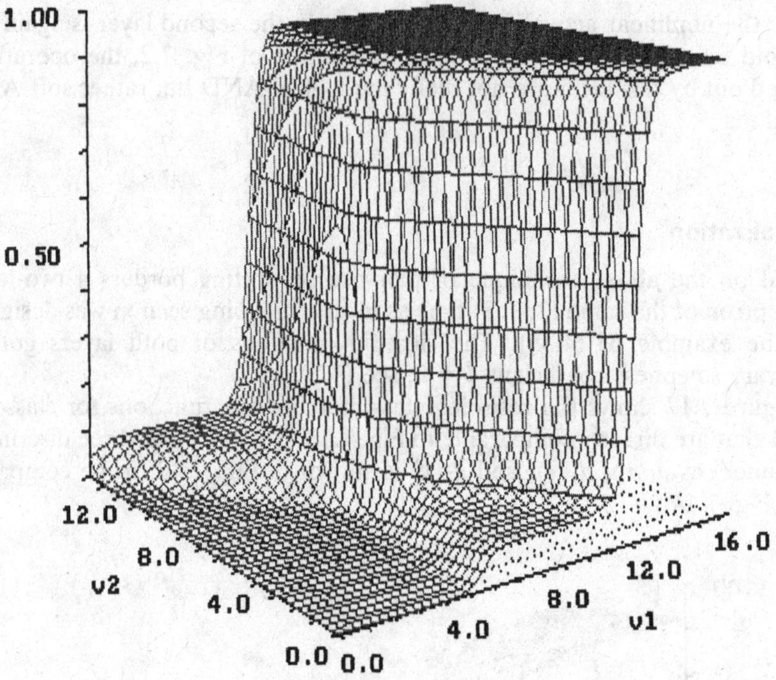

(b)

Figure 7.17. (*Continued*)

To complete the comparisons we have used the same 10,000-sample learning set, from which the (2, 3, 3) perceptron was trained by backpropagation, for measuring the performance parameters ϵ and S^2 as measured during backpropagation. The resulting diagrams are shown in Figs. 7.19 and 7.20.

It can clearly be seen that the (2, 3, 3) perceptron designed from the idea of pairwise separating basis functions compares favorably with that derived from backpropagation learning. The curves for the backpropagation solution approach those for the constructed solution from above and become almost coincident after sufficient learning time.

The solutions found, however, are far from being identical, which is not unlikely to happen since there may exist several local minima with comparable performance into which, depending on the initialization, backpropagation may lead and due to the fact that the constructed solution aims not at an optimum solution but rather at a useful one. These differences become visible in Fig. 7.21, showing the distribution in decision space **D** generated by the (2, 3, 3) perceptron designed from the idea of pairwise borders.

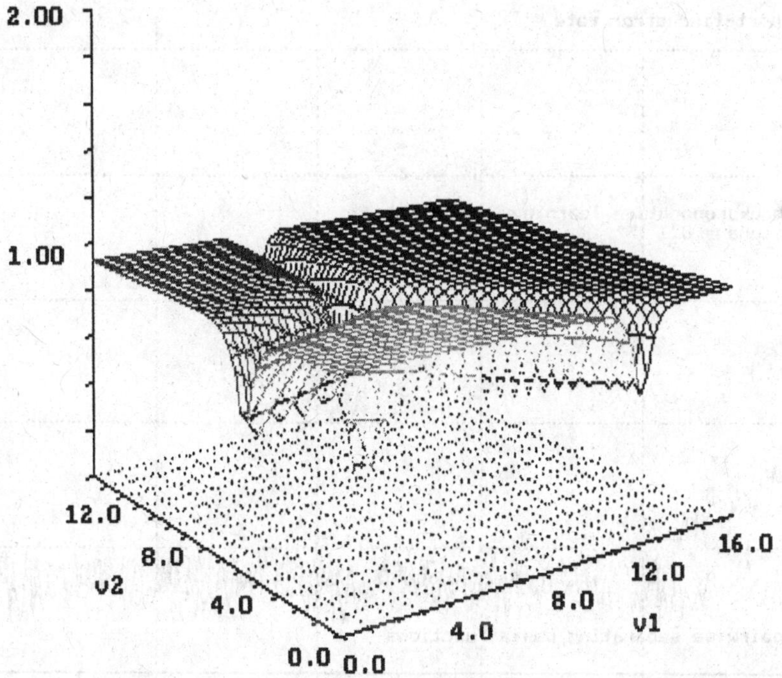

Figure 7.18. Three-dimensional plot of three discriminant functions generated by (2, 3, 3) perceptron constructed from idea of pairwise separating borders between class regions in form of max[$d_0(\mathbf{v})$, $d_1(\mathbf{v})$, $d_2(\mathbf{v})$]. Compare with Fig. 7.14.

7.9 PROPERTIES OF MULTILAYER PERCEPTRON REGRESSION

The multilayer perceptron is a powerful structure for designing functional approximations and shares the property of being a *universal approximator* with the polynomial regression approach provided that neither limitations on the number M of hidden perceptron nodes or limitations on the polynomial degree G are imposed.

Since neither of these requirements will be fulfilled in practice, the question remains of how close we will come to the optimum (Bayes solution) under given restrictions for a given pattern classification task. This question cannot be answered other than empirically by performing classifier adaptation and test. And the answer is valid only for the investigated case.

Besides these general similarities, however, the different approaches must necessarily exhibit certain basic differences that derive from their fundamental design principles.

The most relevant property of multilayer perceptron regression is that the resulting discriminant functions $d_k(\mathbf{v})$ are limited to the range [0 . . 1] due to the sigmoidal mapping of the output values (see Figs. 7.4 and 7.5) resulting in two consequences:

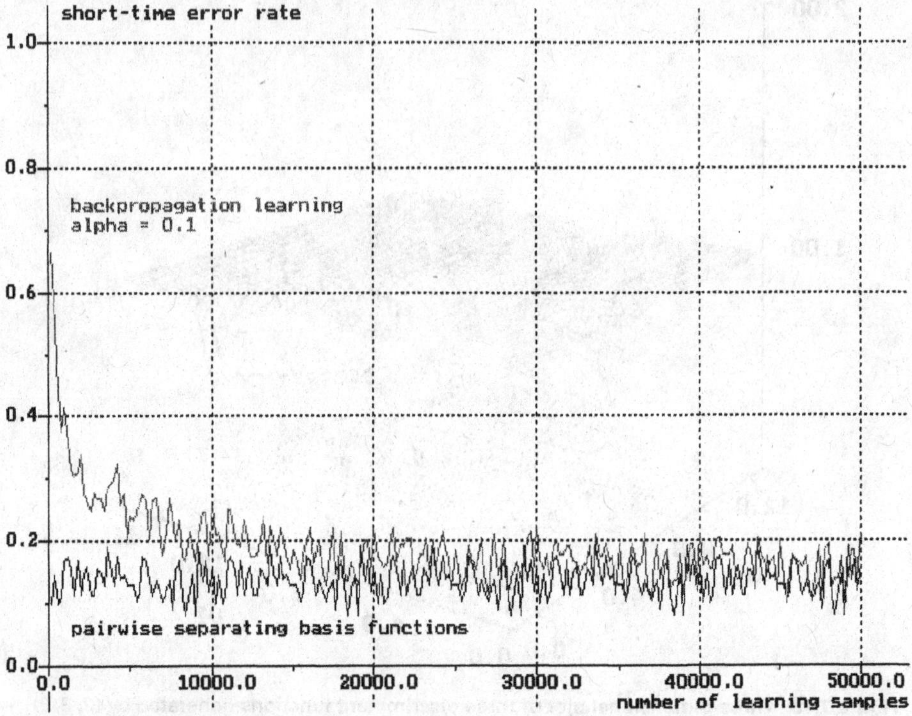

Figure 7.19. Perceptron backpropagation learning compared with construction of pairwise separating basis functions. Abscissa represents five epochs of presentation of 10,000-sample learning set and vertical axis shows short-time error rate ϵ, blockwise measured for every 200 consecutive samples. Curve for $\alpha = 0.1$ is taken from Fig. 7.11. Bottom curve belongs to construction with pairwise borders with learning deactivated.

- Far-off input values, that is, input vectors **v** stemming from regions in measurement space not populated by the learning set, are mapped into discriminant vectors **d** looking as reliable as those from the learning set region.
- The error contribution, that is, the effect on the weight-updating procedure, is maximum for those measurement vectors **v** coming from regions of ambiguous class membership and generating discriminant values $d_k(\mathbf{v}) \approx 0.5$. Pattern vectors classified correctly and with high discriminant values approaching $d_k(\mathbf{v}) = 1.0$ as well as those classified incorrectly but also with high discriminant value for any of the other classes and thus approaching $d_k(\mathbf{v}) = 0.0$ for the own class have vanishing influence on the learning procedure. This is due to the term (7.6),

$$\frac{\partial \sigma}{\partial x} = \sigma(x)[1 - \sigma(x)]$$

occurring in every component of ∇F; see Section 7.6.

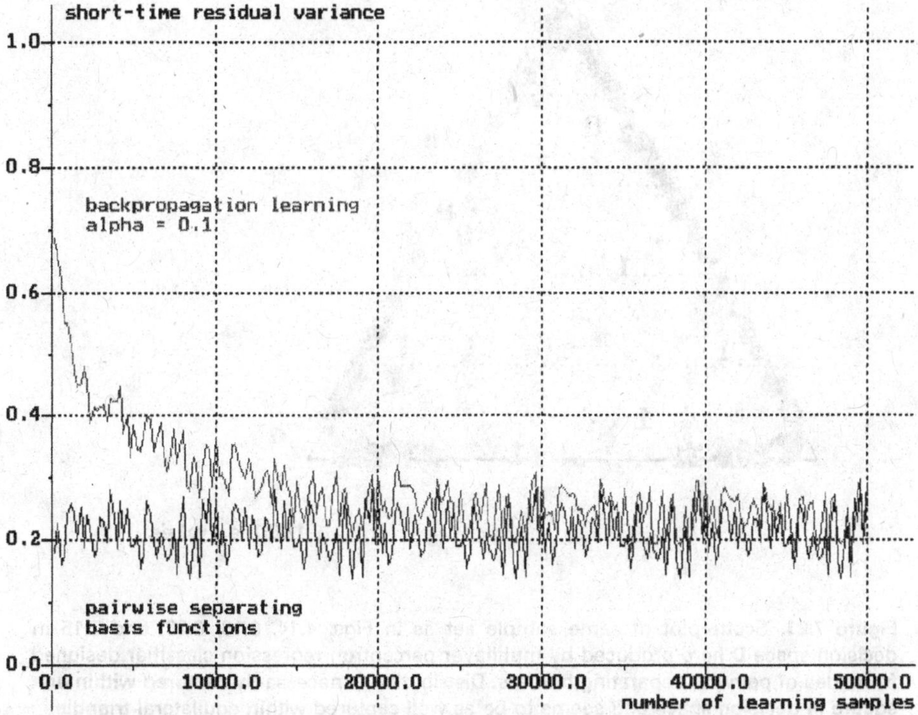

Figure 7.20. Perceptron backpropagation learning compared with construction of pairwise separating basis functions. Abscissa represents five epochs of presentation of 10,000-sample learning set and vertical axis shows short-time residual variance S^2, blockwise measured for every 200 consecutive samples. Curve for $\alpha = 0.1$ is taken from Fig. 7.12. Bottom curve belongs to construction with pairwise borders with learning deactivated.

The first observation makes it difficult to discriminate between pattern vectors **v** belonging to the task at hand and those that are simply garbage patterns. We will return to this problem later in Section 10.2.

The second observation is able to explain the difference between Figs. 6.23 and 7.13. Whereas the polynomial regression classifier (see Fig. 6.14) takes care of those members of class 2 falling behind the class 0 distribution as seen from the class 2 center, the multilayer perceptron classifier ignores the far-off members of class 2 and positions the border between classes 0 and 2 in that region of the measurement space where both distributions meet between their centers of probability mass; see Figs. 4.6 and 4.10.

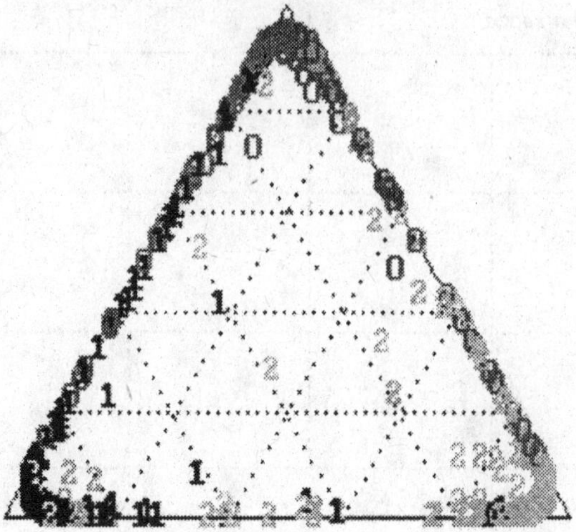

Figure 7.21. Scatterplot of same sample set as in Figs. 4.14, 6.16, 6.26, and 7.15 in decision space **D** here produced by multilayer perceptron regression classifier designed from idea of pairwise separating borders. Distribution is necessarily captured within unit square in decision space and seems to be as well captured within equilateral triangle.

Another peculiarity of the multilayer perceptron already mentioned in Section 7.6 is the problem of symmetries. We have seen that during the learning procedure the different hidden variables take certain roles, for example the role of distinguishing between two certain classes. These roles are not at all predefined but evolve during learning triggered by the incidentalness of the initialization. Basically, each of the hidden variables can take any of the roles. In order to constitute a well-balanced crew, however, no one of the players should take a role already occupied by one of the others.

The notion of symmetry describes the inherent ambiguity of which player may take which role. Since all of them are completely interchangeable, we arrive at a combinatorial manifold of equivalent solutions. Which of these solutions is approached depends on the initialization. There are nontrivial initializations possible representing points of unstable equilibrium that the backpropagation learning rule is unable to leave. A multilayer perceptron initialized with all zero weights, for example, is in such an unstable equilibrium state and will not start learning. Undesired initializations are avoided by starting the learning procedure with random values.

7.10 MODIFICATIONS OF MULTILAYER PERCEPTRON

What we have discussed so far is the multilayer perceptron in its straightforward form. All of the input nodes of each layer are completely connected to all of its output nodes; compare Fig. 7.6. This regular structure allows the design of pattern classifiers with large numbers of weights. A large number of free parameters holds the promise of great flexibility and adaptability but bears the risk of *overfitting* if the number of learning samples does not keep pace with the number of weights.

The effect of overfitting is typically encountered if the learning set size is too small in relation to the number of free parameters: In that case the samples contained in the learning set are perfectly learned, but the classifier renders higher error rates with any test set different from the learning set. Overfitting is not limited to the multilayer perceptron but can be observed with any type of pattern classifier when the learning set is too small to be statistically representative for the task at hand. We will return to this topic in Section 10.5.

In order to counter the risk of overfitting, several variations to the basic concept of multilayer perceptron regression have been proposed with the aim of reducing the number of free parameters without sacrificing the generality of the structure. Among theses ideas are the construction of incomplete networks and weight sharing.

Incomplete Networks

The basic idea of constructing *incomplete networks* is to connect the output nodes of one layer to only a selected subset of its input nodes. Since in most of the applications the measurement data are gained by sampling one- or two-dimensional continuous signals, the components of the input vector **v** own neighborhood relations allowing local neighborhood groups to be defined within the set of measurements. Think, for example, of functions of time such as sampled speech signals or of functions of the two-dimensional plane such as scanned images.

Incomplete networks are then designed by deriving the output variables from only a certain local neighborhood in the set of input variables. This is exemplified in Fig. 7.22 for a single perceptron layer with N input and M output nodes. Depending on the size of the local neighborhood and on the degree of thinning of the output nodes, remarkable reductions in the number of weights can be achieved. Under the name *time delay neural networks* (TDNN) [WAI1989] this technique has found wide distribution in time signal processing, especially in speech recognition. The idea is easily transferred to the processing of images.

The technique of Fig. 7.22 can be applied to the first layer of the multilayer perceptron as well as to any of the subsequent layers. Incomplete networks are often associated with the idea of generating local features from the raw

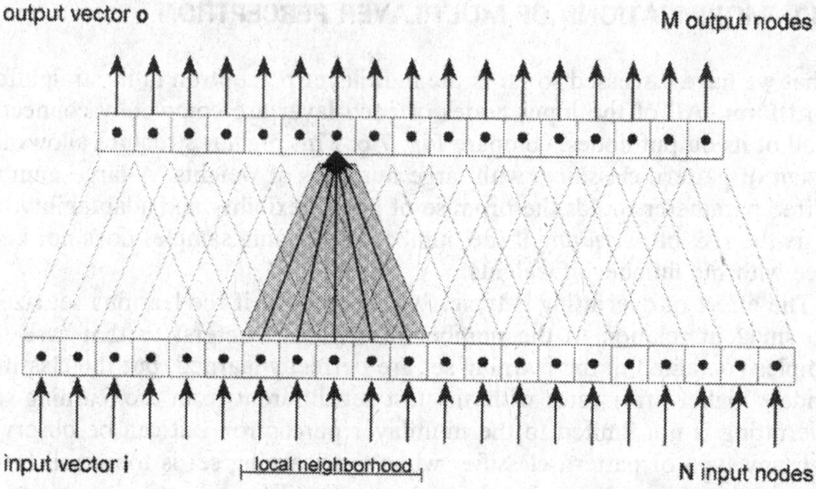

Figure 7.22. Incompletely connected perceptron layer. Each *M* output node has access only to local neighborhood within set of *N* input nodes. Number of weights contained in this layer is thus considerably reduced. Modifications are possible by omitting selected outputs nodes so that overlap of local neighborhood fields is diminished. Same idea can easily be transferred to two-dimensional arrays of input variables as gained from dealing with scanned images.

measurement data; compare Chapter 9. The construction is then motivated by the observation that the sequence of layers generates features having access to local neighborhoods within the set of input variables, whose size increases from layer to layer. The idea is that the features will, with increasing scope, exhibit increasing discriminative power. Following these design conceptions often the number of perceptron layers is chosen larger than 2.

Weight Sharing

Another closely related approach is that of *weight sharing*. The idea of a local neighborhood leads to the grouping of weights. Each of the output variables of the considered perceptron layer is computed from a certain group of its input variables. In terms of deriving features from measurements (see Section 1.4), this can be viewed as computing a feature variable from a certain group of raw measurements.

In general the groups of weights will be different for all of the output nodes, leading to the interpretation that at different positions in the considered perceptron layer different features are computed; compare Fig. 7.22. In certain cases, however, it may be desired that all or at least some the output nodes are looking for the same feature in the input data, which are allowed to occur at different localizations in the input data field. In such a case the arrangement of weights can be forced to be identical for all the feature detectors. Since then the corresponding weights share the same value, this technique is called weight sharing.

The idea of weight sharing can easily be integrated into the weight-updating rule of perceptron learning (7.30) as a kind of additional constraint. After each updating step the weights, which, according to the designer's decision, should be identical, are set equal, for example by averaging and using the average for all of them. This forces the gradient descent search to find a solution obeying the additional constraint.

Modified Optimization Criteria

These considerations show that the gradient descent procedure of multilayer perceptron learning is easily accessible to modifications. As long as the properties of being continuous and differentiable are retained, any criterion function other than *least mean square* can be applied without changing the general structure of the learning procedure. All that then needs to be done is to calculate the partial derivatives with respect to all of the variables contained in the construction in the same way as is carried out in Section 7.6 for the least mean-square criterion function.

This opens a whole field of possibilities, beginning with the use of exponents different from 2 in the criterion function of (3.1) and ending with the use of quite different convex mathematical functions. Another possibility is augmenting the criterion function by introducing supplementary optimization goals.

As an example for this approach, we will consider the goal of keeping the amounts the perceptron weights assume small during learning. What especially shall be avoided is that some of the weights become so large as to dominate the others.

This requirement is easily expressed by

$$G = \sum_{\text{all weights}} [a_{nm}^{\langle h \rangle}]^2 \stackrel{!}{=} \min \tag{7.40}$$

Introducing the additional optimization goal G into the criterion function F_j (7.19) of singular learning together with a weighting coefficient κ, we get

$$F_{j,\text{modified}} = F_j + \kappa G \tag{7.41}$$

The weighting coefficient κ determines the relative importance of G compared with the already existing optimization goal F_j and is deliberately adjusted. The partial derivative of $F_{j,\text{modified}}$ with respect to $a_{nm}^{\langle h \rangle}$ comes out to be

$$\frac{\partial F_{j,\text{modified}}}{\partial a_{nm}^{\langle h \rangle}} = \frac{\partial F_j}{\partial a_{nm}^{\langle h \rangle}} + 2\kappa a_{nm}^{\langle h \rangle} \tag{7.42}$$

Making use of this expression in the learning rule (7.30) of singular backpropagation, we arrive at the modified update rule

$$a_{nm}^{\langle h \rangle} \Leftarrow a_{nm}^{\langle h \rangle} - \alpha \left[\frac{\partial F}{\partial a_{nm}^{\langle h \rangle}} + 2\kappa a_{nm}^{\langle h \rangle} \right] = (1 - 2\alpha\kappa) a_{nm}^{\langle h \rangle} - \alpha \frac{\partial F}{\partial a_{nm}^{\langle h \rangle}} \tag{7.43}$$

which is almost identical to that of (7.30), except for the fact that here each weight is decreased by a certain amount before being updated according to its error contribution.

Comment

We have discussed here only a very few modifications, but even these show that a wide variety of starting points exists for potential variations to be applied to the multilayer perceptron structure and its learning rule.

This openness to modifications has been a major source of inspiration for many experimenters searching for the best of all conceivable structures. It must however be noted that the effect achieved depends on the specific application and its peculiarities. General statements concerning the superiority of a certain approach are hardly obtainable, especially if, which is often the case, the necessary relation between learning and test set size and the number of free parameters is disregarded.

8

RADIAL BASIS FUNCTIONS

The two approaches discussed in Chapters 6 and 7 have, among others, one property in common: Their basis functions are not local but extend across the entire measurement space. In contrast, the radial basis functions approach to be discussed here relies on local basis functions that, due to their inherent design principles, are bound to vanish with increasing distance from their centers in measurement space.

The basic idea is quite simple and straightforward. The learning set {**v**, **y**} is considered to be the sampled version of some continuous function **y**(**v**) that is not explicitly known. What we are looking for is an approximation **d**(**v**) to be constructed from the samples {[**v**, **y**]} and coming close to the true function **y**(**v**).

Think, for a moment, of the extremely simplified case that both variables **v** and **y** are one dimensional. The situation is then rather similar to what we know from one dimensional digital signal processing. Some continuous function $y(v)$ is sampled at regular intervals, and the task to be solved is to produce some reconstruction $d(v)$ of the continuous function from the samples $\{[v, y]\}$ (*support points*). Let us assume that the function $y(v)$ is sampled with high enough sampling frequency. Then the solution is simply to apply an appropriate low-pass filter to the sequence of spikes. Low-pass filtering changes every spike into a point spread function given by the impulse response function of the low-pass filter and renders the approximating smooth function $d(v)$ as the additive superposition of all the smoothed spikes [OPS1975].

This idea can easily be transferred from 1-space into *N*-space. Each of the *J* samples, $j = 1, \ldots, J$, representing spikes with value $\mathbf{y}_j$ at position $\mathbf{v}_j$ in measurement space is replaced by a suitable point spread function $x_j(\mathbf{v})$

vanishing with increasing distance from $\mathbf{v}_j$ weighted with the value $\mathbf{y}_j$ at the position $\mathbf{v}_j$. The linear combination of all point spread functions

$$\mathbf{d}(\mathbf{v}) = \sum_{j=1}^{J} \mathbf{y}_j x_j(\mathbf{v}) \tag{8.1}$$

renders the approximation $\mathbf{d}(\mathbf{v})$.

Besides the difference in dimensions, the situation in measurement space is not as simple as in the signal-processing example. The main complication comes from the fact that sampling here is far from regular and not at all ruled by any theoretically based sampling theorem. We must, instead, cope with random sampling and are never sure that the samples are adequately close to each other.

These complications can be partly countered by letting the coefficients $\mathbf{c}_j$ of the linear combination be free parameters of the construction to be optimized during learning,

$$\mathbf{d}(\mathbf{v}) = \sum_{j=1}^{J} \mathbf{c}_j x_j(\mathbf{v}) \tag{8.2}$$

and preferably by least mean-square optimization.

This kind of approach corresponds to the concept of functional approximation introduced in Chapter 5. Of the two choices—the system of basis functions $x_j(\mathbf{v})$, $j = 1, \ldots, J$, either predetermined (5.3) or themselves dependent on adjustable parameters (5.2)—we will in the following mainly consider the second. This case not only applies to the use of the same point spread function for each of the support points $[v_j, \mathbf{y}_j]$, $j = 1, \ldots, J$, but also comprises the use of differently tailored point spread functions $x_j(\mathbf{v})$ at the different support point positions.

The above equation can be rearranged by combining all of the individual point spread functions $x_j(\mathbf{v})$ into one vector $\mathbf{x}(\mathbf{v})$ and correspondingly all of the column vectors $\mathbf{c}_j$ into one matrix $\mathbf{A}$:

$$\mathbf{x}^T = (x_1 \quad x_2 \quad \cdots \quad x_J) \qquad \mathbf{A}^T = (\mathbf{c}_1 \quad \mathbf{c}_2 \quad \cdots \quad \mathbf{c}_J) \tag{8.3}$$

Doing so, we find then that we arrive at the same general type of estimating function (6.7) thoroughly dealt with in Chapter 6:

$$\mathbf{d}(\mathbf{v}) = \mathbf{A}^T\mathbf{x}(\mathbf{v})$$

However, one small difference should be mentioned. The radial basis function vector $\mathbf{x}(\mathbf{v})$ here does not include a constant term 1, a fact that has certain consequences regarding the properties of the solution: compare Section 6.2. With such a constant term missing in $\mathbf{x}(\mathbf{v})$ the resulting discriminant function $\mathbf{d}(\mathbf{v})$ loses the property of its components summing to 1. Otherwise it would not be possible for $\mathbf{d}(\mathbf{v})$ to collapse completely to $\mathbf{d} \to \mathbf{0}$ in regions of the measurement space far off from the learning sample set.

The approach we have just been following was to establish a least mean-square estimation for $\mathbf{y}$ from $\mathbf{v}$. We know from Chapter 3 that this approach leads us in the context of pattern classification, with $\mathbf{y}$ defined by (1.5) to $\mathbf{d}(\mathbf{v})$ an approximation to $\mathbf{p}$, the *vector of a posteriori probabilities* (3.10).

In the introduction to Chapter 3 we have stated that two different ways are possible to derive estimations for the statistical laws needed for optimum pattern classification: estimates for either the a posteriori probabilities $\text{prob}(\omega|\mathbf{v})$ or the class specific probabilities $\text{prob}(\mathbf{v}|\omega)$. In Chapter 4 we found statistical model fitting by adjusting the parameters of predefined distribution functions to be the adequate technique for estimating class-specific probabilities, and in Chapters 6 and 7 we relied on least mean-square functional approximation for estimating a posteriori probabilities.

The following considerations will show that from the concept of radial basis functions not only estimations for the a posteriori probabilities can be derived but as well estimations for the class-specific probabilities.

The analogy of one-dimensional signal processing provided us with the concept of the point spread function. The single sample $[\mathbf{v}, \mathbf{y}]$ taken from the learning set describes a kind of experience that, strictly speaking, is valid only for that distinct point $\mathbf{v}$ in measurement space for which it was observed. This locally limited validity is by the point spread function carried on into a certain local neighborhood. Thus in a very simple way the effect of interpolation is achieved, limiting at the same time the extrapolating effect in an easily controllable manner. By taking the sum over all the smoothed point functions, the whole approach transforms the sampled representation of a certain function into its smoothed continuous version.

This concept was under the name of Parzen window estimation rather early introduced into pattern recognition ([PAR1962], [DUH1973]). The Parzen window technique uses a Gaussian kernel as the smoothing element. The same idea experiences a kind of rebirth under the label radial basis function approximation.

In the following we will at first look at the techniques of nearest-neighbor and restricted-neighborhood classification from the viewpoint of kernel functions. This will provide us with some insights into understanding what is going on with the radial basis functions concept.

8.1 RELATIONS TO NEAREST-NEIGHBOR AND RESTRICTED-NEIGHBORHOOD TECHNIQUES

The nearest-neighbor principle is one of the most obvious and best studied [DAS1990] techniques for pattern classification. At first glance it seems to have nothing to do with the decision-theoretic approach or with the idea of class-specific and a posteriori probabilities or with the radial basis function concept.

Nearest-neighbor classification simply takes the learning set $\{\mathbf{v}, \mathbf{k}\}$ as a collection of known cases $[\mathbf{v}, k]$ and searches for a given pattern $\mathbf{v}$ to be recognized for the best matching among the precedents $\mathbf{v}_j$. The class label k of the nearest-neighbor $\mathbf{v}_{\mathbf{nearest}}$ is forwarded as the result of the classification.

It must be noted that nearest-neighbor classification needs a metric for measuring distances between the reference vectors $\mathbf{v}_j$ (members of the learning set) and the pattern vector $\mathbf{v}$ to be recognized. Obviously the result depends on the metric chosen. Normally the Euclidean metric is applied,

$$|\mathbf{v} - \mathbf{v}_j|^2 = (\mathbf{v} - \mathbf{v}_j)^T(\mathbf{v} - \mathbf{v}_j) = |\mathbf{v}|^2 - 2\mathbf{v}_j^T\mathbf{v} + |\mathbf{v}_j|^2 \tag{8.4}$$

but depending on the situation, any other metric may be applicable.

Nearest-neighbor classification is a special case of *multireference minimum-distance classification*, the speciality lying in the fact that the whole learning set is used as set of reference vectors.

In terms of everyday commonsense reasoning, nearest-neighbor classification is what we ourselves will do when confronted with unknown situations or an unknown case. We scan our memories for the most similar case and decide in accordance with our past experience. The fact, however, that we need a distance metric for that purpose is not likely to be perceived.

In the field of so-called *machine learning* for expert system applications, nearest-neighbor techniques are known as *case-based reasoning*.

Euclidean One-Nearest-Neighbor Classifier

Minimum Euclidean distance classification divides the whole measurement space into patches, each belonging uniquely to one of the reference vectors $\mathbf{v}_j$. The patch borders are defined by the perpendicular bisectors between neighbored reference points $\mathbf{v}_j$. The situation is illustrated by Fig. 8.1. The concept can, with no fundamental complications, be transferred to higher dimensional spaces [TOU1992]. The resulting patches represent those sections of the measurement space $\mathbf{V}$ having the property that each of their points is closer to the own reference point $\mathbf{v}_j$ than to any of the other $J - 1$ references. A measurement vector $\mathbf{v}$ falling into a certain patch will therefore be classified as a member of the same class k as the reference vector $\mathbf{v}_j$.

Hence, the whole patch receives the label k_j of its reference vector $\mathbf{v}_j$ and becomes thus part of the respective class region. It is useful to consider each patch as a subclass region and the whole class region of a certain class k as the union of all subclass regions with the label k.

We have, throughout this book, made intensive use of the concept of functional approximation. The idea was that pattern classification essentially requires the design of a discriminant function $\mathbf{d}(\mathbf{v})$ capable of mapping any

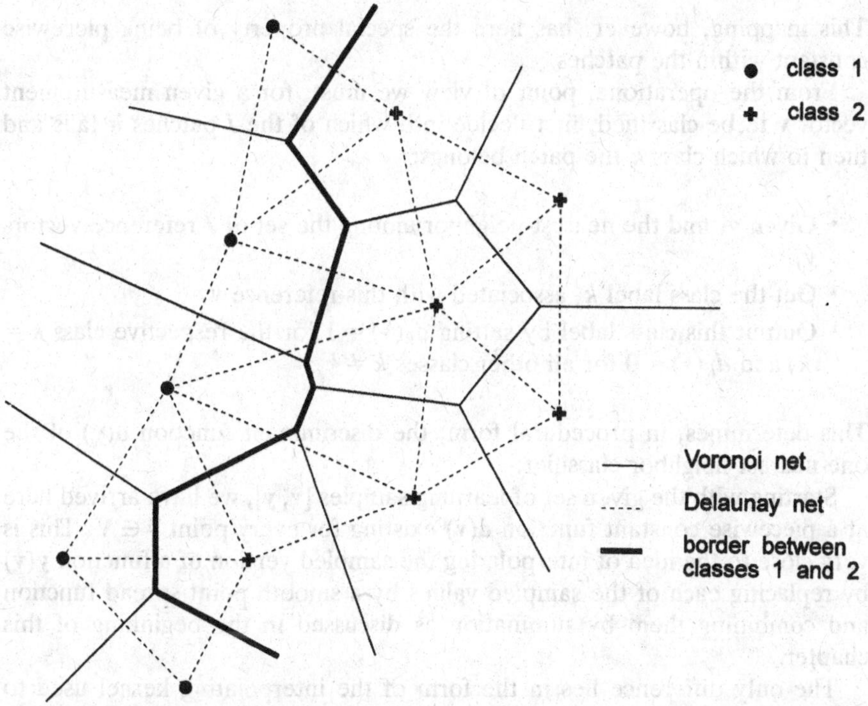

Figure 8.1. Nearest-neighbor classification in two-dimensional measurement space. Reference points become corner points of large number of small triangles spanned by each reference point and its two nearest neighbors. Resulting network of triangles, in two dimensions, is called *Delaunay net* and the whole procedure *Delaunay triangularization.* Perpendicular to triangle's edges run borders of polygonal patches delimiting local neighborhood of each reference point $\mathbf{v}_j$. Resulting network of polygons is called *Voronoi net.* If as in example shown several neighbored references carry same class label, class border follows selection of Voronoi net line segments and becomes itself an irregular polygon.

given measurement vector $\mathbf{v}$ into the corresponding discriminant vector $\mathbf{d}$ from which the class label k could be easily be derived; see Fig. 1.5.

The same viewpoint of functional approximation can be applied here, and the facts concerning the class membership of the regions and subregions can be expressed by a function $d_k(\mathbf{v})$ having the value 1 for points $\mathbf{v} \in \mathbf{V}$ belonging to patches being subclass regions of class k and the value 0 for patches belonging to any other class other than k:

$$d_k(\mathbf{v}) = \begin{cases} 1 & \text{for } \mathbf{v} \in \text{patch belonging to class } k \\ 0 & \text{otherwise} \end{cases} \tag{8.5}$$

Since we have K of these class membership functions, we arrive at a mapping $\mathbf{v} \rightarrow \mathbf{d}$ comparable to the mappings $\mathbf{d}(\mathbf{v})$ dealt with in the foregoing chapters.

This mapping, however, has here the special property of being piecewise constant within the patches.

From the operational point of view we must, for a given measurement vector $\mathbf{v}$ to be classified, first decide into which of the J patches it falls and then to which class k the patch belongs:

- Given $\mathbf{v}$, find the nearest-neighbor among the set of J reference vectors $\mathbf{v}_j$.
- Get the class label k_j associated with this reference $\mathbf{v}_j$.
- Output this class label by setting $d_k(\mathbf{v}) = 1$ for the respective class $k = k_j$ and $d_k(\mathbf{v}) = 0$ for all other classes $k \neq k_j$.

This determines, in procedural form, the discriminant function $\mathbf{d}(\mathbf{v})$ of the one-nearest-neighbor classifier.

Starting with the given set of learning samples $[\mathbf{v}, \mathbf{y}]$, we have arrived here at a piecewise constant function $\mathbf{d}(\mathbf{v})$ existing for every point $\mathbf{v} \in \mathbf{V}$. This is very close to the idea of interpolating the sampled version of a function $\mathbf{y}(\mathbf{v})$ by replacing each of the sampled values by a smooth point spread function and combining them by summation as discussed in the beginning of this chapter.

The only difference lies in the form of the interpolating kernel used to replace the sample $[\mathbf{v}_j, \mathbf{y}_j]$. The kernel function is here piecewise constant over the polygonal domain determined by the corresponding Voronoi cell and has the value $\mathbf{y}_j$ inside the patch and the value $\mathbf{0}$ outside; see Fig. 8.2. The kernel functions of different patches have different shapes since the underlying patches in general are different polygons.

The idea of functional approximation contains the summation, or linear

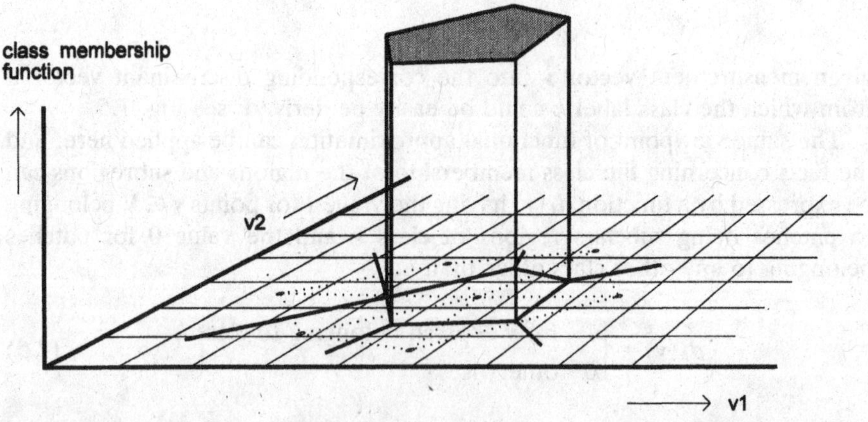

Figure 8.2. Polygon-shaped kernel function belonging to nearest-neighbor approach. Kernel function, centered at $\mathbf{v}_j$, has only two values, **0** outside patch and $\mathbf{y}_j$ inside.

combination, of all the individual basis functions. In terms of the radial basis functions approach this means the summation of all the individual point spread functions. The same summation must be applied to the J piecewise constant kernel functions belonging to the J patches of nearest-neighbor classification. The summation combines all of the J local functions to one general function $\mathbf{d}(\mathbf{v})$. Since the kernel functions are mutually orthogonal, the summation is simply the composition of the J local kernels.

The concept of one-nearest-neighbor classification is easily understood and easy to apply to any kind of classification task. If no limits are set to the number of reference points, one-nearest-neighbor classification comes close to the optimum in performance (the Bayes classifier), whereby the 1NN error rate is bounded to be

$$\epsilon_{\text{Bayes}} \leq \epsilon_{1NN} \leq 2\epsilon_{\text{Bayes}}$$

([DUH1973], [FUK1985]). This makes it a valuable reference for assessing the degree of difficulty of any given practical recognition task.

From a practical point of view, however, it is quite obvious that use of the entire, normally large, learning set $[\mathbf{v}_j, \mathbf{y}_j]$, $j = 1, \ldots, J$, as the set of reference vectors is likely to be oversized. Actually, we need only those reference points close to the class boundaries since all the others do not have any impact on the borderline position and orientation.

Indeed, proper selection of reference points from the given learning set can reduce the computational effort for any classification scheme relying on a set of support points for functional approximation. Generally, for interpolating sampled functions the distances between support points may be larger in flat regions and must be smaller in regions of higher gradients of the function to be approximated.

Comments

Even if the Euclidean one-nearest-neighbor classifier has a number of convincing advantages, it is not often used in practical application.

The pros are as follows: It is powerful, easy to implement, and ready to work whenever the set of references is loaded. It can easily be parallelized since the J distances between the input vector $\mathbf{v}$ and the J references $\mathbf{v}_j$ can be computed in parallel.

The main con is being lavish with the computational resources. In regions of penetrating class-specific probabilities prob(k|$\mathbf{v}$) the one-nearest-neighbor classifier establishes countless small patches belonging alternately to competing classes with increasing number of references.

The reason for this behavior lies in the fact that in the one-nearest-neighbor classifier the step of estimating prob(k|$\mathbf{v}$) is completely omitted and instead the all-or-nothing decision function (8.5) is directly computed;

compare Fig. 1.4. Hence any ambiguity of the decision is hidden behind a kind of arbitrariness leading to waste in computational effort.

Restricted-Neighborhood Classifier

A pattern classification technique closely related to nearest-neighbor classification is *restricted-neighborhood classification*, of which the restricted Coulomb energy network (RCE) is a prominent example [RCE1982].

The idea here is to represent the distribution $\{\mathbf{v}, k\}$ by a smaller number L of reference vectors $\mathbf{v}_l$. For the pattern $\mathbf{v}$ to be recognized, all distances between $\mathbf{v}$ and all of the $\mathbf{v}_l$ are computed in the same way as for the nearest-neighbor classifier. Different from the nearest-neighbor case, the distances are not searched for the minimum, instead, whenever $\mathbf{v}$ falls close enough to one of the references $\mathbf{v}_l$, it is accepted as a member of the respective class.

What is close enough is determined by a suitable threshold that is not necessarily the same for all of the references. The set of references is gained from the learning set by a clustering procedure that introduces a new cluster when a learning sample is not accepted by the existing ones and reduces the size of an existing cluster when a learning sample is erroneously accepted by a cluster not belonging to the correct class.

In measurement space each reference determines a hyperspherical neighborhood centered at the reference point and with the radius given by the acceptance threshold (Fig. 8.3). The distribution $\{\mathbf{v}|k\}$ as defined by the learning set is completely covered by the acceptance regions of its respective set of references. The spheres (in two dimensions circles) belonging to different classes may touch but do not overlap.

At the expense of an especially with higher dimensions fast increasing number L of references the whole construction is capable of representing rather complicated distributions in measurement space and has the special property of generating closed class regions. Whenever a pattern vector $\mathbf{v}$ from a far-off region in measurement space is observed (garbage pattern; compare Section 10.2), it will not be accepted. Reject regions also are likely to occur between the class regions.

From a statistical point of view the concept of restricted neighborhood classification can be viewed as generating a binary approximation for $\text{prob}(\mathbf{v}|k)$ rendering logical predicates "Accepted as member of class k" for the K classes to be distinguished. This technique cares only for class regions and has no provisions for overlapping class-specific probabilities $\text{prob}(\mathbf{v}|k)$ that are likely to happen in many practical classification tasks. In regions in measurement space with penetrating class-specific distributions a mixture of smaller acceptance spheres for the competing classes will emerge. In this aspect the restricted-neighborhood classifier behaves just as the one-nearest-neighbor classifier.

In terms of functional approximation the interpolation properties of re-

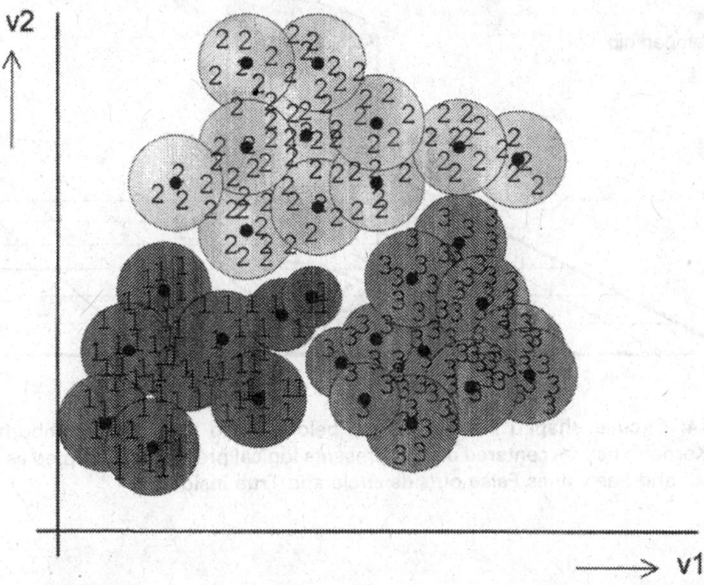

Figure 8.3. Subdivision of measurement space into class regions and reject region (the universe of everything else) by restricted neighborhood technique. Class regions generated by overlapping circular (in the general case hyperspherical) acceptance regions, each determined by one of the L reference vectors together with corresponding acceptance radius.

stricted-neighborhood classification can be visualized similar to Fig. 8.2. The point spread function is here two valued, as in the case of nearest-neighborhood classification, and provides the value False outside and the value True inside the circular region around the reference vector position $\mathbf{v}_l$; see Fig. 8.4.

The combination of the individual contributions to the overall class membership function can in this case not be performed by linear combination but must be accomplished by the logical operation Boolean OR. This operation, however, is easily implemented by linear threshold logic (compare Section 7.1 and especially Fig. 7.2) and turns out to be again a summation followed by the nonlinear operation of thresholding at a suitable level.

The resulting procedure can be represented in the form of a neural network comparable to Figs. 6.1, 6.2, and 7.6, as shown in Fig. 8.5. To each of the L references $\mathbf{v}_l$ corresponds a distance-measuring unit. The dominant operation in computing the Euclidean distances between $\mathbf{v}$ and $\mathbf{v}_l$ is calculating the scalar product $\mathbf{v}_l^T\mathbf{v}$ between both vectors; compare (8.4). Additionally the two expressions $|\mathbf{v}|^2$ and $|\mathbf{v}_l|^2$ have to be calculated. Of these $|\mathbf{v}|^2$ is independent of l and does not influence the decision, if additionally all

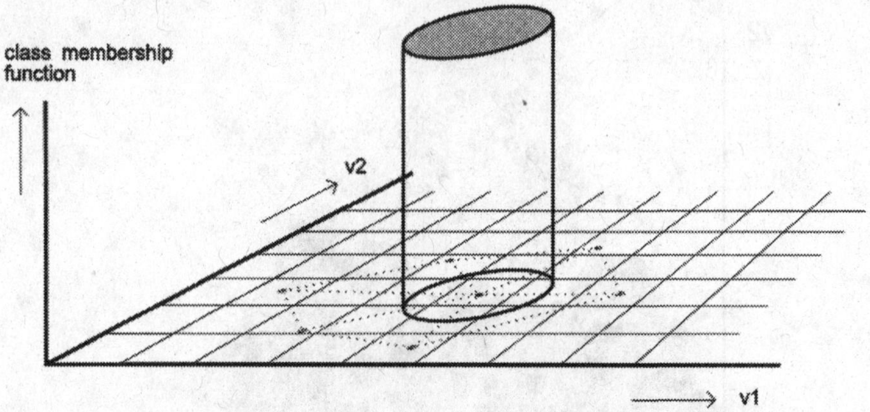

Figure 8.4. Circular shaped kernel function belonging to restricted neighborhood approach. Kernel function, centered at $\mathbf{v}_l$, represents logical predicate "Accepted as member of class k" and has values False outside circle and True inside.

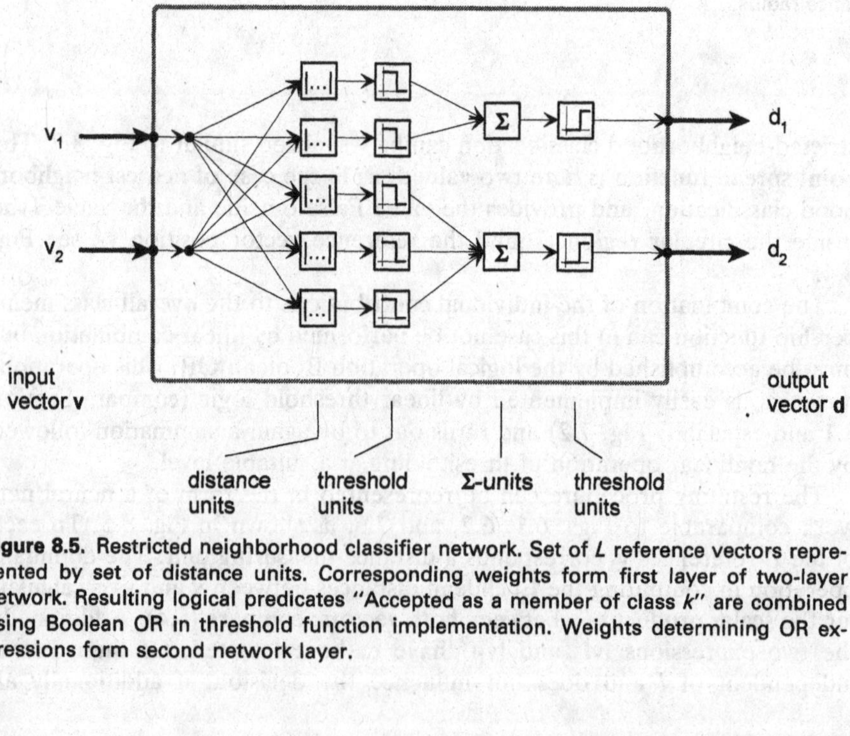

Figure 8.5. Restricted neighborhood classifier network. Set of L reference vectors represented by set of distance units. Corresponding weights form first layer of two-layer network. Resulting logical predicates "Accepted as a member of class k" are combined using Boolean OR in threshold function implementation. Weights determining OR expressions form second network layer.

reference vectors $\mathbf{v}_l$ have the same magnitude both terms $|\mathbf{v}|^2$ and $|\mathbf{v}_l|^2$ can be ignored. This situation occurs, for example, if $\mathbf{v}$ and $\mathbf{v}_l$ are binary valued and their components are represented by $\{-1, +1\}$, which is always possible if they are binary. The distance units are followed by threshhold units rendering a value representing True (normally 1) if the distance is less than the threshold and another value (normally 0) otherwise.

Both functions—distance measuring based on the scalar product, with the necessary completions for computing the Euclidean distance, and thresholding—are just what the model neuron of Section 7.1 does; compare (7.1). It should be noted that regardless of how difficult and computation intensive the distance-measuring procedure may be, it has become usual to also call such a distance-measuring unit an artificial neuron.

Euclidean *k*-Nearest-Neighbor Classifier

Both the one-nearest-neighbor classifier and the restricted-neighborhood classifier of the preceding sections have the property of rendering hard decisions. A given measurement vector $\mathbf{v}$ of unknown class membership is uniquely assigned to one certain class $\hat{k}$. Any indication of whether this decision was made in an ambiguous or in a clear situation is totally suppressed. This is not the adequate reaction for most of the pattern classification applications.

The concept of nearest-neighbor classification, however, can easily be generalized to provide this kind of information. This is illustrated by Fig. 8.6. The technique is known under the name of *k*-nearest-neighbor classification [DUH1973]. In order to avoid confusion with k, the class label, and K, the number of classes, as consistently used throughout this book, we will in the following use the slightly deviating denotation of Q-nearest-neighbor classification.

The Q-nearest neighbor technique renders a local estimate $\mathbf{d}(\mathbf{v})$ for the vector $\mathbf{p}(\mathbf{v})$ of a posteriori probabilities

$$\mathbf{d}(\mathbf{v}) = \frac{1}{Q} \sum_{q=1}^{Q} \mathbf{y}_{Q\text{-nearest among references}} \tag{8.6}$$

valid at position $\mathbf{v}$ in measurement space and directly to be applied in the decision rules of Chapter 2.

The parameter to be determined is the adequate size of the local neighborhood in terms of the number Q of neighbors to be considered. With too small a value of Q we get unreliable results, but increasing Q destroys the locality of the estimation since also the more far-off reference vectors must be taken into account, if not at the same time the reference set size is increased such that the geometric size of the neigborhood region remains essentially unchanged. Both measures increase the computational burden. In practical application, therefore, it is necessary to find a workable compromise.

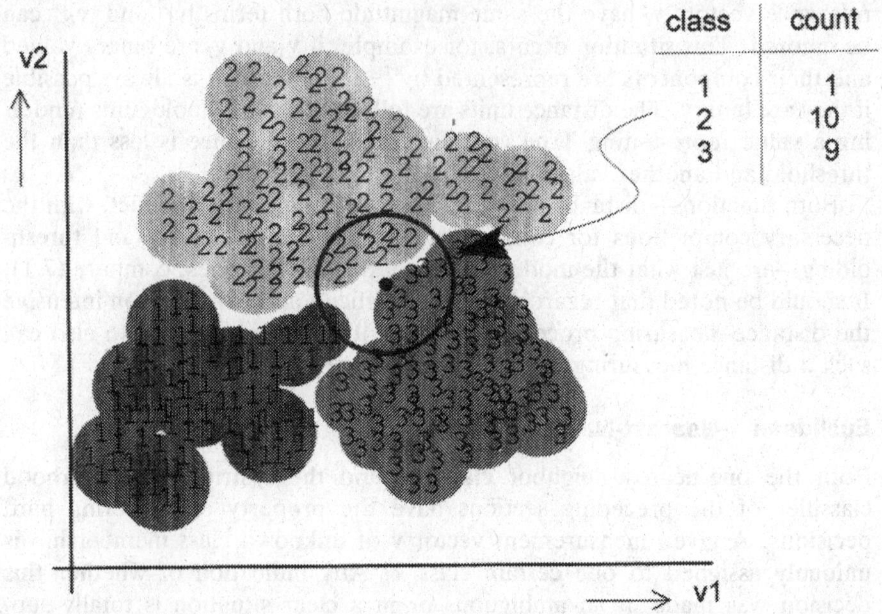

Figure 8.6. The Q-nearest neighbor classifier, providing local estimate for a posteriori probabilities prob(k|**v**). For this purpose spherical neighborhood is determined around given point **v**, marked by black dot. Size of this neighborhood is chosen such that it contains exactly Q nearest neighbors. A a posteriori probability prob(k|**v**) is approximated by counting numbers of representatives of different classes within this neighborhood. In this case we find estimated vector of a posteriori probabilities $\mathbf{d}(\mathbf{v}) = (0.05\ \ 0.50\ \ 0.45)^T$.

A modification is achieved if a weighted form of averaging is used instead of (8.6) giving less influence to the more distant of the Q neighbors and strenghtening the impact of the first nearest neighbor. However, what seems to be a fairly reasonable approach bears the risk of impeding the estimation of $\mathbf{p}(\mathbf{v})$ in those regions of the measurement space where the class-specific distributions penetrate and reference points from different classes occur intermixed. Here the dominating influence of the nearest neighbor counteracts the process of averaging.

Seen from the viewpoint of functional approximation, a peculiarity of nearest-neighbor classification is that the estimating function $\mathbf{d}(\mathbf{v})$ gained from the set of reference vectors is only implicitly determined. For every input vector $\mathbf{v}$ it must be computed from the Q nearest neighbors, and these have first to be searched and found.

8.2 CLUSTERING

Proper selection of reference points is crucial for all of the multireference classifiers discussed in this chapter: nearest-neighbor classifier, restricted-neigborhood classifier, and those derived from the more general concept of radial basis function approximation.

Selection of references from the learning set is a clustering problem, and clustering has a whole area of specific problems and techniques ([BOC1974]), [SPA1983]).

In the context of this chapter, finding a suitable set of reference points is only one of the problems to be solved. The parallel problems are how to determine suitable kernel functions and how to combine them into the final discriminant function. Following the nearest-neighbor and the restricted-neighborhood approaches, some of these problems are implicitly solved as being integral parts of the respective procedure. However, for the general approach of radial basis function approximation these problems must be explicitly solved.

One possibility to tackle the task of reference selection is to define a comprehensive overall functional approximation problem and to treat the number and positions of the references, the shapes of the interpolating kernels, and the coefficients of the linear combination altogether as free parameters of the construction to be optimized by some kind of steepest descent minimum search [POG1989]: compare (5.2).

Another possibility is to separate the two steps of reference selection and classifier design. This leads to the *clustering* approach.

The learning set describes how the probability masses of the K classes to be distinguished are distributed in measurement space for the classification problem at hand. The learning set is assembled by blindly collecting samples $[\mathbf{v}, \mathbf{y}]$ according to the simple rule the more, the better. What we are looking for, however, is a much more economic description of the situation.

The idea is to come to a representation of the probability distributions that is a kind of approximately equidistant sampling of that region in measurement space, which is populated by members of the learning set. We do not need reference points in empty regions or an abundance of references in densely populated parts.

These requirements coincide with what is the goal of *vector quantization*, where a continuous, normally higher dimensional, vector space is to be partitioned into a number of in general irregular quantization intervals such that any vector $\mathbf{v}$ occurring from a stochastic pattern source with given but unknown probability distribution prob($\mathbf{v}$) is mapped into the centroid $\mathbf{v}_l$ of its respective quantization interval and the least mean-square quantization error $E\{|\mathbf{v} - \mathbf{v}_l|^2\}$ is minimum [LBG1980].

The quantization intervals of vector quantization become the patches of nearest-neighbor classification and their centroids the references for which we are looking. The whole procedure results in the partition of the given learning set into subsets and thus in a decomposition of the given distribution into component distributions. Applying comparably simple statistical models to represent the component distributions the complete distribution can be approximately reconstructed from its components by appropriate linear combination.

Depending on the objectives we are pursuing, we can make use of just the set reference points gained from the clustering procedure and the statistical parameters that describe the component distributions.

Clustering procedures suitable for the task of vector quantization should exhibit three properties: The dimensionality of the subspace spanned by the reference vectors to be determined should not be limited in advance; there should be no risk of generating dead clusters, initialized at the start of the procedure or anywhere in between but then remaining empty; and they should work also for large sizes of the learning set.

Vector Quantization Approach

An especially useful technique is illustrated by Figs. 8.7–8.10. The procedure divides the given learning sample in a sequence of steps into subsets corresponding to the clusters for which we are looking.

Each of the clusters is represented by two different reference points serving different purposes, the *seed point* and the *centroid*.

The seed point is needed for deciding which of the points that are members of the overall learning set belong to the considered cluster. They serve as the reference points for a conventional minimum-distance classification procedure, whereby a suitable distance metric is employed, be it Euclidean or not.

The centroid is the mean $\boldsymbol{\mu}_l$ of the set of points actually belonging to the considered cluster. Additionally and parallel to the mean $\boldsymbol{\mu}_l$, the covariance matrix $\mathbf{K}_l$ can be computed for the lth cluster.

The clustering procedure is done in steps. In each step the whole learning set is worked through and each sample is associated to the nearest already existing seed point (in terms of the metric used). From the statistical parameters gained for each cluster a decision is derived about whether to split the present cluster or leave it unsplit. In case of splitting two new seed points are generated directly neighbored to the present cluster mean. Otherwise the cluster mean itself becomes the new seed point. The splitting process is controlled by a suitable threshold ClustThrsh.

The procedure starts with the measurement space origin as the first seed point, resulting in the entire learning set as the first cluster. This is then recursively split into child clusters until no further splittings occur. Due to replacement of the given cluster seed point by the present centroid, unsplit clusters move in the direction of increasing probability density in measurement space until an overall equilibrium is reached. The procedure stops when no more splittings and movements happen.

The process of cluster splitting is controlled by the present cluster size measured in terms of the variance $\text{var}\{\mathbf{v}|l\} = \text{trace}[\mathbf{K}_l]$ of that cluster. Splitting occurs only if

$$\sigma_l = \sqrt{\text{var}\{\mathbf{v}|l\}} > \text{ClustThrsh} \tag{8.7}$$

Generation of new seed points can be accomplished in the simplest case by adding and subtracting a small random vector **r** to the cluster centroid,

$$\mathbf{s} = \boldsymbol{\mu} \pm \mathbf{r} \tag{8.8}$$

or more effectively by using the direction of the eigenvector corresponding to the largest eigenvalue of $\mathbf{K}_l$ for generating the new seed points. Positioning the new seed point in close proximity to the present cluster centroid results in splitting the existing cluster cell without affecting the others. The number of resulting clusters is not bound to be a power of 2 but evolves from the specific parameter settings.

To illustrate this technique, we use again the two-dimensional example of (4.35). What shall be shown here is how the vector quantization procedure treats a given distribution of points in 2-space. The example distribution should not be overly regular. Therefore, by ignoring the class labels, we have formed the union of the three class-specific subsets of (4.35) and taken

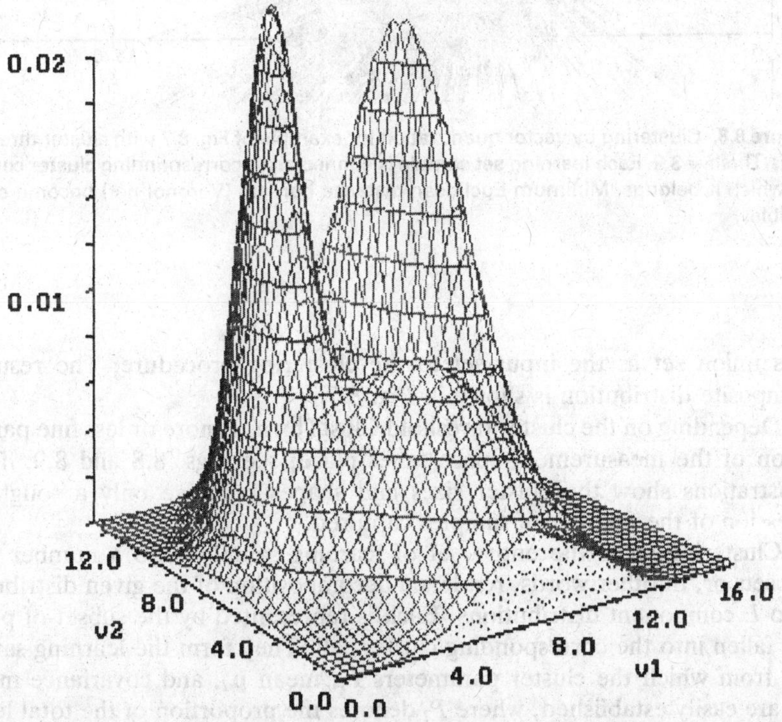

Figure 8.7. Composite distribution illustrating clustering procedure. From this distribution 10,000 samples are drawn as learning set and used for the following exercises with ClustThrsh = 3.2, 1.6.

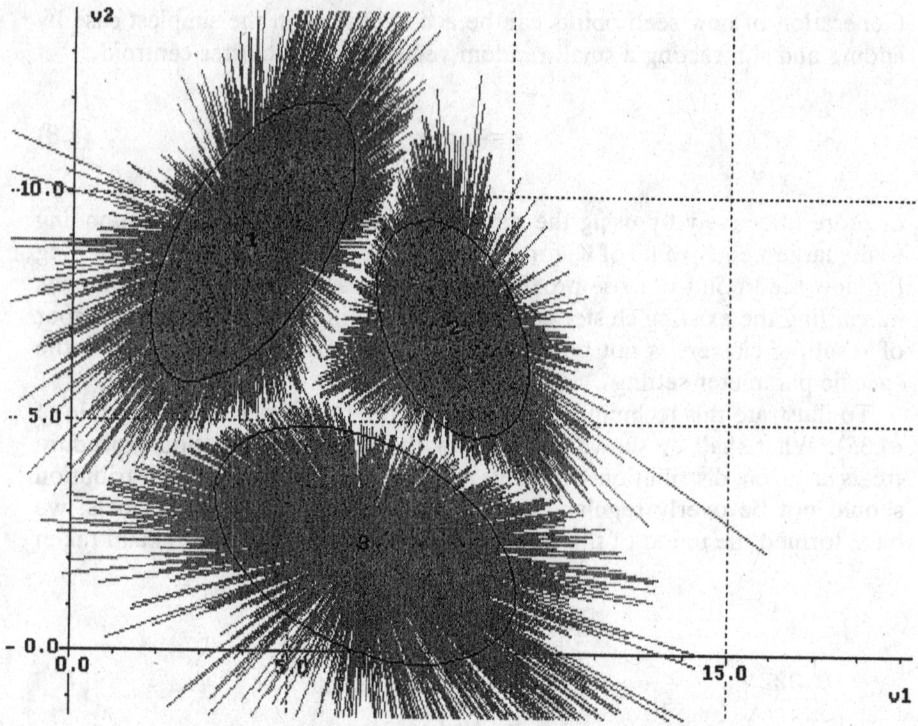

Figure 8.8. Clustering by vector quantization for example of Fig. 8.7 with cluster threshold ClustThrsh = 3.2. Each learning set sample is connected to corresponding cluster centroid to which it belongs. Minimum Euclidean distance borders (Voronoi net) become clearly visible.

this union set as the input set to the clustering procedure. The resulting composite distribution is shown in Fig. 8.7.

Depending on the cluster threshold ClustThrsh, a more or less fine parcellation of the measurement space takes place; see Figs. 8.8 and 8.9. These illustrations show the cluster sizes and shapes but give only a rough impression of the number of samples captured.

Clustering splits the entire set of learning samples into a number L of subsets or, in other words, renders a decomposition of the given distribution into L component distributions. Each is represented by the subset of points set fallen into the corresponding cluster cell. They form the learning sample set from which the cluster parameters P_l, mean $\boldsymbol{\mu}_l$, and covariance matrix $\mathbf{K}_l$ are easily established, where P_l denotes the proportion of the total learning sample captured by the lth cluster.

The concept of decomposed distribution allows us to turn the tables and to reconstruct the original (decomposed) distribution from the component

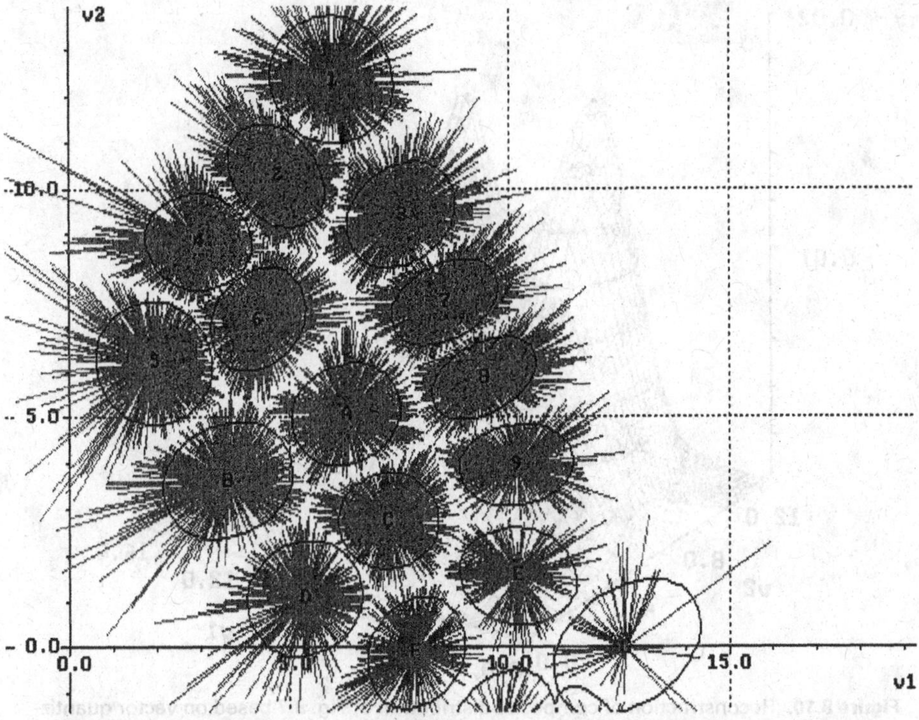

Figure 8.9. Clustering by vector quantization for example of Fig. 8.7 with cluster threshold ClustThrsh = 1.6. Each learning set sample is connected to corresponding cluster centroid to which it belongs. Network of minimum Euclidean distances borders (Voronoi net) becomes clearly visible.

distributions. For this purpose we need a suitable statistical model to represent each of the L component distributions.

A reasonable choice is the normal distribution with parameters given by the cluster parameters mean $\boldsymbol{\mu}_l$ and covariance matrix $\mathbf{K}_l$ of the lth cluster. The L component distribution functions go into a linear combination with weights P_l. The whole procedure renders a useful approximation to prob($\mathbf{v}$), as shown in Fig. 8.10.

The individual distribution prob($\mathbf{v}|l$) representing the lth cluster cell is, depending on the present size of the cluster cell, a more or less small section taken from the wider overall distribution. As a rule, it will not be especially close to the normal distribution since this distribution prob($\mathbf{v}|l$) will be sharply cut off at the cell boundary. Fitting a normal distribution to such an empirical distribution based on the first- and second-order statistical moments will render too slim a model function. We compensated this effect by increasing the measured standard deviations by a certain factor, effectively by multiplying the empirical covariance matrix with the square of this factor.

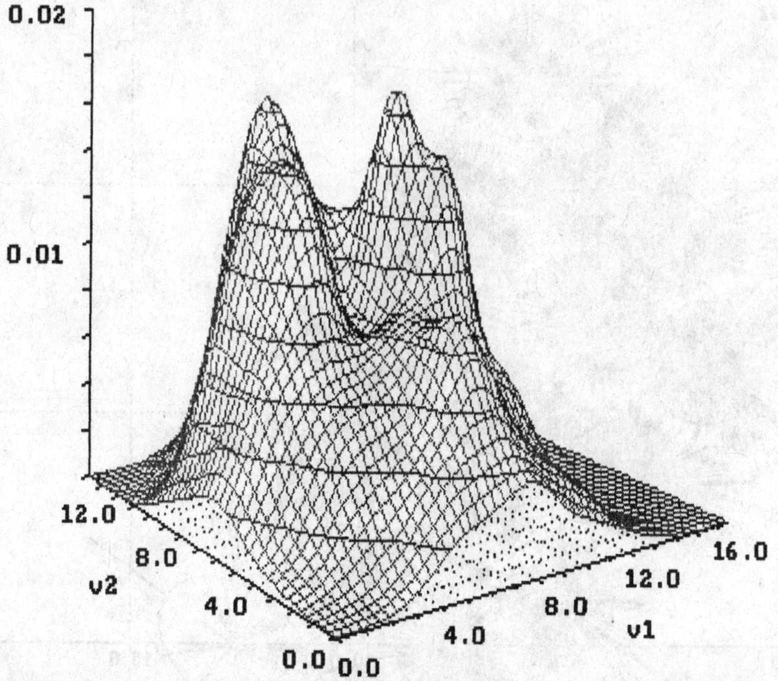

Figure 8.10. Reconstruction of composite distribution of Fig. 8.7 based on vector quantization clustering as shown on Fig. 8.9. In order to come to a smooth reconstruction, measured standard deviations are increased by factor of 1.5. Result resembles reasonably well distribution of Fig. 8.7.

It should be noted that the objective of vector quantization was not to find out which would be the simplest model describing a given statistical situation but rather to provide a partition of the vector space into patches small enough to meet the mean-square reconstruction error requirements but only in those regions of the space where pattern vectors occur at all.

Finding the simplest model is another challenging task and should, ideally, in the case considered here, come out with the three component distributions that make up the composite distribution of Fig. 8.7. Note that the decomposition result of Fig. 8.8 fairly well resembles the three class-specific distributions of the pattern source (4.35).

8.3 RADIAL BASIS FUNCTION APPROXIMATIONS TO prob(v|*k*)

The considerations of the foregoing section led us to a technique of approximating an unknown probability function prob(**v**) from a given learning set that can be viewed as the combination of histogramming and smoothing.

The histogram is established by first partitioning the whole measurement

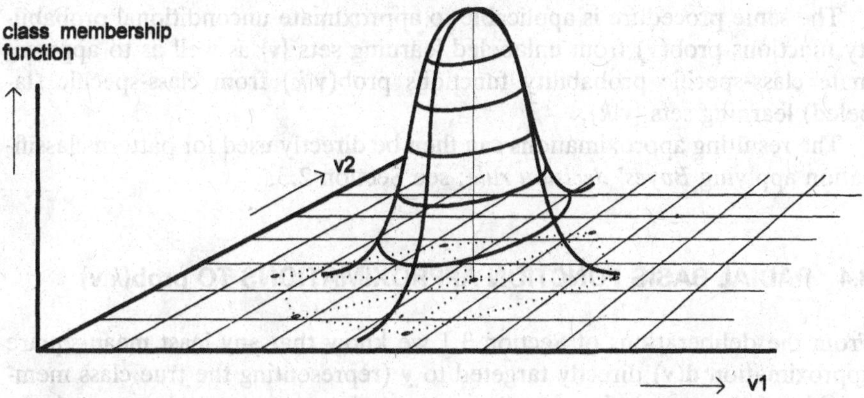

Figure 8.11. Gaussian-shaped kernel function for approximating prob(**v**) from clustering. Kernel function is continuous with its maximum at cluster cell centroid $\boldsymbol{\mu}_l$ and extends unbounded across cluster cell borders.

space into the required number of histogram bins and then counting how much of the learning set falls into each bin. These histogram bins are just the cluster cells determined by vector quantization clustering, and the histogram counts the sizes of the different clusters. Thus, vector quantization clustering provides simultaneously both partitioning and counting.

The result is a sampled representation of the distribution function prob(**v**) with which we are dealing. The samples are given by the cluster cell centroids $\mathbf{v}_l$ and the corresponding cluster cell counts h_l. Thus, the sampled representation is the set of pairs $[\mathbf{v}_l, h_l]$ with $l = 1, \ldots, L$.

The sampled representation must be smoothed in order to come to a continuous approximation. Smoothing requires a kernel function for which the normal distribution function is a good candidate; see Fig. 8.11.

The simplest approach to parameterizing the kernel function is to use uniform width rotational Gaussians. However, from the foregoing section we have learned that good arguments exist for applying individual kernel functions to each of the cluster cells and making use of the cluster cell covariance matrix $\mathbf{K}_l$.

If each of the L cluster cells is represented by a normal distribution function prob($\mathbf{v}|l$), then it carries exactly the probability mass 1 centered at $\boldsymbol{\mu}_l$ but distributed all over the measurement space. The cluster count h_l related to the total number of samples provides an estimation of the a priori probability prob(l) = P_l of the respective component distribution.

The summation over all the L clusters,

$$\text{prob}(\mathbf{v}) = \sum_{l=1}^{L} P_l \text{prob}(\mathbf{v}|l) \tag{8.9}$$

finally renders a legitimate estimation for prob(**v**).

The same procedure is applicable to approximate unconditional probability functions prob(**v**) from unlabeled learning sets {**v**} as well as to approximate class-specific probability functions prob(**v**|k) from class-specific (labeled) learning sets {**v**|k}.

The resulting approximations can then be directly used for pattern classification applying *Bayes' decision rule*; see Section 2.3.

8.4 RADIAL BASIS FUNCTION APPROXIMATIONS TO prob(k|v)

From the deliberations of Section 3.1 we know that any least mean-square approximation **d**(**v**) directly targeted to **y** (representing the true class membership of the pattern [**v**, **y**] to be recognized) comes out to be not only an estimation for the target vector **y** but, at the same time, also an estimation for the vector **p** of a posteriori probabilities. This remains valid even if the approximating function **d**(**v**) is composed of a linear combination of radial basis functions.

Each of the L radial basis functions consists of three parts—the reference vector $\mathbf{v}_l$, some kind of distance-measuring function $g(\cdot)$, and the kernel function $f(\cdot)$— which are combined to give $x_l = f(g(\mathbf{v}, \mathbf{v}_l))$. The usual choice is to take the Euclidean distance for $g(\cdot)$ and the negative exponential function for determining the shape of the kernel $f(\cdot)$. This results in

$$x_l = \exp(-\eta|\mathbf{v} - \mathbf{v}_l|^2) \tag{8.10}$$

which is the mathematical core of the normal distribution function (4.1) and, therefore, is called a Gaussian kernel; see Fig. 8.11.

It should be noted, however, that here no normalizing factor is necessary since it would be completely absorbed in the weights of the linear combination. Another mathematical difference is that the kernel width is controlled by η instead of the standard deviation σ of the equivalent normal distribution:

$$\eta = \frac{1}{2\sigma^2} \tag{8.11}$$

The individual kernel function has thus $N + 1$ parameters: the N components of the reference point $\mathbf{v}_l$ and the width η parameter. The latter is in the simplest case kept constant for all of the L kernel functions.

The linear combination of the L radial basis functions x_l, $l = 1, \ldots, L$, coming from the L reference points with weights $\mathbf{c}_l$ to be optimized gives the estimating function [compare (8.2)]:

$$\mathbf{d}(\mathbf{v}) = \sum_{l=1}^{L} \mathbf{c}_l \mathbf{x}_l(\mathbf{v}) \tag{8.12}$$

which, as shown in the introduction to thischapter using (8.3), can easily be rewritten to render the general form of (6.7), which was thoroughly dealt with in Chapter 6:

$$\mathbf{d}(\mathbf{v}) = \mathbf{A}^T\mathbf{x}(\mathbf{v})$$

Having arrived to this point of the discussion, we find:

- The idea of radial basis functions used for approximating prob(y|v) is a special choice of the set of basis functions for the concept of functional regression.

In combination with the least mean-square optimization (6.11) for adjusting the coefficient matrix **A** from the learning set

$$S^2 = E\{|\mathbf{d}(\mathbf{v}) - \mathbf{y}|^2\} = E\{|\mathbf{A}^T\mathbf{x}(\mathbf{v}) - \mathbf{y}|^2\} = \min_{\mathbf{A}}$$

the concept of radial basis functions opens a variety of new possibilities.

In the simplest case the L reference vectors $\mathbf{v}_l$, $l = 1, \ldots, L$, together with the width parameter η are achieved from vector clustering. The only free parameters are then the coefficients of the linear combination contained in **A**. The solution is straightforward and the results are discussed in Chapter 6.

The next more complicated variant is to use individual width parameters η_l and to include them into the optimization procedure, with the effect that the solution can now no longer be found by solving a linear matrix equation. Solving matrix equations becomes then only a subtask in a comprehensive gradient descent procedure.

The approach can be further generalized by including the L reference vectors $\mathbf{v}_l$ into the optimization process, the Euclidean metric may be substituted by the *Mahalanobis distance* $(\mathbf{v} - \mathbf{v}_l)^T\mathbf{K}_l^{-1}(\mathbf{v} - \mathbf{v}_l)$, and the matrices $\mathbf{K}_l$ of that metric can be included into the set of adjustable parameters. The computational effort is drastically increased with these generalizations.

The resulting pattern classification system can be represented in the form of a neural network structure similar to Figs. 6.1, 6.2, 7.6, and 8.5, as shown in Fig. 8.12.

Outlook

This concludes our journey into three different scientific fields of generating the discriminant function **d**(**v**) of pattern classifiers from the idea of mean-square functional approximation. We started into this expedition in Chapter 5, then traveled through the realms of polynomial regression, multilayer perceptron regression, and radial basis functions in Chapters 6 and 7 and the

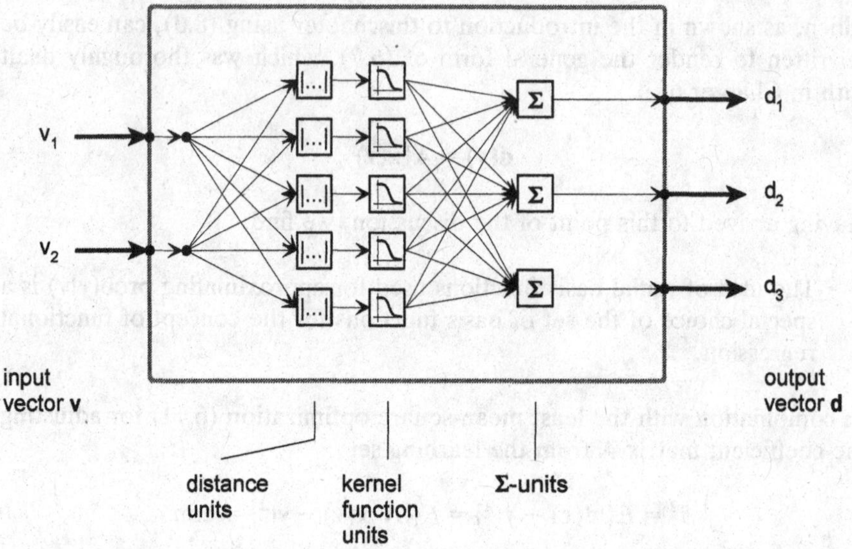

Figure 8.12. Radial basis function network. First layer consists of L distance-measuring units, implementing either Euclidean or more problem-specific distance-measuring functions. These are followed by their corresponding kernel function units determining locality of radial basis functions and forcing them to vanish with increasing distance from kernel center. Final layer provides linear combination of all radial basis functions and generates output vector **d** serving as approximation to **y** and **p**.

present chapter. What we have found on this journey is a network of closely connected ideas that make it difficult to distinguish between what belongs to statistical pattern recognition and what belongs to neural network technology.

In the beginning we stated that the discriminant function $\mathbf{d}(\mathbf{v})$ derived from the learning sample set plays the dominant role in any pattern classification system; compare Section 2.4. However, to make the pattern classification system complete, we must deal with two important questions: first, how to define the set of measurements comprised in the measurement vector $\mathbf{v}$ and, second, how to handle the reject problem, the discussion of which was postponed from Section 2.4.

So far we have been concerned with a single classifier. The last topic to be treated is the question of how more powerful classifiers can be composed from simpler ones. These questions are the topics of the next three chapters.

9

MEASUREMENTS, FEATURES, AND FEATURE SELECTION

In the beginning of this book we introduced pattern classification as the process of mapping observation into meaning, as the process that accepts the measurement vector **v** and returns the discriminant vector **d** and finally the label $\hat{k}$ of the most probable class. This was a rather abstract point of view and allowed us to develop techniques for establishing functions $\mathbf{d}(\mathbf{v})$ and $\hat{k}(\mathbf{d})$ from sets of learning samples without settling the question of which kind of measurement to use for that purpose.

As a consequence, the techniques developed so far work with any kind of measurement data. That being true, it is also quite obvious that these techniques will not work equally well with every kind of measurement data. To the contrary, the choice of measurements has a generally strong influence on the resulting performance: Good measurements are said to be half the success. Whereas theories exist that guide the development of classification techniques, this is not the case for finding good measurements.

The basic difficulties behind these questions stem from the fact that the number of potential measurements that are in some way connected to the events to be classified is practically unlimited; even worse, every linear or nonlinear transformation and combination of primary measurements simply renders a new measurement.

These considerations can also be transferred to the pattern classification system as a whole. We have learned that the classification system establishes a mapping from its input space **V** to the decision space **D** and that this mapping may consist of a sequence of consecutive partial mappings. Measurement transformations may be included or not as the first layer of operations.

This point of view also allows us to consider the whole pattern classifier as being nothing else than a large preprocessing module mapping the given measurement space **V** into a better suited one: $\mathbf{V}_{\text{improved}} \Leftrightarrow \mathbf{D}$. This processing module must then obviously be followed by a subsequent second pattern classifier mapping $\mathbf{V}_{\text{improved}}$ into an also improved decision space $\mathbf{D}_{\text{improved}}$ and designed according to the same principles as the first classifier.

If the first pattern classifier would be optimum—rendering already the vector $\mathbf{p}(\mathbf{v})$ of a posteriori probabilities as the optimum class membership functions—the second classifier would be bound to be the identity mapping and thus be reduced to triviality. However, in the practically relevant non-idealistic case a second classifier, following the first and using its discriminant vector $\mathbf{d}$ as the improved measurement vector $\mathbf{v}_{\text{improved}}$, may indeed improve the overall result.

This is a strange and somewhat irritating observation blurring the conceptual borders between the notions of measurement vector $\mathbf{v}$ and discriminant vector $\mathbf{d}$—strange, in view of the fact that just this discrimination has been the very basis of all our foregoing considerations, irritating in the sense that it seems to lead straight to an endless recursion, shifting the solution of the pattern classification problem into some far distant limit point that can at best be asymptotically approached.

Designing practical pattern classification systems, therefore, is not possible without cutting the Gordian knot and deciding, by experience, engineering knowledge, and general insight into the problem domain, which measurements to use and how to process them into a set of appropriate features.

The distinction between measurements, features, and ultimately discriminant functions is the knack to structure the problem domain that made the pattern classification task at all mathematically treatable. We use the notion of *measurements* when speaking about the raw data and the notion of *features* for those data purposefully prepared to be useful for the classification task.

Thus, in a typical pattern classification system, the measurement vector $\mathbf{v}$ goes into some appropriate preprocessing module and is mapped into a set of more or less discriminating features. The resulting feature vector $\mathbf{w}$ is then input to the pattern classifier proper and mapped into the discriminant vector $\mathbf{d}$.

Whereas the preprocessing module is generally derived from the designer's insight into the problem area or from optimization criteria not directly related to the classification task, the pattern classifier of this last stage in the processing chain is designed according to one of the techniques discussed in the foregoing chapters and thus refers in one sense or the other to the optimization goals of pattern classification (compare Fig. 9.9).

Regardless of the classifier design technique employed, the whole design is in some sense approaching the goal of Bayesian recognition, but under the constraints of its specific construction and therefore, at least in general, not being perfect.

As long as the performance is sufficiently far from being perfect, it may well be advisable to make use of the above considerations and connect the output $\mathbf{d}$ of the given classifier to the input $\mathbf{v}$ of a subsequent one that again must be trained to the same classification task. The imperfections of the first classifier show up in the learning set for the second may at least partially be corrected and thus the overall performance improved.

The primary measurements to be used for classification are in general determined in a most obvious way. So, if the patterns to be recognized are images such as characters, graphical symbols, or any other images containing real-world objects, the raw measurements are usually achieved by spatial sampling, resulting in pixel data, binary black and white, grey value, or three-channel color.

If the patterns are time dependent, the sampling has to happen in time instead of space. Often, as for example in speech recognition, short-time spectral analysis is applied to the sampled speech data, resulting in a vector of spectral intensities that can be sampled at a much lower frequency than the original speech signal. Normally, the event to be classified extends over several scans, resulting in a two-dimensional array of measurement data with its coordinates labeled by time and frequency.

As long as the set of measurement data contains samples coming from points neighbored in space or time or frequency or a similar continuous physical variable, this set contains, implicitly, also the respective mathematical derivatives. These can, but normally need not, be made explicit by taking differences between the neighbored measurements, which is merely a special kind of linear combination. But, linear combination is in a more general form normally already part of the subsequent operations within the pattern classification system and need, therefore, not be explicitly carried out at this state of the procedure. A similar consideration is valid for the integration.

The number of measurement variables determined this way will normally be large. However, the systematic approaches developed in Chapters 4 and 5 for the design of pattern classifiers cannot handle more than a certain limited number of measurements.

The problems with large measurement sets not only are due to computational requirements fast increasing with the size of the measurement vector **v** but also are a consequence of the principle of learning from examples, on which all of the pattern classification approaches discussed in Chapters 4 and 5 rely, sometimes assisted by some kind of statistical modeling. Adjustment of a large number of free parameters from observation data is only then sensible and likely to give reliable results when the number of data points sufficiently exceeds the number of free parameters. Thus, with increasing numbers of measurements, increasing numbers of learning samples will be required.

Therefore, the first step in almost every application is to cut down the number of potential measurements using engineering expertise and domain knowledge and to design appropriate feature extraction and preprocessing techniques. Typically, those variations in measurement data not caused by class membership are neutralized by suitable normalization procedures, such as amplitude variations in speech recognition, variations in position, size, and stroke width, and skew in character recognition, resulting in measurement data being invariant against these variations.

Beyond that, in many applications a variety of more task dependent feature extraction techniques must be provided. A good example is the data compression approach employed for speech recognition where the sampled microphone data is first submitted to short-time spectral analysis and then quantized into a few spectral channels with slow scanning speed and limited amplitude resolution.

Having brought down the number of measurements to a reasonable size, the feature selection techniques of pattern classification become applicable to distinguish between the more and the less promising features. One of the most effective techniques is to let the classifier itself decide which are the most discriminative features.

9.1 EVALUATION OF FEATURES INDIVIDUALLY

The techniques to be developed in the following apply to features as well as to measurements since also the raw measurements can be rank ordered and selected according to some kind of feature selection technique. Therefore, we will use the notation **v** for the vector of variables to be evaluated.

Assume for the following that a comparably large number of potential features $v_c, c = 1, \ldots., C$, is available. They constitute the set of the *candidate features* from which the most powerful subset of features is to be extracted. The selected features will then become the components of the feature vector **v**.

The simplest way of evaluating the discriminative power of the candidate features is to treat each of them separately and to check the performance of the single-measurement classifier working with the candidate feature to be examined. This requires us to design a probing classifier with the candidate feature v_c as input variable and the class label $k = 1, \ldots, K$ as output.

In this case the measurement space of the probing classifier is one dimensional. We need to know the probabilities $\text{prob}(v_c|k)$ and $\text{prob}(k)$. Application of Bayes's rule (2.25) gives then the class regions on the v scale and the resulting error rate ϵ_c is measured by counting the proportion of patterns falling outside their own class region. The recognition rate $\varphi_c = 1 - \epsilon_c$ is a suitable performance score for the candidate feature v_c tested.

Since v_c is a scalar, the K probability functions $\text{prob}(v_c|k)$ can easily be estimated from the learning set by collecting the necessary K histograms. The a priori probabilities $\text{prob}(k)$ are given or also estimated from the learning set.

This technique is fairly simple for moderate number C of candidate features but is computationally expensive if C is large. Hence, we are interested in simplifications. These can be derived from the observation that a feature

v_c is absolutely useless for classification if it turns out to be statistically independent from k. In that case $\text{prob}(k|v_c) = \text{prob}(k)$, the classifier decision fixed for the class with maximum a priori probability $p_{\max}$ and the recognition rate $\varphi_c = p_{\max}$.

Mutual Information

The degree of statistical dependence can be measured with what is called *mutual information* in information theory ([LEW1961], [SCH1968]):

$$T(v, k) = E\left\{ \text{ld} \frac{\text{prob}(v, k)}{\text{prob}(v)\text{prob}(k)} \right\} \tag{9.1}$$

The two arguments v and k of $T(v, k)$ indicate that T describes a relation between the two stochastic variables v and k. For v and k statistically independent, T becomes zero and assumes a maximum for given $\text{prob}(k)$ if v is deterministically related to k. Thus $T(v, k)$ is a suitable performance score for candidate features.

The mutual information $T(v_c, k)$ must also be determined from histograms. By expanding the expectation operator $E\{\cdot\}$ and substituting $\text{prob}(k)$ by P_k and $\text{prob}(v_c|k)$ according to Bayes's law, we get

$$\begin{aligned} T(v_c, k) &= \sum_{k=1}^{K} \sum_{v_c} \text{prob}(v_c, k) \text{ld} \frac{\text{prob}(v_c, k)}{\text{prob}(v_c)\text{prob}(k)} \\ &= \sum_{k=1}^{K} \left[P_k \sum_{v_c} \text{prob}(v_c|k) \text{ld} \frac{\text{prob}(v_c|k)}{\text{prob}(v_c)} \right] \end{aligned} \tag{9.2}$$

In Section 4.5, we have already considered the case that the variable v_c is binary. In this case (9.2) can be remarkably simplified.

With μ_c and μ_{ck} the unconditional and class-conditional expectations of v_c,

$$\mu_c = E\{v_c\} \quad \text{and} \quad \mu_{ck} = E\{v_c|k\} \tag{9.3}$$

the two probabilities $\text{prob}(v_c|k)$ and $\text{prob}(v_c)$ become

$$\begin{aligned} \text{prob}(v_c) &= \begin{cases} 1 - \mu_c & \text{for } v_c = 0 \\ \mu_c & \text{for } v_c = 1 \end{cases} \\ \text{prob}(v_c|k) &= \begin{cases} 1 - \mu_{ck} & \text{for } v_c = 0 \\ \mu_{ck} & \text{for } v_c = 1 \end{cases} \end{aligned} \tag{9.4}$$

Inserting this into the (9.2), we get the mutual information between v_c and k:

$$T(v_c, k) = \sum_{k=1}^{K} P_k \left[(1 - \mu_{ck}) \mathrm{ld} \frac{1 - \mu_{ck}}{1 - \mu_c} + \mu_{ck} \mathrm{ld} \frac{\mu_{ck}}{\mu_c} \right] \tag{9.5}$$

Approximating the binary logarithm $\mathrm{ld}(\cdot)$ by the first two terms of its series expansion,

$$\mathrm{ld}(x) \approx \frac{1}{\ln 2}(x - 1)$$

this can be further simplified to

$$T_{\mathrm{approx}}(v_c, k) = \sum_{k=1}^{K} P_k \frac{1}{\ln 2} \frac{(\mu_c - \mu_{ck})^2}{(1 - \mu_c)\mu_c} \tag{9.6}$$

This expression $T_{\mathrm{approx}}(v_c, k)$ serves as a tool for measuring the ability of a candidate feature v_c to solve a given pattern classification task in the situation that v_c is the only available measurement from which to predict the class membership variable k.

This is a kind of averaged performance score measuring the mean discriminative power of v_c and not taking into account that v_c may be better suited to predict some of the classes and less well to predict the others. If we are interested in measuring the usefulness of v_c for just one certain class k, we can make use of the fact that both expressions $T(v_c, k)$ and $T_{\mathrm{approx}}(v_c, k)$ have the form of a mathematical expectation,

$$T(v_c, k) = \sum_{k=1}^{K} P_k T_k(v_c) = E\{T_k(v_c)\} \tag{9.7}$$

where $T_k(v_c, k)$ can be considered to be the contribution of v_c to predict one certain class k from a set of classes Ω to be discriminated.

Correlation

Another approach in evaluating the discriminative power of the candidate feature v_c is to measure the *correlation* instead of mutual information.

In this case, however, we must use the target vector **y** instead of the class label k to represent the class membership variable ω. The candidate feature variable v_c is in general nonbinary and described by its unconditional and conditional means $\mu_c = E\{v_c\}$ and $\mu_{ck} = E\{v_c|k\}$ and variance $\mathrm{var}(v_c) = E\{(v_c - \mu_c)^2\}$.

Correlation between v_c and **y** is derived from the covariance between v_c and **y** suitably related to the respective variances. Since v_c is scalar and **y** a vector variable, we get a vector $\mathbf{cov}(v_c, \mathbf{y})$ of covariances. The squared magnitude of $\mathbf{cov}(v_c, \mathbf{y})$ is a useful measure of the discriminative power of v_c:

$$U(v_c, k) = |\mathbf{corr}(v_c, \mathbf{y})|^2 = \frac{|\mathbf{cov}(v_c, \mathbf{y})|^2}{\mathrm{var}(v_c)\mathrm{var}(\mathbf{y})} \tag{9.8}$$

The vector of covariances

$$\mathbf{cov}(v_c, \mathbf{y}) = E\{v_c\mathbf{y}\} - E\{v_c\}E\{\mathbf{y}\} \tag{9.9}$$

is determined by the vector of statistical moments

$$E\{v_c\mathbf{y}\} = \sum_k \sum_{v_c} v_c\mathbf{y}\ \mathrm{prob}(v|k)\mathrm{prob}(k) = \sum_k P_k E\{v_c\mathbf{y}|k\} \tag{9.10}$$

Making use of (1.5) we get

$$\mathbf{cov}(v_c, \mathbf{y}) = \begin{pmatrix} P_1E\{v_c|1\} \\ P_2E\{v_c|2\} \\ \vdots \\ P_KE\{v_c|K\} \end{pmatrix} - E\{v_c\}\begin{pmatrix} P_1 \\ P_2 \\ \vdots \\ P_K \end{pmatrix} = \begin{pmatrix} P_1(\mu_{c1} - \mu_c) \\ P_2(\mu_{c2} - \mu_c) \\ \vdots \\ P_K(\mu_{cK} - \mu_c) \end{pmatrix} \tag{9.11}$$

and

$$\begin{aligned} \mathrm{var}(\mathbf{y}) &= \mathrm{trace}[\mathbf{cov}(\mathbf{y}, \mathbf{y})] \\ &= \mathrm{trace}\begin{pmatrix} P_1(1-P_1) & -P_1P_2 & \cdots & -P_1P_K \\ -P_1P_2 & P_2(1-P_2) & \cdots & -P_2P_K \\ \vdots & \vdots & & \vdots \\ -P_1P_K & -P_2P_K & \cdots & P_K(1-P_K) \end{pmatrix} \\ &= \sum_{k=1}^{K} P_k(1-P_k) \end{aligned} \tag{9.12}$$

Compare also (6.60). Inserting these results into (9.8), we get

$$U(v_c, k) = \frac{\sum_{k=1}^{K} P_k^2(\mu_{ck} - \mu_c)^2}{\mathrm{var}(v_c) \sum_{k=1}^{K} P_k(1-P_k)} \tag{9.13}$$

There exist certain conditions that make this expression $U(v_c, k)$ quite similar to what we found in $T(v_c, k)$ from the viewpoint of mutual information. Consider, first, that the K classes are equiprobable ($P_k = 1/K$),

$$U(v_c, k) = \frac{1}{K}\sum_{k=1}^{K} \frac{(\mu_{ck} - \mu_c)^2}{\text{var}(v_c)(K-1)} \tag{9.14}$$

and, second, that v_c is binary resulting in $\text{var}(v_c) = \mu_c(1 - \mu_c)$, compare (9.6),

$$U(v_c, k) = \frac{1}{K}\sum_{k=1}^{K} \frac{1}{K-1} \frac{(\mu_{ck} - \mu_c)^2}{\mu_c(1-\mu)_c} \tag{9.15}$$

Again, $U(v_c, k)$ can be decomposed into class-specific contributions $U_k(v_c)$ of the considered candidate feature v_c to predict the different classes $k = 1, \ldots, K$:

$$U(v_c, k) = \frac{1}{K}\sum_{k=1}^{K} U_k(v_c) \tag{9.16}$$

Relations to Minimum Residual Variance Strategy of Section 6.9

It is interesting to know that evaluating the predictive power of the single candidate feature v_c by measuring the total correlation $U(v_c, k)$ between v_c and $\mathbf{y}$ is exactly what happens in the first two computing steps of the computational procedure described in Section 6.9 if the *minimum residual variance strategy* is applied.

Consider the case that the complete set of candidate features to be evaluated is written into the polynomial vector $\mathbf{x}$ together with one constant term 1; compare Fig. 6.7. Performing the first computing step, this constant term 1 is used as the first accepted predictor variable with the consequence that all of the remaining candidate features as well as the "to-be-predicted" variables are predicted by their respective mean values [see (6.85)], especially the two variables z and $\mathbf{y}$. The estimate for $\mathbf{y}$ was called $\mathbf{d}$. The remaining estimation errors were

$$\Delta z = z - E\{z\} \quad \text{and} \quad \Delta\mathbf{d} = -(\mathbf{y} - E\{\mathbf{y}\})$$

What in Section 6.9 was called z is here the candidate feature v_c. The current values of $\text{var}\{\Delta z\}$ and $\mathbf{cov}\{\Delta z, \Delta\mathbf{d}\}$ at this state of the computing procedure are

$$\text{var}\{\Delta z\} = \text{var}\{v_c\} \quad \text{and} \quad \mathbf{cov}\{\Delta z, \Delta\mathbf{d}\} = \mathbf{cov}\{v_c, \mathbf{y}\}$$

According to Section 6.9, these are exactly the expressions m and $\mathbf{m}$ needed to compute the reduction ΔS^2 of the residual variance to be achieved from using v_c as the only predictor variable within the next computing step: computing step 2 in absolute terms,

$$\Delta S^2 = \frac{|\mathbf{m}|^2}{m} = \frac{|\mathbf{cov}\{v_c, \mathbf{y}\}|^2}{\mathrm{var}\{v_c\}} \tag{9.17}$$

The reduction in residual variance ΔS^2 serves as the selection criterion for candidate variables just as $U(v_c, k)$ is intended to evaluate the discriminative power of candidate features v_c; see (9.8). Omitting the term var{y}, which is irrelevant in this context, both criteria turn out to be identical.

Comments

We find that evaluating the discriminative power of a certain candidate feature variable v_c by mutual entropy (9.2) or by correlation (9.8) has similar results and renders essentially the same results [(9.6), (9.15)] if the candidate feature v_c is binary.

On the other hand, there is the connection to the feature evaluation properties of the minimum residual variance pivot strategy of Section 6.9. However, it should be noted that this identity is valid only for the first computing step controlled by the minimum residual variance strategy.

This makes a major difference between the feature evaluation techniques of this chapter and those of Section 6.9.

Feature selection based on mutual information or on correlation between candidate feature v_c and target vector $\mathbf{y}$, as described here, does not care at all about the correlations among candidate features since this technique deals with each of the candidate features v_c and their relations to $\mathbf{y}$ separately.

Correlations between candidate features are capable of drastically changing the usefulness of feature variables. Highly correlated features must exhibit similar discriminative power scores, but including one of them into the estimating expressions depreciates all the others.

Feature selection according to the techniques of Section 6.9 has the advantage of taking all of the mutual correlations between the feature variables in account. The contribution of one single feature is there evaluated looking into the current situation and taking into account that a certain subset of all the available features is already used for the estimation. This property is a clear plus for the technique of polynomial regression in combination with the direct solution of the linear matrix equation (see Section 6.8) for classifier adaptation.

9.2 RANK-ORDER-BASED FEATURE SELECTION

In practical pattern classification the following decisions are made from the designer's experience and his or her estimation of how useful they are supposed to be for the classification task at hand:

- Kind of raw measurements to use
- Features to derive from the raw measurements
- Kind of preprocessing technique

Typically, the single feature has little discriminative power; hence, taking lots of them improves the chance of coming to a satisfying result but makes it more likely that the feature set as a whole contains correlations and redundancy.

In this situation it is not very helpful to evaluate the potential contribution of the single feature v_c to solve the classification task in isolation as do the usefulness scores $T(v_c, k)$ and $U(v_c, k)$ of the preceding section. An improved measure of usefulness has to consider the mutual dependencies among the features. The decisive question is to determine the contribution of the single feature to solve the classification task after a certain subset of all features is already used for classification.

This is exactly the type of question the technique of minimum residual variance (MS) strategy of Section 6.9 answers. The result is a *rank order among the set of features* with the additional property that those that are linear dependent on others are identified and omitted. The rank order is a by-product of the classifier adaptation procedure and requires the computational effort of solving a linear $C \times C$ matrix, equation with C being the feature set size.

One obvious use to be made of this rank-ordering technique is to start with a set of feature candidates sufficiently larger than intended and to sort out the most promising subset by the rank-ordering procedure.

This technique can also be applied if the size C of the set of candidate features is larger than can be handled by the generalized matrix inversion procedure. In this case the sorting procedure is performed in a sequence of steps. The number of candidate features to be evaluated in one step may be T. The procedure is started with an arbitrary selection of T candidates. The least promising T–L candidates are abandoned, the most promising L completed by another T–L new candidates, and the rank-ordering procedure entered again.

Another useful function of this rank order is to rely the construction of higher order polynomials upon it. The rationale behind this is the idea that feature variables found useful as linear terms of the polynomial discriminant function $\mathbf{d}(\mathbf{v})$ may also prove useful if combined to nonlinear terms. This is a heuristic justified by practical experience and shall be illustrated here for handwritten character recognition.

The measurement vector $\mathbf{v}$ represents the raster image with 16×16 pixels. The character images are centered according to their bounding boxes suitably skew and size normalized in order to fit into the 16×16 raster image. The procedure starts with setting up a complete linear polynomial in $\mathbf{v}$. As a result we gain the rank order for all 256 pixels:

$$\text{rank}[n] = \text{rank order position of pixel } n \qquad n = 1, \ldots, N \tag{9.18}$$

Since the construction of a complete quadratic polynomial would lead to the prohibitive polynomial length $L = 32{,}640$, we are interested in designing incomplete quadratic polynomials. This is done based on two parameters R and D. The first decides which of the linear terms are at all admitted for constructing quadratic terms,

$$\text{rank}[n] \leq R \tag{9.19}$$

and the second decides which pairs n, m of linear terms are allowed to combine into quadratic terms $v_n v_m$,

$$\text{rank}[n]\text{rank}[m]\text{pixeldist}[n, m] \leq D \tag{9.20}$$

where the function pixeldist$[n, m]$ measures the geometric distance between pixel n and pixel m in the raster image plane. This last expression admits combination of individual pixel measurements to quadratic terms whenever either their rank-order position is low or the geometric distance between them is small.

Thus quadratic combinations are favored of those pixel measurements that either are closely neighbored or have proven to be most important for linear classification. In particular, the pure quadratic terms are preferred. Figure 9.1 gives an impression of the resulting polynomial structure $\mathbf{x}(\mathbf{v})$.

In the case of binary measurements $v \in \{0, 1\}$, however, the pure quadratic terms can be completely omitted since then $v^2 = v$. There are numerous modifications to this rule imaginable. The techniques discussed here have a certain resemblance to the GMDH approach discussed elsewhere ([FAR1984], [RSO1989], [GIM1987]).

If the features from which nonlinear polynomial discriminant functions are constructed are themselves rank ordered, which is the case if they are computed by the technique described in Section 9.4, this rank order can again be used to design higher order functions. The simplest way is to admit quadratic combinations among all features up to rank-order position R_2, third-order combinations up to rank-order position R_3, and fourth-order combinations up to position R_4, with R_1 the total number of features and $R_4 < R_3 < R_2 < R_1$.

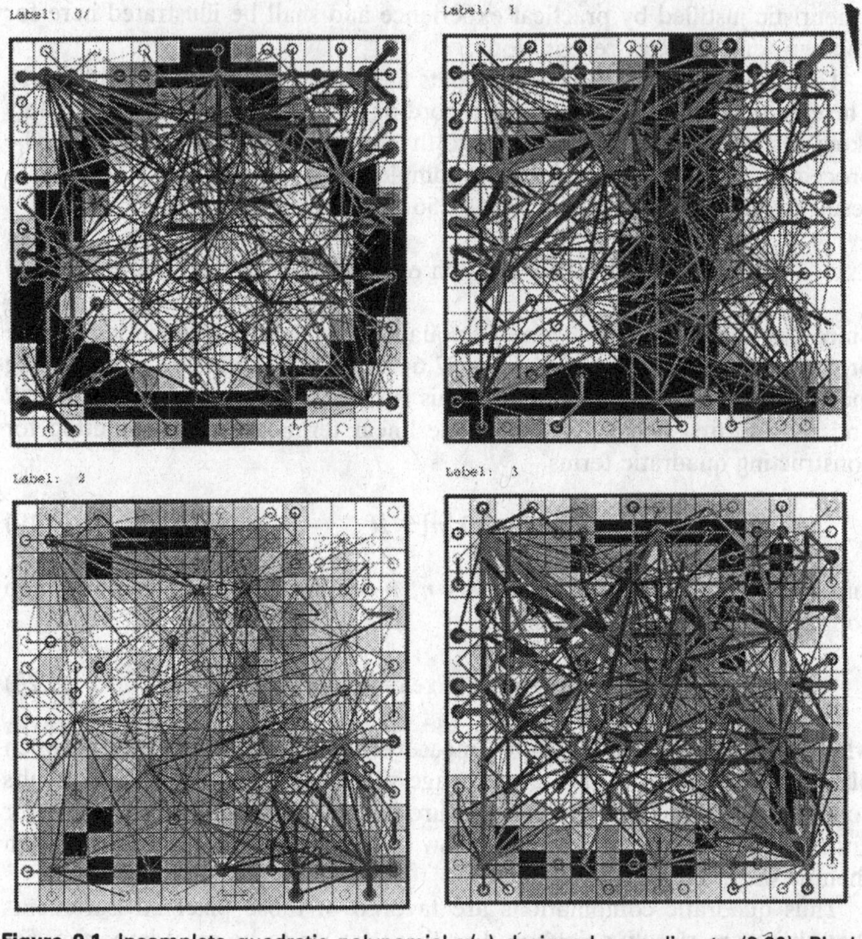

Figure 9.1. Incomplete quadratic polynomial $\mathbf{x}(\mathbf{v})$ designed according to (9.20). Pixels having passed rank$[n] \leq R$ requirement marked by circles. Lines connect pixels combined to quadratic terms. Positive weights shown in light grey and negative weights in dark grey. Linewidth of circles and lines corresponds to magnitude of respective weights in polynomial discriminant functions $d_k(\mathbf{v})$ for the numerals 0 (upper left), 1 (upper right), 2 (lower left), and 3 (lower right). For illustrative purposes polynomial structures are shown before background of individual characters (upper row) and class means (lower row) of respective classes.

9.3 COLLECTIVE EVALUATION OF FEATURE SETS

Once the decisions on which measurements to use and how to preprocess them into feature variables are taken, we arrive at a set of features determining the measurement (or feature) vector $\mathbf{v}$. The next step would then be to perform classifier adaptation based on the learning set and to measure the resulting performance; see Chapter 9.

Sometimes the procedure of feature definition contains one or more parameters remaining open and to be optimized with respect to classifier performance. It may then seem to be to much effort to go through the whole adaptation procedure for every parameter constellation in order to find the optimum. What is wanted, then, instead, is a rough but quick assessment of the discriminative power of the whole set of features.

Such an assessment can be gained by looking into the corresponding feature space $\mathbf{V}$ spanned by the considered set of features and evaluating how separable the given set of classes looks to be in that space. The properties of the given set of classes are in this context determined by the set of learning samples.

Application of the considered feature extraction technique to the learning set renders K class-specific distributions prob($\mathbf{v}|k$), $k = 1, \ldots, K$, in $\mathbf{V}$-space, which may be more or less intermixed or clearly separated depending on the feature set chosen. The evaluation shall be based on certain easy-to-achieve statistical parameters of the K distributions such as the class means $\boldsymbol{\mu}_k$ and the respective covariance matrices $\mathbf{K}_k$, $k = 1, \ldots, K$.

Obviously, the same argument as above of being to computationally expensive holds for the covariance matrix $\mathbf{K}_k$ if the dimension of $\mathbf{V}$ becomes large. However, we will see that for the measure of separability to be developed in the following, we do not need the full covariance matrix $\mathbf{K}_k$; all we need is its trace.

The idea is to compute and relate to each other the variance within the classes and the distances between the class centers.

We denote with V_k^2 the mean-squared *within-class* distance between samples $\mathbf{v}$ of class k and the corresponding class mean $\boldsymbol{\mu}_k$,

$$V_k^2 = E\{|\mathbf{v} - \boldsymbol{\mu}_k|^2|k\} = \text{var}\{\mathbf{v}|k\} = \text{trace}[\mathbf{K}_k] \tag{9.21}$$

and with V^2 the mean of these within-class squared distances,

$$V^2 = \sum_{k=1}^{K} P_k E\{|\mathbf{v} - \boldsymbol{\mu}_k|^2|k\} = \sum_{k=1}^{K} P_k V_k^2 \tag{9.22}$$

which for equiprobable classes $P_k = 1/K$ becomes

$$V^2 = \frac{1}{K} \sum_{k=1}^{K} V_k^2 \tag{9.23}$$

The mean-squared *between-class* distance between the class centers $\boldsymbol{\mu}_k$ and $\boldsymbol{\mu}_j$ of different classes is denoted by D^2. When calculating the mean, we must take into account that the different classes $k = 1, \ldots, K$ occur with different a priori probabilities. The fact, however, that we are just interested in calculating the mean distance between different classes $k \neq j$ must be regarded in the normalizing term before the sum but not in the double sum itself since the distances for these pairs are zero and contribute nothing:

$$D^2 = \frac{1}{1 - \sum_{k=1}^{K} P_k^2} \sum_{k=1}^{K} \sum_{j=1}^{K} P_k P_j |\boldsymbol{\mu}_k - \boldsymbol{\mu}_j|^2 \tag{9.24}$$

For equiprobable classes this expression reduces to

$$D^2 = \frac{1}{K(K-1)} \sum_{k=1}^{K} \sum_{j=1}^{K} |\boldsymbol{\mu}_k - \boldsymbol{\mu}_j|^2 \tag{9.25}$$

From V^2 and D^2 a useful *measure of separability* can be derived as the ratio

$$Q = \frac{V^2}{V^2 + D^2} \qquad 0 \leq Q \leq 1 \tag{9.26}$$

ranging from 0 to 1 and indicating optimum separability of the K classes with $Q \rightarrow 0$ and inseparability with $Q \rightarrow 1$.

Relations to Class-Specific, Pooled, and Common Covariance Matrices

There exist some interesting relations between the expressions V^2 and D^2 as introduced above and the covariance matrices $\mathbf{K}_k$ and $\mathbf{K}_{\text{common}}$ describing properties of the statistical processes $\{\mathbf{v}|k\}$ and $\{\mathbf{v}\}$, respectively.

From the class-specific covariance matrices

$$\mathbf{K}_k = E\{(\mathbf{v} - \boldsymbol{\mu}_k)(\mathbf{v} - \boldsymbol{\mu}_k)^T | k\} \tag{9.27}$$

the so-called *pooled* covariance matrix is derived by averaging

$$\mathbf{K}_{\text{pooled}} = \sum_{k=1}^{K} P_k \mathbf{K}_k = \sum_{k=1}^{K} P_k E\{(\mathbf{v} - \boldsymbol{\mu}_k)(\mathbf{v} - \boldsymbol{\mu}_k)^T | k\} \tag{9.28}$$

whereas the *common* covariance matrix

$$\mathbf{K}_{\text{common}} = \sum_{k=1}^{K} P_k E\{(\mathbf{v} - \boldsymbol{\mu})(\mathbf{v} - \boldsymbol{\mu})^T | k\} \tag{9.29}$$

refers to the process $\{\mathbf{v}\}$, regardless of the class label, with $\boldsymbol{\mu}$ being the common mean $\boldsymbol{\mu} = E\{\mathbf{v}\}$:

$$\boldsymbol{\mu} = \sum_{k=1}^{K} P_k \boldsymbol{\mu}_k \tag{9.30}$$

The common covariance matrix $\mathbf{K}_{\text{common}}$ contains the expression $E\{(\mathbf{v} - \boldsymbol{\mu})(\mathbf{v} - \boldsymbol{\mu})^T | k\}$, which can be transformed into

$$\begin{aligned} E\{(\mathbf{v} - \boldsymbol{\mu})(\mathbf{v} - \boldsymbol{\mu})^T | k\} &= E\{[(\mathbf{v} - \boldsymbol{\mu}_k) - (\boldsymbol{\mu} - \boldsymbol{\mu}_k)][(\mathbf{v} - \boldsymbol{\mu}_k) - (\boldsymbol{\mu} - \boldsymbol{\mu}_k)]^T | k\} \\ &= E\{(\mathbf{v} - \boldsymbol{\mu}_k)(\mathbf{v} - \boldsymbol{\mu}_k)^T | k\} + (\boldsymbol{\mu} - \boldsymbol{\mu}_k)(\boldsymbol{\mu} - \boldsymbol{\mu}_k)^T \\ &= \mathbf{K}_k + (\boldsymbol{\mu} - \boldsymbol{\mu}_k)(\boldsymbol{\mu} - \boldsymbol{\mu}_k)^T \end{aligned} \tag{9.31}$$

Hence we get

$$\begin{aligned} \mathbf{K}_{\text{common}} &= \sum_{k=1}^{K} P_k \mathbf{K}_k + \sum_{k=1}^{K} P_k (\boldsymbol{\mu}_k - \boldsymbol{\mu})(\boldsymbol{\mu}_k - \boldsymbol{\mu})^T \\ &= \mathbf{K}_{\text{pooled}} + \mathbf{K}_{\text{class means}} \end{aligned} \tag{9.32}$$

where $\mathbf{K}_{\text{class means}}$ is the covariance matrix of the K class means $\{\boldsymbol{\mu}_k\}$. Taking the trace of (9.32), we get

$$\text{trace}[\mathbf{K}_{\text{common}}] = \text{trace}[\mathbf{K}_{\text{pooled}}] + \text{trace}[\mathbf{K}_{\text{class means}}] \tag{9.33}$$

Interpretations

All three terms of (9.33) have interesting interpretations. The left-side term is the mean-squared distance between the common mean $\boldsymbol{\mu}$ and all of the samples $\mathbf{v}$ regardless of its class k:

$$\text{trace}[\mathbf{K}_{\text{common}}] = E\{|\mathbf{v} - \boldsymbol{\mu}|^2\} = \text{var}\{\mathbf{v}\} = V_{\text{common}}^2 \tag{9.34}$$

The middle term of (9.33) is the mean-squared distance V^2 introduced above between any of the samples $\mathbf{v}$ and its respective class mean $\boldsymbol{\mu}_k$:

$$\text{trace}[\mathbf{K}_{\text{pooled}}] = \sum_{k=1}^{K} P_k E\{|\mathbf{v} - \boldsymbol{\mu}_k|^2 | k\} = \sum_{k=1}^{K} P_k V_k^2 = E\{\text{var}\{\mathbf{v}|k\}\} = V^2 \tag{9.35}$$

The rightmost term,

$$\text{trace}[\mathbf{K}_{\text{class means}}] = \sum_{k=1}^{K} P_k (\boldsymbol{\mu}_k - \boldsymbol{\mu})^T (\boldsymbol{\mu}_k - \boldsymbol{\mu}) = V_{\text{class means}}^2 \tag{9.36}$$

is the mean-squared distance $V^2_{\text{class means}}$ between any of the class means $\boldsymbol{\mu}_k$ and the common mean $\boldsymbol{\mu}$,

$$V^2_{\text{class means}} = \sum_{k=1}^{K} P_k |\boldsymbol{\mu}_k - \boldsymbol{\mu}|^2 \tag{9.37}$$

which is closely related to the mean-squared *between-class* distance among the class centers $\boldsymbol{\mu}_k$ and $\boldsymbol{\mu}_j$ of different classes as introduced in (9.24):

$$\begin{aligned} D^2 &= \frac{1}{1 - \sum_{k=1}^{K} P_k^2} \sum_{k=1}^{K} \sum_{j=1}^{K} P_k P_j |(\boldsymbol{\mu}_k - \boldsymbol{\mu}) - (\boldsymbol{\mu}_j - \boldsymbol{\mu})|^2 \\ &= \frac{1}{1 - \sum_{k=1}^{K} P_k^2} \sum_{k=1}^{K} \sum_{j=1}^{K} P_k P_j [|\boldsymbol{\mu}_k - \boldsymbol{\mu}|^2 - 2(\boldsymbol{\mu}_k - \boldsymbol{\mu})^T (\boldsymbol{\mu}_j - \boldsymbol{\mu}) + |\boldsymbol{\mu}_j - \boldsymbol{\mu}|^2] \\ &= \frac{2}{1 - \sum_{k=1}^{K} P_k^2} \sum_{k=1}^{K} P_k |\boldsymbol{\mu}_k - \boldsymbol{\mu}|^2 = \frac{2}{1 - \sum_{k=1}^{K} P_k^2} V^2_{\text{class means}} \end{aligned} \tag{9.38}$$

Putting things together, we find

$$\begin{aligned} V^2 &= \text{trace}[\mathbf{K}_{\text{pooled}}] \\ D^2 &= \frac{2}{1 - \sum_{k=1}^{K} P_k^2} [\text{trace}[\mathbf{K}_{\text{comon}}] - \text{trace}[\mathbf{K}_{\text{pooled}}]] \end{aligned} \tag{9.39}$$

and

$$Q = \frac{\text{trace}[\mathbf{K}_{\text{pooled}}]}{\left(1 - \sum_{k=1}^{K} P_k^2\right)^{-1} \left[2\,\text{trace}[\mathbf{K}_{\text{common}}] - \left(1 + \sum_{k=1}^{K} P_k^2\right) \text{trace}[\mathbf{K}_{\text{pooled}}]\right]} \tag{9.40}$$

In the case of binary variables $v_n \in \{0, 1\}$ computation of var{$\mathbf{v}$} and var{$\mathbf{v}|k$} is extremely simplified,

$$\text{var}\{\mathbf{v}\} = \{\mathbf{e} - \boldsymbol{\mu}\}^T \boldsymbol{\mu} = V^2 \qquad \text{var}\{\mathbf{v}|k\} = (\mathbf{e} - \boldsymbol{\mu}_k)^T \boldsymbol{\mu}_k = V_k^2$$

where $\mathbf{e}$ is the N-dimensional vector consisting of N components with value 1, (6.31).

Relations to Minimum-Distance Classification

It is interesting to note that for equiprobable classes $P_k = 1/K$ the denominator of (9.26), $D^2 + V^2$, has the interpretation of being the mean-squared distance between any vector $\mathbf{v}$ coming from the stochastic process $\{\mathbf{v}, k\}$ and all of the class centers $\boldsymbol{\mu}_j$, $j = 1, \ldots, K$, $j \neq k$, excluding that of its own class. This can be shown starting with

$$\begin{aligned} E\{|\mathbf{v} - \boldsymbol{\mu}_j|^2|k\} &= E\{|(\mathbf{v} - \boldsymbol{\mu}_k) + (\boldsymbol{\mu}_k - \boldsymbol{\mu}_j)|^2|k\} \\ &= E\{|\mathbf{v} - \boldsymbol{\mu}_k|^2|k\} + |\boldsymbol{\mu}_k - \boldsymbol{\mu}_j|^2 = V_k^2 + |\boldsymbol{\mu}_k - \boldsymbol{\mu}_j|^2 \end{aligned} \tag{9.41}$$

and taking the average for all values k and j except $k = j$:

$$\begin{aligned} \frac{1}{K(K-1)} \sum_{k=1}^{K} \sum_{\substack{j=1 \\ j \neq k}}^{K} E\{|\mathbf{v} - \boldsymbol{\mu}_j|^2|k\} &= \frac{1}{K(K-1)} \sum_{k=1}^{K} \sum_{\substack{j=1 \\ j \neq k}}^{K} [V_k^2 + |\boldsymbol{\mu}_k - \boldsymbol{\mu}_j|^2] \\ &= \frac{1}{K} \sum_{k=1}^{K} V_k^2 + \frac{1}{K(K-1)} \sum_{k=1}^{K} \sum_{j=1}^{K} |\boldsymbol{\mu}_k - \boldsymbol{\mu}_j|^2 \\ &= V^2 + D^2 \end{aligned} \tag{9.42}$$

Whereas V^2 carries the interpretation of being the mean-squared distance between any vector $\mathbf{v}$ coming from the stochastic process $\{\mathbf{v}, k\}$ and its own class center $\boldsymbol{\mu}_k$, see (9.22).

The measure Q of separability, in this interpretation, is closely related to *minimum Euclidean distance classification* and expresses the relation between the two kinds of average distances relevant in this context, the average distance to the correct reference and the average distance to all of the incorrect references.

Fisher Criterion

Another often used measure of separability is the Fisher criterion

$$F = \sum_{k=1}^{K} P_k(\boldsymbol{\mu}_k - \boldsymbol{\mu})^T \mathbf{K}_{\text{pooled}}^{-1}(\boldsymbol{\mu}_k - \boldsymbol{\mu}) \tag{9.43}$$

relating the distances between the class means $\boldsymbol{\mu}_k$ to the width and orientation of the class-specific distributions as expressed in the "*pooled*" *covariance matrix* having the property of being invariant against linear transformations of the measurement space $\mathbf{V}$.

9.4 PRINCIPAL-AXIS TRANSFORM AND ITS NEURAL COUNTERPART

For most of the practical pattern classification tasks nonlinearity of the discriminant function $\mathbf{d}(\mathbf{v})$ is the key to satisfying solutions. However, in this context nonlinearity must be paid for by computational effort generally fast increasing with the dimensionality of $\mathbf{v}$.

According to (6.2), the following shows for the polynomial regression classifier, the growth of the polynomial length L depending on the polynomial degree G and the dimensionality N of the measurement vector $\mathbf{v}$.

	Polynomial Length L					
Degree G	$N = 10$	$N = 20$	$N = 30$	$N = 40$	$N = 50$	$N = 60$
1	11	21	31	41	51	61
2	66	231	496	861	1,326	1,891
3	286	1,771	5,456	12,341	23,426	39,711

Even for moderate degrees G complete polynomials can only be designed for rather small values of N.

The most straightforward way to reduce the number N of measurements is *selection*. But even this simple-looking procedure results, if we try to reduce N to M, in prohibitively large numbers T of candidate selections to be tested and compared for optimum performance:

$$T = \binom{N}{M} = \frac{N!}{M!(M-N)!} \tag{9.44}$$

Thus, selection also must be guided by heuristics. In Chapter 9 we have discussed some of the possibilities.

In mathematical terms, selection of M measurements from a set of candidate features with size N is *projection*. The N-dimensional measurement space containing the class-specific distributions $\text{prob}(\mathbf{v}|k)$ is by selection projected onto an M-dimensional subspace spanned by the M selected coordinate axes. The question is whether the projected class-specific distributions are, or at least almost are, as separable as the original distributions in N-space. In general, however, it cannot be excluded that what had been separable before may be hopelessly intermingled after the projection.

These considerations directly lead us to the question of what would be the optimum projection. And this question, again, is closely connected with that for the optimum coordinate system since the N-dimensional measurement space we are dealing with may equivalently be described by a multitude of possible coordinate systems and each of them allows another set of projections.

Translation and Rotation of Coordinate System

Spaces are determined by coordinate systems. We must be aware of the fact that the measurement space carrying the stochastic process $\{\mathbf{v}, \mathbf{k}\}$ is determined by the basis vector system established more or less incidentally through the measuring or computational prescriptions on which we decided to rely the whole system design. This need not be the coordinate system optimally suited for projections, and normally it is not.

Finding a better suited coordinate system requires us to analyze the situation in measurement space. We will look into this problem without regarding the classification task, that is, ignoring the class labels. Thus the pattern source $\{\mathbf{v}\}$ generates a distribution of probability mass in N-space centered at $\boldsymbol{\mu} = E\{\mathbf{v}\}$ and with orientations and widths given by the common covariance matrix $\mathbf{K} = E\{(\mathbf{v} - \boldsymbol{\mu})(\mathbf{v} - \boldsymbol{\mu})^T\}$.

This covariance matrix $\mathbf{K}$ determines an orthogonal system of basis vectors (the principal axes), which can be shown to be in several aspects the optimum coordinate system for representing the stochastic process $\{\mathbf{v}\}$.

The covariance matrix $\mathbf{K}$ can be decomposed (4.19) into the product

$$\mathbf{K} = \mathbf{B}\mathbf{D}\mathbf{B}^T$$

of matrices $\mathbf{B}$ and $\mathbf{D}$, where

$$\mathbf{B} = (\mathbf{b}_1 \quad \mathbf{b}_2 \quad \cdots \quad \mathbf{b}_N)$$

is the orthogonal matrix of the eigenvectors of $\mathbf{K}$ (4.16) and

$$\mathbf{D} = \begin{bmatrix} \lambda_1 & 0 & \cdots & 0 \\ 0 & \lambda_2 & \cdots & 0 \\ \vdots & \vdots & & \vdots \\ 0 & 0 & \cdots & \lambda_N \end{bmatrix}$$

is the diagonal matrix of the eigenvalues of $\mathbf{K}$ (4.17): compare Section 4.1.

The N eigenvalue–eigenvector pairs $[\lambda_n, \mathbf{b}_n]$, $n = 1, \ldots, N$, are ordered according to decreasing eigenvalue magnitude. The eigenvectors have unit length and are mutually orthogonal, resulting in $\mathbf{B}^T\mathbf{B} = \mathbf{B}\mathbf{B}^T = \mathbf{I}$.

In the given measurement space a new coordinate system is introduced, translated from the N-space origin into the probability mass center $\boldsymbol{\mu}$ and

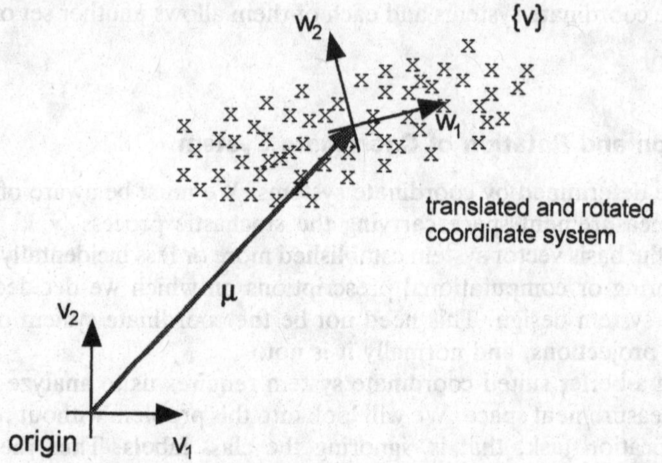

Figure 9.2. Measurement space with given coordinate system together with set {v} of points generated by pattern source. New coordinate system better suited to represent set {v} is gained by translation into center $\boldsymbol{\mu}$ of probability mass and rotation into its principal axes $\mathbf{b}_1, \ldots, \mathbf{b}_N$.

rotated according to the eigenvectors of **K** as represented in the matrix **B** of eigenvectors. See Fig. 9.2.

Known as the *principal-axis transform*, the whole operation can be formally described as a bijective mapping $\mathbf{v} \rightarrow \mathbf{w}$ between the two N-spaces **V** and **W**, where the feature vector **w** is computed from the given measurement vector **v** by

$$\mathbf{w} = \mathbf{B}^T(\mathbf{v} - \boldsymbol{\mu}) \tag{9.45}$$

and, conversely, the measurement vector **v** from the feature vector **w** can be computed by

$$\mathbf{v} = \mathbf{B}\mathbf{w} + \boldsymbol{\mu} \tag{9.46}$$

In N-space **V** there exists the pattern-generating process {**v**} with the stochastic properties

$$\text{Given process } \{\mathbf{v}\}: \quad \begin{cases} E\{\mathbf{v}\} = \boldsymbol{\mu} \\ \mathbf{cov}\{\mathbf{v}, \mathbf{v}\} = \mathbf{K} \end{cases} \tag{9.47}$$

which were used to determine the new coordinate system and the corresponding mapping $\mathbf{v} \rightarrow \mathbf{w}$. From the given stochastic process {**v**} the principal-axis transform generates another stochastic process {**w**} whose stochastic properties directly derive from those of {**v**}. It is easy to show that the stochastic process $\{\mathbf{w}\}$ gained by the transformation is unbiased and uncorrelated:

$$\text{Transformed process } \{\mathbf{w}\}: \quad \begin{cases} E\{\mathbf{w}\} = \mathbf{0} \\ \mathbf{cov}\{\mathbf{w}, \mathbf{w}\} = \mathbf{D} \end{cases} \tag{9.48}$$

The traces of the two covariance matrices **K** and **D** ("before" and "after") are identical,

$$\text{trace}[\mathbf{K}] = \text{trace}[\mathbf{BDB}^T] = \text{trace}[\mathbf{B}^T\mathbf{BD}] = \text{trace}[\mathbf{D}] \tag{9.49}$$

resulting in the fact that both stochastic processes $\{\mathbf{v}\}$ and $\{\mathbf{w}\}$ have the same variances:

$$\text{var}\{\mathbf{v}\} = \text{trace}[\mathbf{K}] = \text{var}\{\mathbf{w}\} = \text{trace}[\mathbf{D}] \tag{9.50}$$

The principal-axis transform fulfills the following optimization criterion: Among all conceivable transformations $\mathbf{v} \rightarrow \mathbf{w}$ of the form given in (9.45) (translations and rotations of the coordinate system) the principal-axis transform has the property of making the individual variances $\text{var}\{w_n\}$ of the transformed feature variables (the main diagonal elements of the covariance matrix $\mathbf{cov}\{\mathbf{w}\}$) maximally nonuniform as measured by the entropy measure of information theory [WAT1970].

We consider in this context the normalized distribution of variances (compare Section 4.2),

$$\text{varnorm}_n = \frac{\text{var}\{w_n\}}{\sum_{n=1}^{N} \text{var}\{w_n\}} = \underset{n}{\text{NormalizeToUnity}}[\text{var}\{w_n\}] \tag{9.51}$$

formally resembling a discrete probability distribution for which the entropy measure

$$H(\text{varnorm}_n) = \sum_{n=1}^{N} \text{varnorm}_n \text{ld}\left(\frac{1}{\text{varnorm}_n}\right) \tag{9.52}$$

can be computed. This expression has values in the range of $[0 \,.\,. \text{ld}(N)]$ and assumes its maximum $\text{ld}(N)$ for uniform values varnorm_n or $\text{var}\{w_n\}$, respectively. On the other hand, the minimum value 0 is assumed if all of the variance of $\{\mathbf{w}\}$ is concentrated in only one dimension, that is, $\text{var}\{v_m\}$ is not zero for some single $m \in \{1, \ldots, N\}$ and is zero for all others, $\text{var}\{v_n\} = 0$ for $n \in \{1, \ldots, N\}$ except for $n = m$. It can be show that the principal-axis transform minimizes $H(\text{varnorm}_n)$ [WAT1970].

Projections Based on New Coordinate System

So far, we have considered the principal-axis transform simply as representing the given N-space by another coordinate system without changing the dimension. In the context considered here, however, the principal axis transform is always combined with projection, which means that only M of the N transformed variables w_n are used as feature variables and the rest are abandoned.

This is mathematically equivalent to using the truncated matrix $\mathbf{B}_M$ consisting of only the M dominant eigenvectors in the transformation rule $\mathbf{v} \rightarrow \mathbf{w}$ instead of the complete eigenvector matrix $\mathbf{B}$,

$$\mathbf{B}_M = (\mathbf{b}_1 \quad \mathbf{b}_2 \quad \cdots \quad \mathbf{b}_M) \qquad M \leq N \tag{9.53}$$

and results in the fact that of the two matrix products $\mathbf{B}_M^T\mathbf{B}_M = \mathbf{I}_M$ and $\mathbf{B}_M\mathbf{B}_M^T \neq \mathbf{I}_N$ only the first renders the M-dimensional identity matrix and the second an $N \times N$ matrix different from the identity matrix except for $M = N$.

Performing the principal-axis transform with the truncated matrix $\mathbf{B}_M$,

$$\mathbf{w}_M = \mathbf{B}_M^T(\mathbf{v} - \boldsymbol{\mu}) \tag{9.54}$$

leads to the dimensionality reduction $N \rightarrow M$ but sacrifices invertibility; in mathematical terms this transformation is called an injective mapping. From the feature vector $\mathbf{w}_M$ the original measurement vector $\mathbf{v}$ can now only be approximately reconstructed,

$$\hat{\mathbf{v}} = \mathbf{B}_M\mathbf{w}_M + \boldsymbol{\mu} \tag{9.55}$$

resulting in the reconstruction error

$$R^2 = E\{|\hat{\mathbf{v}} - \mathbf{v}|^2\} \tag{9.56}$$

Seen from this point of view, the principal-axis transform fulfills another optimization criterion, namely, that of being optimum with respect to the reconstruction error R^2 among all conceivable translations and rotations of the coordinate system for a required dimensionality reduction $N \rightarrow M$ [SCH1977].

The mean of the dimensionality reduced process $\{\mathbf{w}_M\}$ remains the zero vector $E\{\mathbf{w}_M\} = \mathbf{0}$ and its covariance matrix $\mathbf{cov}\{\mathbf{w}_M, \mathbf{w}_M\}$ becomes the truncated diagonal matrix $\mathbf{D}$ of the eigenvalues:

$$\mathbf{cov}\{\mathbf{w}_M, \mathbf{w}_M\} = \mathbf{D}_M = \begin{bmatrix} \lambda_1 & 0 & \cdots & 0 \\ 0 & \lambda_2 & \cdots & 0 \\ \vdots & \vdots & \ddots & \vdots \\ 0 & 0 & \cdots & \lambda_M \end{bmatrix} \qquad M \leq N \tag{9.57}$$

The reconstruction error is computed from

$$\begin{aligned} R^2 &= E\{|\hat{\mathbf{v}} - \mathbf{v}|^2\} = E\{|\mathbf{B}_M \mathbf{w}_M - (\mathbf{v} - \boldsymbol{\mu})|^2\} \\ &= E\{[\mathbf{B}_M \mathbf{w}_M - (\mathbf{v} - \boldsymbol{\mu})]^T [\mathbf{B}_M \mathbf{w}_M - (\mathbf{v} - \boldsymbol{\mu})]\} \\ &= E\{\mathbf{w}_M^T \mathbf{B}_M^T \mathbf{B}_M \mathbf{w}_M\} - 2E\{\mathbf{w}_M^T \mathbf{B}_M^T (\mathbf{v} - \boldsymbol{\mu})\} + E\{(\mathbf{v} - \boldsymbol{\mu})^T (\mathbf{v} - \boldsymbol{\mu})\} \\ &= E\{|\mathbf{v} - \boldsymbol{\mu}|^2\} - E\{|\mathbf{w}_M|^2\} \end{aligned} \tag{9.58}$$

Introducing the variances of $\{\mathbf{v}\}$ and $\{\mathbf{w}_M\}$ and making use of (9.50), we find

$$\begin{aligned} R^2 &= \text{var}\{\mathbf{v}\} - \text{var}\{\mathbf{w}_M\} = \text{var}\{\mathbf{w}\} - \text{var}\{\mathbf{w}_M\} \\ &= \text{trace}[\mathbf{D}] - \text{trace}[\mathbf{D}_M] = \sum_{n=M+1}^{N} \lambda_n \end{aligned} \tag{9.59}$$

The interesting result of these considerations is that the mean-square reconstruction error R^2 is achieved by accumulating those eigenvalues λ_n belonging to the abandoned eigenvectors $\mathbf{b}_n$, $n = M + 1, \ldots, N$. Obviously, the reconstruction error R^2 is minimum if the smallest eigenvalues are accumulated.

The distribution of sizes of the eigenvalues $\lambda_1, \ldots, \lambda_N$ of $\mathbf{K}$ is an intrinsic property of the stochastic process $\{\mathbf{v}\}$ and depends completely on the practical problem at hand. It may well happen that these eigenvalues exhibit a fast decay with increasing order n and even vanish to zero beyond a certain index $n > M$. In such a situation no reconstruction error is to be suffered if all of the eigenvectors above M are omitted; compare Fig. 9.3.

Flat-Galaxy Interpretation

Imagine a three-dimensional measurement space with a distribution of probability mass $\{\mathbf{v}\}$ such as a flat galaxy mainly extending into two dimensions but in general not oriented parallel to the coordinate axes of the given 3-space. The flatness of such a distribution must result in two of the eigenvalues being rather large and similar in size and the third comparably small. Application of the principal-axis transform corresponds to shifting and rotating the coordinate system into the distribution's center and main axes. It is obvious that ignoring the third of the new coordinate axes will not much change the situation.

These concepts can be transferred to higher dimensional spaces. It should be remarked that distributions gained from empirical data in high-dimensional spaces are, as a rule, flat galaxies. In speech and character recognition it has rarely been necessary to work with M larger than 40–50.

The reason is that correlations between the features become more probable and increase in intensity when the number of components of $\mathbf{v}$ is increased with the intention not to lose relevant information.

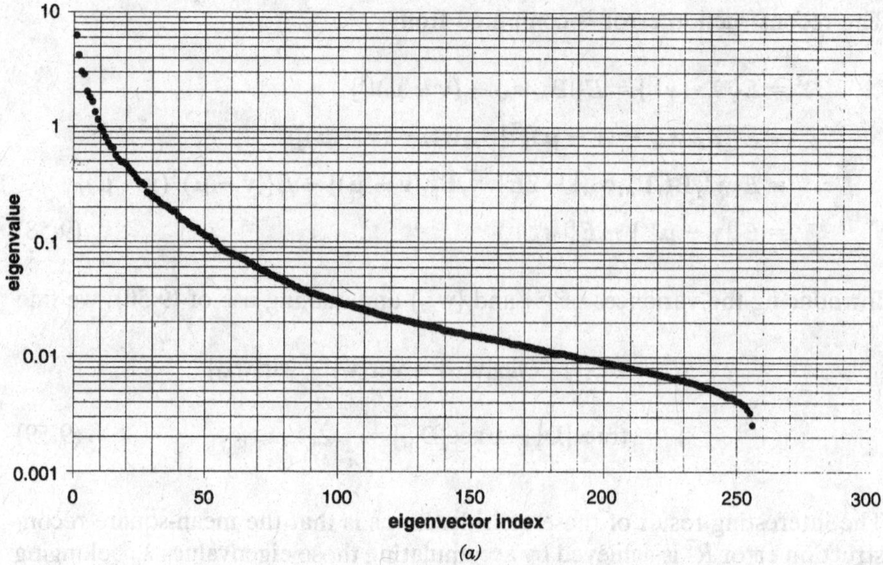

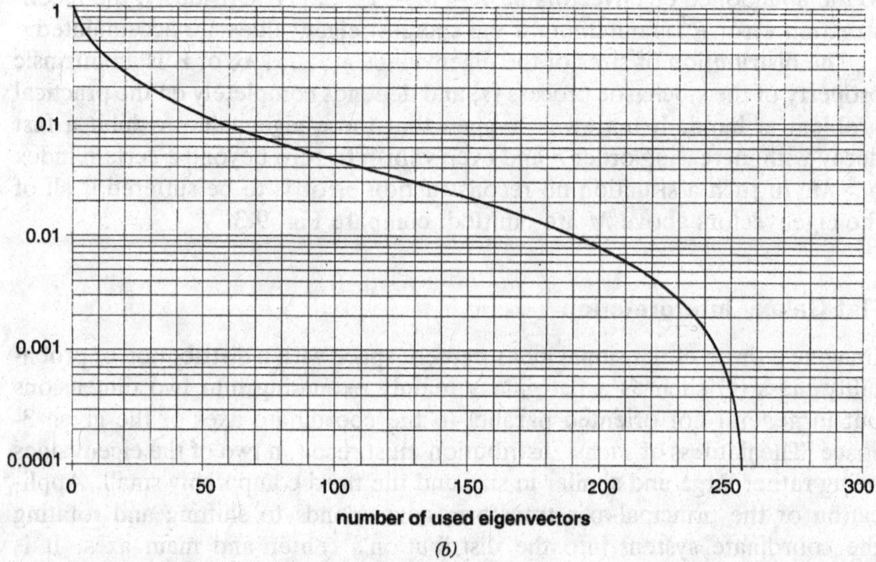

Figure 9.3. Distribution of eigenvalues and resulting reconstruction error R^2 for realistic pattern classification task: recognition of handwritten numerals from their raster images after size and skew normalization. Measurement vector **v** is directly constructed from the 16×16 raster image and is therefore 256-dimensional.

The principal-axis transform is an information-compressing transformation and, due to this property, is used for a variety of applications other than pattern classification. The features achieved by principal-axis transform and concentrated into the feature vector $\mathbf{w}_M$ are unbiased and uncorrelated and hence constitute a useful compact description for the patterns to be classified.

Whitening Transformation

We found it most useful that the principal-axis transform, as discussed in the foregoing sections, compresses the relevant information describing the N-dimensional stochastic process $\{\mathbf{v}\}$ into a smaller number M of feature variables. This property is closely related to another property, namely that of making the variances of $\{\mathbf{w}\}$ maximally different; see (9.52).

There may be reasons to deviate from this trend and try just the opposite way, making the variances of $\mathbf{w}$ all equal. An obvious reason for doing so is to minimize the effect of rounding errors if working with fixed-point arithmetic. The disturbing effect of numeric imprecisions is least if the range of potential values is maximally utilized.

This is easily accomplished by using the square root of the truncated diagonal matrix of eigenvalues $\mathbf{D}_M$ (9.57),

$$\mathbf{D}_M^{1/2} = \begin{bmatrix} \sqrt{\lambda_1} & 0 & \cdots & 0 \\ 0 & \sqrt{\lambda_2} & \cdots & 0 \\ \vdots & \vdots & & \vdots \\ 0 & 0 & \cdots & \sqrt{\lambda_M} \end{bmatrix} \tag{9.60}$$

inverting it and introducing it into the transformation equation of (9.54),

$$\mathbf{w}_M = \mathbf{D}_M^{-1/2}\mathbf{B}_M^T(\mathbf{v} - \boldsymbol{\mu}) \tag{9.61}$$

This has the consequence that all of the transformed feature variables get the same variance $\text{var}\{w_n\} = 1$. The resulting stochastic process $\{\mathbf{w}\}$ is said to be whitened.

Two- and Three-Dimensional Views of High-Dimensional Spaces

The fact that the principal-axis transform positions a task-dependent coordinate system into the measurement space at the relevant position and with the relevant orientation is not only important for the mathematical procedures to follow within the pattern classification system but is as well extremely useful in providing to the human system designer intuitively understandable insights into high-dimensional measurement spaces.

Human capability of interpreting spatial situations is limited to three dimensions since the space of our physical perception is three dimensional.

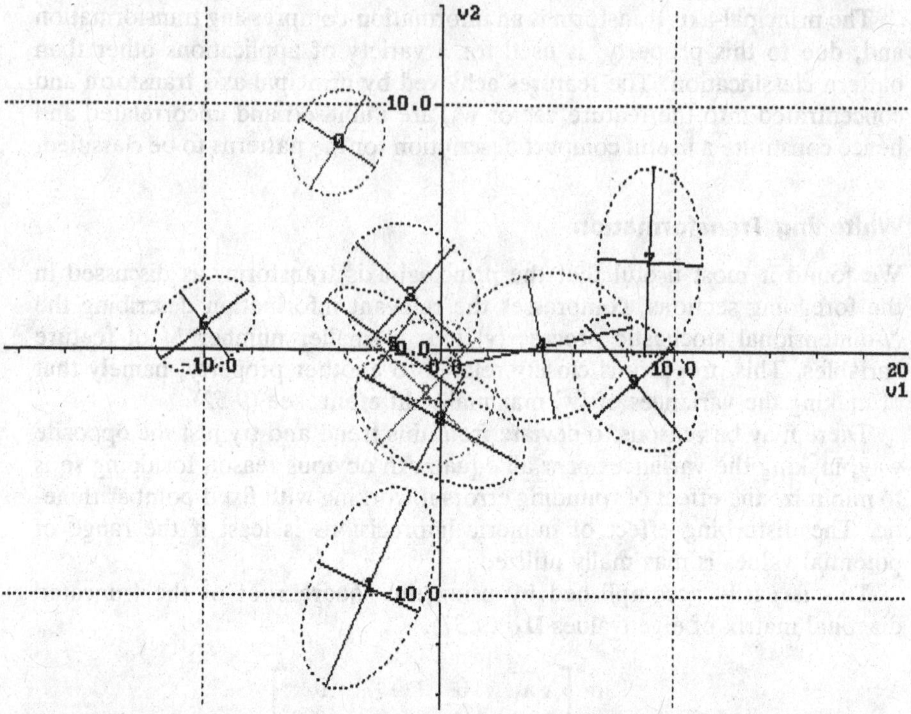

Figure 9.4. Ground view (principal axes 1 and 2) of distribution of 10 numeral classes in measurement space. Class labels *k* are given at class centers. For each of 10 classes class-specific mean $E\{\mathbf{w}|\mathbf{k}\}$ and covariance matrix $\mathbf{cov}\{\mathbf{w}, \mathbf{w}|k\}$ are computed and eigenvectors and eigenvalues determined. Crossing lines represent class-specific eigenvectors with length according to corresponding eigenvalue. Ellipses represent value $Q = 1$ of quadratic form determined by inverse class-specific covariance matrix.

But we are able to navigate in three-dimensional virtual realities presented at graphics workstations and can interpret and understand two-dimensional projections of three-dimensional objects and arrangements such as ground and front views in architecture and mechanical construction.

Relying on these capabilities, we can look into the measurement space, making use of three-dimensional projections gained from the first three of the principal axes or of any other combination of three of the coordinates. Figures 9.4 and 9.5 show the ground view (axes 1 and 2) and the front view (axes 1 and 3) of the distribution in measurement space for the 10 numeral classes of a character recognition task. Each of the classes is represented by their class center and equivalent ellipsoids.

It is rather easy to render three-dimensional computer-generated visualizations from the same kind of data that clearly convey the impression of how the different classes are arranged in measurement space.

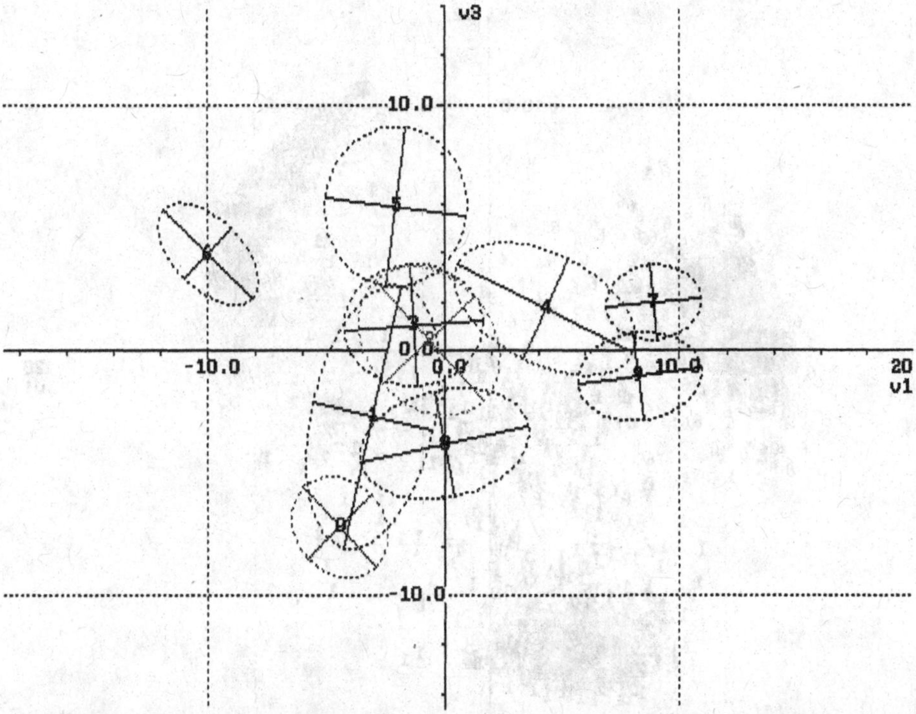

Figure 9.5. Front-view (principal axes 1 and 3) of same distribution of 10 numeral classes in measurement space as in Fig. 9.4. Class labels k are given at class centers. For all 10 classes class-specific mean $E\{\mathbf{w}|k\}$ and covariance matrix $\mathbf{cov}\{\mathbf{w}, \mathbf{w}|k\}$ are computed and eigenvectors and eigenvalues determined. Crossing lines represent class-specific eigenvectors with length according to corresponding eigenvalue. Ellipses represent value $Q = 1$ of quadratic form determined by inverse class-specific covariance matrix.

The visualizations of Figs. 9.4 and 9.5 used ellipsoids to represent the different classes. There is no reason to assume that, in reality, the classes will be ellipsoidally (normally) distributed. This becomes clearly visible in Figs. 9.6 and 9.7, which show the distributions of the three selected classes 1, 6, and 7 from the same example together with their equivalent ellipses for $Q = \{1, 2, 3\}$ and in the same projections as in Figs. 9.4 and 9.5.

The specific shapes of the distributions in Figs. 9.6 and 9.7 mirror the mixture of writing styles present in the underlying set of sample patterns. The ellipsoidal models for the different classes are only able to give a rough description of what really happens in measurement space. Typically the distributions exhibit both areas of high concentration as well as rather flat and wide areas of low but not neglectable class-specific probability mass $\text{prob}(\mathbf{w}|k)$.

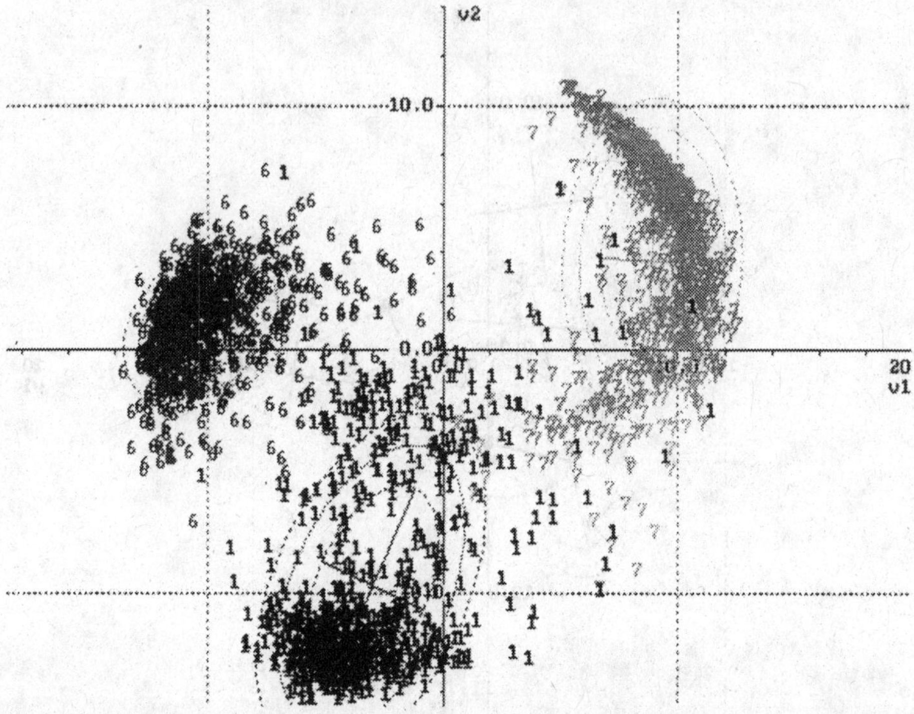

Figure 9.6. Ground view for three classes 1, 6, and 7 in measurement space in same projection as Fig. 9.4. Each class is represented by its class-specific system of eigenvectors together with three equivalent ellipses representing values $Q = 1, 2, 3$ of quadratic form determined by inverse class-specific covariance matrix. Data represent background on which 800 samples per class are plotted.

Reconstruction versus Classification

In the preceding sections we have derived the principal-axis transform from the viewpoint of establishing within the given measurement space a new task-dependent coordinate system. Exchange of one coordinate system for another does not really change the situation if the same full space is considered. All that happens is that things look differently.

Without dimensionality reduction, that is, without projection to lower dimensional spaces, almost nothing is won by switching from $\{\mathbf{v}\}$ to $\{\mathbf{w}\}$. The linear or quadratic polynomial regression classifiers, for example, would have identical results for both cases since any linear transformation $\mathbf{v} \rightarrow \mathbf{w}$ is completely absorbed by the operations of the pattern classifier.

This situation changes remarkably when projection is taken into account and the dimension M of $\mathbf{w}$ is chosen (mostly much) smaller than the dimension of $\mathbf{v}$. Then the expenses for establishing the task-dependent coordinate

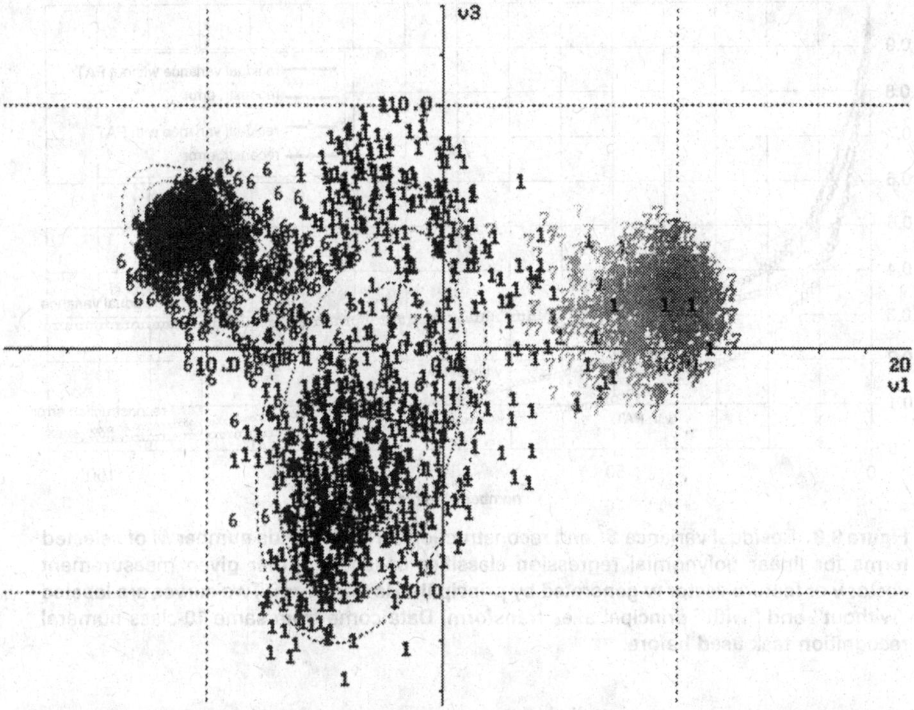

Figure 9.7. Front view for three classes 1, 6, and 7 in measurement space in same projection as Fig. 9.5. Each class is represented by its class-specific system of eigenvectors together with three equivalent ellipses representing values $Q = 1, 2, 3$ of quadratic form determined by inverse class-specific covariance matrix. Data represent background on which 800 samples per class are plotted.

system repay; this is the normal condition under which the principal-axis transform is applied in pattern classification and where its big merits are.

Astonishingly, this is true, although the classification task (the task of distinguishing between the **K** classes) has not at all been considered during the design of this transform. Remember that only the first and second statistical moments of the overall process $\{\mathbf{v}\}$ were taken into account and that no reference was made to the fact that there are K class-specific subprocesses $\{\mathbf{v}|k\}$, $k = 1, \ldots, K$, to be discriminated and making up the stochastic process $\{\mathbf{v}\}$.

This sounds somewhat strange, and many proposals have been made to integrate the classification goals into the optimization criteria for finding the optimum coordinate system [NIE1970]. Practical experience, however, has shown that the features derived from the principal-axis transform are well suited for classification purposes. The diagram of Fig. 9.8 corresponds to that of Fig. 6.10 but shows realistic instead of artificial data. The general appearance of the corresponding curves, however, remains the same.

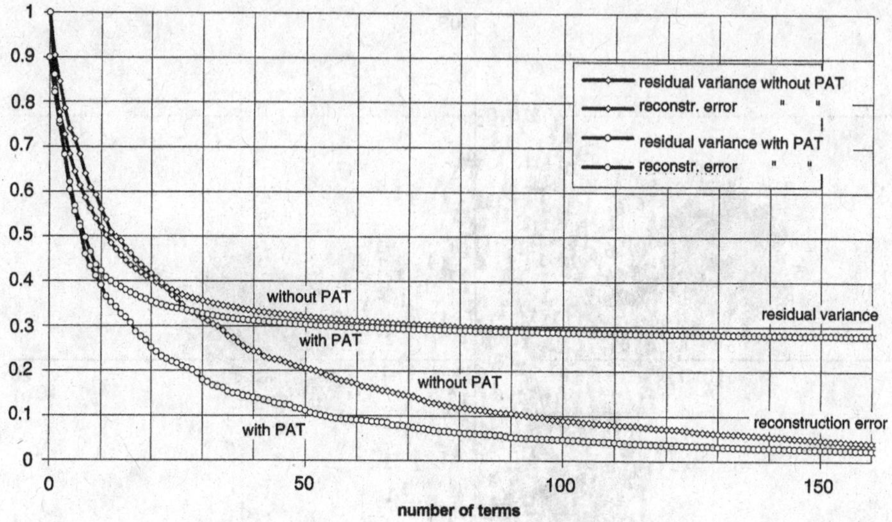

Figure 9.8. Residual variance S^2 and reconstruction error R^2 versus number M of selected terms for linear polynomial regression classifier based on either given measurement vector **v** or feature vector **w** generated by principal-axis transform. Two curves are labeled "without" and "with" principal axes transform. Data come from same 10-class numeral recognition task used before.

The reconstruction error R^2 as a function of the number M of terms used to represent the pattern-generating process $\{\mathbf{v}\}$ monotonically decreases to zero with M approaching $N = \dim[\mathbf{v}]$. The decrease, especially for smaller values of M, is considerably faster for the transformed measurements after the principal axes transform than before.

The residual variance S^2, however, as a function of the same M asymptotically approaches a certain constant level (here, about 0.3) that cannot but be identical without and with the principal-axis transform. Again the decrease is for smaller M much faster for the with than for the without curve. This shows that relying on a certain smaller number M of features gained from principal-axis transform not only provides the necessary information for restoring the original data but also improves the recognition performance compared to using the same number of untransformed measurements.

Another observation concerning the two different viewpoints of reconstruction and classification can be made from Fig. 9.8. Classification needs less information than reconstruction. Notwithstanding the fact that complete reconstruction is always possible whereas error-free classification may not be, we observe that increasing the number M of features beyond a certain value M_{limit} will not pay in terms of classifier performance but keeps paying in terms of the reconstruction error.

The most important advantage gained from applying the principal-axis

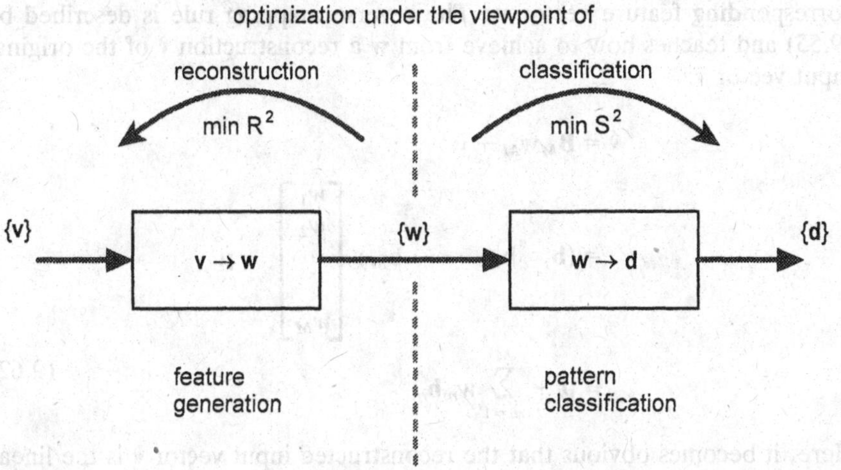

Figure 9.9. System architecture derived from separation between two different optimization points of view, optimization with respect to reconstruction in feature generation, and compression module and optimization with respect to classification in pattern classification module. Feature vector **w** determines interface between two modules.

transform for feature generation and compression is that this leads to a clear-cut overall system design (Fig. 9.9).

The whole pattern classification system, representing a mapping from **v** to **d**, is thus split into the sequence of two subsystem modules. The first module maps the measurement vector **v** into the feature vector **w** and is solely designed from considerations, whether the feature vector **w** carries enough information to reliably restore **v** from **w**. The second module maps **w** into **d** and is solely optimized from the point of view of how to establish a reliable estimation for **d** from **w**.

By introducing this distinction, the overall design process is drastically simplified and made much more effective compared to trials combining both optimization goals already for the step of feature generation. The role the feature vector **w** plays at the interface between the two modules of Fig. 9.9 can be simply stated as to carry as much information as possible about the objects or events to be recognized in a form as condensed as possible.

Reduction to Basic Constituents

The strict separation between the two viewpoints of reconstruction and classification has the consequence that for computing the principal-axis transform the learning set need not be labeled and different classes might be combined without affecting the transformation **v** → **w**, provided that the marginal distribution prob{**v**} does not change.

The transformation rule of (9.54) maps the given input vector **v** into the corresponding feature vector $\mathbf{w}$. The reverse mapping rule is described by (9.55) and teaches how to achieve from $\mathbf{w}$ a reconstruction $\hat{\mathbf{v}}$ of the original input vector $\mathbf{v}$:

$$\begin{aligned}\hat{\mathbf{v}} &= \mathbf{B}_M \mathbf{w}_M + \boldsymbol{\mu} \\ &= (\mathbf{b}_1 \quad \mathbf{b}_2 \quad \cdots \quad \mathbf{b}_M) \begin{bmatrix} w_1 \\ w_2 \\ \vdots \\ w_M \end{bmatrix} + \boldsymbol{\mu} \\ &= \boldsymbol{\mu} + \sum_{m=1}^{M} w_m \mathbf{b}_m \end{aligned} \tag{9.62}$$

Here, it becomes obvious that the reconstructed input vector $\hat{\mathbf{v}}$ is the linear combination of, first, the mean vector $\boldsymbol{\mu}$ and, second, all of the eigenvectors $\mathbf{b}_1, \ldots, \mathbf{b}_M$. The weights of the linear combination are the feature variables $w_1, \ldots, w_M$.

The eigenvectors $\mathbf{b}_1, \ldots, \mathbf{b}_M$ thus turn out to be some kind of basic constituents of the measurement vectors occurring from the pattern source $\{\mathbf{v}\}$. When $\mathbf{v}$ represents a raster image, as in the case of handprint character recognition considered before, the eigenvectors $\mathbf{b}_1, \ldots, \mathbf{b}_M$ are also images, namely those that by proper weighted summation are able to render the original image $\mathbf{v}$ with minimum distortion R^2.

Figure 9.10 shows the collection of the first M eigenvectors belonging to the handprint numeral recognition task used throughout this chapter. Since the measurement vector in this case represents a 16×16 grey value image, so do the eigenvectors. It can be seen that the low-index eigenvectors contribute mainly to the rough (low pass) structures of the image whereas the higher index eigenvectors provide the finer details.

With increasing number M of eigenvectors the reconstruction becomes more accurate. This is shown in Fig. 9.11 for one selected example character raster image.

Neural Principal-Axis Transform

The principal-axis transform is a linear transformation, including translation, controlled by the criterion of minimizing the reconstruction error R^2 between the given measurement vector $\mathbf{v}$ and its reconstruction $\hat{\mathbf{v}}$ from the feature vector $\mathbf{w}$. This is a mathematically well understood technique leading to the standard eigenvector–eigenvalue problem for which mathematical libraries provide a number of solutions at moderate computational expense so that no supercomputers are needed.

In the realm of neural network technology several approaches have been developed for the same purpose, relying completely on the concept of recur-

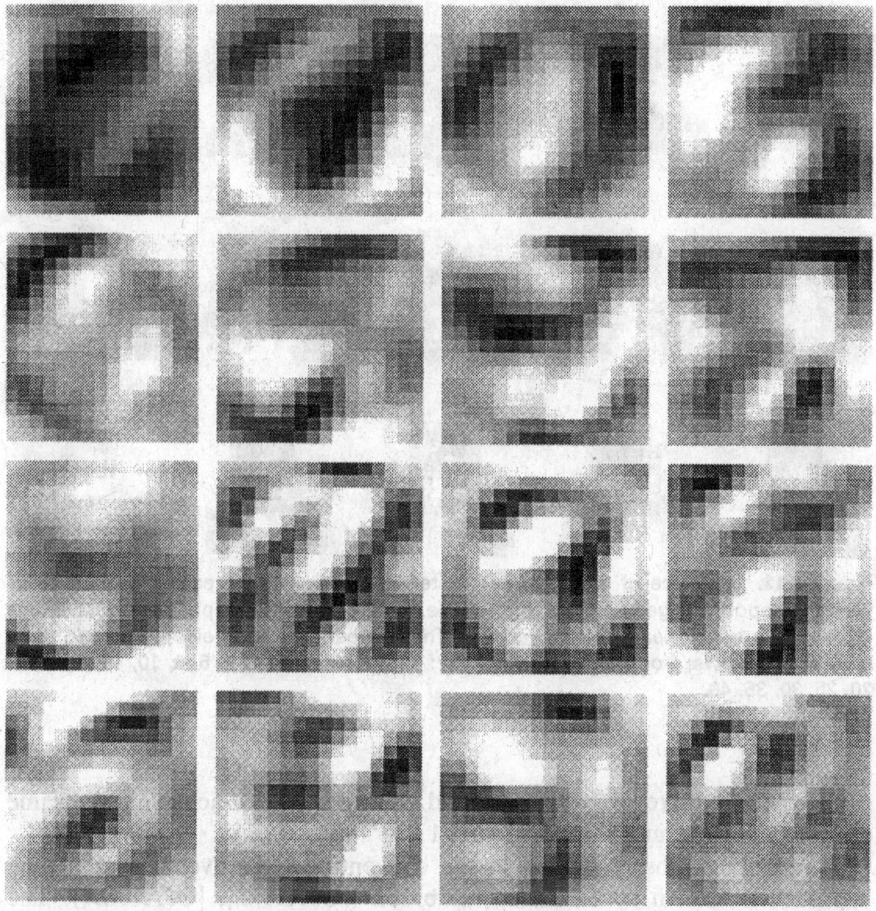

Figure 9.10. Graphical representation of first **M** eigenvectors $\mathbf{b}_1, \ldots, \mathbf{b}_M$ belonging to handprint numeral recognition task, used before, in same format as valid for corresponding measurement vectors **v** (16 × 16 grey value raster images). Since eigenvectors have positive and negative components, zero point grey scale had to be shifted to medium grey level. Thus, "white" corresponds to negative and "black" to positive values. It should be noted that eigenvectors have unit length and undecided sign.

sive learning. This means that all computations are directly based on the sequence of samples as they are consecutively taken from the learning set.

Normally, these recursive learning techniques for feature extraction do not explicitly include translation as the technique described in this section does. In other words, they care for the eigenvectors of the moment matrix $E\{\mathbf{v}\mathbf{v}^T\}$ and not for those of the covariance matrix $\mathbf{K} = \mathbf{cov}\{\mathbf{v}, \mathbf{v}\}$. This, however, does not make a difference if only the process $\{\mathbf{v}\}$ of measurement vectors is made unbiased by explicitly subtracting the mean $\boldsymbol{\mu} = E\{\mathbf{v}\}$ before going into recursive feature extraction. The mean needed for that purpose

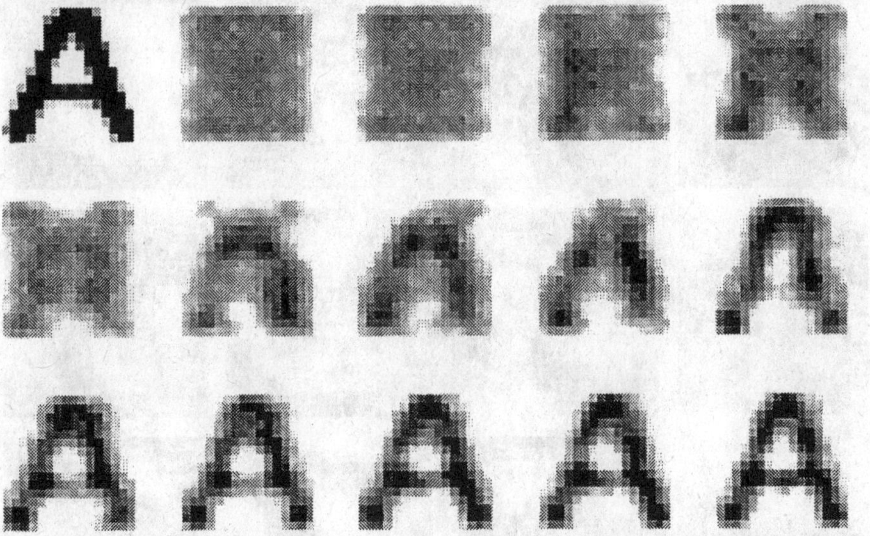

Figure 9.11. Sequence of reconstructed raster images $\hat{\mathbf{v}}$ with increasing number M of vector components gained from one single feature vector **w**. Upper leftmost image represents original measurement vector **v**. The number M of used eigenvectors in three rows is as follows: from left to right: upper: 1, 2, 3, 4; middle: 5, 6, 8, 10, 15; bottom: 20, 25, 30, 35, 40.

can also easily be recursively estimated. Another way of achieving the same effect is using the augmented vector $(1 \quad \mathbf{v})^T$ instead of **v**.

A technique closely related to the conventional eigenvector–eigenvalue approach is known as backward inhibition ([OJA1982], [OJA1989]). The basic structure is only able to compute the dominant eigenvector, that belonging to the largest eigenvalue. After the first eigenvector $\mathbf{b}_1$ and the corresponding coefficient w_1 have been found, the eigenvector is weighted with w_1 subtracted from the input data and the learning process entered again for computing the next eigenvector [HRY1992].

Another technique is directly derived from the concept of the two-layer perceptron with the measurement vector **v** as input vector. This perceptron is given a number M of hidden nodes much smaller than the input vector dimension N. The idea is to force the two-layer perceptron to generate at its output nodes an approximation $\hat{\mathbf{v}}$ to the given input vector **v**.

This can, in general, be achieved by using v as the target vector **y** and applying the same mathematics as Chapter 7, resulting in the same type of learning rules as developed there. See Fig. 9.12. The whole structure renders a least mean-square reconstruction error estimate $\hat{\mathbf{v}}$ for **v** under the constraints of the given perceptron structure. After having trained the network, the vector **w** of the hidden variables is used as the feature vector **w**.

The general feature compression system of Fig. 9.12 works with any kind

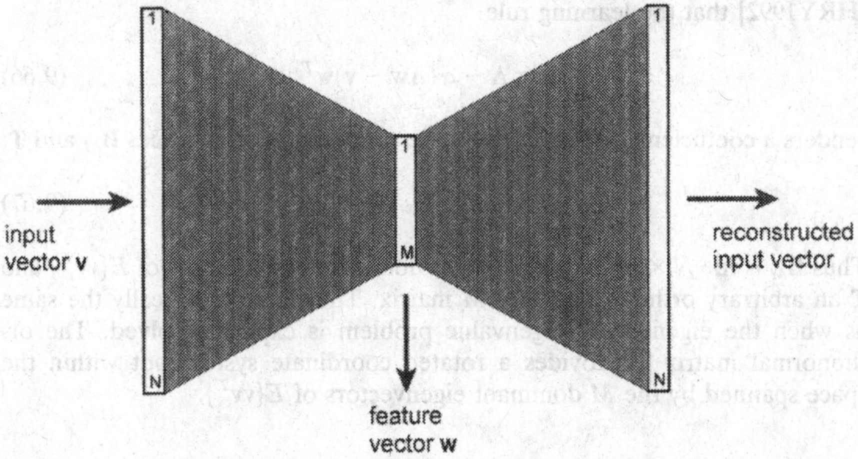

Figure 9.12. Multilayer perceptron-based feature extraction: neural counterpart to principal-axis transform. Output vector **d** is by training procedure forced to become least mean-square approximation to input vector **v**, thus approaching same minimum reconstruction error criterion as is ruling classical principal-axis transform. Dimensionality reduction is accomplished by limiting number of hidden variables to value $M < N$ and using hidden vector **h** as feature vector **w**.

of activation function. If the activation functions are set to be linear in both perceptron layers, the whole structure is considerably simplified and becomes mathematically more similar to the conventional principal-axis approach.

In this case the first layer computes the vector **w** of hidden variables to be used as the feature vector:

$$\mathbf{w} = \mathbf{A}^T\mathbf{v} \tag{9.63}$$

The second layer uses the transpose of the first-layer weight matrix **A** for generating the reconstruction

$$\hat{\mathbf{v}} = \mathbf{A}\mathbf{w} \tag{9.64}$$

The optimization goal is

$$R^2 = E\{|\hat{\mathbf{v}} - \mathbf{v}|^2\} = E\{|\mathbf{A}\mathbf{w} - \mathbf{v}|^2\} = E\{|\mathbf{A}\mathbf{A}^T\mathbf{v} - \mathbf{v}|^2\} \tag{9.65}$$

which would have the trivial solution $\mathbf{A}\mathbf{A}^T = \mathbf{I}$ if M would be allowed to approach N, but this case is definitely excluded. It is shown elsewhere

[HRY1992] that the learning rule

$$\mathbf{A} \Leftarrow \mathbf{A} - \alpha(\mathbf{A}\mathbf{w} - \mathbf{v})\mathbf{w}^T \tag{9.66}$$

renders a coefficient matrix **A** that is the product of two matrices $\mathbf{B}_M$ and **T**:

$$\mathbf{A} = \mathbf{B}_M\mathbf{T} \tag{9.67}$$

Thus $\mathbf{B}_M$ is the $N \times M$ matrix of the M dominant eigenvectors of $E\{\mathbf{v}\mathbf{v}^T\}$ and **T** an arbitrary orthonormal $M \times M$ matrix. The effect is basically the same as when the eigenvector–eigenvalue problem is explicitly solved. The orthonormal matrix **T** provides a rotated coordinate system but within the space spanned by the M dominant eigenvectors of $E\{\mathbf{v}\mathbf{v}^T\}$.

10

REJECT CRITERIA AND CLASSIFIER PERFORMANCE

We have introduced the concept of rejection rather early in this book as a fundamental constituent of risk-minimizing decision making; see Section 2.2. The overall classification system turned out to be clearly separable into a sequence of the rather independent processing steps:

- Calculate the discriminant function $\mathbf{d}(\mathbf{v})$.
- Search for the maximum component of $\mathbf{d}$.
- Reject check.

The question of rejects was postponed, we are now ready to present a detailed discussion of this. The same topic was briefly touched in the context of *confidence mapping* in Section 6.13, where provisions were necessary to check the range of input variables going into functions defined over restricted domains.

Pattern classification is decision making based on observations. The pattern is a pair of values $[\mathbf{v}, k]$ of which only $\mathbf{v}$ is presented to the pattern classification system. The pattern classifier has to derive a decision about the class k for each pattern $\mathbf{v}$ presented. The concept of rejection admits the potential refusal of the decision if the classifier is not certain enough about the case.

It is fundamental realizing that there may be different reasons for such a refusal:

- There is not enough evidence to come to a unique decision since more than one of the class labels appears adequate for the pattern $\mathbf{v}$ presented.

- The pattern classifier must admit never to have seen such a case **v**, which obviously comes from a field outside its competence and therefore must be returned unsolved.

The first of these two reasons is exactly what is considered in statistical decision theory: The *closed-world assumption* holds; the pattern to be recognized comes from one of the legitimate classes and obeys the known or at least approximately known statistical laws governing the application. The individual case can be uncertain since it may well happen that the a posteriori probabilities prob(k|**v**) for the specific pattern vector **v** presented do not indicate a unique decision in the sense that there is not just one a posteriori probability exhibiting a value close to 1 but there are at least two or three of them having values close to $\frac{1}{2}$ or $\frac{1}{3}$, respectively.

The second reason is that something absolutely unforeseen has happened: The closed-world assumption is violated. The pattern vector **v** presented to the pattern classifier does not come from the legitimate classes but represents something else. Consider the example of an optical character recognition (OCR) system developed to read numerals to which an alpha character, or a graphical symbol, or ultimately an absolutely senseless random pattern may be mistakenly presented.

We call the last-mentioned situation the *garbage pattern problem*.

10.1 GARBAGE PATTERN PROBLEM

The pattern space **V** is the universe of all potential patterns. We have seen that the essence of learning in the context of pattern classification is assembling knowledge about how the classes to be distinguished are distributed in pattern space. If we consider the pattern space as a large mass of land (a whole continent), learning from examples simply teaches us where the inhabited regions are and where within them are the settlements of the different classes. Outside these settlements vast areas of terra incognita remain; see Fig. 10.1.

Detecting garbage patterns is of eminent importance for practical application of pattern classification and determines an additional pattern classification problem of its own, namely that of distinguishing the two classes "legitimate" and "garbage" patterns. Referring to what was presented in this book about pattern classifier design, we need to know the probability distributions prob(**v**|legitimate) and prob(**v**|garbage) of those two classes together with their a priori probabilities prob(garbage) and prob(legitimate) = 1 − prob(garbage) or should at least have been given a sufficiently large set of learning samples coming from both classes.

From the already given learning sample for the legitimate classes to be discriminated, we know all we need to know about the class "legitimate":

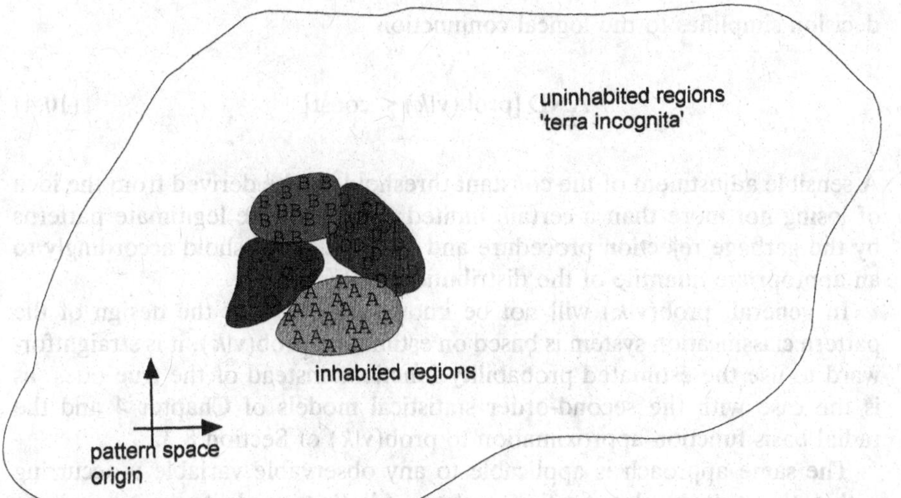

Figure 10.1. Illustration of notions of inhabited and uninhabited regions in pattern space.

$$\text{prob}(\mathbf{v}|\text{legitimate}) = \sum_{k=1}^{K} P_k \text{prob}(\mathbf{v}|k) \tag{10.1}$$

Such knowledge is totally lacking for the class "anything else". The best we can do in this situation is to rely on the uniformity assumption, stating that the class "garbage" is uniformly distributed over the whole pattern space **V**, resulting in

$$\text{prob}(\mathbf{v}|\text{garbage}) = \text{const} \tag{10.2}$$

Bayes's decision rule (2.25) requires us to decide for "garbage" if

$$\text{prob}(\mathbf{v}|\text{legitimate}) < \frac{\text{prob(garbage)}}{\text{1-prob(garbage)}} \text{prob}(\mathbf{v}|\text{garbage}) = \text{const} \tag{10.3}$$

Regardless of whether the a priori probability prob(garbage) is estimated or simply ignored, and thus the decision rule is changed into the maximum-likelihood decision rule (2.26), the "garbage" decision requires us to compare prob(**v**|legitimate) with a constant threshold.

Based on the assumption that near the outside border of the inhabited region only one class-specific probability prob(**v**|k) is nonzero, the garbage decision simplifies to the logical conjunction

$$\operatorname*{AND}_{k=1}^{K} [\text{prob}(\mathbf{v}|k) < \text{const}] \tag{10.4}$$

A sensible adjustment of the constant threshold can be derived from the idea of losing not more than a certain limited portion of the legitimate patterns by the garbage rejection procedure and setting the threshold accordingly to an appropriate quantile of the distribution prob($\mathbf{v}|k$).

In general, prob($\mathbf{v}|k$) will not be known explicitly. If the design of the pattern classification system is based on estimating prob($\mathbf{v}|k$), it is straightforward to use the estimated probability functions instead of the true ones, as is the case with the second-order statistical models of Chapter 4 and the radial basis function approximation to prob($\mathbf{v}|k$) of Section 8.3.

The same approach is applicable to any observable variable υ occurring within the pattern classification system. All that needs to be done is to assemble empirical knowledge about the statistical behavior of that variable υ typically in the form of histograms from which the necessary quantiles can easily be derived. A technique of this kind is described in Section 6.13 dealing with the confidence mapping approach.

It should be noted that the different approaches to arrive at estimations of either prob($\mathbf{v}|k$) or prob($k|\mathbf{v}$) discussed in the preceding chapters are differently well suited for detecting and rejecting garbage patterns.

Things would be easy if the true class-specific probabilities prob($\mathbf{v}|k$) would be known since then all of the necessary statistical information would be directly accessible. The property of being well suited for garbage pattern reject transfers to the techniques working with approximations for prob($\mathbf{v}|k$) even if the approximation is not excessively faithful. Consider, for example, the empirical distribution of class 7 in Fig. 9.6. Modeling this empirical distribution by a two-dimensional normal distribution provides only a quite rough description of the actual situation. The fact, however, remains that far-off pattern vectors $\mathbf{v}$ are easily detected due to their large distance from the class center and the correspondingly vanishing value of $\text{prob}_{\text{estimated}}(\mathbf{v}|k)$.

Things are not as simple with the techniques generating approximations to the a posteriori probabilities prob($k|\mathbf{v}$). The crucial point is that prob($k|\mathbf{v}$) is mathematically undefined in regions where prob($\mathbf{v}$) = 0, and these are just the uninhabited regions of the pattern space $\mathbf{V}$. The estimating functions $d_k(\mathbf{v})$ are allowed to treat these regions deliberately according to their own preferences.

The more we proceed into the far-off uninhabited regions of the measurement space, the more is the behavior of the estimating functions determined by intrinsic properties typical for the family of functions underlying the approximation and the less it is determined by properties of the learning set.

The optimization procedure, being the real core of parameter learning, forces the estimating functions $d_k(\mathbf{v})$ to go more or less accurately through the given points [v, p] in the inhabited region of the pattern space. This is true regardless of the type of basis functions used for the approximation. Outside this region, however, the differences between the techniques discussed in the preceding chapters become dominant. The estimating functions gained from the polynomial regression approach quickly run to plus or minus infinity, those gained from the multilayer perceptron approach stay at values 0 or 1, whereas those gained from the radial basis functions approach vanish quickly to 0:

	Inhabited Regions	Uninhabited Regions
Polynomial regression	Close to $\text{prob}(k\vert\mathbf{v})$	$\rightarrow [-\infty, +\infty]$
Multilayer perceptron	Close to $\text{prob}(k\vert\mathbf{v})$	$\rightarrow [0, 1]$
Radial basis functions	Close to $\text{prob}(k\vert\mathbf{v})$	$\rightarrow 0$

(10.5)

The friendliest behavior with respect to garbage pattern detection exhibits the radial basis functions approach. Outside the inhabited regions the estimated a posteriori probabilities altogether vanish to zero. The least suited technique in this respect is the multilayer perceptron approach since its estimations, due to the underlying design principles, are forced to render values coming from the same range [0 . . 1] as in the inhabited regions. It is therefore impossible to detect garbage patterns from observing the estimations $d_k(\mathbf{v})$. The polynomial regression approach renders estimations quickly, leaving the allowed interval [0 . . 1] when $\mathbf{v}$ moves into the outside areas in V-space with the exception of small stripes along the class boundaries that normally extend into the uninhabited regions; compare Fig. 4.11. Garbage detection criteria can in this case easily be derived from observing the range of values $d_k(\mathbf{v})$. The same is true for the multilayer perceptron approach if in the last layer of the multilayer perceptron the sigmoidal mapping is omitted.

10.2 REJECT CRITERIA

The two types of reasons for a reject (insufficient evidence or suspicion of being garbage) must be ultimately treated by the same reject check procedure. We will, in the following, look into the arsenal of reject criteria with the intention of developing an intuitive understanding of how they work and to which degree they might be able to cope with both kinds of problems

The Bayes decision rule, as introduced in Chapter 2 in the context of statistical decision theory, embodied already a reject rule, namely, find the maximum of $\text{prob}(k|\mathbf{v})$ but check before forwarding the index k whether the maximum found exceeds a certain threshold value β or not; compare (2.21). Due to the decision-theoretic conceptions this reject rule is optimum for the case of insufficient evidence if the closed-world assumption holds and if the a posteriori probabilities are known.

Normally, these are just not known but must be approximated, or estimated, in some way. This book deals with a number of approaches to establish such estimations based on the given learning set. This led to the conception of a mapping $\mathbf{v} \rightarrow \mathbf{d}$ from measurement space $\mathbf{V}$ into decision space $\mathbf{D}$, with $\mathbf{d}(\mathbf{v})$ being the vector of estimated a posteriori probabilities to be used in Bayes's decision rule as if they were the true values.

The true vector $\mathbf{p}$ of a posteriori probabilities has certain properties (compare Section 6.7), which may be lost in the approximation $\mathbf{d}$. These effects are best illustrated in the decision space $\mathbf{D}$. For this purpose we consider the case of $K = 3$ classes to be distinguished and look into the corresponding decision space $\mathbf{D}$ (Fig. 10.2); compare Figs. 1.4, 6.4, and 6.5.

This decision space for $K = 3$ classes is spanned by the three target vectors

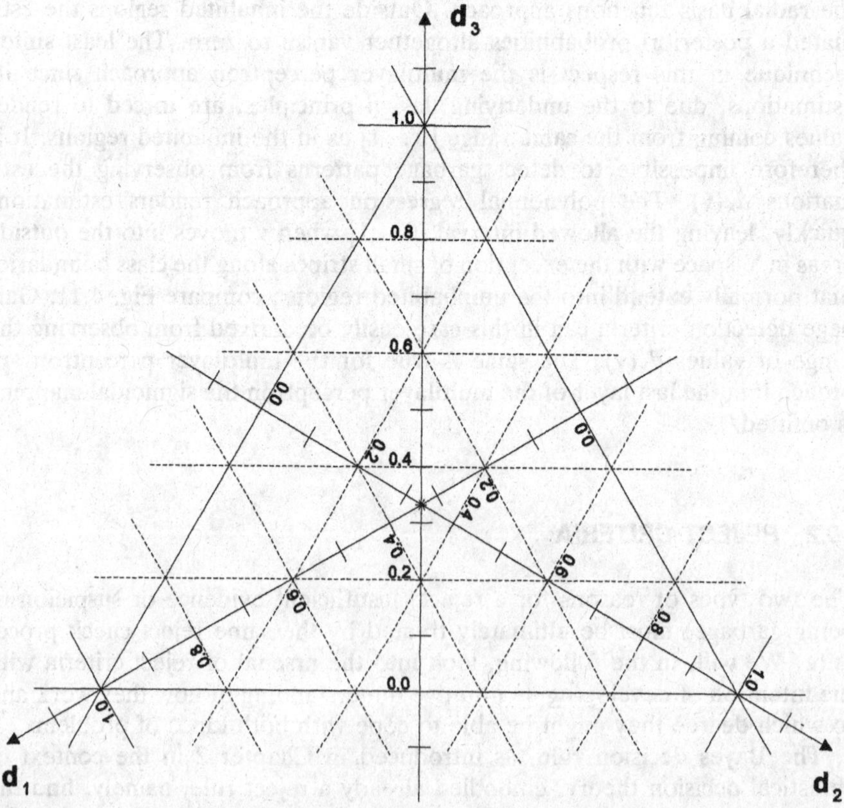

Figure 10.2. Two-dimensional decision space **D** for three-class case, $K = 3$. Triangular coordinate system is valid for three-dimensional vectors **d** having *sum equal-unity* property.

$\mathbf{y}_1$, $\mathbf{y}_2$, $\mathbf{y}_3$, determining an equilateral triangle in 3-space that can be put into the two-dimensional drawing plane with the three corners representing the tops of the three target vectors.

In the case of the optimum discriminant function $\mathbf{d}(\mathbf{v}) = \mathbf{p}(\mathbf{v})$ the set of all possible vectors **d** is completely contained within the triangle's plane and inside the triangle. If we are dealing with estimations instead of the true a posteriori probabilities, the discriminant vector **d** are likely to fall outside the triangle's interior or leave the triangle's plane. Both deviations from the ideal can be corrected by suitable projections and mappings: compare (7.35) and Section 6.13.

Thus, we find that the decision space is essentially $(K-1)$-dimensional. It is straightforward to transfer the conceptions exemplified here for only $K = 3$ classes to higher dimensions.

With the discriminant vector **d** given, the decision about the most probable class is derived by searching for the maximum component of **d** and the reject decision by investigating the distribution of the component values. There are several reject criteria imaginable. The simplest and most often used are the following [SCH1973]:

$$\text{MAX criterion:} \qquad d_{\mathbf{max}} < \text{threshold} \tag{10.6}$$

$$\text{DIF criterion:} \qquad d_{\mathbf{max}} - d_{\mathbf{secondmax}} < \text{threshold} \tag{10.7}$$

$$\text{RAD criterion:} \qquad r^2_{\mathbf{min}} > \text{threshold} \tag{10.8}$$

where $r^2_{\mathbf{min}}$ denotes the minimum among the squared Euclidean distances between **d** and the set of target vectors $\mathbf{y}_1, \ldots, \mathbf{y}_K$; compare (3.12).

The MAX criterion implements exactly what the Bayes decision rule teaches; see Fig. 10.3. The resulting reject region is a triangle oriented opposite to the decision space triangle and emerging from the decision triangle's center for threshold values $> \frac{1}{3}$. In the general case the triangles become K-corner simplices and the minimum effective threshold $1/K$. This type of reject criterion cares only for legitimate patterns **v**. It can be equipped with the capability of rejecting garbage patterns if at the same time also the minimum of the components of **d** is checked, thus enclosing the decision triangle by a parallel but wider triangle. We call this additional test the MIN criterion; see Fig. 10.4.

$$\text{MIN criterion:} \quad d_{\mathbf{min}} < \text{threshold} \tag{10.9}$$

The reject threshold is in this case a negative value.

It should be mentioned that the garbage rejection technique that is part of the confidence mapping procedure described in Section 6.13 provides a similar kind of garbage reject but with the specialty that minimum and maximum thresholds determine acceptance regions on each of the K d_k scales separately.

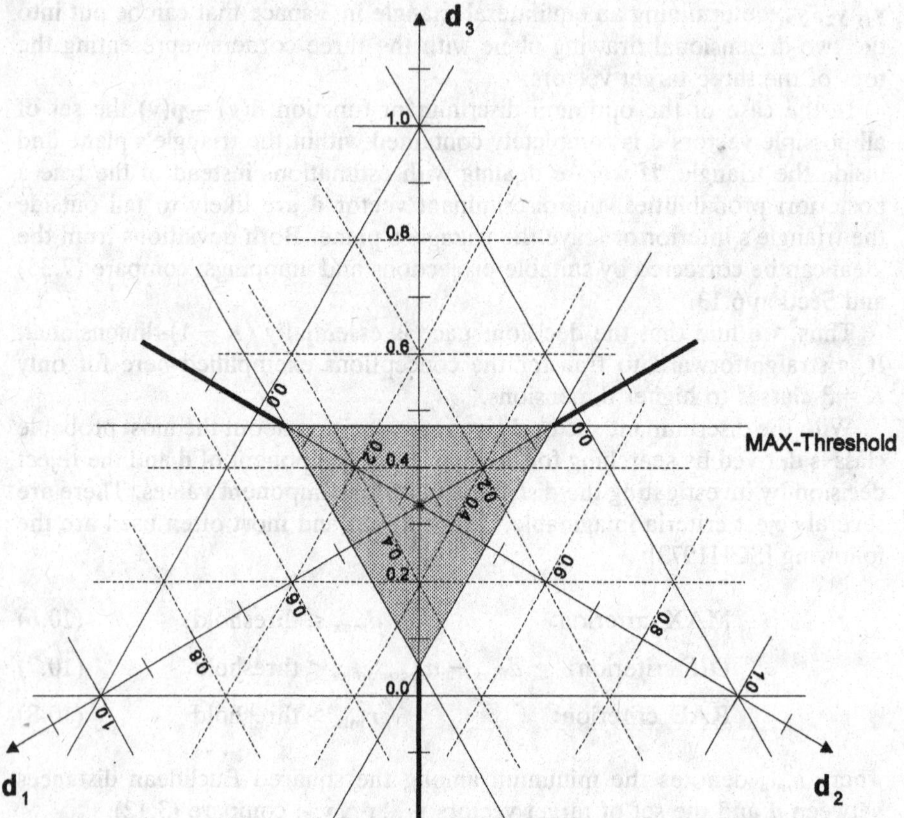

Figure 10.3. Two-dimensional decision space **D** for three-class case. Reject region determined by MAX criterion. Reject region caused by rejecting patterns whenever maximum component of **d** is smaller than required minimum shown as shaded triangle in center area of the decision triangle.

Whereas the MAX criterion establishes an island of no man's land in that region of the decision space where all of the classes are almost equally probable but leaves the borders between each pair of classes unprotected, the DIF criterion separates each class region from all of the others by a stripe of no man's land along the class boundaries; see Fig. 10.5. This technique has the property that small variations of **d** cannot change the class membership of **d**, or **v** respectively, without going through the reject state. As long as the mapping **v** → **d** is continuous or quasi-continuous, the same is valid for **v** with the effect that the class regions in measurement space **V** are also wrapped in no man's land and thus isolated from each other.

The DIF criterion can, as the MAX criterion, be combined with the MIN criterion to provide the capability of rejecting garbage patterns.

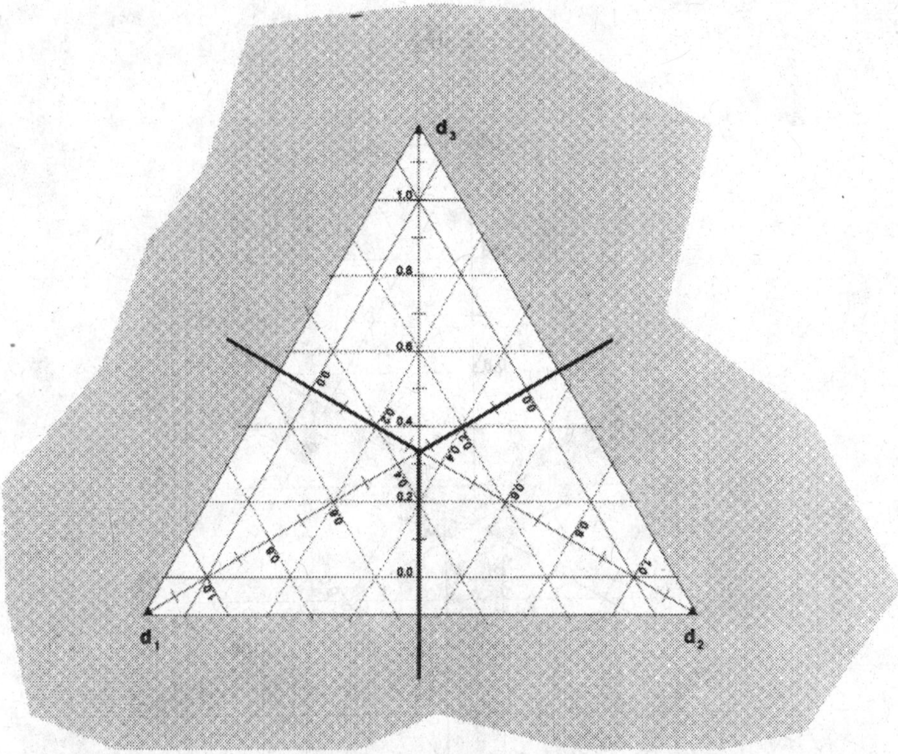

Figure 10.4. Two-dimensional decision space **D** for three-class case. Reject region determined by MIN criterion. Reject region caused by rejecting patterns whenever minimum component of **d** is smaller than threshold is shown as shaded region enclosing decision triangle and having triangular opening parallel to decision triangle.

The third of the three reject criteria (the RAD criterion) is motivated by the close relationship between the kth component d_k of the discriminant vector $\mathbf{d}$ and its squared Euclidean distance r_k^2 to the target vector $\mathbf{y}_k$ of the corresponding class k; compare (3.12). Minimization of the squared Euclidean distance between estimation $\mathbf{d}$ and the true target vector $\mathbf{y}$ has been the goal of all *least mean-square learning techniques*. It is, therefore, most convincing to use the minimum $r_k^2 = r_{\min}^2$ between $\mathbf{d}$ and the closest of the target vectors $\mathbf{y}_k$, $k = 1, \ldots, K$, as reject criterion; see Fig. 10.6.

The specific value of the reject criterion RAD determines whether the class regions are completely embedded in isolating no man's land or directly touch along the class borders. Independent of the number K of classes the accept circles touch for

$$r_{\min}^2 = \tfrac{1}{2} \quad \text{corresponding to} \quad r_{\min} = \sqrt{\tfrac{1}{2}} \approx 0.7 \tag{10.10}$$

The RAD criterion has the property of generating closed accept regions and

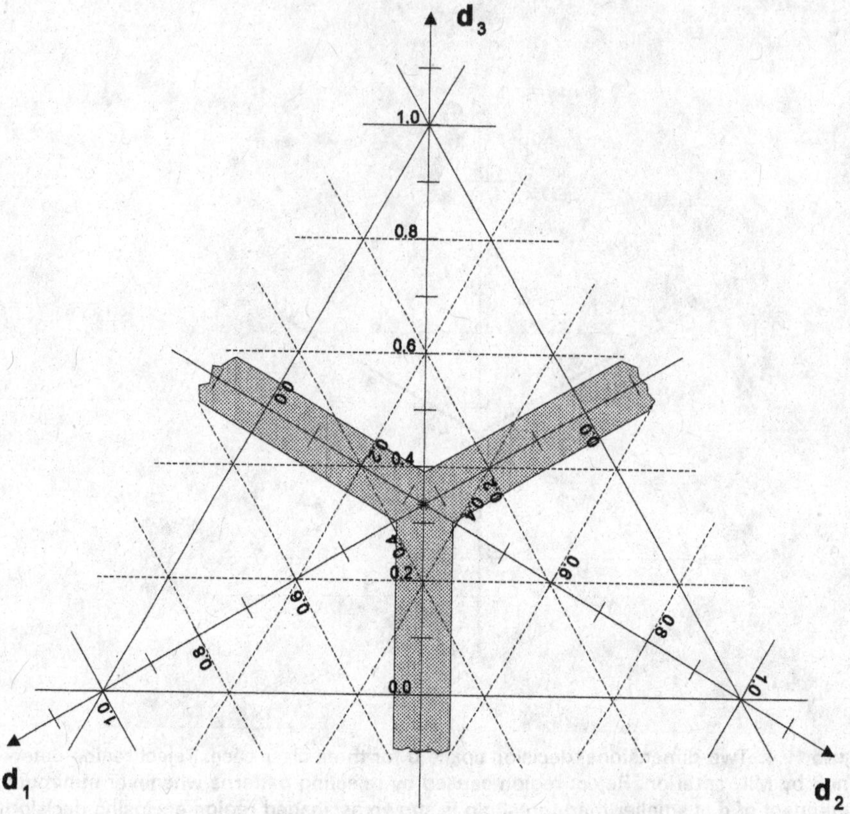

Figure 10.5. Two-dimensional decision space **D** for three-class case. Reject region determined by DIF criterion. Reject region caused by rejecting patterns whenever difference between maximum and second-maximum component of **d** is smaller than required minimum is shown as shaded region along class boundaries.

is thus capable of rejecting ambiguous as well as garbage patterns similar to the MAX and DIF criteria if combined with the MIN criterion.

These properties become especially efficient if **d** is gained from polynomial regression or from multilayer perceptron regression with omitted nonlinearity in the last perceptron layer since then garbage patterns typically cause the discriminant functions $d_k(\mathbf{v})$ to assume values clearly outside the $[0\,..\,1]$ interval; see (10.5).

10.3 AMBIGUOUS PATTERNS AND SETS OF ALTERNATIVES

In practical application, pattern classification is often only part of a larger knowledge-processing activity. Think of the task of automatic reading ad-

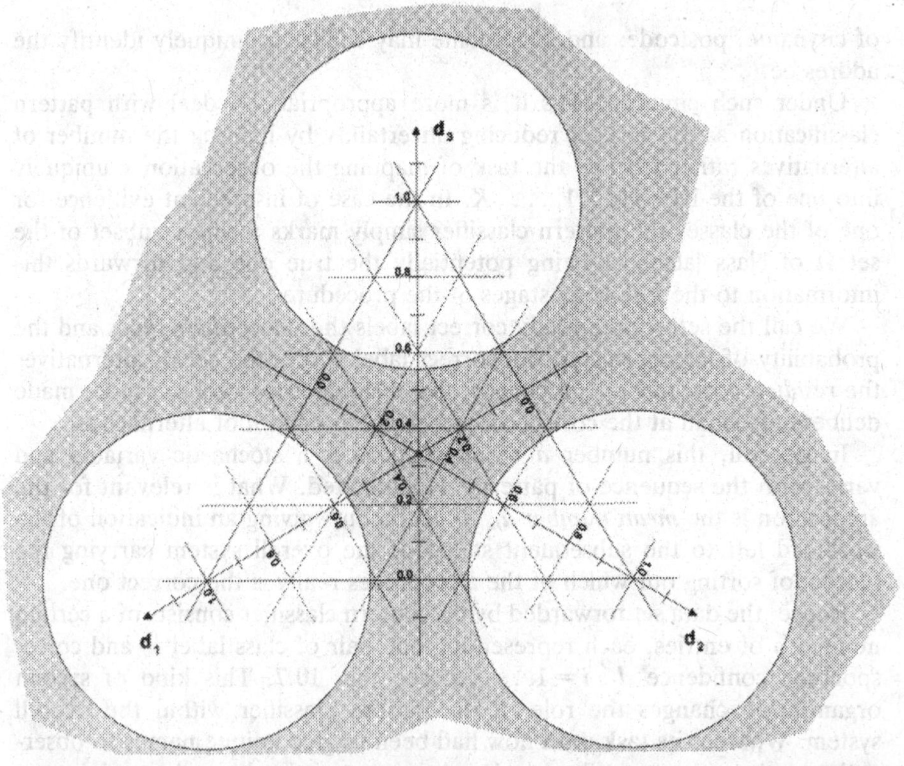

Figure 10.6. Two-dimensional decision space **D** for three-class case. Reject region determined by RAD criterion. Reject region caused by rejecting patterns whenever (squared) Euclidean distance between discriminant vector **d** and nearest target point **y** exceeds admitted maximum shown as shaded region enclosing class reference points and generating, in this case, isolated accept regions for *K* classes.

dresses from every-day mailpieces. Such an application requires us to collect numerous bits of knowledge and to tie them properly together in order to construct a sensible whole, beginning with the task of finding the address area on the mailpiece, separating characters from background, recognizing the character images, recognizing the words formed by the characters, and understanding them by matching them with the logical primitives of the application such as streetname, cityname, post office box number, zip code, building name, company name, and so on.

Pattern classification connects the two worlds of subsymbolic and symbolic processing and provides the primitives for subsequent symbolic reasoning. Typically, perfect recognition on the classification level is neither possible nor necessary. In the above-mentioned example, we may have had difficulties in recognizing every letter of cityname, but even then the name of the city can often be uniquely restored from the rest of the letters knowing that it is a city in a certain state of the United States. Or, more complicated, pieces of cityname, postcode, and streetname may suffice to uniquely identify the addressee.

Under such circumstances it is more appropriate to deal with pattern classification as the task of reducing uncertainty by limiting the number of alternatives rather than as the task of mapping the observation **v** uniquely into one of the labels $k = 1, \ldots, K$. In the case of insufficient evidence for one of the classes the pattern classifier simply marks a whole subset of the set Ω of class labels as being potentially the true one and forwards this information to the following stages of the procedure.

We call the set of potentially correct labels the *set of alternatives* and the probability of having missed the correct label within the set of alternatives the *residual error rate* ϵ_r. Obviously, this residual error rate ϵ_r can be made deliberately small at the cost of an increasing number a of alternatives.

In general, this number a of alternatives is a stochastic variable and varies with the sequence of patterns {**v**} presented. What is relevant for the application is the *mean number* a_m *of alternatives* giving an indication of the workload left to the subsequent stages of the overall system carrying the burden of sorting out which of the alternatives really is the correct one.

Hence, the data set forwarded by the pattern classifier consists of a certain number a of entries, each representing one pair of class label k_i and corresponding confidence d_i, $i = 1, \ldots, a$; see Fig. 10.7. This kind of system organization changes the role of the pattern classifier within the overall system. Whereas its task until now had been to give unique names to observations **v**, it now acts similar to a human expert stating his or her opinion on the presented case and accompanying his or her judgments k_i with subjective probabilities d_i.

In order to be useful for subsequent reasoning the confidences should have the property of being consistent with empirical experience. This means that, on average, of all the judgments with a confidence value of d (e.g., $d =$

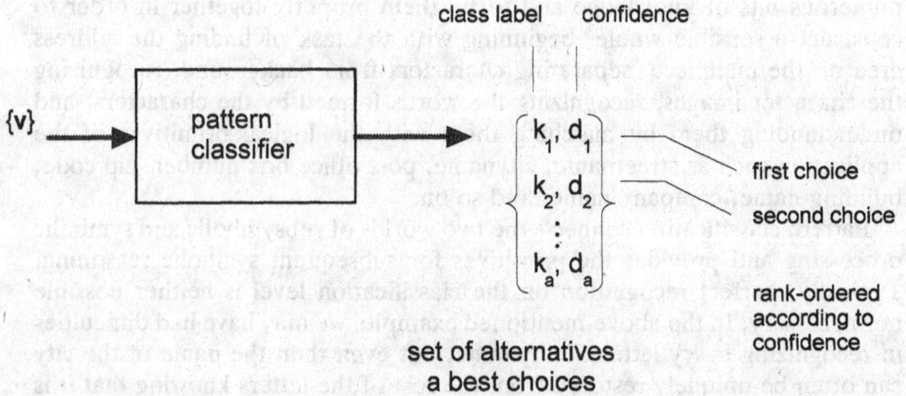

Figure 10.7. Pattern classification as task of forming sets of alternatives.

80%), the same percentage d (again 80%) of judgments should be correct. This is achieved by the technique of confidence mapping, introduced in Section 6.13.

Relations between Reject and Forming Sets of Alternatives

In the introduction to the present chapter we have discussed the two reasons for reject; suspicion of being garbage and insufficient evidence. The first reason can only be treated by reject, whereas the second allows us to apply both measures, reject and forming sets of alternatives.

Garbage patterns, representing anything else except the legitimate classes, are objects that definitely cannot be treated in any reasonable way by the pattern classifier. They must be rejected; forming sets of alternatives for garbage patterns is senseless. Garbage patterns remaining undetected fake legitimate patterns and lead to uninterpretable results.

The second reason, ambiguity due to insufficient evidence, can be treated by both techniques, reject and forming sets of alternatives. In terms of forwarding sets of alternatives, the reject corresponds to forwarding the complete set Ω of class labels as the set of alternatives. In other words, reject as the complete refusal of giving any judgment to the presented case in effect is the same as setting the joker. The reject sets the number of alternatives to $a = K$.

Rejection is a comparably coarse tool of handling ambiguities. Forwarding adequately small sets of alternatives, therefore, is the more intelligent way of dealing with insufficient evidence. However, it must be mentioned that forming sets of alternatives is only then sensible if there are at all any subsequent stages of symbolic reasoning capable of resolving the ambiguities and thus completing the decision.

10.4 CONTROLLING NUMBER OF ALTERNATIVES

The number a of alternatives determines the ambiguity left and consequently has a strong impact on the computational effort in the subsequent stages of the overall system. It should, on average, be as small as possible, which requires us to make it dependent on the actual case.

There are two convincing approaches to decide on the number a of alternatives. The first is based on geometric considerations in decision space, whereas the second argues with confidences and probabilities.

Introduction of Multiple-Class Target Points in Decision Space

The decision space, as introduced in Section 1.4 and used throughout this book, is equipped with K target points corresponding to unique decisions for each of the K classes. The corresponding target vector $\mathbf{y}$ has one single component with value 1 and all others with value 0:

$$\mathbf{y}_{\text{unique}} = (\cdots \quad 0 \quad 1 \quad 0 \quad \cdots)^T \tag{10.11}$$

Alternatives shall be formed if two or more classes compete and seem to be equally probable. This type of event can be expressed by introducing appropriate multiple-class target vectors $\mathbf{y}_{\text{multiple classes}}$ that for the case of two rivaling classes have two components with value $\frac{1}{2}$ and for three rivaling classes have correspondingly three components with value $\frac{1}{3}$:

$$\begin{aligned} \mathbf{y}_{\text{pair of classes}} &= (\cdots \quad 0 \quad \tfrac{1}{2} \quad 0 \quad \cdots \quad 0 \quad \tfrac{1}{2} \quad 0 \quad \cdots)^T \\ \mathbf{y}_{\text{triple of classes}} &= (\cdots \quad 0 \quad \tfrac{1}{3} \quad 0 \quad \cdots \quad 0 \quad \tfrac{1}{3} \quad 0 \cdots \quad 0 \quad \tfrac{1}{3} \quad 0 \quad \cdots)^T \end{aligned} \tag{10.12}$$

The concept transfers easily to an arbitrary number $a \leq K$ of alternatives. The newly introduced target vectors $\mathbf{y}_{\text{multiple classes}}$ retain the same sum-equal-unity property of $\mathbf{e}^T\mathbf{y}_{\text{multiple classes}} = 1$ as the original ones, $\mathbf{e}^T\mathbf{y}_{\text{unique}} = 1$, and hence represent points belonging to the $(K-1)$-dimensional subspace spanned by the K unique target vectors $\mathbf{y}_{\text{unique}}$.

This situation is illustrated by Fig. 10.8 for the case of $K = 3$ classes;

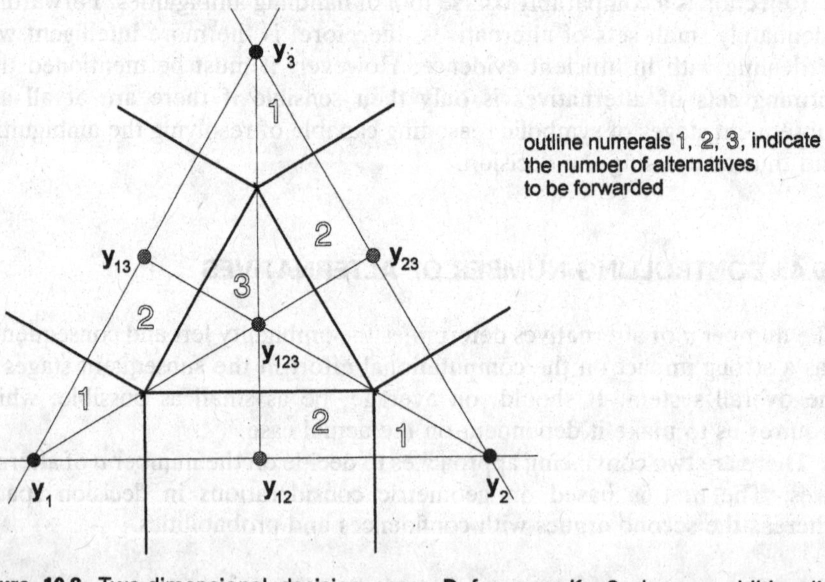

Figure 10.8. Two-dimensional decision space **D** for case $K = 3$ classes, additionally equipped with multiple-class target points for two and three rivaling classes. Decision space is subdivided into patches of different numbers a of alternatives according to Euclidean nearest-neighbor rule whereby set of multiple-class target vectors serves as set of references. Locally valid number a of alternatives indicated by outline numerals.

compare Figs. 10.2–10.6. The additional target points are shown as points of the decision triangle. To each of them belongs a certain set of alternatives. The simple idea is to apply the nearest-neighbor rule, find among the augmented set of target vectors $\mathbf{y}_{\text{multiple classes}}$ that target vector $\mathbf{y}$ being closest to the present discriminant vector $\mathbf{d}$, and forward the respective set of alternatives. Thus, the decision space $\mathbf{D}$ is partitioned into a large number of Voronoi cells each accompanied with a different set, and potentially also different number, of alternatives. The decision on the actual number a of alternatives requires us to compute the squared Euclidean distances between $\mathbf{v}$ and all of the multiple-class target vectors $\mathbf{y}_{\text{multiple classes}}$.

The class labels to be included into the set of alternatives are easily determined from the rank-ordered components of $\mathbf{d}$ since the fact that the nearest neighbor among, for example, the triple-class reference points $\mathbf{y}_{\text{triple classes}}$ is $\mathbf{y}_{ijk}$ implies that $\mathbf{y}_i$, $\mathbf{y}_j$, and $\mathbf{y}_k$ are the three nearest neighbors of $\mathbf{d}$ among the set of unique target vectors $\mathbf{y}_{\text{unique}}$. These relations are valid for any number a of alternatives. And we know from (3.12) that the rank order according to decreasing values of d_k corresponds to the rank order according to increasing r_k. Hence the ith nearest neighbor of $\mathbf{d}$ among the unique target vectors is found by searching the ith-largest component of $\mathbf{d}$.

It should be stressed that deciding about the number a of alternatives in the specific case requires us to compute the Euclidean distances between the given discriminant vector $\mathbf{d}$ and all of the old and new target vectors $\mathbf{y}$. At first glance this seems to be a computationally expensive task since the total number NumbTgt of target vectors for a system allowed to generate a maximum of A alternatives grows quickly with the number of classes K:

$$\text{NumbTgt} = \sum_{a=1}^{A} \binom{K}{a} \tag{10.13}$$

We will see that the whole procedure can be remarkably simplified.

The squared Euclidean distance between $\mathbf{d}$ and one of the NumbTgt target vectors $\mathbf{y}_{a\text{-tuple of classes}}$ representing exactly a alternatives is given by

$$r_a^2 = |\mathbf{d} - \mathbf{y}_{a\text{-tuple of classes}}|^2 = |\mathbf{d}^2 - 2\mathbf{d}^T\mathbf{y}_{a\text{-tuple of classes}} + |\mathbf{y}_{a\text{-tuple of classes}}|^2 \tag{10.14}$$

Considering the definition (10.12) of $\mathbf{y}_{a\text{-tuple of classes}}$, we arrive at

$$r_a^2 = |\mathbf{d}|^2 - \frac{1}{a}\left(2 \sum_{\substack{k \in \text{set of} \\ \text{alternatives}}} d_k - 1\right) \tag{10.15}$$

The search for the minimum distance among all NumbTgt distances is accomplished in two steps. We look first for the minimum distance for a fixed number a of alternatives and compare then the resulting A distances for $a = 1, \ldots, A$ for minimum.

The minimum among r_a^2 for fixed a is easily found by taking in (10.15) the sum over the a maximum components of $\mathbf{d}$. For this purpose the rank-ordered version of the given discriminant vector $\mathbf{d}$ is generated,

$$\mathbf{d}_{\text{rank-ordered}} = (d_{\max} \quad d_{\text{secondmax}} \quad \cdots \quad d_{\min})^T \tag{10.16}$$

and the minimum $r_{a,\min}^2$ computed as

$$r_{a,\min}^2 = |\mathbf{d}|^2 - \frac{1}{a}\left(2 \sum_{i=1}^{a} d_{i\text{th max}} - 1\right) \tag{10.17}$$

The minimum search among the A values $r_{a,\min}^2$ is unaffected by monotonic mappings such as subtraction of $|\mathbf{d}|^2$ and division by -2, which only changes the minimum search into a maximum search. Thus we arrive at a sequence of A numbers $f[a]$, the maximum of which decides on the number a of alternatives,

$$f[a] = \frac{1}{a}\left(\sum_{i=1}^{a} d_{i\text{th max}} - \tfrac{1}{2}\right) \tag{10.18}$$

The optimum number a of alternatives is easily found by searching the largest among the A items $f[a]$. Since the discriminant vector $\mathbf{d}$ is already rank ordered, we need only take the a top components of $\mathbf{d}_{\text{rank ordered}}$ and forward them as the set of the a alternatives.

It should be remarked that the additional target vectors $\mathbf{y}_{\text{multiple classes}}$ are used only for determining the classifier output and not for classifier adaptation.

The above technique of forming sets of alternatives based on multiple-class target vectors and nearest-neighbor classification completely controls what happens if a certain discriminant vector $\mathbf{d}$ is encountered. In each individual case the number a of alternatives generated as well as whether the set of alternatives contains the correct class label or not are completely determined. The size of the set of alternatives cannot, within this framework, be arbitrarily increased in order to reduce the probability of error at the cost of an increasing number of alternatives or vice versa.

Thus, running a given pattern classifier $\mathbf{d}(\mathbf{v})$ with a given pattern source $\{\mathbf{v}, k\}$ results in a fixed pair of values $[\epsilon_r, a_m]$ of residual error rate ϵ_r and mean number a_m of alternatives. Without introducing additional heuristics for shifting the decision boundaries in decision space, no trade-off between residual error rate ϵ_r and mean number a_m of alternatives can be achieved.

Weighing Out Confidences

The drawback of a certain inflexibility is avoided if another technique for generating sets of alternatives is applied. The idea is based on the assumption that the components d_k of the discriminant vector **d** are confidence values in the sense that the decision for the respective class will be correct with probability d_k.

The discriminant vector **d** is an estimate for the vector **p** of a posteriori probabilities. If the ideal case is $\mathbf{d} = \mathbf{p}$ and $d_k = \text{prob}(k|\mathbf{v})$, then the components d_k of the discriminant vector **d** obviously have this property. In the realistic case **d** is only an approximation for **p** and the consistency of confidences is normally destroyed. It can, however, be restored by applying the technique of confidence mapping described in Section 6.13 with the result that the estimations d_k, even if not the true a posteriori probabilities, represent the probabilities of the decisions for the respective classes to be correct.

The K classes to be discriminated are members of the mutually exclusive set Ω of classes. The pattern classifier provides for any given measurement vector **v** the discriminant vector $\mathbf{d}(\mathbf{v})$ with components rank ordered in decreasing size [compare (10.16)]:

$$d_{\text{rank-ordered}} = (d_{\max} \quad \mathbf{d}_{\text{second max}} \quad \cdots \quad d_{\min})^T$$

We are now able to set the number a of alternatives deliberately to any value between 1 and K and to compute the probability of the true class label k to be contained within the selected set of alternatives,

$$\text{prob(true class label } k \in \text{set of alternatives)} = \sum_{i=1}^{a} d_{i\text{th max}} \tag{10.19}$$

and the probability of having missed the correct decision,

$$\text{prob(true class label } k \notin \text{set of alternatives)} = \sum_{i=a+1}^{K} d_{i\text{th max}} \tag{10.20}$$

The probability of being correct approaches unity if the number of alternatives is increased to $a = K$.

Thus, for each of the individual decisions the trade-off is known between the probability of not missing the true class label k among the set of alternatives and the actual size a of this set. It is a straightforward idea to take as many of the rank-ordered candidates as is necessary to move accumulated confidence mass above a certain threshold:

$$\sum_{i=1}^{a} \mathrm{d}_{i\text{th max}} > \text{CnfThrsh} \tag{10.21}$$

Since the procedure has much in common with weighing out goods, it is called weighing out confidences.

The vector $\mathbf{d}_{\text{rank-ordered}}$ of rank-ordered confidences carries a distribution of probability mass that completely depends on the specific situation. Normally, the forwarded sum of confidences will be remarkably higher than the required threshold value CnfThrsh.

The case considered here, the components of **d** being *consistent confidence* values, has an interesting consequence for the mathematical expectation of the $\mathbf{d}_{\text{rank-ordered}}$ vector of rank-ordered confidences,

$$\overline{\mathbf{d}_{\text{rank-ordered}}} = E\{\mathbf{d}_{\text{rank-ordered}}\} \tag{10.22}$$

which can practically be gained by connecting the pattern classifier to the pattern source (it was trained for) and taking the average.

The components of $\overline{\mathbf{d}_{\text{rank-ordered}}}$ have the interpretation

$$\overline{\mathbf{d}_{\text{rank-ordered}}} = \begin{pmatrix} \overline{d_{\max}} \\ \overline{d_{\text{second max}}} \\ \vdots \\ \overline{d_{\min}} \end{pmatrix} = \begin{pmatrix} \text{prob(first choice = correct)} \\ \text{prob(second choice = correct)} \\ \vdots \\ \text{prob}(K\text{th choice = correct}) \end{pmatrix} \tag{10.23}$$

For a fixed number a of alternatives we find therefrom the probability for the set of alternatives to contain the correct class label just by taking the sum over the first a components of $\overline{\mathbf{d}_{\text{rank-ordered}}}$ and the probability of missing the correct label by taking the sum over the rest.

Actually the number a of alternatives is not fixed but varies, according to (10.21), with the individual case. Under these circumstances the residual error rate ϵ_r can be derived from averaging the forwarded accumulated confidence

$$1 - E\left\{\sum_{i=1}^{a} d_{i\text{th max}}(\mathbf{v})\right\} = \epsilon_r \tag{10.24}$$

together with the average number of alternatives

$$E\{a\} = a_m \tag{10.25}$$

Both variables are connected in the form of a trade-off characteristic. By varying the confidence threshold CnfThrsh, the residual error rate ϵ_r can be exchanged for the mean number a_m of alternatives.

As pointed out before, the dependencies between the components of **d** and the probabilities of being correct are valid under the conditions that, first, the discriminant vector **d** contains consistent confidences and, second, the classifier is working on the pattern source for which it was trained.

In general, these probabilities are not computed this way but are rather separately measured by counting frequencies of the respective events, as will be discussed in the following section.

10.5 PERFORMANCE MEASURING AND OPERATING CHARACTERISTICS

We have so far developed a variety of different techniques for constructing pattern classifiers based on the principle of learning from examples. We will now look into how those pattern classifiers behave in practical application. For this purpose, let us briefly recapitulate the line of argumentation that led us to this point.

Pattern classification is giving names to observations. Patterns are pairs of values $[\mathbf{v}, k]$, where **v** describes what is known about the pattern in terms of physical measurements (or derivations thereof) and k is the class label representing the name of the pattern. This "true" class label k must be distinguished from the estimation $\hat{k}$, which, to generate from the observation **v**, is the task of the pattern classifier.

How **v** and k are related is described by the learning sample set. Classifiers are trainable systems capable of extracting from the learning set what they need to know to make their decisions $\hat{k}$ match the true class label k in most cases. Whenever $\hat{k} \neq k$, an error is counted. Minimization of the resulting error rate ϵ has been the natural goal of all of the classifier design techniques discussed.

The essence of the pattern classification (irrespective of the specific technique applied) turned out to consist of the following sequence of steps:

1. Perform a functional mapping $\mathbf{v} \rightarrow \mathbf{d}$.
2. Derive the estimated class label $\hat{k}$ from the discriminant vector **d** based on the minimum-distance principle.

The mapping $\mathbf{v} \rightarrow \mathbf{d}$ carries all of the flexibility necessary to make the same concept applicable to different applications and has therefore been the object of *learning from examples*. The application is represented by the stochastic process $\{\mathbf{v}, k\}$. Training the classifier is performed by adapting the mapping $\mathbf{v} \rightarrow \mathbf{d}$ to make it optimally fit the requirements of the considered application, as described by the stochastic process $\{\mathbf{v}, k\}$.

The following must be emphasized:

- The mapping $\mathbf{v} \rightarrow \mathbf{d}$ itself, although derived from statistical concepts, is by no means stochastic.

The whole pattern classifier is a deterministic system.

Almost all of the difficulties of pattern classification stem from the fact that nothing is known about the stochastic process $\{\mathbf{v}, k\}$ except what can be learned from observing and analyzing sample sets. We have called the collection of samples on which this learning is based the learning set.

Reclassification and Generalization

Once the design of the pattern classifier is completed, we want to know how well it performs on its actual task. One obvious possibility is to use the learning set again for checking classifier performance. This is called *reclassification*, in contrast to *generalization*, where an independent set of test samples is used.

It is extremely important to differentiate between reclassification and generalization since some of the classifier concepts are so mighty that they completely learn what is presented to them during the learning phase even if the probability distributions of the different classes penetrate and classification errors are in reality unavoidable.

Think of the nearest-neighbor classifier using the whole learning set as a set of references and let us exclude the unlikely singular case that incidentally the same measurement vector $\mathbf{v}$ occurs exactly twice or more with different labels within the learning set. Checking classifier performance on the learning set must then in each case find the pattern vector $\mathbf{v}$ itself as its nearest neighbor and deliver the correct class label. If the class-specific probabilities $\text{prob}(\mathbf{v}|k)$ really penetrate, checking the same classifier with an independent test set, errors must show up. Note that what we are just considering is a clear case of *overfitting*.

The following must be clearly understood:

- The only performance measure we are really interested in is performance under generalization conditions.

The classifier is developed for a certain application, and this application is represented by a stochastic source $\{\mathbf{v}, k\}$. The learning set is a random sample drawn from the pattern source. In practical application the trained classifier is connected to the stochastic pattern source and is confronted with newly drawn samples. Pattern classification in the field is checking classifier performance under generalization conditions.

Every performance measure derived from checking the classifier with a certain test set generates a random observation. This observation follows a certain probability distribution that, in the simplest case, can be described by the mean and variance or standard deviation, respectively. Consider, for example, that we are trying to measure the generalization error rate ϵ. In order to get an impression of that distribution $\text{prob}(\epsilon)$, a number of repetitions of the same experiment is required, counting the relative number of errors with different, and independently drawn, test sets:

- Measuring performance parameters under reclassification conditions tends to underestimate error rates and overestimate performance. Measuring the same performance parameters under generalization conditions but with too small test sets gives unreliable results.

Obviously, measuring performance data based on test sets with the intention to check the effect of learning is only sensible if learning and test sets are drawn from the same stochastic process $\{\mathbf{v}, k\}$ and if this stochastic process did not change between extracting these sets.

In practical application the situation is often not so clear-cut. The pattern source $\{\mathbf{v}, k\}$ can be fluctuating and nonstationary. Often it is questionable whether the application is at all adequately represented by just one homogeneous stochastic process or if a multitude of different pattern sources should be considered. In view of the normally large number of free parameters to be adjusted by learning from examples, the learning set sizes are often smaller than they ought to be. The same problem occurs with the test sets, especially if the demand for several independent test sets is brought into the discussion.

Learning and Test Set Sizes

A fundamental question is that for the necessary size of learning and test sets to come to reliable results ([ALL1966], [GBD1992]). Leaving the case of extreme overfitting, occurring with the nearest-neighbor classifier if the entire learning set is used as set of reference vectors, out of account, classifier performance can be measured both ways using the learning set as the test set (reclassification) as well as using independently drawn test sets (generalization). From a practical point of view the size of the learning set is sufficiently large if the performance scores gained from reclassification and those gained from repeated generalization measurements converge to the same figure.

Independent of the classifier design technique applied, reclassification and generalization performance measurements tend to become drastically different for decreasing learning and test set sizes. This effect is called *overfitting* and is caused by the fact that the approximating functions are capable of going more or less precisely through the small number of points given by a small learning set. This is exactly the same effect as observable in two-dimensional curve fitting when a collection of too few points is given in the two-dimensional plane and the fitting curve has too many free parameters.

Many efforts have been devoted to deriving numerical bounds on the required learning set sizes ([MCL1992], [DER1990]). In view of the fact, however, that each practical application is different and no general statistical model exists from which to derive these bounds, the practician is left with the problem of empirically finding out how large his or her learning sets must be.

Statistical Measures Describing Deterministic System

We have stated above that the pattern classification system is a deterministic system. Obviously it is only interesting and useful in connection with the stochastic process $\{\mathbf{v}, k\}$. Hence we have to use statistical tools, not only for training the classifier, but also when evaluating how successful the development has been. This leads to performance measurements based on sample sets delivering performance measures such as error rate, reject rate, and similar data.

Commonly, these stochastic performance data are associated more with the pattern classifier than with the pattern source. It is, however, important to realize that performance measures of this kind describe neither properties of the pattern classifier itself nor properties of the pattern source but rather describe properties of a combination of both pattern source and pattern classifier.

Jackknifing and Leave One Out

Normally, when the development of a pattern classifier is started, the pattern classification task is represented by a given set of sample patterns of a certain but fixed size. We must be aware of the fact that based on this total set of samples two different tasks have to be solved:

- Classifier training
- Classifier evaluation

This requires some sort of partitioning of the total set of samples into at least one learning set to be used for classifier training and another set constituting the test set. Thus, a compromise must be found between reliable learning and reliable testing.

The standard way of proceeding is to divide the given sample set into learning and test sets, often simply by using half of them for learning and the other half for testing. There are several possibilities to come to such a division, and accordingly numbers of pairs [learning set, test set] are derivable from the same given set of samples. The statistical nature of the whole learning and test problem is best taken into account if more than just one classifier is derived from the given sample set and is evaluated using more than just one test set.

The motivation proceeding in this way is to better exploit the limited resources of the given sample set and to gain information about the robustness of the results of classifier adaptation during classifier development.

Classifier learning is improved with increasing learning set size. This observation recommends that we do not use the simple half-to-half partitioning scheme but, instead, make the learning set larger than the test set.

A common technique called *jackknifing* [MCL1992] is to partition the total sample set into S subsets of equal size and to use all but one of them for learning and the remaining one for testing. Since there are S such assignments, S possible classifiers and the same number of error rate measurements are achieved. The average error rate serves as estimation for the true error rate; the standard deviation characterizes the reliability of this performance measure. If the number of subsets S is increased to L, the number of samples, the procedure is called *leave one out*.

It should be remarked that even if we are trying, as we do here, to make more intelligent use of the given sample set, we are in a certain sense bound to the given set of samples. Also, the so-called independent test set, although explicitly excluded from the learning procedure, becomes implicitly involved in classifier learning since we learn from this test set how well the trained classifier does its job.

The conceptual distinction between learning and test sets vanishes completely if eventually the test set results are used for selecting the classifier with optimum performance among a group of competing classifiers, for example, due to certain parameter variations applied during classifier learning.

Sometimes, therefore, a partitioning scheme into more than just learning and test sets is applied. The learning set is used for learning, a first test set is used for parameter optimization during learning, often called cross-validation, and a second test set is used for deriving reliable performance data.

Variability of Error Rate Measurements

Obviously, we are interested in pattern classifiers exhibiting low error rates. And measuring low error rates is only then sensible when the number of samples is large enough to render statistically significant numbers of errors and when the required large test sets are reliably labeled. These requirements altogether make classifier evaluation a complex and expensive task.

Error rate measurements check pattern classifier performance on the given pattern source. Driven by the stochastic pattern source $\{\mathbf{v}, k\}$ at its input the pattern classifier generates at its output a stochastic process {err} of Boolean predicates recording whether its decisions have been right or wrong. The combination of pattern source and classifier is characterized by a certain error rate ϵ that, however, is unknown and not directly measurable.

All we can observe is that if we send n pattern vectors $\mathbf{v}$ to the classifier input, a certain number m of errors are recorded at its output. Keeping n fixed and repeating this kind of experiment several times, we find that m is a stochastic variable coming from the stochastic process $\{m\}$. We call the relation

$$\frac{m}{n} = \epsilon_{\text{empirical}} \tag{10.26}$$

the empirical error rate, which again is a stochastic variable coming from the stochastic process $\{\epsilon_{\text{empirical}}\}$.

Repeated error measurements, each with a fresh test set of n patterns $\{\mathbf{v}, k\}$, on the same arrangement of pattern source and pattern classifier will result in varying empirical error rates $\epsilon_{\text{empirical}}$ except for unbounded sample size n. What we are interested in is the range of variation depending on the sample size n.

Even if we do not know much about the stochastic laws governing the pattern source, the situation considered here is quite well defined in statistical terms. Irrespective of which pattern source is connected to which type of classifier, the stochastic process $\{m\}$ follows the binomial distribution

$$\begin{aligned} \text{prob}(m|n, \epsilon) &= \text{binomial distribution} \\ &= \binom{n}{m} \epsilon^m (1-\epsilon)^{n-m} \end{aligned} \tag{10.27}$$

with ϵ the true error rate of the system under test. Since m is an integer variable, $\text{prob}(m|n, \epsilon)$ is a discrete distribution function. The same is true for the empirical error rate $\epsilon_{\text{empirical}}$ for which the discrete distribution function is derived from the above equation, making use of (10.26):

$$\text{prob}(\epsilon_{\text{empirical}}|n, \epsilon) = \binom{n}{n\epsilon_{\text{empirical}}} \epsilon^{n\epsilon_{\text{empirical}}} (1-\epsilon)^{n(1-\epsilon_{\text{empirical}})} \tag{10.28}$$

For larger values of n it is more convenient to treat $\epsilon_{\text{empirical}}$ as a continuous variable coming from the continuous range of values [0 . . 1]. The distribution of $\epsilon_{\text{empirical}}$ is then equivalently described by the probability density function

$$\text{probdens}(\epsilon_{\text{empirical}}|n, \epsilon) = n \binom{n}{n\epsilon_{\text{empirical}}} \epsilon^{n\epsilon_{\text{empirical}}} (1-\epsilon)^{n(1-\epsilon_{\text{empirical}})} \tag{10.29}$$

The mean and variance of the error count $\{m\}$ are known for the binomial distribution to be

$$E\{m\} = n\epsilon \quad \text{and} \quad \text{var}\{m\} = n\epsilon(1-\epsilon) \tag{10.30}$$

Then the mean and variance of the empirical error rate $\{\epsilon_{\text{empirical}}\}$ are derived:

$$E\{\epsilon_{\text{empirical}}\} = \epsilon \quad \text{and} \quad \text{var}\{\epsilon_{\text{empirical}}\} = \frac{1}{n}\epsilon(1-\epsilon) \tag{10.31}$$

We find that for large n the variance vanishes and the empirical error rate converges to the true error rate, which is what it was to be supposed.

The imprecision of error rate measurements is best expressed by the standard deviation

$$\sigma = \sqrt{\text{var}\{\epsilon_{\text{empirical}}\}} = \sqrt{\frac{1}{n}\epsilon(1-\epsilon)} \tag{10.32}$$

Consider that we are interested in measuring $\epsilon_{\text{empirical}}$ with a certain relative precision

$$\sigma = \tau\epsilon \tag{10.33}$$

for example with the tolerance set to $\tau = 0.1$.

Combining (10.32) and (10.33), we find the required sample size

$$n_{\text{required}} = \frac{1-\epsilon}{\tau^2\epsilon} \tag{10.34}$$

These considerations lead to remarkably large values of n. The example of true error rate $\epsilon = 1\%$ and tolerance $\tau = 10\%$ requires a test set size of about 10,000 to bring the empirical error rate $\epsilon_{\text{empirical}}$ into the $\pm\sigma$ interval of [0.9% . . 1.1%]. Since the model distribution of (10.29) for large n approaches the normal distribution, we know that the empirical error rate $\epsilon_{\text{empirical}}$ will be observed within this interval in just somewhat less than 70% of all the cases.

These relations shall be demonstrated by appropriately evaluating some experimental data already used earlier in this book; compare Fig. 6.31. In this experiment a certain classifier was used for classifying a comparably large test set of 10,000 samples. Every 200 consecutive samples the error rate $\epsilon_{\text{empirical}}$ was measured and recorded. Whereas in Fig. 6.31 the sequence

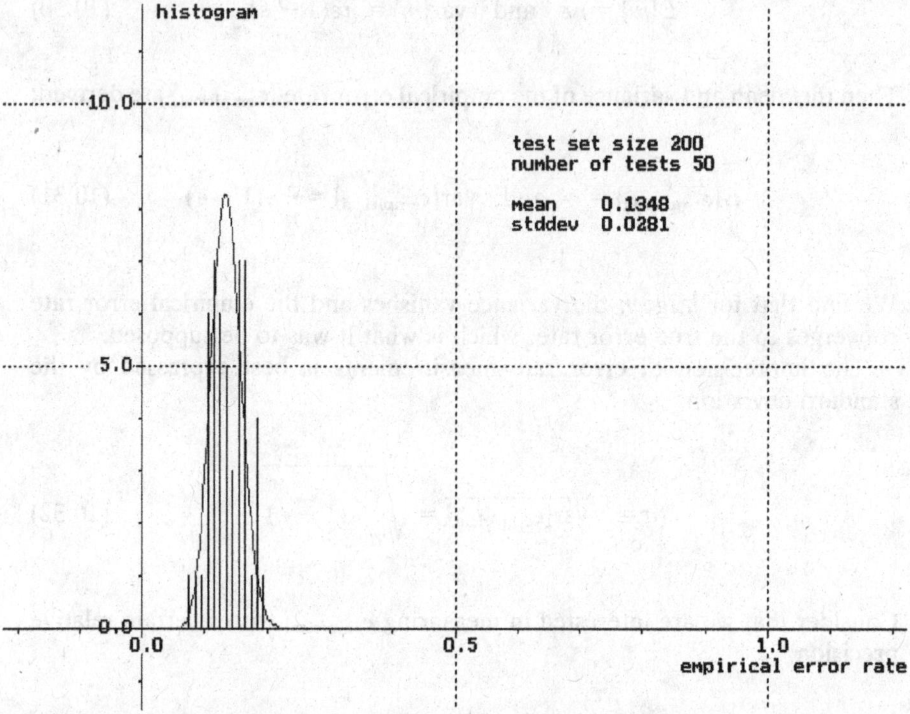

Figure 10.9. Demonstration of stochastic variability of error rate measurements. Data taken from experiment reported in Fig. 6.31. Empirical error rate $\epsilon_{\text{empirical}}$ measured for each 200 consecutive samples over total of 10,000 patterns. Histogram of 50 individual error measurements shown together with theoretical distribution of empirical error rate derived from binomial distribution.

of the 50 resulting individual error rate measurements is shown, Fig. 10.9 represents the distribution of $\epsilon_{\text{empirical}}$ in the form of a histogram together with the model distribution derived from (10.29).

Error and Reject Rates Depending on Reject Threshold

Counting the number of errors is only one part of the story. What we are also interested in is how the probability of errors can be reduced by introducing rejects and alternatives.

Rejects are caused by reject criteria as discussed in Section 10.2. Typically, the reject criterion is one dimensional and rejection is induced when the criterion passes a certain threshold in one or the other direction.

The general procedure shall be exemplified using the RAD criterion of (10.8). The notation of (10.8) uses the squared Euclidean distance $r^2_{\min}$ between the discriminant vector **d** and the nearest among the K unique target vectors $\mathbf{y}_k$ as reject criterion. The effect remains completely unchanged if instead the Euclidean distance r itself is used and the threshold is appropriately adjusted:

$$r = \sqrt{\min_k[|\mathbf{d} - \mathbf{y}_k|^2]} = \sqrt{1 + |\mathbf{d}|^2 - 2d_{\max}} \tag{10.35}$$

The pattern classifier maps every input pattern $\mathbf{v}$ into the corresponding discriminant vector $\mathbf{d}$, which again, according to the above equation, is uniquely mapped into the criterion variable r. Thus, from the stochastic input process $\{\mathbf{v}, k\}$ a stochastic process $\{r, k\}$ is derived. Since it is the task of the pattern classifier to generate estimations $\hat{k}$ for the class label k, we can observe at the classifier output the three-variable stochastic process $\{r, k, \hat{k}\}$. By comparing k and $\hat{k}$, the Boolean predicate err is derived:

$$\text{err} = \begin{cases} 0 & k = \hat{k} \\ 1 & \text{else} \end{cases} \tag{10.36}$$

which allows us to also observe the stochastic process $\{r, \text{err}\}$.

The relevant probability functions are as follows:

$$\begin{array}{ll} \text{prob}(r) & \text{Distribution of } r \text{ regardless of } \hat{k} \text{ being} \\ & \text{correct or incorrect} \\ \text{prob}(r, \text{err} = 1) & \text{Distribution of } r \text{ and } \hat{k} \text{ being incorrect} \end{array} \tag{10.37}$$

Reject rate ρ and error rate ϵ are easily computed according to

$$\rho = \int_{r > \text{RjctThrh}} \text{prob}(r)\, dr \qquad \epsilon = \int_{r \leq \text{RjctThrh}} \text{prob}(r, \text{err} = 1)\, dr \tag{10.38}$$

Practically the probability functions prob(r) and prob(r, err = 1) are approximated by histograms hist[r] and hist[r, err = 1] and reject and error rates computed as functions of the reject threshold RjctThrsh = rad by summation instead of integration:

$$\rho(\text{rad}) = \sum_{r > \text{rad}} \text{hist}[r] \qquad \epsilon(\text{rad}) = \sum_{r \leq \text{rad}} \text{hist}[r, \text{err} = 1] \tag{10.39}$$

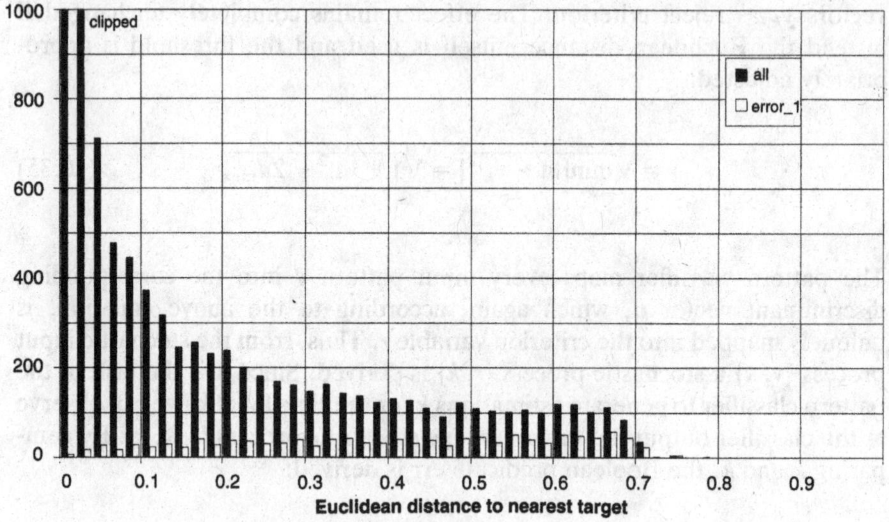

Figure 10.10. Histograms showing distributions of $\{r\}$ and $\{r, \text{err} = 1\}$ over r-scale. Data taken from three-class example of (4.35) applying in this case optimum classifier that makes full use of the fact that three classes are normally distributed in **V**-space and thus generates vector **p** of a posteriori probabilities for discriminant vector **d**. Resulting distributions in **D**-space shown in Fig. 4.14. Due to penetration of probability functions prob($\mathbf{v}|k$) in **V**-space both histograms extend over almost same range of values $r = [0 .. 0.7]$ but with extremely changing likelihood ratio.

The histograms hist[r] and hist[r, err = 1] are shown in Fig. 10.10. The experimental data used for this figure come from the two-dimensional three-class example introduced in Chapter 4 and refers to the optimum imaginable classifier delivering the vector **p** of a posteriori probabilities as the discriminant vector **d**. In this case, the stochastic process $\{\mathbf{d}, k\}$ is bound to fall completely inside the equilateral triangle spanned by the three target vectors $\mathbf{y}_0$, $\mathbf{y}_1$, $\mathbf{y}_2$. We also know that most of the probability mass of $\{\mathbf{v}, k\}$ is concentrated along the sides of the triangle and that the maximum value r can assume within the triangle is limited.

For the general case of K classes to be discriminated the maximum distance within the K vertices decision space **D** is given by

$$r_{\max} = \sqrt{1 - \frac{1}{K}} \tag{10.40}$$

which for the case of $K = 3$ leads to the limits

$$r \leq \sqrt{\tfrac{1}{2}} = 0.707 \quad \text{along triangle's sides}$$
$$r \leq \sqrt{\tfrac{1}{2}} = 0.816 \quad \text{in triangle's center}$$

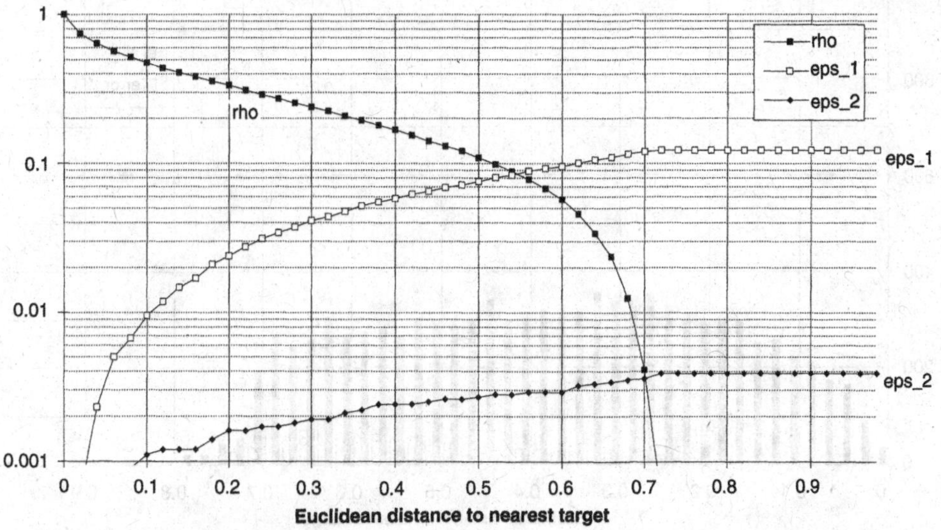

Figure 10.11. Reject rate ρ and error rates ϵ_1 and ϵ_2 computed from histograms of Fig. 10.10 according to (10.39). Two error rate functions ϵ_1(rad) and ϵ_2(rad) correspond to error definitions of (10.41), error is counted for ϵ_1 if classifier's first choice is incorrect and for ϵ_2 if neither first nor second choice is correct.

These conditions are responsible for the comparably abrupt ending of the histograms of Fig. 10.10 above a value of about 0.72 on the r scale. Compare for this discussion Fig. 4.14: The triangle's center is almost empty; only along the triangle's sides do a few points occur with r just above 0.707.

According to (10.39) the error and reject rates as functions of the reject threshold rad are computed from the histograms. The result is shown in Fig. 10.11.

In Section 10.3 we discussed the possibility of forming sets of alternatives. The pattern classifier delivers the rank-ordered discriminant vector $\mathbf{d}_{\text{rank-ordered}}$, see Fig. 10.7 and (10.16). An interesting question is what the probability is of having missed the true class label k among the first a choices.

This question can easily be answered for any number of alternatives $a = [1, \ldots, A]$ by collecting the appropriate histograms hist$[r, \text{err_}a = 1]$ if a generalized error definition as compared with (10.36) is applied:

$$\text{err\_}a = \begin{cases} 0 & \text{if } k \in \{\text{first } a \text{ choices}\} \\ 1 & \text{else} \end{cases} \tag{10.41}$$

Figure 10.11 shows the two error rate curves ϵ_1(rad) and ϵ_2(rad) together with the reject rate curve ρ(rad). Thereby ϵ_a indicates the probability of an error of type err_a.

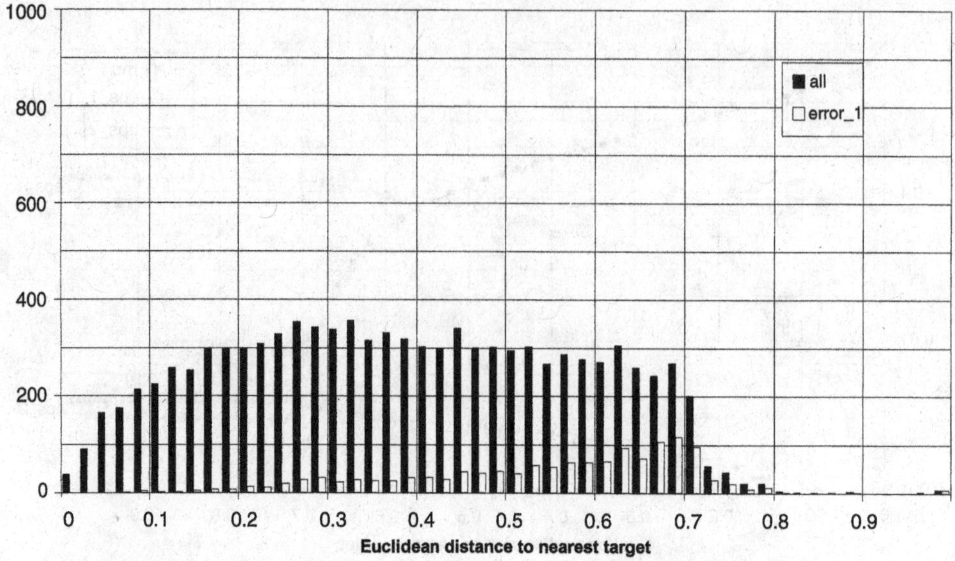

Figure 10.12. Same histograms as in Fig. 10.10, here for second-degree polynomial regression classifier applied to same three-class example of (4.35) and used in Section 6.11 for illustration purposes. Histograms show distributions of $\{r\}$ and $\{r, \text{err} = 1\}$ over r-scale. Corresponding distributions in **D**-space shown in Fig. 6.16. Both histograms extend over almost same range of values $r = [0..0.7]$, but due to imperfections of polynomial approximation, precise hits (those with vanishing distance r to nearest target **y**) are comparably seldom; compare Fig. 10.10.

In Section 10.4 we derived some relations between the components of the average $\overline{\mathbf{d}_{\text{rank-ordered}}}$ of the rank-ordered vector discriminant **d** and the probabilities of the ith choice of being correct; see (10.23). The mean rank-ordered discriminant vector gained from the same experimental data as presented in Figs. 10.10 and 10.13 with the same sample set size 10,000 came out to be

$$\overline{\mathbf{d}_{\text{rank-ordered}}} = \begin{pmatrix} 0.874 \\ 0.122 \\ 0.004 \end{pmatrix} \tag{10.42}$$

which neatly matches forced recognition (no rejects) error rates $\epsilon_{1,\max} = 0.123$ and $\epsilon_{2,\max} = 0.004$, shown in Fig. 10.13.

Note that the data of (10.42) is derived from the learning data only without really checking the classifier performance by counting errors. In the case of the optimum classifier used for this experiment the mean rank-ordered discriminant vector $\overline{\mathbf{d}_{\text{rank-ordered}}}$ provides reliable estimations for the empirical error rates.

Figures 10.12 and 10.13 show the same representations again for the

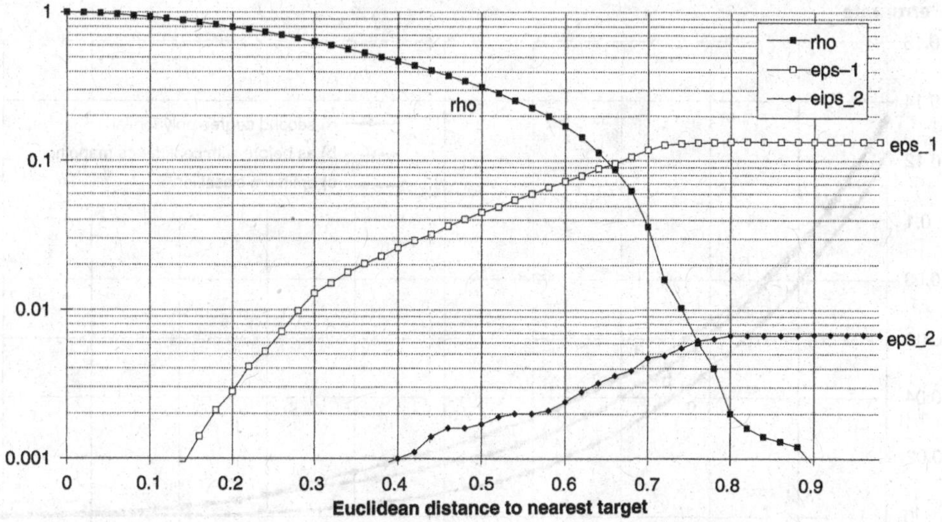

Figure 10.13. Reject rate ρ and error rates ϵ_1 and ϵ_2 computed from histograms of Fig. 10.12 according to (10.39). Two error rate functions ϵ_1(rad) and ϵ_2(rad) correspond to error definitions of (10.41); error is counted for ϵ_1 if classifier's first choice is incorrect and for ϵ_2 if neither first nor second choice is correct.

example of (4.35) but for the quadratic regression classifier as used for visualization in Section 6.11. The general appearance is quite similar; except, that the polynomial approximation is less able to generate precise hits, which already became visible in Fig. 6.16. Another observation is that both error functions in Fig. 10.13 reach slightly higher values for $\rho \to 0$ and that the distance between them is somewhat smaller than in Fig. 10.13.

The mean rank-ordered discriminant vector $\overline{\mathbf{d}_{\text{rank-ordered}}}$ gained from the same experimental data as presented in Figs. 10.12 and 10.13 with the same sample set size 10,000 comes here out to be

$$\overline{\mathbf{d}_{\text{rank-ordered}}} = \begin{pmatrix} 0.767 \\ 0.226 \\ 0.006 \end{pmatrix} \tag{10.43}$$

which does not match well the error rates $\epsilon_{1,\max} = 0.134$ and $\epsilon_{2,\max} = 0.007$ of Fig. 10.13. Obviously, in the case of the only approximately optimum polynomial classifier the mean rank-ordered discriminant vector $\overline{\mathbf{d}_{\text{rank-ordered}}}$ provides too pessimistic an estimation of classifier performance and significantly overestimates the empirical error rates.

These imbalances are corrected if the discriminant vector $\mathbf{d}$ generated by the polynomial classifier is further processed by the confidence mapping

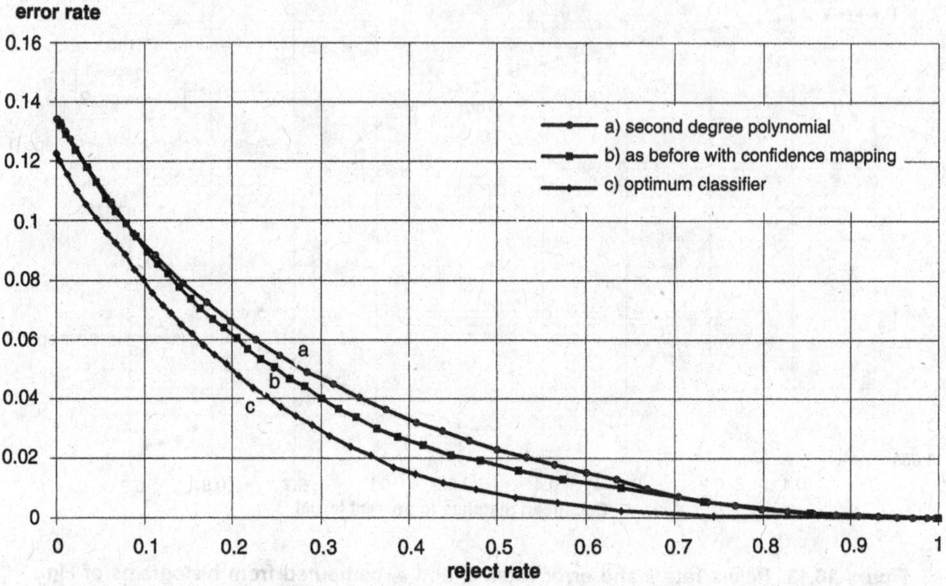

Figure 10.14. Operating characteristic $\epsilon(\rho)$ of pattern classification system. Abscissa represents reject rate ρ and ordinate shows resulting error rate ϵ. Any point on operating characteristic can be arbitrarily chosen by proper adjustment of reject threshold rad. Three curves correspond to three types of classifier considered so far: (*a*) second-degree polynomial regression classifier as in Figs. 10.12 and 10.13; (*b*) same as (*a*) but improved by subsequent confidence mapping; (*c*) optimum classifier computing vector of a posteriori probabilities **p** as in Figs. 10.10 and 10.13.

technique of Section 6.13. This experiment renders the mean rank-ordered discriminant vector

$$\overline{\mathbf{d}_{\text{rank-ordered}}} = \begin{pmatrix} 0.854 \\ 0.132 \\ 0.010 \end{pmatrix} \tag{10.44}$$

which again matches quite well the error rates $\epsilon_{1,\max} = 0.137$ and $\epsilon_{2,\max} = 0.006$ of the corresponding test run.

The plots of Figs. 10.11 and 10.13 show the functions $\rho(\text{rad})$ and $\epsilon(\text{rad}) = \epsilon_1(\text{rad})$, with the index 1 omitted, connected by the common argument rad. Eliminating the parameter rad we arrive at the so-called *operating characteristic* $\epsilon(\rho)$, which represents the functional relationship between reject and error rates; see Fig. 10.14. By proper adjustment of the reject threshold rad, any arbitrary point on the curve $\epsilon(\rho)$ can be chosen as the operating point of the pattern classification system. This parameter adjust-

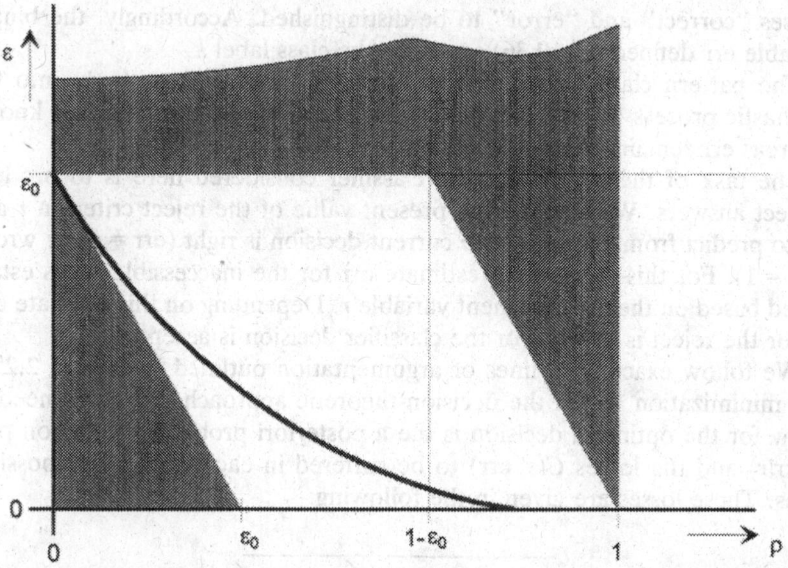

Figure 10.15. Admissible range of functions $\epsilon(\rho)$ in (ϵ, ρ)-plane. Value ϵ_0 indicates forced recognition error rate: maximum value that ϵ assumes if no rejections are allowed to occur, $\rho = 0$.

ment is normally left to the application, depending on whether rejects or errors are more undesired.

The operating characteristic $\epsilon(\rho)$ is a monotonically decreasing curve but, normally, has the property of reducing ϵ much slower than ρ increases, as obviously is the case in Fig. 10.14. In other words:

- For each error avoided in general, a certain number of otherwise correct decisions must be sacrified.

Independent of the specific case, the function $\epsilon(\rho)$ is bound to lie in the nonshaded area of Fig. 10.15.

Optimizing Reject Threshold

The selection of the optimum operating point on the operation characteristic $\epsilon(\rho)$ can again be viewed as an optimization problem fitting neatly into the framework of statistical decision theory, as discussed in Chapter 2.

In the following we will make direct use of the results derived in Chapter 2 and treat the reject problem as a classification problem with the reject criterion r being the one-dimensional measurement variable and the two classes "correct" and "error" to be distinguished. Accordingly, the binary variable err defined in (10.36) serves as the class label k.

The pattern classification system maps its input process $\{\mathbf{v}, k\}$ into the stochastic process $\{r, \text{err}\}$, but during the actual application only r is known whereas err remains inaccessible.

The task of the special pattern classifier considered here is to produce correct answers. We observe the present value of the reject criterion r and try to predict from r whether the current decision is right (err = 0) or wrong (err = 1). For this purpose an estimate $\widehat{\text{err}}$ for the inaccessible err is established based on the measurement variable r. Depending on this estimate $\widehat{\text{err}}$, either the reject is induced or the classifier decision is accepted.

We follow exactly the lines of argumentation outlined in Section 2.2 on risk minimization within the decision-theoretic approach. What we need to know for the optimum decision is the a posteriori probability function prob(err$|r$) and the losses $C(r, \text{err})$ to be suffered in each of the four possible cases. These losses are given in the following:

	$\widehat{\text{err}}$	
err	0	1
0	0	C_r
1	C_f	C_r

No loss occurs if the pattern classifier's decision is correct (err = 0) and the error estimation is $\widehat{\text{err}} = 0$. The loss C_f must be suffered if the decision is actually wrong (err = 1) but the error was not detected ($\widehat{\text{err}} = 0$) and the loss C_r if the error estimation indicates an error ($\widehat{\text{err}} = 1$) regardless of whether the decision was actually correct or not.

Note that in this application the loss assignment is different from the symmetric loss matrix $\mathbf{C}$ of (2.10).

The probability function prob(err$|r$) is derived from

$$\text{prob}(\text{err}|r) = \frac{\text{prob}(\text{err}, r)}{\text{prob}(r)} \tag{10.45}$$

Since err is Boolean, it suffices to know

$$\text{prob}(\text{err} = 1|r) = \frac{\text{prob}(\text{err} = 1, r)}{\text{prob}(r)} \tag{10.46}$$

For practical purposes prob(err = 1, r) = prob(r, err = 1) and prob(r) are approximated from the corresponding histograms; compare the preceding section. Both histograms hist[r] and hist[r, err = 1] have already been considered as the necessary source of information for deriving the ϵ(rad), ρ(rad), and $\epsilon(\rho)$ functions above [see (10.37)]:

$$\text{prob}(\text{err} = 1|r) \approx \frac{\text{hist}[r, \text{err} = 1]}{\text{hist}[r]} \tag{10.47}$$

According to (2.17), the risk vector **r** here comes out to be

$$\mathbf{r} = \mathbf{C}^T\mathbf{p} = \begin{pmatrix} C_f \text{prob}(\text{err} = 1|r) \\ C_r \end{pmatrix} \tag{10.48}$$

where the first component of **r** corresponds to err = 0 and the second to err = 1. The optimum reject decision is that with minimum risk:

$$\text{Decide for reject if:} \quad C_r < C_f \text{prob}(\text{err} = 1|r)$$

Together with (10.46) this simplifies to

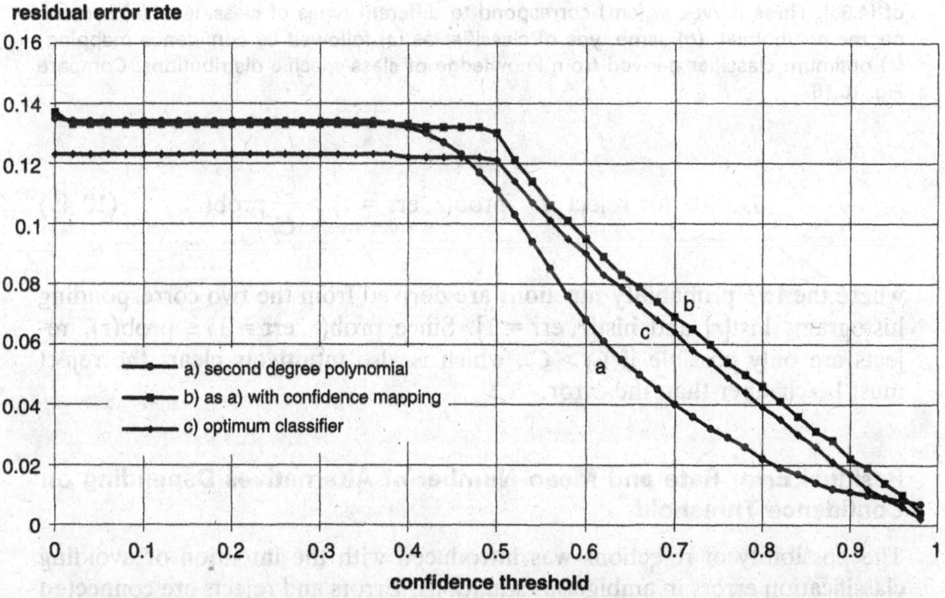

Figure 10.16. Residual error rate ϵ_r as function of confidence threshold cnf for same experimental situation as in Fig. 10.14. Pattern source is three-class example of (4.35). Three curves ϵ_r(cnf) correspond to different types of classifiers: (*a*) second degree polynomial; (*b*) same type of classifier as (*a*) followed by confidence mapping; (*c*) optimum classifier derived from knowledge of class-specific distributions. Compare Fig. 10.17.

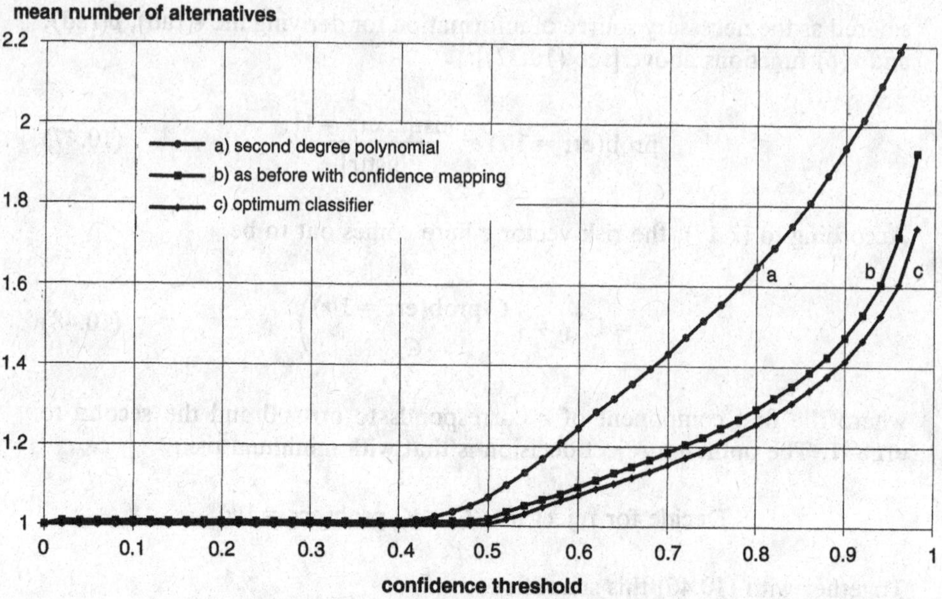

Figure 10.17. Mean number a_m of alternatives as function of confidence threshold cnf for same experimental situation as in Fig. 10.14. Pattern source is three-class example of (4.35). Three curves a_m(cnf) correspond to different types of classifiers: (*a*) second-degree polynomial; (*b*) same type of classifier as (*a*) followed by confidence mapping; (*c*) optimum classifier derived from knowledge of class-specific distributions. Compare Fig. 10.16.

$$\text{Decide for reject if:} \quad \text{prob}(r, \text{err} = 1) > \frac{C_r}{C_f}\,\text{prob}(r) \qquad (10.49)$$

where the two probability functions are derived from the two corresponding histograms hist[r] and hist[r, err = 1]. Since prob(r, err = 1) $\leq$ prob(r), rejects are only possible if $C_f > C_r$, which is also intuitively clear; the reject must be cheaper than the error.

Residual Error Rate and Mean Number of Alternatives Depending on Confidence Threshold

The possibility of rejections was introduced with the intention of avoiding classification errors in ambiguous situations. Errors and rejects are connected by a trade-off relation $\epsilon(\rho)$. We have seen that this trade-off function $\epsilon(\rho)$ can be measured in a single test run applying the given pattern classifier $\mathbf{d}(\mathbf{v})$ to the given pattern source $\{\mathbf{v}, k\}$ and collecting appropriate histograms. The operating characteristic $\epsilon(\rho)$ describes a property of the pattern source–pattern classifier pair.

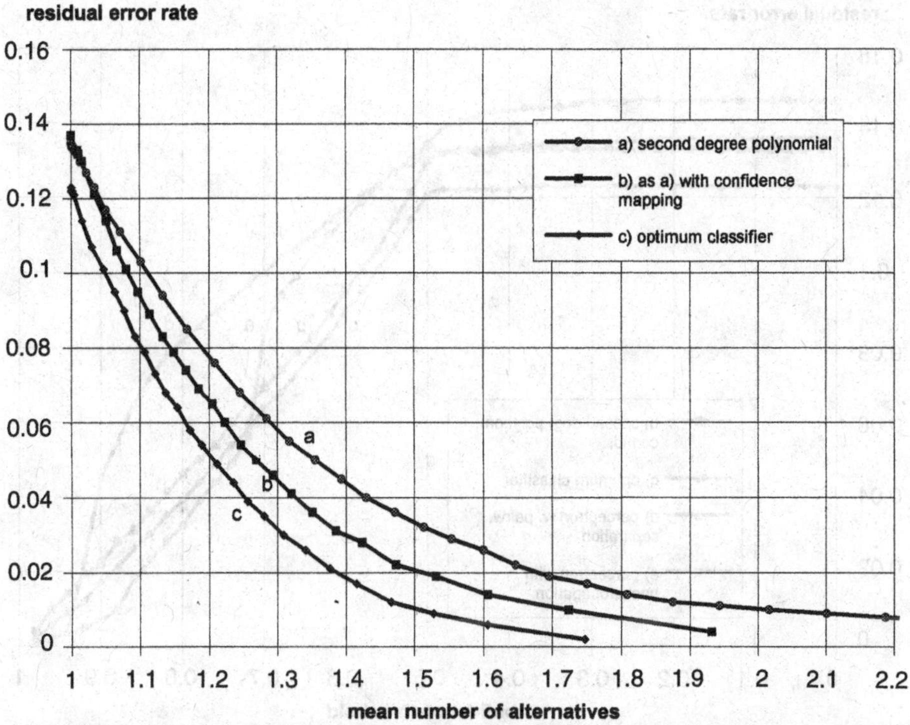

Figure 10.18. Functional relationship between residual error ϵ_r rate and mean number a_m of alternatives gained from representations in Figs. 10.16 and 10.17 for same three cases: (*a*) second-degree polynomial classifier; (*b*) same type of classifier as (*a*) followed by confidence mapping; (*c*) optimum classifier derived from knowledge of class-specific distributions.

Deciding for reject was not the only technique discussed above for dealing with ambiguity and avoiding classification errors. In section 10.3 we have introduced the possibility of forwarding sets of alternatives and in Section 10.4 developed the technique of weighing out confidences for controlling the number a of alternatives to be forwarded. In this approach, a trade-off function exists between the residual error rate ϵ_r and the mean number a_m of alternatives. The operating characteristic $\epsilon_r(a_m)$ again describes a property of the pattern source–pattern classifier pair.

Similar to the case of rejection, in this case one single test run of the given pattern classifier $\mathbf{d}(\mathbf{v})$ applied to the pattern source $\{\mathbf{v}, k\}$ suffices to establish the respective trade-off functions.

The idea is as follows. For each pattern $\mathbf{v}$ the rank-ordered discriminant vector $\mathbf{d}$ is computed (10.16):

$$\mathbf{d}_{\text{rank-ordered}} = (d_{\max} \quad d_{\text{second max}} \quad \cdots \quad d_{\min})^T$$

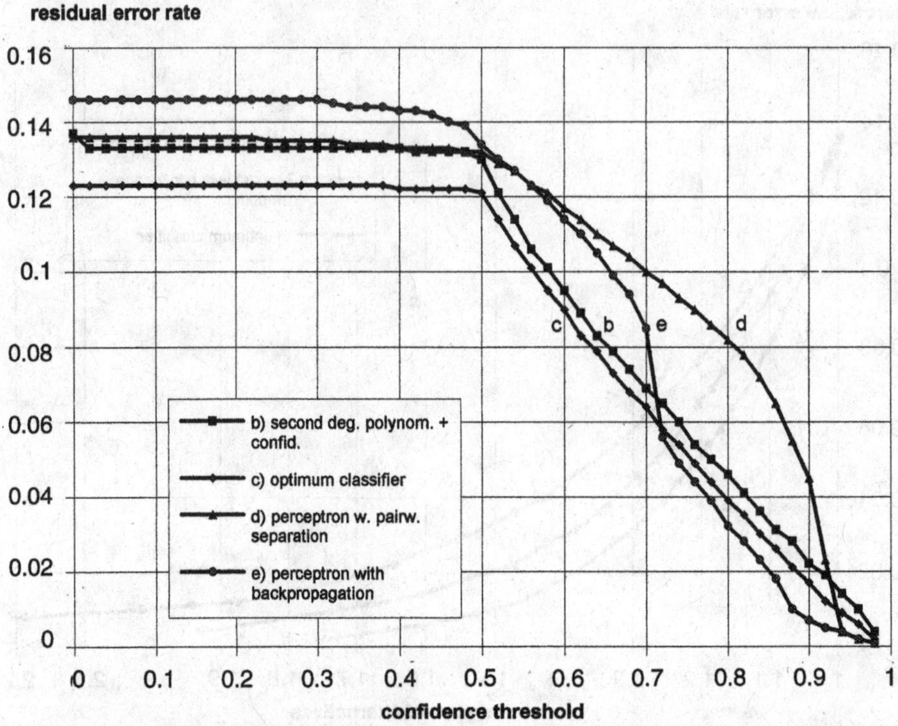

Figure 10.19. Comparison of different types of pattern classifiers based on ϵ_r(cnf) diagram: (*b*) second-degree polynomial followed by confidence mapping; (*c*) reference classifier utilizing statistical knowledge about pattern source; (*d*) multilayer perceptron type classifier designed from concept of pairwise linear separation; (*e*) multilayer perceptron classifier trained by backpropagation.

For a given confidence threshold CnfThrsh = cnf the necessary number a of alternatives is determined according to (10.21). At the same time it is checked whether the true class label k is contained within the set of the a alternatives; compare (10.41). Otherwise an error is recorded. These steps are repeated for a number of different values of cnf and the results accumulated in an appropriate array of counters.

This procedure renders a table from which the functions a_m(cnf) and ϵ_r(cnf) are easily determined. Again the parameter cnf can be eliminated and the functional relationship between residual error rate ϵ_r and mean number a_m of alternatives directly derived.

These relations are illustrated by Figs. 10.16–10.18. These diagrams illustrate how the trade-off between residual error rate and mean number of alternatives for a given pair of pattern source $\{\mathbf{v}, k\}$ and pattern classifier $\mathbf{d}(\mathbf{v})$ can be visualized and, at the same time, demonstrate that visualizations

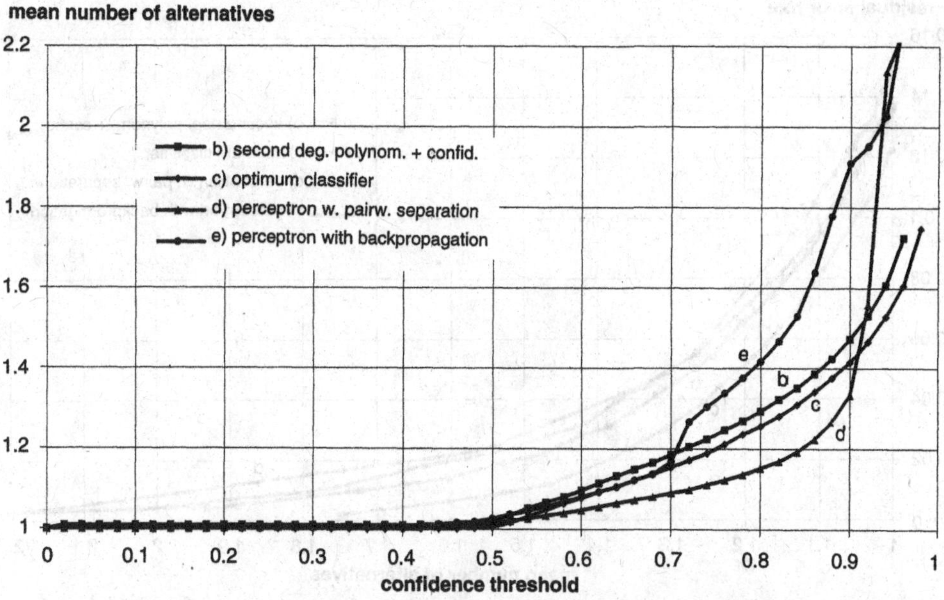

Figure 10.20. Comparison of different types of pattern classifiers based on a_m(cnf) diagram: (*b*) second-degree polynomial followed by confidence mapping; (*c*) reference classifier utilizing statistical knowledge about pattern source; (*d*) multilayer perceptron type classifier designed from concept of pairwise linear separation; (*e*) multilayer perceptron classifier trained by backpropagation.

of this kind are valuable tools for comparisons between different pattern classifier design techniques and different pattern classification tasks.

In this sense, Figs. 10.16 and 10.17 demonstrate the effect of the technique of confidence mapping, as introduced in Section 6.13. We observe that the functions ϵ_r(cnf) and a_m(cnf) measured for the second-degree polynomial classifier (*a*) show a significantly different appearance compared with the ideal curves *c*; confidence mapping (*b*) makes them considerably more similar to *c*. Although the functions ϵ_f(cnf) and a_m(cnf) gained from the approximation (*b*) show slightly higher error rates and slightly higher mean number of alternatives for the same value of cnf compared with the reference (*c*), the general appearance is close to *c*.

Eliminating the parameter cnf from ϵ_r(cnf) and a_m(cnf) provides a representation of classifier performance data well suited for comparison among different classifier design techniques and different pattern sources. The resulting trade-off function $\epsilon_r(a_m)$ between residual error rate and mean number of alternatives is shown in Fig. 10.18. Again a positive effect becomes visible of combining polynomial classification with confidence mapping.

Comparing this result with the operating characteristic $\epsilon(\rho)$ derived for the concept of rejection and shown in Fig. 10.14, we observe that improvements

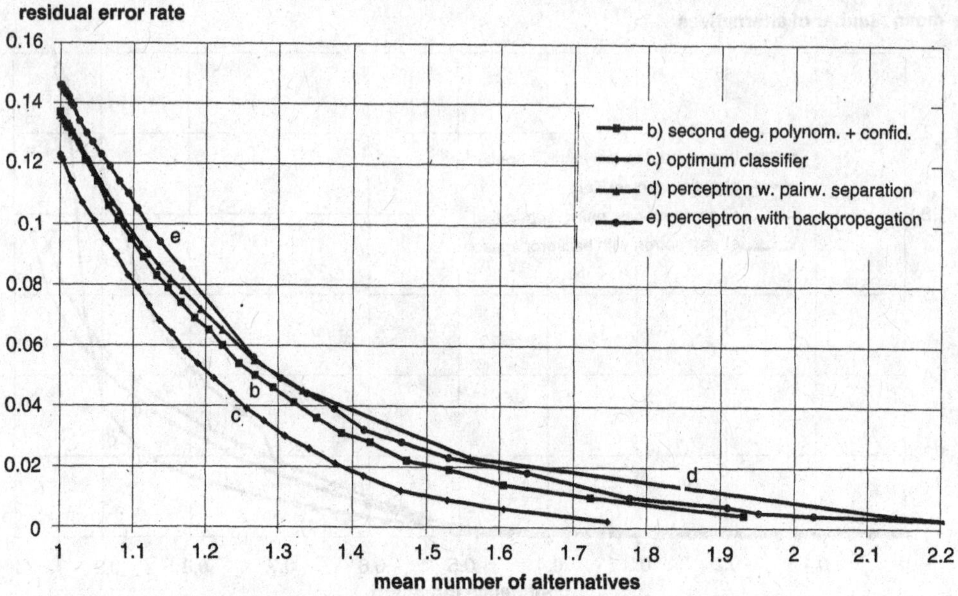

Figure 10.21. Comparison of different types of pattern classifiers based on $\epsilon_r(a_m)$ diagram: (*b*) second-degree polynomial followed by confidence mapping; (*c*) reference classifier utilizing statistical knowledge about pattern source; (*d*) multilayer perceptron type classifier designed from concept of pairwise linear separation; (*e*) multilayer perceptron classifier trained by backpropagation.

relative to the reference (*c*) gained from confidence mapping (*b*) applied to the polynomial regression classifier (*a*) become visible mainly in the $\epsilon_r(a_m)$ diagram of Fig. 10.18 and not so much in the $\epsilon(\rho)$ diagram of Fig. 10.14.

The reason is that in Fig. 10.14 only the first-choice component of the rank-ordered discriminant vector contributes to the result. The technique of confidence mapping is hardly capable of improving the estimations in situations of strong competition between just two of the classes to be distinguished but is, however, well capable of pushing back those third and higher order choices that have nonvanishing estimations due only to the imperfections of the estimating procedure.

These arguments are backed by directly looking into the corresponding decision space scatterplots of Figs. 4.14, 6.16, and 6.26, where we observe that the interior of the decision triangle is cleaned by confidence mapping. We know that estimations **d** falling along the triangle's sides or close to them correspond to the case of two conflicting classes, whereas the triangle's interior corresponds to the situation of three conflicting classes.

The same kind of presentation as in Figs.10.16–10.18 is utilized in Figs. 10.19–10.21 in order to compare the different classifier design techniques discussed in Chapters 6 and 7. Cases *b* and *c* are the same as in the diagrams above. Additionally considered here are the cases *d* and *e*. Both belong to classifiers of the multilayer perceptron type. Case *e* corresponds to the example used for Fig. 7.15 and is trained by backpropagation with learning factor $\alpha = 0.1$, whereas case *d* belongs to the experiment of Section 7.8 of *constructive design of the perceptron basis functions*; compare Fig. 7.21.

Again it is confirmed that the backpropagation classifier of Section 7.7 and the multilayer perceptron designed from the concept of pairwise linear separation of Section 7.8 exhibit the same performance in terms of the $\epsilon_r(a_m)$ diagram, even if their $\epsilon_r(\text{cnf})$ and $a_m(\text{cnf})$ diagrams remarkably differ with each other and specifically from reference *c*.

It would indeed be possible to apply the technique of confidence mapping to multilayer perceptron type classifiers and bring thus the respective curves closer to the reference, but this was not done here. Applying confidence mapping to multilayer perceptrons is the replacement of the predetermined last layer nonlinear activation function by another, statistically adapted, nonlinear function to be trained after the perceptron training is finished.

The results of Figs. 10.19–10.21 show how these diagrams can be used for comparison but are not intended to testify to the superiority of one specific technique for pattern classifier design over another. Visualizations of this kind are able to provide insights into the properties of the different classifier design techniques and allow us to form judgments about which technique or which combination of techniques is appropriate for which purpose.

11

COMBINING CLASSIFIERS

We have learned that pattern classification would be an easy task if the stochastic laws governing the pattern source $\{\mathbf{v}, k\}$ would be known since then we would be able to compute for every pattern $\mathbf{v}$ presented the vector $\mathbf{p}$ of à posteriori probabilities carrying all of the necessary information for deriving the optimum decision.

Unfortunately the mapping $\mathbf{v} \to \mathbf{p}$ is generally unknown. All we can do is to collect sample sets from the pattern source $\{\mathbf{v}, k\}$ and try to recover the unknown mapping $\mathbf{v} \to \mathbf{p}$ from such sample sets. This approach renders a mapping $\mathbf{v} \to \mathbf{d}$, with $\mathbf{d}$ being a substitute for the unknown $\mathbf{p}$ but with the property of, in some sense, coming as close to the true $\mathbf{p}$ as possible. A simple and most obvious measure of deviation between $\mathbf{d}$ and $\mathbf{p}$ is the squared Euclidean distance $|\mathbf{d} - \mathbf{p}|^2$ and minimization of this deviation is a most convincing approach.

We have also learned (see Section 6.3) that using the target vector $\mathbf{y}$ instead of the generally unknown vector $\mathbf{p}$ of a posteriori probabilities in the learning procedure and minimizing the squared Euclidean distance $|\mathbf{d} - \mathbf{y}|^2$ render exactly the same result of $\mathbf{d}(\mathbf{v})$, the least mean-square approximation to $\mathbf{p}(\mathbf{v})$ under the constraints of the predefined general structure of the mapping $\mathbf{v} \to \mathbf{d}$.

Letting the functional approximation $\mathbf{d}(\mathbf{v})$ depend on the learning set $\{[\mathbf{v}, k]\}$ brings the matter of interpolation and extrapolation into the game. What we are interested in, then, is to arrive at an interpolation that is smooth in areas of the measurement space $\mathbf{V}$ populated by the learning set as well capable of following the actual variations of $\mathbf{p}(\mathbf{v})$.

The preceding chapters of this book have developed a number of different approaches to establish such approximate mappings $\mathbf{d}(\mathbf{v})$ from the learning set. Each of these techniques has its own characteristics inherited from its basic design principles and resulting in different interpolating and extrapolating behavior, different ability to follow the changes of $\mathbf{p}(\mathbf{v})$, and different smoothness in V-space.

Different pattern classifiers trained for the same application $\{\mathbf{v}, k\}$ can be viewed as approximations from different directions to the same goal, just as different starting points are possible to reach the same peak in a mountainous territory. Therefore, different pattern classifiers, derived from different concepts, using different sets of measurements, or designed with different constellations of their basic design parameters tend to behave differently in the individual case, even if they may exhibit the same long-term error rates.

Under these circumstances combining different pattern classifiers developed for the same task bears the promise of improving the overall performance, just as in everyday life more than one expert is consulted if a difficult case is to be settled. Since different pattern classifiers have different strengths and different weaknesses, classifier combination must be led by the goal of making the respective strengths effective and repelling the deficiencies.

The following sections deal with several different and differently motivated techniques for classifier combination. What they have in common is that from a group of individual classifiers a larger entity is formed that behaves, from a blackbox point of view, as a single classifier. The techniques described in the following are applicable to any kind of classifier design concept but will, for the sake of simplification, be exemplified here only by the polynomial regression classifier.

The chapter is organized according to the basic principles of classifier combination. Two or more classifiers may be concatenated so that the output of one of them becomes the input to another, or may work in parallel on the same input data, including the case that the different classifiers use different subsets of the same set of input data. The latter variant is the more common. Separate sections are devoted to two of them: hierarchical classifier and classifier networks.

11.1 CONCATENATING CLASSIFIERS

The individual classifier Clsf_i has input vector $\mathbf{v}_i$ and output vector $\mathbf{d}_i$ and provides the mapping $\mathbf{d}_i(\mathbf{v}_i) = \mathbf{A}_i^T\mathbf{x}_i(\mathbf{v}_i)$. The simplest way of combining two classifiers, Clsf_1 and Clsf_2, is to connect the output $\mathbf{d}_1$ of Clsf_1 to the input $\mathbf{v}_2$ of Clsf_2, resulting in $\mathbf{v}_2 \equiv \mathbf{d}_1$. Viewed from input $\mathbf{v} \equiv \mathbf{v}_1$ to output $\mathbf{d} \equiv \mathbf{d}_2$, the combination functions as a single classifier Clsf implementing the overall mapping

$$\mathbf{d}(\mathbf{v}) = \mathbf{d}_2(\mathbf{d}_1(\mathbf{v})) = \mathbf{A}_2^T\mathbf{x}_2(\mathbf{A}_1^T\mathbf{x}_1(\mathbf{v})) \tag{11.1}$$

The general structure is quite similar to that of the multilayer perceptron, as shown in Fig. 7.5, the difference lying in the fact that whereas the coefficient matrices $\mathbf{A}_i$ of the multilayer perceptron are optimized simultaneously within one total optimization procedure minimizing $S^2 = E\{|\mathbf{d}(\mathbf{v}) - \mathbf{y}|^2\}$, here each of the $\mathbf{A}_i$ is trained separately and one after the other.

Let the first classifier Clsf_1 be already trained to the given classification task $\{\mathbf{v}, k\}$. We try to improve the classification system by treating $\mathbf{d}_1$ as measurement vector $\mathbf{v}_2$ for Clsf_2.

Consider, first, Clsf_2 to be chosen to be a linear classifier:

$$\mathbf{x}_2 = \begin{pmatrix} 1 \\ \mathbf{v}_2 \end{pmatrix} = \begin{pmatrix} 1 \\ \mathbf{d}_1 \end{pmatrix} \tag{11.2}$$

In this case adaptation of Clsf_2, according to (6.20), requires us to solve the linear matrix equation

$$E\{\mathbf{x}_2\mathbf{x}_2^T\}\mathbf{A}_2 = E\{\mathbf{x}_2\mathbf{y}^T\} \tag{11.3}$$

which here becomes

$$\begin{pmatrix} 1 & E\{\mathbf{d}_1^T\} \\ E\{\mathbf{d}_1\} & E\{\mathbf{d}_1\mathbf{d}_1^T\} \end{pmatrix}\mathbf{A}_2 = \begin{pmatrix} E\{\mathbf{y}^T\} \\ E\{\mathbf{d}_1\,\mathbf{y}^T\} \end{pmatrix} \tag{11.4}$$

We know from (6.30) and (6.49) that for the trained system Clsf_1

$$E\{\mathbf{d}_1\} = E\{\mathbf{y}\} \quad \text{and} \quad E\{\mathbf{d}_1\mathbf{d}_1^T\} = E\{\mathbf{d}_1\mathbf{y}^T\} \tag{11.5}$$

is valid and hence

$$\begin{pmatrix} 1 & E\{\mathbf{y}^T\} \\ E\{\mathbf{y}\} & E\{\mathbf{d}_1\mathbf{y}^T\} \end{pmatrix}\mathbf{A}_2 = \begin{pmatrix} E\{\mathbf{y}^T\} \\ E\{\mathbf{d}_1\mathbf{y}^T\} \end{pmatrix} \tag{11.6}$$

which holds for

$$\mathbf{A}_2 = \begin{pmatrix} \mathbf{0}^T \\ \mathbf{I} \end{pmatrix} \quad \text{and} \quad \mathbf{d}_2 = \mathbf{A}_2^T\mathbf{x}_2 = \mathbf{v}_2 \tag{11.7}$$

This result shows that no improvements are possible by using a linear classifier for Clsf_2 since in that case the mapping $\mathbf{d}_2(\mathbf{v}_2)$ simplifies to the identity mapping $\mathbf{d}_2 = \mathbf{v}_2$.

The situation changes if $Clsf_2$ is chosen to be a nonlinear classifier. This case has a certain potential of improving the overall system performance, except $Clsf_1$ would already be optimum in the sense of rendering the vector **p** of a posteriori probabilities.

What happens is that the type of basis functions employed for establishing the estimations contained in **d** is changed. Consider the case that both classifiers $Clsf_1$ and $Clsf_2$ are second-degree polynomial classifiers. The combined classifier Clsf becomes one of fourth degree but, however, without having full access to all of the correspondent coefficients. Another interpretation is that the linear system of class borders in the decision space $\mathbf{D}_1$ of $Clsf_1$ is replaced by another system not bound to be linear.

Classifier Tuning

If the first pattern classifier $Clsf_1$ is already optimally trained to its task, this technique does not look so promising. It has, however, proved to be a useful tool for *classifier tuning*.

Consider the case that $Clsf_1$ is some general-purpose classifier working fairly well for a broader class of applications but is not perfect for its current job. Combining the given classifier $Clsf_1$ with $Clsf_2$ and using $Clsf_2$ as a kind of "afterburner" allows us to achieve the desired task-dependent specialization without being forced to restart the comparably expensive learning procedure for $Clsf_1$ [FRA1991a].

This kind of tuning technique competes, first, with classifier iteration as described in Section 6.14 and, second, with recursive learning as discussed in Section 6.13 in the context of polynomial regression and in Section 7.6 in the context of multilayer perceptron regression since recursive learning is an intrinsic property of backpropagation learning.

Another interesting facet of this kind of tuning technique is that it applies not only to the properties of the stochastic process $\{\mathbf{v}, k\}$, which may now be different from those valid when $Clsf_1$ was trained, but also to changes in the composition of the set Ω of class labels.

The simplest case is that of Ω_2 being a subset of the set Ω_1 of class labels belonging to $Clsf_1$. In this situation already a linear classifier $Clsf_2$ makes sense, deriving its estimations $d_k(\mathbf{v})$ from linear combinations of the given estimations contained in $\mathbf{d}_1$ and thus redistributing the given probability masses based on the knowledge that the set of allowed classes Ω_1 is reduced to a certain subset Ω_2.

Astonishingly, to a certain degree also the reverse situation is manageable with Ω_2 being a superset of Ω_1. In such a case the discriminant vector $\mathbf{d}_1$ of $Clsf_1$ serves as the feature vector $\mathbf{v}_2$ for $Clsf_2$. This classifier $Clsf_2$ exploits the similarities of **v** to all of the classes contained in Ω_1 for inferring the similarities of **v** to all of the newly introduced classes.

11.2 CLASSIFIERS WORKING IN PARALLEL

We will now consider the case that the same set of measurement data **v** is input to all classifiers Clsf_i, $i = 1, \ldots, I$. Thus, the group of classifiers to be combined can be viewed as a group of experts looking into the same problem from their individual points of view and stating their opinions about the present case in the form of their discriminant vectors $\mathbf{d}_i$. The central task to be solved here is the combination of different experts' votes related to the same frame of discernment.

Besides working on the same measurement vector **v**, the different classifiers may be specialized in some way. Obvious possibilities are that they employ different subsets of the total set of measurements, use different kinds of transformations for transforming measurements into features, spend differently much computational effort, or rely on different classifier design concepts.

Combination of Fast Low-Performance with Slow High-Performance Classifiers

An interesting case of classifier combination is that of combining classifiers that have different polynomial length L, and therefore exhibit different discriminative power at different computational expense. Such a sequence of classifiers with increasing discriminative power can easily be derived from the mathematical process of classifier adaptation according to the minimum residual variance strategy of Section 6.9; see Fig. 11.1.

The natural arrangement of these classifiers is to let the cheapest and least perfect answer first and the most powerful and most expensive last (Fig. 11.2). The different reject thresholds rad_1 to rad_3 are individually adjusted according to the operating characteristic of Fig. 11.1; thus that the respective classifier is prevented from giving a positive response whenever its competence is overcharged.

All the classifiers operate on the same measurement vector **v** but are (except for the first one) activated only on demand. The percentage being activated is determined by the reject rate of the preceding classifier. The advantage of this construction is to render an overall classifier Clsf as powerful as the best of the partial classifiers but at reduced average computational cost.

Voting

Another reasonable construction is that of combining a group of classifiers having equal competence and equal rights. Under these circumstances, what we are looking for is a rule for combining the different experts' votes into one consolidated vote **d** or into one consolidated decision k.

The similarity of this situation to that of a group of human experts deliber-

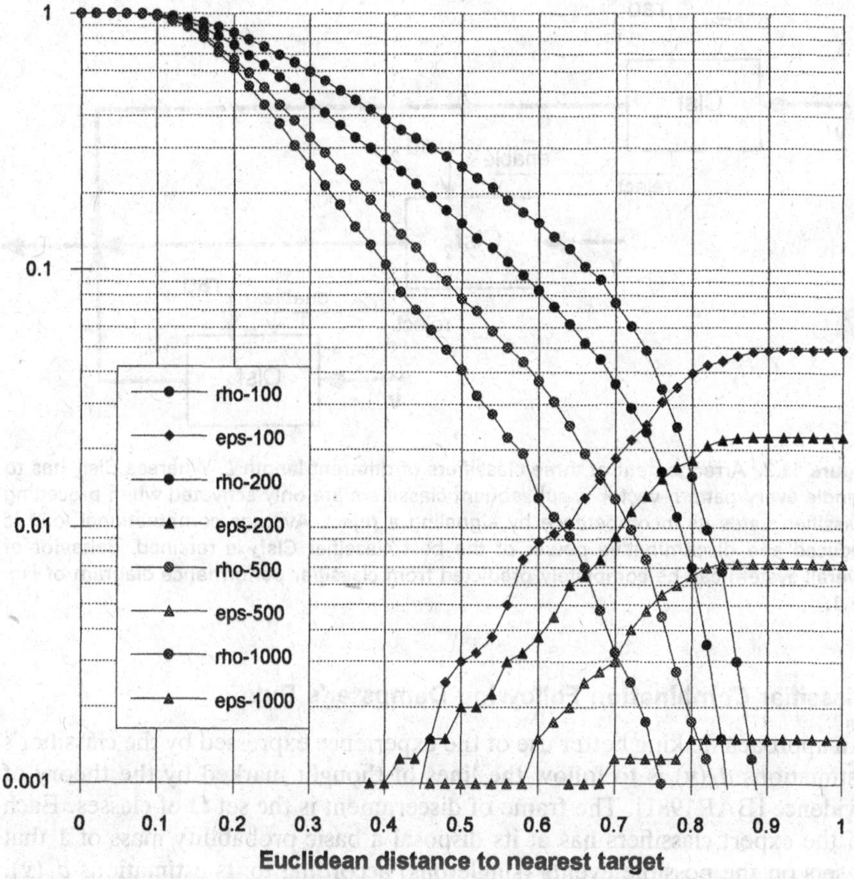

Figure 11.1. Classifier performance diagram for sequence of polynomial regression classifiers of different polynomial length $L = [100, 200, 500, 1000]$. Data taken from handprint numeral example. Classifiers are gained as intermediate results from one single classifier adaptation procedure. Diagram shows that with suitable reject threshold RjctThrsh = rad error rate ϵ(rad) can in any case be made arbitrarily small at the expense of a certain reject rate ρ(rad); compare Fig. 10.13.

ating on a complicated case and often unable to come to a unanimous decision suggests that we apply democratic voting principles. If only two experts are asked, their votes are accepted if coincident; otherwise the whole case is rejected. If more than two experts are in the game, the techniques of simple or qualified majority voting may be applied.

Voting techniques apply when different experts have already come to decision and arbitration takes place on the level of class labels rather than on the level of discriminant vectors **d**. These techniques are, appropriately generalized, applicable also if the individual classifiers forward sets of alternatives instead of first-choice decisions.

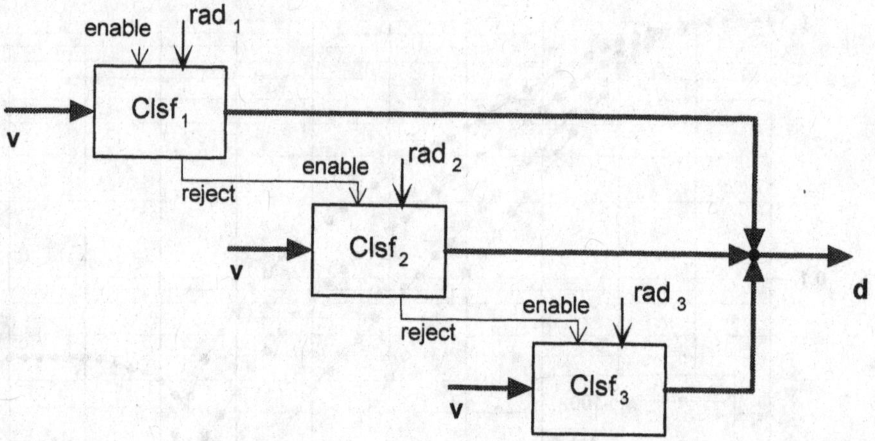

Figure 11.2. Arrangement of three classifiers of different length L. Whereas $Clsf_1$ has to handle every pattern vector **v**, subsequent classifiers are only activated when preceding classifier states its incompetence by signaling a reject. Average computational load is reduced and discriminative power of the best classifier $Clsf_3$ is retained. Behavior of overall system can be completely predicted from classifier performance diagram of Fig. 11.1.

Classifier Combination Following Dempster's Rule

An approach making better use of the experience expressed by the classifier's estimations $d_k(\mathbf{v})$ is to follow the lines of thought marked by the theory of evidence [BAR1981]. The frame of discernment is the set Ω of classes. Each of the expert classifiers has at its disposal a basic probability mass of 1 that it sets on the possible events (singletons) according to its estimations $d_k(\mathbf{v})$. The combination of two or more experts' opinions is brought about following Dempster's rule, to be explained by Fig. 11.3.

The whole procedure is based on the assumption of independence of the two experts. The degree of consent in favor of one certain class k is expressed by the product of the individual votes $d_{k,\text{expert\_1}} \cdot d_{k,\text{expert\_2}}$ generated by the two experts for the respective class. By applying the NormalizeToUnity operation [compare (4.33)], a combined discriminant vector $\mathbf{d}_{\text{combined}}$ is gained with components

$$d_{k,\text{combined}} = \underset{k}{\text{NormalizeToUnity}}[d_{k,\text{expert\_1}} \cdot \mathrm{d}_{k,\text{expert\_2}}] \tag{11.8}$$

The combined discriminant vector $\mathbf{d}_{\text{combined}}$ can be treated as any discriminant vector $\mathbf{d}$ coming from a single classifier and can be processed further to generate rejections or sets of alternatives. The procedure can be easily extended to more than two cooperating experts.

The combination based on Dempster's rule has some quite acceptable

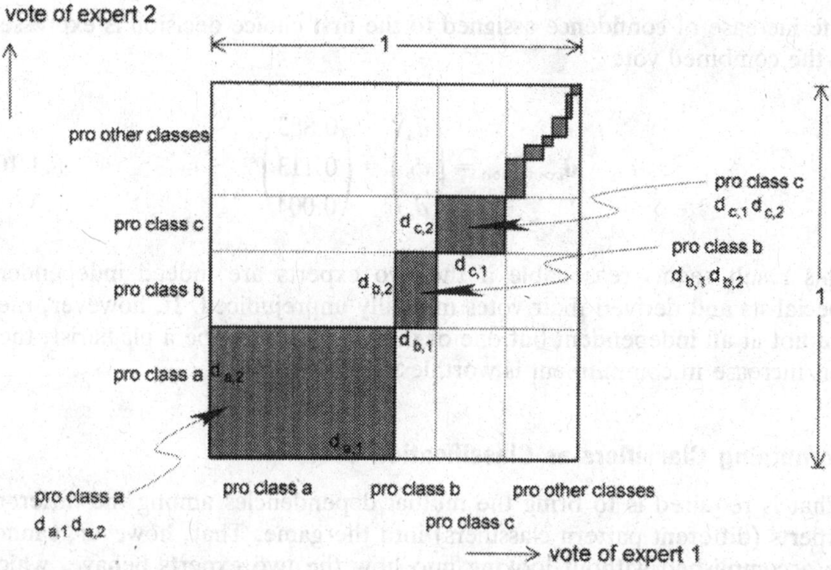

Figure 11.3. Orthogonal combination of votes following Dempster's rule. Unit square is divided along both axes in accordance with estimations $d_{k,\text{expert\_1}}$ and $d_{k,\text{expert\_2}}$ of two experts. Thus unit square is split into K^2 more or less extended rectangles corresponding to all possible pairwise combinations of $k_{\text{expert\_1}}$ and $k_{\text{expert\_2}}$. Area of each rectangle is given by product of $d_{k,\text{expert\_1}}$ and $d_{k,\text{expert\_2}}$. Whereas most regions belong to unequal class labels $k_{\text{expert\_1}} \neq k_{\text{expert\_2}}$ and express contradiction, shaded rectangles belong to matching class labels $k_{\text{expert\_1}} = k_{\text{expert\_2}} = k$. Their area determines credit combination of both experts' votes gives to respective class k. Applying NormalizeToUnity operation (4.33) of Section 4 to these numbers, combined votes $d_{k,\text{combined}}$ for different classes $k = 1, \ldots, K$ are gained.

properties: It takes into account the fuzziness of experts' votes, putting less confidence in less decided votes; it draws its conclusions solely from the present $\mathbf{d}_{\text{expert\_1}}$ and $\mathbf{d}_{\text{expert\_2}}$ data; and it gives no penalties to that pattern classifier weaker in the average. Voting according to Dempster's rule is easy to implement and requires no additional learning or adaptation.

One of its drawbacks is the questionable assumption of independence and orthogonality. We are used to believing that an answer to a difficult question becomes more reliable if more than one expert votes for the same option. This kind of anticipation is confirmed by the combination rule of (11.8).

Consider the example of two experts independently coming to the same conclusion:

$$\mathbf{d}_{\text{expert\_1}} = \begin{pmatrix} d_a \\ d_b \\ d_c \end{pmatrix} = \begin{pmatrix} 0.70 \\ 0.25 \\ 0.05 \end{pmatrix} \quad \text{and} \quad \mathbf{d}_{\text{expert\_2}} = \begin{pmatrix} d_a \\ d_b \\ d_c \end{pmatrix} = \begin{pmatrix} 0.70 \\ 0.25 \\ 0.05 \end{pmatrix} \tag{11.9}$$

The increase of confidence assigned to the first choice decision is expressed in the combined vote

$$\mathbf{d}_{\text{combined}} = \begin{pmatrix} d_a \\ d_b \\ d_c \end{pmatrix} = \begin{pmatrix} 0.883 \\ 0.113 \\ 0.004 \end{pmatrix} \tag{11.10}$$

This result seems reasonable if the two experts are indeed independent specialists and derived their votes mutually unprejudiced. If, however, they are not at all independent but one of them turns out to be a plagiarist, then this increase in commitment is worthless and deceptive.

Combining Classifiers as Classification Task

What is required is to bring the mutual dependencies among the different experts (different pattern classifiers) into the game. That, however, cannot be accomplished without looking into how the two experts behave, which requires learning and adaptation.

This leads us to the concept that combining the votes of different classifiers working in parallel, be they independent or not, is again a classification task. Following this idea we come to the arrangement of classifiers shown in Fig. 11.4.

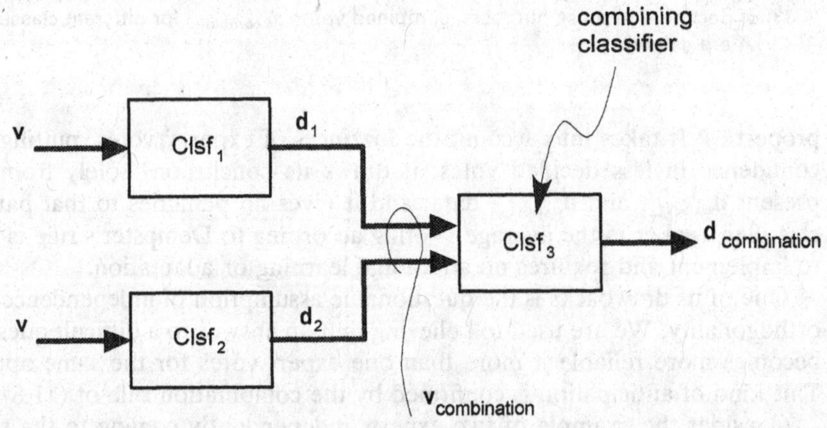

Figure 11.4. Combination of classifiers viewed as classification task. Classifiers Clsf_1 and Clsf_2 are both trained to the same pattern source $\{\mathbf{v}, k\}$ and work on the same input data $\mathbf{v}$ but have a different view on the pattern classification problem due to different measurement transformations, design principles, or choice of fundamental design parameters. The two discriminant vectors $\mathbf{d}_1$ and $\mathbf{d}_2$ as produced by two classifiers Clsf_1 and Clsf_2 constitute measurement vector $\mathbf{v}_3$ for a third classifier Clsf_3, merging votes $\mathbf{d}_1$ and $\mathbf{d}_2$ of the two experts Clsf_1 and Clsf_2 into one combined vote $\mathbf{d}_3$.

The general approach is very similar to that discussed in Section 11.1 in the context of classifier concatenation. The difference here is that Clsf_3 is concatenated with two preceding classifiers, Clsf_1 and Clsf_2, acting as modules that prepare the measurement data for the merging classifier Clsf_3.

Merging of the measurement data for Clsf_3 is easily accomplished by concatenating the two discriminant vectors $\mathbf{d}_1$ and $\mathbf{d}_2$ into

$$\mathbf{v}_3 = \begin{pmatrix} \mathbf{d}_1 \\ \mathbf{d}_2 \end{pmatrix} = \mathbf{v}_{\text{combined}} \tag{11.11}$$

After having been trained to their tasks, the two pattern classifiers Clsf_1 and Clsf_2 constitute fixed mappings $\mathbf{v} \to \mathbf{d}_1$ and $\mathbf{v} \to \mathbf{d}_2$. According to (11.11), the given stochastic process $\{\mathbf{v}, k\}$ is mapped into the stochastic process $\{\mathbf{v}_{\text{combined}}, k\}$ acting as the pattern source for training the combining classifier Clsf_3. And this combining classifier Clsf_3, during its own learning process, adapts to the peculiarities and imperfections of the two classifier experts Clsf_1 and Clsf_2 and hence acquires the capability of making more of their votes.

Classifier training for the combining classifier Clsf_3 is accomplished by any of the classifier design techniques discussed in the preceding chapters of this book. The simplest case is that of using a linear classifier:

$$\mathbf{x}_3 = \begin{pmatrix} 1 \\ \mathbf{v}_3 \end{pmatrix} = \begin{pmatrix} 1 \\ \mathbf{d}_1 \\ \mathbf{d}_2 \end{pmatrix} \tag{11.12}$$

The adaptation of Clsf_3 requires that we solve the matrix equation (6.20),

$$E\{\mathbf{x}_3\mathbf{x}_3^T\}\mathbf{A}_3 = E\{\mathbf{x}_3\mathbf{y}^T\} \tag{11.13}$$

which, together with (11.12), can be written as

$$\begin{pmatrix} 1 & E\{\mathbf{d}_1^T\} & E\{\mathbf{d}_2^T\} \\ E\{\mathbf{d}_1\} & E\{\mathbf{d}_1\mathbf{d}_1^T\} & E\{\mathbf{d}_1\mathbf{d}_2^T\} \\ E\{\mathbf{d}_2\} & E\{\mathbf{d}_2\mathbf{d}_1^T\} & E\{\mathbf{d}_2\mathbf{d}_2^T\} \end{pmatrix} \mathbf{A}_3 = \begin{pmatrix} E\{\mathbf{y}^T\} \\ E\{\mathbf{d}_1\mathbf{y}^T\} \\ E\{\mathbf{d}_2\mathbf{y}^T\} \end{pmatrix} \tag{11.14}$$

Most of the statistical moments contained in the above equation are already known from the learning processes for Clsf_1 and Clsf_2 [compare (6.30) and (6.49)]:

$$\begin{aligned} E\{\mathbf{d}_1\} &= E\{\mathbf{y}\} \\ E\{\mathbf{d}_1\mathbf{d}_1^T\} &= E\{\mathbf{d}_1\mathbf{y}^T\} = \mathbf{A}_1 E\{\mathbf{x}_1\mathbf{y}^T\} \end{aligned} \tag{11.15}$$

$$\begin{aligned} E\{\mathbf{d}_2\} &= E\{\mathbf{y}\} \\ E\{\mathbf{d}_2\mathbf{d}_2^T\} &= E\{\mathbf{d}_2\mathbf{y}^T\} = \mathbf{A}_2 E\{\mathbf{x}_2\mathbf{y}^T\} \end{aligned} \tag{11.16}$$

The data of (11.15) and (11.16) were either already used for the adaptation of the classifiers Clsf_1 and Clsf_2 or were the result thereof, as the two coefficient matrices $\mathbf{A}_1$ and $\mathbf{A}_2$, where $\mathbf{x}_1$ and $\mathbf{x}_2$ stand for the two polynomial structures applied.

The only new information needed for adaptation of Clsf_3 is that contained in

$$E\{\mathbf{d}_1\mathbf{d}_2^T\} = \mathbf{A}_1 E\{\mathbf{x}_1, \mathbf{x}_2^T\}\mathbf{A}_2^T \tag{11.17}$$

reflecting the mutual correlation between $\mathbf{d}_1$ and $\mathbf{d}_2$ or $\mathbf{x}_1$ and $\mathbf{x}_2$, respectively.

Let us consider the extreme case that, due to their different design, the two views on the classification task taken from the viewpoints of the two classifiers Clsf_1 and Clsf_2 are so different that $\mathbf{d}_1$ and $\mathbf{d}_2$ can be treated as being uncorrelated. Then

$$E\{\mathbf{d}_1\mathbf{d}_2^T\} = \mathrm{E}\{\mathbf{d}_1\}E\{\mathbf{d}_2^T\} = E\{\mathbf{y}\}E\{\mathbf{y}^T\} \tag{11.18}$$

is valid. For this case (11.14) can be considerably simplified. Taking into account equations (11.15) and (11.16), we get

$$\begin{pmatrix} 1 & E\{\mathbf{y}^T\} & E\{\mathbf{y}^T\} \\ E\{\mathbf{y}\} & E\{\mathbf{d}_1\mathbf{y}^T\} & E\{\mathbf{y}\}E\{\mathbf{y}^T\} \\ E\{\mathbf{y}\} & E\{\mathbf{y}\}E\{\mathbf{y}^T\} & E\{\mathbf{d}_2\mathbf{y}^T\} \end{pmatrix} \mathbf{A}_3 = \begin{pmatrix} E\{\mathbf{y}^T\} \\ E\{\mathbf{d}_1\mathbf{y}^T\} \\ E\{\mathbf{d}_2\mathbf{y}^T\} \end{pmatrix} \tag{11.19}$$

This matrix equation is solved by

$$\mathbf{A}_3 = \begin{pmatrix} -E\{\mathbf{y}^T\} \\ I \\ I \end{pmatrix} \tag{11.20}$$

resulting in the combined discriminant vector $\mathbf{d}_{\text{combined}}$:

$$\begin{aligned} \mathbf{d}_3 &= \mathbf{A}_3^T\mathbf{x}_3 \\ &= \mathbf{d}_1 + \mathbf{d}_2 - E\{\mathbf{y}\} \\ &= E\{\mathbf{y}\} + (\mathbf{d}_1 - E\{\mathbf{y}\}) + (\mathbf{d}_2 - E\{\mathbf{y}\}) \end{aligned} \tag{11.21}$$

Remarkably, the combined vote $\mathbf{d}_{\text{combined}}$ is achieved, not by averaging the two votes $\mathbf{d}_1$ and $\mathbf{d}_2$, but by relating them to the common average $E\{\mathbf{d}_1\} = E\{\mathbf{d}_2\} = E\{\mathbf{d}_3\} = E\{\mathbf{y}\}$ and taking the sum.

Using the same example as before (11.9),

$$\mathbf{d}_{\text{expert\_1}} = \mathbf{d}_{\text{expert\_2}} = \begin{pmatrix} 0.70 \\ 0.25 \\ 0.05 \end{pmatrix} \tag{11.22}$$

we arrive for this case of "independent" experts at the combined vote of

$$\mathbf{d}_{\text{combined}} = \begin{pmatrix} 1.0\bar{6} \\ 0.1\bar{6} \\ -0.2\bar{3} \end{pmatrix} \tag{11.23}$$

Again the property of least mean-square estimation becomes visible to generate estimations not bound to the [0 . . 1] interval; compare Fig. 6.5. These votes can be transformed into legitimate confidence values applying the technique of confidence mapping (Section 6.13).

In general, however, no assumptions as (11.18), about the two classifiers Clsf_1 and Clsf_2, of being uncorrelated will be made, but instead the coefficient matrix $\mathbf{A}_3$ of the combining classifier Clsf_3 will be computed according to the standard procedure.

Should one of the two classifiers turn out to be a plagiarist, resulting in $\mathbf{d}_1 = \mathbf{d}_2$ and establishing a multiple linear dependence among the components of $\mathbf{x}_3$, this event would be detected during the adaptation procedure and the linear dependent terms eliminated.

Combination of pattern classifiers by introducing the combining classifier operating on their estimations was exemplified here for the case of two classifiers to be combined. Extension for the case of more than two is straightforward.

11.3 HIERARCHICAL CLASSIFIERS

One of the factors making classification difficult is the number K of classes to be distinguished. This is due not only to the obvious effect that with increasing number of classes the potential grows for conflicts between the classes but also to the increasing complexity of the optimum discriminant functions $\text{prob}(k|\mathbf{v})$. Practical pattern classifiers cannot work with these optimum discriminant functions but must rely on approximations $d_k(\mathbf{v})$ of one kind or another. Depending on the type of approximation the capability of $d_k(\mathbf{v})$ to follow $\text{prob}(k|\mathbf{v})$ may be more or less quickly brought to its limits.

One way to escape this consequence of a growing number of classes is to organize the classification system as a hierarchy of classifiers. Consider the case that the set Ω of classes can be split into two subsets Ω_1 and Ω_2 having the property that members of Ω_1 are almost never confused with members of Ω_2 and vice versa when presented to a classifier being trained for the full set Ω of classes. It would then be most straightforward to cut down the number of classes by separating the whole problem into two subproblems and to design a structure of three classifiers, the first one with the task of distinguishing between the two subsets Ω_1 and Ω_2 and the other two with the tasks of distinguishing between the classes contained in each subset.

The same concept can recursively be applied to the already determined subsets; thus a whole tree of classifiers evolves.

There exists an abundance of different concepts for designing hierarchical classifiers. Most of the designs try to use as few measurements as possible in the individual nodes of the classifier tree. In contrast, we will look at this problem from the position that every node has access to the complete set of measurements and may use it either completely or partially depending on its own needs. What we are trying to do here is to derive the whole design from a statistical point of view.

Operations of Individual Node Classifier

The general concept of hierarchical classification is explained by Fig. 11.5. The basic principles of the design will be outlined starting from the assumption that all pattern classifiers constituting the classifier tree are optimum in the Bayes sense: compute a posteriori probabilities with respect to $\mathbf{v}$ [SCH1984].

Each classifier works on a certain set Ω_{in} of classes splitting it into a certain number S of mutually exclusive subsets $\Omega_{\text{out},s}$ of classes, $s = 1, \ldots, S$. At the root node is $\Omega_{\text{in}} = \Omega$, whereas at the leaf nodes the subsets $\Omega_{\text{out},s}$ are one-element sets each containing one single class (singletons).

Formally, for the input and output sets of each classifier holds

$$\Omega_{\text{out},s} \subset \Omega_{\text{in}} \quad \text{and} \quad \Omega_{\text{out},s} \cap \Omega_{\text{in}} = \Omega_{\text{out},s} \tag{11.24}$$

This constitutes a hierarchy of subsets and a correspondent hierarchy of classifier labels. At the highest level of this hierarchy (at the level of the given set Ω of classes), the K class-specific distributions $\text{prob}(\mathbf{v}|k)$ together with the corresponding a priori probabilities $\text{prob}(k)$ are assumed to be known. They describe the statistical properties of the pattern source $\{\mathbf{v}, \Omega\}$ on the level of the complete set Ω of classes.

The respective statistical properties $\{\mathbf{v}, \Omega_{\text{subset}}\}$ on some lower level are derived from

$$\begin{aligned} \text{prob}(\Omega_{\text{subset}}) &= \sum_{k \in \Omega_{\text{subset}}} \text{prob}(k) \\ \text{prob}(\mathbf{v}|\Omega_{\text{subset}}) &= \sum_{k \in \Omega_{\text{subset}}} \frac{\text{prob}(k)}{\text{prob}(\Omega_{\text{subset}})} \text{prob}(\mathbf{v}|k) \end{aligned} \tag{11.25}$$

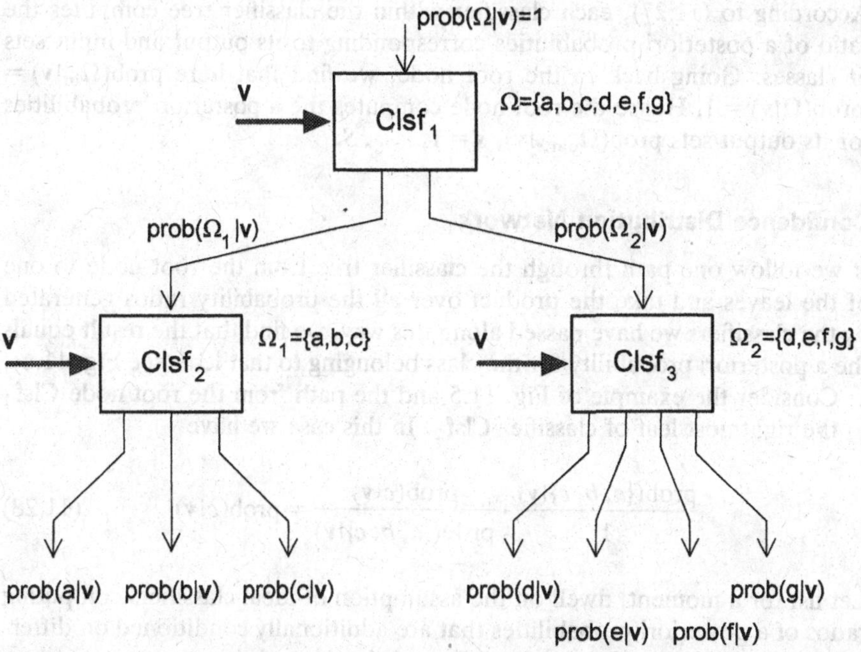

Figure 11.5. Basic principles of hierarchical classification for example of $K = 7$ with set Ω of classes given by $\{a, b, c, d, e, f, g\}$ and divided into two subsets $\Omega_1 = \{a, b, c\}$ and $\Omega_2 = \{d, e, f, g\}$. Hierarchical classification system consists of three classifiers. Root classifier Clsf_1 computes a posteriori probabilities $\mathrm{prob}(\Omega_1|\mathbf{v})$ and $\mathrm{prob}(\Omega_2|\mathbf{v})$. Two leaf classifiers Clsf_2 and Clsf_3 have task of computing $\mathrm{prob}(a|\Omega_1, \mathbf{v}), \ldots, \mathrm{prob}(c|\Omega_1, \mathbf{v})$ and $\mathrm{prob}(d|\Omega_2, \mathbf{v}), \ldots, \mathrm{prob}(g|\Omega_2, \mathbf{v})$. Mathematics given in text.

This is just the statistical knowledge we need to know to compute the a posteriori probabilities at the level of one certain classifier operating under the condition that only those classes have to be considered that are contained in its input set Ω_{in}:

$$\mathrm{prob}(\Omega_{\mathrm{out},s}|\Omega_{\mathrm{in}}, \mathbf{v}) = \frac{\mathrm{prob}(\Omega_{\mathrm{out},s}, \Omega_{\mathrm{in}}, \mathbf{v})}{\mathrm{prob}(\Omega_{\mathrm{in}}, \mathbf{v})} \tag{11.26}$$

Making use of (11.24), this simplifies to

$$\begin{aligned}\mathrm{prob}(\Omega_{\mathrm{out},s}|\Omega_{\mathrm{in}}, \mathbf{v}) &= \frac{\mathrm{prob}(\Omega_{\mathrm{out},s}, \mathbf{v})}{\mathrm{prob}(\Omega_{\mathrm{in}}, \mathbf{v})} \\ &= \frac{\mathrm{prob}(\Omega_{\mathrm{out},s}|\mathbf{v})\mathrm{prob}(\mathbf{v})}{\mathrm{prob}(\Omega_{\mathrm{in}}|\mathbf{v})\mathrm{prob}(\mathbf{v})} \\ &= \frac{\mathrm{prob}(\Omega_{\mathrm{out},s}|\mathbf{v})}{\mathrm{prob}(\Omega_{\mathrm{in}}|\mathbf{v})}\end{aligned} \tag{11.27}$$

According to (11.27), each classifier within the classifier tree computes the ratio of a posteriori probabilities corresponding to its output and input sets of classes. Going back to the root node, we find that here $\text{prob}(\Omega_{\text{in}}|\mathbf{v}) = \text{prob}(\Omega|\mathbf{v}) = 1$. Hence the root node computes the a posteriori probabilities for its output sets $\text{prob}(\Omega_{\text{out},s}|\mathbf{v})$, $s = 1, \ldots, S$.

Confidence Distribution Network

If we follow one path through the classifier tree from the root node to one of the leaves and take the product over all the probability ratios generated by the classifiers we have passed along this way, we find that the result equals the a posteriori probability for the class belonging to that leaf (see Fig. 11.6).

Consider the example of Fig. 11.5 and the path from the root node Clsf_1 to the rightmost leaf of classifier Clsf_2. In this case we have

$$\frac{\text{prob}(\{a, b, c\}|\mathbf{v})}{1} \cdot \frac{\text{prob}(c|\mathbf{v})}{\text{prob}(\{a, b, c\}|\mathbf{v})} = \text{prob}(c|\mathbf{v}) \tag{11.28}$$

Let us, for a moment, dwell on the assumption of ideal classifiers computing ratios of a posteriori probabilities that are additionally conditioned on differently composed sets of class labels. From this point of view the tree structure is more a flow diagram of a certain procedure for calculating a posteriori probabilities than a tree classifier.

Given the input pattern $\mathbf{v}$, all of the probability ratios have to be computed

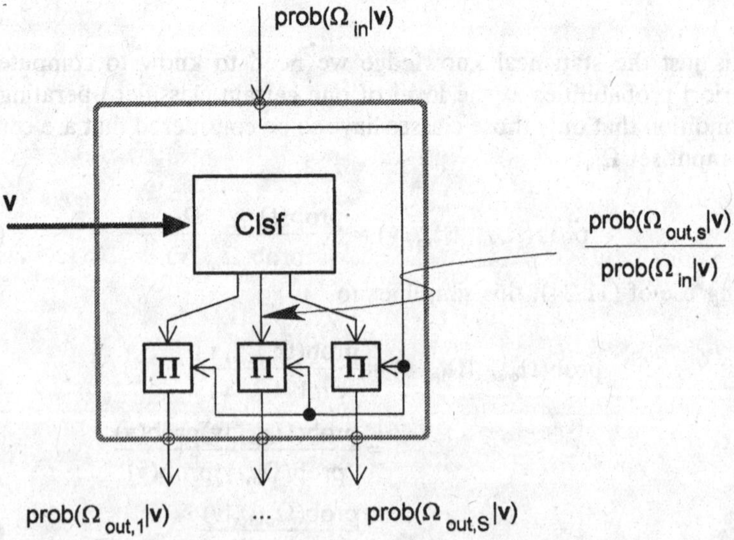

Figure 11.6. Internal structure of each node classifier of tree classifier system of Fig. 11.5.

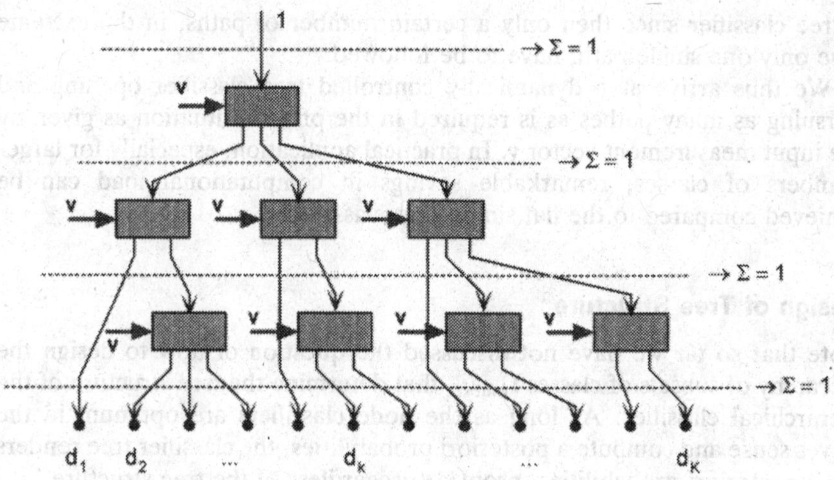

Figure 11.7. Cross sections through tree render sum = 1 at every level.

and properly multiplied in order to obtain the final results prob(k|**v**) at the tree's leaves. In contrast, the idea of a tree classifier is commonly associated with the concept of a switching network, opening only one of the paths from the root node to hopefully the correct leaf node.

The whole scheme considered here works as a confidence distribution network fed with the probability mass 1 at the root node and distributing this probability mass through the tree nodes until it reaches the leaf nodes. The classifier nodes act as a kind of valve directing different quantities of their input mass to their output ports. Making use of the statistical knowledge represented by the probability functions given above, the valves are controlled by the input pattern **v**. See Fig. 11.7.

It is interesting to observe that summing the probability masses over all crossed paths in every horizontal cross section through the tree renders again the value 1. Another observation is worth mentioning. The values along each path from the root to one of the leaves decrease monotonically. This means that whenever one of these values has fallen below a threshold, it can never be larger.

Pruning Classifier Tree

The results at the tree's leaves are the a posteriori probabilities prob(k|**v**). Since we are searching for the maximum among these values, or at least for the larger ones, we need not care for the smaller values. This fact allows us to prune the tree and close a path as soon as its value falls below a certain threshold. Pruning lets the computational scheme of Fig. 11.7 look more like a tree classifier since then only a certain number of paths, in the extreme case only one single path, have to be followed.

We thus arrive at a dynamically controlled tree classifier opening and pursuing as many pathes as is required in the present situation as given by the input measurement vector **v**. In practical application, especially for larger numbers of classes, remarkable savings in computational load can be achieved compared to the flat single-shot classifier.

Design of Tree Structure

Note that so far we have not discussed the question of how to design the hierarchy of subsets of classes Ω_{subset} that determine the tree structure of the hierarchical classifier. As long as the node classifiers are optimum in the Bayes sense and compute a posteriori probabilities, the classifier tree renders the a posteriori probabilities, $\text{prob}(k|\mathbf{v})$ regardless of the tree structure.

The tree structure becomes important, however, even in this idealized case if pruning is considered. In order to keep the computational load low, we are interested in coming to a clear separation between subclasses at the earliest steps of the procedure, which means that at each node, whenever possible, one of the output paths should have a value close to 1 and all the others values close to 0 for all values of **v** relevant for the considered node.

The node classifier maps the input vector **v** into the S-dimensional discriminant vector **d** representing in this case the ratio of a posteriori probabilities (11.27)

$$d_s = \text{prob}(\Omega_{\text{out},s}|\Omega_{\text{in}}, \mathbf{v}) = \frac{\text{prob}(\Omega_{\text{out},s}|\mathbf{v})}{\text{prob}(\Omega_{\text{in}}|\mathbf{v})} \quad \text{for} \quad s = 1, \ldots, S \tag{11.29}$$

The degree of uniqueness of this specific discriminant vector **d** can be measured either by one of the measures introduced as reject criteria in Chapter 10 or by using the *entropy* measure

$$H(\mathbf{d}) = \sum_{s=1}^{S} d_s \text{ld}\left(\frac{1}{d_s}\right) \tag{11.30}$$

which assumes its maximum $\text{ld}(S)$ for uniform values $d_s = 1/S$ and takes on the minimum value zero if all the probability mass is concentrated in one of the components of **d** being $d_s = 1$ and all the others are zero. It must be mentioned that in contrast to the reject criteria of Chapter 10, the entropy measure of (11.30) can only be applied if the discriminant vector **d** has the properties of a vector of probabilities; compare (6.74) and (6.75).

As long as the number K of classes remains moderate and each node has only two output channels, the situation can be systematically treated. For

$S = 2$ the number NumbPart of different partitions of the K classes contained in Ω_{in} to the two output channels $\Omega_{\text{out},1}$ and $\Omega_{\text{out},2}$ is given by

$$\text{NumbPart} = \begin{cases} \displaystyle\sum_{i=1}^{K/2-1} \binom{K}{i} + \frac{1}{2}\binom{K}{\frac{K}{2}} & K = \text{even} \\ \displaystyle\sum_{i=1}^{K/2-1} \binom{K}{i} & K = \text{odd} \end{cases} \tag{11.31}$$

which simplifies to

$$\text{NumbPart} = 2^{k-1} - 1 \tag{11.32}$$

The idea is to compute the K-class classifier and connect it to the pattern source $\{\mathbf{v}, k\}$. Each resulting K-class discriminant vector $\mathbf{d}_{K\text{-class}}$ can be mapped into the corresponding two-channel discriminant vector $\mathbf{d}_{2\text{-channel}}$ according to the different possible assignment schemes:

$$d_{\text{out},1} = \sum_{k\in\Omega_1} d_k \quad \text{and} \quad d_{\text{out},2} = \sum_{k\in\Omega_2} d_k \tag{11.33}$$

Averaging the performance measures for each of the assignment schemes renders the desired selection criteria.

For larger numbers of classes this technique becomes impractical. A useful approach is then to look into the *confusion matrix* of the complete K-class classifier and to evaluate the different assignment schemes by counting the remaining errors.

The confusion matrix of the K-class classifier contains the following elements:

$$\begin{aligned} \text{confus}[k, j] = {} & \text{relative frequency of patterns coming from class } k \\ & \text{and being recognized as members of class } j \end{aligned} \tag{11.34}$$

The assignment scheme distributes the K classes of Ω_{in} into the two sets $\Omega_{\text{out},1}$ and $\Omega_{\text{out},2}$. A grouping error is counted if k and j do not belong to the same group,

$$\text{Error rate}_{\text{assignment}} = \sum_{\substack{k\in\Omega_1 \wedge j\in\Omega_2 \\ \vee k\in\Omega_2 \wedge j\in\Omega_1}} \text{confus}[k, j] \tag{11.35}$$

and the assignment scheme giving the minimum grouping error rate is selected.

For even larger numbers K of classes to be distinguished clustering techniques based on the class means in measurement space are in use [SCH1984].

Adaptation of Node Classifiers

For the preceding considerations each node classifier within the decision tree had access to the same measurement vector $\mathbf{v}$. This does not exclude the fact that each classifier makes completely different use of these measurement data.

In general, each node classifier may be of a different type, apply different measurement transformations, and use different measurement extracts. This specialization evolves with the design of the classifier tree, which begins at the tree root and recursively determines the task for each node classifier. Depending on the specific complexities of these classification tasks, different node classifiers may require different computational effort.

When the tree classifier is constructed from polynomial regression classifiers, substantial savings in the adaptation procedure can be gained if the same measurement transformation $\mathbf{v} \to \mathbf{w}$ and the same draft polynomial $\mathbf{w} \to \mathbf{x}$ is used (compare Section 6.9) for all node classifiers but admitting different polynomial length L for the different nodes. In this case all statistical moment matrices necessary to compute the node classifiers on the different hierarchical levels are easily computed from the class-specific moment matrices $\mathbf{M}_k = E\{\mathbf{z}\mathbf{z}^T | k\}$ by appropriate linear combination:

$$\begin{aligned} \mathbf{M}_{\text{subset}} = E\{\mathbf{z}\mathbf{z}^T | \Omega_{\text{subset}}\} &= \sum_{k \in \Omega_{\text{subset}}} \frac{P_k}{\sum\limits_{k \in \Omega_{\text{subset}}} P_k} E\{\mathbf{z}\mathbf{z}^T | k\} \\ &= \sum_{k \in \Omega_{\text{subset}}} \alpha_k \mathbf{M}_k \end{aligned} \tag{11.36}$$

with the weights of the linear combination given by

$$\alpha_k = \frac{P_k}{\sum\limits_{k \in \Omega_{\text{subset}}} P_k} \tag{11.37}$$

The process of mixing subset-specific moment matrices moves bottom up in the classifier tree of Fig. 11.7 from the leaves to the root node.

We have used the assumption of ideal classifiers calculating a posteriori probabilities for developing the idea of hierarchical classification. In practical application, however, the node classifiers are nonideal and the mathematical properties derived so far are only approximately valid. When using polynomial regression classifiers as node classifiers, each should be followed by its own confidence mapping procedure in order to make the discriminant functions contained in **d** legitimate and consistent estimations for the unknown a posteriori probabilities.

Comments

It should be stressed that dividing the recognition task over a larger number of node classifiers within the hierarchical classifier tree does not increase the total computational effort. We compare for this purpose the case of the flat single-shot polynomial regression classifier recognizing K classes in one step to the case of an arbitrarily structured classifier tree employing several node classifiers of the same type.

Making use of the SumToUnity condition, the *single-shot classifier* needs $K - 1$ polynomials to compute K discriminant functions $d_k(\mathbf{v})$. It is easily verified that the same number of discriminant functions is needed for the hierarchical classifier regardless of the tree structure.

The operating tree classifier acts as a kind of decision tree but running in a dynamic soft-decision mode. Depending on the specific distribution of confidences on each of the tree levels, only one single or a multitude of paths are opened to be followed further.

Hierarchical classification allows us to allocate the computational effort to that of the node classifiers carrying the heaviest burden with respect to the difficulty of the recognition task.

The advantages of hierarchical classification over the single-shot classifier are mainly two:

- Improved discriminative power, due more or less to preventing the imperfections of the approximations to unknown statistical laws to become effective
- Speed-up, due to early closing of those paths of the classifier tree that will render hopelessly small values.

A question requiring special consideration in the context of hierarchical classification is that of how to detect and reject garbage patterns. This question is easiest answered for the root classifier since this classifier is trained on the complete classification task and has thus seen the complete stochastic process $\{\mathbf{v}, k\}$ for $k = 1, \ldots, K$, whereas the node classifiers on the subsequent hierarchical levels know only the stochastic properties of their respective classes as determined by their respective input sets Ω_{in}.

Garbage rejection relies on rejecting everything lying outside the statistical experience in terms of quantiles of certain distributions empirically measured during classifier adaptation; see Section 10.1. At the root node this may be the histogram of the reject criterion RAD or the collection of histograms accumulated for confidence mapping of the generated discriminant vector **d**; see Section 6.13. If on this level a pattern **v** is detected as lying outside the boundaries of the classifier's statistical experience, a garbage reject is induced.

Each subsequent node of the tree classifier guards one path leading to a certain subset of classes. It has at its disposal the corresponding statistical knowledge. On this level whenever a pattern **v** is detected as lying outside the boundaries of statistical experience, the respective path is closed and a "not mine" flag set. If all the paths of the tree are closed, the pattern must be rejected as being garbage.

11.4 CLASSIFIER NETWORKS

One of the properties of hierarchical classification is breaking down the complete pattern classification task into a number of smaller tasks that are easier to solve than the monolithic original one. Especially, close to the leaves of the classifier tree we find node classifiers highly specialized in the task of distinguishing among only a very small number of classes (often only two).

If breaking down the pattern classification task into smaller subtasks is a general advantage, then the optimum would be to rely completely on pairwise classification [BER1983]. In Section 7.8 we found a clear hint that relying on pairwise separation is a powerful approach. This is the approach we will follow now. The basic idea will again be explained, starting with the assumption that we work with ideal classifiers.

Given the pattern **v** to be classified, we need to know the a posteriori probabilities prob($k|\mathbf{v}$) for all $k = 1, \ldots, K$. This can be written [OBE1990]

$$\text{prob}(k|\mathbf{v}) = \frac{P_k \text{prob}(\mathbf{v}|k)}{\sum_{j=1}^{K} P_j \text{prob}(\mathbf{v}|j)} = \frac{1}{1 + \sum_{\substack{j=1 \\ j \neq k}}^{K} \frac{P_j \text{prob}(\mathbf{v}|j)}{P_k \text{prob}(\mathbf{v}|k)}} = \frac{1}{1 + \sum_{\substack{j=1 \\ j \neq k}}^{K} \frac{P_j}{P_k} \text{lik}(j, k, \mathbf{v})} \tag{11.38}$$

The relevant expression is the likelihood ratio

$$\text{lik}(j, k, \mathbf{v}) = \frac{\text{prob}(\mathbf{v}|j)}{\text{prob}(\mathbf{v}|k)} \tag{11.39}$$

which can be provided by a classifier trained to discriminate between the two classes k and j and computing the a posteriori probability for class k:

$$d_{kj} = \text{prob}(k|\mathbf{v}, \{j, k\}) = \frac{P_k \text{prob}(\mathbf{v}|k)}{P_k \text{prob}(\mathbf{v}|k) + P_j \text{prob}(\mathbf{v}|j)} = \frac{1}{1 + (P_j/P_k)\text{lik}(j, k, \mathbf{v})} \tag{11.40}$$

Stated another way, the same two-class classifier provides the a posteriori probability for class j:

$$d_{jk} = \text{prob}(j\,|\,\mathbf{v}, \{j, k\}) = 1 - d_{kj} \tag{11.41}$$

From (11.40) the likelihood ratio needed for (11.38) is derived:

$$\frac{P_j}{P_k}\,\text{lik}(j, k, \mathbf{v}) = \frac{1}{d_{kj}} - 1 \tag{11.42}$$

Inserting this into (11.38), we arrive at

$$d_k = \text{prob}(k\,|\,\mathbf{v}) = \left(1 + \sum_{\substack{j=1\\ j\neq k}}^{K} \left(\frac{1}{d_{kj}} - 1\right)\right)^{-1} \tag{11.43}$$

This is an interesting expression worthy of comment since it connects the a posteriori probability $d_k = \text{prob}(k\,|\,\mathbf{v})$ for class k given the measurement vector $\mathbf{v}$ and valid for the task of discriminating among all K classes contained in Ω with the a posteriori probabilities $d_{kj} = \text{prob}(k\,|\,\mathbf{v}, \{j, k\})$ gained from the $K - 1$ pairwise classifiers trained to discriminate class k from the $K - 1$ classes, $j = 1, \ldots, K, j \neq k$.

These pairwise classifiers have an extremely narrow view into the problem but are highly specialized experts. This is specifically relevant if the ideal Bayesian classifiers, as is necessary for any practical application, are replaced by real classifiers providing only estimations to a posteriori probabilities. Unavoidable imperfections of the approximation technique have the least impact on the resulting estimations if only two classes have to be considered.

Relying the estimation of $d_k = \text{prob}(k\,|\,\mathbf{v})$ on pairwise classifiers as in (11.43) bears the promise of rendering results that are closer to the optimum and more reliable. These advantages, however, must be paid for by computational effort that increases with the number K of classes to be distinguished, since the number of pairwise classifiers is given by

$$\text{NumbClsf} = \binom{K}{2} \tag{11.44}$$

The relation between $d_k = \text{prob}(k\,|\,\mathbf{v})$ and the pairwise estimations $d_{kj} =$

prob$(k|\mathbf{v}, \{j, k\})$ of (11.43) can be reformulated into

$$\left(\frac{1}{d_k} - 1\right) = \sum_{\substack{j=1 \\ j \neq k}}^{K} \left(\frac{1}{d_{kj}} - 1\right) \tag{11.45}$$

and remarkably simplified by introducing the nonlinear transformation

$$t(x) = \frac{1}{x} - 1 = \frac{1-x}{x} \tag{11.46}$$

together with its inverse

$$t^{-1}(x) = \frac{1}{x+1} \tag{11.47}$$

Making use of the transformation $t(\cdot)$ and its inverse $t^{-1}(\cdot)$, the K-class estimation d_k is gained from the $K-1$ pairwise estimations d_{kj} by

$$d_k = t^{-1}\left(\sum_{j \neq k} t(d_{kj})\right) \tag{11.48}$$

The nonlinear transformation $t(\cdot)$ moves the task of combining the $K-1$ pairwise estimations d_{kj} into a representation where the rule of combination is linear and the whole task is accomplished by summation. The results must then be mapped back into the original representation of confidences by the inverse transformation $t^{-1}(\cdot)$.

Combination of Pairwise Estimations Viewed as Combination of Experts' Votes

Equation (11.48) is a remarkably simple expression that suggests a look at the problem of combining pairwise estimations d_{kj} from the viewpoint of combining the votes of experts in a way similar to Section 11.2.

The whole classifier network consists of a group of experts that are highly specialized but have an extremely limited scope of expertise. Each has knowledge about only two classes and can, based on this knowledge, if asked for an opinion of the presented case $\mathbf{v}$, give answers of one of the two following types

- "seems to be mine but may be anything else" or
- "definitely not mine".

Thus, if the pairwise classifier responsible for the two classes k and j maps the given measurement vector $\mathbf{v}$ into the estimation $d_{kj} = 1$, then this fact must be interpreted as "definitely not class j but possibly class k".

The essence of computing $d_k = \text{prob}(k|\mathbf{v})$ from the $K-1$ two-class estimates $d_{kj} = \text{prob}(k|\mathbf{v}, \{j, k\})$, according to (11.48), is combining the votes of those experts able to contribute to this process of forming a common opinion since they have learned something about class k.

The rule of combination (11.48) is kind of soft AND operation. Only if all of the experts d_{kj}, $j = 1, \ldots, K$ except for $j = k$, contribute $d_{kj} = 1$ is the result $d_k = 1$ generated. If but one of the experts decides for $d_{kj} = 0$, the result is $d_k = 0$.

There are several possibilities for designing soft AND functions, all converging to the Boolean AND if the input variables are bound to be either 0 or 1 but exhibiting different transient behavior in between. It must be noted that the rule of combination (11.48) is mathematically derived and makes no use of heuristics such as the questionable assumption of independence of the experts' views.

The rule of combination (11.48) is exact when the pairwise estimations d_{kj} are the true a posteriori probabilities and is approximate to the degree as these estimations are themselves approximations.

Note that of the pairwise classifiers only those qualified for the job contribute to forming the common opinion concerning class k. The others, being indeed unable to produce a sensible vote, are simply not asked.

Combination Network

The procedure is illustrated by Fig. 11.8. The size of the combination network grows with K^2 and becomes quickly larger with increasing number K of classes. There are, however, several possibilities for reducing the computational effort.

The individual pairwise classifiers may be of any type. If polynomial regression classifiers are applied, similar arguments are valid, as in Section 11.3, with the hierarchical classifier. Using the same measurement transformation $\mathbf{v} \rightarrow \mathbf{w}$ and the same draft polynomial structure $\mathbf{w} \rightarrow \mathbf{x}$ leads to an efficient organization of the computational procedure since then all of the necessary $K(K-1)/2$ pairwise moment matrices $\mathbf{M}_{kj}$ can be derived from the same set of K class-specific moment matrices $\mathbf{M}_k = E\{\mathbf{z}\mathbf{z}^T|k\}$:

$$\mathbf{M}_{kj} = E\{\mathbf{z}\mathbf{z}^T|k, j\} = \frac{1}{P_k + P_j}[P_k E\{\mathbf{z}\mathbf{z}^T|k\} + P_j E\{\mathbf{z}\mathbf{z}^T|j\}]$$

$$= \frac{1}{P_k + P_j}[P_k \mathbf{M}_k + P_j \mathbf{M}_j] \qquad (11.49)$$

The rank-ordering feature of the minimum residual variance strategy (Section 6.9) offers the opportunity of shortening the polynomial length L for those

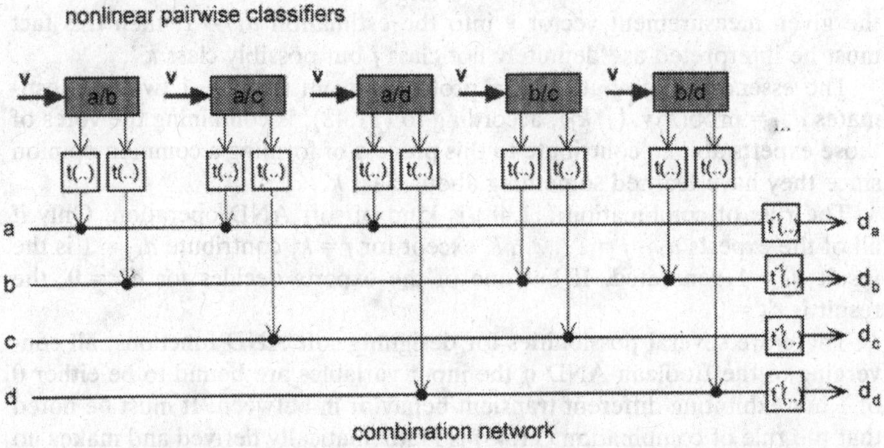

Figure 11.8. Combining votes of pairwise classifiers according to (11.48). Each classifier provides two estimations d_{kj} and $d_{jk} = d_{kj} - 1$ gained from restricted statistical knowledge of only two classes k and j. These estimations are approximations to respective a posteriori probabilities. Individual contributions are mapped by $t(\cdot)$ and accumulated according to respective class labels. Result is again mapped by inverse transformation $t^{-1}(\cdot)$.

pairwise classifiers that separate easily distinguished classes. Note that before going into the combination network the estimations generated by the pairwise classifiers have to be brought into the [0 . . 1] interval by confidence mapping: see Section 6.13.

The whole structure of Fig. 11.8 determines a kind of Voronoi network consisting of nonlinear boundary segments between class regions in measurement space. If the number of classes is large, there will be certain pairwise boundaries that are completely redundant. Redundant boundaries are those separating far distant classes in measurement space that are themselves separated by other classes between them.

Therefore, those pairwise classifiers that during the learning procedure are detected as having the simpler jobs are likely to be redundant. One of the indicators of a simple classification task is the vanishing residual variance S^2 observed while solving the system of linear equations (Section 6.8); another is a clear separation of the eigen and fremd histograms collected for confidence mapping (Section 6.13). Redundant pairwise classifiers are ignored in the combination rule (11.48). In other words, redundant classifiers can be completely omitted in the structure of Fig. 11.8, without disturbing the results.

Remarkable dynamic speed-ups can be gained during operation of the pattern classifier by closing early those of the horizontal collecting lines of Fig. 11.8. which are likely to render vanishing results.

Special Advantages

One important advantage of classifiers consisting of networks of pairwise classifiers, compared to most other types of classifiers, except the nearest-neighbor classifier, is that they allow fast switching of their set Ω of classes. Provided that all of the needed pairwise classifiers are computed in advance, a network classifier for an arbitrary set Ω of classes is configured on-line simply by appropriately addressing the necessary subset of pairwise classifiers.

This feature makes the classifier network especially useful for cooperation with a full-scale single-shot or hierarchical classifier responsible for the complete set Ω of classes. The full-scale classifier and the network classifier together form a kind of working team consisting of a generalist and a large number of extremely specialized specialists.

The generalist classifier gets the task of generating sets of alternatives containing the correct class label with sufficiently high probability. Running such a system in practical application gives rise to the sets of alternatives with varying composition of class labels and requires fast switching of the set of class labels for the network classifier employed to resolve the ambiguities.

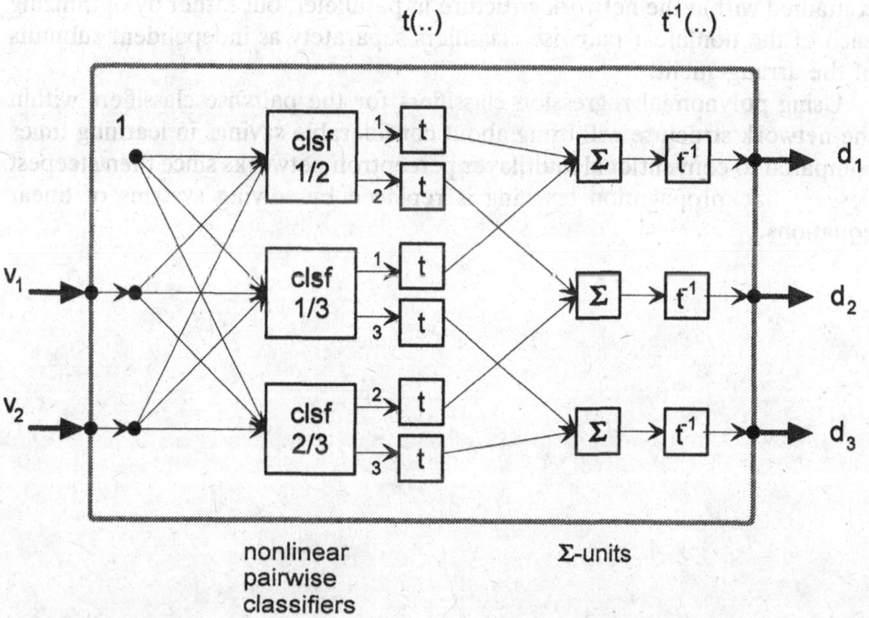

Figure 11.9. Neural network representation of network of pairwise classifiers shown in Fig. 11.8 but with different numbers of classes and for only two input variables in order to make representation comparable to Figs. 6.1 and 7.6.

Relations to Multilayer Perceptron

We have already mentioned the relations existing between multilayer perceptron classifiers and networks of pairwise classifiers. This relationship shall be emphasized by changing the graphical representation of Fig. 11.8. Within the network of pairwise classifiers a large number of pairwise estimations is generated that are then combined by the combination network to render the output values.

The whole structure can be redrawn so that the collection of pairwise estimations becomes the hidden layer of a neural network structure: see Fig. 11.9. Compared to Fig. 7.6, here the first layer computes linear or nonlinear functions of the input vector **v** depending on the type of polynomial used. These are then additionally nonlinearly mapped by the confidence mapping function. The second layer together with the nonlinear transformations $t(\cdot)$ and $t^{-1}(\cdot)$ implements a kind of soft AND operation, reducing to the Boolean AND if all the pairwise estimations assume values 0 or 1.

Note that the network structure of Fig. 11.9 contains as subunits the nonlinear pairwise classifiers that are preferably designed as polynomial regression classifiers. The overall solution is put into the form of a feedforward neural network but is distinguished from that by the fact that learning here is not executed by steepest descent, applied to the entire set of coefficients contained within the network structure in parallelel, but rather by optimizing each of the nonlinear pairwise classifiers separately as independent subunits of the arrangement.

Using polynomial regression classifiers for the pairwise classifiers within the network structure will bring about considerable savings in learning times compared to conventional multilayer perceptron networks since then steepest descent backpropagation learning is replaced by solving systems of linear equations.

12 CONCLUSION

It was the author's intention to lead the reader along a guided tour through the realm pattern classification to a number of different viewpoints, each showing a different aspect of the same problem area. Along this path a collection of concepts and algorithms was assembled, some stemming from the arsenal of traditional pattern recognition and others motivated by what is known about how the biological neuron and the brain function. Although often considered to be fundamentally contradictory approaches, all these concepts have the same mathematical-statistical core founded on the principles of mathematical optimization.

Pattern classification, regardless of whether it is looked at from a traditional or neural point of view, is an essentially statistical problem. The neural network wave did not really revolutionize the science of pattern classification, since the mathematical-statistical core remained untouched, but indeed brought a wealth of new techniques and an enormous push in motivation and creativity.

The increased interest in questions related to learning, perception, and cognition together with the fast accelerating potential of computers and computation released an unprecedented scientific activity in pattern classification and pattern understanding in different application fields and gave rise to a host of different approaches, making it a challenging task to relate them to each other and to the basic theoretical concepts.

Pattern classification is in a certain sense part of the engineering sciences. In the science of mathematical statistics, it is only narrow subfield, with the specialty that the pattern space is normally high-dimensional, that little is known about the underlying statistics, that what can be known must be extracted from sample sets, and that the required large numbers of samples are often difficult to provide and heuristics are needed to fill the gaps.

The fundamental idea of learning from examples underlying the whole field has the consequence that evaluation, performance measuring, and comparison of different competing approaches are only possible by testing with examples. This makes the whole discipline dependent on the application. No indication of classifier performance is sensible unless the specific application is also indicated for which these data are valid.

It follows directly, then, that the goal of practical pattern classification cannot be in finding a universal solution for a universal task. Instead, pattern classification is the universal approach to solving a diversity of different application tasks, all having their own solutions.

Think of just the simple example of recognizing characters. Practical character classifiers have to deal with different collections of fonts, styles of handwriting, ranges of print quality, and compositions of the set of classes. Development of pattern classifiers, therefore, must start with clarifying the application, determining what the properties of the pattern source are, before the pattern classifier can be trained for its specific task.

At first glance, this seems to be in contrast to our own experience of human reading ability as a universal competence, which in a certain sense shall be mimicked by the technical system, but it is not. Comparing technical recognition tasks with human abilities is inspiring and often provides the first idea to the solution. However, this comparison can as well be misleading and deceptive since we are almost unable to separate the comparably constrained low-level recognition tasks, which some technical systems shall solve, from our own comprehensive understanding and from all the reasoning capabilities (conscious or unreflected) we find implemented in our minds.

The adequate theoretical framework for solving pattern classification tasks is statistical decision theory. The essence of learning from examples is establishing estimations for the relevant probability laws governing the application. Quite different constructions are possible serving the same purpose. These different constructions have, due to their basic design principles, different intrinsic properties.

In the preceding chapters we have outlined what we consider to be the most important approaches. An attempt was made to convey how they are motivated and their lines of argumentation. The different degrees of detail were determined by the intention to develop a fundamental understanding of their properties and to make possible the purposeful construction of recognition systems from the presented algorithms.

Special emphasis was put on making visible how closely related the different approaches are. This should especially have made clear that there is no magic [DUI1994] with the artificial neural network approach, sometimes claimed to be a fundamentally new methodology for solving the unsolved problems of statistical pattern classification.

In the discussions on whether neural networks are just a new version of statistical pattern classifiers, the notion of generalization and the claim of the superior generalization capability of neural network approaches have played a special role.

In statistical pattern classification the relation of sample set size and number of trainable parameters has long been a special research topic. It is well understood that the larger is the number of free parameters, the larger the size of the training sample must be. The only way to lessen the requirements on the learning sample set size is to introduce statistical (or other) modeling consistent with the properties of the application. For classifiers designed following the technique of mean-square functional approximation (Chapter 5), this concerns the choice of the set of basis functions.

Knowing the type of basis functions underlying the multilayer perceptron approach (Section 7.5), we understand that a reasonably functioning pattern classifier of this type can be derived from a comparably small learning set. The reason is twofold: First, the sigmoidal basis functions exhibit an exceptionally friendly behavior, and, second, the steepest descent learning procedure is not so susceptible to overfitting since it needs so much time to find precisely the optimum for the learning set.

In contrast, the polynomial regression classifier must, due its perfect adaptatation, exhibit the extreme case of overfitting as long as the number of training samples is smaller than the polynomial length. However, the same behavior of extreme overfitting would be observed with the multilayer perceptron under the following circumstances: Omit the nonlinearity at the last layer output, freeze the values of all weights in the layers before the last layer, and replace the gradient descent learning procedure by generalized inverse matrix inversion.

Another point worthy of note is modularization. The preceding chapters have not only developed a toolbox of algorithms but have also shown that powerful pattern classifiers may themselves be composed of arrangements of simpler ones. This kind of organization breaks the overall optimization task down into a number of partial optimizations easier to handle but requires the development of a theory of classifier architecture. Modularization carries the promise of improved performance for two reasons: First, the smaller classifiers have less parameters resulting in faster and better solutions and, second, due to the simplified tasks of these classifiers, some of the imperfections concerning estimation and approximation can be withheld from becoming effective.

Classifiers cooperating in a modularized organization or part of a larger reasoning system do not communicate in the (hard decision) single best choice mode but forward sets of alternatives composed of pattern label – confidence pairs. To make communication between the modules effective and free of misunderstanding, these confidences must be consistent and measured on a common scale within the entire system (see Section 6.13).

13

STATMOD PROGRAM: DESCRIPTION OF ftp PACKAGE

A simple three-class example in two dimensions is used throughout the book to illustrate the fundamental ideas that in practice may be applied to much more complicated and much higher-dimensional cases. The illustrations derived from this example are almost completely generated using a set of programs developed by the author for the following purposes: to study some simple examples of pattern classification tasks; to solve these pattern classification tasks using the mathematical approaches described in the book; and to produce easily understandable graphical representations illustrating what happens in the different stages of the pattern classification procedures.

The set of programs does not claim to be a professional software package, nor is it directly applicable to large-size real-world pattern classification problems, but may well be of interest to those readers wishing to look a little deeper behind the algorithms presented and to manipulate their parameters.

The whole set of programs is written in Borland Pascal. The package on the Wiley server contains the program sources together with the complete set of software modules (units in Borland Pascal) as well as the executable files and a number of data files. Please refer to the end of this appendix for information on how to download the STATMOD program files from the Wiley ftp site.

13.1 DESCRIPTION OF ANALYSIS TOOLS

The goal of gaining directly interpretable views into measurement and decision spaces prevents work with real world pattern classification tasks which normally reside in high-dimensional pattern spaces. Therefore, the whole package is limited to the case of the

2-dimensional measurement space

which can be directly viewed on the screen with points marked as pattern samples, class regions as colored area, and class borders as contour lines. The restriction to the 2-dimensional measurement space also allows us to generate projective 3d-plots of arbitrary functions over the measurement space, such as, class conditional probability density functions, a posteriori probability functions, class-membership functions, and functional representations of class label or number of alternatives.

The core of the package is the statistical model of the pattern source. The name STATMOD derives from *stat*istical *mod*el.

The statistical model is an external ASCII data structure that can be easily changed by any text editor. The statistical model defines the number of classes, their names (labels), their a priori probabilities, and their class-conditional probabilities. Since only one type of probability distribution function is implemented, the

normal probability function

provisions are made to allow more complex class-conditional distribution functions by introducing a two-stage hierarchy. Each class consists of a number (at least one) of subclasses. Every subclass is normally distributed.

The sequence of measurement vectors generated by the pattern source can be directly taken from the random generator and processed or stored in files and read again from these files. This construction also allows us to include real-world data from any practical application provided that this data is also two-dimensional or suitably projected in two dimensions.

The package provides different techniques for classifier generation. Since the artificial data is basically Gaussian, the Bayes classifier making use of this knowledge establishes the reference. This kind of classifier can be computed directly from the statistical model or from statistical moments collected from sample sets. Essentially two types of least mean square classifiers are provided, based on polynomial regression and multilayer perceptron regression. For both types of classifiers several modifications are possible.

The reference classifier based on the assumption, or knowledge, of Gaussian class-specific distributions is a quadratic classifier. The class boundaries turn out to be quadratic functions in measurement space. For comparison, the polynomial regression classifier within STATMOD also uses complete quadratic polynomials for defining the polynomial structure. The multilayer perceptron regression classifiers may have any number of hidden layers and hidden variables within certain size limitations.

The central program is STM and provides the statistical model, two-dimensional displays of the measurement space, the necessary tools for classifier adaptation (Gaussian reference classifier and polynomial regression classifier), and tools for measuring and visualizing classifier performance. The associated programs serve special purposes: recursive classifier adaptation for the multilayer perceptron as well as for the polynomial regression classifier (NNT), visualization of recursive classifier adaptation procedures over the epochs of learning (PLOTREK), visualization of distributions in decision space (DCSP), projective 3d-visualization of functions of the measurement space (PROJ), clustering following the vector quantization approach (CLUST), analysis and modeling of one-dimensional histograms as needed in the context of confidence mapping (MDLHST), and three further programs for generating special variants of improved polynomial classifiers (QMX, QMY, PKX).

These programs have been incrementally developed and also improved over time. However, the author must admit not to have checked all of the possible branches. The system, however, has proved to be a useful tool for producing visualizations of the mathematical processes occurring in pattern classification systems. These visualizations have been intensively used in courses on "Statistical Pattern Classification" which the author taught at Darmstadt Technical University during recent years.

13.2 HOW TO GET THE STATMOD FILES

The programs are written in Borland Pascal for DOS and can be started as full screen programs under Windows. The details of installation and use are described in the STATMOD description files to be found together with the package you can download from the Wiley ftp server.

The STATMOD package is located on the ftp server of John Wiley & Sons STM (Scientific, Technical, and Medical) division. Please read the README file in the STATMOD area before downloading and installing the files. The file has information about the current version of the program and discusses any special commands you will need to use when installing the program.

The files can be accessed through either a standard ftp program or the ftp client of a Web browser using the http protocol. To gain ftp access, type the following at your ftp command prompt:

ftp:/ftp/wiley.com

When asked for your name, log in as

anonymous

The files are located in the **public/sci_tech_med** directory. Be sure to also download and read the README file.

You can also access the files from an ftp client of a Web browser through the following address:

http://www.wiley.com/sci-tech.html

You will see a listing for STATMOD on the Web page.

The documentation files are formatted for Windows-based word processors. If you need further information about downloading the files, you can reach Wiley's technical support line at 212-850-6194.

REFERENCES

[AGA1966] A. E. Albert and L. A. Gardner, *Stochastic Approximation and Nonlinear Regression*, Research Monograph 42. MIT Press, Cambridge, MA, 1966.

[ALB1972] A. E. Albert, *Regression and the Moore–Penrose Pseudoinverse*, Academic, New York, 1997.

[ALL1966] D. C. Allais, The Problem of Too Many Measurements in Pattern Recognition and Prediction, *IEEE International Convention Record* 7, March 1966, pp. 124–130.

[BAR1981] J. A. Barnett, Computational Methods for a Mathematical Theory of Evidence, in American Association for Artificial Intelligence (ed.) Menlo Park, California, *Proceedings of the Seventh International Joint Conference on Artificial Intelligence*, Vancouver, 1981.

[BER1983] L. Bernhardt, *Zur Klassifizierung vieler Musterklassen mit wenigen Merkmalen*, in H. Kazmierczak (ed.), *Proceedings 5. DAGM Symposium*, Karlsruhe, 1983, pp. 255–260. VDE-Verlag, Berlin, 1983.

[BOC1974] H. Bock, *Automatische Klassifikation*, Vandenhoeck & Ruprecht, Göttingen, 1974.

[DAS1990] B. Dasarathy, *Nearest Neighbor Pattern Classification Techniques*, IEEE Computer Society Press, Los Alamitos, CA, 1990.

[DER1990] M. M. Desu and D. Raghavarao, *Sample Size Methodology*, Academic, San Diego, 1990.

[DUH1973] R. O. Duda and P. E. Hart, *Pattern Classification and Scene Analysis*, Wiley, New York, 1973.

[DUI1994] R. P. W. Duin, Superlearning and Neural Network Magic, *Pattern Recognition Letters* **15**, 1994, pp. 215–217.

[DVO1956] A. Dvoretzki, On Stochastic Approximation, in Jerzy Neyman (ed.), *Proceedings of the Third Berkeley Symposium on Mathematical Statistics and Probability*, University of California Press, Vol. 1, Berkeley, CA, 1956, pp. 39–55.

[FAR1984] S. J. Farlow (ed.), *Self-Organizing Methods in Modelling, GMDH-Type Algorithms*, Dekker, New York, 1984.

[FRA1991a] J. Franke, Experiments on the CENPARMI Data Set with Different Structured Classifiers, in *Proceedings of the Fifth Advanced Technology*

Conference of the USPS, United States Postal Service, Washington, 1991, pp. A167–A181.

[FRA1991b] J. Franke, On the Functional Classifier, in Association Francaise pour la Cybernetique Economique et Technique (AFCET), Paris, *Proceedings of the First International Conference on Document Analysis and Recognition*, St. Malo, 1991, pp. 481–489.

[FUK1985] K. Fukanaga, The Estimation of the Bayes Error by the *K*-Nearest Neighbor Approach, in L. Kamal and A. Rosenfeld (eds.), *Progress in Pattern Recognition*, Vol. 2, Elsevier Science Amsterdam, North Holland, 1985, pp. 169–188.

[GAL1968] R. G. Gallager, *Information Theory and Reliable Communication*, Wiley, New York, 1968.

[GBD1992] S. Geman, E. Bienenstock, and R. Doursat, Neural Networks and the Bias/Variance Dilemma, *Neural Computation* **4**, 1992, pp. 1–58.

[GIM1987] C. L. Giles and T. Maxwell, Learning, Invariance, and Generalization in High-Order Neural Networks, *Applied Optics* **26**, 1987, pp. 4972–4978.

[HOF1985] D. R. Hofstadter, *Metamagical Themes: Questing for the Essence of Mind and Pattern*, Basic Books, New York, 1985.

[HRY1992] T. Hrycej, *Modular Learning in Neural Networks*, Wiley Sixth-Generation Computer Technology Series, Wiley, New York, 1992.

[HSW1989] K. Hornik, M. Stinchcombe, and H. White, Multilayer Feedforward Networks Are Universal Approximators, *Neural Networks*, **2**, 1989, pp. 359–366.

[KRE1991] U. Kressel, The Impact of the Learning-Set Size in Handwritten-Digit Recognition, in T. Kohonen, K. Mäkisara, O. Simula, J. Kaugas (eds.), *Proceedings of the International Conference on Neural Networks*, (ICANN-91) Espoo, Finland, June 1991. Elsevier Science Publishers, Amsterdam, pp. 1685–1689.

[LBG1980] Y. Linde, A. Buzo, and R. Gray, An Algorithm for Vector Quantizer Design, *IEEE Transactions on Communications*, **28**, 1980, pp. 84–95.

[LEW1961] P. M. Lewis, The Characteristic Selection Problem in Recognition Systems, General Electric Research Report 61-RL-2796, Schenectady, N.Y., August 1961.

[LIP1988] R. P. Lippmann, An Introduction to Computing with Neural Nets, *Computer Architecture News* **16**, 1988, pp. 7–25.

[MCL1992] G. J. McLachlan, *Discrimant Analysis and Statistical Pattern Recognition*, Wiley Series in Probability and Mathematical Statistics, Wiley, New York, 1992.

[MCP1943] W. S. McCulloch and W. Pitts, A Logical Calculus of the Ideas Immanent in Nervous Activity, *Bulletin of Mathematical Biophysics* **5**, 1943, pp. 115–133.

[NIE1970] H. Niemann, Mustererkennung mit orthonormalen Reihenentwicklungen, *Nachrichtentechnische Zeitschrift* **6**, 1970, pp. 308–313.

[NIL1965] N. J. Nilson, *Learning Machines*, McGraw-Hill, New York, 1965.

Reprinted with an Introduction by T. J. Sejnowski and H. White, Morgan Kaufmann, San Mateo, CA, 1990.

[NOV1963] A. Novikoff, On Convergence Proofs for Perceptrons, in *Proceedings of the Symposium on Mathematical Theory of Automata*, Polytechnic Press, Brooklyn, N.Y., 1963, pp. 615–622.

[OBE1990] M. Oberländer, Schienenregel zur Berechnung der K Rückschluss wahrscheinlichkeiten, Daimler-Benz Research, Ulm, Internal Note, August 1990.

[OJA1982] E. Oja, A Simplified Neuron Model as a Principal Component Analyzer, *Journal of Mathematical Biology* **15**, 1982, pp. 267–273.

[OJA1989] E. Oja, Neural Networks, Principal Components, and Subspaces, *International Journal of Neural Systems* **1**, 1989, pp. 61–68.

[OPS1975] A. W. Oppenheim and R. W. Schafer, *Digital Signal Processing*, Prentice-Hall, London, 1975.

[PAO1989] Y.-H. Pao, The Functional Link Net: Basis for an Integrated Neural-Net Computing Environment, in Yoh-Han Pao (ed.) *Adaptive Pattern Recognition and Neural Networks*, Addison-Wesley, Reading, MA, 1989, pp. 197–222.

[PAR1962] E. Parzen, On Estimation of a Probability Density Function and Mode, Annals of Mathematical Statistics **33**, 1962, pp. 1065–1076.

[POG1989] T. Poggio and F. Girosi, A Theory of Networks for Approximation and Learning, MIT Artificial Intelligence Laboratory Memo 1140, Cambridge, MA, 1989.

[RAO1973] C. R. Rao, *Linear Statistical Inference and Its Applications*, Wiley, New York, 1973.

[RCE1982] D. L. Reilly, L. N. Cooper, and C. Elbaum, A Neural Model for Category Learning, *Biological Cybernetics* **45** 1982, pp. 35–41.

[RHW1986] D. E. Rumelhart, G. E. Hinton, and R. J. Williams, Learning Internal Representation by Error Propagation, *Parellel Distributed Processing*, Vol. 1, MIT Press, Cambridge, MA, 1986.

[RSO1989] M. B. Reid, L. Spirikovska, and E. Ocha, Simultaneous Position, Scale, and Rotation Invariant Pattern Classification using Third-Order Neural Networks, *Neural Networks* **1**, 1988, pp. 154–159.

[ROS1957] F. Rosenblatt, The Perceptron: A Perceiving and Recognizing Automaton, Report 85-460-1, Cornell Aeronautical Laboratory, Ithaca, NY, 1957.

[SCH1968] J. Schürmann, Die Transinformation als Bedeutungsmass in der Zeichenerkennung, *Archiv der Elektronischen Übertragung* **22**, 1968, pp. 498–501.

[SCH1972] D. Becker and J. Schürmann, Zur verstärkten Berücksichtigung schlecht erkennbarer Zeichen in der Lernstichprobe, *Wissenschaftliche Berichte AEG-Telefunken* **45**, 1972, pp. 97–105.

[SCH1973] J. Schürmann, Zur Zurückweisung zweifelhafter Zeichen, *Nachrichtentechnische Zeitschrift* 1973, **26**, Heft 3, pp. 137–144.

[SCH1977] J. Schürmann, *Polynomklassifikatoren*, Oldenbourg, München, 1977.

[SCH1984] J. Schürmann and W. Doster, A Decision Theoretic Approach to Hierarchical Classifier Design, *Pattern Recognition* **17**(3), 1984, pp. 359–369.

[SEB1962] G. S. Sebestyen, *Decision Making Processes in Pattern Recognition*, MacMillan, New York, 1962.

[SPA1983] H. Späth, *Cluster-Formation and Analyse*, Oldenbourg, München, 1983.

[TOU1992] G. T. Toussaint (ed.), Special Issue on Computational Geometry, *Proceedings of the IEEE*, September 1992.

[WAI1989] A. Waibel, Modular Construction of Time Delay Neural Networks for Speech Recognition, *Neural Computation* **1**, 1990, pp. 39–46.

[WAT1970] S. Watanabe, Feature Compression, in *Advances of Information System Science*, Vol. 3, Plenum, New York, 1970.

[WER1974] P. Werbos, Beyond Regression: New Techniques for Prediction and Analysis in the Behavioral Sciences, Ph.D. Dissertation, Harvard University, Cambridge, MA, November 1974.

[WES1968] J. R. Westlake, *A Handbook of Numerical Matrix Inversion and Solution of Linear Equations*, Wiley, New York, 1968.

[WHI1992] H. White, *Artificial Neural Networks: Approximation and Learning Theory*, Blackwell, Cambridge MA, 1992.

INDEX

9 780471 135340